Rethinking Africa's 'Globalization'

Volume 1
The Intellectual Challenges

PAUL TIYAMBE ZELEZA

Africa World Press, Inc.

P.O. Box 1892   P.O. Box 48
Trenton, NJ 08607   Asmara, ERITREA

Africa World Press, Inc.

P.O. Box 1892
Trenton, NJ 08607

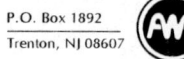 

P.O. Box 48
Asmara, ERITREA

Africa World Press, Inc. First Edition, 2003

Text and Cover Design: Roger Dormann

ISBN: 1-59221-037-6 Cloth
       1-59221-038-4 Paper

The Cataloging-in-Publication Data is available from Library of Congress.

Contents

Preface

This book, and the volume that follows, represent my attempts to understand what globalization, as a process and a project, means for Africa, for the study of Africa, for African universities and intellectuals. It is motivated by my belief that one of the intellectuals' key roles is to make sense of the times and the world in which they live and through that to contribute to meaningful action for progressive change. I also believe that Africa is an integral, indeed, indispensable part of the world, and I am suspicious of discourses that seek to claim its irrelevance, whether with rightist glee, leftist gloom, or postmodernist despair. I have always been disturbed by the tendency to reduce Africa into a descriptive appendage of theoretical formulations manufactured in other historical contexts and discursive climes. Recently, there has been a growing popularity of idealist and dehistoricized analyses and readings of African societies and cultures that take Afropessimism in dangerous new directions. Specifically, I seek to contest current discourses of globalization, postcolonial Africa, and intellectual production, and reaffirm that materialist analysis still matters, political economy still matters, serious empirical research still matters, and Africa will always matter both on its own terms and as an integral part of an unevenly and incompletely integrated world.

As a historian and an African, I am struck by today's infatuation with globalization as it recalls previous infatuations with civilization in the late nineteenth century and modernization in the mid-twentieth century, both of which failed to realize their teleological and universalizing ambitions because they ignored their Eurocentric biases and benefits that made them processes and ideologies subject to contingency and contestation. I remain unconvinced by the strong version of the globalization thesis that the processes identified with contemporary globalization are new, omnipresent, and ineluctable, let alone universally beneficial. Globalization is certainly not endowed with the indispensability and immutability of nature. As a historical and social construct, it remains subject to countervailing social forces and struggles. Indeed, it seems to me that we must try to differentiate the historical and ideological registers of globalization and Africa's links with it, neither overestimating its strengths and the weaknesses of its victims nor underestimating its rapacities and the resistances against it, in order to produce analyses that are not disabling, that do not stifle our rationality and imaginations for African development and a truly decent global society.

This is not to argue that the interconnections in our contemporary world are necessarily similar to those of the past, but that we must eschew the totalizing pretensions and presentist periodization of globalization discourses. It is a little ironic that the tendency to overstate the radical universality, novelty, and consequentiality of contemporary events is characteristic of modernist thought, which the discourses of both globalization and the "posts" seek to disprove. Despite appearances to the contrary, these discourses lack historical depth and geographical breadth. It is often not clear what is really new about globalization as a concept and a process, how the multiple networks of connection between cultures, countries and continents, individuals, institutions and ideologies, or social movements and imaginations are specifically unified and different from the past, and the extent to which they are universal, crossing all borders, and penetrating all spaces on a truly global scale. As a concept, globalization seems to have the explanatory vision from a jetliner high in the clouds: Spatialities and temporaralities on the ground are collapsed into fuzzy fragments and stripped of their complexities and specificities.

It seems to me that the discourses of globalization and the "posts" are also mistaken in denying the efficacy of the nation-state as a meaningful space, and of its ideological mediator, nationalism, as a material agency in shaping contemporary culture and politics in various parts of the world. Globalization supposedly dissolves the nation while the "posts" dismiss nationalism as shibboleths of discredited geographies and histories. Among many scholars, especially in the North, and some in the South, nationalism is derided or distrusted for its alleged primordial pathologies. No attempt is made to distinguish the problematics and projects of nationalism, between the repressive nationalism of imperialism and the progressive nationalism of anticolonial resistance, between the nationalisms that have led to colonial conquest and genocide and those that have sought decolonization and emancipation for oppressed nations and communities, between struggles for domination and struggles for liberation, between the reactionary, reformist, or revolutionary goals of different nationalisms.

The wholesale repudiation of nationalism, and its proudest moment, decolonization—whether in the name of the juggernaut of globalization or the anti-foundationalism of the "posts"—is ultimately a disavowal of history, an act of wilful amnesia against the past and the future. Against the past because it forgets, in the case of Africa, that the progressive nationalist project, which is far from realization, has always had many dimensions in terms of its social and spatial referents. Some post-colonial critics dismiss nationalism because of its alleged mimetism and elitism, that it was an elite project derived from the master-narrative of European nationalism and colonial discourse. This is not a new or radical proposition: It echoes the charges of colonial ideologues at the height of empire that Africa had no history outside Europe, and that the misguided nationalists were misleading the innocent masses, as if the masses had no material interests and imagination for a social order different from the colonial one and were not invested in elements of the nationalist project led or articulated by the elites. It is simply self-saving mystification, if not anti-intellectualist, to claim as some do, that as intellectuals we can never understand what the subalterns say, think, or desire.

Nationalism is not simply a representational discourse, it also involves concrete struggles about material resources and moral possibilities. The African nationalist imaginary, despite its internal inconsistencies and contestations, sought to achieve, in Thandika Mkandawire's (1997a) register, decolonization, nation-building, development, democracy, and regional integration. In other words, in spatial terms it was a nationalist, regionalist, and internationalist nationalism; in social terms a democratic and developmentalist nationalism. Even a cursory glance at the archive of African nationalism shows that since the 19th century African nationalists were as concerned with their specific societies as they were about Pan-Africanism and other internationalist movements and ideologies. The reasons for this lie in the fact that the experiences of colonialism and imperialism were experienced on local, regional, and international scales, so that they were simultaneously localizing, regionalizing, and internationalizing. The fact that the dreams of African nationalism have yet to be achieved is not an argument for their irrelevance.

The case for concrete and specific analyses of Africa cannot be overstated. For some an engagement with African histories and interconnections internally and externally is eschewed by the continent's alleged marginality from globalization or the apparent collapse of the foundational metanarratives of nationalism and development. It has become popular, in the specious names of reflexivity and theorization, to write and to read Africa through personal anecdotes and philosophical speculations in which empirical research and objectivity are treated as suspect romantic leftovers of discredited Enlightenment rationality. Such views represent another denial, this time of intellectual practice itself and of intellectuals as agents of illumination and social criticism, whose specific practice is or should be to challenge power and dominant paradigms of knowledge, to crystallize the memories and experiences of the oppressed, and to produce countertruths.

This, then, is the objective of the book: to contest the dominant discourse of our times—globalization—from the vantage point of Africa and African intellectuals. I present my reflections on the processes and prospects of globalizing Africa and Africanizing globalization. This is a two pronged agenda, concrete and conceptual, examining the developmental implications of globalization for Africa and the intellectual challenges of doing so. In this volume, I largely focus on the latter, the responses, both institutionally and ideologically, to contemporary globalization among intellectuals. Specifically, I look at trends in higher education, the internationalization of African universities, intellectuals and African studies, the bitter contestations over the construction of the continent's pasts and presents among scholars on both sides of the Atlantic, which connects as much as it divides the students of Africa, and the problems and prospects of rewriting and reconfiguring this most bewildering and misunderstood of places.

In short, this book provides a critique of the myths and meanings, promises and perils of globalization, postcoloniality, and other currently popular discourses, interrogating what they entail for Africa and African studies. The book reaffirms the importance of progressive nationalism, Pan-Africanism, and internationalism for Africa's reconstruction, an enterprise in which African universities and intellectuals have a critical role to play. Migrant African intellectuals in the North have a responsibility, it will be argued, to promote radical transnational literacy and conversations that subvert rather than strengthen the cultural and ideological forces of global capitalism in the North and thus reinforce the subordination of the South, including Africa. Like most intellectual explorations, this is a journey in progress, guided by previous intellectual quests, my ideological tendencies, and other personal idiosyncracies.

The chapters in the book originate from lectures, seminars, and conference presentations at various locations around the world. Let me take this opportunity to thank all the organizers of these events and the numerous people who attended and whose questions, comments, criticisms, and even occasional sneers helped me immeasurably to rethink and to refine my ideas. Various versions of Chapter 1 were presented at the International Conference on Globalization, at the Institute of West-Asian and African Studies of the Chinese Academy of Social Sciences in Beijing; at a seminar in the Agrarian

Program at Yale University; and as public lectures at the University of Delaware and the University of Oregon. I would like to thank Professor Yang Lihua in Beijing, James C. Scott at Yale, Wunyabari Maloba at Delaware, and Stephen Wooten and Steve Shankman at Oregon for their kind invitations.

Portions of Chapters 2 and 3 were presented as a keynote address at the International Conference on Historical and Social Science Research in Malawi: Problems and Prospects, sponsored by the University of Malawi and the Nordiska Africa Institute; as conference papers at meetings organized by the Ford Foundation in Johannesburg, Durban, and Nairobi that brought together some of the leading administrators and experts of African higher education. Let me express my gratitude to Professors Kings Phiri in Malawi and Hari Englund in Sweden for being such wonderful hosts, and to Dr. Gerry Salole and Professor Tade Aina, the Southern African representative and East African deputy representative of the Ford Foundation, respectively, for their generosity and critical appraisal of my presentations.

Chapter 4 has seen various incarnations at Ohio State University, the University of California at Los Angeles (where the presentation was published in *Ufahamu*), University of California at San Diego, Kenyatta University and Maseno University College (where the presentation was published as an occasional paper) in Kenya, the University of Cape Town, and Cairo University (where the presentation will be published in Arabic). My visits were facilitated by Professors Isaac Mowoe and Alamin Mazrui at Ohio, Edmund Keller at UCLA, Benetta Jules-Rosette at San Diego, Eric Aseka at Kenyatta, Bethwell A. Ogot at Maseno, Mahmood Mamdani at UCT, and Hamdi Abdulrahman at Cairo University. To all of them, my deepest thanks for their intellectual collegiality and personal kindness.

Chapter 5 was first presented at a colloquium held at the Center for African Studies at the University of Illinois at Urbana-Champaign (UIUC), organized by one of my colleagues, Zine Magubane, who has edited a collection of the papers at the colloquium, including a shorter and different version of this chapter. It was a truly interdisciplinary seminar, and I enjoyed the sharp exchanges between those of us who still remain wedded to old historical materialism and our more trendy literary colleagues.

Chapter 6 was encouraged by Professors Toyin Falola and E. S. Atieno-Odhiambo, who asked me to write it as an introduction to the collection of Professor Ogot's papers. Chapter 7 was inspired by outrage after I saw Henry Louis Gates's atrocious television series—*Wonders of the African World*—and further fueled by a seminar at UIUC and impassioned presentations at the 1999 Annual Meeting of the African Studies Association. I collaborated with Zine Magubane on a different version of the essay. Zine has been a marvelous friend and colleague, and I am indebted to her inspiration, sharp intellect, and comments on Chapters 5 and 7.

The essays that constitute Chapter 8 have been retained as they were originally presented, the first three as keynote addresses at the Zimbabwe International Book Fair, the fourth as an open letter circulated over several e-mail discussion lists in response to an outrageous editorial in Codesria Bulletin by Achille Mbembe, then CODESRIA's executive secretary, before his ignominious ouster, and the final one is an essay that Philip Altbach asked me to write for his Bellagio Series in Publishing. I cannot fully convey my appreciation to Tricia Mbanga and Miriam Bhamare of the Zimbabwe International Book Fair for their magnanimity in inviting me year after year to participate in this great market square of African books, publishing, and learning. Thanks to the book fair I have had the rare opportunity to meet some of Africa's greatest writers and thinkers, as well as many young budding intellects and artists, who carry our collective hopes for a more critical and enlightened humanity on the continent.

The University of Illinois at Urbana-Champaign has been a hospitable intellectual home for me. My mind and curiosity have been well nourished by the countless public lectures, seminars, conferences, symposia, and colloquia that the Center for African Studies, which has been my privilege to direct for the last six years, regularly organizes. As a result of these forums my intellectual and interdisciplinary horizons have expanded enormously. The privilege of meeting hundreds of eminent visiting scholars, activists, and students from all over the world, including from Africa, has been incalculable. I am particularly grateful to the research assistants I have worked with over the last few years: Tunde Braimah, Maimouna Barro, Amanuel Bereket, Brian Bunyan, and Bertin Kouadio, all diligent and delightful; and if they were occasionally overburdened by sudden demands for materials for yet another paper for a conference or seminar, or to meet a publication deadline, they never complained. I am particularly proud of the fact that all but one have proceeded to pursue Ph.D.'s and I have no doubt they will make fine scholars. Through my engagement with the Center for African Studies I have come to understand more clearly the challenges, complexities, contradictions, and possibilities that face international education in the United States, especially as it pertains to Africa. It is doubtful whether I would have written this book, certainly not in the

manner it is, without my experiences at UIUC. Several colleagues commented specifically on some of the chapters. Kwaku Korang and Adlai Murdoch
gave me their considerable insights on postcolonial theory, the subject of
Chapter 5. The fact that I still do not fully understand what all the excitement
about the "posts" is about is of course not for their lack of trying. There are
many more, who have been a source of encouragement and critical support
over the years, as colleagues and friends, such as Alma Gottlieb, Don Crum-
mey, Eyamba Bokamba, Alex Winter-Nelson, Ezekiel Kalipeni, Romanus Ejiaga, and Al Kagan.

Beyond the cornfields of central Illinois, I am fortunate to receive intellectual sustenance from a network of friends, who have always been generous
with their time and conversations. For this book, in particular, I am indebted
to Dickson Eyoh in Toronto, who read almost all the chapters at various stages
of gestation and ever so gently pushed me to clarify and defend my views. I
have also benefited from the intellectual wisdom of Tade Aina in Cairo,
Thandika Mkandawire in Geneva, and Mahmood Mamdani in New York for
discussions or their thoughts on the repertoire of ideas that inform this book
and the subsequent volume.

My greatest debt of gratitude, however, is owed to Cassandra Rachel
Veney, whose intellectual partnership and sparkle and personal warmth and
companionship, helped nurture the writing of this book. A woman of great
intellect and charm, Veney has an acute sense of the ties that bind Africa and
its diaspora. Above all, she has the heart and soul that nurtures and enriches
my private life. To her, and to my daughter, soon to be eighteen, the age she
has been since six, and to my late mother and my sister, the four women who
have shared their lives and taught me the infinite joys of belonging, this book
is dedicated, with love.

Champaign, Illinois, 18 October, 2001

Chapter 1

Globalization, Africa, and Intellectuals

Introduction

Globalization seems to be everywhere, as rhetoric and reality, as process and project. It is propagated simultaneously as an intellectual concept and an ideological commodity, describing concrete conditions and prescribing particular futures. Used by scholars, artists, politicians, businesspeople, and the media to refer to a wide range of complex and contradictory processes and phenomena characterizing contemporary history, it has become a powerful but malleable metaphor that accommodates widely divergent theoretical, empirical, and ideological paradigms, positions, and possibilities. For its triumphalist supporters, globalization is celebrated as inevitable and progressive, indeed, as marking the end of history as we have known it; while for its detractors it reinforces global economic inequalities, political disenfranchisement, and environmental degradation.

Clearly, globalization generates both anxiety and excitement, sometimes within the same individuals or institutions. Depending on how it is defined and perceived, globalization has its advocates, adversaries, and ambivalents. The advocates and beneficiaries of globalization are found among the ascending countries and technocrats, the dominant economic enterprises and commercial classes; while the adversaries are concentrated in the dominated countries among peasants, workers, and small businesses. Those ambivalent about globalization consist of classes and enterprises that both win and lose from specific policies. Intellectuals are not immune from the conflicted perceptions and prognoses engendered by globalization: Some are exhilarated by its promises, others frightened by its perils, and many are worried about its implications for their own craft, for globalization as a research paradigm and a paradigm of research threatens to decompose the old social and spatial units of analysis, and it overwhelms the explanatory power of the conceptual toolkit of many social science and humanities disciplines.

It behooves me, in this chapter, to state what I understand by globalization and intellectuals and what the two mean for Africa. The chapter is divided into three major parts. The first part comments briefly on encounters between Africa and globalization, a subject that will be dealt with in greater detail and in its various dimensions in subsequent chapters in this and the next volume. The second examines the conflicting meanings of globalization, especially its technological, cultural, economic, and political features, arguing that while international connections have indeed grown in speed and intensity, we Africans should desist from assuming that globalization is either complete or an uncontrollable force before which we must stand beguiled and becalmed with impotent resignation. The text wades through some of the vast literature on the subject trying to strip fantasy from fact, expectations from evidence, inferences of isolated facts from context and common sense. My critique is guided by an abiding concern for the implications of contemporary processes of globalization for the distribution of power and wealth, which is becoming ever more unequal, but which is also being contested and will continue to be contested in ever more passionate, and occasionally desperate, ways.

Finally, the third part focuses on the role of intellectuals: How are they being transformed by the forces of globalization in higher education and how are they responding to this new, grand narrative of our times. For "committed" intellectuals in or from Africa and the South more generally, where the national project of development, democratization, decolonization, and self-determination is far from complete, the articulation of progressive nationalism, predicated on progressive regionalism and internationalism, is more important than ever. The South needs insurgent intellectuals who promote our understanding and capacity to act, who neither overestimate the strengths of globalization and the weaknesses of its victims nor underestimate its rapacities and its resistances.

2

Remapping Africa

Let us begin with the obvious. Africa is a place, a material and imagined place, or rather a configuration of places, an embodiment of spaces that are socially produced and produce the social. Its material and symbolic boundaries are constantly shifting, for Africa's spatiality, like all spaces, encompasses the vast intricacies, the incredible complexities, and interlocking and dispersive networks of relations at every scale from the local to the global (Zeleza and Kalipeni, 1999). Africa, in short, is a geography, a history, a reality and an imaginary of places, peoples, and positions, both an invented intellectual construct and an object of intellectual inquiry. What is Africa in the brave new world of contemporary globalization? What are its new cartographic and cognitive boundaries, its internal and external networks? What is the intellectuals' role in clarifying and mapping Africa's place in this reconfigured world?

Two powerful metaphors dominate current intellectual and ideological, policy and popular discourses about Africa. It is claimed, with various degrees of glee and gloom, that Africa is marginal and in crisis both in epistemological and economic terms, that African polities, economies, societies, and studies are irrelevant to globalization. Over the last decade, there have been vigorous debates about the dimensions and dynamics of Africa's alleged marginality and crisis. What strikes me, as a historian, however, is not how new these debates are, but how old they are, and that we have heard them before. When wasn't Africa seen as marginal and in crisis? The language of crisis and marginality, so deeply embedded in the Western imaginary since the tragic encounter between Africa and Europe in modern times, with the onset of the Atlantic slave trade, is attractive for its equal opportunity ideological possibilities: To those on the Right, if we can still use that cliché, it evokes a death wish for a continent seen as beyond the pale of humanity; while for the Left, it kindles the sympathies of redemption for the downtrodden.

Thus, both Africa and globalization evoke powerful images, of historical irrelevance and inevitability, human destitution and development, economic privation and progress, one forever mired in the pathologies of its "backwardness" and the other marching forward to the limitless possibilities of the future; two states of being, two modes of social and spatial organization, splendidly isolated from each other. Africa is widely seen as one huge mess of deprivation, disease, despotism, and destructive conflicts, with little to contribute to globalization, which its delirious advocates hail as marking the end

3

of the tyrannies of history, geography, and the state. Through these images and myths African histories and futures are condemned, those of globalization celebrated, and particular visions of society and the global order are constructed and consumed. Thus, globalization is as much an ideology, a kind of universal elixir, utilized by varied groups to sell their own economic, political, and intellectual interests, as it is a chronicle of actual historical processes, an attempt to capture contemporary trends in economy, technology, culture, and politics. Its persuasive power rests in its very porousness, its capacity to mean all things to all manner of people, as promise or peril, something beneficial or baneful, that will bring global deliverance or devastation.

As a historian and as an African, I do not share the view that globalization is either new, or that Africa is marginalized from it. I believe Africa matters. It has always mattered. It certainly matters to the Africans themselves, over 800 millions of them who live across this massive continent from Cape to Cairo, Senegal to Somalia, who are unlikely to commit mass suicide any time soon; nor is their beloved continent likely to disappear into the sea somewhere. It also matters to the African diasporas, both the historic diaspora created through the slave trades of the last millennium across the Atlantic Ocean, the Mediterranean Sea, and the Indian Ocean as well as the contemporary diaspora dispersed by the depredations of colonial and postcolonial misrule. It matters to millions more, either for reasons of trade, security, religion, culture, or curiosity. Its study will always matter to the Africans themselves and to all those invested in understanding and finding solutions to the continent's myriad challenges, from those cocooned in the universities and the international agencies, to those involved in the continent's vibrant organized civil society, from NGOs to professional associations.

It seems to me we need to differentiate between the historical and ideological registers of globalization and Africa's links with it. Understood as a historical process, the world has been globalizing for a long time, although the process accelerated rapidly during the course of the twentieth century. Africa has been an integral part of these processes, central to the construction of the modern world in all its ramifications—economic, political, cultural, and discursive—over the last half millennium. This is not to argue, however, that Africa's engagements with and contributions to globalization have necessarily been beneficial to its peoples. On the contrary, Africans have paid a high price over the last half millennium in the construction of a more integrated world. Samir Amin (2001) makes this point forcefully. The notion of Africa's marginalization which implies, on the one hand, that the continent, or much of it, is out of the global system or integrated into it only superficially, and on the other, that the poverty of African peoples is precisely the result of their not being sufficiently integrated into the global system, is not borne out by the facts.

To take just one measure: Africa's ratio of extra regional trade to GDP is the highest in the world. In 1990 it was 45.6 percent, compared to 12.8 percent for Europe, 13.2 percent for North America, 15.2 percent for Asia, and 23.7 percent for Latin America. On this score, Africa is even more integrated in the global system than any other region in the developed or developing world. Yet it remains the poorest. Are the two connected? Is there something wrong in the way Africa is integrated? When people talk about Africa's marginalization, they do not refer to the high levels of Africa's global trade, but to its relatively small volume. The questions ought not be about the degree to which Africa is integrated, for Africa is highly integrated. Rather the questions ought to be about the manner of Africa's integration, why its integration over the last five hundred years has produced little autocentered development, i.e., economies that are simultaneously inward looking and open, are integrated in the global system in an active not passive way, shaping but not always adjusting to it. The Atlantic slave trade and colonialism initiated Africa's integration into the world capitalist system in a most destructive way, while the devastating regime of structural adjustment during the 1980s and 1990s derailed the feeble attempts at autocentered development that some of Africa's more enlightened postcolonial states tried to initiate.

Samir Amin regards globalization as the manifestation of contemporary capitalism's chaos, which "is visible in all regions of the world and in all facets of the political, social and ideological crisis" (Amin, 1997: 2). This crisis comes after the collapse of the postwar regime of accumulation (1945-90), which, in turn, succeeded the age of industrial capitalism and colonialism (1800-1945), itself an outgrowth of mercantilism that lasted from the fifteenth to eighteenth centuries and was fashioned by the hegemony of merchant capital in the dominant Atlantic centers and by the creation of peripheral zones in the Americas, to which Africa supplied slave labor. In short, in Amin's view, capitalism has a long history of expansion and uneven development. The era of global disorder since 1990, which is called globalization, is "responsible for the erosion of the three subsystems that formed the basis of postwar growth (the national welfare state in the West, the national bourgeois project of Bandung in the Third World, and Sovietism in the Eastern bloc" (Amin, 1997:34). Globalization is further characterized by the emergence of new technological, financial, ecological, media and communication, and military monopolies.

Globalization via the market, Amin insists, is a reactionary utopia that must be countered "by developing an alternative humanistic project of globalization consistent with a socialist perspective" (Amin, 1997: 5) based on a new global political system that would organize disarmament, provide equitable access to the planet's resources, negotiate open and flexible economic relationships between the world's major regions, and begin negotiations for the correct management of the global/national dialectic in the areas of communication, culture, and political policy. That there are obstacles to this vision from the North cannot be gainsaid, but it is imperative in the meantime to relaunch the development of the South by restructuring international financial and trade institutions regulating the global financial markets. He urges the intelligentsia not to abdicate its responsibilities. He is particularly critical of Northern intellectuals who have adopted the faddish postmodern critiques of capitalism. "I consider postmodernism," he writes, "a non-starter, in the sense that beyond its hype it offers no conceptual instruments capable of transcending the capitalist framework; neither does it demonstrate any capacity to inspire an innovative design for social change " (Amin, 1997: 136).

The insights of the postmodernists, he scoffs, may "look fresh to readers previously impressed by the assumptions of bourgeois essentialism, economism, and teleology. For those of us who never swallowed such assumptions, however, they represent nothing fresher than one more trip along the boundaries of bourgeois thought" (Amin, 1997: 137). Indeed, the "posts" have left open the entry of neoconservative communalist ideologies and contributed to the massive retreat by left-wing intellectuals in the North "from a characteristically naive enthusiasm for the Third World to a pro-imperialist stance now hardly distinguishable from Third World-bashing" (Amin, 1997: 144). It is the duty of intellectuals in the South, he admonishes, to deconstruct new justificatory rhetoric of globalization, "thus laying bare its functional connections with tactical and strategic objectives of crisis management....In Africa, it is time to breathe new life into the concepts of pan-Africanism and pan-Arabism, pushed off center-stage by the earlier successes of the development process, now that the hollowness of those past successes is so clear" (Amin, 1997: 149-150).

Amin's sweeping historical overview and impassioned critique of capitalist globalization is shared by many other African intellectuals. Dani Nabudere (2000) also argues that contemporary globalization is neither new nor "a unilinear phenomenon proceeding in some predictable fashion, progressively moving from one state to another on a kind of evolutionary grid. On the contrary, it is recognized that globalization now proceeds unevenly in the same way that capitalist modernization proceeded in the earlier phases even within Europe" (Nabudere, 2000: 11). However, unlike Amin, he believes that globalization "is first and foremost a cultural project and then an economic and political one" (Nabudere, 2000: 52). He contends that it is a process driven by the West, which has supplanted the globalizations of other civilizations, including that of the Soviet-led communist movement. He traces its origins to the Christian universalism of the Crusades and the trading voyages of the European Middle Ages, through the scientific stage of the early modern period, to the subsequent eras of the industrial and capitalist revolution, capitalist imperialism, and internationalization. The latter stage was first characterized by multilateralization and now by so-called globalization, which is marked by denationalization, deregulation, and the expansion of a post-Fordist economic system. For Africa globalization has meant structural adjustment programs, which have derailed postindependence development efforts and led to what he calls the "third colonial occupation," distinguished by the downsizing of the postcolonial state and downgrading of democracy. One of the consequences has been the growth of traditionalism, the "neo-traditionalism, which the political elites resort to in the form of neo-tribalism, and post-traditionalism that the masses of the people use as an instrument of struggle for cultural integrity and freedom" (Nabudere, 2000: 53).

The disastrous consequences of contemporary capitalist globalization for Africa are outlined in graphic details by Thandika Mkandawire (1997a, 1998a, 2000), who vigorously contests the neoclassical explanations of the African economic crisis of the 1980s and 1990s, which seek to absolve external factors, principally the international financial institutions, and blame the crisis on internal factors, such as poor natural conditions and human resources and political conflicts, and especially policy failures. While conceding that indeed African states made mistakes, Mkandawire is dismissive of the voluntaristic analyses of state policy offered by the World Bank and its academic friends. He puts greater emphasis on the role of structural and external factors, specifically the global capitalist crisis of the 1970s and 1980s, which led to the declining terms of trade for Africa and brought other external shocks, and the role of misguided policy advice often by the same Western individuals and institutions now criticizing the African states.

Analyses of globalization and Africa are dismal, he believes, because most of the nuances that characterize the debate elsewhere "disappear; as a result, the dominant view emphasizes the hyper-globalists on one hand and the incomprehensible marginalization of the continent on the other....Globalization is figuratively portrayed as an unstoppable train that African nations fail to board at their peril. No time is allowed to make special arrangements before one's departure....Threatening language is used to caution those who, for some reason, may not be ready for the 'trip.' Thus, Africans are reminded that they are at a crossroads. Either Africa takes 'appropriate measures' (read IMF/World Bank policies) or it will continue to be marginalized into oblivion. In the famous words of Margaret Thatcher: 'there is no alternative' to adjustment to the exigencies of globalization" (Mkandawire, 1997a: 74). This is globalization as naked ideology. He cautions that "there are at least two possible *wrong* ways of reacting to [globalization]—either by escaping into xenophobic 'fundamentalism,' or 'nativist,' positions or by engaging in blind celebration of the 'universal' by an uncritical embrace of globalization. Both reactions would constitute two ways of being lost, and both responses are, alas, evident in Africa. Another approach is to acknowledge these processes and rethink how to strategically engage with them in order to shield or further one's own agenda" (Mkandawire, 1997a: 101 emphasis original). This agenda, he insists and I agree, must be rooted in the unfinished historical and humanistic tasks of progressive African nationalism: decolonization, development, democracy, nation-building, and regional integration, duly revised to reflect the changed times.

For many African intellectuals, therefore, globalization is seen as a destructive phenomenon and a coercive ideology from the North that, despite some of its novelties, is only slightly different from previous forms and phases of capitalist imperialism. They refuse to be fooled by the delirious boasts of the globalists that we are all globalized now. As the renowned Nigerian political economist Claude Ake (1995: 22-3) reminds us, "it is not an abstract universal that is magically emerging everywhere; it is concrete particulars that are being globalized. What is globalized is not Yoruba but

English, not Turkish pop culture but American, not Senegalese technology but Japanese and German." It has always been the insufferable arrogance of the North, he observes, to conflate "its own model of society with the ideal state of being. In the 1960s, this was epitomized in the rather premature proclamation of the end of ideology. That this turned out to be a costly mistake did not apparently matter. For in the heady triumphalism of the post-Cold War era the claim has been revived, and it is more dogmatic and grander: The real and the ideal have become one in the contemporary North; history is over" (Ake: 1995: 21).

For Ake, then, "uneven globalization is not only a process but also an ongoing structuration of power...[it] is the hierarchization of the world—economically, politically, and culturally—and the crystallizing of a domination. It is a domination constituted essentially by economic power" (Ake, 1995: 23). Since the East-West cleavage has disappeared, the North-South divide "is all the more conspicuous now for having the field alone and all the more important for being reconstituted by the peculiar dynamics of the post-Cold War world," although, he stresses, "the saliency of the North-South dichotomy does not underplay the contradictory and even conflictual plurality of each of these formations. Cultural differences have survived the uniformizing effect of capitalism even in the North, where it has been most successful" (Ake, 1997: 24). Contemporary globalization, he predicts, will not survive "without solving the problem of uneven development and the poverty of much of the world's population. The North would do well to resist the temptation that it can appropriate at will and pay no heed to even development and the rule of law in global governance. The ghetto is too large and the haven it inhabits is small and shrinking. A policy of policing the status quo is feasible, but only in circumstances that effectively repudiate civilization." (Ake, 1995: 42). Like Amin, Ake is critical of the postmodern consciousness celebrated by many Northern intellectuals "that eschews all epiphanies and sees no faith, only pluralities, differences, contradictions, and archaeologies of knowledge that validate themselves arbitrarily....The poor countries are luckier. Development remains a plausible cause and poverty a great enemy" (Ake, 1995: 23).

The argument that African intellectuals should beware of Northern discourses of globalization is stated unequivocally by Tade Aina (1997). "Just as globalization is about power relations and the construction of hegemonic order, [Northern] analyses rely on constructs that reflect and express a view and realization of that power, of that world, of those who construct it, and the place from which they perceive it...the globalization theories imagine and envision the world within a limited scope which is place-determined in terms of privileging a particular Eurocentric (Northern) positioning or understanding which undervalues, ignores or rejects non-European, non-Northern visions and knowledge. Backed by the very global power being studied," he notes wryly, "these discourses succeed in imposing on the rest of the world, particularly the South, their outline of the visions and imaginations of the globe. This in itself reflects the uneven power relations we are talking about" (Aina, 1997: 19). While the bulk of "the 'West-centered' analyses," he observes, "emphasize the 'time-space compression,' 'shrinking world,' new technologies, integrated markets, global inter-dependence and global flows albeit within a framework implicitly underwritten by Western dominance, 'non-West knowledges' struggle with two related sets of elements," namely, "the question of inequality, unevenness and injustice embodied in the New World Order....Related to this and concretely illustrated by the economic restructuring process embodied in the Structural Adjustment Programs (SAPs) is the question of what globalization means for economic development and whether this is still a possibility for African economies" (Aina, 1997: 20-21).

To be sure, there are African intellectuals who accept globalization as "an omnipresent and inescapable fact" and even welcome it for its potential to liberate African economies, politics, and social sciences from the suffocating grip of statist nationalism. One of the proponents of this argument has been Achille Mbembe who, in 1997, becoming executive secretary of CODESRIA, Africa's premier social science organization, embarked on an ambitious program of "globalizing" the African social sciences on the premise that "the things we have been used to are dead. Others reformed. Others still re-emerge in forms that have never been imagined before. We can no longer continue to resolutely apply the same old categories of analysis of things which have gone astray....Thus, we will no longer waste time," he announced, "refuting, sometimes awkwardly, the often erroneous interpretations produced elsewhere by others" (Mbembe, 1998: 3). We now lived, he declared, in "a world made up of fragments, of floating signs, of open texts, of flexible economies and ever-moving meanings" (Mbembe, 1998: 5). He immediately convened a series of conferences on the theme of "globalization and the Social Sciences in Africa," where unfortunately little clarity emerged on what globalization actually entails for Africa and the social sciences.[1]

Clearly, Africa and globalization have a long and unhappy history together. Africa's purported marginalization from globalization hardly means that the continent is not integrated into the world as such, but that it is integrated in a subordinate position. The degree of this subordination may have changed in recent decades, but its basic structure has not altered fundamentally since the emergence of the modern world system. In a large sense, then, for Africa globalization represents an old problem in new contexts: the hegemony of Northern processes, practices, and perspectives. Part of the intellectual challenge is to contest this provincialization of world history, to transcend the writing of histories of the South as transitional narratives to globalization, much as once their histories were written as transitional narratives to modernity, as histories of absences, of lack, of becoming. How is globalization understood in the North? We now turn to that question.

Selling Globalization

Ever since the concept of globalization entered academic circles in the 1980s, debates have centered on its characteristics, origins, implications, and trajectory. However, there is no agreement about what it actually means. Globalization seems to defy the definitional capacity of "the established disciplines," laments Frederic Jameson (1998a: xi), "as a sign of the emergence of a new kind of social phenomenon." It is, he continues, "an unclassifiable topic, which is the intellectual property of no specific field, yet which seems to concern politics and economics in immediate ways, but just as immediately culture and sociology, not to speak of information and the media, or ecology, or consumerism and daily life." One way to begin mapping this proverbial elephant is to eschew narrow disciplinary approaches and try to be multidisciplinary. In this chapter, I attempt to touch the elephant in several parts in an effort to get a better picture of its shape and contours.

There have of course always been brave souls in the jungle of academia who are not daunted by the challenges of definition. Jameson (1998b: 15) himself, who thinks we are living in the postmodern age, believes "that globalization is a communicational concept, which alternately masks and transmits cultural or economic meaning." For Roland Robertson (1992: 177-8), contemporary globalization entails "the twofold process of the particularization of the universal and the universalization of the particular," which merely begs questions about the scale on which the universal and particular are themselves defined. Scott Lash and John Urry (1994: 4) offer a more ambitious definition, that the "contemporary global order, or disorder, is...a structure of flows, a de-centered set of signs in space," a post-Fordist era characterized by "'reflexive production' and 'reflexive consumption'...[and] aesthetic reflexivity." Less ponderous is David Harvey (1989) for whom globalization is characterized by time-space compression. Anthony Giddens (1990) tries to go a little further, claiming that time and space have become compressed through the processes of "distanciation" and "disembeding." The former refers to "the conditions under which time and space are organized so as to connect presence and absence" and the latter the ways in which social relations are restructured "across indefinite spans of time-space" (Giddens, 1990: 14, 21).

Underlying all these definitions, is a sense that the contemporary world is somehow different from the past, that we live in an increasingly interdependent, deterritorialized world, created by the emergence of new transnational information and computer technologies which tear asunder the spatial-temporal divides and distances of the past and shrink the world, if not into a global village, then into neighborhoods that are more familiar with each other. In short, new economic, political, and cultural geographies are emerging that create a world of enhanced locational substitutability in which territorially based institutions, especially nations-states, diminish as barriers to the flows of goods, services, information, capital, technology, and people. But there is no agreement on the nature or degree of the differences, or on the past from which globalization has arisen or divorced itself. In a sense, then, globalization is still searching for its appropriate past, as much as it is seeking its assured futures (Bindé , 2001; Shami, 2001). My own inclination, from my location as a historian and as an African, is to trace contemporary globalization to the global histories of colonialism and neocolonialism and to prefer a future in which development, in its temporal and spatial dimensions, in its material and moral terms, is more evenly distributed across the world.

Thus, the debates on globalization have centered on its purported historical origins, its technological, cultural, economic, and political dimensions. Dating globalization has proved quite vexing. To its advocates, globalization is seen as a new phenomenon involving a fundamental restructuring of the global system that is both inevitable and irreversible. Although some may concede that the process is still in its formative stages, and that it is difficult to capture the exact shape and contours of the emerging postindustrial, postmodern, or postcapitalist world, the hyperglobalists believe that globalization is the wave of the future, and that a new global socioeconomic system is emerging from the crumbling old order of accumulation and social organization. They predict the end of the nation-state and foresee the emergence of global civilization (Ohmae, 1990; Horseman and Marshall, 1994; Burbach, et al. 1997; Piven and Cloward, 1998; Harris, 1998; Sivanandan, 1998; Davis, 1998).

The excitement of the hyperglobalists is well captured in Jeffrey Sachs's breathless opening in an article for the influential American periodical, *Foreign Affairs* (1995: 50): "The 1990s is one of the great watershed decades in economic history. The postwar division of the world economy into the First, Second, and Third Worlds has ended. Not only has communism collapsed, but other ideologies of state-led development that were prevalent in the Third World for decades have fallen into disrepute. If the United States and the other industrial countries act with wisdom, they have a chance to consolidate a global capitalist world system, with profound benefits for both the rich and the poor countries." There might even be poetic benevolence in globalization, Robert Wright (2000: 56) believes, in that "globalization, at least to judge by its effects on income and the effect of income on happiness, is good for the poor and, if anything, bad for the rich."

To the sceptics, mostly found among neo-Marxists, dependistas, and nationalists from the South, there is really nothing new about globalization. It looks, tastes, sounds, and smells like the age-old world capitalist system, with its insatiable capacity for conquest, domination, exploitation, and the production of inequality, disorder, and crises. Globalization, they aver, is merely a polite way of saying imperialism, or the world capitalist system, or Western modernization, in these neoliberal times, for the present highly internationalized economy is neither unprecedented nor truly global, since it continues to be dominated by the major economic powers of Europe, North America, and Japan. Contemporary globalization might be different in quantitative terms but not in terms of its fundamental structures or the units of analysis that define the process. Indeed, it is contingent and susceptible to interruptions and ruptures as has happened in previous globalization cycles. For example, between 1914 and 1945, and some would say until the collapse of the Soviet Union, war, revolutions, and economic nationalism reversed a century's progress in integrating economies. For the sceptics, then, there is little that is new in the global system, and globalization is largely a myth, one that turns contemporary trends of economic internationalization into immutable forces of nature before which governments and societies are utterly powerless (Hall, 1991a; Zevin, 1992; Johnson, 1992; Hirst and Thompson, 1996; Marshall, 1996; Amin, 1997; Veseth, 1998, Petras, 1999).

Finally, there are the so-called transformationalists who argue that contemporary patterns of globalization surpass those of earlier epochs in terms of the extensity of global networks, the intensity and impact of global interconnectedness, and the velocity of global flows. The contemporary era presents a historically unique confluence, to quote Held et al.(1999: 425), "of patterns of globalization in the domains of politics, law and governance, military affairs, cultural linkages and human migrations, in all dimensions of economic activity and in shared global environmental threats." In short, the transformationalists seek a middle ground between the hyperglobalists and skeptics by recognizing that globalization is transforming state power and world politics, that transactions and interdependence among countries have accelerated and intensified, and that the patterns of economic growth and cultural formation are undergoing important changes (Underhill, 1994; Holm and Sorensen, 1995; Boyer and Drache, 1996; Weiss, 1997, Held et al., 1999).

We must resist the temptation to see globalization the way "civilization" or "modernization" used to be presented, as inevitable and one-dimensional and immune to interruptive upheavals and reversals. As an African historian, I tend to agree with those who take the broader temporal and spatial view, that the world has been globalizing for a long time, that the intensity and extent of international interactions across continents, countries, communities, and cultures has been growing—amidst setbacks and strife—for centuries, although they accelerated in the twentieth century, especially after the Second World War and more recently with the end of the cold war. In my view, the term globalization is best understood as the expansion of global capitalism that is subject to age-old processes and patterns of capitalist accumulation with all their social and spatial inequities and divisions of labor.

The technological revolution is widely seen as the motor of contemporary globalization. There have been spectacular advances in computing power and telecommunications that have transformed the ease, speed, quantity, and quality of global information flows and, combined with significant improvements in physical transport systems, have led to sharp falls in communication and transportation costs. Economically, this has made it easier to expand trade and to bring many goods and services not previously traded into circulation, improved the capacity of multinational corporations (MNCs) to coordinate their activities, enhanced the mobility of capital and the integration of financial markets, and turned information into an increasingly valuable asset and commodity. Culturally and politically, it is said the technological revolution has strengthened transnational cultural communications and formations, facilitated networking among resistance movements against dictatorial states as well as institutions promoting globalization itself, and helped to democratize the production and dissemination of information.

For an intellectual migrant like me, working in an American research university, the joys of being able to read African newspapers on the Internet, to communicate with family and friends in distant lands by inexpensive e-mail, and to download journal articles and other research materials, including many used to write this book, is incalculable. But one has to be clear that the privileges of the "network society," as Manuel Castells (1996) calls it, are enjoyed by a global minority. Access to the new technologies and the information society is filtered through the unyielding hierarchies of location, class, gender, and generation. The divides between the technological haves and have nots, between the information rich and information poor, are huge and deepening.[2] While ideological divisions have become muted, "a more intractable division is taking hold, this time based on technology. A small part of the globe, accounting for some 15 percent of the earth's population, provides nearly all of the world's technology innovations. A second part, involving perhaps half of the world's population, is able to adopt these technologies in production and consumption. The remaining part, covering around a third of the world's population, is technologically disconnected, neither innovating at home nor adopting foreign technologies" (Sachs, 2000: 81).

The technologically excluded regions are concentrated in the South, including large parts of Africa. In these countries the structures of technological innovation and adaptation, which elsewhere involve academia, government, and industry working in harness, are weak. This provides one more reason, as discussed in Chapters 2 and 3, to revitalize African universities and to promote effective academic exchanges between the North and the South, and to engage seriously the African intellectual diaspora with the continent. The technological and information divides mean that much of the celebrated "global consciousness" supposedly spawned by globalization is imbued with Northern values and ideologies, since the Northern countries dominate the technological revolution (Nazer, 1999). The role of technology in economic globalization also needs to be examined more critically. Between 1970 and 2000, rates of growth for the world economy as a whole and in many countries, including most of the industrialized countries in western Europe and North America, were actually lower than over the preceding thirty years.

Thus, while the so-called "new technologies" may be different from those in the past and may enable the transmission and accumulation of information more rapidly and in greater quantities than before, "that in itself has not led to either a new class structure or provided a new economic dynamic or state structure. The new technologies are embedded in pre-existing classes, nation-states and the larger constraints and imperatives of the capitalist system. The notion of information as 'the new capital' is, of course, nonsense as is the idea that the mass of new information and the glorified clerks feeding and processing information are the new captains of the economy" (Petras, 1999: 17). It is also important to emphasize that these technologies only make it possible to move capital, goods, and services across the globe, but "market imperfections in the international economy still exist. The degree to which liberalization has occurred is the result of a very political process of bargaining and competition among the more powerful states over how institutions that govern the international economy are constructed....Technological changes only raise the possibility of greater integration; power and politics determine how it proceeds" (Daves, 2000: 115).

Cultures of Globalization

Similar care needs to be taken in analyzing the cultural dynamics and effects of globalization. All too often, discourses of cultural globalization or transnationalization simply universalize the experiences and anxieties of the elite. As Doreen Massey (1994) has so perceptively suggested, the unsettling discovery of the dislocations of globalization among social theorists and commentators in the North is elitist and sometimes racist in that it reflects their apprehension of loss of control as their local streets and neighborhoods are "invaded" by cultural imports and communities from the former colonial world. For peoples who were once enslaved and colonized the feelings and realities of being dislocated, placeless, and invaded is nothing new. On the other hand, celebrations of cultural globalization are sometimes heard loudest among scholars from the South translocated to the North in what are essentially narratives of cosmopolitan self-aggrandizement, or among scholars of Northern progeny seeking to advertise their multicultural sensibilities.

Analyses of cultural globalization seek to map out the flows of information, ideas, imaginations, visions, values, and tastes "mediated through mobile individuals, symbolic tokens and electronic simulations" (Waters, 1995: 126). It is argued that these flows not only link together previously separated cultures, forcing them to relativize themselves against each other that lead to self-reflexive examinations and cultural adaptation; they also facilitate the development of new or syncretic transnational cultures. Globalization, it is claimed, restructures social identities constructed around religion, nationhood, and ethnicity as well as other social structures and markers. These identities are often simultaneously reinvigorated and decoupled from locality. Debate has centered on what characterizes cultural globalization as process, policy, and product. As process, there are questions about the nature and directionality of the cultural flows; as policy the issue is identifying the agents that drive it; and as product there is dispute on whether it leads to cultural hegemonization, homogenization, heterogenization, or hybridization.

The conceptual challenges of deciphering the processes of cultural globalization begin with unpacking the concept of global culture itself. What does it mean? How does it compare to local, ethnic, or national cultures, which are based on shared stories and memories? Besides the media-mediated signs and symbols, what are the myths and memories, stories and symbols, events and experiences, heroes and histories that underpin global culture? The proponents of global culture claim to transcend the state-centrist paradigm and tend to associate its emergence to the increased interpenetration of cultures, heightened global consciousness, the emergence of a global civil society, and the spread of consumerism, involving the commoditization and consumption of popular culture, brand names, and dreams of the good life (Robertson, 1992; Sklair, 1991; Lury, 1996; Friedman, 1997; Macnaghten and Urry, 1998). Skeptics emphasize the incompleteness and contingency of these characterizations, that global culture does not exist in its unitary or multicultural form, or that where elements of it exist they are shallow and inauthentic (Lull, 1995; Barker, 1999; Miyoshi, 1998; Street, 1997). Paul Hirst and Graheme Thompson (1996) go so far as to argue that the notion of globalization in the domains of culture or politics ceases to be sustainable or threatening without the notion of a truly globalized economy, which they believe does not yet exist.

In short, global culture is often defined and debated less in terms of what it is than in terms of its process and prospects. Analyses of the process of cultural globalization tend to be colored by implicit convictions as to whether its impact is deep or superficial, progressive or retrogressive, liberating or destructive for local and national cultures. The common assumption is that the cultural flows are predominantly from the North to the South, the West to the rest. Indeed, to many people much of the global cultural traffic is commodified Anglophone culture, or to be even more precise, American popular culture. Even Europeans, especially the French, have long expressed concern that American mass culture is eroding and dissolving their cultures and traditions (Morley and Robins, 1995). The more peripheral cultures of the South, it is argued, are forced to adjust through what Hannerz (1991) calls "creolization" (see also Mohammadi, 1997; Boyd-Barret, 1997). According to this view, then, it is in the South that accommodations to Northern-derived and driven cultural globalization are made. This perspective tends to be dismissed on three grounds.

First, South-North flows have increased, from foods and music, to clothing styles and languages (Axford, 1995). Consequently, creolization, i.e., cultural hybridization, or cultural synchronization is also taking place in the North. For some, this process is concentrated in the interstices of mass culture and given the official imprimatur of multiculturalism, but for M. Featherstone (1993), the "third cultures," as he calls them, are promoted by firms and professions that are increasingly autonomous from the nation state and have global frames of reference, necessitating their development of flexible organizational practices and modes of orientation that take into account the particularities of local cultures. What emerges is a global cross-over culture, a North-South melange (Featherston et al., 1995). Second, it ignores regional processes that mediate, and sometimes supplant, the North-South cultural flows. For example, to quote Arjun Appadurai (1996a: 32), "for the people of Iran Jaya, Indonesianization may be more worrisome than Americanization, as Japanization may be for Koreans, Indianization for Sri Lankans, Vietnamization for Cambodians, and Russianization for the people of Soviet Armenia and the Baltic republics...for polities of smaller scale, there is always a fear of cultural absorption by polities of larger scale, especially those that are nearby. One man's imagined community is another man's prison."

In fact, for Appadurai, the new global cultural economy cannot be understood in the simple terms of centers and peripheries, push or pull models, surpluses and deficits, or producers and consumers. He proposes that global cultural flows are ubiquitous and disjunctive, and involve the flows of people, technology, financial information, media images and information, and ideologies and world views, i.e., what he terms, ethnoscapes, technospaces, financescapes, mediascapes, and ideoscapes. Disjunctures have become central to the politics of global culture because of the sheer speed, scale, and volume of each of these flows, which in turn lead to disjunctures between nation and state, cultural homogenization and cultural heterogenization. Appadurai's model is undoubtedly one of the most innovative, offering insights into contemporary globalization as a process that involves complex and dynamic interactions over a wide range of social spheres and spatial scales.

Clearly, cultural globalization is produced by many flows that are carried on by a variety of agents; but not all flows and agents are equal. Globalization may indeed be characterized by disjunctive flows, but the question still remains: what drives them? Claiming that the contemporary configuration of cultural forms possess "no Euclidean boundaries, structures, or regularities," or that they are "overlapping in ways that have been discussed only in pure mathematics (in set theory, for example) and in biology (in the language of polythetic classifications)...[or] something like the human version of the theory that some scientists are calling chaos theory" (Appadurai, 1996a: 46) is unnecessary mystification. In fact, this does not stop Appadurai from urging us "to pay special attention to the relation between mass mediation and migration, the two facts that underpin my sense of the cultural politics of the global modern" (Appadurai, 1996a: 21). Appadurai's "radical emphasis on dispersion and decenteredness relativizes domination and masks the persisting geopolitical inequalities between and across regions, nations, and localities" (Ching, 2001: 295).

Contemporary globalization is a product of concrete histories of global capitalism and is primarily driven by technological and economic forces, which no amount of culturalism, with or without pretentious allusions to science, can hide. Cultural globalization is not simply an amorphous process, it is facilitated by the new technologies and the corporate infrastructures within which they operate. The most tangible forms of cultural globalization are comprised of consumer goods, icons, and symbols transmitted by information and telecommunication technologies from television to the internet. By and large, both the products and the technologies are either from the North or controlled by Northern corporations. The principal agents of cultural globalization are pop music, television, cinema, and tourism (Held et al., 1999).

Each of these sectors, in terms of their global reach, are controlled by large Northern corporations even if, as is the case with cinema, the South may be the major producer. And so it is America's Hollywood, not India's Bollywood, that dominates global cinema, even on airlines flying to and from the South! Thus, the global cultural industries are limited to a few sectors and forms that are selected and marketed by multinational corporations for profit. There has been growing concentration in the production—hardware, software, and content—and distribution of information and entertainment as larger conglomerates emerge (van Ginneken, 1998).

The corporate dominance of the North in cultural globalization is evident in the case of "world music," one of the celebrated examples of cultural flows from the South to the North. First discovered by academics as "ethnomusicology," the marked musical "other" of European music, "world music" entered popular culture from the 1980s when some well-known musicians from the United States and Europe, such as Paul Simon, backed by powerful record companies, began prospecting for new sounds and inspiration in the South. Sensing a new market for consumers seeking more product choice and consumer-friendly multiculturalism, the music industry consolidated its hold on world music, which had become fully commoditized by the 1990s, to the chagrin of many "ethnomusicologists." The world music parlayed by the music industry, sought to "market danceable ethnicity and exotic alterity," to quote Steven Feld (2001: 195). As it was blended and mixed, aura became authenticity, caricature represented creativity, dominance substituted for difference. Feld (2001: 211) concludes: "That these blends and mixings are celebrated as liberatory and inspiring, that they unquestionably bring pleasure and stimulation to many, retells a story of the affinities of moderns and primitives. Like varieties of primitivism well chronicled in other domains...world music creates a voyage of discovery, a sonic experience of contact, and auditory deflowering that penetrates the harmony of difference."

The story of world music makes clear the disagreements on the impact of cultural globalization. To many, both its critics and supporters, cultural globalization essentially entails Westernization or even Americanization. Its impact is seen in terms of cultural imperialism or cultural modernization, that cultural globalization is reinforcing the hegemony of the North and leading to cultural homogenization and destroying local cultural autonomy and authenticity. Jameson (1998b) believes that the violence of American cultural imperialism is impervious to the resistances of what he calls the postmodernist inventions of neo-Confucianism and Islamic and Hindu fundamentalism and worries that it overwhelms even "wealthy and culturally elegant" Europe. But the cultural imperialism thesis has its opponents. Peter Berger (2000) notes that American popular culture, which so many rail against, is only one of the four faces of global culture. The other three are, first, the "Davos" culture of the international business elite, named after Davos, Switzerland, the city where the world economic summit meets; second, the "faculty club culture" of the Western intelligentsia; and third, evangelical Protestantism. "To put it graphically," he writes, "if the 'Davos culture' tries to sell computer systems in India, the 'faculty club culture' tries to promote feminism or environmentalism," while the evangelicals try to sell religion (Berger, 2000: 422). The four faces are each distinctive and relate in complex ways and differ in their level of American domination.

Others are more adamant. David Rothkopf (2000: 450) believes that the spread of American cultural symbols and icons is positive, because it promotes integration and international understanding. Indeed, it is a measure of the progress of civilization, for, unlike all other cultures, "American culture is an amalgam of influences and approaches from around the world. It is melded—consciously in many cases—into a social medium that allows individual freedoms and cultures to thrive." Warming to his subject, Rothkopf continues, "Americans should not deny the fact that of all nations in the history of the world, theirs is the most just, the most tolerant, the most willing to constantly reassess and improve itself, and the best model of our time." Though less chauvinistic, John Tomlinson (1991: 175) rejects the idea that globalization promotes cultural imperialism, arguing that unlike imperialism, globalization is a "far less coherent or culturally directed process...globalization suggests the interconnection and interdependency of all global global areas which happens in a far less purposeful way." Indeed, as a disorganized process, globalization weakens the cultural coherence of all individual nation-states, including the economically powerful ones. This view is echoed by Alan Scott (1997) for whom globalization's processes of standardization and diversification, unification and fragmentation are occurring in the absence of either a cultural or an economic hegemony.

The notion that the United States is as culturally vulnerable as Somalia, that Americans are as powerless as Albanians, or that American culture is offering a selfless service to the world is quite amusing. The issue is not why cultural particulars from the United States or the North are universally popular, but what makes them become dominant particulars in the first place. People in the South need not be dupes for cultural imperialism to exist. They do not dance to Tupac because they have been fooled or forced to do so, but they are more likely to know him, still very much alive despite his death, than singers in other parts of the South, unless they, too, are marketed by the corporations that broker global cultural trade and traffic. For African youths, the fact that Tupac is African American may reinforce their self-identification with him and enhances his popularity. In short, American culture is not always seen as European, itself a source of product differentiation for global cultural capital. This is only to suggest the complexities of cultural imperialism. We also need to go beyond simplistic notions that Northern hegemony entails local cultural destruction. People in the South may consume or crave Coke, Macdonalds, and Madonna, but that is not how they spend their entire day; they are busy working and living with family and friends and talking to each other and dreaming, not in English or French or German or Japanese, but largely in their own languages. When they consume the imported products and seductive images, their pleasures and meanings are processed and perceived through the complex filters and registers of their own culture. It is well to remember that in the vast rural hinterlands of the South, and even in the sprawling urban shanties, people have no access to television to watch Madonna videos, computers to surf the Internet, or the incomes to afford McDonald's hamburgers. For genres and imports that are language intensive, such as TV programs and films, language can pose considerable barriers to straightforward cultural importation (Straubhaar, 1997). Moreover, the power of states to mediate foreign cultural forms and influences through educational and other policies should not be underestimated (Featherstone, 1996).

In other words, "local cultures"—a term notoriously difficult to define—none of which can claim to be pure or static, are far more resilient and adaptable than the champions or critics of cultural globalization often allow, and people, even poor ones, are not passive receptacles of alien cultural products. Anxieties and celebrations are often based on anecdotal evidence, for little empirical research has actually been conducted on the specific impact of cultural flows (O'Sullivan et al., 1994; Friedman, 1997; Beynon and Dunkerley, 2000). In fact, the global-local nexus is constantly being reproduced in complex ways. Globalizing and localizing dynamics go hand in hand sometimes as part of deliberate global corporate strategy, but also because responses to globalization can reinforce the politics of place, lead to the revitalization of locality (Morley and Robins, 1995; Taylor et al., 1995; Tehranian and Tehranian, 1997; Tehranian, 1999; Czetkovich and Kellner, 1997). Juxtaposed between the globalizing and localizing tendencies are growing impulses towards regionalism, which represents an attempt to mediate the pressures for the transnationalization of capital and the historic territorialization of the national economy (Ching, 2001).

Instead of destroying local culture, foreign cultural influences can provide the technological and symbolic resources for cultural revival or the ideological impetus for cultural reaffirmation and resistance, at local and regional levels, or even globally, as is evident in the rise of national and transnational ethnic rebellions, religious fundamentalisms, nationalisms, and new social movements (Robertson and Chirico, 1985; Tomlinson, 1991; Axtmann, 1997; Lechner, 1993; Beyer, 1994). The growth of the new peasant movements in many parts of the South, including Africa, which will be examined in greater detail in Volume Two, attests to the growth of cultural and political resistance, either against exploitative globalization or failed modernization, or both (Eder, 1993; Ray, 1993; Omvedt, 1993; Burgmann, 1993; Sklair, 1998; Veltmeyer, 1997; Mittelman, 1998; McMichael, 1996); and following the 11 September 2001 terrorist attacks on the World Trade Center in New York and the Pentagon in Washington, the existence of a global terrorist network is evident.

Nevertheless, it is still a lot easier to make a case for the hegemony of the North in the traffic of global cultural symbols and products than for cultural homogenization. This is of course not to deny that certain cultural forms have growing universal appeal, especially among young people, thanks to global marketing by multinational corporations, or that foods and fashions from the South have become local staples in the North, especially in the "global cities"; but even those forms, such as rap or reggae music, are received, interpreted, and reproduced in different ways in different countries and contexts. In short, the spatial contours of place and location and the social markers of class, age, and gender, not to mention the memories of history and religion, still influence the patterns and processes of cultural assimilation and adaptation.

Instead of homogenization, then, many argue that cultural globalization is leading to, as Jan Pieterse (1995: 64) puts it, the hybridization of already hybrid cultures. However, cultural hybridization itself needs to be analyzed carefully, whether it is a long-term cultural process, as a practice to ensure survival or as a marketing strategy (Kapur, 1998). As Pieterse notes, it undermines neither Western hegemony nor existing relations of power. We must always question, James Lull (1995) implores us, on whose terms and for what purposes do cultural hybrids develop. Racist punks might enjoy eating Indian curry in the day and beating Indians in the dark. The African diaspora knows this story only too well; cultural hybridization did not bring, and has yet to bring, racial equality with their compatriots of European descent, whether in the United States or Brazil, despite the global commodification of the glamorized blackness of a Michael Jackson, a Michael Jordan, or a Pele.

It is clear that conceptualizing and mapping cultural globalization is quite problematic. All too often, the discourse of cultural globalization, as is the case with other globalization discourses, is trapped in the binaries of homogenization and fragmentation, centralization and decentralization, universalism and particularism, and globalization and localization. While there is no doubt that cultural interconnectedness is increasing, there is nothing new about this. Efforts to construct grand theories of cultural globalization tend to be marred by culturalist and other ideological biases. If cultural globalization means a cultural order or cultural flows unmarked by unequal flows between social and spatial hierarchies and structures of economic and political power, then we will await its coming for a long time, indeed.

Economics of Globalization

Culture is not the only domain where there is little agreement on globalization. In fact, debate is as heated as ever about its economic and political dimensions. By the end of the 1990s, the wind of triumphalism had begun to go out of the hyperglobalists' sails. In a lead story on globalization, *The Economist* (2000) warned that while the anti-capitalist protesters who have wrecked meetings of the international financial institutions in various capitals "are wrong about most things...they are right on two matters, and the importance of these points would be difficult to exaggerate. The protesters are right that the most pressing moral, political and economic issue of our time is third-world poverty. And they are right that the tide of 'globalization', powerful as the engines driving it may be, can be turned back. The fact that both these things are true is what makes the protesters—and crucially, the strand of popular opinion that sympathizes with them—so terribly dangerous. International economic integration," the article stressed, "is not an ineluctable process, as many of its most enthusiastic advocates appear to believe. It is only one, the best, of many possible futures for the world economy; others may be chosen, and are even coming to seem more likely," although choices other than capitalist globalization would represent "an unparalleled catastrophe for the planet's most desperate people...."

A few months later, *Business Week* (2000: 74), another influential periodical for the monied elites, concurred in a cover story on global capitalism. It began: "It's hard to figure how a term [globalization] that once connoted so much good for the world has fallen into such disrepute." The weekly noted that while exports had surged for two decades and foreign investment expanded, growth had been uneven, and that poverty was still widespread. It commended the antiglobalization protesters for having helped "to kick-start a profound rethinking about globalization among governments, mainstream economists, and corporations that, until recently, was carried on mostly in obscure think tanks. This reassessment," the article continued, "is badly overdue. In the late 20th century, global capitalism was pushed by leaps in technology, the failure of socialism, and East Asia's seemingly miraculous success. Now it's time to get realistic. The plain truth is that market liberalization by itself does not lift all boats, and in some cases, it has caused severe damage. What's more, there is no point denying that multinationals have contributed to labor, environmental, and human rights abuses...the global economy is pretty much still in the robber baron age."

The article went on to warn that "if global capitalism's flaws aren't addressed, the backlash could grow more severe. Already, momentum for new international free-trade deals has been stopped cold." The article argued that unless the world's poor saw benefits from globalization, political support for it would erode, and it would unravel as "previous golden ages of global capitalism, such as the one at the turn of the 19th century, unraveled. It all adds up to a breakdown of what was known as the Washington Consensus, the world view pushed aggressively by the U.S. Treasury, the IMF, and the World Bank in the early 1990s. This dictum held that all countries should open their markets to trade, direct investment, and short-term capital as quickly as possible. The transition would be painful, but inevitably, prosperity would result. In hindsight, it was a naive and self-interested view...Even the IMF now warns that a high degree of openness to global capital can be dangerous for some developing nations" (*Business Week*, 2000: 75).

Before the limits and contradictions of global capitalism were discovered by some of its ideologues and globalization assumed its current scholarly vogue, proponents of Marxist, dependency, and world systems theories had mapped out the cartographies of capitalist expansion, which emphasized the economic and exploitative dimensions of the emerging capitalist global village. While economics remains critical to the formulations of globalization, recent globalization theories more explicitly incorporate the political and cultural aspects of transnational connections and global convergences. Malcolm Waters (1995: 95) goes so far as to declare the demise of the era of "political economy" and the dawn of the era of "cultural economy." Globalization is seen as a process and a period of exceptionally intensive and integrative material, political, and symbolic exchanges and heightened global consciousness or reflexivity that decompose the territorial boundaries and autonomies of national economies, states, and cultures.

Nevertheles, economics remains the queen of globalization discourses. Five key indicators are used to demonstrate the increasing globalization of the world economy: trade, investment, financial exchanges, production, and consumption. The arguments are that world trade and investment have expanded rapidly; world financial markets have become more integrated and financial flows have exploded; world production is increasingly dominated by multinationals and flexible organizational practices; and a global consumer culture is emerging that homogenizes consumer tastes. Indeed, commodity production is becoming dematerialized as more workers become engaged in the production of commodified services rather than material commodities. In short, the world has entered a new economic era characterized by, to quote Gary Gereffi (1997: 53), "a fundamental shift toward an integrated and coordinated global division of labor in production and trade. Today the most dynamic industries are organized in transnational production systems....As almost every factor of production—money, technology, information, and goods—moves effortlessly across borders, the very idea of distinct U.S., Japanese, or German economies is virtually meaningless." But the empirical evidence for some of the economic trends, as for those associated with the political and cultural aspects of globalization, remains quite mixed. The tendency has been to extrapolate developments in the world of global finance to cover all forms of capital.

National economies, Paul Krugman (1996) insists, are still very much alive, and in the North what happens domestically with productivity determines rates of income growth. He views much of globalization rhetoric as "globaloney" (see also Hanke, 1996). Even without underestimating the impact of the global economy on national economies, especially in the South, it is clear that the world is still far from being a single economy. Not even the developed economies function as an integrated whole. "Even with the revolution in transportation and communication," Dani Rodrik (1997: 20) writes, "and the substantial progress made in trade liberalization over the last three decades, national economies remain remarkably isolated from each other," which means that "most governments in the industrial world are not nearly as shackled by economic globalization as is commonly believed." For example, trade between Canada and the U.S. is among the freest in the world and only minimally hampered by transport and communications costs, yet "trade between a Canadian province and a U.S. state (that is, international trade) is on average 20 times smaller than trade between two Canadian provinces (that is, intranational trade). Clearly, the U.S. and Canadian markets remain substantially delinked from each other. And if this is true of U.S.-Canadian trade, it must be all the more true of other bilateral trade relationships." Thus, while it is true that there has been increased international exchange of goods, services, and capital, economistic arguments that this is unprecedented or leading to economic convergence either in terms of economic performance or productivity are unconvincing. Regional and national histories, politics, and patterns of development still matter (Stallings, 1995; Berger and Dore, 1996; Keohane and Milner, 1996; Loriaux et al., 1997).

Critics have pointed out that while trade has indeed grown faster than world output since the Second World War, trade as a percentage of GDP remains small for most countries. The United States, the current locomotive of globalization, exports only a little over 10 percent of its GDP. Moreover, the rate of growth in world trade is lower than that experienced between 1880 and 1913. In fact, by the end of the 1990s world trade, estimated at 31 percent of world output, was below the level reached in 1913, which stood at 33 percent. Evaluating recent economic performance in a historical perspective Baker et al. (1998; also see Zalewski, 2000) show that similar levels of trade and direct foreign investment were common during the early 1900s, except that power has now shifted from the nation-states to private enterprises, which has weakened the ability of governments to mitigate some of the negative consequences of increased integration such as wage stagnation and greater inequality. Hirst and Thompson (1996) go so far as to argue that some aspects of the international economy are less open than they were before 1914.

Similarly, Paul Streeten (1998: 14) believes if "integration implies the adoption of policies by separate countries as if they were a single political unit...the world was more integrated at the end of the nineteenth century than it is today." The relative share of the developed and developing regions has also not changed significantly since the nineteenth century despite periodic fluctuations and shifts in intergroup and intragroup trade. The main changes, argues Ankie Hoogvelt (1997: 75), have been towards "a modestly thickening network of economic exchanges within the core, a significant redistribution of trade participation within the core, the graduation of a small number of peripheral nations with a comparatively small population base to 'core' status, but above all to a declining economic interaction between core and periphery, both relative to aggregate world trade and relative to total populations participating in the thickening network."

This does not mean, however, that important shifts have not occurred in international trade that result in serious consequences. Most remarkable, perhaps, is the expansion of trade in services—from travel, retailing, nursing, cleaning, engineering, legal and accountancy services, to telecommunications and multimedia services—which has extended international competition into areas that were previously nontradable and that penetrate deeper into national societies and can mold cultural values and national identities than a movement of goods. Not surprisingly, services and intellectual property issues have increasingly come to dominate international trade negotiations and disputes. Some of the popular anxieties about globalization are undoubtedly fueled by the expansion of international trade into domains that were previously sheltered behind national borders. Also important, even if still largely unacknowledged in national trade policies and accounts, is the fact that the level of intraindustry, as compared to interindustry, trade has expanded due to growing specialization within multinational corporations, which means that there are large parts of the economy where it is difficult to disentangle "national" exports and "foreign" imports. This implies that much of international trade occurs outside the market (Champlin and Olson, 1999).

The role of multinational companies in the world economy and in the process of globalization is of course quite complex. Some see them as the harbingers of a borderless world. It is common to come across comparisons of corporations and countries, i.e., claims that General Motors is bigger than Switzerland, Pakistan, and South Africa, or that 51 of the 100 largest economies are not countries but corporations (Kaplan, 2000: 206). The comparisons are meant to suggest that corporations are becoming more powerful than, and independent of, governments, a fact to be condemned or celebrated according to one's ideological predilections. The comparisons are bogus, declares *The Economist* (29 September 2001: 14), because national income, which is a measure of value added, "cannot be compared with a company's sales (equal to value added plus the cost of inputs)." And it asks rhetorically: "The value added of Microsoft is a little over $20 billion a year, about the same as the national income of Uruguay. Does this make it remotely plausible that Bill Gates has more sway over the people of Uruguay than their government does? ...But those are specious comparisons, you might reply. Of course, Bill Gates is less powerful than the government of Uruguay in Uruguay, but Mr. Gates exercises his power, such as it is, globally...Well then, where, exactly is Mr. Gates supposed to be as powerful in relation to government as the alarming comparison between value added and national income implies?...the power that Mr Gates exercises globally is over Microsoft. Every government he ever meets is more powerful than he is in relation to its own citizens."

Although *The Economist,* of course, seeks to exculpate MNCs of wielding excessive power, it raises critical questions about the relationship between corporate power and state power. Specifically, there is a widespread assumption that there is a growing divorce between multinational corporations from states or governments. Michael Tanzer (1995: 1-2) declares categorically: "While it is true that Exxon, Bayer, and Toyota sell and invest all over the world and that their primary goal is to make money for their shareholders, this does not make each of them independent of its home country...today, as throughout history, the power of the state has always been used to pressure other countries to reduce barriers to the companies' exports or investments...The fact that we are now in a slow-growth or stagnant era, with fierce and growing economic rivalries, means that the state-company linkage is more important than ever." Indeed, despite all the hoopla about globalization, Andrew Mair (1997: 65) contends, MNCs "remain focused primarily in their home country (in terms of output and sales turnover, locus of most innovation, and leadership mentality) with relatively weak strategic and operational linkages among countries." And when they invest abroad, Timothy Koechlin (1995: 96) observes, "they are more likely to invest in countries that are dependent on their home country for credit, export markets, technology, imports, and/or aid."

The conclusion is inescapable, the thesis of the postnational, stateless, or global enterprise operating in a borderless world, unencumbered by the regulatory constraints of states and the production and consumption particularities of location, is more of a normative wish than a description of reality. Multinational firms that are truly global, whose resources, production, investments, and markets are evenly spread around the globe, rather than concentrated in their countries of origin, are still relatively rare, for the simple reason that, as Michael Veseth (1998: 188) quips, "the rumors of the deaths of distance and the state and culture and the individual all are exaggerated." In fact, globalization does not mean MNCs will have to become less but more multicultural, because "legal and political systems, cultures, individual tastes, business practices, product safety requirements, and environmental standards will continue to differ among countries and often be sharply altered for years to come, demanding countless and rapid adjustments by international businesses" (Hormats, 1999: 37). To be sure, the MNCs have increased their share of world trade and investment since the end of the Second World War: In 1988, they accounted for 75 percent of international commodity trade and 80 percent of international exchanges of technology and managerial skills, but only 8 percent of gross world product (Dunning, 1993:14-15; Doremus, et.al., 1998). Despite their rising commercial dominance, the fact still remains that MNCs still control a relatively small share of global production.

Thus, globalization has not entailed the unprecedented expansion of trade and the dominance of multinational corporations in global production, let alone the integration of real territorial economies worldwide and the mobility of all factors of production, including labor. As James Mittleman (1997b: 229) reminds us, "the compression of time and space is limited because flows of capital and technology must eventually touch down in distinct places." In short, increased economic flows do not necessarily mean that contemporary economic places are losing their status as places and becoming a mere space of flows, for many economic activities enjoy local unsubstitutabilty, because they are dependent on resources and assets such as labor, information, conventions of interaction and relation-specific skills that are territorialized. "The mere existence of large-scale international flows," Michael Storper (1997: 36) argues, does not lead directly to a conclusion that a productive activity is deterritorialized. A point further developed by Meric Gertler (1997: 58), who argues that the social and spatial embeddedness of industrial capital remains considerable, and that there are "real and continuing limits to the effectiveness with which capital, in the form of leading-edge machinery and production systems, can move over long distances."

It appears, then, that while it is true that the production of commodified services has expanded enormously and the Fordist system of mass production has increasingly given way to flexible production and organizational practices, especially in the North, industrial capital retains its significance, and the logic of capitalist accumulation remains intact. Revealingly, despite the growing mobility of capital, labor continues to be trapped within its national borders. The flow of labor at the global level lags far behind the flows of capital and commodities. In fact, there was hardly any change in the proportion of migrants in the world population between 1965 and 1990; their percentage remained at 2.3 during this period (Zlotnik, 1999: 23). Thus, the closing decades of the twentieth century witnessed little of the mass migration the world saw at the end of the nineteenth century.

The most compelling face of economic globalization can be seen in the growing integration of financial markets and in the velocity of movement of capital that have been facilitated by the computer revolution. The hypermobility of capital, some claim, is leading to the withering of boundaries and the power of the state as governments lose control over foreign exchange markets that trade over a trillion dollars a day (Bluestone and Harrison, 1982; Reich, 1991). The reality is of course a lot more complex. To begin with, as Gordon Clark and Kevin O'Connor (1997) contend, despite all their mobility, the very design and production of financial services and products are profoundly influenced by the location of the provider. Clark and O'Connor believe that this is not only because of persistent time-space distances between markets, systematic differences in countries' economic structures, or differences in regulatory regimes; financial products often have a distinct spatial configuration of information in their design. In short, "the geography of places shapes the operation of financial markets and the global economy primarily because of the geography of information that is embedded in the provision of specific financial products. There is, in effect, a robust territoriality to the global financial industry" (Clark and O'Connor, 1997).

It is also important to remember that the much trumpeted capital flows do not consist largely of direct foreign investment (DFI) but of speculative capital that is often divorced from real economies. As Paul Streeten (1998:18) observes, "in 1971 about 90 percent of all foreign exchange transactions were to finance trade and long-term investment, and only 10 percent were speculative. Today these percentages are reversed: well over 90 percent are speculative." Thus, most of the international financial flows are not directly related to the growth of productive forces, although of course crashes in the financial markets or stock exchange can have a major impact on the real economy. In fact, David Felix (1998) claims that increased financial speculation and volatility has been a contributing factor to economic stagnation since the early 1970s, and many have blamed the Asian crisis of the late 1990s on speculative mania (Woo, 2000; Altman, 2000). The financial crises of the late 1990s dented the economic credibility of neoliberalism in many intellectual circles, although it remained a potent doctrine among politicians, including followers of the so-called "third way" (Hutton and Giddens, 2000). Even George Soros (1998), the much-reviled or much-admired financial operator, expressed alarm at the ungovernability of unregulated financial markets, which were wrecking havoc on entire countries and economies, in the North and the South, and threatening to destroy global capitalism. He joined the chorus calling for the international regulation of global financial markets (Synott, 2000; van Wolferen, 2000).

As for direct foreign investment, while flows have also risen substantially and affect patterns of regional and national development, the case for "investment globalization" tends to be overstated. Capital is not yet entirely free to cross national borders in its search for the highest returns. Most domestic savings stay at home regardless of higher rates of return abroad, and when they are invested abroad, they are skittish and run at the first sign of danger. Not only is the great bulk of investment in most countries domestic investment undertaken by domestic firms, foreign investment is often linked to and spurred by domestic savings. Direct foreign investment has been and remains a small share of overall investment. For example, the ratio of DFI to all domestic investment for the largest eight recipients of international direct investment between 1960 and 1990, accounting for 89 percent of the world stock of DFI, averaged only 4 percent (Koechlin, 1995). This data also shows that DFI is concentrated among the industrialized countries. There has in fact been a geographic redirection of DFI "away from the periphery and into the core of the system," so that, argues Hoogvelt (1997: 77), by the mid-1990s, 91.5 percent of all foreign direct investment went to only 28 percent of the world's population.

Thus the South's share of DFI actually declined between the 1960s and

1980s. At the end of the 1990s, 80 percent of direct foreign investment, which had soared to $400 billion yearly, went to only 10 countries, while 100 countries averaged just $100 million each year (*Business Week*, 2000: 76). Clearly, the increased velocity and volume of financial flows were quite selective and left many countries behind. Moreover, the proportion of DFI, as a share of international trade, did not represent a significant departure from the pattern before the Second World War. In fact, some estimates indicate that the stock of world direct foreign investment "fell from around 9 percent of the global GDP in 1913 to less than half of that figure and had not recovered its earlier importance, even by 1990" (Cable, 1995: 31).

Comprehensive analyses of economic globalization ought to go beyond measuring the flows of trade and capital, and include the flows of other factors of production, such as labor, land in the form of international real estate investments, entrepreneurship, and intellectual property. These flows should be examined at five distinct but interconnected levels: the global, international regions, countries, industries, and firms (Hart and Prakash, 1995; Prakash and Hart, 1999). Such analyses will clearly reveal glaring globalization mismatches across factor flows, thus demonstrating the unevenness, incompleteness, and contingent nature of current globalization processes, which may be subject to sudden cessation or reversals. Even more importantly, it ought to be understood that globalization is not simply an extension of markets or an expansion of financial flows; rather it is a process that involves complex cultural and political institutions.

Perhaps more significant than the actual economic flows is the imposition of global market discipline, the apparent imperative of maintaining "international competitiveness," which either compels governments or has been used by them as a justification to deregulate economies and privatize public enterprises, changes that have entailed the erosion of long-standing social bargains embodied in labor contracts and social welfare programs. Globalization and its ideology of neoliberalism or the free market, imposed everywhere through structural adjustment policies and programs with all the neo-classical zeal that the international financial institutions can muster, has reinforced the asymmetry between capital and labor. It has deepened the inequality in bargaining power between them: Employers can move abroad or threaten, but employees cannot. Much of the tension generated by and in opposition to globalization is fueled by the fact that while working people require more social insurance against the actual and perceived ravages of globalization, governments have been retreating and curtailing their social obligations.

The transformation of class power overwhelmingly in favor of capital against labor is one of the key factors underpinning the growth of international economic flows and the emergence of globalization as a legitimating ideology. Globalization is facilitated by, and justifies, the ascendancy of the export classes whose profits depend on lowering labor costs at home and exploiting new frontiers abroad. Besides providing external outlets and removing the internal constraints imposed by labor-capital relations, mediated by a postwar welfare state, the globalization of the late twentieth century was also stimulated by the increase of international competition as old industrialized and newly industrializing economies sought to grow themselves out of the global economic crisis of the 1970s and early 1980s. The apparent novelty of globalization arises from the simultaneous collapse of the dominant ideologies of inward directed development—from Keynesianism, socialism, and corporatism—which subordinated external exchanges and investments to the growth of protected domestic industries and markets.

Politics of Globalization

Much of the debate on globalization also centers on the extent to which a new global political and military order has emerged. Few now talk confidently of President Bush's "New World Order," or believe in Francis Fukuyama's (1989, 1992) hasty declaration about "the end of history" proclaimed in the heady days following the collapse of the Berlin Wall. Fukuyama's triumphalist thesis declared that the end of communism marked the historical exhaustion of viable alternatives to Western liberalism, even if international conflicts might persist, especially between states, and ethnic and nationalist conflicts might increase. The posthistorical world would be a sad time, because it would have none of history's exciting struggles and dramas, and perhaps centuries of boredom would eventually ignite history again! Others were not so sure. History was certainly not over in the apocalyptic predictions of Samuel Huntington's (1993, 1996) "clash of civilizations," Benjamin Barber's (1992, 1996) "Jihad vs. McWorld," and Robert Kaplan's (1994) "coming anarchy."

Huntington baldly argued that for the relevant future, there would be no universal civilization, but a world of different civilizations, which would clash unless they learned to coexist with each other. Global conflict would no longer be caused by ideological or economic forces, but by cultural divi-

34

sions along the fault lines dividing the world's major civilizations. Civilizational identities, he contended, are less mutable and less easily compromised and resolved than political and economic ones. Civilizational consciousness and antagonisms were increasing because the world was becoming a smaller place and interactions between people of different civilizations were increasing, processes of economic modernization were uprooting people from local identities, the extraordinary power of the West was greatly resented, and economic regionalism was increasing.

For Barber, the world faced two possible futures, both bleak and undemocratic. One was the Jihad world of blood-stained hypernationalism, religious fundamentalisms, tribalized consciousness, and the incivilities of identity politics. The other was the McWorld of fast food, fast music, and fast computers, a commercially homogeneous global system driven by transnational, transideological, and transcultural market, resource, information-technology, and ecological imperatives. Neither was democratic, for the McWorld would promote the antipolitics of globalism, and the Jihad world the antipolitics of tribalization. His guess, though, was that globalization would eventually vanquish retribalization. Kaplan was not so sure. The future lay in West Africa, he proclaimed, a dying region collapsing under the weight of pathological anarchy spawned by rampant epidemics, overpopulation, unprovoked crime, scarcity of resources, refugee migrations, the erosion of nation-states and international borders, marauding private armies, and drug cartels.

These ghastly visions reflected a sense of moral panic among Western commentators as post-cold war triumphalism ebbed in the aftermath of the East Asian economic meltdown and the Russian implosion of 1997-99, and the stubborn trail of bloodshed, violence, civil conflicts, and terrorism from the Balkans to Rwanda to the United States itself, most of which proved impervious to the regulatory capacity of the lone superpower, or the United Nations, or the ubiquitous international financial institutions. Critics pointed out the follies of each of these grand predictions. For example, Eisuke Sakakibara (1995) argues that what we have witnessed since the demise of the cold war is not the end of history but of progressivism, both of socialism and the neoclassical dream itself, the belief that there is only one ideal end, thanks to the unpredictable forces of globalization and environmental constraints. Yahya Sadowski (1998) finds that chaos theory, the notion that globalization is leading to social disruptions, as manifested through either Samuel

Huntington's clash of civilization or Robert Kaplan's pathologies of ethnona-tionalism, is analytically fuzzy and cannot stand the test of evidence. His cri-tique of the ethnocentric and conspiratorial theories of Huntington and Kaplan is apt, although his own view of globalization lacks theoretical rigor.

Fouad Ajami (1993) has accused Huntington of creating specious civi-lizational systems and borders and of exaggerating the prevalence of civiliza-tional identities, because he underestimates the global dimensions and tenac-ity of modernity and secularism and the power of the state. It is states that control civilizations, not civilizations that control states, Ajami insists. For Michael Klare (2000: 133), the glaring reality of our times is that "many of the most severe and persistent threats to global peace and stability are aris-ing not from conflicts between major political entities but from increased discord within states, societies, and civilizations along ethnic, racial, reli-gious, linguistic, caste, or class lines." These conflicts are largely fueled by widening divisions in the distribution of wealth and resources, rather than stoked by primordial ethnic hatreds, as depicted by the media and politicians keen to absolve themselves of responsibility. It is in fact politicians and their intellectual allies who often manufacture and manipulate ethnicity and race, cynically strip diversity of its positive possibilities and turn it into an incen-diary source of conflict (Bowen, 2000; DeVotta, 2000).

Thus, what is mindless about the violence engulfing many parts of the world, argues David Keen (2000), is not the violence itself, but the analysis that "can be actively—and even sometimes intentionally—disabling." The apparent "chaos" of today's world is driven, and depicted as such, by power-ful vested interests keen on maintaining a patently unequal social order that is beneficial to them. From the inner cities of the North to the shanty towns of the South, the redneck militias of the United States and the warlords of Somalia, we are witnessing, according to Keen, the equivalent of the privati-zation of social services, namely, the privatization of war and security. Unrepentant neo-Marxists everywhere and nationalists in the South have long insisted that globalization is and will lead to more global disorder and chaos because of its failure to develop new forms of political and social organization going beyond the nation state; to reconcile the growth of indus-trialization in parts of the Asian and Latin American periphery with the pur-suit of global growth; and to develop a relationship, rather than an exclu-sionary one, with the African periphery.

This is a message that finds support in Kofi Annan (2000), the UN

Secretary General. He observes with the concern of an impassioned international civil servant, that globalization is rapidly losing its luster in many parts of the world because of the global inequalities it is perceived to be engendering. "Throughout much of the developing world," he observes, there is growing anger, resentment, and resistance arising out of the "feeling that globalization is a false God foisted on weaker states by the capitalist centers of the West. Globalization is seen, not as a term describing objective reality, but as an ideology of predatory capitalism" (Annan, 2000: 127). The backlash against globalization is manifested in a rising tide of nationalism, growing appeal of illiberal solutions, and the politics of populism. "If globalization is to succeed," he concludes, "it must succeed for poor and rich alike. It must deliver rights no less than riches. It must provide social justice and equity no less than economic prosperity and enhanced communication ...politics are at the root of globalization's difficulties and politics will be at the heart of any solutions" (Annan, 2000: 129-30).

For many observers, then, the late twentieth century and early twenty-first century will be remembered as the era of the "globalization of poverty," "marked by the collapse of productive systems in the developing world, the demise of national institutions and the disintegration of health and education programs" (Chossudovsky, 1998: 293). Moreover, instead of encouraging peace and security and international interdependence, globalization has reinforced inequalities, polarizations, chauvenisms, and conflicts within and among nations. It encourages a widespread but uneven tendency toward the decomposition of civil society and traditional political formations that as Robert Cox (1997: 27) states, "is accompanied by a resurgent affirmation of identities (defined by, for example, religion, ethnicity, or gender) and an emphasis on locality rather than wider political authorities." James Roesneau (2000) in fact believes that the processes of chaos and fragmentation are so pervasive and generic that one is apt to say we live, not in an age of globalization, but in an age of fragmentation. The case for political globalization does not, however, according to its proponents, lie in normative assumptions about peace and stability. Ian Clark (1997) has argued forcefully that the twentieth century has been an age of globalization and of fragmentation, that the two are sides of the same coin.

For some analysts, globalization does not entail the end of locality, but the production of localities on sites and scales that are increasingly globalized. In other words, we live in a world of "glocalization" in which the local and global are mutually constituted and reproduced (Robertson, 1995; Luke, 1995; Swyngedouw, 1997). Political and economic processes involve rescalings both upward to the supranational or global scales and downwards to smaller units including communities and individuals. Strategies of global localization are widely used by key forms of industrial, service, and financial capital. These rescalings "are invariably contested and the outcome varies considerably from scale to scale, both horizontally and vertically, depending on the type, degree, and content of the scale transgression, its downscaling or upscaling" (Swyngedouw, 1997: 156).

Specifically, the debate on political globalization has centered on the relationship between globalization and state power and globalization and democratization. The contention is that the national state has declined as transnational economic and cultural interactions have grown, which have reduced the redistributive capacities and legitimacy of the state; as areas of traditional state responsibility have become increasingly coordinated by or been ceded to international and regional political units and organizations; as a system of global governance has emerged to deal with global problems, such as human rights, the environment, development and inequality, peace and order, and what O'Neill (1990) calls "globalizing panics," such as AIDS, which respect neither territorial boundaries nor the problem-solving capacity of any state; as world cities have become increasingly and self-consciously transnational actors with their own agendas, worldviews, and networks; and as global civil society and reflexivity have spread thanks to the rapid expansion of international organizations and the tendency of politicians to blame national problems on global forces (Held, 1991; Crook et al., 1992; Ohmae, 1990; Altenstetter and Bjorkman, 1997; Yach and Bettcher 1998; Bauman, 1998; Falk, 1999; Knox, 1995; Sassen, 1991, 2001; Marcuse and van Kempen, 2000).

Clearly, the scope of state sovereignty and the shape of international relations and political culture have undergone significant changes. But pronouncements about the impending death of the state, welcomed by some elements of both the Right and the Left—the former because it wants to discipline labor and other recalcitrant national social forces and the latter as proof that world capitalism exists and that national struggles are futile—appear premature. To begin with, states have not been disappearing but multiplying. There were more states in the 1990s than ever before in history. Paul Hirst (1997) believes that states will continue to have three key roles, whatever other functions they may gain or lose. They will retain a role as regulator providing legitimacy for international economic regulations and stability to financial markets; as orchestrators of social cohesion and economic cooperation between major social interests at the national level; and as guarantors of the rule of law, and enabling plural communities to exist without excessive conflict.

Moreover, as has been suggested by Streeten (1993, 1998) and Rodrik (1996), globalization has led to and needs bigger rather than smaller government. Countries that have taken greater advantage of world markets, as measured by the share of trade in GDP, have larger governments, as measured by the share of government expenditure in GDP. The point is that in a world still divided by nation-states, the more countries globalize the more governments act "as insulators against external shocks, as a kind of insurance against external risk, a way of alleviating market distortions" (Streeten, 1998: 41). Witness how quickly the much maligned "big government" came back in the United States, even among Republicans, following the crisis engendered by the 11 September 2001 terrorist attacks, as *The Economist* (September 29, 2001: 35-6) noted with bemusement. The same issue also observed that "governments around the world on average are now collecting slightly more in taxes—not just in absolute terms, but as a proportion of their bigger economies than they did ten years ago. This is true of the G7 countries, and of the smaller OECD economies as well." The level of government receipts as a share of GDP rose from about 40 percent in 1990 to 42 percent in 2000 for the G7, and for the OECD countries as a whole from 42 percent to nearly 44 percent (*The Economist*, 29 September, 2001: 14-18).

Death wishes for the state are ideological in that they are partly based on the assumption that state intervention in the global market "makes things worse rather than better—an argument that ignores the fact that states frequently intervene on behalf of capital itself" (Foster, 2000: 20). It stands to reason that globalization is not occurring in spite of states, but often with their active participation or complicity, which can be tempered if not withdrawn (Herod et al., 1998). State policies and prevailing national political and institutional conditions have a direct impact on patterns of foreign investment. Peter Marcuse (2000: 25) goes so far as to argue that "the importance of state action in enabling the capitalist system of the industrialized world to function is increased, not reduced, as that system spreads internationally. If states do not control the movement of capital or of goods, it is not because they cannot but because they will not—it is an abdication of state power, not a lack of that power. The very importance attached by international business interests to the WTO, tariff agreements, the government enforcement of contractual rights and the protection of intellectual property interests attest to the continuing if not growing importance of the state."

Indeed, the idea that all governments are necessarily powerless to control the forces of capitalism "serves only to mystify and mythologize the workings of the world system and to reify the restructuring that has taken place. As is well recognized, it is the states of the South that have suffered the most from the global discipline" (Wilkin, 1997: 24). Global political power, whether among states or the much-vaunted international organizations, remains firmly in the hands of the North. But even in the South the coercive and repressive propensities of the state have increased as its capacities to administer welfare and security have declined. States everywhere still enjoy enormous power to stem the mobility of its citizens and to deny migrants the rights of citizenship, as anyone who has ever dealt with dour immigration officials knows. Indeed, today global migrations are subject to more stringent internal and international controls and surveillance than ever before.

That the nation-state is very much alive, as the object of power and desire, can even be seen in the case of the Olympics, an event that is as globalized and corporatized as any. Nationalism thrives at the games themselves, as well as in the way they are reported and received. The interest of broadcasters and audiences in almost every country is first and foremost drawn to the performance of their own athletes, then followed by athletes of allied countries, whether based on the real or imagined affinities of region, religion, race, or ideology (Bernstein, 2000).

The relationship between globalization and democracy is equally complicated. The number of "democratic" states has increased as globalization has spread, which would seem to suggest a conjunctural, if not causal, connection between the two. In fact, there are those who attribute the spread of democracy in Africa in the 1990s to the demonstration effects of communism's extinction in central and eastern Europe and to the examples of western democracies, transmitted to Africans through CNN and the conditionalities of the international financial institutions (Zeleza, 1997a, 1999a). Nonetheless, many of these democracies, like the older and truncated democracies elsewhere, are minimalist, reducing democracy to periodic electoral contests, unencumbered by any developmentalist and distributive objectives.

The rise of "illiberal democracy," as Fareed Zakaria (2000) calls it, is often seen as peculiar to the South and the former communist world. Zakaria believes that this spreading virus can be overcome if, "instead of searching for new lands to democratize and new places to hold elections," the United States works "to consolidate democracy where it has taken root and to encourage the gradual development of constitutional liberalism across the globe" (Zakaria, 2000: 194). During the 2000 U. S. elections the world saw what this much-vaunted liberal constitutionalism amounts to with stories of voting irregularities and the selection of the president by the unelected branch of government—the Supreme Court (Veney and Zeleza, 2000). The ever cynical and ethnocentric Kaplan (2000) argues that democracy cannot thrive in the backwaters of the South and in the former Soviet empire, which lack the social and economic achievements that have sustained it in the United States, although he is worried by the rise of corporate oligarchies. He is far less concerned about the withdrawal of large numbers of people from the electoral process. "The last thing America needs," he avows, "is more voters—particularly badly educated and alienated ones—with a passion for politics" (Kaplan, 2000: 210). That the two might be connected—rising corporate control and electoral disenfranchisement—misses this arrogant advocate of aristocratic democracy.

In so far as globalization represents an increase in the power of capital over other social classes, it contributes to the shrinkage of democracy. As capital and neoliberal ideology become more dominant and the social movements of workers, peasants, and other social classes weaken, the sphere of private and unaccountable decision making expands while that of public and accountable decision making diminishes. Until recently when antiglobalization protests caught the attention of the media, policy makers, and the global corporate elite, resistance to globalization was dismissed as the rantings of fringe radicals. It became even fashionable among academic critics of globalization to point out that while capital was becoming increasingly globalized and a global regime of economic governance was emerging, policed by the international financial institutions, workers and peasants remained localized and unable to develop equivalent global networks of resistance and empowerment (Mengisteab, 1999). The "old geographies of democracy," to borrow a term from Murray Law (1997), were shifting as the scales of political representation and economic organization became incongruous. The power of people to influence policy democratically at the national level was reduced by globalization, yet at the global level there were no democratic institutions to enable people to control or influence their destiny. The apparent mismatch in the scales of capital formation and social struggle was reproduced in the "politics of resistance" literature which seemed to revel in the militant particularisms of localized protests, loyalties, and identity politics (Sklair, 1998; Brass, 1997).

There is no doubt that labor has been battered by capital, which has been strengthened by the neoliberal doctrines and the exit options provided by globalization, reinforced by the assaults of the state and corporations on unionization and the restructuring of work through casualization, informalization, and housewifization (Broad, 1995). Workers have yet to develop new effective strategies or repertoires of power, as Frances Piven and Richard Cloward (2000) call them, to counter the aggressive new elite repertoires. Despite the myths of an all-powerful juggernaut of globalization, the fact remains that "employers still need workers; politicians still need voters," and workers are slowly acquiring new repertoires of resistance that take advantage of the very "vulnerabilities created by globalization and lean production....Industrial restructuring, with its extended chains of production, can make employers more, not less, vulnerable to work stoppages. Moreover, in a number of these instances, workers demonstrated their ability to reach across borders and inspire secondary actions that increased the leverage of work stoppages in one country. Experiences such as these, if they are nourished by labor lore and not buried by neoliberal propaganda, are perhaps the basis for a revival of a belief in labor power" (Piven and Cloward, 2000: 414, 423).

There is growing evidence of the emergence of new worker-community-consumer alliances, student and human rights groups' anti-sweatshop campaigns that have targeted specific companies, such as the footwear giant Nike, as well as the resurgence of strikes against austerity measures. In 2000, for example, general strikes rocked Argentina, Uruguay, Nigeria, and South Africa (Brecher et al., 2000a). International labor cooperation, organized around particular conflicts or for long-term alliances, also seems to be growing. All these stirrings broke into global consciousness between 30 November and 3 December 1999 in the port city of Seattle, which has its own long history of labor struggles (Levi and Olson, 2000). Since then international demonstrations have followed all meetings of the WTO, IMF, World Bank, the G7, and other organs of capitalist globalization and began reframing the debate about globalization, whose advocates have been put increasingly on the defensive and forced to change some of their rhetoric. *The Economist* (29 September 2001: 14) asking, in a lead article: "Is globalization doomed?" expressed their collective alarm. The magazine went on to blame governments and businesses for having made a poor case for globalization.

The "Battle of Seattle" in 1999 and other antiglobalization protests since then have demonstrated that there is a growing global resistance movement to capitalist globalization, and the growth of globalization from below (Brecher et al., 2000a, 2000b; Keck and Sikkink, 1998). Richard Falk (1999: 30) even forecasts that "transnational social forces seem on the verge of forming some kind of global civil society over the course of the next several decades, providing a foundation for the project of 'global democracy'." The point is that capitalist globalization in its various historical phases has neither bestowed democracy on the world nor does it foreclose prospects for democratic struggles at local, national, and international levels. This is to suggest that our analyses of globalization must pursue a dual analytical agenda, mapping out the capital logic of globalization and the logic of struggle by the powerless, disenfranchised, dislocated, and immiserated working peoples of globalization. Globalization discourses have tended to be elitist in that they usually portray the emergence of the global economy as the sole creation of capital. This ignores the active roles that various social groups and movements play, especially labor, "in shaping the historical geography of the global economy" (Herod, 1997: 170) both as direct agents through the creation of their own transnational networks, and through their resistance, which shapes the terrain of globalization. For example, American organized labor promoted internationalization by establishing independent links with labor movements in other countries to serve its own interests and by articulating the positions of American foreign policy and capital (Zeleza, 1987a, 1987b; Herod, 1997).

The role of labor in the current conjuncture of globalization needs to be considered thoughtfully, because as Glenn Adler (1997: 118) has argued, "without taking labor seriously as an actor in the GDL [global division of labor] it is difficult to assess where challenges are likely to emerge, as well as the substance of such challenges and their likelihood of success." The profound optimism of the right and pessimism of the left that current patterns of globalization are irreversible seems based less on an actual analysis of counter-hegemonic projects than on an unfounded fatalism. In other words, globalization is not a mechanical and uncontested process of capitalist expansion. It involves and implicates labor and other social groups who challenge, mediate, and restructure the processes of globalization at various spatial levels. It is not a coincidence that in the 1980s and 1990s there were unprecedented struggles against authoritarianism and for democracy, which were inspired more by the ravages and recessions brought by globalization to large masses of people, than by its successes and benefits. It is also important to note that many of the social movements resisting globalization were themselves becoming increasingly globalized, facilitated by the very technologies of globalization (Mittelman, 1997a).

In short, focusing on social movements and their struggles offers possibilities for conceptualizing alternative visions and structures to bring about sustainable development and democratization. The project of change and struggle must involve, as Stephen Gill (1997: 205) claims, "'double democratization'—of government and political life, at both local and global levels. Efforts need to be intensified to substantially democratize more internationalized forms of state and an embryonic global civil society. In this sense, the neoliberal globalization tendency will continue to be countervailed politically—it is neither inevitable nor an 'end of history,' as some of its advocates and apologists seek to claim." Thus globalization is not simply a process, but an ideology based on the assumption that the forces and structures constituting globalization are both inevitable and beneficial. "The ideology of globalization," argues Cox (1997: 23), leaves "understood but unstated the need for repressive police and military force to prevent destabilization of the world economy by outbursts of protest from the disadvantaged outsiders." Globalization should be understood as an uneven process of historical development, whose trajectory is continuous, uncertain, and unpredictable, not the culmination of some predetermined phenomenon. Much of the changes associated with it are occurring between the more developed countries rather than involving a geographical reorganization of production across the age-old North-South divide. As such, it is premature to speak of a global economy, or of a global society, although there are ever-growing and thickening circuits of globalization. As Saskia Sassen (1997: 34) puts it, "We cannot take the existence of a global economic system as a given, but rather we need to examine the particular ways the conditions for economic globalization are produced." It is a myth to assume that globalization "embodies a teleology, or a predetermined logic with an imputed final state—a global village, a worldwide economy, a world government, and so on," maintains Mittelman

(1997b: 233). It is certainly not "an ineluctable trend, a juggernaut rolling into a new millennium."

The analytical emphasis on globalization has tended to be on changes in the sphere of capital as an exchange relation, in the globalization of markets, and less on capital as a production relation, in the spatial and social contexts of production. This is to suggest that as before in history, when people traded over ever-expanding geographical distances, the commodities they traded were produced in specific places, and the lives of the producers were embedded in those places. Not much has changed even in the current era of so-called "symbolic exchanges." The production of the symbolic, let alone the material, commodities of globalization has not transcended geography—even as their flows accelerate—the historical geography of capitalism that differentiates and hierarchizes the world between winners and losers, the rich and poor, within and across the territorial boundaries of nation-states, regions, and the world.

Intellectual Engagements

Economically, globalization has brought enormous benefits to certain countries and classes, but has brought great misery to others. It is generally recognized that it has been bad for most of Africa and in many parts of the world for workers and the poor, who have seen the income gap with the rich widen, economic insecurities increase, and social dislocations deepen. Unemployment and underemployment have grown for the new underclass of people without the education and skills demanded by the knowledge-based information economy. Generally, globalization has failed to produce rates of growth predicted by its protagonists. A. S. Bhalla and Albert Berry (1998: 174) note that "the growth rates for all regions outside Asia were much faster during 1966-73 than during 1974-90 and 1991-93. The growth rates for South Asia were about the same in the early 1990s as in 1966-73 but slower than during 1974-90. The forecasts for all the regions show that growth rates during 1995-2005 will be much lower than during 1966-73."

At this point, I would like to discuss the role of intellectuals at this historical conjuncture. Universities and intellectuals have been critical institutional and analytical purveyors of globalization. They are powerful ideological machines organized around disciplinary frameworks that seek to colonize and to dismantle singular practices, and that historically have advanced through a more thorough subjection of their objects of study to what Alberto

Moreiras (1998: 81) calls "the global epistemological power/knowledge grid." Intellectuals have to ask themselves, to what extent are they factors of the contemporary global system, with its insatiable appetites and capacities to absorb and commodify discursive opposition and cultural difference? What do pedagogy, activism, and research mean, asks Appadurai (2001), in this new era of globalization? What kinds of connections and collaborations should intellectuals be constructing across the globe and to what purpose? What are the political agendas of our discourses of globalization? How do our disciplines, perspectives, and practices contest or confirm globalization, turn us into either saboteurs or talk show hosts for global capitalism?

Intellectuals, in my view, cannot be innocent bystanders in the great battles for or against capitalist globalization. Accustomed to analyzing others, intellectuals ought to turn their gaze upon themselves occasionally, wiping the fogs of self-idealization from their mirrors, to become more self-reflexive. There are many myths about intellectuals, foremost among them, that they are more rational and objective than the poor unthinking masses, because they float above particular social interests and possess special powers of social criticism. Romantic notions of intellectual rationality, detachment, and marginality persist, despite all the evidence to the contrary that intellectuals have become increasingly attached to, and are reproduced through, powerful cultural institutions and industries—prominent universities, foundations, publishing houses, and the mass media—all of them, in various ways, connected to big government and big corporations, which demand and reward conformity. In short, intellectuals are not outsiders always opposed to the status quo.

Indeed, throughout history, and certainly during the twentieth century, intellectuals have been legislators of freedom as much as tyranny, conquest and liberation, progressive and repressive ideas. It is common in the North to bemoan the fact that intellectuals introduced, popularized, or defended totalitarian ideologies and systems, from fascism and Nazism to communist authoritarianism. For Africans and others in the former colonial world, western imperialism and colonialism belong to this hall of infamy, indeed preceded and outlived the oppressive regimes of the twentieth century. European intellectuals authorized imperialism, while governments executed it, and industrialists benefitted from it. As Edward Said (1993) has passionately argued, the savage, destructive, and all-encompassing energies of Eurocentricism, articulated by the intellectuals and artists of Europe, penetrated all sectors of European society, from the state to social movements, including workers' and women's movements, and propelled or facilitated and sustained, the imperial and colonial conquests of Europe's inferiorized "others" across the globe.

Closer to our own times, he argues, the crude, reductionist, and coarsely racist representations of the Arab world reproduced in the media helped make the Gulf War popular among Americans, and, one could add, account for their indifference to the plight of the Palestinian people in the occupied territories. Most American intellectuals, Said avers, have blissfully avoided "the major, I would say, determining political horizon of modern Western culture, namely imperialism" (Said, 1993: 60). This is not an affliction of only policy-oriented intellectuals who have internalized the norms of the state, but also those who consider themselves "progressive." The latter have been "defanged" by "the American university, with its munificence, utopian sanctuary, and remarkable diversity....Jargons of an almost unimaginable rebarbativeness dominate their styles. Cults like post-modernism, discourse analysis, New Historicism, deconstruction, neo-pragmatism transport them into the country of the blue; an astonishing sense of weightlessness with regard to the gravity of history and individual responsibility fritters away attention to public matters, and to public discourse" (Said, 1993: 303).

The conditions of intellectual public engagement are changing in quite complex and contradictory ways. Today the state and capitalism are "backed by an unusually large number of intellectuals in the West and East" (Kuryluk, 1995: 33), yet at the same time there is a growing feeling that intellectuals are increasingly devalued. Reductions in government support for universities are seen as evidence of a growing disdain for academics' contribution to the business of governing collective life; driven by the need to "marketize" the universities themselves and to reduce spaces for public debate and discourse, all dictated by the neoliberal ideological fever that has gripped governments, with its distaste for critical theoretical knowledge and its preference for "practical" and "craft" knowledge (Wood and Clifford, 1999; Smyth and Hattam, 2000). Intellectual life is increasingly characterized by what I would call corporatization, academicization, and technicalization.

There has been a growing incorporation of civic-minded intellectuals into the policy-making apparatuses, professionalization of intellectuals as academics, and greater demand for technical proficiency and productivity. As shown in Chapter 3, corporatization manifests itself in changes in university management as well as in the growing involvement by private corporations in existing higher education institutions and in creating their own. Consequently, the monopoly long enjoyed by the universities in knowledge production is fast eroding. Also, the humanities and social sciences are losing out to the professional, technological, and scientific fields on their own campuses in the rapidly growing virtual universities and in the corporate-owned institutions and research centers. Whether out of defiance or ignorance or indifference to these changes, many humanists and social scientists fiddle with the proverbial chairs on their sinking decks, talking to themselves in self-referential, turgid, and ephemeral debates that are more concerned with the diagnosis of texts than of the times, of the safe politics of the sign than the severe politics of society.

This is to suggest that the conditions for intellectual production and engagement have changed, in some cases for the worse. Needless to say, these changes and the responses to them occur unevenly, in different combinations and concentrations, and with different implications for different countries. If one may be permitted to make a generalization, in the North the intellectual landscape has been profoundly transformed by the end of the cold war and the demise of the intellectual left; while in the South intellectuals remain preoccupied with questions of nationalism and development in an age that worships at the alter of untrammeled markets, and that is intolerant of autonomous development paths. I will briefly examine these shifts in a few select countries both in the North and the South, if only to underscore the fact that African patterns and the challenges that confront African intellectuals are not unique.

The pressures for corporatization in the United States were reinforced by the cold war. Chapter 4 will show that the area studies project, the bedrock of international education in the American academy, was invigorated and increasingly financed out of national security concerns. The effort to thwart communism was so consuming that the CIA, Frances Saunders (1999) informs us, spent vast sums of money—principally through the Congress for Cultural Freedom (CCF)—often laundered through both established organizations such as the Rockefeller and Ford foundations, the American Council of Learned Societies, the Modern Languages Association, the Metropolitan Opera, and the Museum of Modern Art, and front organizations, such as the Farfield Foundation, to promote numerous American and foreign intellectuals, artists, and journals, especially those on the noncommunist left. The passengers on the C.I.A. gravy train is a veritable who's who of American and European intellectuals, artists, and journals. The tentacles of the CIA extended to Africa, where the literary journal *Transition* was founded in Uganda with funds from the CCF "to undermine Communism's claims in the former colonial world" (Sharlett, 2000: A20).[3]

In the meantime, intellectuals increasingly turned into academics as the universities emerged as the centers of intellectual production, the principal locus of intellectual life. As Russell Jacoby (1987) noted in his book *The Last Intellectuals,* which popularized the term "public intellectual," the unaffiliated intellectual became quite rare. Some have argued that as intellectuals became academics they became less intellectual for their intellectual wings were clipped by the exactions of tenure and specialization. As universities became more corporatized, academics gradually lost their mission. Laments Masao Miyoshi (1998: 267): "Once professors presumably professed; they are now merely professionals." Despite a shared fidelity to ideas, it can be said that intellectuals and academics differ in terms of their audience, craft, and aesthetics. The audience of academics is disproportionately composed of other academics and students, while intellectuals seeks to speak to a wider educated public. Academics also tend to be specialists who know a lot about a little and whose curiosity is confined to narrow designated areas, while intellectuals are generalists who enjoy the freedom of unchanneled curiosity and revel in the power of untrammeled social thought.

An academic is a farmer—to use Jack Miles (1999) memorable metaphor—who has a field that he tries to cultivate well. An intellectual is a hunter who does not have a field but a quarry that he pursues across as many fields as necessary, often losing sight of it altogether. Even their approach to writing varies. To most academics writing is valued for its instrumental value, as a tool to get the job done; it is seen as a practical art, so that "to compliment a great scholar on his beautiful style is, in the usual case, as much a breach of decorum as complimenting him on his complexion" (Miles, 1999: 315). In fact, the more academic the discourse, as is the case with the "posts" that will be discussed in Chapter 5, the more difficult and convoluted the writing and the higher the reputation of those who speak in such impenetrable tongues. In contrast, intellectuals, who see writing as a fine art, value both substance and style, complexity expressed with clarity.

When American academics venture beyond their campuses to speak to a general audience through the media they are called public intellectuals. In reality, they are public academics dabbling in journalism while maintaining their academic positions. According to Joseph Epstein (2000: 46), who idealizes the traditional intellectuals of days gone by, the new public intellectuals are "academic specialist[s] who can write the op-ed piece or do the political talk show...[or] someone vaguely intelligent who happens to appear before the public" on TV. The ones with truly interesting or radical things to say, such as the indefatigable linguist and social critic Noam Chomsky, are rarely seen in the public media. Unlike many of their predecessors, or counterparts in developing countries where conditions often demand serious intellectual engagement, the so-called American public intellectuals, as depicted in Chapter 7, are often disconnected from organized social constituencies or movements and are uninterested in articulating profoundly transformative social agendas or projects.

There are of course many ways and bases of distinguishing intellectuals. Aleksandr Iurevich (2000) divides contemporary Russian intellectuals into three types—ideologues, reformers, and service personnel—who differ in their ability to develop and to defend dominant doctrines and ideas. In France, Michel Winock (Oppenheim, 2001: B9) also identifies three types, whom he calls the professional, specific, and anonymous intellectuals, defined in terms of their relative range of expertise and solicitation by the media. In the United States, Aronowitz and Giroux (1985) differentiate between four groups—the hegemonic, accommodating, critical, and transformative intellectuals—distinguished in a descending order of support for the establishment. In Latin America, according to Karl Zimmerer (2000), intellectuals either see themselves as social critic-commentators or social-reformer-activists, images that are often paired, among social scientists, with academic and applied work, respectively. In African discourses, there is a tendency to make broad distinctions between "radical" or "committed" scholars, who espouse revolutionary philosophies and programs, and "reactionary" or "reformist" scholars, who support the status quo or seek piecemeal changes.

Public intellectuals, in my view, are those who provide actionable knowledge, offer social critique for social action, and exhort action for social aims. They are thinkers who are unafraid to prick power and to prod the conscience of society against injustices. They cultivate and practice a critical sensibility, framed around self-reflection, scepticism, refusal, imagination, and unlearning. In other words, they exercise reflexive engagement about the social and political implications of the knowledge they produce; are committed to a constant interrogation of categories and metaphors of discourses circulating in the public sphere, including their own; refuse to surrender to despair; seek to sustain a resistant position; believe in social agency and the possibilities of change; and systematically strive to unlearn privileges and oppressive discourses and to reclaim silenced and subjugated knowledges (Abascál-Hildebrand, 1999a, 199b; Smyth and Hattam, 2000).

Before the end of the cold war, socialism provided Western intellectuals who were critical of their own societies analytical and ideological armor. Indeed, to the chagrin of many on the Right, in those days the term intellectual seemed to be reserved for the Left, who delighted in criticizing their own societies. The misguided, if feigned, estrangement of the leftist intellectuals, Paul Hollander (1998; 2000) and other critics charge, was rooted in the academic subculture that valorizes the intellectual as an outsider and a social critic. It also reflected a desperate search by intellectuals suffering from the pangs and pains of secularization for new gods, a new moral and social order, which they claimed to find in the ultimately doomed communist and socialist revolutions, whose cast of champions kept shifting from the Soviet Union, China, to Cuba, Vietnam, and the assorted revolutionary experiments of Africa.

Marxism gave leftist intellectuals, the critics maintain, theoretical conceit and moral certainties, an outlet to express their aversion to capitalism, with all its materialism and consumerism, if not for modernity itself. They were attracted to Marxism because it promised material progress with social justice and cohesion, modernity without alienation. By criticizing their own societies and idealizing socialisms elsewhere, the Left could display their alienation and their capacity for critical thinking and questioning as well as their high moral concerns for equality, justice, social well-being, adding a sense of community, meaning, and purpose. They had the best of all possible worlds that living in a rich, democratic society could allow: the luxury of criticism, idealism, passion, and political commitment combined with security, material and status rewards, safety, and group support.

Whatever the merits of some of these revisionist critiques, there is no doubt that they express the triumphalism of the Right and the capitulation of the Left following the demise of the Soviet Union and the extinction of "actually existing socialism" as a credible alternative to global capitalism. They are intended to silence serious criticisms of Western societies at home and abroad, to forestall censure of global capitalism. In response some on the left have abandoned their old faith altogether and have joined the right-wing bandwagon and backlash, many have found solace in the gentle ideals of social democracy and picked new, fancy causes; others have fallen prey to the various "posts" parading in the academy; a few still hope that, from the ashes of twentieth century socialism, there will emerge a new, more open, less economistic, deterministic and deductive Marxism fit for the twenty-first century (Callari et al., 1995). It is this sense of abdication by the left and exultation by the right, the apparent foreclosure of global systemic options, that Fukuyama celebrated in his end of history thesis.

Clearly, the collapse of socialism led to a profound intellectual crisis in certain circles in the North. "Where are the young left intellectuals?" Kevin Mattson (1999: 53) asks with evident anguish. "Name a young left writer or thinker who is in his or her 30s," he laments, "and is known to a wide readership or audience. You probably can't name too many. Now, think of how disparate and broken down the American left is today—struggling on within the work of a few organizations, lone politicians, and the remnants of protest movements. Maybe," he continues, "there is a connection between these two things. Without young left intellectuals providing any vision that goes beyond local struggles for justice, the left remains a polyglot of movements without clear direction."

Young academics lucky enough to obtain university tenure-track jobs are left little room for either sustained thought or for public engagement by the punishing demands of the publish or perish syndrome. Those who seek refuge elsewhere find little intellectual nourishment and radical sustenance: Countercultures have increasingly become commodified avenues for self-expression; the think tanks are mostly havens of conservatives, and the media and the publishing world shun serious critics of the corporate control of American culture and politics. In a political culture where even the term "liberal" became a dirty word, "political correctness," a weapon to intimidate progressives (Berman, 1992; Bauman, 1993); and many women, especially young ones, refuse to be called feminists (Mandle, 2000; Rothenberg, 2000; Howe, 2000),[4] for a young academic identifying herself as left-wing courts professional suicide.[5] But the Right still insists that unrepentant Left intellectuals dominate the campuses (Bloom, 1988; Kimball, 1990; D'Souza, 1991, 2000; Gelenter, 1997).

This sense of intellectual angst and drift is of course not restricted to the Left or to the United States. It is evident in other parts of the North as well.

In France, where the term intellectual emerged during the Dreyfus affair of 1898 that galvanized the spirit of collective social conscience among the French intelligentsia, and where intellectuals have long been taken and have taken themselves very seriously, intellectuals are apparently engulfed by a growing sense of irrelevance and marginality. They complain that their influence seems to be decreasing at the same time as their visibility is increasing, a tribute to the supremacy and superficiality of the media that dictates the public agenda more than ever before. Indeed, the media increasingly anoints intellectuals who compete for media visibility, and respect, thus creating a vicious circle (Guidice, 1997).

Soul-searching reached a crescendo when Regis Debray (2001), an intellectual of impeccable activist credentials, declared with typical Gallic hyperbole that the French intellectual was dead. He contends that the historicotechno circumstances of globalization are creating "fast food" intellectuals, characterized by "collective autism, bombast of presentation to the point of unreality, moral narcissism, a chronic lack of sober foresight, and total immersion in instantaneousness....Instantism reflects the promotion of the immediate, the apotheosis of the microsecond, nowness and hotness of the newest arrival in a society based on capital flows, mutabilities and metamorphoses rather than on constancy and stability of durable goods and services" (Debray, 2001: 60). He warns against the digital intellectual of tomorrow who will be "more hyper-specialized, less dependent on immediate reception, freer toward opinion...also more segmented and less 'public,' less a citizen, attached to a community of birth or interests, with a diminished ambition to be universal. Digitized communication risks presenting us," Debray concludes, "with a fragmented and patchy world, even parochial, statistical and egotistical all at once, exchanging the common welfare for collective constituencies or interest groups of the like-minded. Such communication already directs a steady assault at the viewing-listening e-public through channels of thematic, regional, confessional and ethnic content" (Debray, 2001: 62).

Critics have pointed out that Debray's announcement of the death of the French intellectual is premature. At issue is not their demise, but their diminished cohesiveness as the community has fractured into Winock's "professional intellectuals," "specific intellectuals," and "anonymous intellectuals." The intellectual Debray mourns is the committed activist, who used to march on the streets and fight for the big causes, but who now finds himself isolated in a world of television and computers and on campuses dominated by those who reject the Enlightenment ideals of rationality and progress that sustained the Left (Oppenheim, 2001). Despite their different prognoses on the health of the French intellectual, Debray and his critics seem to agree that the public intellectual has lost much of his public audience and his expressive authority within the universities themselves.

The same seems to be happening in Britain, where some commentators wonder loudly, "Are intellectuals useless?" (Llyod, 1998), or lament "the lost intellectuals of Blair's Britain" (Sivier, 1997). A climate of anti-intellectualism, we are told, has been spreading as the "universities are now supposed to be centers of industry, as well as academia. They're not, however, supposed to be producing academics" (Sivier, 1997: 188). Indeed, it would appear that as new centers of knowledge have emerged outside the academy, including think tanks, which siphon policy advisers from the universities for the political parties, "intellectuals have lost their monopoly of knowledge—which is a good thing; but they have also lost their independence, which is damaging to their moral authority" (Lloyd, 1998: 12).

The intellectual left began losing its steam and seductions under Margaret Thatcher's resolute conservatism, which was bolstered by combative right-wing think tanks, and the ferocious attacks from former fellow travelers like Paul Johnson (1990: 342), who excoriated intellectuals as a class for perpetrating the "worst despotisms of all,", namely, "the heartless tyranny of ideas" imposed in one heinous scheme after another on hapless humanity throughout the twentieth century. Intellectual descent continued under Tony Blair's fuzzy "third way" neoliberalism. That even a Perry Anderson, the doyen of the British left and a flag bearer of the unaffiliated intellectuals, would pack his bags and finally settle at a university—the University of California at Los Angeles—is viewed as a sign of how far the British public intellectual has lost his autonomy and influence (Skidelsky, 1999).

In Eastern Europe the dramatic changes of 1989 transformed the role of intellectuals. The demise of communist authoritarianism was facilitated by the struggles of many courageous intellectuals such as Vaclav Havel. Where are these intellectuals now? Are they still important, asks Slavenka Drakulic (1999). He gives a troubled answer: "It seems that they have lost their importance and the leading position in their societies. If so, I would say that is rather normal: the more normal the society, the less need for public moralists, redeemers, or intellectual heroes. On the other hand, these societies are still far removed from normalcy and the transition to democracy is far from over.

In every postcommunist country, a tough struggle between authoritarian and liberal forces is going on and the outcome is not certain. Perhaps the critical intellectuals were written off too early, in the belief that democracy will take care of itself" (Drakulic, 1999: 276). Indeed, in some parts of Eastern Europe reactionary intellectuals, such as Radovan Karadzic, a psychiatrist and poet and an indicted war criminal, have played a major role in stoking the memories of inter-ethnic hatreds that have ravaged the former Yugoslavia.

These professors of death, like their counterparts in Rwanda and elsewhere in Africa, discussed in Chapter 2, and all those who have supported the killing impulses of imperialism, are a grim reminder that intellectuals are not, by their vocation, necessarily on the side of the angels. Nor do they always make more enlightened politicians as is clear in Russia, where there has apparently been a "a mass departure of scholars for politics. Although this kind of 'brain drain' cannot compare in scale with other types, such as the emigration of Russian researchers and their entry into business, it is comparable to them in importance, for it has an appreciable effect on both academics and politics" (Iurevich, 2000). Scholars are attracted to politics in pursuit of noble goals—"saving the fatherland" and improving society—and crass desires for power, fame, and wealth. Besides becoming politicians, scholars have also entered politics as consultants and advisors. For their part, Russian politicians seem to have a penchant for academic degrees, which they seek for the aura of disinterested expertise it gives them in a career that is still viewed as dirty. The result is that Russian politics is the most "degree heavy" in the world. The will to truth meets the will to power.

However, neither the universities nor Russian politics have benefitted much from the union. Politics remains muddled, mired between democratization and authoritarianism. The academics-turned politicians, most of whom were not very successful academics, are "ruthless towards their former colleagues...they not only do not lobby to defend their colleagues' interests but, on the contrary, often act against them. Thus, for example, many Duma members who hold advanced academic degrees regularly vote against spending on research, while former scholars working for the executive branch cut research funds even more drastically" (Iurevich, 2000: 33). As funds are reduced, pressures to create independent research centers and consultancies increase, a phenomenon with which African scholars are only too familiar. Since politicians mostly seek public opinion surveys, the research centers that have mushroomed have largely been formed by scholars in the social science disciplines of sociology, economics, and political science, thereby turning the tables on the natural, technical, and medical sciences which were once considered the "real" sciences.

The challenges of maintaining intellectual autonomy that confront intellectuals in Asian countries would also be quite familiar to African intellectuals. They center mostly around issues of autonomy both from the state and from Western hegemony. Globalization, Renato Constantino (1997, 2000) warns, threatens to turn Asian intellectuals into what he calls "comprador intellectuals." He notes that two traditions have characterized intellectuals' responses in the South to the hegemonic discourses of the North. On the one hand, "centuries of miseducation under imperial taskmasters have left a legacy of dependence which frequently manifests itself in an uncritical acceptance of Northern ideas and ready acquiescence to Northern prescriptions." On the other hand, "intellectuals of the South have also been conditioned not to be too quickly taken in by what the North has to offer because of their exposure to the liberation struggles of their countries. Mass memories about colonial oppression always linger in the interstices of social history. Assertions of indigenous wisdom, despite colonial impositions, constitute counter-intellectual efforts against the dominant thought. These articulations contributed vastly to the sense of nation which became a cultural defense and at the same time the focal point of the national struggle" (Constantino, 1997: 275).

The hegemonic discourse of neoliberalism—propagated by the Northern centers of power, principally the transnational corporations, the multilateral institutions, Northern governments and their powerful groupings such as the G-7—justifies globalization in the interests of the North at the expense of the South, vast swathes of which have been devastated by structural adjustment programs. Globalization and the North are of course routinely absolved by their defenders of responsibility for the persistent crises of the South. Such is the level of conceptual denial, it has been charged, that arrogant economic technocrats in the North largely blame the Asian financial crisis of the late 1990s, among the tigers previously praised for their economic miracle, on "crony capitalism," or the failure of "Asian values" more generally, terms that shift focus from the ill effects of deregulation and speculative mania to rampant corruption in Asia itself (Karel van Wolferen, 1999; Lim, 1998).

The power of intellectuals to contest neo-liberal ideology and its mystifications is being undermined, Constantino argues, by the disappearance of critical intellectuals and the emergence of comprador intellectuals, who are products of the growing takeover of universities by global corporations "through the endowments they provide, the researchers they fund and the faculty consultants they pamper with large fees. Through such largesse, they are able to set the directions of curricular development, get the information they require, and tap the expertise which can ensure their competitiveness." (Constantino, 1997: 79). Radical intellectuals in Asia, he insists, have a responsibility to expose both the comprador intellectuals and the bitter truths about globalization, often in contradiction with the propaganda of their own governments, as part of the struggle to inaugurate an Asian renaissance that is neither a replication of Europe nor the Asian past.

The battle of the intellectuals is particularly critical in China, given the country's size, importance, and its protracted and problematic transition from communism to capitalism. Like intellectuals in many parts of the world, Chinese intellectuals are divided in their relation to the state and in their international orientations. This is contrary to the perspective, based on simplistic patron-client models popular in some Northern quarters, that claims "Chinese intellectuals have no autonomy: they are merely spokesmen of political leaders and they can carry out intellectual activities only under some kind of political patronage" (Ma, 1998: 50). More recently, it has become common to attribute intellectual dissident activities in China and locate the base for intellectual autonomy, in the international attention dissident scholars receive, especially in the United States.

International support has of course helped some individuals, but the expansion of intellectual space in China owes a lot more to internal transformations, including the economic and higher education reforms that have been undertaken. Indeed, the widespread belief that all Chinese intellectuals "suffer persecution under the Communist regime, support reform and hope for the democratization of the country," Liu Binyan (1996: 384) tells us, "has actually never been true. While the scholars who colluded with the Gang of Four have been throughly discredited as extreme leftists, those who cooperated with the conservatives in the 1980s included not only leftist scholars, but also liberals. However, it was only in the 1990s, after the failure of the Tiananmen movement, that this actual state of affairs gradually came to light." China's single-minded pursuit of economic reforms unaccompanied by commensurate political reforms, has engendered an unprecedented open internal debate and dissension among Chinese intellectuals.

Accompanying the growing debates and assertiveness by Chinese intellectuals in the 1990s, was a rising nationalistic discourse, which superseded, according to Suisheng Zhao (1997), the antitraditionalism that dominated Chinese intellectual circles in the 1980s. The anti-traditionalists criticized traditional Chinese culture and national character as obstacles to modernization, and often exhibited a "pro-Western complex." At one level the attack on tradition may have been tactical, where culture was used as "a euphemism for political institutions that were too dangerous to attack openly...In spite of their heavy attack on Chinese history and tradition, most anti-traditionalists remained in their heart deeply nationalist. Their critique or even cynical treatment of their own past was one way of yearning for the re-creation of China's national greatness" (Zhao, 1997: 728). Following the end of the cold war, and the decline of communist ideology in China itself, the Chinese Communist Party increasingly staked its legitimacy on its role as the guardian of economic reform and national pride. Rapid economic growth boosted Chinese self-confidence, while increased contacts with the West, where tens of thousands of Chinese students flocked to study, and undisguised Western concerns about China's rise, lessened Chinese romanticization of the West.

Although nationalism obviously does not appeal to all Chinese intellectuals, and nationalist discourse is the source of ideological clashes and heated debates, most Chinese intellectuals are committed, Zhao (1997: 736) contends, "to make China rich and strong. China's reformist and revolutionary movements over the past century have essentially been born of the struggle to make the dream true." This is a dream African intellectuals also understand only too well. As will be demonstrated in several chapters in Volume Two, most African intellectuals, despite all their differences—and there are many, sometimes violently so—are committed to the three D's that have guided African nationalist thought since the nineteenth century: decolonization, development, and self-determination, although there has never been agreement on what each specifically entails.

The idea of nationalism evokes different intellectual reactions in different parts of the world. As K. S. Jomo (2000: 338) notes, "under more developed or advanced capitalism, nationalism is usually associated with chauvenism, reactionary jingoism, racism and even fascism, for obvious historical reasons. Some dissenters to this predominant view (e.g., Hobsbawm) have sought to assert the progressive potential and possibilities of patriotism, arguing that the left has incorrectly conceded this sphere to the right. The situation in the Third World, however, has been quite different with the general presumption being that nationalism was, in and of itself, basically progressive, though some exceptions might have been reluctantly conceded. Nationalism was primarily seen as a legitimate, in fact, necessarily progressive response to imperialism, whether or not it involved formal colonial rule." Given the failures of the postcolonial nationalist states, nationalism has lost some of its popularity in certain intellectual circles in the South.

Nevertheless, struggles for development and against global inequities and the unprecedented power of international corporations and financial institutions have renewed, now that socialism is in a deep coma, and are articulated in the language of economic nationalism. The idea of development, or the recent trope of sustainable development, remains central to the imaginary of the underdeveloped regions of the world. In fact, the project of development as a social good and development as a project that sustains academics have become more important than ever in so far as globalization in general recasts discourses about development and globalization in higher education restructures the conditions of intellectual production and reproduction. In many parts of the South, as will be shown in the case of Africa in the next chapter, thanks to the neoliberal reforms of structural adjustment, university wages are so low that many academics are forced to engage in consultancies, the bulk of which focus on development work, broadly defined.

In Bolivia, for example, we are told that "by the 1990s, nearly all social scientists with academic appointments...had come to rely on applied or contract work as a means of securing income. The 'NGO-ization' of social science work in Bolivia...was tied to development initiatives that were hoped to lessen the international donors who increasingly favored NGOs and preferred to avoid, at the most, to co-manage with government agencies and existing social organizations such as the worker unions and peasant leagues" (Zimmerer, 2000: 182). Critical intellectual work suffers as academics become fiercely competitive hustlers expected to confirm the prescriptions of the funders, and their reports, which gather dust in NGO and donor offices, replace publications that circulate in the public domain.

Thus, the consultancy syndrome, which on the surface appears to connect academics to the "real" world and blurs the academic-applied distinction, in effect represents the commercialization and deradicalization of academic work. Similarly, the unprecedented NGO boom, which has saved many academics from penury, stifles and fragments old social movements as much as it opens new spaces for civil society in the South and subordinates them to the singular demands of globalization and to the North in new ways (Zeleza and McConnaughay, 2002). Academics in the North also increasingly depend on external commercial sources, if not for their survival, for their research, so that they, too, have to juggle with the contradiction of being simultaneously implicated in corporate and neoliberal state agendas and talking back against their funders as critical intellectuals, of speaking truthfully to the powers that feed them.

In short, while the specificities of intellectual production, reproduction, and engagement might differ from one country to another, in the South and the North, some of the challenges are quite similar. There is, if you will, a globalization of assaults against intellectuals. Besides the imperative of making sense of the world, intellectuals, therefore, have a corporate interest to understand the conditions in which they find themselves in different parts of the world in order to devise strategies to respond to them as collectively and creatively as possible.

Conclusion

Globalization demands close attention from intellectuals, both analytical and political, because it is the dominant question of our age and a source of some of the changes reshaping the conditions of intellectual production. We must try to explain the flows and conjunctures and the actual workings of contemporary global capitalism, stripped of its ideological mystifications, which have been sprouting with the wild abandon of poisonous mushrooms. We must unravel the struggles against it; find, name, and analyze the voices from below, increasingly coalesced around transnational advocacy networks, pitted against globalization in its current configurations, and imagine alternatives that are more humane, more equitable, more sustainable, more democratic.

The implications of globalization for the social sciences are particularly acute. Long tied to the confines of the nation state and the disciplines, the spatial and conceptual complexities of our contemporary world demand international and interdisciplinary perspectives. Disciplinary anxieties are rising in the Eurocentric American academy and efforts to develop more comparative approaches are emerging from psychology, and anthropology to law, sociology, literary and cultural studies (Martinez, 1998). I agree with Emmanuel Wallerstein (1999: 154-5) that "we social scientists must totally transform ourselves or we shall become socially irrelevant and relegated to some minor corner of some minor academy condemned to while away our time in meaning-less rituals as the last monks of a forgotten god." Appadurai (2001) is also right that we must rethink the meanings of pedagogy, activism, and research in this new phase of globalization, specifically those of us located in the so-called area studies; we must develop new ways of internationalizing and democratizing research about globalization itself, and I would add, about other aspects of the human experience as well. We must seek to promote greater awareness and cross-fertilization between the research cultures, priorities, and styles of different regions as part of the struggle to promote knowledge of globalization that is derived from the globalization of knowledge.

Above all, we must regain our faith in, as Wallerstein advises, substantive rationality, abandon Eurocentricism, push for the epistemological reunification of the cultures of the humanities and the sciences, and reaffirm the possibility of applying human intelligence to human problems in order to achieve human potential in the continuing struggle for the good society. We must reclaim the nobler role of intellectuals as activist social critics, sufficiently equipped with analytical skills to explain the past and make sense of the present, and endowed with the moral imagination to envision a better future, to dream for what Richard Rorty (1997) calls a decent global society that contains dozens of worldviews. As African intellectuals we have a responsibility to bring to globalization discourses the experiences and expectations of our societies, and refrain from becoming mindless parrots for Northern perspectives, preoccupations, and paradigms, not in pursuit of narrow nationalisms or the dangerous myths and essentialisms of what Paul Gilroy (2000) calls raciology, but as part of the struggle to create a global civilization in which we as Africans, for so long victims of oppressive forces emanating from elsewhere, can feel at home.

Endnotes

1. One of these conferences was organized jointly with the South African Human Sciences Research Council and University of the Witwatersrand in Johannesburg in September 1998 where, interestingly enough, no black South African intellectuals were invited and other African intellectuals, including myself, were invited to be discussants of presentations by mostly postmodernist Northern scholars! Another was CODESRIA's 9th General Assembly in December 1998 held in Dakar, which was by most accounts, the worst general assembly in CODESRIA's history in terms of organization and intellectual import, perhaps demonstrating that globalization without clear local anchors is untenable. A vast amount of literature has emerged on globalization and Africa that examines the political, economic, cultural, and security implications. See for example, the studies by Kidane Mengisteab (1996), Keller and Rothchild (1996), and Richard Mshomba (2000). One of the most sensible interventions is by the historian Frederick Cooper (2001: 189), who declares categorically that "African history reveals the inadequacy of the concept of globalization."

2. For a detailed examination of the development and impact of information and telecommunication technologies in Africa see Paul Tiyambe Zeleza, Ilesami Adesida, and Ibulaimu Kakoma, eds. (2002).

3. The CIA also published and distributed books, organized high-profile academic conferences, and supported art exhibitions to promote abstract expressionism and vanquish socialist realism! The intellectuals and artists who, wittingly or unwittingly, received C.I.A. support included the philosophers Bertrand Russell and Isaiah Berlin; historian Arthur Schlesinger; poets Stephen Spender, Robert Lowell, T. S. Elliot and Cszelaw Milosz; painters Mark Rothko and Jackson Pollock; musicians Dizzy Gillespie, Leontyne Price and Nicolas Nabokov; novelists George Orwell, Arthur Koestler, Milovan Djilas, Vladimir Nabokov, Isak Dinesen, Peter Mathiessen, Robert Warren and Mary McCarthy; and critics Lionel and Diana Trilling, Irving Kristol, Melvin Lasky, and Sidney Hook. The journals that benefitted from CIA programs included *The Partisan Review, The Hudson Review,* the *Sewanee Review, Poetry, Daedalus, The Kenyon Review,* and *Encounter* in England, *Der Monat* in West

Germany, *Preuves* in France, *Transition* in Uganda, and several others elsewhere. Reviewers of Saunders' book have generally been unsympathetic: some have expressed mild surprise at the extent to which the CIA had set itself up as a national endowment for the arts (Lapham, 2000), bemusement that she lacks the sympathetic imagination for the realities of the time (Beauchamp, 2001; Coleman, 1999), fails to understand that the CIA campaign was designed to subsidize not suppress ideas, that it did not compromise anyone's intellectual freedom even if some may have been duped (De Neufville (2000; Draper, 2000), and that she displays typical leftist arrogance and a failure to appreciate that the West won the cold war after all because organizations like the CIA have done good work (Puddington, 2000).

4. Some African Americans prefer the term womanist to feminist in a gesture of discursive and racial difference. See Allan (1995).

5. Robert Johnston (2000) reports his dismay at discovering, during graduate student struggles for unionization at Yale (graduate student TA's do a lot of teaching on American campuses) that his colleagues, who "had produced prodigious amounts of wonderful—and plenty of left-wing—scholarship" showed either opposition, hostility, or apathy to student unionization efforts.

Chapter 2

African Universities and Intellectuals: Promises, Perils, and Politics

Introduction

Politics affects all our lives, our social relations and practices as citizens and academics, as creators and consumers of cultures and commodities, as the producers, practitioners, and prey of power, as objects and subjects of knowledge. Each social and spatial sphere has its own politics, its own production, practices, and performances of power, from the family to the firm, the school to the state, the local neighborhood to the United Nations, always filtered and enacted through the contexts, complexities, and contradictions of class, gender, ethnicity, nationality, religion, and other social markers. This chapter examines the promises, perils, and politics of African universities and intellectuals, arguing that in most African countries the development of universities has been firmly tied to the vagaries of state politics and policies, the shifting missions and mandates of international donor agencies, and the unpredictable demands and dislocations of civil society. Equally critical are the internal challenges, the cultures of the universities themselves, their goals and governance, management of resources and infrastructures, their capacities to pursue intellectual excellence and equity, political autonomy and public accountability, local relevance and international recognition. Specifically, African social scientists have been caught in the bind of addressing African realities in borrowed languages and paradigms, conversing with each other through publications and media controlled by foreign academic communities, and producing prescriptive knowledge for the political kingdom, which four decades after its invention is still to realize its triple dreams of development, democracy, and self-determination.

If, as rumored, we have entered the new age of globalization and of the knowledge economy, where the protection of national boundaries and production of raw materials are no longer critical for the wealth or poverty of nations, then higher education has to be seen as "basic education" in a world where research and development is more critical than ever. Let me hasten to add that as a historian, I do not think globalization began the other day with CNN or yesterday with the Internet. The challenge for Africa's intellectuals, leaders, and assorted friends is to map out modes of integration onto an unfolding global system that will maximize, not further marginalize, the interests of the continent's peoples and polities, economies and environments, societies and cultures.

This chapter is divided into four parts. The first outlines the remarkable growth of African universities since independence. The second looks at the role external forces, i.e., forces outside the universities, principally the state, foreign donors, and civil society have played in the development of African universities and in the execution of social science research. The third part examines the challenges within the universities themselves and some of the recent reforms that are being implemented. The final part focuses more specifically on the conditions and commitments of African intellectuals. While many of the intellectuals referred to in this chapter are connected to universities, as argued in chapter 1, not all intellectuals are confined to, nor even products of, the universities.

The Promises of Uhuru

The educational achievements of independent Africa are as impressive as the challenges are intimidating. In 1960, the putative year of African independence, only 9 percent of the African population was literate, rising to about 60 percent four decades later. Taking the sub-Saharan region alone, excluding North Africa, gross enrolment ratios rose from 45 percent in 1965 to 74 percent in 1995 for primary schools, from 5 percent to 35 percent for secondary schools, and from 1 percent to 3 percent for tertiary institutions. The equivalent figures for North Africa and the so-called Middle East were 62 percent to 94 percent for primary schools, 20 percent to 62 percent for secondary schools, and 3 percent to 15 percent for tertiary institutions (World Bank, 2000: 107). Thus, many more schools and universities were established in the first four decades after colonialism than in a century of imperial rule.

When the colonial powers departed, the bulk of African countries did not even have a single university. Indeed, in many countries the number of university graduates could be counted in the dozens, perhaps hundreds, but rarely in the thousands. At independence in 1960, populous Nigeria had one lonely university at Ibadan, one of the four regional university colleges, modeled on Oxbridge, that Britain belatedly set up in 1948 in its African colonies to produce skilled professional elites to serve a maturing colonial capitalism and to save it from the dangerous agitation of the nationalist masses. The other three institutions of higher learning were the University College of Ghana, the University College of Khartoum, and Makerere University College (Ajayi et al., 1996; Nwauwa, 1997). Four decades later Nigeria boasted forty-three universities, thirty of them founded after 1978 during the oil boom years, as well as sixty-nine polytechnics, colleges of technology and of education. Twenty-nine of the universities were federal, eleven state, and three private. Altogether, student enrollment rose from 2,000 in 1960 to 404,969 in 1995, a phenomenal growth by any standard (Eribo, 1996: 64; Ejiaga, 2001: 4). By the mid-1990s, Sudan had thirty-six universities, a third of them private, many focused on specific skills (Morna, 1995).

Similar impressive achievements were recorded in the three East African countries of Kenya, Tanzania, and Uganda, which initially shared Makerere University College and later the University of East Africa. As national identities burgeoned and developmental ambitions rose, the university split into three national universities in 1970 Three decades later the number of universities in each of the three countries had skyrocketed. For example, formerly socialist Tanzania had established nine universities, seven university colleges, and twelve other institutions of higher learning (Mkunde, 2001: 28). The expansion of higher education in Kenya was equally spectacular. By 2000 there were six public universities, eight private universities, four national polytechnics, and dozens of technological, professional, and educational institutions, and research institutes and centers. Enrollment in Kenyan universities rose quite sharply from 12,986 in 1980 to 67,371 in 1995 (World Bank, 2000: 111). Uganda also witnessed a remarkable growth in the number of higher education institutions, so that by the beginning of 2001 there were fifteen universities, four public and eleven private, eleven national teachers' colleges, fourteen paramedical schools, six polytechnics and technical colleges, 6 colleges of commerce, and a handful of other colleges specializing in forestry, hotel management, and so on. The expansion in student enrolment can be seen in the case of Makerere, the country's flagship university, which rose from the ashes from the mid-1990s. Undergraduate enrollment at Makerere increased from 9,231 in 1996 to 16,289 in 2000, and graduate enrollment from 1,144 to 1,540 (Ssebuwufu, 2001: 19).

Rapid growth in university enrollments was witnessed across the continent. Altogether, the number of tertiary students in Africa more than trebled from 782,503 in 1975 to 3,461,822 in 1995, an average increase of 17 percent per annum, compared to an average world growth rate of 5 percent. The largest concentration of university students was in Egypt (850,051 in 1995), followed by South Africa (617,897), Nigeria (404,969), Algeria (347,410), and Morocco (294,502) (World Bank, 2000: 111). Between them the five countries accounted for nearly three-quarters of African students in tertiary institutions. In contrast, there were 23 countries with fewer than 10,000 university students in 1995. Thus, the size and scale of university systems varied enormously among African countries. Cairo University with its 155,000 students and nearly 8,000 faculty members—making it one of the largest universities in the world—had more students and academics than many of these countries combined.

There were also sharp gender differentials in terms of access to university education. While several countries had managed to attain gender parity at the primary and secondary levels by 2000, very few had managed to do so at the tertiary level. The exceptions were Botswana, Lesotho, Swaziland, Namibia, and South Africa. Females made up 34 percent, 22 percent and 12 percent of primary, secondary, and tertiary level students across the continent as a whole (Meena, 2001: 4-5). To be sure, gradual improvements were recorded in some countries. For example, at Makerere female admissions increased from 27 percent in 1990-91 to about 40 percent in 1999-2000 (Ssebuwufu, 2001: 19), while at the University of Dar es Salaam, where an affirmative action program for female students was introduced, it increased from 13 percent to 16 percent between 1994 and 1997 (Meena, 2001: 7).

The gender gap also manifested itself in fields of study and faculty distribution. Women were concentrated in the humanities and social sciences, while they were grossly underrepresented in the sciences and most of the professional fields. Between 1994 and 1997 female enrollment in the sciences as a percentage of the total female enrollment in the tertiary sector ranged from 6.5 percent in Chad, 9.1 percent in Tanzania, 12.6 percent in Benin, 14 percent in Zimbabwe, and 16.7 percent in Uganda, to 32.4 percent in Tunisia, and 36.8 percent in South Africa (UNDP, 2000: 258). The percentage of female faculty was even lower than that of female students, even in countries that had achieved enrollment gender parity. At the University of Dar es Salaam in Tanzania, for instance, women made up 11 percent of the faculty in 1999/2000 (down from 12.5 percent in 1997/98), while at Abdou Moumouni University in Niger they made up only 9.7% (Meena, 2001: 12). Needless to say, the female academics were crowded in the lower ranks and in the humanities and "soft" social science disciplines.

As multi-ethnic, sometimes multi-racial, and invariably class societies, access to university education in African countries was further differentiated according to ethnicity, race, and class, as well as, in some cases, to religious and cultural affiliations. Class became increasingly salient as the African middle classes grew after independence, in many cases thanks to the establishment or expansion of university education itself, and sought to reproduce themselves. When I attended the University of Malawi in the early 1970s many of my fellow students were from rural and peasant backgrounds, few were from the then minuscule middle class. Today, it is our children, the children of middle class parents who tend to predominate. Incidentally, the ravages of structural adjustment programs, which have pauperized many sections of the middle classes, have reinforced the chase for middle class credentials that university degrees provide. Thanks to massive currency devaluations these credentials can no longer be obtained easily from abroad, hence the intense pressure to expand university education at the same time as financial resources have diminished. Expansion has also been prompted by political calculations to spread the fruits of uhuru across regions and ethnic groups. Thus, much of the expansion noted above was based on a mismatch between enrollments and resources, leading to growth without development, to use a phrase from the development literature of the 1970s. There were severe strains on physical and pedagogical infrastructures, which resulted in declining quality and morale. To many of the academics subsisting on teaching overload and starvation wages, their universities were no better than glorified highschools.

The mix of gender, race, and class as differentiating and discriminatory markers of access to higher education are particularly potent in postapartheid South Africa. Apartheid institutionalized racial hierarchies and inequalities at all levels of the educational system and created an unwieldy and costly bureaucracy. Demands for educational reform and redress ranked high after 1994. Postapartheid South Africa found itself with well-endowed white universities, that had little moral and political legitimacy, and poorly endowed black universities that had little academic credibility (Moja and Cloete, 1996). The challenges of transforming and rationalizing this racialized and structurally differentiated system, while protecting academic freedom and raising the quality of teaching and learning, were truly Herculean (Cloete and Bunting, 2000; Higgins, 2000; Vidovitch et al., 2000). By the end of the decade, much had changed in the social composition and curricula of universities, indeed a new institutional landscape was emerging and the old category differences were disappearing.[1] However, a lot more remained to be done to create a system that would serve the new democratic order and the humanistic values of the liberation movements, and that would meet the challenges of economic and social development in a new globalized environment.

Using the old apartheid designations, between 1993 and 1999 African tertiary enrollment increased from 40 percent to 59 percent, while it declined from 47 percent to 29 percent for whites, remained steady at 7 percent for Indians, and declined slightly from 6 percent to 5 percent for coloreds. The changes in student composition occurred in a context in which enrollments in the historically black or disadvantaged institutions fell sharply—by 22 percent between 1998 and 2000, while they rose 6 percent in the historically white universities (HWUs), implying a demographic drift from the former to the latter. By 2000, black students constituted half of the students at the HWUs taken together, and they were in the clear majority at four, were even at one, and close to half in two, and were less than a third at only two others.[2] The proportion of black students was even higher at the historically white technikons, reaching 76 percent in 2000. Overall enrollments, however, fell short of projections because of poor highschool graduation results, financial constraints, and declining retention rates. The latter is variously attributed to the fact that large numbers of students from the enrollment bulge of the mid-1990s graduated, high failure rates for poorly prepared students and financial constraints for good students, and fewer students pursuing graduate studies immediately after completion (Balintulo,

2000; Cloete and Bunting, 2000: 9-16).

Changes in faculty composition were much slower. Between 1993 and 1998, the numbers of African faculty increased from 7 percent to 12 percent, 4 percent to 5 percent for Indians, and remained steady at 3 percent for coloreds. These averages, of course, hide significant differences among universities. In 1999, blacks constituted 5 percent of the full-time academic staff and 6 percent of the executive and support professionals at the historically white Afrikaans universities, 21 percent and 27 percent at the historically white English universities, and 60 percent and 65 percent at the historically black universities. University administrators in the HWUs sought refuge in arguments that qualified black academics were simply not there, or they preferred better paying jobs in industry and government, or could not adjust to the universities' institutional culture. They were reluctant to admit that there were severe shortcomings with the institutional culture itself that alienated many black academics, including those already there, hence their high turnover. The difficulties of retention not only affected South African blacks, but also immigrant intellectuals from other parts of the continent, whose numbers increased, who were often appalled by the institutional racism and intellectual myopia of the South African universities. One of the most renowned cases is that of the struggle between the eminent Ugandan political scientist, Mahmood Mamdani, and his colleagues at the University of Cape Town regarding the composition of an African Studies curriculum (Mamdani, 1998a, 1998b; also see Chachage, 1999).

The HWUs formed "transformation forums" to respond to demands by African students and academics for changes in the composition, curricula, and culture of the universities, but the affirmative action programs showed limited results either because of poor conception or poor implementation or both. Responses to affirmative action range from support to opposition. As in the United States, although they are obvious historical, demographic, and political differences between the two countries, the supporters of affirmative action see it as a means to address past or current discrimination and to promote diversity among students and faculty, while its opponents reject it as "reverse discrimination" or for stigmatizing its beneficiaries. Such is the ambivalence that the University of Stellenbosch, the bastion of Afrikaner intellectuals who designed apartheid as an affirmative action program for poor whites, refused to use the term affirmative action for its program, preferring to call it "staff broadening policy." No wonder that in 1995

71

Stellenbosch had only five black academics, one more than in 1983 (Lindsay, 1997; Mabokela, 2000; Vergnani, 1998; Hugo, 1998).

Also unequal were changes in the gender gap, although affirmative action programs adopted by most universities were primarily concerned with addressing racial inequalities. Female enrollments increased by 44 percent between 1993 and 1999, from 202,000 in 1993 to 291,000 in 1999, while male enrollments reached a peak of 305,000 in 1995 and declined to 273,000, so that in 1999 female representation was 52 percent, up from 43 percent in 1993. The number of female faculty in the universities rose relatively slowly, from 30 percent in 1992 to 35 percent in 1999, the bulk of them swamped at the rank of lecturer and below. In fact, women outnumbered men at these ranks, while men vastly outnumbered women at the higher ranks from senior lecturer to full professor (Balintulo, 2000; Cloete and Bunting, 2000). Despite their rising numbers, South African female academics found themselves, as elsewhere, marginalized and excluded in the predominantly masculinist institutional cultures and discursive regimes of higher education. This being South Africa, however, female academic identities and careers were also marked by race and class, which complicated gender relations and solidarities, leading to the bitter contestations between white and black women feminists over questions of representation—the underrepresentation of black women academics, the misrepresentation of black women's experience by white women, and the claims by women academics to represent the broader women's movement (Daymond, 1996; Walker, 1997; 1998; Hassim and Walker, 1998; Allan, 2001).

The rapid expansion of education across the continent not only led to a massive improvement in the African human capital stock, it also laid the institutional basis for the social production of African intellectual capacities, communities, and commitments. But the constraints, contradictions, and confusions of African education remained daunting; indeed, they deepened as one country after another faced the recessions of development and democracy, conditions exacerbated by the imposition of draconian structural adjustment programs (SAPs), which threatened to decompose the social fruits of *uhuru*. Despite the massive educational expansion since independence, Africa remains the least educated continent in the world, with a gross higher education enrollment ration of less than 5 percent, as compared to 10 percent for the low-and middle-income countries and 58 percent for the high income countries.

The Perils of Dependency

As with other social phenomena, the educational enterprise in Africa is, therefore, a tale of triumphs, trials, and tribulations, a stirring and searing story of perpetual struggle punctuated by sporadic successes and setbacks. From the 1980s, the setbacks outweighed the successes, as the struggles for the reproduction, regulation, and relevance of university education faced unprecedented challenges that were, simultaneously, institutional and intellectual, political and pecuniary, moral and managerial. Three powerful external forces set the conditions and contexts for African universities as sites and systems of knowledge production. They are: the state, international donor agencies, and civil society. All three exerted, in various measures, pecuniary and political pressures that affected the operations of universities, including research.

Most obvious is the role of the state. At their inception the vast majority of African universities were public institutions created, financed, and controlled by the state. Although a few universities existed before the twentieth century, including the ancient Islamic universities of northern Africa and Western-style universities in West Africa and South Africa, the current wave of university construction began during the twilight years of colonial rule. The post-Second World War universities were small in size, dominated by expatriates, and created in the curricula image of Oxbridge or the Sorbonne, although they were seen more as teaching than research institutions. By design and default they were regional universities. The explosion of universities after independence did little to alter their technocratic mission inherited from the colonial university, although it was now reconfigured to facilitate the realization of the dreams of uhuru: development and nation-building. To be sure, efforts were made with varying degrees of seriousness and success to domesticate and nationalize school structures, syllabuses, standards, and staff. Nonetheless, the celebration and excitement hid an uncomfortable reality, that the universities were, according to a memorable phrase by Thandika Mkandawire's (1997b:17), "born in chains." One set of chains was institutional, the other intellectual.

Institutionally, the universities were held on a tight leash by the state, which saw them simultaneously as cathedrals of cultural authenticity and local assembly plants of Western modernity. The role of the state remained one of control rather than of supervision. In short, governments sought to manage universities "in the same way they managed roads, the army, or customs....The tendency of politicians to intervene in higher education left many institutions hostage to factional policies, with decisions on student selection, faculty appointments and promotions, curriculum design, and similar matters made on political grounds rather than on merit" (World Bank, 2000: 63). Initially, many African academics bought the developmentalist mission, not simply because the universities were fiscally dependent on the state, or that the postcolonial leviathan could whip them into submission; rather they, too, were intoxicated by the immense possibilities of national independence, whatever their preferred ideological fix, whether socialism, capitalism, or a concoction of the two. Moreover, at the time the moral and intellectual credentials of the nationalists were high, and the academics always felt compromised in their gaudy Oxbridge gowns. After all, far more universities were established in the first twenty-five years of independence than in a century of colonial neglect; but the totalizing language of nationalism brooked no opposition to the national will incarnated in the state. Nation-building and developmentalism became the central paradigms in African and Africanist research. National memories and uniformities were invented. Each social science discipline, from anthropology and history to economics and political science, sought to chronicle the teleological march of African cultures, societies, economies, and polities from "tradition" to "modernity," from the pitfalls of underdevelopment to the possibilities of development, from colonial lack to postcolonial fulfilment, from the stasis of being to the agency of becoming.

Thus, in the heady years immediately after independence academics were as enchanted as the nationalist leaders were by the totalizing dreams of nation-building and development and contributed, advertently or not, to the construction of an authoritarian ideological edifice that would later consume them. Many of them also believed in the importance of basic research as a means of not only writing Africa into the empirical and theoretical corpus of the imported Eurocentric disciplines, but of promoting scientific and technological development. Relations turned sour as the challenges of nation-building and development proved intractable, as authoritarianism grew and as African studies became more radicalized. To be sure, traffic between the classroom and the cabinet continued. Indeed, it could be argued that the rising tensions in university-state relations reflected the narcissism of minor difference; an intraclass struggle by the elite for the hearts and minds of African peoples.

To be sure, there were also structural forces at work. The missions of the political class and the intelligentsia began to diverge as the technocratic agenda assigned to the universities to produce skilled professionals and workers for the indiginization of the state bureaucracy and the "formal" economy was increasingly achieved given the small size of most African countries and economies and as economic growth slowed down from the mid-1970s. The university lost its mission, at least in the eyes of those who pulled the purse strings. Reinforcing the divergence was the nationalization of the university labor market in the 1970s as the interterritorial universities, such as the University of East Africa, the University of Botswana, Lesotho, and Swaziland, and the regional university systems in Francophone Africa were dissolved into national universities, which enabled the state to tighten its hold over the universities. Subsequent expansion and Africanization of staff and curriculum did not halt the slide towards the parochialization and politicization of African universities, nor was it always translated into the development of an organic intelligentsia, that is intellectuals who were seen as critical to the articulation of the state project. Then in the 1980s structural adjustment programs were imposed with neo-classical zeal by the World Bank and IMF. These programs forced or facilitated states to reduce their fiscal responsibilities to the universities. The combined effect was to undermine the autonomy of academics and the capacities of universities to support basic research.

Besides the fact that the state was suspicious and dismissive of academics, often seeing them as purveyors of "foreign ideology," repressive politics left little room for the latter to occupy public space or to engage in critical discourse openly. Moreover, the tendency by some African rulers to see themselves as philosopher kings reduced intellectual work to sycophancy. They underestimated the intellectual and political complexity of the processes of building and developing the political kingdom. For its part, much African academic research appeared to the state functionaries "irrelevant," either because it was not "applied" research, or because African academics were adversarial, especially those who expected imminent revolution, or because they blindly followed western research themes that did not address local conditions. Also, African governments relied on foreign expatriates for development models and research. The relatively easy access to foreign expertise, bankrolled by the international financial institutions and donor agencies, enabled Africa's repressive governments to lower the short-term costs of intellectual repression, which led to the ironic situation whereby these governments could only access their own academics through donor-contracted reports (Mkandawire 1999; Mazrui, 1978; Diouf and Mamdani, 1994; Ngara, 1995; Ajayi et al., 1996; and Prah, 1997).

These trends worsened in the "lost decade" of the 1980s. Tendentious studies questioned the cost-effectiveness of universities, arguing that higher education offered lower private and social returns than primary education, so that public interest in universities was substantially lower than in primary schools. So powerful did this misguided gospel become that at least one country "seriously contemplated closing its only university as a matter of policy and many others maintained an ambivalent attitude towards the tertiary sector" (Smallwood and Maliyamkono, 1996: 326). The rate-of-return studies were based on narrow and dubious calculations, which now, even the World Bank itself acknowledges. They "treat educated people," to quote a report cosponsored by the Bank and UNESCO,

> "as valuable only through their higher earnings and greater tax revenues extracted by society. But educated people clearly have many other effects on society: educated people are well positioned to be economic and social entrepreneurs, having a far-reaching impact on the economic and social well-being of their communities. They are also vital to creating an environment in which economic development is possible. Good governance, strong institutions, and a developed infrastructure are all needed if business is to thrive—and none of these is possible without highly educated people. Finally, rate-of-return analysis entirely misses the impact of university-based research on the economy—a far-reaching social benefit that is at the heart of any argument for developing strong higher education systems." (World Bank, 2000: 39).

If this critique is any indication, it appears that the World Bank's fidelity to educational voodoo-economics might be changing, although that seems unlikely, as the damage has already been done.

Clearly, foreign donors have had a profound impact on African universities and research. Their role increased rapidly from the 1980s as state support diminished, for there were no other major alternative sources of research funds, not from industry, or alumni, as is common in the United States; foreign industry conducted the bulk of its research back home, while the African bourgeoisie was too mired in "primitive accumulation" and had yet to develop the habits of public institutional charity. In many countries the "Link," as K. F. Hirji (1990: 9-16) calls relations with foreign donors, became indispensable for research funding, conferences, the provision of equipment, books, and much-needed income. Their relative freedom from domestic political constraints also enabled them to fund research themes that no local authority would consider. Moreover, because of their high standing and influence they sometimes shielded their research grantees from harassment and persecution by the local authorities. In certain circumstances they were even able to offer support and haven to fleeing or beleaguered scholars.

The volume and value of support from the major foundations for African universities and research has been quite considerable. For example, the Ford Foundation alone made 259 grants totaling $52.7 million between 1990 and 1999 in fifteen African countries to universities and NGOs.[3] According to Teboho Moja (2000), these grants supported a wide range of research activities, teaching and curriculum innovation, university administrative reform, staff development, and community development. Much of the research was in the social sciences and policy-oriented. It was disseminated through conferences, workshops, and publications. While lauding the foundation for its activities, Moja (2000: 29) argues that "support to research in Africa has been mainly for applied research that addressed issues of concern to society. Africa has not been a significant contributor or beneficiary of the knowledge revolution. Countries in Africa like other developing countries have fallen behind in their ability to create or access knowledge needed for modernizing economies." Specifically, she noted that knowledge developed with foundation support "is seldom distributed through the electronic media," and that "there is also limited interaction amongst grant recipients working in the same area to exchange ideas and improve the quality of their work" (Moja, 2000: 27).

This critical assessment is echoed by David Court, a long-serving representative of the Rockefeller Foundation in Nairobi. The Rockefeller Foundation spent $33.1 million in funding African research during the same period, much of it in the biomedical and agricultural sciences. He candidly admits that the relationship between the donor and the recipient is inherently unequal. "One has resources, the other would like them. In order to gain access the applicant can hardly avoid adjusting the manner of his approach to accord with the known or perceived preferences of the donor in a process of self-restriction and hence reduction of freedom" (Court, 1990: 9). Needless to say, "changes in donor interests are bound to provoke a corresponding response by scholars leading them to take on topics which are of lower personal or institutional priority than those on the external agendas" (Court, 1990: 10).

Thus the donors frequently set the research agenda, often based on the research priorities and paradigms in their home countries. Despite periodic shifts in topics and emphasis, research supported by external donors has tended towards applied social science at the expense of basic research. The work of many African social scientists has been reduced to consultancy and short-term contract work, which "usually appears in reports that do not become part of the public domain or open to wider intellectual discourse" (Court, 1990:10). Undoubtedly this has contributed to, to quote Mkandawire (1989:12), "the creation of fragmented and non-cumulative social science...the executive summaries and reports replace articles and books." In the process the continent's ability to define itself and the quality of African scholarship may have suffered. Donors have succeeded in turning many of Africa's brightest social scientists into what James Petras (1990:7) calls, with reference to Latin American intellectuals, institutional intellectual entrepreneurs who "live in an externally dependent world, sheltered by payments in hard currency and income derived independently of local circumstances...[and] write for and work within the confines of other institutional intellectuals, their overseas patrons [and] their international conferences...."

African academics cannot, of course, be entirely blamed for moonlighting in the worlds of consultancies and the informal sector faced as they are by low pay and recruitment and of reward structures marred by corruption, patronage, and politicization. I vividly recall when teaching in Kenya in the 1980s, the juggling I had to do to cling to a rapidly evaporating middle class lifestyle. In addition to my formal job at Kenyatta University, I also taught courses thirty miles away at the Catholic University of Eastern Africa, and learned to hustle my talents to foundations on projects that meant little to me as a historian. Needless to say, my research suffered. In my six years at the Kenyatta University I witnessed the research and teaching environment deteriorate at the same time as the university system, both public and private, was undergoing unbridled, unplanned, and often chaotic expansion. Classrooms became overcrowded, teaching loads expanded, research funds virtually dried up, and political intervention intensified as the Moi regime was faced with an increasingly restive civil society and political opposition.

To these challenges academics responded in several ways. There was the internal and external "brain drain" as they fled from the universities to other sectors at home or to universities abroad, or turned into consultancy hustlers and informal sector hawkers. Prematurely retired or part-time university academics established an intellectually vibrant and autonomous academic NGO sector, composed of continental, subregional, and national research networks and organizations– one of the most exciting developments on the African intellectual scene in the 1980s and 1990s. In the social sciences such organizations as the Dakar-based Council for the Development of Social Science Research in Africa (CODESRIA), the Addis Ababa-based Organization of Social Science Research in Eastern Africa (OSSREA), the Harare-based Southern African Political Economy Series (SAPES) Trust, and the Center for Basic Research (CBR) in Uganda were founded or expanded. Some of the best work in the African social sciences was increasingly produced by academics connected to these research institutes and networks.

The natural sciences were even better organized and funded. In addition to the numerous African branches of international research centers, including many sponsored by UN agencies, there were the centers founded by African scientists. Among them the International Centre for Research in Agroforestry (ICRAF) founded in1977; the world-famous International Center of Insect Physiology and Ecology (ICIPE), founded in 1970 but incorporated as an intergovernmental organization in 1986; and the African Academy of Sciences established in 1985, all founded in Nairobi, the last two by the renowned Kenyan scientist Thomas Odhiambo, a former professor at the University of Nairobi. Most of these institutes and centers, unlike the universities, have state of the art equipment and are on the cutting edge of research in their respective fields.

Thus, the independent research centers increasingly became central players on the African research landscape and in the production, dissemination, and consumption of scholarly knowledge. They were products of both the successes and failures of African universities. Undoubtedly, they provided crucial support for basic and applied research, much of it conducted by, or subcontracted to, especially in the social sciences, university-based academics. They also offered training, internships, and fellowships to graduate students, particularly in the natural sciences. Nevertheless, their facilities for research and training were too limited to serve as a realistic alternative to the universities. Moreover, most of these centers were largely dependent on foreign funding agencies. Thus, while they helped expand intellectual and ideological spaces, they substituted dependency on the state for dependency on foreign donors that imposed its own constraints.

The "brain drain" from the universities was not confined to the independent research centers or to other occupations in the private and public sectors. It also extended to increased academic mobility across countries, a subject discussed in the next chapter. The majority of African academics of course, remained in their countries and tried to fight for better conditions of work and living. In the 1980s and 1990s, strikes and other protests by both students and staff increased. During the five and half years that I taught at Kenyatta University, there was a major student strike every academic year, which led to closure of the campus for varying lengths of time. Underlying the protests were broad political, economic, and social causes, although they were often triggered by campus complaints against administrative authoritarianism and poor living and learning conditions.[4] Several years after I left, between November 1993 and 1994, about 3,700 faculty at Kenya's then four public universities, including Kenyatta, went on strike when the government refused to register their union despite the apparent liberalization of the political system (Atteh, 1996: 38).

Some of the most spirited academic and democratic struggles took place in Nigeria under Babangida's and Abacha's tyrannical regimes. Over three dozen riots occurred between 1980 and 1996, including the widespread student crisis in 1988, the antistructural adjustment riots in 1989, and the prodemocracy riots between 1990 and 1993. The strike wave resumed later in the decade as the prodemocracy movement mobilized against Abacha's unprecedented reign of terror. Faculty protests were spearheaded by powerful academic unions that, in the 1970s, concentrated on promoting the rights, needs, and aspirations of the rapidly expanding professoriate, and, in the 1980s, protected them from the deepening crisis in the university system (Jega, 1996). Campus and nationwide faculty strikes and other forms of protest increasingly became common. In one university the faculty resigned en masse to protest the unfair dismissal and harassment of some of their colleagues.

The state responded to student and faculty protests with both the sticks of repression and the carrots of reform or cooptation. In 1991, for example, rioting students were shot and killed at the universities of Yaounde in Cameroon and Lubumbashi in the former Zaire, while in Gabon, Togo,

Swaziland, Nigeria, and Côte d'Ivoire many students were beaten, arrested, and detained (Domatob, 1996: 32). In Nigeria, between 1985 and 1993, more than 100 students were killed, 1,000 were imprisoned, and hundreds more suspended. Soon after, the National Association of Nigerian Students and the Academic Staff Union of Universities were banned. Striking faculty members were treated no better. In May 1992 when the universities were closed for six months, hundreds of faculty were fired, imprisoned, and evicted from their houses (Atteh, 1996: 38).

As they were harassing and persecuting their own faculty, some governments turned to international scabs, the ubiquitous development experts provided by bilateral and multilateral aid donors. According to some estimates, by the mid-1980s, there were as many as 100,000 foreign experts working in the sub-Saharan region alone, excluding North Africa, some of them in the universities. None of the repressive measures succeeded in stemming the rising tide of opposition to authoritarian rule. In short, universities became hotbeds of the struggles for democracy, which, from the 1980s, began to rock one African country after another. But not all students and faculty protests and activism were progressive. Some were incited by cynical politicians and agents provocateur. Most tragically, on Nigerian campuses violent student cults terrorized fellow students and faculty, committing acts of rape, murder, and wanton destruction of property. The fact that they targeted student union leaders and radical academics, were well-armed, included among their members children of powerful people, and were treated with leniency by Nigeria's fierce police and autocratic university administrations led many to believe that the cults, which originally started as social clubs, were patronized by the military regime and vice-chancellors anxious to destroy student unionism (Babaleye, 1998; Jason, 1998; *Tempo*, 1999).

Besides coercive state control and growing donor dependency, African academics have also had to contend with the sanctions and sanctimoniousness of civil society. Forgetting for one minute the arcane debates about the meaning of civil society in the African context (Mamdani, 1995; Comaroff, 1999), African academics clearly are linked to various social groups whose interests and prejudices they often articulate. As knowledge workers, they are both connected to and divorced from working people; connected through their socialization and representation of the various groups they identify with, and divorced because of the social distance engendered by the nature of academic work and the cultural distance generated by the use of European languages, which they share with the political class, but which are not the languages of ordinary people's day-to-day social communication. As Ali Mazrui (1994: 21) reminds us, outside of North Africa the concept of an African Marxist, economist, physicist, or any other scientist who does not speak a European language, or an academic conference conducted primarily in an African language is, for the time being, "sociologically impossible."

Virtually all of Africa's fifty-four countries are multicultural, multiethnic, multilingual, and multi-religious thanks to the fiat of European colonial map making. This calls for creative management and negotiation of the jostling social forces, to which African academics are tied. Universities and research agendas are not immune from the structured social inscriptions of civil society, whether of ethnicity, gender, or class. Cultural groups and norms have been known to place constraints on "permissible" fields of study and discourse. As is well known, numerous overt and covert limitations are placed on research and discussion of women's and gender issues (Imam, Mama and Sow, 1997). Also common have been restrictions on questions of sexuality frowned upon by both Christian and Islamic extremists. Religious questions usually provoke ire from the groups concerned. Thus, despite their linkages to the state through employment and civil society through socialization, African academics often find themselves being "organic" to neither.

The case of Algeria demonstrates the complex interpenetration of the repressive capacities and propensities of both the state and civil society. It also shows how reactionary forces unleashed by struggles for democracy can appropriate the political space opened up if the democratic movement has no social project fundamentally different from that of the discredited regime. Once acclaimed as a model of Third World socialist development, state repression in Algeria gave way to religious persecution and detentions were replaced by assassinations. Rocked by riots in 1988 once the flow of petrodollars slumped, which had sustained the bureaucratic system, the shell of autocracy cracked. The future, it seemed, belonged to the popular movement, to democracy. The intellectuals were a cheerful lot; but their "epistemological optimism," as Ali El Kenzi (1996: 45) calls it, proved premature. Obsessed with state violence and violations of freedom, they failed to see and to scrutinize the tyrannical impulses of the Islamists. In fact, both they and the state were taken by surprise. To the state, it was the left, the activist intellectuals, who posed a threat, and so it concentrated its terrorizing surveillance on them; indeed, it promoted the expansion of religious activity as a counterbalance and an outlet for mounting social and political discontent. Using their vast network of mosques, educational and charitable associations, the Islamists seized more public and rhetorical space, turning popular discourse from the economic and social to the religious and moral. For them conquest of state power was only part of the journey towards the systematic transformation of society, of its representations and values. They wanted a cultural revolution. Secular intellectuals, as bearers of a contrary cultural formation, as masters of competing social meanings, endangered the hegemonic ambitions of the Islamists and became their prime targets.

There is no clearer indication that, for better or worse, universities are an integral part of their societies than the impact of the HIV/AIDS pandemic on African universities. A report on HIV/AIDS in seven universities in six countries,[5] commissioned by the Association for the Development of Education in Africa (ADEA), makes grim reading (Kelly, 2001). The report notes that although no one knows for sure HIV/AIDS morbidity rates at the seven universities, given the cloak of secrecy, silence, denial, and fear of stigmatization and discrimination, there are enough indications that the universities have not been spared. Campus mortality rates have increased, and although it would be rash to attribute everything to AIDS, they are higher than they ever were before the pandemic. For example, the universities of Zambia and Nairobi have been experiencing an average monthly death rate of three and four to six people, respectively, higher than before. Altogether, the former reported 352 deaths in the period from 1990 to1999, of whom two-thirds were male and one-third female, and one-eighth were academic and the rest nonacademic. While AIDS-related student deaths are also reported, its real impact tends to unfold after they have graduated and entered the workforce.

To be sure, HIV/AIDS impacts the affected universities directly and indirectly. They incur more direct costs through increased financial outlays for benefits, recruiting, training and health programs, indirect costs from absenteeism and lowered workforce productivity, and systemic costs from reduced overall skills, experience, and morale. Teaching and research are also affected as experienced staff are lost and workloads increase for others. The economic, social, and demographic impact of the pandemic on the wider society also affects the universities. Taking care of family members suffering from HIV/AIDS reduces household incomes that might be invested in education, while AIDS deaths leave behind growing numbers of orphans who have limited resources for education. While the demographic impact of HIV/AIDS might reduce enrollment pressures on the universities, it raises dependency ratios—a smaller proportion of people in their productive years supporting larger numbers of young and elderly persons—thereby reducing productive investments. In short, the pandemic reduces human, physical, and social capital, which diminishes economic growth, and when combined with rising competing claims for health care and other needs, could lead to the availability of fewer public resources for education in general and for higher education in particular.

Despite its gravity, the universities have not responded adequately to the crisis. Many provide information and education on HIV/AIDS to students through their health services and clinics, which also supply condoms and counseling. Student welfare associations, AIDS societies, and anti-AIDS clubs have also emerged on some campuses to sensitize students, increase awareness, and provide peer support. Because of these efforts, student awareness of the existence and transmission patterns of HIV/AIDS has increased, although many students still continue to exhibit attitudes of denial, fatalism, or misguided invincibility. At the same time, university medical services tend to be terribly understaffed and underresourced. Even as university AIDS research has increased, unfortunately, the disease and its impact have yet to be integrated into relevant sections of the curriculum.

At the heart of the problem is the fact that, with some notable exceptions, university responses tend to be adhoc and piecemeal. On many campuses there has been a lack of coordination and commitment from the top, without which it is difficult to develop a strategic approach and to lay out clear targets for action. Where university leadership has adopted proactive strategies the disease has been contained. The Kelly Report recommends that universities embark on a two-pronged strategy: first, an inward-looking strategy aimed at self-preservation by protecting the functioning of the university as an AIDS affected institution; and second, an outward-looking strategy that seeks to use the university's enormous research capabilities to help design cohesive national policies and strategies for combating the disease. The HIV/AIDS pandemic offers a supreme test of how effectively African universities can respond to emerging challenges and needs and turn its relations with external constituencies from destructive dependencies to constructive collaborations.

Internal Challenges and Reforms

Besides the "external" forces outlined above, African academics have also been confronted by numerous internal challenges, configured around issues of governance and management, resources and accountability, production and dissemination of knowledge, and access and equity. African universities have been characterized by authoritarianism, partly as a reflection of prevailing state authoritarianism itself and the fact that in many cases senior university administrators are state appointees, who, in turn, appoint unit heads down the administrative hierarchy. A particularly egregious example of this was the appointment of military officers as vice-chancellors of several Nigerian universities. Not only did these officers lack experience in or commitment to higher education, many were corrupt. They also destroyed traditional democratic structures of university governance and encouraged violence on the campuses, playing different factions of students against one another to maintain control. Military rule facilitated the imposition of structural adjustment on the university sector, which resulted in a gradual shift of educational values away from knowledge and learning and the notion of education as an investment to a focus on technical and remedial education. Moreover, the administration of Nigerian universities became increasingly centralized as power was concentrated in the National Universities Commission (NUC), which controlled major aspects of university management, from setting student enrollment targets and courses of study, to academic and staff salaries and the selection of vice-chancellors (Benedict et al., 2000).

The late Nigerian political scientist Claude Ake (1994) has reminded us that state authoritarianism in Africa should not be exaggerated, for the coercive capacities of the postcolonial state are weakened by the limited ideological hegemony that the political class enjoys. Academics themselves shoulder some of the blame for the prevalence of authoritarianism and erosion of academic freedom. Besotted by opportunism, careerism, parochialism, factionalism, and ideological intolerance, intellectuals have often weakened their collective defense against state assaults, and by defining academic freedom in narrow and elitist terms as a professional right unencumbered by social responsibility, they forfeit popular support. The road to academic freedom must begin with honest self-criticism among the intellectuals themselves, of their practices and values. For Ake academic freedom without internal institutional democratization is inadequate.

It needs to be followed, Joseph Ki-Zerbo (1994) has argued, by a renewed commitment to social responsibility through the creation of vibrant and integrated intellectual associations, groups and communities on national, regional, and continental levels that, in turn, must actively participate in wider struggles for democracy. The question of social responsibility dominates African discourses on academic freedom. The reasons for this lie in the acute politicization of African social formations, a product of long histories of struggle against the barbarities of the slave trade, colonialism, and postcolonial misrule. The powerful pull of such memories, and the strong links maintained by the small band of academics to the cultures and communities of civil society and their class affinities to the ruling elite, is what makes them see themselves either in the "magisterial" role of a revolutionary vanguard or in a "ministerial" one of facilitating progressive change, to use Ki-Zerbo's (1994) interesting metaphors. Rarely do they perceive themselves solely as academics. Intellectualism for intellectualism's sake is often regarded as a sign of petty-bourgeois self-indulgence. It is this valorization of the "public intellectual" that gives African academic debates about social responsibility their urgency.

It is not surprising, therefore, that among the major international declarations that have been adopted in various regions of the world in the last two decades on academic freedom, the Kampala Declaration, adopted by African intellectuals in 1990, is perhaps the most forthright on linking "Intellectual Freedom and Social Responsibility," to invoke its very title. Part of the preamble states: "The struggle for intellectual freedom is an integral part of the struggle of our people for democracy and human rights. Just as popular forces are waging a struggle for democracy and human rights, so are African academics, intellectuals, students and other members of the intelligentsia deeply involved in their own struggles for intellectual and academic freedom." Notice the reference to both intellectual and academic freedom. The title of the declaration, in fact, speaks of "intellectual" rather than "academic" freedom.

Thus, African universities have been weighed down by their own institutional constraints. The decision-making process tends to be discretionary and authoritarian. Universities have often been characterized by a top-down authoritarian administrative structure, poor communication, and strained relations between administration and teaching faculty. When combined with the meager funding at many of the universities, the proximity of faculty housing on or near campus, and the politicization of campus life, the result is internal bitterness, tension, resentment, and divisiveness that can be quite disruptive (Mathieu, 1996). From the 1980s, while funding constraints indeed became severe, the financial plight of many universities was often compounded by top-level corruption and mismanagement. As resources meant for teaching and research were frittered away in the conspicuous consumption of the university administrative elite with their chauffeur-driven cars and special allowances, or filtered through a maze of patron-client networks that rewarded sycophants and marginalized independent-minded scholars, buildings decayed, libraries and laboratory facilities deteriorated, and the culture of learning and knowledge production degenerated. In the worst cases, the patronage system determined the allocation of positions and appointments, departmental budgets and individual salaries, promotions and rewards, teaching loads and research facilities, sabbaticals and conference travel, housing and allowances, and routine services including conflict-free scheduling, computerized class rosters, grade sheets, and transcript compilation. (Nelson, 1996a; Domatob, 1996; Peil, 1996; Kirkaldy, 1996).

Numerous studies have pointed out that many universities were remiss even in areas that constitute their core mission of teaching, research, and public service. Strategic planning, data management, curricular reform, and staff development suffered from neglect. In a situation where funding levels were erratic, state intervention a constant threat, and independence and innovation frowned upon, strategic planning was often seen as an exercise in futility. For example, in 1986, Nigeria's NUC, in collaboration with the World Bank, asked universities to produce strategic plans, but five years later only the University of Ibadan had done so, although we are assured that as universities have gained greater autonomy under Obasanjo's democratic government elected in 1999, they are reviving long-moribund academic planning committees to start the process (Benedict, 2000: 7). The problems of data management are captured most poignantly in a story about the University of Nsukka's acting registrar who did not know how many students were enrolled in his university and couldn't offer a precise ratio of graduate to undergraduate students. Apparently it also took six weeks to register students for courses. The situation in other African universities may not be as bad, but there is an enormous need for automation, accuracy, protection, and security of university records.

As books disappeared from university bookstores and libraries, students read less, became more dependent on their teachers, and intellectual lethargy spread. On a 1996 visit to Chancellor College, the main campus of the

University of Malawi, where I received my undergraduate education, I was shocked to find that the bookstore had been closed and the building was being turned into offices. It was from that very bookstore that I had, over four years of intellectual engagement and excitement, acquired books, those incredible treasures of the mind and the proudest possessions of my college life, which set me on a lifelong journey of reading, study, and critical reflection. In response to this travesty of book-hungry universities, it is reported that in Nigeria a handout culture has developed, whereby students have come to depend on typed notes from their lecturers, who charge an appropriate fee to line their indigent pockets (Olukoshi, 2001: 5). In the Democratic Republic of the Congo we are told "students have no textbooks, and professors must dictate their notes or copy them onto a blackboard" (World Bank, 2000: 25). In short, learning and curricula reform suffered as many library shelves became empty of current journals, books, and monographs and lagged awfully behind in the acquisition of modern information technologies or were filled with discarded miscellanea of Western libraries, out-of-date texts, and unwanted publishers' remainders (Zeleza, 1997a: Chapter 4).

For their part, science laboratories were littered with broken down or incompatible and outdated equipment dumped by sympathetic international donors and Western universities. Some of the continent's once great research universities became cruel caricatures of their proud pasts. Universities in Eastern and Southern Africa reportedly spent an average of 4 percent of their small and declining budgets on research and 4.3 percent on libraries (Ngara, 1995: 122). In the 1990s, overall government support for research and development accounted for 0.2 percent of gross domestic product (Deen, 1999). Not surprisingly, in 1995 scholars on the entire continent published 9,075 papers in the sciences and social sciences and received 72,233 citations in 1993-97, a mere 1.2 percent and 0.5 percent, respectively, of world publications and citations in the two fields (World Bank: 2000: 127).

The research gap was part of a much wider technology gap. Many of the continent's universities lagged behind in the deployment, utilization, and exploitation of information and communications technologies (ICT). The challenges were at both the national and university level. While African governments in the 1990s gradually came to recognize the importance of the "information revolution" for development, they were slow in developing the appropriate policies and in making or encouraging the necessary investments in the sector. For many universities, ICT was simply one more item on the long queue of desperate needs. A 1998 survey by the Association of African Universities found that only 52 of the 232 academic and research institutions that responded had full internet access, while the rest had access that was "inadequate" (Useem, 1999: A52). Internet access was generally limited to faculty and graduate students (Ajayi, 2000).

There have been rapid changes since then, however, thanks to massive investments. In November 2000, all fifty four African countries were finally brought online when Eritrea obtained a local internet connection. According to Mike Jensen (2001),[6] the number of African internet subscribers reached 1.3 million, and since each computer with an internet or email connection supports a range of three to five users, he estimates there were somewhere around 4 million internet users, that is one user for every 200 people, compared to a world average of one user for every 30 people. This was far behind the 1 in 3 ratio in North America and Europe, but ahead of some regions in the developing world.[7] There were huge discrepancies in internet connectivity among African countries, and between rural and urban areas, and men and women. For example, 750,000 of the internet subscribers were in South Africa and 250,000 in North Africa, leaving about 300,000 in the remaining forty-eight countries.

The internet was still largely confined to the major cities, although in a growing number of countries there were points of presence (POPs) in smaller towns, and local call charges for accessing the internet became increasingly common, as did kiosks, cybercafes, and other forms of public internet access. As in the old colonial days though, when telephones were routed through the imperial capitals, almost all the international internet circuits in Africa, with the exception of some internet service providers (ISPs) in southern Africa, were connected to the USA or to Europe. As a result most African internet sites were hosted on servers in these countries. Equally troubling, African internet content development remained low, although it was growing rapidly, especially for the news media. Dependency on the North extended to funding for ICT capacity building initiatives and training.[8]

Information and Communication Technology has been successfully integrated in some of the better endowed universities in southern Africa and North Africa.[9] For example, at the University of Namibia all faculty and staff are linked to the campus internet network, video conferencing facilities are available for interactive video classes between students at the main campus and the satellite campuses, the library is being transformed into a high-tech

ICT information resource center, and a Knowledge Center is being set up for online distance education (Kiangi and Mshigeni, 2001). Among the universities that have made significant ICT advances in North Africa is Al Akhawayn University in Ifrane, Morocco, established in 1995 (Clark and Lai, 1998). On the whole, however, African universities have not been central to ICT development in the region, although in some cases they were among the first to introduce the internet in their countries (Adubifa, 2000). Many do not have reliable campus backbones and local area networks, and while most African universities have websites, the Internet and e-mail are rarely used for curriculum development, teaching, learning, and research. By the end of 2000, my own alma mater, the University of Malawi, still did not have its own website!

The challenge, it seems to me, is not only to develop ICT infrastructure and capacities in African universities, but also to increase African intellectual content. Failure to do so is to condemn African students to intellectual backwardness and dependency, both of which constitute a monumental crime against Africa's development and future. Students in the poorer African universities are indeed increasingly exposed to knowledge that is not only intellectually outdated but irrelevant for the job market. Universities have become, to quote a pithy comment by Paulin Hountodji (2001: 2), the Beninois philosopher and a former minister of education, "huge factories for a product still unknown twenty years ago: the unemployment of cadres and learned people. There is an increasing gap between the university curricula and the amount of knowledge and know-how required by the new job-market. Given the saturation of the civil service, new jobs can only be found today in the private sector which also has to be developed." Instead of preparing students for the changing conditions of professional life, "enrolling as a student has become more and more often a way to put oneself on the sidelines and postpone the time when one is considered as an unemployed graduate. Not so long ago in Benin, people used to enrol again and again, migrating from one department to another up to the age of 30 and more, just because they didn't know what else to do."

Staff training and development did not fare well either in many African universities. The use of masters degree students as teachers for prolonged periods without further training became quite common. Adebayo Olukoshi (2001: 4), one of Africa's most intellectually stimulating younger scholars and the new head of CODESRIA, laments the situation in his native

Nigeria: Graduate students "were overworked and given responsibility for courses for which they were hardly qualified. The entire staff-in-training programme that was once a feature of universities collapsed; mentoring of junior faculty by senior colleagues had also become a rarity." Many universities were dominated by two generations of postindependence scholars, the first generation trained mostly abroad—in regional or Western universities—in the 1950s and 1960s, and the third generation trained locally in the late 1980s and 1990s. Missing was the crucial second generation, trained both at home and abroad in the 1970s and early 1980s, scholars of my generation who were able, given their life cycle and qualifications, to migrate to greener pastures in independent research centers, NGOs, and consultancies at home, or overseas. For example, in Nigeria between 1992 and 1995, the number of lecturers dropped by 6.8 percent, i.e., from 12,977 to 12,064 (Oni, 2000: 15). Thus, African universities that had been the engines of capacity building for the civil service and economy, now often lacked capacity. The case, in the mid-1990s, of a three-person history department at the once renowned University of Ghana in Legon teaching 300 students was not unusual (Peil, 1996: 53). Nor was it in the political science and economics departments at Bayero University in Kano in the late 1990s, where only three and four of seventeen faculty members of each, respectively, had Ph.D.'s (Benedict, 2000: 9).

As for public service, despite all the rhetoric on its importance, few African universities developed effective programs of public outreach, e.g., advertizing what they did and informing the increasingly literate public of what universities could provide, as a way both to counter the anti-intellectualist propaganda of governments and some segments of civil society and as a way to mobilize and garner widespread support for a highly valuable national resource. More often than not, public service was reduced to profitable consultancies, not public engagement and education, and valued more as a source of desperately needed funds than in terms of public accountability and the need to break the "town and gown" divide, or the "village and varsity" divide for the rural-based universities. Until recently, even the consultancies were largely ad hoc and uncoordinated, driven by the interests of individuals leaving behind little institutional benefits. With a few notable exceptions, supplemental funds for public universities came from the so-called donors, rather than from alumni, let alone from income generating projects based on the exploitation of the university's capacity to produce knowledge. A distinction ought to be made, argues Emmanuel Ngara (1995: 124), "between activities aimed at promoting excellence in fundamental, applied and developmental research on the one hand, and on the other, legitimate activities directed at both producing knowledge for the sake of solving the problems of particular industries and generating funds for the university."

The separation of the research and consultancy function in "selling knowledge" that Ngara advocates, finds few adherents among African universities desperate to raise funds by any means necessary. Donors, of course, constitute an important source of funds, but in most cases their contributions are target specific and nonrecurring. An endowment culture for public institutions has yet to take root among Africa's bourgeois and middle classes, many of them beneficiaries of the largess of the state-financed universities, although alumni associations exist or are emerging in several countries. Universities are increasingly resorting to four main income-generating strategies. First, introducing or increasing student fees. For various, and sometimes contradictory, reasons this has been met by stiff resistance from students, their families, and politicians. The nationalist social contract engendered expectations that education should be provided at minimal or no cost to students, although in reality a significant and growing portion of the financial costs of education was increasingly borne by families, whose resources were severely strained by the disastrous effects of structural adjustment. Alternatively, foreign students were charged higher fees to subsidize local students, as did the University of Khartoum, which charged students from its oil-rich neighbors $6,000 and Sudanese students $2 (Morna, 1995).

Second, many universities began introducing demand-driven courses for which students were willing to pay, mostly in the professional fields, especially in business, management, health, environmental, agribusiness, communication, and technology studies. These programs attracted many people who were already employed and keen to acquire new skills or certificates to advance their careers. The "executive programs" are sometimes part of the curriculum and taken by regular students, or they are offered in satellite campuses in the cities and specifically tailored for the clientele with little regard to academic integrity or quality. To facilitate this process and as a part of curricula reform, universities that operated on the rigid academic year calendar increasingly switched to a more flexible and user-friendly semester system. Third, the commercialization of some service units and university space became popular. The first allowed universities to reduce staffing and salary expenditures, while the second enabled them to earn rental incomes from unutilized space. The services contracted to private operators often include cleaning and catering services, while university facilities like halls of residence and conference rooms might be rented for private functions during weekends and vacations, or university-owned land leased for farming and other activities. Fourth, universities started creating limited liability companies to undertake consultancies and commissioned projects and commercialize university-generated knowledge and products.

Some of the newer universities experimented with innovative programs of engaging the public in the very design of their academic programs. For example, in 1991 after the long war of liberation from Ethiopia, the University of Asmara, Eritrea, developed what is called a "dual linkage model", in which each college has a joint steering committee with its stakeholders in the public and private sectors. The committee helps identify specific challenges, designs the curricula and joint research projects required to address them, and provides quality control for teaching and research programs. The work of the committees also enables the university to participate in the preparation and review of the strategic sectoral development plans (Yisak, 2001). In Namibia, the University of Namibia deliberately set out to establish a Northern campus that would be fully integrated into a community of over 800,000 people of mixed incomes and economic activities, of poor social and physical infrastructure, and recovering from war. The aim was to provide both quality university education and to assist in the development of the region. The university and an educational consultant firm it had hired from the United States formed a joint committee with community representatives who decided on the location, structure, and programs of the campus. They decided that both academic and community development programs would be offered, and they developed a list of these programs based on long-term planning and in-depth analysis of the sociopolitical reality. When established the campus received overwhelming community support, which it used to leverage additional government funding (Katjavivi, 2001).

There is no doubt that internal reform measures have rescued some universities from financial penury. For example, Makerere increased its internally generated revenues from Uganda Shs. 5.07 billion (US $3 million) in 1996 to Uganda Shs. 17 billion (US $10 million) in 1999 out of a total budget of $28 million. By then over 80 percent of the students were already privately sponsored and only 20 percent were on government scholarships.

The university hopes to match the government contribution by 2002-2003. The funds enabled the university to raise salaries and to improve retirement benefits, thus making it possible to attract and retain faculty and to reduce the high turnover of the 1970s and 1980s, to expand the staff development program, to establish a maintenance fund for repairs of dilapidated campus buildings and roads, to create a research and publication fund, to improve students welfare by restocking laboratories, libraries, lecture theaters and for expanding teaching space, and to embark on an ambitious information technology program (Ssebuwufu, 2001). Similar reforms enabled the University of Dar es Salaam to generate 12 percent of its operating budget, which it hopes to raise to 20 percent, thus halting the decline and beginning the improvement of its operations (Mkunde, 2001). In Nigeria, the University of Lagos reportedly raised 59 percent of its funds internally, and many other Nigerian universities raised up to 10 percent.

The results of these reforms should not be exaggerated. Both Makerere and Dar es Salaam, which I am familiar with and last visited in July-August 2000 for a project evaluation, still have a long way to go before they can meet the expectations of their own faculty and students, let alone international standards. This caution is shared by Sylvia Tamale (2001), a faculty member at Makerere who is still awaiting her dream university, one characterized by "authentic" African values, small, well-equipped classes; a vibrant research culture; a decentralized, effective, and accountable administrative system, gender equality, and autonomy from the state. At Dar es Salaam students went on strike in late 2000, complaining about low stipends for books and poor accommodation, which resulted in a temporary suspension of all the students (Bollag, 2001a)

In the case of both Makerere and Dar es Salaam the financial reforms were preceded and accompanied by administrative reforms predicated on greater democratization of internal governance, decentralization of decision making, and management planning and efficiency. Legislative changes were also proposed giving universities more autonomy and giving them freedom to make their own decisions. Even slated for removal was the head of state as titular head of public universities. Lagos owed its success less to far-reaching reforms than to its location in one of Africa's most vibrant commercial centers, although Nigerian universities have been undergoing significant reforms since the inauguration of the Obasanjo administration. Not only are salaries being increased (by about 300 percent in 2000) although they still remain low, the rhetoric of accountability, efficiency, and relevance is also increasingly heard on Nigerian campuses (Ejiaga, 2001); but the administration of the university sector is also being decentralized as the role of the NUC is reduced and universities assume more powers and autonomy in exchange for an expected raise of 30 percent of their operating budgets, incidentally a figure hatched by the World Bank and other so-called donors!

The changes that strengthen internal democratic governance and signal a shift from state control to state regulation ought to be welcomed; but the state should not be allowed to abdicate its responsibility of providing the bulk of the funds for public education. In the so-called new knowledge economy and era of globalization, university education is more crucial than ever for development and national and regional competitiveness. Given their concentration of scientific, technical, and human resources, African universities are vital to solving specific problems that confront African societies. However, universities are not simply utilitarian machines or agents of development, let alone corporations in gowns, they are also reservoirs of creativity and knowledge production, centers where critical consciousness is cultivated, an engaged and informed national and global citizenry is formed, a sense of humanism is fostered, and the aesthetics of cultural innovation, appreciation, and tolerance are nourished. At their best, then, universities are institutions that seek to solve practical problems and to encourage lofty contemplation, to pursue pure and applied research, and to accommodate those with pragmatic minds and poetic souls.

The corporatist model informing some of the reforms threatens to push universities into a straightjacket that is as dangerous as the discredited model of state control and authoritarian developmentalism. The fact that the World Bank (1988, 1994, 2000) is pushing the new model, as always in the inestimable names of, this time, institutional differentiation, financial diversification, quality assurance, vocational relevance, economic competitiveness, privatization and equity, should be enough reason for pause. Not only are many of the bank's recommendations warmed over conclusions from the past, their universality recall the intolerant menu of structural adjustment programs that served the same fare regardless of a country's specific needs. Nor are the structural reforms suggested all that new; higher education in much of Africa is already differentiated. And while private universities ought to be encouraged, they cannot provide a realistic alternative to the massive needs of human resource development in Africa.[10] Even in the world's quintessential capitalist country, the United States, public universities account for the bulk of tertiary enrollments and training, and the major private universities receive huge amounts of state funding for research. Among the Asian tigers, usually thrown in the face of Africans as examples of the possibilities of privatization, private universities are often subsidized by the state. In cases where private universities are new and not subject to powerful external public constituencies, they tend to focus on narrow and profitable fields. The challenge is to treat the university sector itself, and the entire educational system, as an integrated whole, not as a disparate collection of competing institutions with different rates of return.

Specifically with regards to funding, the issue is not simply one of diversification of sources, but of their adequacy and efficiency, not simply calculated in narrow accounting terms but in broad social terms. As Njabulo Ndebele (2001: 2), the new vice-chancellor of the University of Cape Town, puts it so poetically: Our notion of accountability must not be "in the first instance, to political or financial imperatives, but more significantly to the public imagination." Certainly governments need to invest even more, not less, if African higher education is to recover and flourish. Also, it is mistaken to raise user charges on the assumption that rates of return for higher education are high, when in fact they have been declining since the 1980s, thanks to falling incomes spurred by structural adjustment. No wonder, in Kenya, for example, 75 percent of university graduates who had benefitted from student loan schemes since 1974 had not repaid the money by 1997 (Ogot, 2001: 260). Expecting substantial increases in alumni and other private contributions without significant changes in the tax code that would allow significant tax deductions for the contributors as is the case, say, in the United States, is unrealistic.

The financial reforms that have been undertaken are reinforcing differentiations between and within universities. For example, in the easily commercialized disciplines, such as the Business School at Makerere, a professor earns up to $3,000 (compared to $64 ten years earlier) a month, several times what a professor in the arts disciplines earns. While Lagos generates three-fifths of its operating budget, the University of Sokoto generates only 0.6 percent, and many of Nigeria's rural-based universities have little chance of raising funds from "executive programs." In fact, because of their very location they are expected to provide infrastructural services (including housing, schools, medical facilities, and even electric power and transportation) to their staff and to neighboring communities, which universities in large cities do not have to do (Ejiaga, 2001). A very different and demanding form of public service indeed.

Genealogies and Burdens of African Intellectuals

Administrative and fiscal reforms are not enough in themselves to revitalize Africa's universities and to turn them into centers of global excellence. The issue of knowledge production also needs to be tackled. I have written extensively elsewhere (Zeleza, 1997a) of the need for African universities and intellectual communities to overcome the historical handicaps of intellectual dependence, to Africanize global scholarship and globalize African scholarship, to produce knowledge that addresses and explains the problems and possibilities facing the peoples, economies, societies, and cultures of this infinitely varied and complex of continents. At stake in this context, then, is the question of African intellectual autonomy and authority.

Clearly, this involves not only struggles against the authoritarian predilections and practices of the state, civil society, and the academy itself, but it is also an epistemological one against paradigms, theories, and methodologies that inferiorize, misrepresent, and oversimplify African experiences, conditions, and realities. Many studies have been published in recent years on the propensity of all the major social science and humanities disciplines for universalizing Western experiences, often highly idealized, into metatheoretical constructs to analyze other societies. The result is that these societies are seen in terms of lack, in terms of absences, as caricatures or eternal "others" of the West. These critiques, of course, differ in their intensity and resolutions. The most enlightened ones, in my view, eschew the Afrocentric fantasies of what Kwame Anthony Appiah (1992) calls "nativist handwaving," sentiments shared by V.Y. Mudimbe (1992, 1994), who has done much to unravel the invention of Africa through the social imaginary of the Western epistemological order. According to Archie Mafeje (1994), the struggle for academic freedom and intellectual authority in Africa and in African studies entails jettisoning Eurocentric theories and paradigms and developing authentic African intellectual discourses, without falling into the trap of an essentializing cultural revivalism that homogenizes Africa's diverse cultures and histories and poses them in binary opposition to other cultures and histories.

As a professional formation, African intellectuals have complex histories that have yet to be written. As with other discourses on the continent, African intellectuals are often discussed through the stifling prisms of color and colonialism, i.e., in racialized and imperialized terms, whereby Africa is understood as the sub-Saharan concoction and its preoccupations with colonialism and its legacies (Mamdani, 1994; Mafeje, 1994; Nwauwa, 1997; Zachernuk, 1999, 2000; Falola, 2001). This is, of course, not to deny that Africa does indeed include the so-called sub-Sahara region, and that African intellectuals have thought and written extensively on the effects of the encounter with a colonizing Europe. Rather, it is to point out that Africa also includes North Africa and intellectual traditions in indigenous languages, including Arabic, as well as in the religious idiom of Islam, which antedated the European moment and connect to it and contest it in ways that differ from African intellectual tendencies and trajectories more directly spawned by the European encounter.

In a suggestive study on Senegalese intellectuals, Mamadou Diouf (1994) demonstrates that the assumption that African intellectuals are a product of the colonial or postcolonial periods is not applicable even to so-called sub-Saharan Africa, let alone to Africa as a whole. Tracing the changing relations between intellectuals and the state in Senegal from the days of the great Sudanic empires to the present, he shows that the intellectual strata created by the colonial state existed alongside a much older indigenous one, which colonialism unsuccessfully sought to domesticate and to neutralize. Muslim intellectuals survive to this day alongside the intellectual strata that traces its origins to colonialism. Colonial intellectuals were tied to the fortunes of state capital and its developmentalist ambitions, notwithstanding their flirtation with the seemingly opposed ideologies of Senghor's Negritude, Diop's Neo-Phaoronism, and Marxism.

As the crisis of modernization became more apparent, they sought refuge in the pretensions of technocratic solutions, thereby weakening their ability to contest structural adjustment programs in the politicized terrain of national politics, now increasingly filled by the intellectuals from the precolonial tradition who "have moved increasingly into the modern economic sector" and now "occupy a central position in all possible strategies in Senegalese society, because they are perfectly articulate in French, Wolof and Arabic, smoothly skilled in operating simultaneously in all the codes and in the milieux associated with them" (Diouf, 1994: 239). Thus, what is described as the fragmentation of the intellectuals refers to the modern school of intellectuals who have been less successful in determining their fate. Hence, they are now "falling back on a more professional definition of their role, with a consequent distancing from the state" (Diouf, 1994: 241). Their struggle for academic freedom, therefore, represents not simply a search for intellectual and institutional autonomy but also a new self-image and mission. The connections, contrasts, and contestations between the two intellectual traditions, the ancient and modern ones, are complex and deserve more comprehensive inquiries.

Intellectuals in North Africa are heirs to a long Muslim-Arab tradition. Today, there is a tendency among many scholars, ignorant of this tradition, to equate Islam with fundamentalism. Religious fundamentalism is of course not peculiar to Islam. Indeed, as Amin Khan (1994) shows in his highly textured analysis of Algerian intellectuals, during the brilliant classical phase of Islamic civilization, intellectual freedom flourished, before scholasticism developed and Islam became a handmaiden of Turkish domination. Later, under French rule, there were efforts to crush that freedom. The new intellectual strata created by colonialism was divorced from the masses, although they played an active role in the liberation movement. The ferocity of the struggle for liberation brooked little opposition and debate. Always suspect in the eyes of those steeped in a defensive and increasingly conservative Islam, the secular intellectuals sought to buy acceptance by acquiescing to nationalist populism, for which they were rewarded after independence with incorporation into the state apparatuses of an oil booming economy.

Indeed, the secular intellectuals became organic to the state, as they became preoccupied with charting its developmentalist and nation-building projects as well as their own advancement. Given their modernist orientation and ambitions for the country, they ignored the simmering cultural schisms and discontents, preferring to perceive culture in the technical and bureaucratic terms of "schooling plus speeches on the retrieval of national identity....Presented in this form, culture got hijacked by Arab-Muslim ideologues" (Khan, 1994: 284). The failure of the state and modernist intellectuals to develop a coherent cultural policy that recognized the country's internal ethnic and linguistic divisions, instead of sweeping them under the fiction of national unity, proved costly. As the lights of nationalism began to dim with time, under the cloud of a failing modernization, Islamic fundamentalists moved to occupy "the jagged cracks between identity and modernity, consensus and democracy, authority and legitimacy" (Khan, 1994: 295).

The opposition in North Africa is not of course simply between Islamists and secular intellectuals. The Islamists are frequently opposed by other Muslim intellectuals and institutions. Nowhere is this better expressed than in Egypt, where Al-Azhar, the oldest surviving university in the world, finds itself delicately placed between the state and the Islamists who are opposed to the state. As the appeal of Islamism has increased, the government has increasingly sought to bolster its religious legitimacy and marginalize the Islamist opposition by mobilizing Islamic symbols, among them the relatively moderate but highly authoritative ancient Muslim institution of higher learning, Al-Azhar. Beginning with Nasser's regime, the state has repeatedly called upon Al-Azhar to justify campaigns against Islamists and to support legislation that might otherwise arouse religious opposition. In return, significant administrative duties have been transferred to Al-Azhar, giving it a free hand to speak on religious matters—including most recently control of all private mosques, which are vital in the recruitment and organization of the Islamists—as well as a significant say in areas of social policy (Barraclough, 1998). As the state has ceded more power to Al-Azhar, the latter has made inroads into broader domains of public discourse, the result of which has been growing censorship, the marginalization of secular intellectuals, some of whom have even been murdered or persecuted after being pronounced as apostate by the prominent ulama of Al-Azhar (Durac, 1999; Castillo, 2001). In October 1994, an attempt was even made on the life of the great Egyptian novelist and Nobel laureate Naguib Mahfouz, a passionate defender of science, socialism, and social justice whose writings and public statements are widely viewed as blasphemous (Najjar, 1998). These acts have provoked the secular intelligentsia to mobilize and to speak out against the Islamists and Al-Azhar. In May 2000, they formed the Association of Egyptian Independent Intellectuals (Hesse, 1995; Adel, 2000).

Ideological and analytical divisions are of course not confined to the opposition between secular and religious intellectuals. In fact, they have always existed among Africa's secular intellectuals. Several chapters of Volume Two examine in detail some of the different orientations and trajectories of African secular intellectuals. One chapter discusses the middle class intelligentsia, which played a crucial role in the imagination and invention of the postcolonial state during the first moment of decolonization in the 1950s and 1960s and in the second moment of democratization from the 1980s and 1990s, and the different, and in many cases conflicting, visions and agendas that were articulated, for example, by academic and literary intellectuals, and by proponents of different developmentalist and democratic models, which reflected the different social movements the intellectuals straddled and their divergent material and discursive regimes. Another chapter in Volume Two focuses on the history of the fervent longing by African thinkers and social activists for an African renaissance, the historical and contemporary conceptualizations of the idea, the contexts that occasioned its resurrection in the 1990s, contestations over it, and its construction in terms of spatial and social referents.

In the chapter at hand, however, I would like to comment on African intellectuals' engagements with various critical moments, including the 1990s, a period of bewildering extremes for Africa. It saw the rise of mass movements and mass revolts driven by democratic and developmentalist ideals, as well as mass murder and mass poverty perpetrated by desperate regimes and discredited global agencies. A decade of unparalleled political change and epic victories against oppression was also one marked by stubborn continuities and unprecedented violence and genocide. The pace of change was so rapid, the cast of players and stakeholders so numerous that it is difficult to tell a coherent story, certainly not a single or simple story beloved by those who see Africa as one, either because they have no time for understanding its astonishing diversities or because they wish to impose an emancipatory pan-African solidarity. These struggles and changes paralleled, in their quantitative scope and qualitative dimension, those that occurred in the 1950s and 1960s, when most African countries gained their independence from colonial rule. Representing the pluralization of associational life and the expansion of political space, the democratic wave represented the latest moment of accelerated change in a long history of struggles for freedom; an exceptionally complex moment often driven by unpredictable events and new social movements and visions, anchored in the specific histories and conditions of each country, where national, regional, and international forces converged unevenly and inconsistently, and where economic and political crises reinforced each other, altering the terrain of state-civil society relationships, the structures of governance, and the claims of citizenship.

While numerous studies have been produced on aspects associated with this moment, its full historical weight has yet, in my view, to be fully grasped. This is partly because the drama is still unfolding, although journalists and social scientists who suffer from the short attention span of channel-surfing intellectualism, hopping from one crisis and continent through CNN and from one fancy theory to another, have already declared that it is over. Historians are more patient; they will pronounce their verdict several decades from now, after probing the dusty archives and foggy oral memories of the various protagonists. Clearly, the struggles for democracy have yielded both successes and failures, compromises with the past and concessions to the future. Numerous dictatorships have fallen and elections have become as frequent as coups once were. Meanwhile, several transitions have been aborted, some are still tenuous, several intransigent regimes remain, most sadly for me in the country of my own birth, Zimbabwe,[11] those who only a few years ago were seen as the "new generation of leaders" have shown their true tyrannical colors. The regional wars they have been fighting, from the Horn and the Great Lakes region to Liberia and Sierra Leone, mark the consummation of their autocracy and the militarism that may finally consume them. These wars and conflicts are an integral part of Africa's bumpy road to the future, of Africa's renaissance, in which old and new visions compete to rename and redraw the political cartography and culture of Nkrumah's kingdom.

Political liberalization and democratization have certainly offered African scholars unprecedented opportunities to re-examine their societies and revisit their histories without the blinkers of nationalist dogma and misguided developmentalism. What are the implications of this new moment for historical and social science research, the fields with which I am most familiar? Let us take the case of Malawi, my home country. Only a decade ago whole areas of historical and social science research in the country were taboo. As Owen Kalinga (1998), one of Malawi's leading historians has shown, the Banda regime profoundly affected the production of history in Malawi, from the adoption of the name Malawi itself as a correction of the colonial designation, Nyasaland, and as a gesture of territorial claims in the region. Critical to the propagation of a new version of Malawi history was the Cabinet Crisis of 1964. Mentioning the names of the Cabinet "rebels" was "illegal" and could "lead to one's detention in one of the notorious camps that were mushrooming in the country. Their role in the anti-colonial struggle was being deliberately obliterated from the memories of Malawians" (Kalinga, 1998: 540).

Consequently, in re-enactments of the country's history in the media and at public rallies Malawi's recent political history was distorted, and Banda's role exaggerated. This resulted in the strange spectacle in which, for example, during Martyrs Day celebrations, on 3 March, references "would be made to the anti-colonial struggles, but no mention would be made of the people and activities of the 1950s which had directly contributed to independence" (Kalinga, 1998: 541). The Banda regime did not hesitate to manufacture precolonial versions of history as well to manipulate contemporary politics, most glaringly in the deposition of Chief Mwase, in the powerful central region, who had fallen out of favor with Banda. "The President justified his action on the basis that people had misunderstood Chewa history....Banda's version won the day and henceforth was expected to be taught in schools and colleges" (Kalinga, 1998: 544). Besides threats of incarceration and the public performances of history, the Banda regime tried to control the production of history through strict controls of access to the National Archives.

The fact that Kalinga was able to write and to publish this paper is a testimony to the political changes that had taken place in Malawi since 1994, when the Banda regime fell from power. Indeed, the conference, where this chapter was first presented, would not have been held. Yet it would be too easy for us as historians and as intellectuals to gaze back and attribute all the deformities of Malawi's political culture on Banda's tyrannical shoulders. As I have argued elsewhere (Zeleza, 1997a: Chapter 16), it is quite evident that in many ways, large and small, Malawian intellectuals not only conceded political space to the state, but sometimes assisted in authenticating its authoritarianism. In the early 1990s, close college friends of mine such as Ken Lipenga, a gifted writer who has yet to realize his promise, sold his talents to tyranny during his ill-fated stint as editor of the country's only daily newspaper by writing inflammatory editorials against students and church leaders clamoring for political change. Another writer, James Ng'ombe, for example, became managing director of the country's leading publisher; and Steve Chimombo, also a writer, happily connived with power by publishing uncritical literary drivel, by keeping quiet, or by denouncing their fellow writers who had been detained, such as Jack Mapanje, the renowned poet, or those who had gone into exile, such as myself. When Banda's regime lost the historic elections of 1994, many of the regime's intellectual supporters quickly changed sides and became, overnight, praise singers of the new regime. Lipenga turned up as a speech writer for the new president, Bakili Muluzi, before being elevated to a cabinet position. Mapanje and I politely turned down cabinet appointments, because we did not believe the struggle for democracy was over. Certainly the fact that many of the new leaders were recycled politicians from the Banda era was cause for concern. Critical vigilance was essential.

We have to face up to these ugly truths if our criticisms of the Banda regime are to be morally credible. The regime was spawned by the specific histories of Malawian nationalism and decolonization and the configuration of social forces and perceived developmentalist imperatives. It tapped into, and reshaped, the existing regional, ethnic, class, religious, and gender dynamics of Malawian society. Thus, the culture of authoritarianism, which sustained censorship, was reproduced at many sites, in the home, in the schools, at the work place, in a complex spiral leading to, and reverberating from, a state headed by an infallible Life-President. The state also had its intellectual propagandists; all those writers and scholars who justified or overlooked the regime's acts of terror, whether in the misguided names of tradition or development or for sheer personal advancement. Clearly, oppression has multiple faces, requiring triple interrogations from progressive intellectuals: We need to maintain permanent vigilance against the state itself, against the intolerant potentialities of civil society, of tradition, religion, and popular culture and against ourselves, our ideological and careerist tendencies for complicity with unproductive power.

The 1994 transformations in Malawi did not catch the world's imagination as did the momentous events in South Africa or in Rwanda in the same year. In the former, there was the triumph of change; in the latter, the tragedy of carnage. In both countries history and intellectuals played a key role. Afrikaner intellectuals propagated and perpetrated the vicious crime of apartheid, whose demise the world celebrated, while in Rwanda Hutu intellectuals fomented and fueled the genocidal horror that shocked the world. The role of South Africa's white supremacist Afrikaner Broederbond as the intellectual architects of apartheid is well known. Less appreciated is the fact that the intellectual proponents of apartheid, at home and abroad, often justified it as an adaptation of the European liberal tradition (Sanders, 1999). They framed the racial "question" in terms of multinationalism, that racial separation promoted the principle of national self-determination, which would prevent a single group dominating the others and allow the full development of each, thus ensuring political liberty for all groups in their respective national homelands. We all know, of course, that this was a monstrous lie to disenfranchise the majority black population and to prop up white supremacy.

However, separatist racial ideology was not a monopoly of irredeemably bigoted Afrikaner followers of the Broederbond. As I have argued elsewhere (Zeleza, 1997a: 91-93), it was at the heart of South African liberalism, anchored as it was on notions of cultural pluralism, which allowed liberal historians and social scientists who became dominant in the English-speaking universities from the 1920s to see South Africa primarily in terms of race and culture and to depict its history as a series of cultural interactions between groups with different, and for many incompatible, cultural and civilizational endowments. Liberal historiography and scholarship advanced highly racialized and idealistic analyses that essentialized the country's racial and ethnic groups, and that anthropologized African cultures, thereby denying Africans historical agency. The social devastations and dislocations of racial segregation on the Africans could be explained away as the inevitable pangs of "modernization" and "detribalization." Racial inequalities were normalized in so far as they were portrayed as products of cultural differences, rather than economic exploitation, for in the liberal tradition the modernizing economy was inherently rational, efficient, and nonascriptive, that is, color-blind. This promoted reformist complacency, for if apartheid were merely a racial ideology quite separate from the capitalist economic system, the latter's liberalizing and integrative propensities would render it obsolete as soon as the "natives" became fully modernized. Assigning the "racial question" to the realms of African culture and Afrikaner ideology absolved both the economically dominant English South Africans and capitalism from the sins of apartheid. Indeed, the strict separation drawn between capitalism and race, culture and class, power and production sanitized the evolving system of racial capitalism and justified the analytical invisibility accorded to African resistance, struggles, and aspirations. Histories of the University of Witwatersrand, the self-styled bastion of liberalism, written after the end of apartheid by sympathetic insiders (Murray, 1997; Shear, 1996; Lewsen, 1996), reveal beyond doubt the fraudulence of South African liberalism even before the strictures of apartheid, that is was largely ineffectual rhetoric not matched by its deeds, practices, and performance (Phillips, 2000).

South Africa was forced to confront the memories of apartheid during the hearings of the Truth and Reconciliation Commission. It was a dramatic and painful confrontation with history, an encounter between the histories of repression and the histories of struggle, an attempt to repudiate the former and reaffirm the latter, supported by moral and material demands for restitution and reparations, but the South African reconciliation drama after 1994 also represented an encounter between different intellectual traditions. African nationalist thought and visions, captured most poignantly in the debate about the African renaissance, were stripped of their marginality and increasingly valorized. Since 1990, when the transition from apartheid became inevitable, South African intellectuals, regardless of race, discipline, theoretical inclination, or ideology, have had to deal with, whether publicly or privately, the unsettling legacies and demands of their collective and individual pasts and futures, although forgetting is quite tempting for many as shown by the popularity of postmodernism in some quarters, a subject discussed below in Chapter 5.

Moments of political transition have not always been conducive to confronting historical memories productively and to substituting the pains of the past with the possibilities of the future. Rwanda is a dreadful reminder of the incendiary powers of selective remembering and forgetting and the murderous role intellectuals can play. In South Africa, memories of repression and resistance were mobilized against organized state terror on behalf of a racial minority, while Rwanda's incipient democratic movement was thwarted by bloody attacks unleashed by a crumbling state, assisted by its intellectual cabal, against its unarmed citizenry. As in imperial Europe, Nazi Germany, apartheid South Africa, and elsewhere where fascist terror has reared its ugly head, intellectuals in Rwanda wrote the script for genocide. In the episode on Rwanda in the documentary *Hopes on the Horizon* Laurent Nkusi, a University of Rwanda history professor who lost his family in the genocide, laments the role played by his departmental colleague and chairman, Ferdinand Nahimana, who was "among those people teaching hatred on the radio." The film's narrator continues: "Following the genocide, the teaching of Rwandan history was suspended in 1996 by the government. A group at the university had decided to probe to see if they could map out a new future for their country."[12]

History was used by historians and other Hutu intellectuals to stoke memories of hatred and fear of mutual annihilation among the Tutsi and Hutu. The fact that the two communities share more commonalities than differences, that they speak the same language, have similar religious traditions, occupy the same geographical space, and have been governed for centuries by the same aristocracy, had to be forgotten. The irreconcilable differences between the two communities had to be manufactured, the annihilation of the Tutsis justified. The "murderous professors," as Michael Chege (1996-97) calls them in his passionate indictment of Africa's unscrupulous intellectuals, concocted the fantasy of Hutu ethnic superiority and the falla-cy that the Tutsis were immigrants from Ethiopia who had exploited the Hutu and abused their hospitality, so that it was time to ship this malignant minority back home via the Nile, dead or alive. As befitting a modern infamy planned and perpetrated by intellectuals (not by the "tribal" savagery of the Western media), radio and television (not some "talking drums") became the medium of death. Supported by a beleaguered authoritarian state dominated by a narrow-minded ethnic elite, which felt threatened by popular insurgent democratic forces, the regime's loyalist intellectuals broad-casted their fraudulent histories and messages inciting the Hutu majority with hatred and murderous violence against the Tutsis.

After President Habyarimana was killed in a mysterious plane crash at Kigali airport on 4 April 1994, the order to commence the carnage came on the infamous Radio Mille Collines. In a matter of weeks it was all over, i.e., the mass killing of 850,000 Tutsis, a genocide executed with swift ferocity that stupefied Africa and the world. The Tutsis were indeed "shipped back home," multitudes of mutilated and bloated bodies floated and suffocated the fresh waters of the Kagera River that empties into Lake Victoria, from where the Nile begins its long winding journey to the north, where it is joined by several tributaries, one of which hails from Ethiopia. The genocide was soon followed by the refugee exodus as the Tutsi-led RPF captured power in Kigala. It was now the turn of Tutsi intellectuals to fabricate new history and geography as the RPF followed Hutu extremists and their sym-pathizers all the way into the Congo Democratic Republic. As the Rwanda crisis spilled into the Congo, it added fuel to the incendiary maelstrom engulfing Mobutu's banal dictatorship. Before long, Rwanda became embroiled in the regional conflagration over the Congo, which sucked in several countries in Eastern and Southern Africa. To be sure, these conflicts were caused by powerful political, economic, and strategic interests, but the fact still remains that in Rwanda many intellectuals played a despicable role as professors of death.

Even in impoverished African universities, such behavior shows that what intellectuals do really matters; that historical and social science writing have real consequences on real peoples' lives. The impassioned warning that Chege (1996-97) made about some intellectuals' dangerous flirtations with ethnic hatred in his native Kenya needs to be taken seriously. The Moi regime is supported by establishment intellectuals, many of them my colleagues in the History Department at Kenyatta: Men such as Henry Mwanzi and William Ochieng' eventually left the academy to become propaganda chiefs for the ruling party and the president's office, respectively. These intellectual sycophants have unabashedly falsified Kenyan history, singled out the Kikuyu, who constitute the largest and wealthiest ethnic group in the country, although politically marginalized, for scurrilous attacks. As Chege notes, like their intellectual counterparts in Rwanda, they smear the hated Kikuyu with the stereotypes of "greed," "land grabbing," and "racial miscegenation."

Similarly, Nigerian dictators have had their indefatigable intellectual supporters, demonstrating once again that intellectuals are as attracted as they are repelled by naked power. The seductions of power have lured many of them to sing and dance for the soldiers, excusing their brutalities and thievery, exonerating their lies, and exculpating their sins. Motivated by greed and opportunism, indifference or fear, or confusion and censorship, these poets of the barracks sought to justify, to legitimate, and to authorize the arbitrary, perverse power of the gun. Two books published on Nigerian politics in the mid-1990s demonstrate the divergent positions that Nigerian intellectuals took in the 1980s and 1990s in the face of deepening political and economic crisis. The book by Olagunju, et al. (*Transition to Democracy in Nigeria,* 1993) is an extended scholarly praise-song by the apologists of the Nigerian military. It is in fact dedicated to Babangida, the wily and ruthless military dictator who held Nigeria in bondage for eight long years, whom they call a historical figure in "the Hegelian sense." Mesmerized by the apparent fortune of serving as advisers and acolytes to such a figure, the authors muster all their collective intellectual prowess to confound critics and to celebrate Babangida's political and administrative genius, intellectual brilliance and vision, personal probity and charm.

As it behooves academics, they phrase and punctuate their praise-song with just enough convoluted concepts, controversies, and contrived complexities. They argue that for political transitions to succeed the right institutions must be created, the appropriate policies designed, and the proper lessons learned by the public. Transition to democracy is, in short, essentially a "designing problem" and a "learning process." Who, then, is best equipped to design, teach, and ensure a successful transition project? The highly disciplined and nonpartisan military of course! The thesis is stated boldly: "We attempt in this book to explore and explain ...[that] much more so than previous military and civilian regimes in post-independence Nigeria, the Babangida Administration has pursued an integrated, multi-dimensional, bold and complex project of economic, cultural, political and social reconstruction as short-term strategies for the long-term objective of democratizing the Nigerian polity and socioeconomic structures" (Olagunju et al., 1993: 20).

It is downhill from here onwards. History is shamelessly reconstructed and subverted to project, in reverse, the democratic mission of the military, for whom the Babangida regime constitutes its ultimate incarnation. By a theoretical sleight of hand, the military is portrayed as "very much part of the civil society in the country" (Olagunju et al., 1993: 28); indeed, the most conscious, not to say armed, custodian of civil society, of the country's proud "heritage of mainstream liberal democratic thought and federalist ideology"(Olagunju et al., 1993: 29), so that "military intervention has a necessarily restorative, democratic objective"(Olagunju et al., 1993: 32). In their view all military interventions in Nigeria were spawned by this revivalist calling, to clean up the mess left behind by the structural deformities of previous constitutional arrangements, the trail of flammable regional and ethnic rivalries, widespread election fraud, economic decline and mismanagement, and a culture of kleptocracy left behind by corrupt competitive party politics. As a firm believer in the virtues of liberalism, federalism and democracy, Babangida, they tell us, was forced to overthrow Buhari's regime in August 1985, when the latter reneged on the issue of transition to democracy, which it had promised after overthrowing Shagari's degenerate civilian government in December 1983. The nauseating tale goes on and on.

Mercifully, Nigeria also boasts of scholars who are truly committed to both intellectual excellence and democratic values and to the pursuit of meaningful development for their country. We meet a few of them in the book edited by Adejumobi and Momoh (*The Political Economy of Military Rule, 1984-1993,* 1995). To be sure, there are occasional echoes of the apologetic and militarist line in the book; but most of the contributors succeed in demonstrating the criminality of the Buhari and especially of the Babangida regimes and how both these dictatorships flirted with then robbed the country of its aspirations for development and democracy in a relentless pursuit for power and privilege for a decadent political class. In organization and temperament, one contributor argues, the military is authoritarian and incapable of fostering democracy. The emperor has no clothes in these narratives. "We had," Momoh (1995: 17) writes of Babangida's regime, "a dictatorship headed by a military junta which was foxy and fraudulent and therefore used state resources in pursuit of a transition programme with the deliberate objective of undermining it or indeed subverting it."

Emerging at a particular conjuncture, and out of a specific constellation of social forces, the authors contend, this dictatorship reflected and accelerated the process of the privatization and appropriation of the state by a structural adjustment program (SAP) class that expanded and prospered from buying public enterprises on the cheap and from making easy money from juggling the foreign exchange rate, while withdrawing from the provision of social services. Contrary to the libertarian discourse of structural adjustment, SAPs required extreme state coercion, since it entailed massive devaluations not only of the naira but of the jobs, livelihoods and hopes of peasants, workers, and the professional middle classes. Opponents, real and imaginary, were persecuted, opportunists coopted, and the restive masses occasionally bribed with populist rhetoric and dispensations as the Babangida regime carried out its class project of consolidating dominant class interests, both metropolitan and local.

With admirable clarity the various contributors explain the transformations taking place in Nigeria's political economy in the 1980s and early 1990s, the political maneuvers behind the smoke and mirrors of the transition program, for example, how the creation of states was used as an instrument in intraelite struggles for bureaucratic placement, advancement, and enrichment, and how to manipulate popular desires for the equitable distribution of resources and power among and between regions and ethnic groups. Further, it is shown that as with most tyrannies in underdeveloped countries, Babangida's regime exhibited a schizophrenic face, flexing iron muscles at home and grinning sheepishly to imperialism abroad.

Clearly, African intellectuals are not cut from the same cloth. The challenge of intellectual production, therefore, is as much about revitalizing universities from decline as it is about rescuing African intellectuals from supporting despotism. Most African universities have yet to recover from the debilitating deprivations of the 1980s and 1990s. In fact, political democratization riding on the coattails of economic liberalization has often meant less, not more, resources for the universities. Encouraged to acquire a new corporatist ethos and to sharpen their entrepreneurial skills, universities are expected to raise additional funds by hiking fees and by doing applied research for the private sector. This, added to the persistent teaching pressures, threatens to erode even further the universities' mission for basic research. While the problems of declining funding and increasing corporatization also afflict universities in the North, in Africa the effects are much worse for universities lacking long histories and traditions of scholarly production and the protective networks of generations of generous alumni.

If left unchecked, the current trends will reinforce the international intellectual division of labor whereby African universities and social scientists will continue to import appropriate packages of "universal" theory and, at best, export empirical data; to be consumers of advanced research conducted in the universities of the North. The African academic enterprise has long suffered from a culture of imported scientific consumerism. This culture, established during the colonial era, spread after independence despite rhetorical protestations to the contrary and ritual obeisance to local cognitive needs. African academics continue to exhibit strong tendencies of what Paulin Hountodji (1997) has called "theoretical extroversion," the feverish importation of paradigms, problematics, and perspectives and the search for legitimation and respectability from the intellectual establishments of the North. Research is the lifeblood of the intellectual enterprise, the process through which ideas and insights, technologies and techniques, old and new, are nurtured and nourished, tried and tested, developed and discarded. In the so-called "new knowledge economy," research is even more important than ever, allowing a country not only to generate new knowledge, but also effectively to process knowledge produced elsewhere and to engage in productive scholarly and scientific commerce and competition with other nations. Only the future will tell whether the recent economic and political changes that have taken place in African countries will strengthen African universities and research capacities.

What, then, should the research agenda be for African intellectuals such as historians and social scientists? Of course, I would not dare suggest a laundry list even if space permitted, which thankfully, it does not. If I can venture a prediction, both the empirical subject matter and theoretical paradigms will continue to be as diverse as the disciplines and the locations and ideologies of the researchers; I would hope that African social science scholarship will be inspired by a burning desire to address the pressing issues of the times, to deepen our understanding of our economies, politics, cultures, societies, ecologies, legal systems, moral orders, gender relations—the list is endless—in order to bring about progressive and sustainable change. As for historians, they must continue expanding the temporal and spatial horizons of African histories, to tell large and small stories of our multiple pasts. We must try to resist the seductions of post-something sophistries parading in some sections of the western academy and being propagated by the likes of Achille Mbembe, CODESRIA's discredited and ousted executive secretary. In this endeavor, African migrant academics could play a positive role, a subject examined in the next chapter.

Conclusion: Envisioning African Universities

The need to revitalize African universities is quite self-evident, but it requires serious rethinking that goes beyond technical restructuring aimed at immediate problem solving. It is indeed gratifying for those of us committed to the existence of vibrant African universities that the silly and dangerous notion that universities are an irrelevant and expensive luxury for poor Africa, a notion popularized by the World Bank in the 1980s, is finally dead. As already indicated, the World Bank now swears on the critical importance of universities for Africa's development in the twenty-first century. The foundations have followed suit, although not all had really believed in the bank's old canard (Lively, 1999). In April 2000, the four American foundations—Ford, Rockefeller, Carnegie, and MacArthur—announced a $100 million five-year initiative to revitalize select universities in West, East and Southern Africa (Bollag, 2000). Soon after the Ford Foundation created a new ten-year $300 million worldwide program to underwrite 3,500 graduate student fellowships for students from Africa, Latin America, Asia, and Russia (Bernstein, 2001). Conferences on African universities have become increasingly common on the continent itself and among Africa's friends abroad, some of which I have attended or organized.[13] Organizations such as the Association of African Universities (1991a, 1991b, 1995, 2001) and UNESCO (1992a, 1992b, 1993, 1995, 1997, 1998a, 1998b) have also weighed in with weighty reports and declarations.

A cynic, and Africa encourages cynicism, might regard this flurry of activity as cyclical, fueled this time by a temporary millennial frenzy. Whatever the cause or likely duration of these initiatives, much of the renewed interest in African universities shown by African governments, international agencies, foundations, and African universities themselves is focused on reforming rather than fundamentally reconstructing them. This is partly understandable given the dire straights many African universities find themselves in. Nevertheless, there is also a crying need for bold visions to drive the restructuring of African universities. This is to suggest there is relatively little "visioning" and "imagining" of what the "African university" ought to be. Living in an age that distrusts the future, either because of the influence of the "posts" that rail against teleological narratives, or because of triumphant global capitalism that claims the end of alternatives, the "vision thing" seems to be a relic of socialist planning or poetic affectation.

I found myself in precisely this quandary when I was invited to participate in a conference on visioning the African university in 2050. The organizers were deliberately vague, allowing us to be as concrete or as creative as we wished in describing our imagined university and to focus on whatever caught our fancy, from its physical structure, location, and functions to its dominant values and relationships. I decided to write a short story about the vice-chancellor of a high-tech university, a renowned female scientist who has a remarkable personal and social history, and whose campus embodies a lifelong vision of what a university should be. She is being presented an award for her research achievements by the president of a United States of Africa, who also happens to be a woman (Zeleza, 2001).

Other visions were even more elaborate. Many dreamed of truly decolonized, democratized, and decentralized universities, whether as physical or virtual entities; universities that are autonomous yet accountable, committed to the pursuit of intellectual excellence yet rooted in their communities, effectively managed internally yet working closely with all stakeholders; universities that are Africanized in their staffing, values, pedagogy, epistemologies, and instructional languages yet are capable of competing globally, contributing to the global pool of knowledge, and responding quickly and effectively to global changes and emerging local needs; universities that attract students and faculty from across the continent and the diaspora, and that participate in extensive academic exchanges with universities in other parts of the world; universities that provide inclusive education, where access is open regardless of physical or class disabilities or various cultural and social affiliations; universities with ample and up-to-date learning facilities, instructional technologies, and well-equipped libraries and laboratories, manageable student-teacher ratios, that provide multiple entry and exit

113

points as well as individual and group enrollments for lifelong and flexible learning; universities with vibrant communities of scholars, where public seminars, lectures and debates flourish, research and publishing are valued but not subjected to the mindless "publish and perish" syndrome, and where African scholars can engage in "idle contemplation" as well as provide solutions to practical problems; universities where gender is mainstreamed, curricula are innovative and not trapped in the old parochial disciplinary divisions or the current faddish interdisciplinary fields, and which produce students who are literate in the major fields of knowledge, innovative and entrepreneurial, as well as critical thinkers and citizens; universities where the professors are highly trained and motivated and productive but also include practitioners from other sectors; universities, in short, that are the spearhead of the African renaissance.[14]

Bold visions, indeed, although some were marred by the perennial anguish of assuming there is an essential Africanness that needs to be recuperated for the universities to rediscover their true mission. There will always be many types of African universities, their Africanness arising not from some spurious traditional essence, but from their very spatial and social situatedness in contemporary Africa. This is to argue for forward-looking dreams, rather than Afrocentric fantasies of glorious pasts. Nevertheless, little will be achieved if African states do not take the lead in re-investing in African higher education. They have a crucial role to play in mobilizing national and international efforts. It would be a good idea if part of the funds saved from any debt forgiveness were earmarked specifically for the universities and strategic research initiatives. Managers of African universities also have critical responsibilities; to address the issues of accountability and corruption, to promote teaching and research excellence, to devise creative ways of diversifying sources of funding, and to be keenly aware of new trends in international education, and to forge partnerships that promote both capacity-building and capacity-utilization, effectively utilizing African capacities wherever they may be located, in independent research centers, neighboring countries, or outside the continent. At stake is our survival and well-being as a global people.

As intellectuals, we must articulate clear agendas for African societies and peoples, especially as the continent encounters new processes of globalization. These agendas must be rooted in the unfinished tasks of progressive African nationalism—development, democratization, and self-determination—revised to reflect different contexts and changing circumstances. In the current wave of globalization, as before, Africa is intimately involved, more as a passenger than the driver. Without strong, well-funded universities and research programs, we will continue being passengers. If our history is not to continue repeating itself, in which weakness condemned our ancestors to slavery and colonization, and if our offspring are not to be condemned to similar fates of exploitation and humiliation, we need to become drivers as well.

Endnotes

1. According to the report by the Centre for Higher Education Transformation written by Cloete and Bunting (2000) the old category differences in South African higher education were between advantaged and disadvantaged, Afrikaans and English, university and technikon. The new landscape is divided between what they call entrepreneurial expanding institutions; traditional elite institutions; emerging stable institutions; uncertain-unstable institutions; and crisis ridden institutions. Government funding for higher education between 1995 and 1999 increased by 5 percent in real rands; as a proportion of total government expenditure the increase was from 2.6 percent to 3.0 percent, and from 12 percent to 14 percent as a percentage of total government expenditure on education.

2. In descending order, the enrollments were as follows: Natal (79 percent), Rhodes (56 percent), Pretoria Extension: Contact Only (56 percent), Wits (54 percent), Rand Afrikaans (50 percent), Cape Town (48 percent), Potchefstroom (47 percent), Stellenbosch (32 percent), Pretoria: Contact (23 percent). Free State was 46 percent in 1999, see Balintulo (2001). The drop in student numbers at the HBUs or HDIs (Historically disadvantaged institutions) was pronounced at the University of the North, where numbers fell from 13,800 in 1995 to 7,800 in 2000. The situation at this and other HDIs was apparently brought about by student inability or reluctance to pay fees and widespread corruption. Declining enrollment was also reported for the institutions providing distance education, namely, the University of South Africa and Technikon

South Africa, where numbers dropped by 41,000 students between 1995 and 1999, while residential institutions increased their residential students by 31,000, which suggests that the growth of distance education by the latter was largely responsible for the declines at the former institutions. See Vergnani (1998a, 1998b, 2000a, 2000b).

3. This is small when compared to funds raised by the average US research university. For example, Johns Hopkins University, the top institution in federal research-and-development expenditures, raised $724.5 million in fiscal 1997. Iowa State University which raised $52.9 million, compared to the $52.7 spent by the Ford Foundation over ten years, ranked eighty-sixth among U.S. universities. See *The Chronicle of Higher Education* at http://chronicle.com/weekly/almanac/1999/facts/13money.htm

4. For two detailed and interesting studies on student strikes in Burkina Faso and Côte d'Ivoire, see Christopher Wise (1998) and Cyril Dadieh (1996), respectively.

5. They are: University of Benin in Benin; University of Ghana in Ghana; University of Nairobi in Kenya; Jomo Kenyatta University of Agriculture and Technology also in Kenya; University of Namibia in Namibia; University of the Western Cape in South Africa; and the University of Zambia in Zambia. The lack of "hard" statistics has not prevented estimates from being banded about, for example, that 20-30 percent of the students at the University of Nairobi are infected, according to Burton Bollag (2001b) writing in *The Chronicle of Higher Education*. Bollag's article elicited a fierce denial from Mori Kandeh (2001) that, like the Western media in general, Bollag had exaggerated the incidence of AIDS on the continent and in the universities, whose faculties, he argued, were decimated more by the brain drain to the West than AIDS. Yes, the Western media tends to sensationalize and pathologize Africa, but that does not mean the HIV/AIDS pandemic is not real. The difficulties of establishing effective AIDS-prevention programs in one West African country, Benin, are recounted by Benjamin Lawreence (2001).

6. Mike Jensen is an independent consultant based in South Africa who

specializes on African Internet issues and maintains a comprehensive website on the subject (http://www3.sn.apc.org/africa)

7. In Latin America and in the Caribbean there was one internet user for every 125 people, in South East Asia and the Pacific 1 in 250, among the Arab states 1 in 500, and in South Asia 1 in 2500 (Jensen, 2001).

8. Jensen's website lists all the major continental (twelve), sub-regional (six), international (eighteen), national/local (thirty-three) agencies and private sector and foundations (twenty-five) involved in the development of ICTs in Africa in 2001 and the specific programs and projects they support. Most are either from, or are funded by, the North.

9. Websites from the two regions dominate in terms of quality web content, according to a report on the top fifty African Websites by Noel Yavo (1999). The websites were evaluated in the categories of education, sciences, culture, community development, and public information.

10. The explosion in private universities can partly be explained by pressures for higher education that the public universities have been unable to meet, growing demands for specialized education, and calls from the elite, dissatisfied with declining standards and frequent closures of public universities, for quality and internationally recognized education for their children (Nwamuo, 2001).

11. The tale of state assaults against academic freedom in Zimbabwe is a sad one indeed. The government has, through legislation and naked repression, systematically, undermined the institutional autonomy of the university, all in a desperate effort to silence student and faculty protest, a part of the pro-democracy movement, against a misguided and authoritarian regime that has failed to deliver on the promises of the liberation struggle. Many of the state officials bent on taming the University of Zimbabwe are former students and lecturers at the university, including the regime's propaganda chief, Jonathan Moyo, formerly a lecturer in political science, appointed minister of information in 2000. For a succinct summary of the attacks against academic freedom up to the turn of the 1990s, see Cheater (1991).

12. Hopes on the Horizon Film Project, Script, 16 May 2000: 21. The Rwanda genocide has elicited fierce debate among scholars as to its causes, courses, and consequences. One of the questions in the debate is whether the elites, including the intellectuals, were the perpetrators of the genocide, or whether it was also a project of both the masses and the governing elite as Mamdani (2001) believes it was. Others emphasize the role of treacherous elites, or the homicidal masses, or regional factors (see Sharlet, 2001). I believe no one single factor by itself can explain such a complex and ghastly event as the genocide, but here I am simply pointing out the culpability of the intellectuals.

13. I have attended several meetings organized by the Ford and MacArthur foundations, and the Center for African Studies at the University of Illinois, of which I am director, is organizing its 2002 Annual Spring Symposium on the theme "African Universities in the 21st Century" in conjunction with the university's College of Education, the Association of African Universities, and CODESRIA.

14. The African Higher Education Retreat was sponsored by the Ford Foundation and held in Durban, South Africa, May 29 -June 1, 2001. This is a summary of some of the papers listed below which were written for the retreat, although the deliberations themselves departed from normal intellectual discourse and were more akin to an NGO palaver: Salih (2001; Tamale (2001; Katjavivi (2001); Manuh (2001; Iskandar (2001) Olukoshi (2001); Vubo (2001); Yizengaw (2001); Coffie (2001); Ouma (2001); Diaw (2001); Abagi (2001); Semambo (2001); Tabifor (2001); and Mwangi (2000).

Chapter 3

International Academic Exchanges: Patterns and Possibilities

Introduction

The previous chapter examined the various challenges that face African universities and the attempts that have been and are being made to revitalize them. It was noted that the internal and external "brain drain" has been one of the key manifestations of the crisis facing many African universities as some of their academic members migrate to greener pastures at home and abroad; at home to public or private sectors or to the emerging NGO academic sector of independent research centers and institutes, and abroad to universities in the neighboring countries or in the North. Thus, Africa's academic exchanges flow in three directions: within countries, among countries, and across continents. They take several forms, including the physical mobility of academic staff and students, networking in terms of research and libraries, and collaboration in the areas of curricula development, programs, seminars and conferences.

The question of Africa's brain drain to the North raises troubling questions among African intellectuals, university administrators, and policy makers, questions about African development and globalization, national education and internationalization, intellectual autonomy and transnational engagements. I believe that any meaningful program of revitalizing African universities and of promoting their research capacities must seek ways of forging and institutionalizing close and constant collaborations, contacts, and

119

conversations between African academics in the national universities, the independent research centers, and in the foreign universities, both those in other African countries and in the North. More broadly, this chapter seeks to examine the role that partnerships with Northern universities and academic communities can play in this process of revitalization under the current configurations of globalization. This is to suggest that African universities, which are largely patterned on European and American models, have always had relations, despite periodic fluctuations, with universities in the North.

This chapter is divided into five sections. The first briefly examines the general implications of globalization for higher education; the second, academic exchanges and mobility within the continent itself are looked at; the third, the processes and patterns of African intellectual migrations to the North are analyzed. Particular attention is given to the question of the African brain drain, as manifested, for example, by rates of return of African graduate students. The fourth part focuses on the dynamics and dimensions of Africa's international academic exchanges, particularly with American universities. Briefly discussed are some of the exchange models that have developed between the two regions in terms of student and faculty mobility and research collaborations. The final section makes suggestions on how to build productive linkages across the Atlantic using Africa's own intellectual diaspora.

Higher Education and Globalization

It is a cliche of our times that we live in an age of globalization. Globalization can be seen as a new and self-defining reality. As indicated in the two previous chapters, I do not think globalization is really new or beneficent, or that it entails homogenization. Stripped of their celebratory or condemnatory verbiage, globalization discourses refer to the intensification of international connections, contacts, and communication, and the growth of a more interdependent world integrated by new information and communication technologies. Nonetheless it is a process fraught with contradictions. The globalization of financial markets and transnational corporations is accompanied by economic regionalization and informalization; cultural transnationalism spreads simultaneously with rising cultural chauvenism and fragmentation; states are said to be declining as they proliferate and increase their internal repressive capacities; and certainties about the materiality of globalization are trailed by crises of knowledge about the world where we live.

The apparently relentless march of globalization, whether defined as a historical process describing concrete conditions or as an ideological project prescribing particular futures, forces a new reckoning for every sector and institution. Hence, the proliferation of studies on globalization and the economy, or culture, or politics, or education. Numerous studies have appeared and conferences organized to examine globalization in education. This is a large and exciting subject that I have no intention of discussing in detail except to identify some of the key debates. At one level the links between globalization and higher education are obvious. It would not be an exaggeration to argue that research conducted by the world's universities has helped produce globalization as a constellation of material and imaginary, spatial and symbolic processes, while globalization is simultaneously producing new contexts and imperatives for intellectual communities. In other words, universities are both a cause and manifestation of globalization, in that they have always aspired to be globalized and they are globalizing institutions.

More difficult to identify are the specific implications of current processes and projects of globalization for higher education. Needless to say, since there is no agreement on what constitutes globalization, the manifestations and trends of globalization in higher education are in serious dispute, as regards their extent, efficacy, and ethics (Currie and Newson, 1998; Scott, 1998). Paradoxes abound. Universities are experiencing rapid growth in the face of reduced resources; they are prey to too much and too little state intervention; they are research institutions producing an ever declining share of research; and they are purveyors of internationalization that penalize international exchanges through differential fees, for example. Much of the analysis and debate seem to center on six key trends in higher education that are connected to contemporary technological, economic, and ideological transformations. If the information and communication technologies constitute the motor of these changes, transnational firms drive them, and neoliberal discourse provides the fuel. I have identified the six key trends dubbing them the six Cs: corporatization of management, collectivization of access, commercialization of learning, commodification of knowledge, computerization of education, and connectivity of institutions. These trends are not new of course, but they have become more urgent and more complex, and they manifest themselves unevenly in different world regions.

Corporatization of management refers to the adoption of business models for the organization and administration of higher education institutions. As we saw in the last chapter, governmental donors press universities into the discourse of accountability and entrepreneurship, obliging them to undertake new budgetary strategies and to expand and diversify their sources of funds to become more efficient, productive, and relevant. Critics point out that the reigning ideology of free market capitalism increasingly sees education not primarily as a social good or as a human right, but as an economic investment, a training ground for cogs in the machine of industry and the new information economy, not a haven for socializing students to the community, to the life of the mind, or to a profession. Universities are turned into mills to produce and retool entrepreneurs and information operatives, instead of oases to nurture the values of democratic citizenship (Spring, 1998; Kempner, 2000; Newman, 2000). The dangers of corporatization are real, but some of the critics are blinded by false nostalgia, forgetting how insular, authoritarian, and even corrupt university management was, and still is in many instances, not to mention sexist or racist. The challenge is to devise new administrative systems that increase efficiency, transparency, accountability, and democratic governance.

By collectivization of access I mean the growing massification of higher education, the perception that education is a lifelong learning process, and the increasing collaborations between universities and, or interventions in university affairs by, stakeholders in the public and private sectors, which has resulted in the reconfiguration, some would say erosion, of traditional notions and values of university autonomy, academic freedom, liberal education, and quality (Tangian, 2001; Duderstadt, 1999/2000; Sacks, 1996). The upsurge in higher education reflects the expansion of the youth population, the growth of middle class incomes and aspirations, the creeping credentialism in professions and occupations, and the rising demand for knowledge-based skills and jobs. Given the rapid economic changes, the separation between education and career as chronologically distinct phases of life are crumbling, and the two mesh, as one writer colorfully puts it, "as the horizontal and vertical threads of a single piece of fabric, as interwoven, as inextricably combined" (Reinsch, 1996: 593).

Thus, universities are adapting to the demands of continuing education for workers in the knowledge-based industries by restructuring their courses, making them part-time and modular. Consequently, universities are becoming more diversified in their programs and student composition. Already, in some countries, older working students outnumber younger students. According to Peter Jarvis (1999: 52), "this is true of most North

American and UK universities. In the UK, for instance, the Higher Education Funding Council reported that there were many more people studying in universities who were over the age of 21 years than there were traditional undergraduate students in 1993." As the worlds of academe and work converge ever more closely, universities are increasingly seen as advanced vocational schools, subject to market responsiveness and social accountability rather than the old notions of autonomy and academic freedom. I would argue that while the expansion of access to universities is welcome and some vocationalization is unavoidable, care must be taken to ensure that universities retain and realize their role as sanctuaries of critical reflection and basic research.

Commercialization of learning refers to the rapid expansion of private universities, the increased involvement of private enterprise in the provision of higher education, and the establishment of "executive" programs in public universities. Thus we are seeing the rise of what some call the "market-oriented university" (Buchbinder, 1993; Buchbinder and Newson, 1992), the "entrepreneurial university" (Clark, 1995), or the "consumer university" (Barrow, 1997). Besides the spectacular growth of private universities related to the rising demand for higher education and the ever-changing needs of the knowledge-based economy, corporate universities are emerging. These are universities that are created by large industries or transnational corporations

> from Disney and McDonalds to Motorola in the USA and Body Shop, British Aerospace and BT in the UK. Transnational corporations have the knowledge, the finance and the employees to provide specialized teaching and learning—but significantly they are not only training their own employees and some institutions, such as Arthur D. Little Institute in the USA, are now engaged in initial preparation of workers without any guarantee that they will get a job in the company on successful completion of the studies. This is a new idea—but throughout the history of the university there have been different founders of universities—the church, the state and now the large corporations (Jarvis, 1999: 54).

These changes are eroding the monopoly that universities have long enjoyed over the resources and privileges of intellectual production. In addition to the universities, the sites of scholarly knowledge production now include state agencies, private corporations, and independent think tanks or research centers and networks. The connections between these institutions are exceedingly complex, but partnerships are being formed, indeed encouraged, and many academics rotate among them with varying degrees of comfort and ease.

All these developments reinforce the commodification of knowledge, as reflected in the increasing production, sponsorship, and dissemination of research by commercial enterprises and for-profit institutions or companies established by faculty, the tendency to apply intellectual property rights and copyright to research and instructional materials, and raises of student charges. The more education and research are regarded as economic investments, the more their costs and returns are calculated according to market and proprietary principles. State subsidies have been reduced or removed in many countries and student tuition rates raised to reflect the "real" costs of tertiary education. Universities are also setting up research parks on their campuses, often partnered with industry. Faculty members, especially in science and technology, to quote Stanley Ikenberry (2001: 35), former president of the American Council on Education, "live dual lives as professors and CEOs of start-up companies. Major pharmaceutical companies lock up research agreements with entire academic departments."

In the United States, industry has become an important source of research funds as federal expenditure on research and development has declined. For example, in 1999 federal agencies accounted for only 26.7 percent of the $247 billion that the nation spent on R&D, compared to 65 percent in the early 1960s (Greenberg, 2001). In the meantime, companies sponsored a growing proportion of research performed by the universities, rising to $2.2 billion in 1999 or 9.4 percent of the universities' research expenditures (Basinger, 2001). Critics contend that such ties "threaten to undermine both the objectivity of researchers and the safety of human subjects in medical studies" (Brainard, 2000: A31). These dangers are evident in medical research funded by the drug companies, which sometimes try to influence the interpretation of research findings or even bar publication of disagreeable results (Guterman, 2001). Such practices forced editors from the world's leading medical journals "to adopt a policy that would allow them to refuse to publish any drug company-sponsored studies in which the scientific independence of the involved researchers was not guaranteed" (Kellogg, 2001). The stakes are indeed high as was apparent at a meeting of more than 700 officials from universities and companies to discuss the growing support that corporations were providing for academic research. The participants failed to reach agreement (Brainard, 2001). Several universities, however, have adopted conflict-of-interest guidelines, and some advocates for integrity in science have set up a website to list academic scientists conducting industry-sponsored research (Blumenstyk, 2001a; http://integrityin-science.org).

It is not always compelling to attribute all these trends to contemporary globalization, but in the area of the new information and communication technologies (ICT) the impact of globalization seems incontrovertible. The computerization of education involves the incorporation of ICT into the knowledge activities of teaching, research, and publication. Much of the debate on globalization in higher education centers on the educational impact of ICT. Opinions differ sharply. Before outlining them, it should be noted that until recently online education was mostly confined to the United States, and English was the language of instruction. The ascendancy of English, although begun long before, the ICT revolution accelerated it. So dominant did English become as the lingua franca of academia that 95 percent of the 925,000 scientific articles published in 1997 were written in English (Bollag, 2000). This "linguistic imperialism" troubled many people in countries where English was not widely spoken or used. So did the U. S. grip on online education.

Challenges were soon mounted. In early 2001, presidents of Canadian colleges and universities and senior business executives announced an ambitious plan to invest heavily in online education (Carnevale, 2001a). Across the Atlantic, in August 2001, Britain unveiled plans to establish a national virtual university owned by a consortium of British universities (Carr, 2001a). This came a few months after the European Union adopted a three-year $13.3 billion "eLearning Action Plan" aimed at broadening digital literacy in Europe and contesting American supremacy (Birchard, 2001). Further east, China reported that it intended to have five million students in 50 to 100 online colleges by 2005, up from 38 colleges and 240,000 students in March 2001 (Walfish, 2001). China's online programs involve collaborations between universities and publicly traded high-tech companies, a clear example of the ubiquity of university-industry alliances even in a nominally communist country. African leaders of higher education generally believe that the adoption of the new technologies is critical for the revitalization of African universities and for national economic and social development, sentiments that have been expressed at numerous regional and international conferences (Niang, 1997; African Regional Consultation, 1997; UNESCO, 1998, 2000).

However, not everyone is enthusiastic about the benefits of online education. In Asia, we are told, Thailand and Japan still put a premium on the socialization of student-teacher classroom interactions and are lukewarm towards virtual universities (Brender, 2001; *The Chronicle of Higher Education,* June 29, 2001: A 28). Even the United States' southern neighbor, Mexico, faced with aggressive American institutions flocking to enroll Mexican students in online education programs, apparently fear that internationalizing its education may come to mean Americanizing it (*The Chronicle of Higher Education,* 22 September 2000: A41).

It is of course in the United States, where online education is most developed, that some of the most heated debates are heard. To its supporters, ICT offers limitless possibilities to expand, democratize, and globalize university education, assuming of course that access to computers and online services is available. Skeptics, however, question whether the primary motive behind the craze for online education lies in the universities' educational interests or vendor companies' aggressive marketing, in profit rather than pedagogy. They point out that drop out rates are 10 to 20 percent higher for online courses than for traditional courses, although there is no agreement as to whether this is because the teachers are inexperienced in online teaching, or because the students who take them in the first place have busy schedules (Blumenstyk, 1999; Carr, 2000; Young, 2000).

The debate has centered on two issues, first, the cost and profitability of online education, and second, its pedagogical benefits. The jury is still out on both issues. Six studies assessing online education at six universities indicate that online programs are neither cheap to produce nor as profitable as originally anticipated. Some are breaking even, some are losing money, and very few are making money (Carr, 2001b). As the realization has dawned that online programs are not cash cows, some universities have scaled back or even closed the for-profit distance education companies they had set with such great expectations, as Temple University did in mid-2001 (Blumenstyk, 2001b). On the question of quality, the American Federation of Teachers believes that it is compromised in programs driven by business interests (Carnevale, 2001b). A study by sixteen professors at the University of Illinois concluded that online education shows both promise and peril because while good teaching can occur online, it is often more costly and time-consuming than traditional classroom teaching (Young, 2000). Another study sponsored by the National Education Association indicates that distance learning can be quality learning only if colleges and universities recognize the students' needs (Carnevale, 2000).

We need to go beyond narrow financial calculations and the polar options of boosterism and rejectionism, as Nicholas Burbules and Thomas Callister (2000) call them. They argue, and I agree, that the positive and negative potential of the new technologies must be faced squarely by universities and academics, with the aim of harnessing the positive, and safeguarding their role as creators and certifiers of authoritative scholarship. Instead of wholesale embrace or dismissal, it is more productive to determine which technologies are useful for which students, for which subject matters, and for which purposes. Engagement with the new technologies allows universities to provide their students with critical technoliteracy, democratized and customized higher learning, and help to shape the emerging ICT educational regime, e.g., the tension between pedagogical and proprietary norms.

Since they are both repositories of information and media for knowledge production, the new technologies are not merely "delivery systems" that pass through colleges and universities, leaving their core values either unchanged or destroyed. Rather, the new technologies are an integral part of the complex and contradictory changes taking place in the conflicted terrain of higher education. If tapped carefully and creatively they hold exciting possibilities for removing the spatiotemporal constraints that limit access for nontraditional students, promote student interaction and cooperative learning, pedagogical experimentation, collaborative research, and transnational exchanges. They can blur the distinctions between on-campus and off-campus teaching, between residential and distance education. In short, the impact of ICT is ambiguous because, like all technologies, it is not simply an innocuous tool, in this case a potential educational tool, but "a political economy and field of power, a new nexus of human-machine relations and a force for remaking the conditions constitutive of subjectivity" (Tuathail and McCormick, 1998: 347). The impact of ICT depends on its design and the technoculture it embodies and promises, the prevailing structural and institutional contexts in which it performs, and the broader material conditions and social relations in which it is articulated.

Finally, there has been increased connectivity of institutions that pertains to the increased emphasis on institutional cooperation and coordination within and across countries, a process facilitated by ICT, competition from the new corporate interlopers of higher education, the rising costs of maintaining such expensive infrastructures as libraries, and pressures from students and for internationalization. International education cooperation involves activities ranging from academic mobility, internationalization of curricula and programs, networking and linking arrangements to research collaboration and joint publishing. To be effective, academic exchanges have to be truly reciprocal and mutually beneficial, based on shared planning, implementation, and evaluation processes. Unfortunately, this has not been the case for Africa.

This chapter explores the linkages within Africa and between Africa and the North. Africa's educational linkages with other regions of the South are hardly discussed not because they are unimportant but because they are relatively underdeveloped. South-South scholarly cooperation is in fact imperative because, as Mohammed Hassan (2000), the head of the Third World Academy of Sciences has argued, these regions have much to learn from each other and need to work together to reduce the huge gap between the North and the South in the production and utilization of scientific and technological knowledge. South-South cooperation also provides a more propitious platform for building North-South linkages. To many African scholars intra-African institutional partnerships are indeed seen as a prerequisite for fruitful exchanges with other world regions (Fobih, 1999; Hill, 1999; Camara, 2000).

Continental Travels

There are few reliable studies on academic mobility and exchanges within and among African countries, but general patterns can be discerned. In the days when there were a handful of regional universities, exchanges of staff, students, and curricula flourished. Staff and students came from many countries within each region and beyond. Indeed, the academic staff was often dominated by expatriates from the former colonial powers and the curricula was patterned on European models. There were tensions between regionalization and internationalization, between Pan-African dreams and Eurocentric designs. In the face of nationalisms that distrusted regional integration as much as they disliked neo-colonial dependency, the system was unsustainable.

With the establishment of national universities after independence, the old patterns of regional and international academic exchanges began to change. Generally, the nationalization of universities posed a more immediate threat to regional than to international mobility. If the national universities no longer produced regional or Pan-African elites, the bourgeoning middle classes they bred typically received their undergraduate degrees at home and graduate degrees abroad, mostly in the North. Thus, until recently both internal and regional academic mobility were quite limited in most African countries. Internal mobility was limited for academic staff in countries with one national university and elsewhere too because the uniform conditions of service imposed on the universities by governments hampered their differentiation and the emergence of a competitive academic labor market.

The situation began to change as universities expanded in number, state control diminished, and private universities emerged. In Kenya, for example, I witnessed the growth of a relatively vibrant academic labor market from the late 1980s following the establishment of new public and private universities. Since the universities grew faster than there were academic staff, many of us soon learned to manipulate the situation to our advantage for promotions and salary raises. Regional migrations also began to increase as rates of economic growth among African countries fell and became more differentiated. Some of the movements followed the old trails of colonial regionalism. To quote Smallwood and Maliyamkono (1996: 322):

> The old Central African Federation and East African Community left a legacy of staff and student mobility of which traces still exist. Uganda and Tanzania exchange students under the East Africa Inter-University Council, and the new private universities in Kenya have begun to attract students from neighboring countries. Zambia and Tanzania exchange students in medicine and mining, and in southern Africa the smaller SADCC members send students to their larger SADCC neighbors, notably to Zimbabwe and to Tanzania and Kenya. In the Francophone countries of West Africa there is also a shared legacy that should encourage interuniversity cooperation. The extent of student and staff mobility across French-English language barriers is very limited although it does occur, students from Burundi exchange with students from Tanzania, for example, but only to study English and French respectively. Mobility between

Anglophone Southern and Eastern Africa and West Africa is also very limited.

In North Africa, Egyptian universities have signed hundreds of academic cooperation agreements involving student and faculty exchanges and secondments, joint degrees, and curricula, research and technical collaboration, mostly with universities in the region and the Arab world. Both Cairo University and Al-Azhar University attract students from West and East Africa (Nkrumah, 2001). While Egypt is at the center of academic exchanges in North Africa, Nigeria was the magnet in West Africa during the oil boom years, while postapartheid South Africa has become the hub in Southern Africa. Nigeria even earmarked 5 percent of total university enrollment for foreign students and entered into bilateral education agreements with about thirty countries, most of them on the continent. In 1989-90, however, there were only 678 foreign students out of a quota target of 8,600. Between 60 to 70 percent of the foreign students came from Cameroon, and the rest trickled from other African countries, as well as from India, Pakistan, and Sri Lanka. Very few were from developed countries (Akinpelu, 1994: 111).

Similarly, the University of Ghana does not meet the 10 percent it allocates to foreign students. But the University of Ougadougou claims that foreign students constitute 10 percent of its enrollment (*AAU Newsletter*, 4, 2-3, 1998: 7). Other universities that apparently attract large numbers of foreign students are the International University of Africa in Khartoum, which prides itself on being a Pan-African institution, drawing students from over fifty countries (*AAU Newsletter*, 4, 2-3, 1998: 14); Burkina Faso's Polytechnic University of Bobo-Dioulasso, established in 1997, where 14 percent of the students in 1999 were foreign; and Egypt's Misr University for Science and Technology, established in 1996, drew more than 25 percent of its students from abroad in 1999 (*AAU Newsletter*, 6, 2, 2000: 7-8).

Many of the academics who have migrated to universities in other African countries tend to do so on their own accord, as labor migrants fleeing repression or deteriorating economic conditions, rather than as part of structured schemes of short-term or long-term reciprocal faculty exchanges. Not surprisingly, they are often subject to the hostility accorded to immigrants or refugees (Zeleza, 1997a: Chapter 2). In short, Africa lacks the highly structured and effective academic exchange programs that have been established in the European Union since the mid-1980s, such as ERAS-

MUS, a student and faculty exchange program that involves 1,500 institutions and over 100,000 students annually; COMETT created to support university-industry cooperation through training partnerships, of which there were 205 in 1993-94 involving 3,500 firms and 1,500 institutions of higher learning (Frost-Smith, 1994); LINGUA, designed to boost the learning of foreign languages in educational institutions and the workplace; and TEMPUS, formed in 1990 to promote university cooperation with Central and Eastern Europe.[1]

Structurally, the European programs emphasize the creation and development of networks, mobility of people, and joint innovative projects as a means of achieving systematic and sustainable cooperation. Besides research collaboration, these programs have facilitated the emergence of new types of qualification and certification for academic work, including joint and double degree programs and curricula reform. This has been made possible by the existence of a favorable political climate in the region, as well as the presence of a powerful central coordinating body in the form of the European Union which makes available considerable financial resources. Also, the Western European countries are comparatively small in size and live in very close proximity to one another which reduces communication costs, and the economic and cultural differences between them are not as pronounced as they are in Africa and other world regions. The programs themselves were carefully designed to meet specific objectives and the universities were fully consulted to ensure that the demand for the services actually existed. Moreover, they were built on pre-existing networks of resource persons and activities and the participants feeling a sense of ownership and they are well-marketed.[2]

While such comprehensive cooperative programs have yet to emerge in Africa, academic cooperation has grown across the continent, principally through research networks, computer networks, and library networks. There has been an explosion of research centers and networks that seek to promote and coordinate research among African scholars and sometimes to provide graduate training. Some were mentioned in the previous chapter, such as CODESRIA, OSSREA, and SAPES in the social sciences, and ICRAF and ICIPE in the sciences. They all maintain active links with the universities. For example, ICIPE has an Insect Science Program that involves twenty-two African institutions, and SAPES offers a joint masters' degree in policy studies with several universities in Tanzania, Zimbabwe, Mozambique, Malawi, and South Africa.

Perhaps the most ambitious organization devoted to building African research capacities is the African Capacity Building Foundation (ACBF), established in 1991 and based in Harare. The ACBF was founded by the African Development Bank, the World Bank, and the UNDP, with the support of fourteen African countries and nine developed countries. Its initial mandate was to help build capacity in the area of macroeconomic policy analysis and development management. In 1999 the ACBF's scope was expanded, and it was asked to devise programs to reverse the brain drain and encourage the retention and intensive use of existing capacity. Since its inception, the Foundation has worked with policy analysis units and supported research and training programs and institutions at national and regional levels. By September 2000, it had awarded fifty-nine grants totaling $110 million; seventeen of the fifty-nine were for training projects. It has been claimed that the training programs have enhanced graduate economics education in some 33 departments of economics across the continent (http://www.acbf-pact.org/; Osundina, 1995). Among the regional research networks supported by the ACBF is the African Economic Research Consortium (AERC), established in 1988 to strengthen economic policy research. The consortium networks individual researchers and also supports a collaborative master's program involving twenty universities in fifteen Anglophone countries, and has an active publishing program, which by 2000 had issued more than 100 books and monographs (http://www.world-bank.org/wb/aerc/aerc.htm). The Francophone equivalent of AERC is the Programme de Troisième Cycle Inter-universitaire (PTCI), which runs a collaborative master's among thirteen universities.

Many of the regional networks for training and research are sponsored by the Association of African Universities (AAU). They include the University Science, Humanities and Engineering Partnerships in Africa (USHEPiA), coordinated by the University of Cape Town; the M.A. Program in Renewable Energy Systems at the University of Science and Technology in Ghana; Research on Semi-Arid Agriculture in Dakar; the master's program and research in distance education at the University of Namibia; Network for Environmental Bio-Technology at the University of Ouagadougou; the Network for Accountancy Programs at the University of South Africa; and the master's program on Human Rights Law in Africa at the University of Pretoria (ADEA Working Group on Higher Education, 1998: 7-8). The organization of the Human Rights Law program shows how these programs are structured. Established in 2000, it brings thirty students from all over the continent, who are taught by instructors from across the continent and abroad. After the first six months the students have a choice of continuing at the Center for Human Rights in Pretoria or completing the second six months at a selected number of other law faculties on the continent (*AAU Newsletter*, 5, 2, 1999: 18-19).

The AAU has been at the forefront of promoting interuniversity cooperation since its creation in 1967 in Rabat, Morocco. By 2001 its membership had grown from 34 to more than 170 universities drawn from 43 countries. However, its work is often hampered by inadequate financial and administrative resources. Besides establishing and coordinating the research networks listed above, the AAU also runs leadership and management training programs, and provides special services designed to promote academic mobility among its members.[3] The scale of these services should, however, not be exaggerated. In 1999-2000, only ten awards each were given for staff exchanges, graduate scholarships, and theses research with funds donated by German and American agencies (*AAU Newsletter*, 5, 3, 1999: 10). Another indication of the small-scale nature of its operations and its external financial dependency is the fact that when it decided to establish an endowment fund, it set its sights on raising $10 million, to which the Ford Foundation promised to contribute $2 million (*AAU Newsletter*, 5, 2, 1999: 15).

There are also several networks that coordinate work on, or by, women researchers; networks such as the Association of African Women for Research and Development, formed in 1977 (AAWORD, 2000), and the Women in Science and Technology in Africa Network founded in 1997 from a joint AAU/UNESCO project for women in science and technology (*AAU Newsletter*, 5, 2, 1997: 12). Another well-known organization is the Forum for African Women Educationalists, founded in 1992, which brings together African women ministers of education, vice chancellors and other senior policy makers to design gender-sensitive policies and mainstream gender in educational plans and programs (Meena, 2001: 15-18).

Computer networks and collaborative distance education programs have also become increasingly important. They are opening new learning frontiers for African students and some see them as a means of curbing student migrations overseas in search of educational opportunities (Darkwa and Mazibuko, 2000: Mwaura, 1999; Schlegel, 1994). In South and Southern Africa, for example, Uninet, created and managed by the Foundation for

Research Development, connects universities, polytechnics, and research centers to each other and the Internet (Knoch, 1997; http://www.frd.ac.za/uninet.html). Possibly the best-known online education project is the African Virtual University (AVU), established by the World Bank in 1997 to provide semester-long courses in the sciences and engineering.

By 2001, the AVU had established learning centers at twenty-six universities in fifteen countries. It had delivered some 3,500 hours of instructional programs, registered over 24,000 students, and provided 1,000 personal computers. The AVU also provided a digital library with 2,000 full-text journals, a web site, and e-mail accounts, and other web-based services. Typically, the AVU classrooms have "between 25-30 students, sitting at their desks watching the broadcast on large screen projections, television monitors or computers. During the class, students have the opportunity for real-time interaction with the instructor using phone lines or e-mail. This framework allows a student in Rwanda, for example, to pose a question to a professor in Togo or Paris that can be heard and commented upon by students in Benin and Senegal" (www.avu.org/).

While many welcome the facilities and opportunities the AVU offers for multimedia teaching and learning, some are critical of its access, relevance, and sustainability. AVU programs are quite expensive and inaccessible to poor students. Maurice Amutabi (2001: 3) informs us that Kenyatta University in Nairobi, the AVU headquarters, "was closed in October 2000 because students rioted over e-mail charges imposed by the institution (a mere Ksh.500=less than $10) per term to use AVU facilities." The fact that most of the courses and curricula are designed in American and European universities, and the instructors speak with unfamiliar foreign accents, also raises concerns about the relevance of the teaching and learning processes. The involvement of the World Bank, the same institution that has imposed draconian structural adjustment programs upon African countries, breeds concerns about the sustainability of the project should the bank withdraw its support. After all, Africa is littered with projects abandoned by donors as they move on to the next craze in "development assistance."

In August 2001, the AVU Board announced the end of the pilot phase and the launch of a full operational phase in which new accredited degree and diploma programs would be delivered. It promised a more focused and African-based operation in which African universities would be more involved in the development and delivery of courses. The program itself would be divided into two tracks, an academic channel offering undergraduate students degrees in computer science and electrical and computer engineering and a business and technology channel delivering short courses in management, information technology, foreign languages, and an executive MBA. The AVU would become an independent entity and establish centers in more countries in both private and public universities and to private franchises housed in corporations and NGOs. An ambitious agenda of commercialized education indeed.

The third area of cooperation is libraries. It has always been recognized that libraries are indispensable to university teaching and research, although rhetoric has often not been matched by funding. In fact, libraries took the brunt of the university funding crisis discussed in the previous chapter. The information revolution and globalization have reinforced the challenges facing African university libraries. There is a need not only to move from conventional to electronic libraries, but to improve library cooperation at national, regional, and international levels, all of which require expensive investments in retooling library staff and establishing ICT infrastructures (Asamoah-Hassan and Bannerman, 2001). Predictably, library cooperation has advanced faster within the more developed countries on the continent than between countries.

With its relatively large economy and university system, South Africa has made the most progress. Several library consortia have been created to facilitate cooperation and resource sharing. These include the Cape Library Cooperative founded in 1993 among five university libraries in the Western Cape (http://www.adamstor.ac.za/Academic/Calico/portal.htm); the Eastern Seabord Association of Tertiary Institutions, founded in 1992 by universities and technikons in the Eastern Cape (http://www.esati.org.za); the Foundation of Tertiary Institutions in the Northern Metropolis formed in 1996 by seven universities and five technikons in the Gauteng province (http://sunsite.wits.ac.za/gaelic/fotim.html); the Free State Libraries and Information Consortium also formed in 1996 by four universities, a technikon, a public library and a technical library (http://www.uovs.ac.za/lib/frelico/index.htm); and the Confederation of Open Learning Institutions of South Africa, founded by the national universities and technikons providing distance education (http://www.colisa.ac.za/index.html).

Cooperative library networks or projects at regional or continental levels are relatively rare. The few initiatives have been led either by South African institutions, the Association of African Universities (AAU), or external institutions. In November 1999, Technikon South Africa provided an initial sponsorship of R1 million to set up the African Digital Library, available around the clock to Internet users in Africa only (http://www.AfricaEducation.org/adl). The library was established jointly with the AAU and a private American company (Howard and West, 2000). Another, quite overdue, initiative is the Database of African Theses and Dissertations (DATAD) project, launched in 1998 to create capacity in African universities for the collection, management, and dissemination of theses and dissertations electronically, in order to promote, highlight, and improve accessibility to the work of African scholars both within and outside the continent (http://www.aau.org/datad/). A feasibility study covering eighteen universities identified more than 30,000 theses and estimated that these universities produced 6,000 new theses every year (*AAU Newsletter*, 4, 2-3, 1998: 3). An academic treasure trove indeed.

Transatlantic Voyages

African academic mobility has of course not been confined to the continent. During the colonial period Europe was the chosen destination of many Africans seeking higher education. After independence, Africans continued to trek to the former imperial metropolises for higher education or to work, although few became university professors. African skilled and intellectual migrations to Europe persist and seem to have increased in recent times. Even larger are the migrations of African students and academics to the United States. There is little doubt that African academic migration to the U.S. have grown as university conditions in Africa have deteriorated. These migrations are part of a complex tapestry of international academic relations between Africa and the U.S., which will be examined in greater detail in the next section.

As will be demonstrated in Volume Two, African migrations to the North have grown rapidly in the last two decades. The migrants include highly skilled professionals, including intellectuals. According to Kofi Apraku's (1991: 5) study of migrants to the United States in the 1980s, 58 percent of the respondents held Ph.D. or M.D. degrees and an additional 19 percent had master's degrees; 20.2 percent were university professors in their home country prior to migration; 11.3 percent were economists; 8.1 percent were medical officers; 7.3 percent were engineers; 6.4 percent were researchers; and the rest belonged to other professions. Politicians were a paltry 2.4 percent. Recent studies show that the African "brain drain" to the North has accelerated. According to United Nations estimates, between 1960 and 1975 some 27,000 well-educated Africans departed for the North, another 40,000 between 1975 and 1984, reaching 80,000 in 1987, and an average 20,000 every year since 1990 (Johnson, 2000). Egypt alone lost 45,000 scientists after 1950 (www.arabicnews.com).

Opening a conference on the brain drain organized by the United Nations Economic Commission for Africa (UNECA), Lalla Ben Barka (2000: 2), the deputy secretary, drove the point home by noting that in the mid-1990s, there were "more than 21,000 Nigerian doctors practicing in the United States alone while Nigeria's health system suffers from an acute lack of medical personnel; 60 percent of all Ghanaian doctors trained locally in the 1980s had left the country, while in Sudan, 17 percent of doctors and dentists, 20 percent of university lecturers, 30 percent of engineers in 1978 alone had gone to work abroad." The *West Africa* (1995: 1433) magazine bemoaned the fact that while there were "an estimated 100,000 highly qualified educated Africans working in Western Europe and North America," there were "about 100,000 expatriates from the developed countries employed in sub-Saharan Africa," costing $4 billion annually to maintain, or about 35 percent of the region's official development assistance. A tragic testimony to the asymmetries of global migration flows.

The African intellectual migrants are a part of the rising tide of global skilled migration, a category that is not well defined, but is assumed to take many forms, including "brain drain," professional transients, skilled permanent migrants, and business transfers.[4] "The geographical circulation of intellectual elites and the resulting de-or multi-nationalization of knowledge," Iredale (1999: 90) notes, "is a phenomenon of the twentieth century....A global labor market now exists in some occupations where a person's skill is his/her greatest asset to be bought and sold." Not surprisingly, the attention paid to skilled migration has increased both in sending and receiving countries. The former seek to devise policies to curb the outflow of skilled emigrants, encourage their return, and pursue compensation from the industrialized countries; while the latter are concerned with developing migration selection policies that facilitate the entry of temporary or permanent skilled immigrants and ensure their successful labor market integration.

Theoretical explanations for skilled migration echo many of the conventional migration theories that will be examined in greater detail in Volume Two. The first is the micro-level human capital approach that contends individuals move to maximize gains from the investment in their education and training. The second is the macro-level structuralist neo-Marxist perspective that emphasizes the operations of unequal development between core and periphery countries. Finally, there is the "structuration" approach that stresses the important role of international agents, regional policies, and global networks. Skilled migration can be examined in terms of its motivation, spatiality, mechanisms, and temporality.

Skilled migrants are motivated to move for various reasons, such as fleeing from oppressive regimes, or through direct and indirect inducements from foreign governments, industries, or agencies (Appleyard, 1991; Simanovsky et al., 1996). Spatially, they move from South to North, North to South, or within each zone. The mechanisms or channels of migration include personal networks, the internal labor markets of multinational corporations, or movements with the assistance of international recruitment agencies (Findlay, 1995; Findlay et al., 1996). The stay of the skilled migrants may be permanent, temporary, or circulatory. In addition, skilled migration flows are affected by the nature of the migrants' reception and integration into the host countries.

The migration of African intellectuals is a product of conditions in both Africa and the North. Economic, social, political, and educational developments in Africa have conspired to generate emigration pressures, while the skill-selective and wealth-selective immigration policies of the Northern countries have offered opportunities for highly skilled Africans to migrate. The migration flows have been sustained by the intricate and intense educational networks that link universities in Africa and those in the North, the recruitment drives and inducements of various institutions and organizations, and the cumulative traditions of migration that have emerged as skilled migration has expanded. Like international migrants from other regions, African professional migrants have increasingly become part of transitional communities involved directly and indirectly in both home and host countries, in ways that have an impact on, to quote Hamilton and Chinchilla (1996:198), "economic and political processes in the sending and receiving countries and relations between them which may reinforce or challenge existing relations of power within and between countries."

African intellectual migration to the North is an outgrowth of complex movements of African intellectuals in the continent itself within and between countries. African intellectuals are members of complex networks linking universities and independent research centers in Africa to those in the North through training, publications, and research funding. Ali Mazrui's (1978) suggestion that African universities functioned as branches of multinational corporations remains apt despite strenuous efforts at indigenization. In other words, African universities still derive their organizational and scholarly models from the North. Large numbers of students continue to be sent to the North for graduate training; research themes are not only influenced by Northern fads, but much of African research is funded by foundations and agencies from the North; and Northern media dominate scholarly publications and set the standards. It is this complex web of dependent institutional, intellectual, and ideological linkages between Africa and the North that facilitates and sustains the flows of migrant African intellectuals.

This is of course not peculiar to Africa. Almost everywhere the four major institutional sites of scholarly production, namely, state agencies, private corporations, the universities, and independent think tanks or research centers are often connected, at home and abroad, in complex ways through funding, networks of personnel and shared research inquiries and interests. In short, academics, through the very nature of their work and institutional affiliations, belong to potentially globalized and globalizing networks. African scholars can be found in three major sites: the continent's universities, independent research centers, and institutions in the North. These sites, as spaces and centers of scholarly knowledge production, are interlinked in complex and contradictory ways. The conditions and linkages between the universities and research centers and networks on the continent are relatively well known. The least understood of Africa's triple intellectual formation are the migrant intellectuals in the North, a community that needs to be examined for its own sake, and more importantly, because it offers African scholarship a unique entry and insertion into global research networks and engagements with historic African diaspora communities. It is, in my view, a crucial link in the chain of activities and agencies essential for Pan-African solidarity and struggle.

As shown in Chapter 2, the challenges and dilemmas of African universities became more evident as the nationalist dreams of development, democracy, and self-determination evaporated in the face of the mounting recessions of economic growth and political governance. As the social contract of independence crumbled, a process exacerbated by draconian and deflationary structural adjustment programs, struggles for new conditions of living, for the "second independence," gathered momentum. Increasingly persecuted and pauperized, academics left the splendid isolation of their brick towers and joined the entrepreneurial and restive world of the informal sector and the marching masses. In the meantime, new sites of scholarly production began to emerge. In short, the funding crisis of the universities created both the need and the space for the creation of new sites of intellectual production and reproduction.

Most visibly, there was the proliferation of independent research centers; the emergence of what can be called an academic NGO sector. Much has been written about NGOs either as reservoirs of entrepreneurial energies from which a truly developmental bourgeoisie will emerge, or arenas where democratic civilities of associational life are learned. The reality is of course far more complicated than such wishful analyses might suggest. As with the other NGOs, the academic NGOs have had complex and often contradictory relations with the state and foreign capital. Their aspirations for, and rhetoric of, independence and indigeneity have often been compromised by the realities of financing. A few can be characterized as FONGOs (Foreign-Organized NGOs), many are FFONGO's (Foreign-Financed NGOs), and some are suspect GONGOs (Government-Organized NGOs).

This is not to deny or dismiss the enormous work performed by these organizations. It is merely to point out the dependent relationship between the research centers that mushroomed from the 1980s and the foreign funding agencies, sometimes mediated by the state itself. In short, while the centers' establishment expanded intellectual and ideological spaces, this did not automatically entail the decolonization of African scholarship. Indeed, the opposite may have been the case. It is not uncommon for the donor agencies to impose research themes that reflect the policy and paradigmatic fads of their home countries and scholarly communities rather than the perceived priorities and problems of the African researchers themselves. This is to suggest that the need for transparency, accountability, and mutual respect in relations between African research centers and external donors should be paramount.

The research centers are organized on national, subregional, or continental levels. Regardless of such differences, most of the centers are interdisciplinary, and only a few appear to operate within more traditional disciplinary boundaries. With proliferation has come unevenness in quality. Some of these centers are no more than glorified consultancy agencies, happy to collude with their clients in confirming policy decisions already made. Others, often against great odds, seek to maintain high standards of scholarly research and networking. Constantly replenished by the intellectual energies and ambitions of scholars exiled from their repressive countries or impoverished universities, the latter seek to transcend the debilitating limitations of research narrowly focused on the bounded fictions of specific disciplines and nation-states, in an era when intellectual understanding and effective policy formulation demands interdisciplinarity and regional cooperation. Thus, the regional and continental research institutions have become central players on the African research landscape and in the production, dissemination, and consumption of scholarly knowledge.

These centers are products of both the successes and failures of African universities. In these days of Afropessimism it is often forgotten that while there were universities during the colonial period, the bulk of the educated class in contemporary Africa, including the majority of the academics and researchers, were trained in the universities that were established or expanded after independence. Independence, therefore, set the basis for the rise of African scholarly communities capable of developing their own intellectual trajectories. The fiscal and intellectual crises of the universities from the 1980s, nevertheless created propitious conditions for the formation and growth of independent research centers that took their research themes and theoretical cues less from the ideological predilections of the postcolonial state and more from the seductive dreams of Pan-Africanism and the stubborn demands of globalization. For these centers, regional cooperation became an important research paradigm and paradigm of research. They represented the pluralization of African intellectual life, which is a thoroughly good thing. Gone were the days when universities monopolized intellectual labor and production.

The brain drain to the North was part of these complex processes of intellectual mobility and transformation. As might be expected, the motivations and morality of African academics and professionals traversing the Atlantic and the Mediterranean are in serious dispute. Whatever one's position, they represent an intellectual reality and resource that needs to be acknowledged and utilized. Even if they are not the advance armies of Edward Said's (1993) Third World "voyagers into" the belly of the North, or

Ali Mazrui's (1978) Pan-African forces of "counter-penetration," Africa's migrant intellectuals constitute a presence that reflect, and can promote, Africa's global intellectual presence.

Much of what is known about African migrant intellectuals in the North is anecdotal. Little systematic research has been conducted on their demographic and social composition, occupational and institutional affiliations, let alone ideological orientations and personal intentions. Comprehensive data and analyses of African migrant intellectuals in the North is essential in order to understand the full magnitude of Africa's brain drain to the North and to devise meaningful policies to deal with it. A good beginning in collecting this data has been made in the study conducted by the US Social Science Research Council on the rates of return of African Ph.D.'s trained in North America between 1986 and 1996 (Pires, et.al., 1999). Despite its limitations[5], the study yields invaluable information on trends in the production and distribution of African intellectuals in North America in the 1980s and 1990s.

The data revealed that 57 percent returned to their countries of origin, a further 5 percent to other African countries, for a total return rate to Africa of 62 percent. Altogether, 36 percent stayed in North America, and the remaining 2 percent went to Europe and elsewhere. Despite annual fluctuations, there was no well-defined trend in the return and stay rates of African graduates during this period. Interestingly, the rate of return was almost the inverse of the stated intentions of the Ph.D. recipients: In an NSF Survey of Earned Doctorates for the 1986-1996 period only 35 percent had expressed an intention to return to their home countries and 1 percent to another African country. The authors speculate that some graduates only return temporarily, while many others "who initially intend to stay encounter difficulties (financial, legal, familiar) in actually doing so, and ultimately return to their home countries" (Pires et al., 1999:11). It could also reflect changes in employment opportunities and other circumstances in the home countries of the recipients in the course of their training.

Variations in rates of return were conditioned by a complex set of factors. Politics was one. Thus, while the Tanzanian economy was not stronger than that of Nigeria, more Tanzanians (79 percent) returned home than Nigerians (34 percent) partly because of Tanzania's relative political stability as compared with Nigeria's political turbulence. Economic and institutional factors also played a role. Kenya was no less politically unstable than Cameroon, but more Kenyans (65 percent) returned home as compared to

Cameroonians (33 percent), no doubt because of "Kenya's stronger economy, the relative strength and number of universities and independent research centers, and the presence of many international organizations that provide employment opportunities" (Pires et al., 1999:14). Return rates also appear to have been affected by the relative size of immigrant populations, which might explain why more than twice as many Ugandans (79 percent) returned as did Ghanaians (34 percent), despite the fact that the two countries had similar levels of political stability, types of political regimes, and rates of economic growth. Ghana's immigrant population in the United States was larger than Uganda's, which provided the networks and social capital for the graduates to study and stay as shown by the fact that the vast majority of Ugandans studied using funding from international agencies, unlike Ghanaians who sponsored themselves or were funded by North American universities.

This suggests that rates of return were relatively higher for those who were sponsored by governments, official agencies, and private foundations: 73 percent for those funded by their home governments; 75 percent for those funded by private foundations; and 90 percent for those funded by U.S. government agencies. Perhaps reflecting its tighter employment market return rates were even higher in Canada: 89 percent for those funded by CIDA, 95 percent for IDRC, and 100 percent for the Canadian Commonwealth.[6] In contrast, only 28 percent of those who sponsored themselves and 50 percent of those who received North American university funds returned. The reasons for this are not far to seek. Recipients of government or foundation sponsorship are usually admitted into Canada and the United States on temporary non-immigrant visas, and they also tend to be well-established professionals in their home countries. Conversely, those who receive university funding or fund themselves are under no obligation to return. Moreover, the latter tend to take longer to complete their studies and they acquire the experience and develop the social networks, often through teaching and research assistantships, that facilitate their employment in North American universities and colleges after graduation.

Return rates were also affected by age at graduation. Only 36 percent of those who graduated in the 20-29 year-old age group returned home as compared to 58 percent for those in the 40-49 age group because older recipients were more likely than the younger ones to have more established careers and family responsibilities to which they would return to. There were no demonstrable differences in return rates according to gender, although only 19 percent of the Ph.D. recipients in the survey sample were female. The graduates' field of study also had an impact on return. Rates of return to Africa was highest (70 percent) for the life sciences; followed by the social sciences (65 percent); education (62 percent); the physical sciences (56 percent); the humanities (54 percent); professional services (also 54 percent); and Engineering (45 percent). The relatively low return rate for engineering, the physical sciences, and professional services might be attributed to high demand in North America, while for the humanities it might be attributed to the low demand in Africa. The converse may help explain the high return rates for the life sciences, social sciences, and education, namely, "a relatively low demand in North America and a relatively high demand in the region [Africa]...those fields with high return rates in our survey do loosely correlate with those fields prioritized by funding programs. Moreover, these programs frequently select for advanced training those Africans working on projects they are funding, and often hold open their jobs (or better ones) until their return" (Pires et al., 1999: 19-21).

Clearly, rates of return were positively correlated with levels of political stability and rates of economic growth at home, previous patterns of immigration to North America, the age and career trajectories of the graduates, their fields of study, and sources of funding. Not surprisingly, Botswana with its political stability, buoyant economy, and low levels of Northern migration, had a high rate of return (94 percent), in contrast to the low rates recorded for Sierra Leone (22 percent) and Liberia (21 percent), countries wrecked by civil war and with relatively large immigrant populations in North America. It is also more likely that Ph.D. recipients from Botswana were sponsored by their government and other agencies than those from Sierra Leone and Liberia.

Rates of return, however, do not tell us everything about the dynamics and impact of the brain drain in this age of growing transnational skilled migrations and improved communication technologies. "We must be cognizant," Piers et al. (1999: 36) argue, "of the possibility that 'return' does not, by definition, accomplish the goals of capacity-building programs, while 'stay' does not, by definition, vitiate the possibility of contributing to at least some of the goals." In short, not all those who return home contribute to Africa's development, nor do all those who stay overseas contribute nothing to their countries' development.

Unequal Exchange

African universities maintain a wide range of relationships with universities in Europe and in North America. Some of the links are between consortia or individual institutions and often involve student and staff exchanges, research collaboration, and assistance in the areas of curriculum development, quality assurance, and university management. The popularity of particular African regions and countries as linkage partners for overseas institutions seems to follow the trails of colonial relations. Thus, universities in Anglophone and Francophone Africa have their strongest linkages with universities in Britain and France, respectively. The academic linkage programs of the other European countries tend to reflect their overall foreign policy ambitions to win new friends and influence educational development in Africa.

The Germans have been particularly aggressive. Their programs are coordinated through the German Academic Exchange Service (DAAD), an association of more than 300 institutions of higher education, mainly funded by the German government. In 1998 alone, DAAD sponsored nearly 2,000 graduate students and scholars from 41 sub-Saharan countries to German universities, and 800 Germans to African universities, mostly to conduct their own research, although 70 went to teach, nearly half for up to 5 years. The exchanges mainly focus on the sciences (http://nairobi. daad.de/subsharan-sec1.htm). Special efforts have been made to strengthen links with the University of Namibia, once a German colony (http://www.unam.na/vcdesk/presjune.html). Also, DAAD operates additional programs in North Africa, through which hundreds of students and academic staff have been trained and exchanged. Some of the collaborations between German and North African universities are quite innovative. For example, the partnership between the universities of Kassel in Germany and Minia in Egypt, signed in 1982, involves joints seminars, workshops, and student supervision. The seminars alternate every two years between the two universities, and all proceedings are published. In order to promote continued cooperation among the alumni of the exchange programs, the German Egypt-Arab Region Inter-Alumni-Net (GEAR) was established in 1999 (http://www.wiz.uni-kassel.de/gear/newsletter/gnews1.htm).

The linkages between African and European universities seem to fluctuate according to the contours of political and social transformations within Africa. During the ugly days of apartheid, for example, South African institutions were generally shunned. The academic boycott was of course an integral part of the cultural and economic sanctions against apartheid. To be sure, it generated passionate and polarized debates and was frequently breached (Haricombe and Lancaster, 1995; Coovadia, 1999). Following the end of apartheid, universities from around the world have been falling over themselves to establish links with South Africa, sometimes to the wry amusement of the South Africans, as I witnessed when I went there in 1994 and 2000 to establish linkages for my universities in Canada and the United States, respectively. The suitors have come from as far as Australia, where many white South Africans fleeing black rule prefer to settle.[7]

On the whole, South African universities have formed more linkages with universities outside than within the continent. For example, by 1997 the University of Natal had one link each with universities in Africa (Egypt), Asia (Malaysia), and Canada, but eight in Europe and fourteen in the United States (http://tony.csd.unp.ac.za/links/links.htm).[8] Many of the linkages with the smaller European countries have been negotiated by national consortia. For example, in March 1996, the Danish Rectors' Conference visited and explored institution-specific linkages with twelve South African universities (http://www.rks.dk/rektorkollegiet/sydafrika/southafr.htm). Between 1991 and 2000, the Norwegian Council of Universities' Committee for Development Research and Education Program, supported by the Norwegian Foreign Ministry, sponsored numerous cooperation agreements and research projects throughout Africa (*AAU Newsletter*, 5, 2, 1999: 7-8). The Nordic institutions often seek not only to forge North-South relations, but also to strengthen South-South linkages, although this is not always achieved, as is clear from the research program in public administration between the universities of Dar es Salaam, Zimbabwe, the Western Cape, and Bergen in Norway (www.siu.no/vev.nsf/).

Besides using resources from governments and their own coffers, European universities have also been adept at using international organizations to foster exchanges with African institutions. For example, through the auspices of the International Association of University Presidents, in 2001 four universities from Denmark, Belgium, and the Netherlands established a program to provide African scholars in 10 East African universities access to full-text articles in 200 online journals (Bollag, 2001c). As European unification has deepened, the European Union has become more assertive in formulating foreign policy for its members, including fostering new types of academic cooperation and exchange with both developed and developing countries.[9] Even as early as the 1970s, scholarships from the European Development Fund enabled many African students to study in Europe. I was one of them.

African and European universities have also made good use of UNESCO programs and networks. One of the most interesting is the UNESCO Chairs Program, launched in 1991, that facilitates twinning, networking, and other linking arrangements among universities. Funded by UNESCO and the participating institutions, the program is centered around "chairs," often visiting professors, around whom a whole range of activities are organized, including research programs, scholarships and fellowships, and staff and student exchanges. Within five years, 163 UNESCO Chairs had been established (30 in sub-Saharan Africa), supported by 750 researchers and others, who organized more than 350 courses, mainly at the graduate level, attended by more than 7,500 students, and 120 seminars, training workshops, symposia, and colloquia attended by more than 6,000 participants. Moreover, more than 50 inter-university networks, varying in size from 3 to 50 institutions, were created, 580 academics and 355 students from the South went to the North for further training, and 240 joint research projects were set up that resulted in the publication of 55 volumes, some 100 articles, and over 150 monographs and reports. Examples of the African networks include a science network created around the UNESCO Chair in Mathematics and Science Education at the University of the Western Cape, involving scientists at universities in South Africa, Zimbabwe, Mozambique, Namibia, the universities of Utrecht in the Netherlands, Lund in Sweden, the Ruhr in Germany, and Porto in Portugal; and the Network of African Teacher Training Institutions, built around the UNESCO Chair at the Ecole Normale Supérior in Dakar (Chitoran, 1996). By 2000, there were 360 chairs and 60 networks.

In addition to the large programs, there are smaller ones organized around the few African studies centers in Europe. One of the most well-known is the Nordic Africa Institute in Upssala, Sweden, founded in 1962. The institute encourages and conducts research and studies on Africa in the Nordic countries, mostly in the humanities and social sciences, and promotes cooperation between African and Nordic researchers. It maintains a modest library (43,000 titles and 700 current periodicals in 1996) and a publication program (forty-nine scholarly books between 1992 and 1996). Since 1982 it has also supported a guest researcher program that brings three to four researchers, mostly from African countries, for two to four months. The guest researchers are expected to work on topics and themes being pursued in the institute's research program. The Institute organizes some of its major seminars and conferences in Africa in collaboration with local universities and research centers. Between 1992 and 1996, for example, sixteen out of the fifty-eight conferences and seminars were held in various African countries (Nêste, 1997). In 2000 I had the privilege of giving the keynote address at the conference organized in Zomba, Malawi, between the institute and the University of Malawi, my alma mater.

It is perhaps with the United States that Africa has its most extensive and complex academic exchanges. With its 4,048 colleges and universities, enrolling 14.8 million students, 2.8 million faculty and staff, and revenues of $197 billion in 1999-2000, the United States has the largest, richest, most diversified and decentralized higher education system in the world.[10] Also large, diverse, and complex is its international knowledge system. In the late 1990s, 30 percent of all foreign students in the world studied in the United States, although this represented a drop of 10 pecent since 1980. These students brought in an estimated $7.5 billion to the U.S. economy every year (Desruisseaux, 1998). In 1999-2000, there were 516,438 foreign students, or 3.5 percent of the total number of students in American colleges and universities.

There is no doubt that international education constitutes an important feature of the American international knowledge system. Broadly, three types of international education programs can be identified: student and faculty exchange programs, short term training programs conducted in the United States for foreign officials, and technical assistance for specific projects. For African universities it is the student and faculty exchange programs that have had the most important impact. Generally, these programs were developed through the area studies project, which was funded both by state and private sources primarily to serve United States interests and only secondarily to promote African development. As one article notes, "with a few notable exceptions—for instance, in agriculture—U.S. institutions did not work to help colleges and universities increase the pace of economic development within their countries (except indirectly, by creating a better-educated citizenry)"(Chapman and Claffey, 1998). The history of the area studies project will be discussed fully in the next chapter.

International academic exchanges in American universities are financed both internally and externally: internally through student fees and faculty sabbaticals and research fellowships, although the latter sometimes recycle resources from the state, the foundations, and other donors. The leading federal agency in promoting higher education partnerships is USAID, which in 1998 provided partial support to more than 115 higher education partnerships involving over 400 universities and colleges in the United States and abroad (Vargas-Baron, 1998: 86). It supported programs in seventeen African countries, which were linked to twenty-three American universities. The bulk of the projects were in health and nutrition, followed by economic development, democratic initiatives, and environment and natural resources (USAID, 1999).

There are clear imbalances in the flow of students and other academic exchanges between the United States and other world regions, including Africa. The imbalances are evident not only in the total numbers involved, but also in the students' regions of origin and destination, their levels, length and fields of study, and social composition. In 1999-2000, there were 516,438 foreign students in the United States, 15 percent higher than in 1993, compared to 129,770 American students abroad, or a mere 0.9 percent of all American students.[11] Thus, there were nearly four times more foreign students in the United States as there were American students abroad. While the majority of foreign students came from Asia (54.4 percent), the majority of American students went to Europe (62.7 percent) accounting for only 15.2 percent of foreign students in the United States—and only 6 percent went to Asia.

As for the levels of study, while 90 percent of the American students abroad were undergraduate, mostly juniors and seniors, and 9 percent graduate, only 46 percent of foreign students were undergraduate and 42 percent were graduate; and the rest were nondegree students. Also, foreign students stayed far longer than did American students. The former often spent years pursuing their degree programs, whereas Americans studying abroad, despite their rising numbers, were staying for shorter periods, mostly for a semester or less (Wheeler, 2000: A74). In 1998-99, 38 percent spent one semester, another 34 percent spent a summer term, and less than 10 percent spent a whole academic year (*The Chronicle of Higher Education*, 10 December 1999).

The imbalances can also be seen in the fields of study. Foreign students largely came to the US for the sciences and professions. In contrast, Americans went abroad for the social sciences and humanities. The top fields of study for foreign students at US institutions in 1999-2000 were business (20 percent), engineering (15 percent), mathematics and computer science (11 percent), social sciences (8 percent), and physical and life sciences (8 percent). For their part, American students concentrated on, in descending order, the social sciences and humanities (35 percent), business (18 percent), foreign languages (8 percent), fine or applied arts (8 percent), physical sciences (7 percent), education (4 percent), health sciences (4 percent), engineering (3 percent), mathematics and computer science (2 percent), agriculture (1 percent), and the rest were in undeclared and other fields. Comparisons of the academic level of the foreign and American students also shows imbalances. The low percentage for foreign languages implies that few American students knew the languages of the countries they visited other than English and reflects the fact that less than 10 percent of American students learn foreign languages.

In terms of social composition, principally gender and race, there were noticeable discrepancies as well. Among the foreign students, 58 percent were men and 42 percent were women, while among the American students, women predominated with 65 percent compared to 35 percent for men. Less comparable, but quite meaningful in the American context is the racial distribution. White students made up 85 percent of the study abroad students, Hispanics 5 percent, Asian-American 4 percent, African-American 3 percent, American Indian 1 percent, and multiracial 1 percent. Thus, American students abroad were predominantly undergraduate, female, and white, who went for short periods to study the social sciences and humanities, while foreign students were largely people of color, graduate, and male, who sought to earn their degrees in the United States in the sciences and the professions.

Academic mobility between Africa and the United States lagged far behind the other regions. In 1999-2000, only two African countries were among the top thirty countries sending students to the U.S. led by Kenya with 5,684 students (at number twenty) and Nigeria with 3,602 (at number twenty-eight). Ghana with 2,127 came in at number forty-five, Egypt with 1,964 at forty-nine, South Africa with 1,962 at fifty, Morocco with 1,607 at fifty-eight, Ethiopia with 1,285 at sixty-three, Zimbabwe with 1,184 at sixty-five, Tanzania with 1,091 at sixty-seven, and Botswana with 1,053 at seventy. Taiwan, fifth on the list, sent nearly one-and-half times as many students to the US as the ten African countries combined. Altogether, Asian countries, led by China, accounted for seven out of the ten leading senders, or 54.4 percent of the total, followed by Europe with 15.2 percent, Latin America 12.1 percent, the Middle East 6.8 percent, Africa 5.9 percent, North America 4.7 percent, and Oceania 0.9 percent.

Even more dismal are the statistics for American students going to Africa. By the mid-1990s, according to a survey conducted by the National Consortium for Study in Africa (NCSA) (Pires et al, 2000: 4), there were 107 programs, most of them created after 1990, sponsored by sixty-eight institutions and consortia in twenty-three African countries. More than half the programs were for single semester or summer session. In 1999-2000, Africa hosted a mere 2.8 percent of American students, the same figure as the Middle East. Only two African countries, South Africa and Ghana ranked among the top thirty destinations; 891 American students went to South Africa, while 627 went to Ghana. Although this represented remarkable increase for the two countries—of 44.4 percent and 29 percent, respectively, over the previous year—their combined total was less than Austria's intake of 1,865, the thirteenth most popular destination for American students.

Similarly, Africa was not a major source or destination for faculty exchanges. African countries accounted for a relatively small percentage of academics visiting American universities: 3 percent, as compared to 2.1 percent for Oceania, 4 percent for the Middle East, 4.4 percent for North America, 6.4 percent for Latin America, 37.7 percent for Asia, and 42.3 percent for Europe. The country with the largest number of foreign scholars at US institutions from Africa was Egypt with 640, compared to the leading country China with 11,854. As with the foreign students, most of the visiting scholars were in the sciences and professions. There were 70,501 of them in 1998-99, eighty-one percent of whom were primarily involved in research, 11 percent in teaching, and 8 percent in both teaching and research. Their leading fields of specialization were the health sciences (26 percent), physical sciences (15 percent), life sciences (15 percent), engineering (13 percent), social sciences (4 percent), agriculture (3 percent), mathematics (3 percent), and computer and information sciences (3 percent) (*The Chronical of Higher Education,* 10 December 1999).

The reasons for the unequal academic exchange between Africa and the United States are quite obvious. Africa remains low on the list of destinations for American students and faculty largely because of the continent's abysmal image, fed by both Africa's own malfeasance and America's inveterate racism. The perennial, powerful, but partial pictures of conflict, disease, and poverty that dominate American media portrayals of Africa act as powerful disincentives for academic mobility from the United States to the continent. Conversely, the racism that devalues everything African in the U.S., which is primarily directed at African Americans, combined with the perilous state of many African universities, reinforces the depreciation of African intellectual institutions and skills, so that Africa is rarely seen as a desirable source of student and faculty exchanges. In other words, not only are African degrees likely to be disparaged, continental Africans pay a cultural tax, i.e., the devaluation of their human capital, in addition to a racial tax that people of color, and especially African Americans, pay in the United Sates.

There are of course more specific reasons that undermine both student and faculty exchanges besides negative images or discouragement from nervous families and friends. The capacity of African universities to accommodate American students and to provide them with adequate housing, healthcare, and safety is thought to be limited. The frequent closures of African campuses because of strikes or political instability do not help. A further deterrence is the lack of desired courses and for students in the sciences, technology, and professional schools resources in these fields are deficient. No less serious are the problems of credit transferability and academic equivalence. On the United States side there is the fact that, according to the NCSA survey, 52 percent of American students who went to Africa in the 1990s did so on programs run by other institutions (Pires et l., 2000: 7). Determining academic equivalence for courses taken in Africa can be problematic whether because of doubts about their quality, especially for those based on the experiential model, or because some African universities are not semesterized. Moreover, there are financial constraints, not the least of which are the rather high travel costs that prevent many relatively poor students from going to Africa (Coffman, 2000).

For their part, African universities are not always enamored by the American students, who they sometimes find poorly prepared academically and culturally, exhibit intolerable racial and class arrogance, and suffer from the safari syndrome and show more interest in being tourists than students. Penina Mlama (2000: 27), in charge of international programs at the University of Dar es Salaam, which has formal links with sixty-one universities in Africa, Asia, and Europe, including eleven from the United States, notes that her university does not experience the same kind of negative "reactions from students from Europe or other parts of the world. It seems to be a problem peculiar to American students....Academic departments have also observed a certain lack of seriousness for studies by some exchange students." She recounts an incident in 1994 when the university was closed because of student disturbances, American students presented an ultimatum to the vice-chancellor demanding its immediate reopening, or they would with-draw and "the university would collapse because it would lose the foreign currency they were bringing to it" (Mlama, 2000: 26). Mwenda Ntaragwi (2000), a Kenyan director of the study abroad program of St. Lawrence University in Nairobi, an island program that operates independently of any university program in the country,[12] finds little difference between the students and the tourists that they so often despise. He argues that study abroad constitutes educational tourism, for "the tourist, ethnographer, or student all share a common characteristic—the drive to acquire. All strive to acquire experience, information, and memories" (Ntaragwi, 2000: 59).[13]

The fact that so few American students come to study the sciences and professions, and that most are concentrated in a limited range of courses in the social sciences and humanities is also a source of complaint by African university officials. At the University of Ghana, for example, we are told that "the most popular courses are in music and dance departments, and virtual-ly every student takes a course in one or the other, or both" (Dolphyne, 2000: 30). The lack of reciprocity in student exchanges is another cause for concern. Because of costs African universities are often unable to send exchange students to their American partners, so that the exchange is one-sided. The University of Ghana, which hosts eighty-five to ninety North American students, reportedly sent its first exchange undergraduate student to the U.S. in 2000 (Dolphyne, 2000: 33). Similarly, hardly any undergrad-uate students have been sent from the University of Zimbabwe, which main-tains 150 links worldwide, in exchange for the dozens of American students it receives (Hill, 1999; Zinyemba, 2000). Thus, to many African university administrators, academic exchanges with American universities reek of patronage rather than reflect partnership.

For student exchange programs to be effective and sustainable genuine reciprocity is imperative. Despite declarations by study abroad administra-tors in the United States, including the NCSA, to increase consultation and collaboration with African universities, raise student numbers, including minorities, develop new programs, and promote cooperation among American universities themselves, academic exchange programs between the

United States and Africa remain unequal (Wiley and Metzler, 2000; Delahanty and Raducha, 2000). African universities try to benefit from these programs by requiring American students to pay for real costs in "hard" currency and by seeking support for graduate training and collaborative research projects. Some have also set up special foreign accounts from "surchages" on the American students, which they use as they see fit (Metzler, 2000). Donations of equipment, books, and other resources are sometimes requested. One-to-one exchanges of undergraduate students are nonetheless rare. Exceptions include the program between the University of Illinois and the University of Cape Town, launched in 2000, but it only involves four students going in each direction.

The relatively low numbers of African students going to the United States can partly be accounted for by American cultural and academic prejudices that prevent them from being actively recruited by U.S. universities. Financial reasons also play a major role. Given the harsh economic conditions in many of their countries, African students lack sponsorship from families and home governments. The sources that prospective African students tend to rely on, namely, scholarships from the US government or international organizations, accounted for a paltry 0.6 percent and 0.5 percent, respectively, of the primary sources of funds for foreign students studying in the United States in 1999-2000. The vast majority of these students relied on personal and family sources (67.1 percent), followed by U.S. College or university (18.9 percent), home government or university (4.59 percent), foreign private sponsor (2.7 percent), current employment (2.3 percent), and/or U.S. private sponsor (2.7 percent) (*The Chronicle of Higher Education*, 17 November 2000).

Notwithstanding the problems and challenges outlined above, the potential value of well-organized and coordinated student exchange programs is clear. When they work, they offer students a rare opportunity to learn about other cultures and societies as well as their own, to overcome negative stereotypes and myths about others, to deepen understanding and knowledge of the challenges of development and globalization, to explore new career possibilities, and to build international friendships, alliances, and networks that might in future be useful (Pires, 2000; Cressey, 2000; Pendleton, 2000; Watkins, 2000; Riggs, 2000; Buschman, 2000). It has been argued that studying in Africa even offers American students useful lessons on America's intractable racial quagmire and helps African Americans come to terms with their identities (Tolliver, 2000; Dawson, 2000; McCoy, 2000). For African universities, the programs can help to internationalize their curricula and student body, expose students to different learning styles, and demystify the world's remaining superpower (Redcliffe and Schackleton, 2000).

Disincentives also exist on both sides of the Atlantic that militate against effective faculty exchanges. For African scholars wishing to go to American universities there is the problem of funds. Also, the fact that so few of them are Americanists or work in reputable scientific institutions confines them to underfunded African studies programs or second-rate American universities. To American academics immersed in the conceits of Euroamericentricism or the universality of science, Africa's intellectual value is not self-evident. Even in the best of circumstances, strong institutional disincentives exist in faculty appointment, promotion, and tenure procedures that discourage American academics from participating in long-term, mutually beneficial relationships with their counterparts abroad. In the highly competitive, publish-or-perish madhouse of the American academy, tenure clocks are known to favor mass production, which often precludes prolonged collaborative research and copublishing with overseas colleagues. Scientists in the research universities do not think they have much to gain by going abroad to work with colleagues in laboratories that are less well-equipped than their own.

This often means that it is academics from the less prestigious universities, and those without tenure, or those marginalized by or committed because of reasons of age, nationality, race, gender, and discipline who might be more willing to engage in scholarly exchanges. In the case of Africa, there are of course the indefatigable Africanists in the social sciences and humanities and the academics of African descent, including the recent diaspora. The Africanists often have no choice but to maintain African connections if they want to remain credible, although this does not always entail fostering meaningful and mutually beneficial relations with their African colleagues. Neither does the behavior of the African diaspora intellectuals always differ from that of the Euroamerican Africanists.

Cultivating collaborations with scientists will require far more resources, including the revitalization of the research labs and other infrastructures in African universities. Within the United States the foundations, national research institutes and councils, and professional associations could play a role in sensitizing universities to the benefits of international education and transforming the reward structures that penalize academic exchange and mobility. The difficulties of establishing new linkages between African and American scholars cannot be underestimated, but the inclusion of foreign scholars in SSRC committees is a move in the right direction (Prewitt, 1996a, 1996b; Kassimir, 1997). Several research funding agencies now require collaboration between American researchers and partners in Africa, or Asia and Latin America, before they can fund a project, although the research priorities and agendas are often set by U.S. based specialists. Encouraging more multinational thematic research involving American and African researchers is long overdue. In short, given their financial and professional muscles, the foundations could facilitate new linkage programs built around joint appointments and funding leaves of absence to work in foreign institutions, international collaborative research competitions, and innovative electronic systems of instruction.

New patterns of academic exchange and mobility between American and African universities are emerging. Three can be identified: (i) the growth of what is called "transnational" education; (ii) globalization of American scholarly societies; and (iii) the expansion of online education. First, transnational education often involves the establishment of overseas university branches. This is of course not new, but the scale is. It is facilitated by the growing privatization of higher education around the world. In countries where education was a state monopoly, in the past American universities would assist in establishing colleges modeled on their own, as the University of Illinois did in the early 1970s in creating an agricultural college in Sierra Leone. Today, "steadily increasing numbers of students are enrollling in local programs offered by foreign institutions, or by local colleges working with overseas partners" (Tugend, 1996).

Branches of American universities are growing in Africa. For example, following legislation authorizing private higher education in Senegal in 1998, it was announced that Suffolk University in Boston would develop a branch in Dakar. In response to this growing phenomenon of "transnational education," in 1995 the Global Alliance for Transnational Education (GATE) was formed to collect information about these institutions and to work with universities and accreditation agencies to define international programs and ensure their high quality, given the fact that too many universities seemed willing to lower their academic standards for overseas programs. By 2000, however, GATE had "become a corporate entity so riddled with conflicts of interest that it may no longer be viable" (Blumenstyk and

McMurtrie, 2000).

Second, a growing number of American scholarly associations are expanding their global reach by aggressively recruiting foreign members. To quote Beth McMurtrie (2000: A53):

> From the Organization of American Historians to the American Mathematical Society, the groups have broadened their membership bases and stepped up collaborations with their counterparts abroad. They recruit foreign scholars to write for their journals, provide technical support for fledgling societies in developing nations, and connect scholars through their Internet offerings. Even scholars that don't try to recruit abroad are finding that more of their members now have foreign addresses.[14]

She attributes this to three factors: American academics are becoming global in their outlook; the collapse of communism opened up communication with Eastern Europe and expanded research there and interest in international research generally; and the powerful impact of the development of the Internet.

With specific reference to Africa, Michael Wolf (1997: B13) notes that "since 1994 the American Bar Association's African Law Initiative has worked with law schools in eight African countries, including the University of Dar es Salaam Faculty of Law. With funding from the United States Information Agency (USIA) and the volunteer participation of deans and professors from American law schools, this project has worked to create "sister law school" linkages between African and American law schools. It has assisted with curriculum development, faculty training in clinical teaching methodologies, and library development."[15] Also using USIA funds the Michigan State University and H-Net conducted Internet training workshops in Southern Africa, which resulted in the creation of a discussion network called H-Safrica (http://www.matrix.msu.edu/connect/finalreport1998.html).

Third, international distance education using the Internet is expanding rapidly, which enables American universities to export curricula and instructional expertise, especially in the lucrative fields of science, engineering, and business (Ercolano, 1996). In a relatively short time, thousands of online programs have been developed by universities across the United States, in which overseas students can enroll. Some are in fact specifically targeted at international students. In 2001, the Illinois Virtual Campus had 2,803 courses and 74 programs offered by the leading universities in the state, among them the flagship system of the University of Illinois. One of the programs, the Global Human Resource Development offered by the College of Education at the university's Champaign-Urbana campus, is a graduate program that targets students in developing countries, including Kenya, where a department in the college has operated a graduate degree program for many years.

As noted earlier, opinions differ on the potential impact of the new information and communication technologies. There can be little doubt that the electronic media revolution offers new possibilities for international scholarly communication. As argued in the previous chapter, African universities have to adopt the new information technologies not only to ensure they are not left further behind, but also to develop innovative exchange programs amongst themselves and with universities in the North. Let me give three examples of such programs. The first is the knowledge exchange and learning partnerships (KELP) initiative, partly funded by U.S. government agencies, the participating institutions, and the private sector, which aims to encourage Africa to Africa to U.S. networking and exchanges. The networks are supposed to encourage multiple-level partnerships and collaborative relationships among universities, research centers, and other higher education institutions, and to be mutually-beneficial to the participating institutions, although they are supposed to be African-led in order to inspire African universities to assume a leadership role in transnational education.

Operationally, the networks are based on, according to Maria Beebe (2001: 19),

> sharing faculty via distance learning; email/discussion from among faculty and student groups; audio/video conferencing between faculty and student groups; and, where, possible, face-to-face faculty and student exchanges between African and American institutions. The network notion is for both African and American faculty members to exchange and develop course or module materials, for both African and American students to discuss material via chat rooms and perhaps even do papers together, and for both sets of faculty members to be available to both sets of students for advising.

One of the networks is the Public Affairs Network, which links the University of Pretoria with several African and American universities, as well as local, provincial, national governmental and nongovernmental bodies.

The challenges involved in transnational online education—course development, teaching, and certification—cannot be underestimated. There are several examples of how this can be done. There is the fascinating collaborative curriculum co-development (CCD) project between Tufts University, Makerere University, and the University of Dar es Salaam. Launched in January 2001, the project seeks to connect international relations students at the three campuses through a shared website using asynchronous learning networks. It aims to promote interactive dialogue among students and to give them a richer and more complex appreciation of the variety of credible paradigms for understanding international relations, as well as to encourage them to use information technology as an important learning resource.

The architects of the project, Pearl Robinson et al. (2001: 4), inform us that unlike the traditional distance learning model in which course content is broadcast from an instructor in one location, in this project instructors at the three institutions collectively

> have developed a metacourse—constructed around a general theme (in this case, regionalism in African International Relations), a core body of knowledge, overlapping readings, and a series of interactive website exercises designed to involve groups of students at the three universities in a common learning plan. Instructors at each site have prepared a syllabus tailored to the particular curricula and programmatic needs of the home institution. Also, students are encouraged to contribute materials of their choosing to the website, thereby initiating discussion threads prompted by their own sense of local policy concerns, current events, or issues that emerge from the CCD interactions.

All the materials involved in, and the knowledge generated by, the interactions between and among the instructors and the students constitute the metacourse.

The third example of collaboration is a conference planned for April

2002, jointly organized by the University of Illinois and CODESRIA, and cosponsored by the Association of African Universities. During the conference each site will interact with the other group of scholars, share keynote addresses and plenary sessions, and engage in real-time exchanges. Using interactive video, instant messaging between participants, creating an online forum or web discussion board for multiple voices and open conversations, and using conference rapporteur for offline discussions, the exchanges and dialogues will be opened up to the broader community. Hearing and seeing presentations at the various locales will foster a more enriched dialogue at each site amongst people who might not otherwise be able to attend the same conference. We expect the video and Internet conferencing will also enable productive linkages to emerge after the conference.

It is quite evident that the demand for international education in both Africa and the North is expanding, but it is an enterprise facing many challenges. Besides the rapid changes in the field of international scholarship and the emergence of new international education specialties, pressures are building on researchers because of the exponential production and flows of knowledge. Demands on the international knowledge system are expanding faster than the available resources. At the height of the Republican-led "Contract With America" isolationist and triumphalist frenzy in the mid-1990s, the U.S. Congress threatened substantial funding cuts to educational and cultural exchanges (Rubin, 1995). To the consternation of many in the study abroad community, the new National Security Education Program required the recipients of its scholarships to serve as federal employees upon return. Critics feared that it turned students into government agents subject to suspicion and attack. While some welcomed it as source of new funds, most Africanists called for its boycott (Dubois, 1998).

Between 1995 and 1998 federally sponsored exchange programs in the U.S. declined by 15 percent and have grown only marginally since (Desruisseaux, 2000). As Philip Altbach (1998) argues, for most colleges and universities "internationalization" is all rhetoric because they lack the resources, will, and strategy. The phony debate between "area studies" and "globalism" that raged in the mid-1990s, as if the two can be divorced, is a sad testimony to the lack clarity as to what internationalization implies, that it is not Americanization, that globalization must be tempered with contextualization (Hall and Tarrow, 1998). As for African universities, trapped by even greater penury, their efforts to build new partnerships with American universities are often frustrated by the sheer size, complexity, and diversity of the U.S. higher educational system, which makes coordination difficult. African universities would be well-served to work more collectively. Above all, they need to exploit their own intellectual diaspora, offering a small way out of the unidirectional globalism of the North and Africa's dependent globalism, of changing the balance of trade in international education (Peterson, 2001).

Towards Brain Mobility

It is easy to see African intellectual migrations to the North as an unmitigated economic, political, and cultural disaster for Africa. Financial remittances from the migrants, while important for their families and communities and sometimes in national balance of payments accounts, do not seem to compensate for the net losses of their productivity and potential contributions to national development. It has also been argued that the intellectual migrations deprive civil society of the organizational political skills of middle class professionals. According to the critics, that explains, why African governments publicly decry the migration of their intellectuals, while they do little to create conditions that would stem the tide.

All this may be true, but it forecloses the possibility that the migrants can also be turned into assets for Africa. The notion of the brain drain is rooted in human capital approaches in which the migration of highly skilled people is seen as a loss to sending countries in so far as returns on the capital invested is assumed to be forfeited. The sending countries have responded by trying to impose restrictive or incentive policies designed to make migration either more difficult or less attractive, or they demand compensation from the receiving countries (Meyer et al. 1997; Gaillard and Gaillard, 1997; Fourie and Joubert, 1998). The persistence of high levels of skilled migration clearly indicates that these policies have not worked. Neither has the return option, which seeks to encourage skilled migrants to return home. The only countries that have succeeded in attracting their skilled migrants back are those that are able to offer them remuneration and conditions comparable to the countries in which they live.

This leaves the diaspora option, which seeks to maximize the potential gains of the brain drain to the sending country by viewing the skilled migrants as a potential network and a pool of useful and beneficial human resources. The challenge becomes how to build expatriate knowledge networks and establish connections between them and their countries of origin, which would allow for the exchange of information and knowledge and the transfer of skills (Granovetter and Swedberg, 1992; Murdock, 1997). Since it is likely that many African skilled migrants may not return, despite the proverbial wishes of migrants to return home "someday," African countries and the migrants themselves need to devise creative strategies that exploit and enhance the potential benefits of African skilled migrations to the North. Attacking the patriotism of the migrants or demanding direct recompense from the Northern countries is not likely to go far given the fact that the migrants are quite committed to their families and countries back home and the racialized assaults of exile often force them to identify even more passionately with Africa's fate. The Northern countries can claim to have trained many of the migrants as well and argue that they do not "cause" migration by pointing to their stringent immigration measures. Thus, it is far more fruitful to concentrate on how African migrants in the North can constitute themselves into an effective network, a lobby for Africa, that actively campaigns for African causes, capable of cultivating old and new alliances and constituencies for Africa, and forming new linkages with their counterparts on the continent.

Africa and its diaspora have not always effectively mobilized to serve and advance each other's interests as has been the case, for example, between the Jewish diaspora and Israel, or increasingly the Chinese diaspora and China. Israel's clout in Washington has less to do with the economic importance of Israel to the United States than with the successes of the powerful Jewish lobby. Similarly, China's rapid economic development in recent decades has been fueled, to a great extent, not by some nameless Western investment as we are often led to believe, but by investment from the overseas Chinese. The new African diaspora and their offspring in the United States can help invigorate the re-awakened interest in Africa among the historic African American diaspora, and serve as a transAtlantic bridge, as cultural mediators between Africa and Africa America, whose communication and knowledge of each other has largely been through the distorted lenses and prejudices of imperialist and racist media.

Migrant African intellectuals, as cultural producers, have an important and specific role to play in brokering relations between Africa and the North, in blackening the Atlantic. They must resist the seductions of the Northern academies to become native ventriloquists, complicit "others" who validate narratives that seek to marginalize Africa. Nor should they let themselves be manipulated as a fifth column in the North's eternal racial wars by disavowing the protracted struggles of historic African diaspora communities for the full citizenship of racial equality, economic empowerment, and political power. Sometimes immigrants from Africa or the Caribbean tend to forget that the roads on which they ride to their jobs in industry or in the academy were paved by those who proceeded them. Solidarity requires respect for each other's struggles and recognition of our splendid diversities anchored on a strategic racial essentialism, in so far as it is the historical racialization of our humanity that has produced and continues to reproduce our collective exploitation and denigration—whether in Africa or in the North.

Migrant African intellectuals should not be seen solely in the magisterial role of cosmopolitan revolutionaries or the ministerial role of teachers subverting the North through counter-penetration. They are both students and teachers of African and Northern societies, cultural workers and producers who should, in solidarity with historic African diaspora communities, construct knowledges of their multiple worlds that demystify the roots of Africa's and diaspora Africa's oppression and exploitation; knowledges that seek to empower their communities; that expose and confront the tyrannies of Northern imperial power and Africa's dictators; that promote respectful conversation between Africa and the North.

Scholarly production and conversation is conducted through publications, conferences, classrooms, and increasingly through the Internet. What should the role be for migrant African intellectuals in African and Africanist scholarly production and discourse? Let me make a few proposals that suggest the possibilities of turning migrant African intellectuals from liabilities into assets for African intellectual development. In days gone by, global migration often entailed permanent relocation or long separation and infrequent encounters with one's native home through mail and the occasional visit. The contemporary revolution in telecommunications and travel has compressed the spatial and temporal distances between home and abroad, thus offering migrants unprecedented opportunities to be transnational, to be people of two worlds, perpetually translocated, physically and culturally, between several countries or several continents. Thus, globalization is not simply facilitating the rapid flows of capital and commodities, but also revitalizing old cultural and community networks, thus strengthening transnational ethnic, racial, and national identities.

It is in this context that the possible contributions of migrant African intellectuals can be examined. Innovative and cost-effective exchange programs that facilitate the periodic flow of migrant African intellectuals from the North to Africa need to be developed. To date, exchange programs have largely focused on Northern scholars coming to Africa, and occasionally African scholars visiting Northern institutions. Too often, the linkages have been one-sided, used by Africanists in the North to underwrite their academic careers, leaving little intellectual benefits for African scholarship. We need to devise programs that specifically target migrant African intellectuals, who constitute an important, but underutilized link in the transfer of technology and intellectual capital from the North to the continent. They have a responsibility to be Africa's intellectual eyes and ears. As we all know, Africa is routinely defamed and denigrated in the popular media and in scholarly publications in the North. Migrant African intellectuals ought to continuously challenge such misrepresentations, particularly among Africanists and other scholars, and to raise the intellectual costs of maligning and misrepresenting Africa.

Let us explore more concretely how new linkages and forms of collaboration can be established between migrant African intellectuals and intellectual communities on the continent around each of the three critical areas of scholarly pursuit: teaching, research, and public service.

Migrant intellectuals can contribute to teaching and training in Africa in five ways. First, through joint appointments in African and Northern universities, which could enable them to teach in Africa periodically. Upon their return to the North they could continue to supervise graduate students and to provide them with access to research materials from the North. In this way, periodic teaching visits would foster continuous interaction with students. Second, as shown earlier, the new information and communication technologies offer unprecedented opportunities for collaborative distance teaching, research, and other activities. The establishment of virtual universities provides a unique opening to link African intellectuals in the North to students and colleagues on the continent. In this context, the AVU needs to be expanded and to incorporate migrant African intellectuals. Third, the latter need to take advantage of study abroad programs sponsored by their institutions and various consortia, encouraging the expansion of these programs in Africa and ensuring that they benefit African students and are not glorified tourist junkets for students from the North. Fourth, migrant

African intellectuals ought to participate actively in existing, or in establishing new, national and regional training and research networks. Finally, it is possible for migrant African intellectuals to contribute to curriculum development in African institutions: informally, through personal contacts; and formally, through linkages between their institutions in the North and African institutions.

Each of these linkages in the teaching domain can foster more fruitful research linkages between African intellectuals within and outside the continent and contribute to the advancement of research and development in Africa. Specifically, there are four ways that migrant African intellectuals can play a productive role in the realm of research. First, joint research projects ought to be pursued more vigorously in a manner that maximizes the "comparative advantage" of each group in terms of access to data, research funds and materials, and theoretical formulations. Quite often, Northern researchers, equipped with fistfuls of dollars and theoretical conceits, descend upon Africa to test their latest pet theories and use their African colleagues as research assistants to collect data. Northern-based African scholars could help in changing the dynamics of such a research culture and promote more equitable relations by openly criticizing exploitative practices and sensitizing universities and foundations that fund African research to promote research that is truly collaborative, from the conception of research problems to the collection and interpretation of data, to the writing and publication of research results.

The initiative announced in 2000 by the Carnegie, Ford, MacArthur, and Rockfeller foundations to provide $100 million for the revitalization of African universities, mentioned in the previous chapter, is welcome but obviously not enough for the task. Ultimately of course, it is massive investment by African governments in higher education that will make a real difference. For the donor initiatives to work, it might be useful to select a few key institutions in each region and strategic areas of research, or to establish centers of excellence, to obtain massive support. It will not do to throw little bits of money at the hundreds of African universities and at all topics imaginable. As much as possible support should be concentrated on large innovative interdisciplinary research themes mainly in the areas of science and technology, that judiciously incorporate the social sciences and humanities. As Michael Chege (1998) has suggested, the foundations and other donors genuinely interested in the revitalization of African universities must openly desist from supporting corrupt institutions and individuals. Moreover, the consultancy syndrome must be curtailed and so must the tendency to rely on expatriates for research, which is often based on ill-disguised contempt for African academics. The appointment of increasing numbers of Africans as program officers and directors in some of the large foundations offers African intellectuals on the continent and in the diaspora an opportunity to promote new North-South research linkages and practices. Similarly, the appointment of Africans in senior administrative positions in African studies programs provides a basis for building new Africanist research cultures. The establishment of mutually beneficial institutional linkages and support between African researchers across the Atlantic constitute the second area in which migrant African intellectuals could advance research in and on Africa.

The third area centers on publication. Coauthorship and copublishing between African scholars and publishers based on the continent and their counterparts in the North should be encouraged. It offers the former wider markets for their ideas and products and helps the latter to focus their research on fundamental questions confronting Africa, thus saving them from the sterile seductions of postsomething theorizing, so beloved among many Northern scholars. As I stress elsewhere (Zeleza, 1997a), and especially in Chapter 8 below, African scholars based in the North should try as much as possible to publish in Africa-based journals and monograph series as a way of building African intellectual capacities and communities and of promoting intellectual conversations across the Atlantic in so far as it will be in their interest to see to it that such publications are marketed and read in the North. The reciprocal responsibility on the part of continentally based scholars and publishers is that they must export well-produced texts of impeccable scholarship. They are unlikely to attract their compatriots based in the North who seek to ascend the slippery poles of tenure and promotion if their publications are shoddy and reinforce the perceived inferiority and marginality of African scholarship. In short, coauthorship and copublication offer possibilities to promote and mainstream African scholarship.

In addition to collaborative research, migrant African intellectuals could contribute to the development of respectful intellectual conversations across the Atlantic through the establishment of extensive general and specialized review periodicals, edited and published jointly in the North and in Africa, in which African and Africanist publications would be routinely reviewed. The review periodicals could also assist in advertizing African books in the

North and vice versa and in breaking the cycle of self-referential solitude that currently characterizes Africanist scholarship. Such scholarly media would help promote more accountability and respectful communication between African and Africanist and other Northern scholarly communities. Today Northern scholars writing on African countries do not need to worry about what their African colleagues think or say, especially if the latter are based on the continent, because they are unlikely to review their work. This promotes intellectual indifference and misconduct, which sometimes includes outright fraud and the falsification of data.

Migrant African intellectuals have a special responsibility to mainstream African scholarship into global scholarship by promoting the consumption of African scholarly texts in the North. This often requires nothing more than simple commitment in so far as university professors have considerable freedom in designing courses and establishing or authorizing reading materials. That African intellectuals in the North must inform themselves of scholarly publications by their colleagues on the continent that could be used as class texts cannot be overemphasized. More challenging is to ensure that African publications are ordered by libraries despite their dwindling acquisition budgets and that they are included in index and citation systems that increasingly act as gateways to research products and inquiries as publications and information explode. Not to be cited by the major indexing services often spells intellectual invisibility or death. Migrant African intellectuals, working in collaboration with Africana librarians, need to push for the inclusion of African publications in these indexes that filter and legitimate scholarly products.

As for public service, migrant African intellectuals can also play several roles. First, there is advocacy. Together with the historic African diaspora communities, and working with groups interested in Africa, they can contribute to the formation of active lobbies for Africa with key public and private constituencies, ranging from governments and the corporate sector to the increasingly influential NGO movement and the media. As intellectuals, they have the capacity to provide coherent analyses and to chart the contours of fruitful relations between Africa and the North. At the very least, African governments and institutions should use them as interpreters of the North. Their work is also essential to minimizing media misrepresentation and marginalization of Africa. This is connected to the second public service function that migrant African intellectuals can perform: being actively engaged in outreach either through existing institutions to which they belong or through new institutions that they can form. Outreach aims to promote informed knowledge and public discourse on Africa. The constituencies for outreach include the institutions and sectors mentioned above, as well as educational institutions, movements with potential international scope, such as labor unions and religious organizations, and various cultural communities, especially those among the historic African diaspora.[16]

Finally, wherever possible the intellectuals, like other migrants, need to participate actively in the politics of both their countries of origin and settlement. Often they tend to be more preoccupied with politics back home than in their new countries, i.e., through fund-raising activities, forming exile political parties, and lobbying in Northern capitals against abhorrent dictatorships and governments. It is important to balance this with engagement in the electoral politics of the North, which often requires taking up citizenship. As their numbers and political voices rise in specific locations, and through coalition building with groups and constituencies favorably disposed towards Africa, the new African diaspora might begin to influence the foreign policies of their adopted countries towards Africa. The role of migrant intellectuals in this endeavor is to map out the trajectories of African political participation in the North and to interrogate the current constructions of citizenship and to articulate new ones that resonate with their transnationalism and the positive possibilities of globalization.

Clearly, effecting these changes and developments requires much more than personal commitment by individuals. Institutional anchors are required to navigate the demanding rigors and rituals of academic life and migrancy. The institutional mechanisms can include both old and new institutions. Better use could be made of existing academic associations and networks, such as the African Studies Association in the United States and CODESRIA in Senegal, to coordinate and develop some of the activities outlined above. Official university associations, such as the Association of African universities also have a role to play. So do international organizations, such as UNECA, whose executive chief has promised to mobilize the African intellectual diaspora to strengthen research networks throughout Africa (Amoako, 1999; Bella, 2000), UNESCO, and UNRISD (United Nations Research Institute for Social Development).

The way forward might require setting up separate organizations that specifically focus on promoting the utilization of migrant African intellectuals in the development of teaching, research, and public service in and on Africa along some of the lines suggested in this chapter. Such organizations could put to much better use some of the funds currently allocated to programs promoting the permanent return and relocation of migrant Africans, or the huge sums spent on technical assistance by often ill-informed or indifferent non-African expatriates. I would like to propose the formation of a North American Pan-African intellectual diaspora network to coordinate exchanges and linkages between African intellectuals in North America and the continent and to promote Africa's educational development.[17] It needs to be recognized that the challenge for Africa is not simply one of capacity building but of capacity utilization too, of finding the most effective ways of fully exploiting the intellectual and technical capacity that has already been built, which for various reasons, is now scattered all over the world.

Numerous expatriate knowledge networks exist, but few are linked to African countries and none to the continent as a whole. According to Mercy Brown (2000), of the forty-one such networks—mostly formed in the late 1980s and early 1990s—worldwide, only six were connected to Africa.[18] Typically, their membership is highly skilled, dispersed, active in the fields of science and technology, and consists of nationals of a particular country living abroad motivated by the desire to contribute their skills and expertise to the development of their countries of origin. They operate as independent, nonpolitical, and nonprofitable organizations and conduct their work by maintaining websites and databases of members' data, organizing specific activities such as newsletters, conferences, and seminars.

The Pan-African intellectual diaspora network I am proposing would do all these things and more. It would seek to link diaspora intellectuals not only to their countries of origin but to other countries across the continent. Specifically, the network would work closely with the Association of African Universities, the African Academy of Sciences, and other international, continental, and regional university associations and research networks, to promote linkages, and to facilitate the transfer of knowledge, information, and skills through physical and virtual mobility, teaching and training, research and publishing, policy analysis and advocacy. Prior to its formation, we need to have better grasp and data on the migrant African academics, information about their qualifications, locations, positions, current types of linkages with African institutions, and their attitudes towards expanding or establishing new linkages. This has to be placed in the larger context of higher education

169

linkages, exchanges, and partnerships within Africa itself and between Africa and the North, a subject on which deeper understanding is also required.

A vibrant culture of intra-African academic exchanges is indispensable to the development of strong and beneficial educational linkages with countries and regions outside the continent. Thus, African universities must articulate policies to promote student recruitment and faculty exchange from other African countries besides the unorganized and individual migrations. Such policies should recognize that foreign students are a cultural, intellectual, and sometimes, financial resource for African countries. They can contribute significantly to the academic experience of local students and research collaboration. As part of this endeavor, managers of Africa's higher education institutions must lobby for the streamlining of visa, taxation, and employment policies and regulations to facilitate entry for bona fide short-term and degree students and to enable these students to maximize their exposure, wherever possible, to local society and culture through internships and employment. The managers of African universities have to be keenly aware of new trends in international education and forge partnerships that promote both capacity-building and capacity-utilization, effectively utilizing African capacities wherever they may be located, including the North.

Conclusion

The rising migration of Africa's professional elites and intellectuals may indeed be a curse if dismissed and ignored, but it can be turned into a blessing if embraced and utilized. It is generated by, and inserts Africa into, contemporary processes of transnationalization and globalization, which follow and reinforce the old trails of Pan-Africanism, for after all, the Atlantic slave trade represented a massive brain and brawn drain from the continent to the Americas. The challenge for Africa, then, is how to rebuild the historic Pan-African project, spawned by the global dispersal and exploitation of African peoples over the centuries, by creatively using the current migratory flows of African peoples, cultures, capacities, and visions and the contemporary revolution in telecommunications and travel technologies. It is an old challenge in a new age that requires responses and solutions that are both old and new.

Clearly, academic exchanges between Africa and the North have a long and complicated history. They have certainly helped to build educational capacities and knowledge on both sides of the Atlantic and the Mediterranean. Nevertheless, the relationship has been unequal in terms of both the flows and the benefits. More Africans, for example, have studied in the United States than Americans have studied in Africa, yet the advantages have not always gone to the African side. Certainly, Africans hardly influence American studies the way Americans dominate African studies both in the United States and within Africa itself; terms of debate about Africa, with all their prescriptive baggage, are often set by American Africanists. This, of course, is merely one reflection of the pervasive relations of dependency between Africa and the United States.

I believe it is possible to transform these relations, to improve the terms of academic discourse and exchange between the North and Africa. This requires the establishment of carefully constructed partnerships that embrace all the key constituencies and components of the academic enterprise, i.e., on the one hand, the stakeholders—students, faculty, and administrators—and on the other the services—teaching, research, publishing, and dissemination. Thus, for African academics, truly effective faculty exchange programs would need to include creating research projects, teaching possibilities, exchanging materials, and publishing outlets. Many of the programs that have been established have been piecemeal, small, and uncoordinated. To improve the traditional linkages and to take advantage of the emerging ones, it is imperative to build new structures of cooperation and collaboration.

African universities need to make better coordinated linkages to, and use of, their "natural" allies in the academies of the North, i.e., the three interrelated constituencies: In addition to the African migrant intellectuals, there are the Africanist associations and the historically black colleges and universities (HBCUs). The associations can be effectively mobilized to lobby governments and the foundations for better international education programs, against immigration restrictions affecting African students and scholars, and to monitor exchange programs that are potentially harmful.[19] For their part, the HBCUs in the United States, are interested in linking up with African institutions, but they have tended to be sidelined because of the marginalization of African Americans in the American academy and society in general and the unwillingness or ignorance on the part of African institutions. The HBCUs are where the majority of African Americans and large numbers of African students receive their higher education, and where many migrant African intellectuals teach. Too often, linkages between U.S. and African educational institutions are confined to the historically white institutions. The signing of a memorandum of understanding between the AAU and the

HBCU Consortium for National and International Education in July 1999 to promote academic exchanges, joint research, and curriculum development, between African universities and the HBCUs is quite encouraging (*AAU Newsletter* 5, 2, 1999: 13-14).[20]

Building new foreign partnerships, mediated by Africa's potential allies, including specifically the African historic and contemporary intellectual diasporas will go a long way toward improving and strengthening the visibility of African research, both on the continent itself and globally, and to turn the brain drain not just into a potential "brain gain," but into "brain mobility." This is essential for Africa's revitalization and renaissance, as well as for the globalization of African scholarship and the Africanization of global scholarship.

Endnotes

1. ERASMUS stands for the European Community Action Schemes for the Mobility of University Students; COMETT for Community Program for Education and Training in the Technology Field; LINGUA for European Cooperation Programmes for Language Teacher Training; and TEMPUS for Trans-European Mobility Scheme for University Studies.

2. These programs of course face specific challenges: They reach only a small fraction of students and faculty; there are imbalances in the flows among countries and regions and according to language, social and geographical origins, and gender; quality of academic programs varies and arrangements for academic recognition and certification need improvement; and so does coordination with other industrial, environmental, and cultural sectors of the European Union. See Alan Smith (1996); Gisela Baumgratz-Gangl (1996); Karl Roeloffs (1996); Ladislav Cerych (1996); and Tamas Lajos (1996).

3. At its Tenth general conference, held in February 2001 the AAU recommended, among other things, to explore ways of establishing regional centers of excellence and to set up regional university accreditation

bodies to oversee standardization in the five regions so as to facilitate student and staff exchange (*AAU Newsletter*, March 2001: 3).

4. Phillipe Garnier (1998) argues that the fastest growing component of skilled migration consists of temporary migrant service providers, that is, migrants who perform services abroad without the intention or right to settle or to seek employment in the host country. They are made up of intercompany transfers; individual service providers and specialists on specific assignments; short-term or business visitors; diplomatic and international personnel.

5. The study covers only Ph.D. recipients from 219 American universities and a couple dozen Canadian universities between 1986 and 1996. Also, only citizens of sub-Saharan African countries at the time of graduation were considered. The rate of return survey was restricted to fifty-four US schools graduating thirty or more Ph.D.'s and fifteen Canadian universities. Completed surveys were received from only twenty-seven of the fifty-four US universities and three of the fifteen Canadian universities. Altogether, the researchers were able to gather adequate data for 1,708 cases, out of an estimated population of 5,537 sub-Saharan African graduates from the selected American and Canadian universities. The authors concede: "Given this situation, a more complete picture of actual career trajectories over time would be of enormous value, as would follow-up interviews with or the distribution of questionnaires to a sample of African Ph.D. recipients in both the Return and Stay categories" (Pires, et al. 1999:9).

6. Nevertheless, CIDA virtually ended its scholarship program for African graduate students (http://www.matrix.msu.edu/sacapacity/reports/part-research.html). Other agencies, such as USAID, have been placing increasing emphasis on short-and medium-term training in technical areas rather than on long-term general academic training (Vargas-Baron, 1998).

7. Immediately after the 1994 democratic elections, the Australian Agency for International Development established the Australia-South African Institutional Links Programme as part of its commitment to develop-

ment cooperation with South Africa in the field of education. Thirty-one projects were funded in the first three rounds, among them a project on university staff development for quality teaching analyzed by Jennifer Weir et al. (2001).

8. Several American universities have special South African programs. Among them are Howard University's extensive linkage program with several South African universities, including the Historically Disadvantaged Institutions (HDIs), called Howard University Republic of South Africa Residency (HURSAR) (http://www.founders. howard.edu/hursap9798.htm); and the University of Michigan's South Africa Initiative for academic exchanges and interdisciplinary seminars (http://www.umich.edu/~saioum/IIJournal.html).

9. Since the mid-1990s, the European Union has signed a series of agreements with various countries. In 1995 the EU signed an agreement with the United States for a permanent transatlantic academic exchange program that would facilitate student and mobility and exchange, increase exchange of knowledge and information in vocational education, and promote the exchange of faculty working on issues related to the EU and relations between the United States and Europe. Initially the program would make grants to between 10 and 15 consortia on each side (see Desruisseaux, 1995a). Similar programs have been established for the United States, Canada, and Mexico (Desruisseaux, 1995b), and in the Pacific Rim between Canada, the United States, Indonesia, Japan, New Zealand, the Philippines, Thailand, and some of the island nations (Cohen, 1996).

10. All figures are from *The Chronicle of Higher Education*, Almanac 2001-2. Of the 4,048 colleges and universities, 41.5 percent are public and the rest are private; 71.6 percent are non-profit and 28.4 percent for profit. For students, using the official racial classification, 1 percent were American Indian, 6.1 percent Asian, 11 percent Black, 8.9 percent Hispanic, 69.4 percent white, and 3.5 percent foreign. Altogether, men constituted 43.9 percent and women 56.1 percent. As for the composition of staff and faculty, 97.3 percent were American citizens and resident aliens, and 2.7 percent were aliens; 57 percent were full-time and

43 percent part-time faculty; 20.7 percent were full-time faculty and 15.3 percent were part-time; 5.2 percent full-time executive, administrative and managerial staff, and 15.3 percent part-time; and the rest were clerical, secretarial, technical, service, and maintenance staff; 63.7 percent of the full-time faculty and 52.2 percent of the part-time faculty were men, compared to 36 percent and 47 percent, respectively, for women; 5.1 percent of the full-time and 4.5 percent of the part-time faculty were black, compared to, respectively, 85.1 percent and 87.6 percent for whites, 5.8 percent and 3.2 percent for Asians, 3.3 percent and 3.7 percent for Hispanics, and 0.7 percent and 1.0 percent for American Indians. As for the sources of revenues, comparing public and private institutions, tuition and fees accounted for 19 percent and 43.0 percent of total revenues for public and private institutions, respectively; federal appropriations and grants and contracts, 11 percent and 13.8 percent; state governments 35.6 percent and 1.9 percent; local governments 3.9 percent and 0.8 percent; private gifts, grants and contracts 4.3 percent and 9.1 percent; endowment income 0.6 percent and 5.2 percent; sales and services 12.5 percent and 12.5 percent; hospitals and other sources 13.1 percent and 13.8 percent, respectively.

11. These figures, unless otherwise stated, are all from the "International Section" of *The Chronicle of Higher Education,* 17 November 2000.

12. American study abroad programs in Africa can be divided into several types. First, there are the stand-alone programs that are run by an American university or group of universities or consortia totally independently of local universities, although local faculty may be used as instructors. In such programs the American students have no formal interactions with local students. Second, there are programs in which American students are brought as a group, often with a resident director appointed by the U.S. university or consortium, and enrolled in local universities. Third, there are the programs that involve American students coming to an African university on their own initiative as individuals.

13. To some study abroad programs are invaluable precisely because, to quote Simeon Kanani (2000), a Kenyan entrepreneur, they "have emerged as

the fastest growing subsector of the [tourism] industry," which in Kenya's case is the country's biggest foreign exchange earner. He notes that the number of credit-award academic study programs in Kenya grew from fifteen in 1998 to twenty-two in 1999, fifteen of the latter group were from the United States, and there were more than eighty other non-credit programs, most of them short two-week or field observation excursions. He operates his Technical Study Tours Ltd., which contracts with study abroad programs of several universities, including the Minnesota Studies in International Development, strictly as a profitable business. Another example of an African entrepreneurial venture in the field of study abroad is the Student and Youth Travel Organization of Ghana founded in 1994 by the M&J Travel and Tours as a nonprofit NGO to facilitate educational travels for Ghanaian students abroad and foreign students in Ghana. The SYTO has established partnerships with numerous American institutions and international study abroad organizations. In 1999, it set up a branch office in the United States (Sandenburgh and Schut, 2000).

14. There is always the danger that American societies, typically larger and more prosperous than their foreign counterparts, may be intrusive and undermine foreign societies. To avoid this, some American groups have created membership agreements with those organizations. Under the agreements, membership in a scholar's home organization earns him or her special privileges, such as a discounted rate on membership in the American society.

15. A related phenomenon is the establishment of overseas research centers to assist visiting American researchers, with funds from the US Department of Education. These centers are often used by locals scholars in the region. In Africa there are three: the West African Research Association, the American Research Center in Egypt, and the American Institute for Maghrib Studies.

16. In the United States these include such important political organizations as the NAACP, the Urban League, Operation PUSH, the Congressional Black Caucus, and TransAfrica, to mention the prominent ones at the national level; and the influential African American churches and other religious organizations.

17. Since writing this chapter, I have learnt that in May 2001, the Independent African Commission and the United Nations University outlined an ambitious program to create multidisciplinary centers of excellence in science, technology, humanities and policy management, an African Millennium Initiative for Science and Technology to link African scientists in the diaspora to their counterparts at home, and a database of African talents both in the diaspora and the continent (http://www.milasfrica.org/accra e.htm). The network I propose would not be restricted to scientists but would include academics and intellectuals in all fields and would specifically target three cohorts of scholars, the junior professors, middle-level professors, and retired professors.

18. Specifically, to the Arab countries (the Network of Arab Scientists and Technologies Abroad), Kenya (Association of Kenyans Abroad), Nigeria (Association of Nigerians Abroad), Morocco (Moroccan Association of Researchers and Scholars Abroad), South Africa (the South African Network of Skills Abroad), and Tunisia (the Tunisian Scientific Consortium). Abebe Kebede (n.d) mentions a few others with more limited scope. See also Teferra (2000).

19. The climate for international scholars and students in the United States deteriorated following the immigration law of 1996. A tracking system of foreign students was introduced in the aftermath of the 1993 bombing of the World Trade Center in New York. Involving the use of fingerprints and detailed computer records to monitor foreign students, it curtails the rights of these students. As for harmful exchanges, many of the students coming to Africa are using National Security Education Program (NSEP) grants that African studies programs and the ASA have universally condemned for compromising the students and the countries they visit because of its national security requirements (Desruisseaux, 1999). Africanists can, and do, individually foster invitations to their home institutions for African students and scholars, lobby their institutions, and gather books and equipment for African universities. These activities are commendable, but there is no substitute for collective and coordinated programs.

20. There are other encouraging signs. In 1995, four medical schools at HBCUs established partnership in the SA Health Care Initiative to improve health care for the disadvantaged in South Africa. As head of one of the participating schools, Dr. Louis Sullivan, president of the Morehouse School of Medicine and former U.S. Secretary of Health said, "Black medical schools in the United States have had to struggle with the very issues with which their South African counterparts are now contending" (*The Chronicle of Higher Education*, 29 September 1995). In 1998 the United Negro College Fund, an organization of thirty-nine private black institutions, won a $21.9 million grant from USIA to help fifteen historically disadvantaged institutions in South Africa with technical assistance and support in curriculum, finance, research, staff development, and student leadership.

Chapter 4

The Pasts and Futures of African Studies in the United States

Introduction

The term "crisis" is much beloved in African studies, smearing all it touches, including the object of its study, Africa, and its own epistemological standing and future. So we hear that African studies, like all area studies programs in the United State, is in a terminal state of crisis. The crisis is seen as something new, spawned by the ideological ramifications of the end of the cold war and the intellectual ravages of globalization. A powerful narrative no doubt, but one that falsifies and simplifies the past as much as it forecloses the unpredictable possibilities of the future. Is there indeed a crisis for African studies and other area studies programs in the United States? Or is it a storm in a teacup, as Michael Watts (1997:185) believes; a peculiarly American debate of no priority for Africans, as Michael Chege (1997:133) contends; a debate inspired, according to Zeleza (1997a:201), by America's "channel-surfing intellectualism in which the temptation to reinvent newness is always great?" Will we a decade from now, as Julius Nyang'oro (1997: 166) reassures us, "realize that the current debate was not about the viability of area studies as such, but rather a nervousness brought about by the fear of shrinking resources in the academy generally?" If in fact there is a crisis, whose crisis is it? What is its trajectory?

As a historian with an aversion to crystal-gazing and apocalyptic speculations parading as knowledge, I am far more comfortable dissecting the past

179

than predicting the future, in untangling and unpacking the messy process-es of change than in reducing them to an omnipotent crisis. Much of the alarm is fueled by Afropessimism, the belief that Africa is condemned to eternal marginality, especially now that it has lost even the dubious atten-tions of pawnship during the cold war. I do not share the view that Africa is marginal, not to the world as a whole, and certainly not to its peoples on the continent and in the diaspora. Priscilla Stone (1997:181) is correct that we must stop asking self-defeating questions: "'Why is African Studies margin-alized, disadvantaged, and impoverished relative to other Area Studies?' This question is no longer relevant if it ever was."

So I prefer to talk of challenges: What are the challenges facing area studies, including African studies? In what ways are they linked to changes in the wider American academy and its international knowledge system? How are these challenges being met? How can they be tackled, tamed, and transcended? These are some of the questions addressed in this chapter: the changing intellectual, institutional, and ideological contexts; social compo-sition, and scholarly cultures of African studies in the United States. A key argument of this chapter is that African studies in the United States is infused with, and operates within the parameters of, America's racial ecolo-gy. The racial divisions in the field are evident to anyone who has ever been engaged with it, although many prefer to ignore them as Deborah Amory (1997) argues. Hence, the racialized genealogies, paradigms, and preoccupa-tions of the field and the conflicting claims between the authorizing dis-courses of objectivity and authenticity. Thus, as an institutional field in the United States, African studies is less about Africa and more about the United States itself; it is as American as any disciplinary or discursive field in the American academy.

This chapter is divided into four parts. The first examines the compet-ing institutional histories of African studies as a field and its racialized social hierarchies. The second looks at the complicated relations between area stud-ies and the shifting projects of the state and the disciplines. The third part outlines the challenges posed by globalization as a process of change and a paradigm of research and by interdisciplinary modes of inquiry and scholar-ship. Finally, the fourth part asks what the social activist agenda of African studies should be.

Histories and Hierarchies

The claims that area studies and African studies are in crisis rest on and repro-duce incomplete histories of the area studies project, which, in turn, lead to inadequate analysis of the nature of the current challenges and ways they might be overcome. It is commonly assumed that the Second World War gave birth "area studies" in the American academy, and the cold war nurtured it, in response to the grueling demands of global confrontation spawned by the two wars. It follows that since the cold war is now over, area studies have lost their *raison d'etre*, knowledge of the world outside Euro-America can be inferred from the universal models of the disciplines, or the homogenizing imperatives of globalization. This narrative is quite appealing to triumphalist right-wingers who think history is over; fiscally minded university administrators seeking programs to cut; and desperate social scientists aspiring to be natural scientists with their rational-choice models. However, this narrative silences other histo-ries. Pearl Robinson (1997:169) eloquently contests this history:

> Debates about the future of African Studies seem to have little to do with the past as I know or have come to under-stand it. What I discern is a profusion of arguments linked to differing standpoints and designed to privilege new hier-archies of access to resources. Virtually all the prevailing reconstructions of African Studies begin with the Cold War and focus on the legacies of government and foundation-funded Area Studies programs. Curiously, such accounts generally omit any reference to the long-standing tradition of African Studies at historically black colleges and univer-sities, only rarely gives a nod to African American profes-sional and lay scholars of Africa, and seldom acknowledge the existence of epistemic communities based in Africa.

Thus, history is used to stake positions, to mark boundaries, to confer authority in the struggle for intellectual, material, and reputational resources as African studies and other area studies programs, indeed, as the academy as a whole is restructured in response to internal institutional and epistemo-logical changes and new global economic and political realignments.

There is no doubt that the Second World War and the cold war had a profound impact on the development of area studies, and that the end of the cold war has brought new contexts. But area studies, certainly African studies, antedated both wars. The roots of the area studies tradition go back to the nineteenth century. According to Burkart Holzner and Matthew Harmon (1998:47):

> Prior to 1900, U.S. "research" about other parts of the world consisted of four traditions: the "classical" tradition, which studied the ancient civilizations of Greece, Rome, and Egypt; the missionary movement, whose proponents traveled to other nations with the intent of encouraging conversion, but who were often anti-intellectual and explicitly limited the scope of inquiry into their host societies; a "scientific racism" tradition that attempted to demonstrate the superiority of whites through comparison with and systematic examination of other races; and, finally, an anecdotal "tradition" of relying on information about non-Western cultures from potentially unreliable travelers.

During the late 1940s and 1950s when area studies became institutionalized, Gilbert Merkx (1995) contends, cold war concerns were often used to achieve long-sought support for higher education in general and long-standing research on the non-Western world in particular.

The area studies project was bolstered by the need to overcome the isolationist and parochial tendencies of the American public and academy, increasingly seen as unbecoming and perilous for a superpower. The American public was woefully uninformed about the rest of the world, especially the newly independent countries of Africa and Asia, where the United States and the Soviet Union were locked in fierce combat to win hearts and minds. The need for information about these countries, including America's turbulent backyard, Latin America, as well as the Soviet bloc, was seen as essential in the struggle for global supremacy between the USA and USSR. Reinforcing the national security imperative was the epistemological imperative to internationalize knowledge in the academy. While the link between social science and area knowledge goes back to the origins of some social science disciplines, such as sociology and anthropology, most of the disciplines remained resolutely ethnocentric, an intellectual deficiency syndrome that worsened as they aspired to "scientific" status and concocted, from American experience, universal models, and theories that magically transcended the realities and diversities of global histories and geographies, cultures and societies, polities and economies. The theoretical conceit and parochialism of the disciplines reflected the imperial provincialism and ignorance of the American public.

Area studies were expected to overcome these deficiencies and to provide the public and academy with information about the non-Western world. It was, therefore, infused with the twists and turns of American foreign policy, the projection of imperial power, in which knowledge of America and the allied West more broadly was lodged within the disciplines, and that of the rest of the world was relegated to the area studies ghetto and inscribed with the pathologies of otherness. Consequently, the United States was not considered an "area," but at the very core of disciplinary knowledges, its experiences and the epistemologies derived from them elevated to manifestations of the universal. So the pernicious fictions were born and bred that area studies was concerned with the parochial and the particular, while American studies, and their civilizational cousins, European studies, were disciplinary parables of the human condition.

The development of area studies was also tied to the fate of ethnic minorities in the United States. The "scientific racism" that colored much of the earlier work on non-Western societies was rooted in racist and discriminatory policies at home against the Native Americans, African Americans, and others. The exclusion of these populations from political and cultural citizenship, from the American mainstream, necessitated the separation of their ancestral cultures and continents from disciplinary narratives. In short, given the centrality of race in American society and politics, the eternal struggles between blacks and whites, African Americans and European Americans, rooted in slavery and segregation, it meant that the privileges and pathologies of the wider American social and intellectual order were refracted and reproduced with a ferocious investment of patronage, passions, and pain in African studies in a manner that was unusual among the area studies programs. The place of Africa in the American social imaginary was inextricably tied to the state of American race relations, so that more often than not, definitions and defamations of Africa were projections of African Americans. The vocabulary used to depict the otherness and failed promises of Africa was often the same as that used for African Americans. This congruence of constructions and condemnations lay at the heart of the future contestations, often bitter, between Africans, African Americans, and European Americans in the study of Africa.

The result was that before the Second World War, except for missionaries and anthropologists, the quintessential discipline of the non-western other, Africa remained an intellectual "dark continent" in the mainstream academy. It also meant Africa would figure centrally in African American popular and intellectual discourses. From the nineteenth Century, African American scholars began to study Africa systematically, in an effort to correct biases and distortions, vindicate the continent's cultures and histories and to restore them to the repertoire of world civilizations, as part of their struggles for emancipation from slavery and later segregation in America. The African American vindicationist and emancipatory tradition of African studies was pan-African in inspiration and orientation. "Rejecting the dichotomies on which Africanist scholarship would later be constructed," Michael West and William Martin (1997:311) state, African American scholars "connected ancient Africa to modern Africa, Africa north of the Sahara to Africa south of the Sahara, and, especially, the African continent to the African diaspora. They tended to concentrate on broad political, religious, and cultural themes that transcended national and continental boundaries in the black world."

Located in the historically black colleges and universities (HBCUs), these scholars were often public intellectuals who saw their work as an integral part of the liberation struggles of Africans and African Americans. The era of the professional academic Africanist had yet to come. Nevertheless, the conceptual and ideological foundations had already been laid: from imperial Europe came the paternalistic focus on the "native" other; from settler America came the preoccupation with "racial" difference; both could trace their roots to Hegel. The racialized discourse of Africa in the American academy and society required and reinforced the Hegelian denial of Africa's historicity and humanity. Hegel's ghost, as Olufemi Taiwo (1997) has argued so passionately, was to cast a permanent pall on African studies programs that emerged from the late 1940s. The Africanists' Africa did not refer to the continent as a whole, but to that truncated concoction known as sub-Saharan Africa. Africa was black, tropical, trapped, as Hegel decreed, in the bosoms of the "undeveloped, unhistorical spirit." The northern part of the continent was removed and recast into the imperial cartography of the Middle East. Middle from whom? the South African writer, Peter Abrahams once asked.

The British, of course! In short, the racialization of Africa reflected the racialization of America, and reproduced the Hegelian and Conradian dismissal and diminution of Africa as the "dark continent," the ultimate other of Europe, of white western civilization.

By the early 1950s, then, there were at least two competing Africas in the American academy and social imaginary; the Africa of the African American scholar-activists and the Africa of the academic Africanists; the Africa of popular struggle and liberation and the Africa of policy formulation and implementation. In one Africa was a civilizational presence; in the other a basket case of absences, a continent awaiting development and modernization. The Africanists's Africa triumphed in the academy, not for its superior intellectual insights, but because it resonated with the predilections of the general public and the prescriptions of the foreign policy establishment. So the history of African studies had to be re-written, the newly institutionalized African studies project sanctified. From then on, in the official histories of African studies, including the most recent by Jane Guyer, *African Studies in the United States* (1996), it became fashionable to ignore the fact that African studies was pioneered in the HBCUs and not in the HWUs (historically white universities), by African American scholar-activists not European American academics and policy wonks (Herskovits, 1958; Baum, 1965; Dressel, 1966; Cowan, 1969; Curtin, 1971; Carter, 1976). The Philip Curtin (1971: 358) 1970 ASA presidential address is typical: "At the end of the Second World War North America had no real community of scholars specializing on Africa."

Silenced were the deliberate efforts by some Africanists to subvert the work of African Americans. For example, in the 1930s Melville Herskovits reportedly helped deny funding for W.E.B. Dubois' Encyclopedia Africana project, while offering (when the ASA was formed in 1957) to help the CIA in any way possible (Martin and West, 1999a: 86-92). In the spurious name of objectivity, Herskovists "regularly advised his African American graduate students not to study in Africa....The fact that white Americans, not black Americans, were thought to possess 'objectivity' in relation to Africa reflects the construction of race relations in the United States, where white constitutes the unmarked category" (Amory, 1997: 110). Thus, wresting paternity of the field from Dubois to Herskovits, from Howard to Northwestern, represented a much larger battle, the incorporation of Africa into the orbit of American foreign policy and cold war calculations, and a paradigmatic shift from posing large civilizational and cultural questions to policy-oriented developmentalist research, from popular engagement to professional encounters with Africa.

The professionalized and developmentalist thrust of African studies from the 1950s reflected wider trends; first, the territorization of poverty and the professionalization and institutionalization of development practice; and second, the commoditization and corporatization of academic culture, which forced and facilitated the divorce of academics from social movements. The momentous discovery that poverty was a peculiar Third World condition amenable to technical and technological fixes, made in the heated postwar context of American-Soviet ideological rivalries and imperial-colonial struggles, allowed the emergence of the development experts and the prescriptive and policy orientation of area studies, especially in African studies since Africa was regarded as the most underdeveloped region (Escobar, 1995; Zeleza, 1997a: Chapter 7). At the same time intellectual life was becoming more professionalized, thanks to the postwar expansion of university education and the growth of middle class comforts, consciousness, and conservatism, all of which spawned a social science research culture that valorized objectivity, detachment, and a mindless chase for theory, as Edward Said (1993: Chapter 4) has complained so bitterly. This expedited the separation of African studies from domestic African American constituencies and reinforced the use of deductive methods and models, in which Africa was reduced to a testing site for theories manufactured with faddish regularity in the American academy.

These competing Africas in the American academy and general public, which were by no means monolithic and unconnected, were complicated from the 1960s following African independence and the explosion in higher education on the continent and the nationalist project to decolonize education and culture, by the entry of African scholars into the fray. Carrying their own baggage of memories of colonial and racial oppression and the developmentalist ambitions of an aspiring nationalist elite, African students and faculty flocking to American campuses in the 1960s, were caught up in the fault lines of America's racial solitudes and the revolutionary fervor of the Civil Rights movement. While they saw common cause between the struggles for independence in Africa and civil rights in America, unlike the generation of the Kwame Nkrumahs and Nnandi Azikiwes, who were educated at the HBCUs, the new generation of African students were increasingly trained at the historically white universities and were more likely to be sponsored by governments and international agencies than sustained by the contributions and civilities of black communities and churches. The contradictions in their structural, social, and spatial positions provoked intense unease and discomfort with the content and composition of African studies.

The result of all this was the confrontation of Montreal in 1969, where a group of African and African American scholars and activists took on the Africanist establishment, demanding "pluralism and parity" (Shepherd, 1969).[1] The Montreal confrontation marked a crucial moment for what it revealed of the institutional and intellectual solitudes in African studies and the legacies it left behind. Organizationally the insurgents, led by the Black Caucus, demanded increased black membership and participation in all phases and operations of the African Studies Association (ASA) (Black Caucus Statements, 1968 and 1969). Intellectually, they called for the inclusion of a pan-Africanist perspective in research themes and the assumption of scholarly authority by African and African Americans. Politically, they insisted on collective commitment to struggles for emancipation in Africa and in the United States from the ravages of imperialist and racist oppression, exploitation, and marginalization (LeMelle, 1969, 1971; Challenor, 1969; Turner and Murapa, 1969; Gappert, 1969; Johnson, 1971; Clarke, 1969, 1976). Many of the affronted "gatekeepers" reacted angrily, charging their opponents with reverse "racialism," or made unabashed defense of professional neutrality and scholarly objectivity, for the "untrammeled pursuit of scholarship and truth," in Nimer's words (Nimer, 1970; van den Berghe, 1969; Burke, 1969a, 1969b; Emerson, 1969;). Others advocated reformist concessions in the name of liberal tolerance (Sklar, 1969), or a strategic leftist compromise (Wallerstein, 1969; Resnick, 1969a, 1969b). Later some white "radicals" accused the Africanist community of being lackeys of imperialism by spying for the American government, pursuing research agendas and themes, for example, on "modernization" that benefitted American business and imperial needs (Chilcote and Legassick, 1971).

The lines of debate drawn by Montreal continued in subsequent years; but the contexts changed. The African Heritage Studies Association (AHSA), formed by the Black Caucus, went its way, and perhaps fewer African Americans entered African studies, opting instead for African American studies. The institutionalization of the domestic racial solitudes was almost complete. There was no resolution of the fundamental institutional, ideological, and intellectual contradictions and constraints facing African studies within and outside the American academy. Rid of the perennial challenges and criticisms from vocal African Americans, minor reforms were made in the structural organization of the ASA, and the Africanist establishment hoped to return to the charmed clubbiness of the past.

Concentrated in the HWUs, rather than the HBCUs, the African American studies movement was both an ally and a foe of African studies. Many a reluctant university administration was forced to establish or to expand African studies programs in direct response to the institutional and epistemological challenges posed by African American students and faculty, inspired by black consciousness, black arts, and the Civil Rights movements more generally, as outlined so cogently by William Banks (1996: Chapters 8-10). Demands for courses on the black experience soon turned into calls for black studies departments, centers, institutes, or programs that should both be independent and involved in community service. To quote Floyd Hayes (1994:154):

> The African American Studies Movement converged with mass movements of protest against the brutalizing effects of social injustice, socioeconomic inequality, racial antagonism, the Vietnam War, and university paternalism....African American students also audaciously called into question the American academy's dominant Eurocentric perspective—the unchallenged assumption that Western European culture is superior, neutral, and normative. Labeling this orientation ethnocentric, African American students charged that Western education, wittingly and otherwise, diminished, distorted, and, in many instances, obliterated the contributions of African peoples to world development generally and the contributions of African Americans to America's development specifically. Therefore, African American students demanded that the university establish courses of study that provided a systematic examination of African and African-descended peoples' experiences.

By challenging Eurocentric paradigms and the rigid barriers between academic disciplines, the African American studies movement helped legitimize the study of non-Western cultures and multidisciplinary and interdisciplinary studies; but by pointing to the configuration of European American power and domination in the American academy, even in African studies, and emphasizing the collective black experience, it challenged African studies as constituted at the time. In short, as Manning Marable (1995) reminds us, the African American studies movement was an integral part of the multiculturalism debate that facilitated the entry of African studies programs and other minority and women studies programs into the academy. It should not be forgotten, Wahneema Lubiano (1996) and Mae Henderson (1996) stress, that the engagement and encounter of African American studies with the disciplines involved contestation and negotiation over the production and construction of knowledge and the exclusionary and hierarchic practices of the academy long before the rise of cultural studies and other deconstruction projects of theorizing about difference, absences, presences, and oppositionality that have become so popular in the American academy over the last two decades.

By the early 1980s, more than 600 of the nation's 3,535 institutions of higher education offered courses in black studies, African American studies, Afro-American studies, or Africana studies. The number had dropped to about 215 by the early 1990s, thanks to internal dissensions, overwork, dwindling administrative support (partly because of mounting attacks against affirmative action), and growing competition for resources by other ethnic studies and thematic studies programs (Philip, 1994:14-19; Pogue, 1993; Manning, 2000a)[2]. Except for the Africana studies programs, most of the black studies programs focused largely on the American experience. Those that incorporated Africa and the African diaspora as a whole tended to adopt pan-African and Afrocentric approaches that found little favor among Africanists in the African studies programs. To be sure, there were vigorous debates over Afrocentricity among African American scholars (Manning, 2000b: Part Three). But whatever their ideological foibles and rigidities, the Afrocentricists were more willing to engage African social thought and seminal thinkers, from Cheikh Anta Diop to Frantz Fanon, than was the case among their Africanist counterparts who tended to ignore African writings and paradigms (Asante, 1987, 1988; Hall, 1991b; Morgan, 1991; Zeleza, 1997a: Chapter 4).

Thus, the divide between African studies and African American studies was institutional and intellectual: Housed in separate, sometimes antagonistic units that often ignored each other, they examined Africa from distinctly different angles. The Africa of African studies was the sub-Saharan contraption examined through the gaze of modernization and development; the Africa of Africana studies was continental and diasporic, focusing on the ancient past and transnational connections among African peoples. The gulf between development and diaspora was deep and unproductive. As Alfred Zack-Williams (1995:349) puts it: "Diasporic studies, which is situated within the tradition of cultural studies, tends to be de-linked from political economy, thus running the risk of a descent into its cultural relativism. Similarly, development studies, with its emphasis on political economy divorced from cultural studies, runs the risk of economic reductionism." Writing from the European vantage point, he notes that "development studies has maintained an ostrich-like detachment from issues of race and diasporan concerns. In the context of African studies, apart from the study of the aberration of apartheid South Africa, African studies is silent on African migration to Europe and the condition of the African diaspora in Europe" (Zack-Williams, 1995:351). The institutional divide was loudly racial: African studies programs were dominated by European Americans and African American studies programs by African Americans.

The entry of increasing numbers of continental African scholars into the African studies fray offered African studies both an opportunity and a challenge. As migrants from predominantly black societies, African migrant intellectuals were not always sensitive to the racial dynamics and demands of American society and the academy; some even internalized the dominant's society's negative stereotypes of African Americans, which often made them accomplices with European Americans in America's eternal racial war, for which they were sometimes rewarded with preferential hirings and promotions over African Americans. By hiring a few continental Africans, African studies programs gained credibility and universities shored up their affirmative action credentials. The Africans, however, were not always so easily placated; their blackness assumed greater salience the longer they stayed in America and as they and their families were forced to negotiate the country's treacherous racial quagmire and their children became African Americans or American Africans, as Ali Mazrui calls the children of first generation African immigrants.

The gravitation towards African American grievances reinforced the Africans' own long-standing grumblings against the marginality of African voices in African studies. Hence, the growing trail, from the late 1960s, of complaints by African scholars resident in the United States about the relevance and reliability, accountability and authority, biases and boundaries, concepts and constructions, definitions and distortions, integrity and imperatives, ideological attachments and intellectual agendas of the Africanist enterprise (Njisane, 1971; Mhone, 1971; Owusu, 1971; Uchendu, 1977; Mudimbe, 1988, 1994; Irele, 1991; Appiah, 1992; Owomoyela, 1994; Mamdani, 1995; Mkandawire, 1997b; Eyoh, 1996; Chege, 1997; Nyang'oro, 1997; Zeleza, 1997a, 1997b). It is quite remarkable that the complaints African scholars made in the 1990s echo those made twenty years earlier. In a comprehensive and biting critique of the Africanist enterprise, first delivered as the Abiola Lecture at the 1996 ASA Annual Meeting, Thandika Mkandawire (1997), former head of CODESRIA, Africa's premier social science organization, outlined seven sources of African discontent with Africanist scholarship. Africans were dissatisfied with the Africanists, he stated, first, for their gatekeeping functions; second, their continued, indeed, increasing primacy given to the deductive method and the use of Africa as a testing ground; third, their patronizing and exploitative use of local research communities; fourth, the international division of labor in which Africanists did most of the "conceptual work" and Africans performed field work; fifth, the failure to establish mutually beneficial and respectful intellectual bridges between the two research communities and the invisibility of African scholarship in Africanist publications; sixth, the preachy and prescriptive approach of most writing about contemporary Africa; and seventh, the disdain for Africa as shown by the accretion of epithets and contemptuous metaphors in describing African conditions, economies, polities, and social classes. For these reasons, the respect and tolerance for non-African writing in Africa was waning, reinforced by the growing inaccessibility of Africanists' work because of high import costs and the rapidly increasing volume of local publications and cross-referencing among African scholars.

The tragic part of Mkandawire's criticisms is that there were hardly any that had not been heard before. In 1971 alone, there were three major critiques of Africanist scholarship published. Mlahleni Njisane (1971: 3) condemns "the strong parallels found between academic meetings of apartheid South Africa on the one hand, and those of the African Studies Association on the other." Despite the fetish made of field research and scientific terminology, he noted the propensity for reliance on anecdotal evidence and demeaning vocabulary when referring to African phenomena. Also in the same year Michael Owusu (1971: 24) argues that "as long as western schol-ars, however liberal-minded and well meaning, dominate the study of African societies and cultures, the results of their research will continue to be disputed by educated Africans—if not on scientific grounds, then on the basis of sentiment and ideology. For Guy Mhone (1971: 8) Africanists could be attacked on two levels.

> The primary or first level of attack is based on the argument that scientific inquiry is not wholly value-free and that it has limits and constraints which ought to be openly accepted by any investiga-tor...The second level of attack is ideological. At this level, Africanists can be attacked either for perpetuating a certain ideology or for excluding particular ideologies from the realm of concern. Africanists as a group can be considered guilty at this level without accusing each one of the conscious perpetuation or exclusion of a specific ideology.

In the repertoire of the Africanists' biases, he singled out their morbid fas-cination with "tribalism," the contrived "distinction between Africa South of the Sahara and North Africa," support for "one-party states" in the name of integration, their propensity for deductive theorization and generalization from western rather than African intellectual traditions, and their cynicism and indifference to African concerns and concepts such as pan-Africanism.

African studies in the United States, admonished Victor Uchendu (1977) several years later, suffered from "a terminal colonial order." Africanists were implicated, whether by choice or by circumstance, in the asymmetrical relations of dependence and domination between Africa and the West, so that their work was treated with suspicion by African scholars. Many continued to treat Africa as a research laboratory, to analyze and to assess the continent through the prism of constantly shifting Eurocentric concepts and theories, to avoid taking principled political positions by hid-ing behind the immoral fiction of academic neutrality. "African studies," he concluded, "is nothing if it provides no service to Africa. It served the inter-ests of colonial governments; it has a responsibility to serve independent Africa, a major consumer and audience of its studies" (Uchendu, 1977: 10).

As for scholarly communication between Africans and Africanists, John H. Clarke (1976:11) pointed out that in reading Africanist publications, "none of the new books on African history [by Africans] are reviewed, and in looking at the books and magazine articles by ASA members, it is rare that the work is even referred to or quoted, positively or negatively." In the 1960s, the indifference to African scholarship was often justified on the grounds that, to quote Robert D. Baum (1965: 43), the Africans "in most cases are not yet ready to perform the kinds of research we feel are necessary. They need time to build up their own resources." In the 1980s, the African university crisis provided an excuse for not consulting African scholarship. In the words of Timothy Shaw (1993: 153), "in such unconducive conditions, there is every prospect that external authors will have superior opportunities both to research and to publish, local book and journal publishers and markets being what they are."

While many African scholars based in the United States bemoaned the persistent pathologization of African societies, cultures, economies, states, polities, and leaders and their own marginality in African studies and that of Africa in the American academy, Ali Mazrui (1978) celebrated the role of the African migrant intellectuals as an academic fifth column of counterpenetration that can subvert Western scholarship. Abiola Irele (1991) sees them as potentially key players—because of their immersion in both African and Western cultures, languages, experiences, and epistemologies—in verifying, validating, and expanding Africanist knowledge; promoting comparative scholarship; and reconfiguring the disciplines and international scholarship.

It was, of course, no secret to the Africanist gatekeepers that their African colleagues were increasingly dissatisfied and frustrated by the asymmetrical relationship between them. As early as 1965 Baum, (1965: 43) had observed that

> Europeans and Americans face increasing African annoyance and suspicion. Africans are disturbed at being regarded as guinea pigs and their countries as laboratories to test scientific hypotheses. They are wearying of visits by team after team of specialists, asking many of the same questions, probing many of the same people, with very little, Africans feel, being received in return for what some of them consider exploitation.

A year later, after a visit sponsored by the ASA to seek closer ties with African scholars, William Hance and Philip Curtin discovered (1966: 24-5)

things we had not known about the African academic
scene, even though both of us have been in Africa at quite
frequent intervals during the past decade or so. Previously,
however, we had gone to Africa with our own research
objectives, had talked to scholars in Africa mainly about
that research, and had found most of our contacts within
the narrower circle of our own disciplines. In the summer
of 1965 we asked scholars in Africa about their work, their
reactions to American research in Africa, and their views
concerning the possibility of more extensive international
cooperation...they see new generations of unformed scholars arriving in ever-increasing numbers. Even the most pro-
American among them are bound to have some questions
about the future.

Smock (1970) saw that future, and it looked ugly. Many American
researchers, he charged, pursued research that had little relevance for Africa,
and that only served to further their own careers. They often displayed insufferable arrogance and unethical behavior:

> How many American political scientists expect ready access
> to the President, Secretary of State, or Chief Justice, along
> with freedom to examine confidential government docu-
> ments, in their studies of the American political system? Yet
> many American scholars believe they have an inherent right
> to any data required to complete their research in Africa.
> Inevitably, this intellectual aggressiveness often results in
> abuse of research privileges....As a result, many [Africans]
> are now resentful of this form of intellectual imperialism
> (Smock, 1970: 24).

This sense of disquiet was still being expressed by some European
American Africanists in the late 1990s. In 1997, Hunt Davis (1997:146)
wrote wryly: "The relationship and interaction between black and white
scholars of Africa have often been uneasy and sometimes openly antagonistic...." Jane Guyer (1997:151) lamented that the major challenge in African

studies continues to be the boundary "between us [Africanists] and intellectual production in Africa....For a variety of reasons, one senses that in African Studies we have not yet arrived at the point at which collegial engagement on a completely egalitarian footing is the norm." Ron Kassimir (1997:161), program director for Africa at the Social Science Research Council (SSRC), conceded: "It must be recognized that Area Studies are also contested from within...there is no consensus on the meaning of 'African Studies.' Its definition is a matter of both epistemological and political debate...African scholars based on the continent often do not recognize the Africa that is analyzed and invoked in ASA [African Studies Association annual meetings] panels." Iris Berger (1997:11), former president of the ASA, tried to be more sanguine in her presidential address at the 1996 ASA Annual Meeting: "Controversies over boundaries and authority are healthy provided that the field's intellectual and organizational vitality emanates as much (or more) from Africa as from other parts of the world."

Grave concern over the racial chasms in African studies was also expressed by African American scholars who had tenaciously maintained their African research interests. In her presidential address to the 1997 ASA Annual Meeting, Gwendolyn Mikell (1999: 1) argued that the Africanist community faced three distinct challenges:

> The first is to overcome the historical hierarchies based on race and nationality that attended the creation and early history of the ASA. These hierarchies pushed many Africanists of color to the margins of our organization. The second challenge is to address the need for mutuality in internal policy relationships regarding Africa, particularly at a time when many American international affairs experts have said that there are no U.S. national interests that link us to Africa and that any such assertions are divisive. However, the third and perhaps most time-sensitive challenge is that of creating mutuality in intra-ASA relationships. We must grow comfortable with the increasing diversity of ASA members.

These sentiments were echoed by Sandra E. Greene (1999) in her presidential address to the 1998 ASA Annual Meeting. She called for a more activist

195

ASA that "must maintain its preeminent role in fostering scholarly exchange, but that the association must also seek to engage in a much more active dialogue with the policy world; it must address issues of concern to academics in Africa, and it must work to encourage greater interest in Africa within and outside the academy" (Greene, 1999: 1).

Political and Disciplinary Conditionalities

Thus, from the 1950s the stage was set for bitter "paternity suits" over African studies as the field entered the segregated corridors of the historically white universities, and the research and reputational rewards rose, bankrolled by the foundations and the federal government, and as the tantalizing possibilities for professional advancement and policy intervention beckoned under Camelot. Born out of America's enduring racial divide, and in the context of the cold war, African studies were imbricated, perhaps more than other area studies, in the explosive tensions of racial politics at home and imperialism abroad. It was dogged by the crisis of legitimacy from the very beginning, by the unresolved questions of its audience, mission, and relevance and by the perennial contestations and cravings for scholarly authority and respectability. Always latent and lacerating, the asymmetries of power in the production and consumption of Africanist knowledge and the contestations over content and canon would periodically erupt into open confrontation. The cast of characters would change, and so would the specific contexts; but the underlying structural conditions, the fundamental text, always remained the same.

Unanchored from its intellectual and cultural moorings in the African American communities, scholarly and popular, and detached by distance and disposition from African societies and social thought, African studies in the United States drifted unsteadily between the treacherous anchors of competing and sometimes complimentary "formulas," as Staniland (1983) has called them. The Washingtonian formula demanded that African studies contribute to the definition, defense, and deployment of American interests and intentions in Africa. The cultural brokerage formula called upon Africanists to act as impartial cultural diplomats, interpreting and mediating representations and encounters between Africa and America. The disciplinary formula promoted Africa as a tropical laboratory to test and to refine the methodological and theoretical frameworks of the disciplines. The development formula championed the cause of developmental policy formulation and intervention. Finally, the solidarity formula implored Africanists to show commitment to African social movements and struggles.

It was an enterprise in which the aspirations for professionalism, policy relevance, and political advocacy jostled for intellectual and moral supremacy. This was of course not peculiar to African studies. Other area studies, indeed, all disciplines, are always negotiating their epistemological identities and social utility; but the potential for convulsion was always greater in the marginalized and isolated Africanist ghetto. The conjuncture of the Civil Rights movement and growing opposition to the Vietnam War in the United States, and the intensifying liberation struggles in settler Africa and the discontents of misguided developmentalism in independent Africa pried open the simmering crisis of Africanist scholarship into the confrontation of Montreal in 1969.

As the intellectual and ideological debates among Africanists were raging, the area studies project as a whole faced new challenges about its overall mission, relations with the disciplines, and funding. Besides resources provided by the universities themselves, funding for area studies came from the foundations, especially the Ford and Rockefeller Foundations, and the federal government under Title VI of the National Defense Education Act passed in 1958. Enacted in the aftermath of the Soviet Sputnik space mission, the first Title VI clearly sought to bind education to national security needs. The original emphasis was on foreign language training rather than area studies. Six priority languages were identified: Chinese, Japanese, Arabic, Hindi-Urdu, Portuguese, and Russian; eighteen other languages as second priority emphasis; and fifty-three additional languages as third priority emphasis (Scarfo, 1998:23). In the first year of the program, $3.5 million was appropriated. The funds were allocated to nineteen centers for teaching foreign languages; one hundred seventy one students received fellowships for studying the six priority languages; and twenty-six research projects were funded, most of them on effective methods of language teaching and the development of teaching materials.

In subsequent reauthorizations of Title VI in the 1960s, both the appropriations and mandates of Title VI expanded. According to Merkx (1998:77), "the high point in Title VI appropriations, controlling for inflation, was reached under the Johnson Administration. Both the Nixon and Reagan Administrations sought to zero-budget Title VI. In both cases, proponents of the specialist training mission were able to rescue Title VI from oblivion, with significant support from the defense and intelligence communities." Despite the rescue efforts, the number of centers funded by Title

VI were cut in half from the 106 that had been established by the late 1960s. Also, new requirements were instituted, including a three-year competitive cycle for centers; funding was provided for centers focusing on western Europe and functional topics and to internationalize general undergraduate curricula; and centers were asked to undertake outreach beyond their immediate faculty and student population.

In the 1980s and early 1990s, new mandates were added to Title VI, e.g., minority recruitment, library acquisitions of foreign materials, and establishment of support for overseas research. Also, centers for international business education were added "as national resource centers in teaching improved techniques, strategies, and methodologies in international business, instruction in critical foreign languages, and other fields to better understand U.S. trading partners, and to conduct research and training in international aspects of trade and commerce" (Scarfo, 1998:25). Thus, from a preoccupation with national defense and security in the 1960s, federal funding for area studies in the 1990s shifted to greater concern for U.S. international economic competitiveness. However, the expansion in the functions of Title VI centers was not matched by increased funding. Adjusted for inflation, Title VI funding fell by 17 percent from $64.2 million in 1967 to $53.3 million in 1995; and funding for Fulbright-Hays programs fell by 56 percent from $13.8 million to $5.8 million during the same period (Kazanjian, 1998:21).

Declining federal funding for area studies since the 1960s raises fundamental questions about the importance of these programs in American foreign policy calculations. By the 1980s, about 95 percent of all funding for foreign language and international studies in the Title VI National Resource Centers was derived from the universities themselves; but as the supporters and beneficiaries of Title VI are quick to point out, "in spite of the relatively small amount of funding awarded a center, the national reputational status among faculty and students and the frequent re-competition is very important to universities in deciding whether to invest in new faculty positions, librarians, library holdings, and other resources for the study areas or fields"(Wiley, 1998:218). While this is correct, the fact remains that area studies programs must compete with other units and departments in universities for the bulk of their funding. The fate of area studies is therefore tied far more firmly to the shifting fiscal and intellectual currents on campuses than to the winds of change in Washington. This requires proponents of area studies to understand and to negotiate the changing political economy of higher education in the United States.

Within the universities, area studies programs, like other interdisciplinary programs, have always faced institutional and intellectual challenges from the disciplines. The disciplines, which tend to focus on the United States, regard area studies, at best, as sources of data to test existing theories and, at worst, as unscientific relics of the Cold War maintained as concessions to political correctness and minority nationalisms. The often-quoted statement by Robert Bates, a rational-choice Africanist, is a typical if extreme example of the disdain for area studies among some in the disciplines: "Within the academy," Bates asserts, "the consensus has formed that area studies has failed to generate scientific knowledge" (quoted in Holzner and Harmon, 1998:38). Comments Holzner and Harmon (1998:38):

> The idea that area studies has not produced scientific knowledge is obviously untrue, indeed comical. It presupposes an unrealistically narrow definition of what science is. By a realistic conception of the nature of science, the disciplined pursuit of increasingly valid knowledge about the world, area studies have made enormous contributions to scientific knowledge, especially through empirical challenges to scientific theories, social and otherwise.

Bates' characterization of the tensions between area studies and what he calls social scientific approaches caricatures, to use his own words, area studies. His suggestion that what he mysteriously calls "analytic narratives" offer "a bridge between the social sciences and Area Studies" show the dangers of acquired intellectually deficient science (Bates, 1997:127).

Bates is an Africanist political scientist of long-standing in the field. Much of the intellectual challenge to area studies has come from political science and its dismal social science cousin, economics. Armed with the reductionist and deductive theories of rational choice models, in the 1950s economics began to banish much of the real world into oblivion, in a relentless pursuit for the rigors of natural science. Economics sought to become more like physics, and political science sought to become more like economics. Both ended up becoming caricatures of their objects of desire. As economics mutated into pale physics, "economic history, the history of economic thought, and development economics [were] largely dropped from the graduate curriculum and replaced by courses in mathematics and modeling. One of the consequences has been a sharp decline in both undergraduate and graduate economics enrollments" (Merkx, 1998:83).

The results have been less than edifying for the external clients of the discipline, for whom there is little correspondence between the theoretical models and the real world, the validating marker of any good theory and policy. To quote Merkx (1998:84):

> Joseph Stiglitz, chairman of the Council of Economic Advisors, states that "It's very clear that the new classical economics is irrelevant." The chairman of the National Association of Business Economists is quoted as saying that "Academic economics has taken a very bad turn in the road. It's very academic, very mathematical, and nothing like as useful to the business community as it could be." The head of the global economics group at Morgan Stanley adds that his company will not hire economics Ph.D.'s unless they also have substantial experience outside academia....In 1991 the Commission on Graduate Education in Economics issued a report saying it feared that universities were turning out a generation of *idiots savant*, skilled in techniques but innocent of real economic issues.

The anxiety is not confined to acquisitive business tycoons averse to the intellectual delights of theorizing, but finds echoes within the profession itself (Kreps, 1997). William Barber (1997:96) informs us that "officers of the American Economic Association—as well as a number of the profession's senior establishment figures—have been at the forefront of some exercises in self-criticism. Economists teaching in liberal arts colleges have been catalytic agents in this process." Robert M. Solow (1997:42), one of those senior figures, perhaps best captures the growing anxieties when he protests that "economics became a self-consciously technical subject, no longer a fit occupation for the gentleman-scholar." He believes that the ambition by economists to behave like physicists faces

> two dangerous pitfalls. The first is the temptation to believe that the laws of economics are like the laws of physics: exact-

ly the same everywhere on earth and at every moment since
Hector was pup. That is certainly true about the behavior of
light and heat. But the part of economics that is independent of history and social context is not only small but dull.
I want to suggest that a second pitfall comes with the imita-
tion of theoretical physics: there is a tendency to underval-
ue keen observation and shrewd generalization, virtues that
I think are more usually practiced by biologists.

Perhaps economists harboring natural science ambitions ought to become
more like biologists.

It is ironic that political science should be moving in the direction of
economics, when the latter's emulation of the natural sciences is coming
under growing attack. This is not the first time political science has joined
the party rather late. In the 1950s and 1960s, the behavioral revolution
gripped the field, as the discipline sought to move toward science, but the
discipline was moving, states Charles Lindblom (1997:231), "to a positivist
model of science at the very time that the model was, in several other quarters, under attack." The rational choice revolution is simply the latest in a
long line of attempts by some in political science to overcome their scientific inferiority complex. In the hands of anxious Africanist political scientists
like Bates, suffering from imagined complexes of Third World methodological and theoretical backwardness, the debilitation becomes both tragic and
farcical. Lindblom (1997:236) believes that "political science has rarely done
and can only rarely do science as conventionally described. Its conventionally scientific aspirations are bound to be disappointed." Rational choice cannot be a universal explanatory theory of all politics. Critics within the discipline itself point out that, to cite Rogers Smith (1997), "the focus on building a universal theory has led rational-choice scholars to ignore empirical
testing or to do it poorly. They contend that the empirically supported contributions of rational choice to our understanding of important political subjects are thus virtually non-existent." For those interested in tackling the politics of gender, race, ethnicity, religion, and the world at large, rational
choice is a method in search of a mission.

The tension between area studies and the disciplines is as old as area
studies programs. As noted already, area studies were established in part to
counter the excessive parochialism of American education, which, it was

believed, was not befitting a superpower—one, moreover, engaged in global mortal combat with the Soviet "evil empire." The area studies approach had a special benefit to the burgeoning corps of Africanists because, except for anthropology, there were very few African specialists in the social sciences and humanities in the historically white universities. But from the very beginning it was understood, to quote Lyman Legters (1964: 3), that:

> The area approach was not an alternative to disciplinary modes of university organization, but rather a means of both focusing and reinforcing disciplinary competence with reference to a particular world region. The device helped to strengthen departments by reminding them of neglected fields and opportunities, and its corollary of multidisciplinary emphasis helped to enable the social sciences and humanities to address themselves more effectively to the many contemporary problems lying on the periphery of individual disciplines....African studies, could, in the usual fashion of latecomers, avoid some of the pitfalls of the earlier area programs, e.g., needless tension between disciplinary and area interest or loyalty.

Thus, conceived as a response to a perceived crisis in American higher education, the role of area studies was to "nourish" the disciplines with empirical data, while remaining subordinate to the epistemological and managerial authority of the disciplines (Rafael, 1994:94-95). Consequently, area studies programs provided little of their own independent instruction, or made faculty appointments. Their primary function became that of coordinating and campaigning for the inclusion and integration of non-Western knowledge and specialists in the disciplines.

The incorporation of area studies on the margins of universities recalled the organization of studies of American minorities. The two were in fact linked. Area studies were established when the civil rights movement was raging and scoring victories, spurring liberal anxieties over desegregation. The National Defense Education Act (NDEA) of 1958, which brought in federal funding for area studies, "was held up by a number of southern congressmen who feared that it would intensify federal intervention on all levels of schooling and thus further hasten desegregation. Only because of the generalized hysteria over the putative technological advances of the Soviets, as represented by the launching of the Sputnik satellites, did liberal cold war ideology manage to contain southern racialist fears and allow for the enactment and subsequent extensions of the NDEA" (Rafael, 1994: 96). Area studies inherited the discourse that depicted African Americans and other minoritized populations as "problems" external to the mainstream but amenable to social science fixes: the newly independent nations became the equivalent of "problematic" American minorities for the area studies project. To the foundations, the objectives and rationale of funding area studies was not always distinguishable from funding social engineering projects among American minorities (Sibley, 1974; Sutton and Smock, 1976; Berman, 1984; Fisher, 1993).

Like all people with dual loyalties, Africanists suffered from acute tensions. Some, of course, managed them skillfully, others did not. But everyone's standing in the disciplinary pecking order was affected by popular and paradigmatic perceptions of Africa; hence, the zeal, excessive in many cases, to demonstrate the theoretical utility of African data, to use Africa as an empirical lab for testing theories manufactured with faddish regularity in the disciplines. Africa furnished the Africanists with empiricist confidence and theoretical insecurity. Given the greater prestige accorded to "theory" in the academy, the survival of the Africanist scholarly enterprise was always in question, vulnerable to theoretical shifts in the disciplines. There were of course disciplinary variations in these permutations. Some responded by stubbornly burying their heads in their beloved African villages; some took to flying on the clouds of theory and joined in area studies bashing; and some feigned surprise at all the commotion, insisting that all was well, that "to a degree unacknowledged by either side in these debates, the study of Africa is already lodged in the core of the modern university," that "research in Africa has shaped the disciplines and thereby shaped our convictions as to what may be universally true" (Bates, Mudimbe, and O'Barr, 1993: xii, xiv).

This reassurance was greeted with weary cynicism in some quarters (Zeleza, 1994a). Declared Martin and West (1995: 25): "A retreat to the defense of African studies by its contribution to the nineteenth-century European divisioning of knowledge into disciplines seems to us shaky grounds on which to defend African intellectual studies," and they somberly warned of the "inexorable downward spiral if not the end of African studies as we have known it for two generations...." The death of African studies due to falling funding and assaults by the disciplines had been predicted before. In 1965, Baum (1965:1) argued that "most scholars now agree that the area studies approach cannot exist without the more theoretical comparative approach...." In 1970, L. Gray Cowan (1970: 346-7) alerted the Africanist community to the fact that Africanists were entering a decade of dwindling resources for area studies, while Roger Yeager (1970) argued that area studies had already served their purpose of ending intellectual ethnocentrism in the American academy, so that they had outlived their usefulness. For Brian M. Fagan (1970) area studies were beginning to die a natural death because of their narrow focus and were being replaced by a greater emphasis on multidisciplinary studies and comparative international research projects of a problem-oriented nature. Donald Wilhelm (1971) called for the replacement of area studies with a new model based on the trinity of thematic, comparative, and multidisciplinary approaches, and the development of research and teaching methods that were cross-disciplinary and cross-national. He also advocated the integration of the natural sciences and technology.

It is clear, therefore, that disciplinary death wishes for area studies are hardly new. Gwendolen Carter (1976: 4) puts it succinctly: "Attacks on 'area studies' as such are spasmodic but perennial. What is puzzling is that 'area' seems to be restricted in these attacks to non-Western data and interests. What about American studies, Soviet studies, even European studies? Are they any less concerned with 'area'? I cannot see why." The reason is simple: Firmly rooted in Eurocentric traditions and an imperializing mission, sanitized and idealized European and American conditions and conceptions, in short, the Western epistemological order constitutes, in the American academy, universal knowledge, against which the rest of the world must be apprehended and appropriated.

The eternal binary oppositions in western social thought, which construct the enduring and destructive fictions of the "West" and its numerous "others," and which are at the root of constructions of American studies as disciplinary knowledge and the study of other regions as "area studies," find new articulations in current debates and discourses about area studies and the disciplines. The dichotomies include traditional area studies versus area-based knowledge, global versus local knowledge, area versus thematic programs, Americo-centric versus international scholarship, basic versus applied research. The high priests of the new intellectual order argue that it is necessary to create new structures through which to pursue international scholarship because of the very success by the area studies in deparochializing the American academy. They also cite the demise of the bipolar perspective of the cold war; the consequent reassessment of priorities and redirection of resources by the private, federal, and state sectors; and the relentless march towards globalization (Heginbotham, 1994; Prewitt, 1996a, 1996b). Lurking in the minds of the intellectual policy establishment is also the concern that while the USA remains the sole superpower, it "does not dictate either the pace or the direction of global change" (Lombardi, 1993: 2).

Following the terrorist attacks of September 11, 2001, the seductive illusion that the rest of the world could be understood on terms defined by the United States ideologically or epistemologically suddenly appeared naive and dangerous. The solipsism of popular paradigms in the American academy—from the fantasies of rational choice in political science to the fictions of postmodernism in the humanities—became all too apparent. The imperative to know the major regions of the world through their own eyes became incontestable. The much-maligned area studies no longer seemed so quaint any more, and debates about globalization and interdisciplinarity were recast.[3] This is as clear a reminder as any of how concrete events and national trauma can shape scholarship and a cautionary tale for those in the American academy who insolently dismiss the preoccupations of scholars from Africa with their own traumas defined around the monumental tragedies of slavery, colonialism, and underdevelopment.

Challenges of Globalization and Interdisciplinarity

It can be seen that area studies in the American academy are beset by many challenges concerning their mission and mandate—intellectual, institutional, and ideological. African studies face many of the same challenges, although they are sometimes articulated in some unique ways because of the specific trajectory of African studies outlined earlier in the chapter. Besides the contestations between Africans—both at home and abroad—African Americans, and European Americans over the protocols of scholarly production and authority, paradigms and perspectives, and the very social composition of African studies, which have plagued and weakened the field in the last few decades, the African studies enterprise, together with the other area studies programs, confront new challenges or old challenges recently repackaged as new. They can be grouped into three broad categories: intellectual, institutional, and what I call civic challenges.

The intellectual challenges can be divided into two: those posed by international studies and those from interdisciplinary studies. If the cold war structured discourses and programs in international education, globalization has now become the guiding force and paradigm. It has become commonplace to argue that we live in an age of globalization, characterized by the rapid and constant flows of commodities, capital, communication, and cultures; ideas, images, individuals, and institutions; and visions, values, vices, and viruses. Globalization, so the argument goes, renders the old structures of organizing and producing knowledge in bounded regions increasingly obsolete[4]. Besides, the cold war is over. In place of area studies, we need international or global studies, or at the very least comparative regional studies. For their part, the Afropessimists believe that because of its economic marginality, Africa has little to gain from globalization, which has redirected attention to the world beyond the borders of North America (Martin and West, 1999b:7).

One can respond to these challenges, especially when they are advanced by university administrations compelled more by cost cutting considerations than arcane theoretical debates, with cries of intellectual indignation by pointing out that globalization is not new, that it is in fact a polite way of saying imperialism, which is as rampant as ever; that it is a term that often serves ideological rather than analytical purposes and seeks to rationalize a new global regime of free market accumulation and exploitation and to silence opposition and criticisms spawned by detailed regional knowledges and experiences; that globalization does not mean homogenization; that globality reproduces locality in new, unpredictable ways that demands more, not less, focused understanding of the world's numerous societies and cultures in all their bewildering complexities; that a lot of comparative work already takes place within the broad regions covered by the area studies. For example, comparing South Africa and Egypt, is as demanding as comparing, say, the United States and Japan. Much of the debate about area studies "today proceeds as if the research of scholars in area studies still focused only on detailed descriptions of individual nations or regions. In the social sciences, the contention that area studies must use knowledge about particular regions to make more broadly applicable generalizations won out 20 years ago. To invoke it again seems little more than a misleading rhetorical exercise" (Hall and Tarrow, 1998:B4).

Indeed, African studies has always been "conducted under the rubric of globalizing frames of reference," as Christopher Lowe (1997a:298-9) argues, including modernization theory, underdevelopment theory, the African diaspora, articulation of modes of production, structural adjustment, theories of globalizing markets and democratization, and theories of postcoloniality. Through those lenses Africa scholars have addressed many inherently global and comparative topics, including the slave trade; colonialism and decolonization; formation of states, classes, and ethnicities; urban growth; religious transformations; and the reconceptualizations of choices and meaningful agency through involvement in labor and commodity markets. The problem for Africa scholars has not been lack of global perspectives or global theory. Rather, the difficulty has been to test and modify the theories and to discover the questionable assumptions underlying them, so as to more adequately describe and interpret African realities.

In short, if Africanist scholarship has any problem at all, it is that Africa has always been globalized without the global being Africanized. In contrast, in American studies, which pass for the disciplines as currently constituted, the global is Americanized, while America is not globalized. The African intellectual condition is produced by global dependence, the American one by global domination. An American can be a professor in most disciplines in the social sciences and humanities without knowing anything about other societies and countries; almost unheard of is an Africanist or African professor who only knows the society s/he studies or comes from. Thus, it is not area studies people, certainly not the Africanists, who need to be internationalized, but those in the ethnocentric disciplines. Proclaims Chege (1997:136-137):

It is also time for North America and Western Europe to be designated as "Area Studies" as well....To that extent, calls for methodological rigor should not be dismissed offhand. The same applies to Western-based scholarship, to the extent that it is prepared to see itself objectively as one more "area" in which theory is validated or rejected. Such an approach would help short-circuit the sterile polemical debate on the relevance, or lack thereof, of Area Studies and still adopt a stridently critical demeanor concerning the reigning concepts of social science.

It is one of the supreme ironies that at the time that globalization and internationalization are in vogue, even among the most parochial of university administrators, death wishes for area studies are heard more loudly than ever, often from people who know little about area studies or from area studies people, such as Bates, eager to refurbish their disciplinary credentials. Thus, while it is true that much may be gained from analyzing global trends, there are also dangers that such a focus threatens to undermine America's already limited knowledge about other nations, diminishing attention to the cultural, historical, and political contexts in particular regions. Peter Hall and Sidney Tarrow (1998:B5) warn:

> The greatest danger in the current debate over area studies is that in the name of studying global trends or advancing overarching theories about them, the next generation of internationally oriented social-science researchers will give short-shrift to area-based empirical knowledge. Driven by shifts in the incentives that foundations offer and discouraged by tight university budgets, graduate students may find themselves echoing the Italian labor leader who tried to dodge domestic issues [about the Italian government's impending pension reform by switching the topic instead to the pressures of globalization]: They may turn to globalization because they don't know what to say about the internal complexities of the societies they are studying.

Part of the problem lies in misunderstanding the international knowledge system in the American academy and the place of area studies within it. Another is that while the corporate pressures for globalization are recognized and even embraced, the demographic pressures of globalization are less well appreciated. Holzner and Harmon (1998:33-4) identify five components of the international knowledge system: The first three of which are specifically aimed at producing knowledge about the world outside the United States, and the other two involve educational and professional activities beyond the country's borders. It is critical for proponents of area studies to have a clear understanding of the system as a whole and how it can become better integrated and improved.

The five components are, first, area and foreign language studies that focus on particular countries and cultures in specific world regions; second, transnational and international studies that deal with phenomena that involve more than one country or world region and the interrelations of events within and across countries; third, global studies that focus on processes that are global in scope or that affect the planetary habitat as the context of all human activities; fourth, international education professions responsible for the mobility of students, scholars, and others across national boundaries; and fifth, scientific and professional activities carried out in international settings. It is important to emphasize that all these components overlap, and that one cannot be removed without undermining the entire system. There can be no meaningful transnational and international studies or global studies without area and language studies, and vice versa. Those who think otherwise need to do a little more traveling, both figuratively (through reading) and literally (outside their comfortable intellectual and residential cocoons). In a masterly speech surveying American social sciences delivered at the 40th Anniversary of Title VI in April 1998, Ken Prewitt, then president of the Social Science Research Council, reported the intellectual anguish of many America-centric social scientists in the recently reorganized SSRC committees, half of whose members are scholars from other regions, when they discover that their overseas colleagues swear by different research methodologies and theories even on the same topic or theme. A small reminder that there are indeed many real worlds outside the United States. If the so-called "universal theories" that parade in the American academy with such self-assurance cannot explain or correspond to those worlds, then such theories are no better than academic fetishes, held more as an act of patriotic faith rather than as intellectual reason.

One of the major forces fueling interest in international education on American campuses is the need to maintain, if not improve, the global economic competitiveness of the United States. While the world in recent years, has experienced many dazzling changes including the end of the cold war, the proliferation of states and transnational social movement organizations, as well as dizzying technological revolutions involving computers and the Internet, waves of migrations, and turbulent social and environmental disruptions, the transformations in the global economy may be more fundamental. In the words of JoAnn McCarthy (1998:66):

The most dramatic changes, however, will take place in shifting economic powers of the world. The list of the G7 countries already misrepresents the leading economic powers since neither the United Kingdom nor Canada currently rank among the top seven. At present, the seven leading powers (in rank order) are: the United States, Japan, China, Germany, France, India, and Italy. By 2020, the seven will most likely be (in order): China, the United States, Japan, India, Indonesia, Germany, and South Korea. The Department of Commerce is predicting a major shift in U.S. exports away from our traditional trading partners in Japan and Europe to ten developing nations known as the Big Emerging Markets. These countries are: China (including Hong Kong and Taiwan), India, Indonesia, South Korea, Mexico, Brazil, Argentina, South Africa, Poland, and Turkey.

Predictions are, of course, always unpredictable. But if the last half century is anything to go by, it would not be rash to expect profound shifts in the global economic and political order in the next half century, although the exact configurations of that order cannot be forecast with precision.

There is ample evidence that American universities are not meeting the training demands for workers with the necessary foreign language skills and knowledge. Merkx (1998:82) estimates the annual demand over the decade for such workers

> at 20,000 business jobs, 6,000 government jobs, and 10,000 education jobs, or an annual demand for 36,000 language or area-trained personnel...[while] a combined total of 25,000 B.A. and M.A. graduates with foreign language or area training enter the job market....These data suggest that even without further growth in patterns of government, business, and educational employment, the production by Title VI centers of personnel with foreign language training or foreign-area skills remains insufficient to meet the nation's needs.

The shortfall is even evident at the university level, where it is estimated 2,100 foreign language or area studies jobs will be needed over the next decade, while projected Ph.D. production in these fields stands at about 1,900. At the very least, then, universities need to supply the personnel trained in foreign language and area studies that are demanded by the economy. Already the federal government spends over $88 million, over one and half times the cost of all Title VI programs, on in-house government foreign language training programs.

It is quite common in Africanist circles permeated with Afropessimism to see Africa as even more marginal in the brave new world of economic globalization than it was in the bad old days of the cold war. It is not sufficiently realized that United States trade with Africa is sizeable and rapidly growing. During the 1992-96 period, four African countries—Angola, Egypt, Nigeria, and South Africa—ranked among the fifty largest U.S. trade partners; U.S. exports to South Africa alone equaled U.S. sales to Russia, and were greater than U.S. exports to all of Eastern Europe. In 1997, U.S. agricultural exports to Africa were valued at $2.3 billion, which were greater than U.S. agricultural exports to Central America, Eastern Europe, and South Asia combined and nearly as large as U.S. agricultural exports to South America, valued at $2.6 billion (National Summit on Africa, 1998a, 1998b). As Africanists continue to decry Africa's economic marginality, American business see new opportunities and push Congress to enact legislation to promote and to safeguard their rising stake in African markets. The disjuncture in perceptions between scholars and capital over Africa's prospects is quite evident at the annual spring meetings of the Association of African Studies Programs and in the deliberations of the controversial National Summit on Africa. The possibilities of academics shaping the corporate agenda are not high; but the growing interest by American business in Africa offers opportunities to quell impressions among university administrators that Africa is more marginal than other regions, therefore African studies programs are not worthy of support. In short, in the struggle for resources, it cannot hurt to temper the excessive Afropessimism and to point out Africa's growing economic importance, even if one might detest the nature of current U.S.-African economic relations.

Economic forces are not alone in exerting pressure for the internationalization of U.S. education. The demographic processes of migration and immigration are going to have a noticeable impact on international studies in general, and area studies in particular. Immigration brings new dynamics in the relationship between area studies and U.S. ethnic populations that are

211

so familiar to Africanists. According to Linda Rodriguez (1998:156),

> the United States is currently experiencing the largest wave of immigration since the 1901-10 period, when 8.8 million people came to the country. In 1910 immigrants represented 14.7% of the total U.S. population....Today, some 24 million immigrants representing 9% of the nation's population reside in the United States.

If current demographic trends persist, it is expected that the percentage of the non-Hispanic white population will progressively drop, falling to about half the total U.S. population by the middle of the twenty-first century. Not only are area studies required to understand the migration flows, but also in addressing the challenges facing immigrant groups, and providing "heritage" knowledge for their offspring.

Working together with the ethnic studies programs, the area studies centers, Carlos Torres (1998:164) believes, "provide the intellectual and cultural tools with which to integrate the diverse heritage of the racial and ethnic groups that are emerging, as the nation's new majority, into a new synthesis of U.S. culture." While the majority of the new immigrants are from Latin America and Asia, African migration has been on the rise as discussed in Volume Two. African studies programs stand to gain from any increased visibility that continued migration might give to area studies and from specific demands for heritage language training and knowledges demanded by the American Africans. The latter will reinforce long-standing agitation by African Americans for African studies relevant to the historic experiences and cultural needs of African peoples on both sides of the Atlantic, thus making the distinction between (foreign) African studies and (domestic) African American studies less salient.

What do all these changes, actual and prospective, mean for African studies and, more broadly, area studies? Area studies programs have to consciously promote and embed inter-regional, cross-continental perspectives in their triple mission of teaching, research, and public service or outreach. To area studies purists, with lifelong commitments to their beloved African villages, this smacks of heresy. For African studies, it may actually represent a road back to the future, to an African studies reconnected to the diasporic and pan-Africanist commitments and the global and civilizational concerns of Dubois, Dike, Diop, and Davidson, away from the prescriptive developmentalism and pedantic chase for the insignificant.

We ought, nevertheless, to be careful not to assume that a magical return to pan-Africanist themes and politics guarantees the future of African studies as Martin and West seem to think. I agree with Sandra Greene's (1999b: 9-10) concerns about whether Martin and West's proposed reconstitution of African Studies as

> the study of Africa in its transnational, transcontinenal and transcultural complexities' ...does justice to the multiple worlds in which Africa has operated, is operating , and will continue to operate in the future? Does a singular focus on linkages defined by "race" and culture really serve African Studies and Africa now and into the future? I think not. I do believe, however, that a Pan-Africanist approach must be one of the central pillars of a broad, self-consciously inclusive approach to the field, an approach that is dynamic and capable of responding to changing currents and trends.

Martin and West's proposition, which I share, is based on sympathies for pan-Africanism and schematic analyses of what they identify as the three traditions in the study of Africa, namely, the Africanist (read European American), transcontinental (read African American), and continental (read sub-Saharan African), which I find simplistic. Certainly, it ignores many continental Africans who have been transcontinental in their approaches and African Americans who have been focused exclusively on the United States. Their argument that the transcontinental tradition is the oldest—dating from the nineteenth century—and therefore most legitimate repeats old Eurocentric myths that the African "natives" did not study themselves until the Europeans, in this case the Westernized African diaspora, cast their intellectual gaze upon them. This echoes what Ali Mazrui (2000a) has called "Black Orientalism" with reference to Henry Louis Gates' film series, *Wonders of the African World,* a subject I discuss at greater length in Chapter 7. Incidentally, Martin and West uphold, as an example of the welcome transformations in fusing African and African American studies, the Department of Afro-American Studies at Harvard headed by Gates, who "has promoted, in a highly celebrated if limited way...black studies programs' original concern with Africa—coalescing a constellation of faculty with transcontinental interests" (Martin and West, 1999b: 29). Martin and West's African studies remains firmly confined to the humanities and social sciences and has no room for the sciences and professions. It, indeed, provides a road back to the past, not to the future.

If carefully done, comparative studies have the potential of liberating the study of Africa from the paradigmatic prison of pathological exceptionalism. Programmatically, this entails promoting closer collaboration among area studies centers and between the latter and domestic ethnic studies programs, such as African American studies, Asian American studies, and Latina/o studies in course offerings and curriculum development; extracurricular activities, such as conferences; organizing joint research projects; and pooling outreach resources. There is already considerable overlap in faculty and student interests in domestic ethnic studies and foreign area studies programs. Cultivating and catering to such interests is not only good academic politics and helps maximize scarce resources, it must be part of a larger objective of simultaneously provincializing and globalizing American studies, that is, stripping the study of American economics, politics, sociology, and culture of its claims to universal truth, to epistemological supremacy.

The composition of area studies programs and institutional incentives for international studies also need to be examined. Deliberate efforts should be made to increase the representation of domestic minorities in area studies in order to build or to strengthen their capacity to pursue teaching, research, or international service careers. Strong disincentives exist in the faculty appointment, promotion, and tenure system that discourages faculty from participating in long-term, mutually beneficial relationships with their counterparts abroad. Tenure clocks are known to favor mass production, which often precludes prolonged collaborative research and copublishing with overseas colleagues; yet, the possibilities for international scholarly communication have never been better with the electronic media revolution, which is gradually spreading to many parts of the world, including Africa.

International cooperation is essential for the successful implementation of educational internationalization in the American academy. It requires the construction of genuinely collaborative research and linkage programs between American scholars and their overseas counterparts. The former must realize that the centers of foreign area scholarship are located in the foreign countries themselves, as much as the United States is the center of American scholarship. Imperial or racial arrogance has often blinded many to this elemental fact, certainly in African studies, where it has been common to equate the material poverty of African nations and universities to the paucity of local scholarly production and probity. I have in mind not simply relations between, say, Africanists and their counterparts on the continent, which obviously need improving, but also between African and American scholars who share thematic interests even if covering different global locations. After all, like their American counterparts working on the United States, African scholars in Africa are more likely to define themselves in disciplinary or interdisciplinary terms than as area studies specialists or as Africanists.

The difficulties of establishing thematic rather than geographic linkages between African and American scholars cannot be underestimated, but the inclusion of foreign scholars in SSRC committees is a move in the right direction (Prewitt, 1996a, 1996b; Kassimir, 1997). For Africanists who have prided themselves on comparative work there is nothing to fear from these changes, as Nyang'oro (1997) and Robinson (1997) stress emphatically. Several research funding agencies now require collaboration between American researchers and partners in Africa, or in Asia and in Latin America, before they can fund a project, although the research priorities and agendas are often set by the U.S.-based scholars. Encouraging multinational thematic research involving American and African researchers is long overdue and would dissolve some of the historic antagonisms between African and Africanist scholars. In my own personal experience, I have rarely encountered difficulties with colleagues who work, say, on Canadian or American history, and I have often wished for more engagement with them for mutually beneficial intellectual conversations.

In addition to the challenges posed by international studies, area studies face competition from interdisciplinary or multidisciplinary studies, which is fueled by internal epistemological transformations taking place within and among the disciplines and the growing conviction by many scholars, and sometimes by university administrators interested in closing small departments, that the nineteenth-century intellectual division of disciplinary knowledge is increasingly becoming obsolete, so that each discipline is incapable, by itself, of explaining the complex and interconnected social, ecological, and physical phenomena and processes. While the importance of interdisciplinarity is widely recognized the meaning of the term is not always clear. To its detractors interdisciplinarity is seen as a threat to disciplinary boundaries, hierarchies, and rigor, while its proponents value it as a creative space between disciplines where new questions are asked, new approaches developed, new understandings advanced, and new fields and disciplines emerge. All too often, these debates are tied to intellectual territoriality and struggles for resources.

Interdisciplinarity needs to be strengthened by giving interdisciplinary units, including international studies, more instructional authority. Critical to this effort is faculty recruitment, retention, and retooling. There is also a need to internationalize many existing interdisciplinary programs in the humanities and social sciences, such as women studies, ethnic studies, and cultural studies, which emerged out of the political and intellectual ferment of the 1960s. Women studies is a good example of an interdisciplinary area that has grown and matured rapidly. On many campuses, however, it is common for women studies programs to focus on American and European women, while African, Asian, and Latin American women are relegated to the less prestigious and applied women-in-development (WID) or gender-and-development (GAD) programs. Interaction between the developmentalist and disciplinary ambitions of the two fields would strengthen the interdisciplinary and international credentials of women studies. Collaborations between ethnic and area studies are also sometimes discouraged, for example, by Title VI funding mandates that require strict separation between (international) area studies and (domestic) ethnic studies and by many proponents of the two fields eager to build and to maintain intellectual identity for programs that are often beleaguered and underfunded; yet, the two fields often attract the same student cohorts and when linked they benefit from intellectual cross-fertilization (Yang, 2000). The development of diaspora studies offers opportunities for effective curricula and programmatic collaborations while maintaining autonomy on campuses where that is the tradition.

Also underdeveloped are relations between area studies and cultural studies. Ivan Karp (1997) complains that the field of cultural studies, as constituted in the American academy, does not always offer an antidote to the cultural arrogance of the disciplines; it merely reproduces it in trendy clothing. He finds it "professionally and personally troubling that the great mass of Third World peoples—especially rural Third World peoples—are simply left out of the Cultural Studies equation, or are treated as an appendage to the cultural activities of minority and Third World peoples who work and live in the urban and Western metropolitan centers" (Kamp, 1997: 287). Interaction between cultural studies and area studies offers opportunities for mutual critique and transformation: making cultural studies more internationally sensitive and international studies more culturally sensitive (Nelson and Gaonkar, 1996; Appadurai, 1996b; Lee, 1995, 1996; Gray, 1996). A field with continuously shifting theoretical and methodological interests and frameworks, cultural studies has had close, complex, and critical relations with a series of more traditional disciplines and interdisciplinary terrains (During, 1993; Grossberg, 1996; Dominguez, 1996; Nelson, 1996; Steinberg, 1996; Ross, 1996). Needed are comparative or cross-cultural perspectives, which can enhance our understanding of the increasingly global nature of cultural production, consumption, and communication. Transnational or international cultural studies strengthen strategic institutional alliances for interdisciplinary studies and add a critical and cosmopolitan inflection to the persistent cultural studies' critiques of the disciplines.

The interdisciplinary scholarship movement, if it grows and becomes more institutionalized, will increasingly dissolve the contrived tension between area studies and the disciplines. While we await the day when all of us will be liberated from the stifling strictures of disciplinary conformity and can begin to enjoy the permissive pleasures of interdisciplinarity, we need to participate in shaping and inserting our beloved Africa into the new architecture of interdisciplinary scholarship. First, we need to be in the forefront of challenging the theoretical, empirical, and ideological shortfalls of specific disciplines, informed by our knowledge of African realities and epistemologies. It is surely not enough to celebrate Africa's contributions to the disciplines without actually demonstrating the role of African thinkers and paradigms as is done in the book *Africa and the Disciplines* (Bates, Mudimbe, O'Barr, 1993).

Second, area studies programs themselves should be made more interdisciplinary in fact, not simply in intent. All too often, these programs function as glorified administrative offices for Title VI and other grant writing, organizing occasional conferences and providing postal addresses for visiting African faculty and perhaps spaces for lonely African students to hang out, with little actual interdisciplinary research and teaching. Area studies programs are dominated by the social sciences and humanities, although there have been considerable shifts in the relative concentration of these disciplines over time. The bulk of the faculty who identify themselves as Africanists are in the social science and humanities disciplines, so are those who dominate African studies conferences. At most Title VI centers the number of core faculty from the natural sciences and professional schools is minuscule.

217

As for conferences, I was struck, as Chair of the National Panels Committee of the 1998 Annual Meeting of the African Studies Association, that out of the 714 presentations accepted in the preliminary program, 115 dealt with current African politics, especially democratization; followed by eighty-eight on colonial and postcolonial history; and sixty-two on cultures and cultural change. The dominance of political science, history, and anthropology was even greater when we include papers in other sections focusing on political, historical, and anthropological themes. Altogether, the three disciplines accounted for about three quarters of the submissions. The remainder was shared by geography with seventy presentations, economics with forty-seven, literature and science with thirty-seven each, and philosophy, four. The low presence of literature and the virtual absence of linguistics might be accounted for by the fact that both disciplines have their own associations, the African Literature Association and the African Language Teachers Association, respectively, which also organize annual conferences. The invisibility of philosophy is a testament to the continued disregard for African thought among Africanists and in philosophy departments (Taiwo, 1997). The strong presence of political scientists, on the other hand, reflects both the modernist and prescriptive preoccupations of Africanist scholarship and their alienation from the paradigmatic center of the discipline.

The preeminence of political science, history, and anthropology in African studies is attenuated when we examine the production of dissertations on Africa by discipline. Data shows that out of the 3,468 Africa-focused dissertations produced in American universities during the 1986-94 period, the three disciplines accounted for 26.4 percent of the total as compared to 30.6 percent for the 1974-87 period (Guyer, 1996:27-45). The two leading disciplines, during both periods, were education and economics and business. Education accounted for 21.4 percent and 15.9 percent and economics and business for 12.4 percent and 11.6 percent of the dissertations produced during 1974-87 and 1986-94, respectively. Also remarkable are the production figures for the professional and scientific disciplines of agriculture, communications, natural and applied sciences, and urban and regional planning. Collectively, these disciplines increased their share from 10.8 percent of the dissertations in 1974-87 to 19.1 percent in 1986-94. Clearly, since at least the 1970s, African studies, with its emphasis on the social sciences and humanities, has not been catering to a large student constituency in the sciences and professional fields. The fact that the majority of the dissertations in these fields are produced by African students—74 percent in agriculture, 71 percent in communications, 64 percent in economics and business, 74 percent in education, 100 percent in law, 93 percent in library science, 75 percent in psychology, and 47 percent in sciences and engineering during the 1986-94 period—while American students predominate in the traditional area studies disciplines reinforces the perception of African studies as academic tourism. This leads to a peculiar situation in which African studies loudly wears its developmentalist credentials as rhetoric without the disciplinary capabilities to sustain development as practice. So the field loses credibility with two critical student constituencies: It fails to satisfy the cultural quests of African Americans and the scientific quests of Africans.

Given the interests of African students in the sciences and professions, broadening African studies to incorporate the natural sciences and professions does not, therefore, simply represent surrender to corporate and academic capitalism but belated responses for relevance to a key constituency. The challenge is how to prevent area studies from becoming maids to the sciences and professions. This is not a problem confined to the area studies. As noted by Stanley Aronowitz (1997:108), "We are experiencing the transformation of nearly all the humanities and many social sciences into services for business, computer technology, and other vocational programs." Efforts must be made to promote mutual engagement between the area studies and the sciences and professions to expand the intellectual tent of African studies, so that it is no longer dominated by anthropologists, historians, political scientists, and others in the humanities and social sciences, without at the same time reducing these disciplines into intellectual attendants. The case for closer intellectual collaboration is compelling, as I have discovered while writing a book on the economic history of Africa in the twentieth century. One cannot fully understand, say, the development of African agriculture and agrarian systems without situating it as much in political ecology as in political economy, in the overall context of fluctuations in the environment and the economy, which requires readings in environmental science and history. In short, a closer integration of the natural sciences and professional studies in area studies programs would expand the campus constituencies of area studies centers in terms of faculty affiliates and alliances and student involvement, including that of foreign students who come more to learn about science than about their own societies.

The intellectual challenges facing area studies can be seen as having institutional dynamics and implications. Increasingly, as already stated, these programs are besieged because of declining funding from their own institutions and from national public and private sources, which is partly a product of the privatization of the economy and the dismantling of the social welfare state and the Fordist social contract of middle class mobility and stability. For programs on the margins of the academy, the fiscal challenges can be debilitating. Funding decisions are tied to political calculations and constituencies, to the rationalities of legitimation. This is why it is imperative for area studies programs to ally themselves firmly with the domestic ethnic studies programs and enlarge their circle of intellectual friends beyond the social sciences and humanities. Also, the question of instructional authority must be addressed. Area studies teaching is often conducted in departments. The challenge for these programs is not to compete with the departments, a losing proposition under the current organizational structure of most universities, but to offer interdisciplinary, comparative, and international courses, including minors, majors, and degree programs that only they are capable of designing and delivering.

Developments in the sciences are instructive in this regard. "The production of graduate education and research in the sciences and engineering," Gary Rhoades and Sheila Slaughter (1997:32) observe, "is taking place in [the] interdisciplinary units, relegating discipline-based departments to the task of educating undergraduates." To be sure,

> such units are better resourced in the sciences and engineering than in the social sciences and humanities. This is predictable, given the supply-side focus on productivity and wealth creation: interdisciplinary units in sciences and engineering center on solving problems and creating commercial products that laypersons see as important; such units in the social sciences and humanities tend to turn problems into verbs (as in, "problematize"), identifying problems and generating textual products that are unrecognizable to laypersons.

The point is this: The relationship between the disciplines and interdisciplinary studies need not be a zero-sum game. It is possible for area studies as interdisciplinary units to carve out curricular space for themselves that is currently unfilled or impaired by the disciplines.

Worldly Engagements

Despite the aspirations of many in the academy, i.e., to isolate themselves from the mundane concerns of the masses in their ivy or ebony towers of idle contemplation or research, the university is, for better or worse, embedded in society and beholden to its collective dreams, as much as it is often ripped apart by the social cleavages of race, gender, ethnicity, and other social markers. The question of the academic community's civic mandates and constituencies, therefore, becomes critical. The extra-academic constituencies of scholarly knowledge production include various segments of the public, the state, and the ubiquitous international community. Much of the reorganization in American universities—in terms of administration, employment, enrollments, and programs—reflects, and is a direct response to, changes in the wider society. The corporate culture of accounting, productivity, downsizing, commercialization, and competitiveness, all grounded in a neoconservative discourse, has invaded university campuses with a vengeance. Reinforcing the universities' own ruthless "research culture," as Zelda Gamson (1997) calls it, the result is the decomposition and recomposition of the academic labor market and the restructuring of programs and governance. The new culture of academic capitalism and supply-side higher education is seen in growing authoritarian managerial control, threats to tenure, rising tuition fees, declining public expenditure, and in the swelling faces of the lumpen-professorate, part-time or nontenure track faculty, whose numbers nearly doubled between 1970 and 1991, increasing from 21.9 percent to 43 percent of the senior instructional workforce (Rhoades and Slaughter, 1997:20; Tirelli, 1997; Zeleza, 1997c).

It is easy to submit to, or rail impotently against, the forces of academic capitalism and supply-side higher education that are restructuring and ravaging the academy. A more productive and difficult response, argues Jeremy Smith (1997:135), is political engagement, born out of the realization that the "crisis in higher education has been paralleled in the wider society by falling wages, welfare cuts, the breakup of communities, huge increases in the prison population, and the commercialization of cultural expression." He challenges professors "to harness themselves to political movements....Professors must engage in the conflict with power that authen-

221

ticity demands—not just in the realm of ideas, but in practical politics" (Smith, 1997:137). In other words, programmatic struggles in the academy reflect, and must be latched on to, wider societal struggles. Smith's counsel would be understood by many in African studies, where the fortunes and misfortunes of the field have been embroiled with domestic and international struggles and transformations. It requires us to pay close attention to, and mobilize, the shifting public constituencies for Africa.

With the end of the cold war, as Martin and West (1995) and West and Martin (1997) have suggested, the Africanists' Africa may be falling apart. Interest in African studies, they observe, even within the academy, is more widespread than ever before. This has little to do with the irresistibility of Africanist academic products. Rather, it is rooted "in the renaissance of Africa interest in Black Communities" (Martin and West, 1995: 25). The Africanists' Africa was linked to cold war Washington, the foundations, and narrow academic networks, and as these wither with the demise of the cold war, that Africa begins to wilt, unable to secure sustenance from the new resurgent Africas. "It is worth pondering why this has taken place," they say. "The most obvious answer is based on the social and political realities of race: those who dominate African studies, the major centers, and the national organizations, are predominantly white and male." It is imperative that the African studies scholars and associations must engage more seriously and systematically African American communities. As Greene (1999: 11) has argued, "African Americans constitute in the U.S. the population that historically has had the most consistent interest in Africa. It is still the population with the greatest interest in Africa, outside the resident population of immigrant Africans."

The African agenda is also increasingly driven by business interests and by popular grassroots organizations in the African American community. Schooled in the civil rights and antiapartheid struggles, African American political leaders, inside and outside Congress, have been in the forefront of the movement to establish, to use President Clinton's words during his 1998 Africa tour, a new political and economic partnership between the United States and Africa. The initiatives of the emerging policy engagement with Africa include not only the deeply flawed Africa Growth and Opportunity Act passed in 2000 but also the growing popularity and importance of the African and African American Summit, and the launching of the National Summit on Africa, which held a series of regional meetings on Africa throughout the coun-

222

try from 1998 to 2000. As might be expected, there are serious conflicts and contradictions among the new constituencies and networks for Africa. How specific African studies programs and associations relate to and utilize them individually and collectively will depend on their institutional histories, and locations and the ideological inclinations of their core faculty and administrators; but engage them they must. In short, Africanists must be more proactive, engage in public debates on Africa, and promote critical and informed discussion about African issues and relations between Africa and the United States.

All this implies the need for activism, taking African studies to the streets.[5] The question is which streets? African streets? American streets? On both sides of the Atlantic there are of course many streets—rural, urban, and suburban streets, as well wall streets and parliamentary streets. Students of Africa can walk any of these streets based on their personal and political locations and inclinations, and material and moral resources, but collectively and cumulatively they must have an agenda as broad as the forces that affect the lives of Africans in all their splendid diversities of class, gender, region, nationality, ethnicity, religion, and culture. Africa is too big and its challenges too immense to accept only one method of engagement, a singular activist position sometimes beloved by impatient idealists and naive radicals, some of whom have never even been to the continent or know it from brief academic tourist encounters.

African studies seems prone to superficial activism, because it tends to attract students and faculty with a missionary mentality; those who believe that they are doing Africa a favor by studying it, joining the field to save this benighted continent either from itself or from its external exploiters. The appropriation of Africa is justified in the name of humanitarianism among those hoping to burnish their multicultural sensibilities and credentials or work for international aid agencies and NGOs, or in terms of revolution among those who missed the restive sixties and seventies and seek refuge from their bourgeois comforts in the possibilities of revolution in the underdeveloped world, or in terms of identity among those who trace their ancestry to Africa and seek to quench their diasporic alienations in Africa's imagined authenticity. Hence, the passionate, politicized, and prescriptive tone of much writing on Africa. I am often struck when grading students essays by how many of them are written as if they are the first to diagnose the problems, that Africans themselves do not adequately know and understand the problems, let alone are capable of resolving them[6]. The most militant among them are opposed to serious intellectual work and regard any attempt to theorize about Africa as a reactionary deviation from engagement with the continent's pressing problems. There are of course many who are attracted to African studies for theoretical reasons, but more often than not it is to use African data to test existing theories. While the former think their work is assisting the cause of African liberation, the latter believe they are bringing intellectual light to the "dark continent."

In the heyday of the African nationalist and American civil rights struggles in the 1950s and 1960s, the streets on the two sides of the Atlantic were a lot closer, and many jumped from one to the other. The same was true for a brief moment when antiapartheid struggles intensified in the 1980s. Since then, however, there has been no single overarching issue or movement to focus the minds of African and American scholar-activists. Africans remain preoccupied with the enduring nationalist dreams and challenges of development, nation building, and democracy, now overlaid by the terrible effects of structural adjustment programs, the debt crisis, and the HIV/AIDS pandemic. In the U.S., racial inequalities issues remain central, increasingly coalesced around the politics and economics of civil rights, social welfare, and the criminal justice system. Nevertheless, connections exist, forged through the rapacious tentacles of globalization that currently structure economic and political inequalities within and between nations, which have provoked countervailing political movements against global capitalism as vividly manifested in demonstrations and riots against the unholy trinity of today's global economic order—the IMF, World Bank, and the WTO. The 1999 Seattle riots awakened Americans to the activities of the gendarmes of global capitalism and galvanized many activists. It is important, however, to remember that such riots had long been common in many African cities, and that African scholar-activists had also been campaigning against the Bretton Woods institutions long before the baton was picked up on American campuses.

This underscores the need for the American Africanist community to strengthen its linkages with African institutions in response to the struggles and changes taking place on the continent and to try to devise and develop programs of intellectual exchange and communication that are equitable and mutually beneficial. In the current era of globalization, Africanists in the USA would also benefit from increased collaboration with Africanists in other parts of the world, including Asia, Europe, the Caribbean, and Latin America. Such engagements would help temper the excessive imperial provincialism of US Africanist scholarship, the tendency to see the world in terms of America's discursive perspectives and racialized preoccupations. It would make clear that the debate about "area studies" is a peculiarly American one and a marker, not of America's outward extroversion, but of its inward introspection, reflecting national narcissism masquerading as universalism. This is what often gives debates about African studies in the U.S. their apocalyptic inflection, as if the death of area studies as they are currently configured in the American academy would somehow lead to the disappearance of the regions concerned. Much as the study of the U.S. within the U.S. continues outside the invisible American studies programs, the study of Africa in African countries is done and will continue to be done outside the equally invisible African studies programs there. Similarly, just as some of us began studying Africa before we joined any African studies programs in the U.S., we will continue doing so after these programs disappear. This is simply to underscore a simple point: American institutions and Africanists have no monopoly on the study of Africa.

In reading debates about African studies over the last few decades, one is struck by the persistence of the same questions. This is amply borne out by comparing the papers in the *Africa Today* of 1969 (Vol.16, Nos. 5 & 6) on the Montreal confrontation with *Issue* of 1995 (Vol.23, No.1) on contemporary trends in African studies. The tone may be different, the writers may be from different generations, but the fundamental issues and conflicts are the same, the sense of dissatisfaction and drift is the same, and the consternation that things are falling apart, that the Africanist enterprise is in crisis pervades both periodicals. A running theme in the latter issue and in Guyer's (1996) prosaic history of African studies in the United States is the fear that Africa and African studies risk becoming more marginalized. The question is, marginalized for whom? Certainly not for people within the continent itself, nor for those of us for whom Africa is not merely an academic "problem," a distant research site that can be abandoned at will, but a permanent and profound existential and intellectual reality. Similarly, the lamentation about dwindling resources must to be stripped of the deceptive solidarity of impending collective penury that it suggests: Who benefitted most when the resources were relatively abundant in the 1960s? In reality, how abundant were the resources in the 1960s?

Conclusion

Clearly, the intellectual and organizational boundaries and constituencies of African studies, and area studies more generally, are shifting rapidly. To some this represents a crisis; it might indeed be a crisis to those who painstakingly constructed the African studies enterprise that we have come to know in the last fifty years, where they have invested so much intellectual, ideological, and even emotional capital. In such proclamations of crisis it is tempting to see millennial frenzy, living as we do on the verge of a new century and a new millennium. To me and to many others the fears that African studies and area studies in general are about to disappear from the American academy are misplaced. Immanuel Wallerstein (1995:23) may be exaggerating when he declares that "the whole disciplinary taxonomy is about to crumble" and with it "the distinction between the two cultures" of the disciplines and area studies, but it cannot be denied that we are living in a moment of transition. Like all such moments, it is full of both danger and opportunity. While remembering the multiple histories of the past, we must seize the tantalizing possibilities of the future: to return African studies to some of its earlier pan-Africanist and global preoccupations; to reconnect it to African American communities; to engage the sciences and professions and to join in the construction of new truly international and interdisciplinary studies programs; and to forge a new partnership with Africa and its scholars.

Ultimately, the sustenance of the study of Africa lies on the continent itself, and it is imperative that new forms of intellectual collaboration be established that reflect and take into account the changing contexts of scholarly knowledge production on the continent. In Chapter 3 above, there was a more detailed examination of the nature of the new linkages that should be created and cultivated. Suffice it to say here that they should encompass all the key stages and structures of knowledge production, from the conception of research themes and organization of collaborative research to publications, review networks, and reward structures. Critical to that dialogue, to the construction of new intellectual triangular trans-Atlantic conversations—between Africa, the United States or the Americas more generally, and Europe—will be African immigrant scholars located in the North, who in their personal and professional lives straddle the three continents, and frequently cross and seek to bridge the Atlantic, so much the source of our historic pain; and so much the spring of our collective liberation and the future of a truly deracialized modernity.

Endnotes

1. For a detailed discussion of the events leading to and following the Montreal confrontation, see Martin and West (1999a: 97-106).

2. The estimates of black studies programs vary quite considerably. Manning (2000a: 10) quotes one estimate placing the number of black studies programs at 800 in the early 1970s and its decline to about 315 by the mid-1990s. Manning also provides a succinct overview of the history of black studies as an intellectual tradition that has undergone various phases over a two hundred year period, although it has retained its descriptive, critical, and prescriptive mission. See also Manning (1995) and the various contributions in the section on "Mapping African American Studies" in Manning (2000b).

3. The sense of anguish, shock, and intellectual drift can be seen in the special issue of the review of *The Chronicle of Higher Education*, "The Fractured Landscape: Reflections on September 11, 2001, and Its Aftermath," 28 September 2001. Also see, the reflections posted on the website of the Social Science Research Council, "After September 11, "Perspective from the Social Sciences," at

4. According to Martinez (1998), globalization is apparently beginning to impact the epistemological, ontological, and methodological bases of the disciplines, from anthropology and sociology to psychology and law.

5. The question of taking African American studies back to the streets has become increasingly critical and has attracted attention in the national education media. See the articles in *The Chronicle of Higher Education* by Jeff Sharlet (1999) and by Alison Schenider (1999).

6. This is tied to widespread ignorance about African intellectual thought, the incredible belief that African intellectuals hardly exist (Zachernuk, 1999).

Chapter 5

The "Posts," History, and African Studies

Introduction

The explosion of the "posts" in the 1980s and 1990s, especially in the academies of the North, led by the holy trinity of poststructuralism, postmodernism, and postcoloniality, with or without hyphens, has been a source of great intellectual energy and excitement as well as concern and confusion. What is one to make of these imperious "posts" that cherish discursive pluralism, contemporary constructions that claim existential and epistemological "afters," critiques of all forms of representation that create new representations, from the vantage positions of history and African studies? Indeed, what is one to make of concepts whose very popularity are derived from and demand the defiance of definition, paradigms that delight in their intellectual eclecticism? For the African historian the "posts" pose peculiar and particular challenges of discipline and domain; the fact that history as a discipline is mistrusted for its metanarratives and methodologies, while Africa, as a spatial domain, is often marginalized from the manufacturing and mappings of the "posts."

The result has been widespread hostility to the "posts" by most African historians, indeed, by many in African studies, certainly among scholars based on the continent. This unease is not confined to Africa. In China, Liu Kang (1998: 165) tells us, "postmodernism, and related theoretical discourses such as postcolonialism, seem to be largely eschewed by the intellectual 'mainstream,' as newly imported Western theoretical shibboleths ill-suited to Chinese situations."

In this chapter I would like to explore the troubled encounter between history and the "posts" in particular and the "posts" and African studies in general. The connections and contestations between these formations are complex and contradictory. At the outset let me make two claims, which are quite predictable, coming from a historian and an African scholar. The first is that the "posts" are not above or beyond, history, that is, they can be historicized: They arose at a particular moment, they mark and characterize, whether as conceptual paradigms or as cultural politics, specific conjunctures that are open to historical inquiry and analysis. The second is that African studies, together with other area studies, and developments in Africa associated with decolonization and struggles against Western hegemony, played a role in the deconstruction and decomposition of the modernist mentalities and methodologies that the "posts" rail against so much.

One could even argue that the fragmentations, ambivalences, contingencies, hybridities, and multiplicities associated with the "posts," as conceptions and conditions, were articulated and experienced, with unsettling urgency and persistence, from the bloody dawn of colonial conquest and the violent negations and negotiations it entailed for the cultural cartographies of African peoples. In a sense, then, Africans saw some of the "posts," through historical forces that were not entirely of their own making, before they were belatedly discovered in the West. In a sense, then, the "posts" bring the South to the North, disrupts and pluralizes both, thereby helping to dismantle, as Trinh T. Minh-ha (1996) has observed, the stubborn myth of the West as a unitary and monolithic category.

At the same time, however, it is important that the "posts" emerged, or were named as such, as discursive systems in Northern institutional locations. The production and promotion of the "posts" from the 1970s and 1980s as Northern intellectual fads, I would argue, gave them a distinctly Western accent, if not grammar, that did not resonate well with the intellectual and ideological languages of the South, even if, as is true of postcolonial theory, some of the leading theorists indeed hailed from the South and were translocated in the North. For many intellectuals in Africa, where the lingering dreams of independence demanded visions of the future anchored on what Thandika Mkandawire (1998a) calls the unfinished historic and humanistic agendas of nationalism, "postsomething" scholarship, as Fred Cooper (1993: 193) once called it, reeked of self-indulgent angst, pretentious theorizing, apolitical posturing, and historical fatigue; it reflected the comforts of scholarly professionalization divorced from the claims of civil society and social movements. Suspicion of the "posts" was of course also quite widespread among the left in the North, at least in the early days before they were defanged by the collapse of "actually existing socialism" in the former Soviet bloc.

Thus, my analysis of the "posts" in this chapter seeks to map out the historical and institutional contexts in which they emerged and developed and the contributions from, and the confrontations with, African studies. The chapter is divided into five sections. The first two sections explore the intellectual histories of postmodernism and postcoloniality. Because postcoloniality has been more important for Africa than postmodernism, I disscuss the former at greater length than the latter. The third section examines the role played by changing institutional practices in Northern academies in popularizing the "posts." The fourth section investigates the engagement of the "posts" with history, and the fifth, an engagement with women studies and African studies within and outside the continent.

The "Posts" of the Rich

I am intrigued by the tensions inherent in the concepts of postmodernism and postcoloniality, between their use as periodizing terms and as typological descriptions; between their chronological and epistemological ambitions; between their culturalist and materialist referents; between literary-textual readings and political-economic analyses of the real world; between aspirations of activist engagement and rhetorical dismissal of commitment for fear of accusations of totalization; between their professed affinities for pluralism, multiplicity, and difference and their tendencies to collapse and homogenize diverse histories, structures, and racial formations, embracing in their generous transhistorical bosom the former imperial powers of Europe, the settler societies of the United States, Canada, Australia, and the ex-colonial countries of Asia and Africa; between the Northern locations of their production and the Southern origins of some of their leading proponents; between their empirical insistence on the representation, inscription, and interpretation of the particular, the local, and the different and their transcendental desire to become another universal, another grand narrative, another set of the great historicultural explanations.

Clearly, the "posts" are riddled with many internal contradictions: They tend to argue against theory building when they themselves advance theoretical positions; they tend to dismiss logic, reason and rationality, yet they do so employing these very tools; they claim to oppose the privileging of any position, to be against truth, but go on to privilege themselves, glibly making truth claims; and they pride themselves in their oppositional criticism and openness, yet they derive their authority from institutionalization in the academy, from the closure that comes with professional specialization.[1] Part of the problem is that each of the "posts" comes in many shapes and forms and with an entourage of advocates and critics who do not always agree on what they are discussing or disputing.

From the 1960s, the spread of the "posts" in Northern academic and popular discourses was tied to new currents and ferment in both scholarship and society, to challenges to the old global social order brought about by decolonization struggles in the South, civil rights and students struggles in the North, the rise of feminism, and the evident crises of socialism and capitalism in the contending blocs of the old cold war. These events and movements were accompanied, in the case of the United States, by the frenzied appropriation of theories manufactured in postwar Europe, from the Marxisms and structuralisms of the early postwar years to the poststructuralisms of the turbulent 60s, as well as by internal restructuring in some disciplines such as history and literature as the "subjugated knowledges" of formerly silenced groups, including the racial minorities, women, and gays claimed public intellectual space. Also, the explosion of popular culture, especially the impact of television, film, music, and sports disrupted the exaltation and exclusivity of high culture. In short, the "posts" reflected and reproduced the fragmentations, uncertainties, and instabilities of the times.

Postmodernism and postcoloniality remain vexing terms that defy easy definitions. What Stuart Hall (1999: 14) once said about the postcolonial—that "it doesn't mean what it obviously means," and that it tumbles from the paradigms where it seems "settled and come[s] loose in your hands"—can be said of postmodernism, which antecedes postcoloniality by several decades. Perry Anderson (1998) traces its origins to the 1930s in the Hispanic interworld, where it was used as an aesthetic category to describe a conservative reflux within modernism itself. When the term emerged twenty years later in the Anglophone world, it apparently did so as an epochal category. The two meanings, the aesthetic and the temporal, were to bedevil postmodernism as the idea developed.

In its epochal guise, mapping the moment of the postmodern is problematic. Arnold Toynbee, the British historian, dated the postmodern age to the 1870s, seeing it as an epoch characterized by the rise of an industrial working class in the West and of modernization in the rest of the world. In contrast, for Charles Olson, an American poet, the postmodern world lay beyond the imperial age of colonization and the industrial revolution. By the end of the 1950s there were several versions of postmodernism. To some it was a negative marker, implying less, not more, than modern and entailing the collapse of the modern ideals of liberalism and socialism. To others postmodernism merely referred to a complex set of antimodernist artistic strategies. "Depending on the artistic discipline, then," writes Hans Bertens (1995: 5), postmodernism came to be seen as "either a radicalization of the self-reflexive moment within modernism, a turning away from narrative and representation, or an explicit return to narrative and representation."

In the 1960s, the idea of postmodernism began to crystallize as scholars and artists from various disciplines focused their analytical gaze more systematically on the concept and the phenomena it sought to capture. To some, postmodernism simply came to be identified with the "attitude" of the 1960s counterculture or the "new sensibility" of the social and artistic avantgarde. Ambitious thinkers like Ihab Hassan, the Egyptian literary critic, sought to envision postmodernism as both an artistic tendency and a social phenomenon. Charles Jencks, an American architect, theorized the eclecticism of postmodern architecture as a style of "double-coding" and seeing postmodernism as a movement involving the liberatory mixture of the old and the new, the high and low, as a world civilization of plural tolerance, identities, and choices.

In the meantime, as postmodernism's flirtation with poststructuralism became an embrace, the former adopted the latter's deconstructionist interrogation of representations and the power inherent in the discourses that surround us. By the 1980s, postmodernism had expanded beyond the arts and humanities to the social sciences and into popular discourse about the postmodern world, seen variously as describing the emergence of a new age, that of postmodernity, or new ways of looking at the world. To some the postmodern condition, to use the term of Jean-Francois Lyotard's (1984) seminal text, was linked to the emergence of a postindustrial society, where knowledge had become the main economic force of production, and it entailed the demise of the "metanarratives" and teleologies of the Enlightenment project. To the followers of Jean Baudrillard, it referred to a hyperreal world of signs and simulations, while to unrepentant Marxists like Frederic Jameson (1991) it implied the cultural logic of late capitalism.

With some notable exceptions, such as Jameson, the idea of the post-modern conformed to the visions and values of the Right that were on ascendancy from the 1970s. The one narrative whose death Lyotard "above all sought to certify was, of course, classical socialism. In subsequent texts, he would extend the list of grand narratives that were now defunct: Christian redemption, Enlightenment progress, Hegelian spirit, Romantic unity, Nazi racism, Keynesian equilibrium. But the commanding referent always remained communism" (Anderson, 1998: 31). Communism, of course, imploded in the 1980s, but far from marking the disappearance of grand narratives, the world fell prey to the most grandiose narrative of all, that of the capitalist market as the universal elixir of liberty and prosperity, to which Lyotard could only respond with metaphysical answers of melancholy.

No less troubling is Baudrillard's totalizing and nihilistic vision. His semiologically inspired analysis of consumer society and the electronic media, for all their insights, paint a nightmarish world of despair. He argues that the commodity and the sign are virtually interchangeable, that the political economy of the sign has superceded the political economy of production, and that this new mode of signification is controlled by the code formed and embodied by the media, which reproduces the hyperreal, a world in which representations are irrelevant, and where the social has disappeared, where thinking and effective action are impossible, and where everything, including production and the political, even if they persist are reduced to meaningless signs. Baudrillard's "later work exhibits all the worst traits of poststructuralism: a contempt for facts and definitions, a style that is equally reluctant to give concessions to the demands of the concrete, and a grand vision that develops distinct metaphysical tones" (Bertens, 1995: 144).

Appropriating some of the insights of Lyotard and Baudrillard and many others, Jameson sought to develop a comprehensive theory that anchored postmodernism firmly in the objective transformations of capitalism and the cultural signals of the new age from the media to the decentered subject; that captured changes in diverse disciplines, the arts, and discourses; that mapped its social bases and geopolitical patterns; and one that avoided moralism by understanding that this was a historical epoch with its own logic. There is much to admire in Jameson's sweeping historical and theoretical exposition, but his periodization of the postmodern, whose emergence he dates to the 1970s, has been questioned by those who date the arrival of late capitalism to the end of the Second World War (Mandel, 1978), or by those who argue that there has been no fundamental break in capitalist organization or in modernist culture (Callinicos, 1989). The global reach of postmodernism has also been questioned. How can postmodernism have meaning for societies where the basic conditions of capitalist modernity have yet to be realized? Jameson insists on the unevenness of capitalist and postmodernist development, but the question still remains "whether this unevenness is too great to sustain any common cultural logic" (Anderson, 1998: 121).

Aijaz Ahmad (1992) queries the very hierarchies of this unevenness embedded in Jameson's construction of "First" and "Third" worlds. He accuses Jameson of reproducing binary opposition between a postmodern "First World" and a nationalist "Third World," of homogenizing the latter into a civilizational "other," of ignoring the cultural heterogeneity of these societies and of their literary products. Moreover, he notes, the two are defined on different grounds, the first in terms of materialist conditions and internal historical connections and the latter "purely in terms of an 'experience' of externally inserted phenomena," namely, the experience of colonialism and imperialism (Ahmad, 1992: 100). Turning the deconstructive tables, Ahmad demonstrates that Jameson's text is gendered and racialized, reflecting his location in the United States, so that his theory of postmodernism is infected with "First World" biases that always depict the "Third World" in terms of lack and becoming, of following where the West has already trodden.

Obviously, postmodernism does not imply the end of modernity everywhere, not even in the so-called West itself, let alone the exhaustion of modernities in the rest of the world. As one vocal postmodernist candidly admits, "the chief signs of modernity have not disappeared", and he proceeds to lists them in detail (Seidman, 1994a: 1).[2] It has in fact been argued that what we are witnessing globally is not postmodernity, but the growth of "alternative modernities" (Ong, 1996; Gaonkar, 2001) "multiple modernities" (Hefner, 1998) or "new modernities" (Robotham, 2000), especially in Asia, leading to the revalorization of Asian knowledges and historiographies, which challenges and supercedes, both in theory and practice, Western modernity, postmodernity, and postcoloniality.

The conceptual problems of postmodernism, its epistemological status, epochal dimensions, and spatial scales have persisted. Postmodernism has continued to elude consensus and clarity, as it has been embraced by different people at different conceptual levels discussing different phenomena. If there is any uniting thread between them, it is the loss of faith in representations and the notions of truth, reality, meaning, and knowledge. Like all newfangled scholarly movements, the "posts" have their charismatic master theorists, who, in the case of the United States, are appropriately imported, like fine wine and perfume, from continental Europe, mostly from France. The stars in the postmodern firmament are Michel Foucault (1976, 1980), with his notion of discourse, and Jacques Derrida (1976), with his deconstruction.

The importation of intellectual rhetoric from France by humanities scholars in the United States is a fascinating subject in itself. In an interesting essay on the rise of Jacques Derrida's stock among American academics, Michèle Lamont (1987) argues that his high reputation had little to do with the intrinsic value of his ideas. He became a brand name to literary scholars facing a disciplinary crisis, because his work, already valorized by the educated French elite, demanding "sophisticated intellectual goods" as a means of distinguishing themselves from the lesser mortals consuming Marxism and other simplified discourses, incorporated "a sophisticated writing style, a distinctive theoretical framework, and a focus on questions defined as both important and concerned with an important philosophical tradition" (Lamont, 1987: 592). Moreover, its "ambiguity" and "adaptability to any text" ensured its marketability. Thus, the American fascination with French philosophy, some believe, can be explained quite easily in concrete sociological terms (Eakin, 1999).

More cynical critics believe that many in the humanities are attracted to the dense and often impenetrable French intellectual style because they have little to say, for "clarity would expose your lack of content" (Dawkins, 1999: 141). According to two physicists, Sokal and Bricmont, the work of many of the revered French philosophers is full of inaccurate and meaningless scientific and pseudoscientific terminology. On Jacques Lacan, the influential psychoanalyst, they say, "although Lacan uses quite a few key words from the mathematical theory of compactness, he mixes them up arbitrarily and without the slightest regard for their meaning. His 'definition' of compactness is not just fake: it is gibberish" (as quoted in Dawkins, 1998: 141). Sokal and Bricmont are equally scathing about Jean Baudrillard, whose work is marked by "a profusion of scientific terms, used with total disregard for their meaning and, above all, in a context where they are manifestly irrelevant. Whether or not one interprets them as metaphors, it is hard to see what role they could play, except to give the appearance of profundity to trite observations about sociology or history" (as quoted in Dawkins, 1998: 141). Sokal, of course, proceeded to play a hoax on *Social Text* by writing an article that was full of scientific nonsense clothed in postmodern babble, but the postmodern crowd did not laugh at this breach of "truth" and authorial "privilege," a sign of how seriously they take themselves.

The postmodern theoretical toolkit has been dominated by discourse, deconstruction, and difference. Discourse is understood to mean a structure of statements, terms, categories, and beliefs that is specific historically, socially and institutionally, through which the contextual construction of social meanings occurs, a process that involves conflict and power and is articulated in organizations and institutions as well as words, all of which constitute a matrix of texts to be read in which knowledge and power are intricately woven. Deconstruction refers to a mode of reading that exposes a text's internal differences, teases out its unfinished and unstable meanings, repressed contradictions, and exposes the interdependence of seemingly dichotomous terms and their meanings, through double reading, which entails the reversal and displacement of binary oppositions, around which Western logocentric thinking and hierarchies of value have been historically organized. The notion that binary oppositions differ and defer to each other, that their meanings are mutually constitutive, that a positive definition rests on the repression of its representational antithesis, that a unitary concept contains its own negations, is central to the concept of difference or "différance," the term coined by Derrida. The argument is that language is indeterminate, and since words do not depend for their meaning on their correspondence to the real, but on their association with other words, in perpetual chain and slippages of signification, meaning is always undecidable and perpetually deferred, which guarantees against interpretive closure essential to any metanarrative.

These claims are both appealing and problematic. For embracing pluralism, multiplicity, and difference and repudiating totalizing Western discourses, postmodernism opened spaces for previously silenced voices, especially of women and peoples from or associated with the South. This was its democratizing effect; but by rejecting large-scale liberation organized around the structured inscriptions of nation, class, and gender as terrorizing leftovers of the Enlightenment, it robbed those same groups of the future. This was its depoliticizing effect. Its support for a cultural politics of difference, as

Cornell West (1994)[3] calls it, is potentially progressive, but its rejection of emancipatory narratives and projects is reactionary. This accounts for much of the complex and contentious relations between the "posts," the disciplines, and various interdisciplinary fields, such as women's studies and African studies (which will be examined later in this chapter) or as African American studies.[4]

The "Posts" of the Poor

Postcoloniality appears to have inherited some of the same intellectual and ideological baggage of postmodernism. As with the latter, there is little agreement among its proponents on what postcoloniality actually means. Employed in a wide range of cultural and literary disciplines, the term has become so diffuse and heterogeneous that it defies definition as to whether it refers primarily to texts and discursive practices, to the construction of subjectivities and identities, or to concrete historical processes. The high-priests of the field themselves, some accredited by choice, others by association, have different preoccupations. Let us take the example of the famous trinity, Edward Said (1979, 1993), Homi Bhabha (1990; 1994), and Gayatri Spivak (1988a; 1999).

Said, whose book *Orientalism* is considered by many a foundational text of postcolonial studies, concentrates on discourse analysis, showing the Eurocentric inventions of "others," the discursive machinations of imperialism, and believes in the liberatory potentialities of nationalism and the diaspora condition. Homi Bhabha's (1994) psychoanalytic postcoloniality rejects Said's emphasis on domination and the binary between the colonizer and colonized, self and other, speaking subject and silent native. He celebrates hybridity and "in-betweenness," that the colonial encounter was full of ambivalences, slippages, and mimicry out of which fluid identities were transacted and negotiated. Gayatri Spivak's (1988a; 1999) Marxist and feminist-inflected deconstruction has steadily moved from colonial discourse analysis to international transcultural studies and has become increasingly critical of postcolonial studies. In her first systematic treatment of the field she flatly declared "that much U.S. academic postcolonialism was bogus" (Spivak, 1999: 358).

It is not surprising, therefore, that the field of postcolonial studies is riddled with squabbles and confusion. As with other metatheoretical discourses, postcolonialists are often as riven by internal sectarian disputes as they are riled by critics who dismiss the whole enterprise for its sins of commission and omission. It seems to me that debates about postcoloniality center on five key areas: its genealogies, boundaries, fields, locations, and ideologies. Genealogies refer to the theoretical and historical origins of postcoloniality as a theoretical construct; boundaries refer to the temporal and spatial scales of postcolonial discourse; fields refer to the units and frameworks of analysis; locations refer to the places where postcolonial discourse and theory are mainly produced and consumed; and ideologies refer to the political orientations and effects of postcoloniality. Needless to say, the import and flavor of these debates have shifted over time and according to location and context.

Postcolonial theory emerged in the Anglo-American academy in the mid-1980s in the wake of the rise of poststructuralism and postmodernism. This raises questions on the relationship between postcoloniality and the other "posts." There are those who argue that they are quite different, that the postmodern is an apolitical description of conditions in advanced capitalist societies, while the postcolonial is concerned with global inequalities and is liberatory. The postcolonial seeks to deconstruct the ideological discourses that naturalize Western hegemonic representations and reformulate the knowledges and identities authored and authorized by colonialism by foregrounding the cultural, problematizing the categories of colony, nation, community, and cultural tradition; dismantling the binaries that divided the world into the West-rest, tradition-modernity, colonizer-colonized, and emphasizing interdependencies and dialectical interconnections. To some, coupling the postcolonial with the postmodern, then, is theoretically, ideologically, and empirically misleading and unproductive (Barker et al., 1994; Mongia, 1996).

Others believe that postcoloniality and postmodernism are interlinked, but disagree on the nature and productivity of the linkage. For Ato Quayson (2000), the two can be analytically and beneficially deployed on questions of marginality and identity. Besides their shared prefix "post" and the attendant temporal and epistemological problematics this raises, both are concerned with representational discourses and offer second-order meditations upon real and imagined conditions, and only by appropriating each other can they fully explain the state of the contemporary world. He urges us to perceive postcolonialism as a process of postcolonializing, to disentangle it "from its implicit dimension of chronological supersession, that aspect of its prefix which suggests that the colonial stage has been surpassed and left behind. It is important to highlight instead a notion of the term as a process of coming-into-being and of struggle *against* colonialism and its after-effects. In this respect the prefix would be fused with the sense invoked by 'anti' " (Quayson, 2000 emphasis original). If so, then why not just call it anticolonialism, especially since resistance seems to be privileged in the construction of the postcolonial? Or call it neocolonialism when discussing contemporary relations of dependency between the ex-colonial and the former imperial powers? This is not to be facetious. It is merely to ask what the concept "postcolonial," whether used in chronological or epistemological terms, adds to the corpus of world systems theories, variously inspired by Marxist, dependency, and modernization paradigms.

Ahmad (1996) and Arif Dirlik (1996) suggest a more sinister and an unproductive union between postcoloniality and postmodernism. For Ahmad, literary postcoloniality emerged as postmodernism's wedge to colonize literatures from the South, so that "what used to be known as 'Third World Literature' gets rechristened as 'postcolonial literature' when the governing theoretical framework shifts from Third World to postmodernism" (Ahmad, 1996: 276). Repudiated were older and more radical conceptions of postcolonialism used in the 1970s, "with specific reference to the type of postcolonial states that arose in Asia and Africa after postwar decolonization" (Ahmad, 1996: 276). Dirlik is even more vehement calling postcoloniality a "progeny of postmodernism," whose popularity "has less to do with its rigorousness as a concept or with the new vistas it has opened up for critical inquiry than it does with the increased visibility of academic intellectuals of Third World origin as pacesetters in cultural criticism"(Dirlik, 1996: 295). Also, thanks to the changing interests of global capitalism that have penetrated the universities through corporatization, "intellectual orientations that earlier were regarded as marginal or subversive" such as multiculturalism, "have acquired a new respectability"(Dirlik, 1996: 305). Postcoloniality, he concludes, is not simply the condition of a comprador intelligentsia, as suggested by Kwame Anthony Appiah (1998), but "the condition of the intelligentsia of global capitalism" (Dirlik, 1996: 315).

Charges by Ahmad and Dirlik that postcoloniality is the invention of a few privileged migrant Indian and Palestinian intellectuals working in the Western metropoles have not gone unanswered. Stuart Hall (1996), the influential proselytizer of cultural studies whose analyses of race, ethnicity, diaspora, identity, and contemporary politics have extended Marxist and postmodernist frameworks (Morley and Chen, 1996), states that Dirlik's "crude ad hominen and ad feminam name-calling disfigures the argument of a distinguished scholar of modern China...," although he agrees with some of Dirlik's charges that postcoloniality derives its philosophical and theoretical grounding from poststructuralism, and its culturalism tends to disavow economic underpinnings of colonial and contemporary social formations. We will explore the question of the location of the production sites and agents of postcolonial theory later.

Before Ahmad and Dirlik had made their acerbic interventions on the theoretical origins and ideological interpellations of postcoloniality, debate centered on the historical and geographical boundaries of postcoloniality. "When exactly," asks Shohat (1996: 325) "does the postcolonial begin?" We can further ask, when will it end, and where is it to be found? Is it the time "after colonialism" (Prakash,1995) or "postcontact?" (Ashcroft, 1989; Lionnet, 1995). Does postcoloniality describe typological conditions and relations that transcend time? Or is it a discursive tendency for deconstruction? In short, does it refer to a temporal "after" or "going beyond," or to an epistemological reconfiguration that privileges culturalist and antifoundational analysis and narratives? Does it encompass every country that Europe colonized, including the settler colonies, such as the United States, later an imperial power in its own right, or indeed, does it apply to all places that were ever colonized throughout the world? Ania Loomba (1998: 1-7) seems to wonder about such questions by foregrounding her discussion of postcoloniality with a survey of both what she calls precapitalist and capitalist colonialisms, European and non-European empires. How much space and time can postcoloniality really handle before it crumbles under the weight into a meaningless term?

The question of postcoloniality's temporarity and spatiality was articulated forcefully in two often-cited essays by Anne McClintock (1994) and Ella Shohat (1996), both first published in 1992. McClintock argued that while postcolonial theory disavows the binaries of Western historicism, it nonetheless postulates the totalizing binary of colonial-postcolonial and reorients and subordinates the world's diverse histories and cultures to the grand march of a monolithic, undifferentiated colonialism, of European time. It confers "on colonialism the prestige of history proper; colonialism is the determining marker of history" (McClintock, 1994: 255). Inequalities of power and privilege within and among nations, regions, classes, and genders are vaporized before the dazzling glare of a homogenizing postcolonialism, despite the ritual obeisance that is made to difference, hybridity, and multiplicity. Abandoning new empowering visions of the future, "without a renewed will to intervene in the unacceptable, we face being becalmed in an historically empty space in which our sole direction is found by gazing back, spellbound, at the epoch behind us, in a perpetual present marked only as 'post'" (McClintock, 1994: 266). Shohat also criticized postcoloniality for its problematic temporarity, both with reference to the past and the present. On the one hand, she charged, its lack of historical specificity collapses and homogenizes diverse chronologies, cultures, histories, structures, and racial formations, homogenizing Asian and African countries and the settler societies of North America and Australasia, while its connotation of an "after" glossed over the continuing depredations of neo-colonialism and global capitalism.

Subsequent contributions to the debate produced little clarity. Some argued against erasing the differences between the colonial experiences of, to quote an earlier intervention by Arun Mukherjee (1990: 2), a self-described "non-white Canadian", "the First World and Third World....They [postcolonial theorists] should remember that we have not been colonized in the same way. 'Race' has made a tremendous difference in how the empire treated us. And these differences, alas, continue to this day." Conflating the colonialist experiences of the First and Third Worlds, she insisted, "is both trivializing of the Third World and exaggerated regarding the (white) Canadian." Others, however, insisted on including the white Canadians, Australians, and New Zealaders as postcolonials (Slemon, 1996; Ashcroft et al., 1989; During, 1985). Peter Hulme (1995:119) urges postcolonialists to find a place even for the United States, which would, he asserts, "affect the shape and definition of the field." He argues that the misgivings about the role of America in postcolonial studies were misplaced, for the term postcolonial should not be reduced to a badge of merit reserved for poor or powerless postcolonial states, and that the "post" in "postcolonial" has both a temporal and critical dimension, making it applicable to a country like the United States, which was once a colony.

Ahmad and Dirlik soon weighed in. To them, postcoloniality offered a crass conceptualization of periods and authors. But Hall, while critical of the careless homogenizing that the universal usage of the concept "postcolonial" encouraged, contends that it was unhelpful to discriminate the uses of the term either by reserving it exclusively to non-Western colonized societies and denying it to white settler colonies or the colonizing societies of the metropoles. He cautions against the nostalgic wish to "return to a clear-cut politics of binary oppositions, where clear 'lines can be drawn in the sand' between the goodies and the baddies" (Hall, 1996: 244). Postcoloniality, he maintains, breaks the old colonizer-colonized binaries of imperial histories, helps us reread colonization as part of an essentially transnational and transcultural global process, and recenters colonization in the official narratives of the West. Nevertheless, he recognizes that Britain, the United States, Canada, Jamaica, Nigeria, India, and Latin America, or Algerians in Algeria and France, could not be "postcolonial" in the same way. Similarly, writing several years later, Quayson (2000: 10-11) distinguishes between the United States and the West more generally and "real" postcolonial societies. "But this does not mean," Hall (1996: 246) writes, "they are not 'post-colonial' in *any way*" (emphasis Hall). But in what ways are they postcolonial? Their postcoloniality was connected to, he suggests, "a general process of decolonization which, like colonialism itself, has marked the colonizing societies as powerfully as the colonized (of course, in different ways)."

True, but not particularly insightful. Who said the colonies and imperial metropoles and settler submetropoles were not connected, whether during colonial rule, decolonization, or after? It seems to me the question is not so much about whether these societies had and continue to have linkages, but the nature of those linkages, the hierarchies and relations of domination embedded in and reproduced by the linkages. The so-called "old histories" of imperialism, against which some postcolonialists rail and for which they seek to provide an alternative periodization, were not always inscribed with simplistic binaries, oblivious to the differentiations and complexities of place, time, class, race, nationality, ethnicity, and gender. Indeed, according to some critics, the histories of empire inspired by postcolonial theory are often sanitized of economic exploitation and social struggle and tend to consist of facile reconstructions of the colonial moment as an infinite series of cultural, if complex, interactions, or "inter-connections," as Catherine Hall (1996: 70) puts it, devoid of historically structured oppositions and struggles.

The questions about the geographical and historical scales of postcoloniality have been tied to debates about its analytical fields and frameworks. One of the few areas of agreement between friends and foes of postcoloniality concerns its culturalist thrust, which is derived from its poststructuralist underpinnings and disciplinary base in English studies. This has been a source of both its strengths and weaknesses. The proponents and opponents of postcoloniality often tend to make extravagant claims about the theoretical novelty or nonsensicality of postcolonial theory. Loomba offers one of the more measured evaluations of postcoloniality for the study of colonialism as a whole and literacy criticism itself. Postcolonial studies, she argues "intensify and sharpen debates about the social fabric, and make it imperative for us to weave the economic realities of colonialism with all that was hitherto excluded from 'hard' social analysis—sexuality, subjectivity, psychology and language. They remind us that the 'real' relations of society do not exist in isolation from its current or ideological categories." (Loomba, 1998: 37).

Postcoloniality, moreover, expands our analytical vocabulary, so that it "is not just a fancy new term for colonialism; it indicates a new way of thinking in which cultural, intellectual, economic or political processes are seen to work together in the formation, perpetuation and dismantling of colonialism. It seeks to widen the scope of studies of colonialism by examining the intersections of ideas and institutions, knowledge and power" (Loomba, 1998: 54). As for literature, postcolonial criticism encourages the complex reading of texts, including of metropolitan fiction, which is shown to have been deeply imbued with the imperial "structure of attitude and reference," as Said (1993) calls it, and the importance of literary texts as materials for historical study. Loomba notes, however, that "postcolonial literature" tends to be confined "to texts written in various Englishes. Secondly, postcolonial studies are located entirely within English studies, a location that not only seriously circumscribes the scope of the former, but also has serious implications for its methodology" (Loomba, 1998: 96).[5]

This circumscription means some claims of analytical innovation by postcolonial critics hardly come as news to people in other disciplines. As Loomba (1998: 54) herself says concerning the intersections of ideas and institutions, knowledge and power, "such a perception is not entirely new, and was in circulation among nationalist ideologues." Nor is it news to Africanist historians such as Megan Vaughan (1991) and Terence Ranger (1983), whose works on colonial medicine and the invention of tradition, Loomba quotes. Indeed, I would argue that anyone familiar with African intellectual history will know that African historians and other scholars were analyzing the complex and contradictory intersections between colonialism and knowledge, the invention of tradition, reconstruction of identities, the nuances of resistance, the connections between colonialism, literature and language, and the role of images, stereotypes and other representations in textual and nontextual media as part of the matrix of colonialism, in short, they discussed and wrote about the cultural, discursive, or representational dimensions of colonialism long before they had heard about Foucault and Derrida and learnt to speak poststructuralism and postmodernism. That does not mean the insights of postcoloniality are useless or not entirely "new," that is, representing recombinations and unexpected juxtapositions that make the familiar strange. Rather, they have specific disciplinary, locational, and ideological provenance and appeal. This is a call for greater theoretical modesty among literary postcolonialists, more serious engagement with other disciplines, and more caution against imperializing and universalizing tendencies.

In fact, critics from within English studies have become increasingly aware of the limitations of the dominant culturalist postcolonial paradigm. Hall (1996: 258), for example, argues that in reaction against deterministic economism associated with reductionist Marxism, there has been "a massive, gigantic and eloquent disavowal" of the economic by discourses of the "posts," "as if, since the economic in its broadest sense definitively does not, as it was supposed to do, 'determine' the real movement of history 'in the last instance,' it does not exist at all! This is a failure of theorization so profound, and (with very few, still very sketchy, exceptions...) so disabling, that in my view, it has enabled much weaker and less conceptually rich paradigms to continue to flourish and dominate the field." This critique has been taken up by literary critics, such as Neil Lazarus (1999), who maintain fidelity to Marxism, or those such as Quayson (2000), who seek a radical mission for a beloved theory in which they have invested so much.

Lazarus (1999: 9) declares with undisguised concern that "most of the work in the subfields of postcolonial studies and 'colonial discourse theory' (and also, I would say, 'ethnic studies' and 'cultural studies') currently being produced in cutting-edge intellectual circles of Europe and North America seems to me to [be]...paying a huge price for its own premature repudiation of systematic theory," which in his view, is Marxism. "My ambition in this book [*Nationalism and Cultural Practice in the Postcolonial World*]," he proclaims, "is to try to alter the existing balance of forces in the field of postcolonial studies, by way of making the field as a whole accountable to philosophical and political claims, interests, and demands, to which (to its own detriment) it is currently little attuned" (Lazarus, 1999: 10). He seeks to liberate postcoloniality from the theoretical protocols and procedures of the dehistoricizing and depoliticizing "posts" by latching them firmly to materialist, realist, and Marxist analysis, while retaining the genuine insights and advances that have been generated within the field, for example, in its consistent critique of Eurocentricism and patriarchy.

As a literary critic of English studies who is located in the North, Lazarus finds himself agreeing and disagreeing with the uncompromising Marxist criticism of postcoloniality advanced by Ahmad, the India-based critic, and by Dirlik, the U.S.-based historian. The rest of his book provides an extended argument for the possibilities of radical readings of both colonialism and the contemporary world, in its institutional and ideological, structural and cultural forms. It consists of wide-ranging Marxist-inspired discourses on modernity, globalization, the "West," reaffirmations of the historic importance of decolonization and the continuing relevance of nationalism for the future, as well as critiques of misappropriations of Fanon by Bhabha (1989) and Christopher Miller (1990), the contributions and inadequacies of subaltern studies, the life and times of C. L. R. James, focused around the tropes of cricket, modernism, and national culture, and the political and cultural economies of Afropop in the age of global capitalism. It is a fascinating exercise, but much of what he writes is readily found in conventional Marxist-oriented historical, sociological, and political analyses of colonialism and cultural globalization, which makes one wonder whether postcoloniality can remain a distinctive field if it incorporates methods and paradigms from Marxism and other disciplines.

For some postcolonialists the aim is precisely to do that, to have postcoloniality become a truly interdisciplinary field. Quayson (2000) underscores this discursive ambition by devoting a whole chapter to an explication and demonstration of interdisciplinarity. While he makes an interesting distinction between instrumental and synoptic interdisciplinarity, the cases he chooses to exhibit his own interdisciplinarity—cursory glances at Theodor Adorno, Achille Mbembe, and Homi Bhabha—leave him firmly stuck in the conventional culturalist and textualist framework of much postcolonial theorizing. The subsequent discussions on topics ranging from history and historiography, African literature and literary criticism, feminism and modernity to postmodernism and postcolonializing Shakespeare are remarkable more for their eclecticism than for any particular insights on each of these topics or in their combination. This kind of interdisciplinarity, i.e., throwing disparate topics together under the same book covers without an analytical structure that binds and illuminates them, is quite inadequate. As indicated in the previous chapter, interdisciplinarity involves more than an individual's or a field's self-declaration of faith in interdisciplinarity; the proof is in the institutional and intellectual pudding (Wissoker, 2000; Garber, 2001).

Much of the early criticism of postcoloniality centered on its perceived affinities to the antifoundationalism of poststructuralism that, it was claimed, made it ideologically depoliticized or depoliticizing. Some of the most trenchant critiques on this score came from Ahmad, Dirlik and E. San Juan (1998). For Ahmad postcoloniality is part of imperialism's ideological armory to weaken and annul struggles for national liberation, democracy, and socialism. The emphasis on hybridity, contingency, decenteredness, and ambivalence stripped "all cultures of their historicity and density," he writes, "reducing them to those lowest common denominators which then become interchangeable, produces not a universal equality of all cultures but the unified culture of a late imperial marketplace that subordinates cultures, consumers and critics alike to a form of untethering and moral loneliness that wallows in the depthlessness and whimsicality of post-modernism" (Ahmad, 1996: 290).

By rejecting the so-called master narratives, including the foundational role of capitalism in history, Dirlik (1996: 315) declares, and dismissing the Third World while remaining obsessed with Eurocentricism, in short, "in their simultaneous repudiation of structure and affirmation of the local in problems of oppression and liberation, [postcolonial critics] have mystified the ways in which totalizing structures persist in the midst of apparent disintegration and fluidity" (Dirlik, 1996: 315). "To put it bluntly," he proclaims, "postcoloniality is designed to avoid making sense of the current crisis and, in the process, to cover up for the origins of postcolonial intellectuals in a global capitalism of which they are not so much victims as beneficiaries" (Dirlik, 1996: 313).

Postcolonial theory, E. San Juan (1998: 9-10) maintains, was culpable of what it claimed to repudiate: mystification, moralism, idealism, and reification, which enabled it to mask "its counterrevolutionary telos by denying its own worldly interests and genealogy. It occludes its own historical determinacy by deploying psychoanalytical and linguistic conceptual frameworks that take market/exchange relations for granted." Postcoloniality reproduced and resonated with, in short, the triumphalist geopolitical and globalization demands of the post-cold war Western metropoles. Its language games of positionalities, articulated through the idioms of hybridity, indeterminancy, multiplicity, and fragmentation, provided ideological registers and celebrations of consumerism and cultural imperialism in that they replicated, not repudiated, the cultural claims and production scheme of flexible, post-Fordist capitalism.

These blanket critiques are not entirely fair, for of course not all postcolonialists are antifoundationalists. The postfoundationalists or nonfoundationalists, such as Satya Mohanty (1997), believe in the possibilities of realist knowledges that can support progressive politics. Said's critical studies of imperialism and support for the national liberation of Palestine are well known. Postcolonial Marxists like Lazarus (1994, 1999) constantly re-affirm the emancipatory potential of the anti-imperialist nationalisms of the South, a position expressed with defiant conviction in Benita Parry's (1994) "two cheers for nativism." The fact still remains, however, that this is not the dominant trend in postcolonial studies, where the tendency has been to deride nationalism, to distrust large-scale resistance and valorize local resistance, or even to emphasize, as Spivak (1988b) did in her famous essay on the subaltern, that the subaltern cannot speak because her voice cannot be recovered and represented by intellectuals, a position that was widely challenged (Parry, 1987; Busia, 1989-90; Mani, 1992). There is no question that these doubts and debates, and especially the work of the subaltern studies group in India, have enriched our understanding of the complexities of resistance (Cooper, 1994), but local resistances have, in the end, to be placed in the larger context of resistance movements against colonialism or global capitalism, if they are not to be reduced to picturesque gyrations of local agency that are glibly celebrated or condemned.

Compared with their Indian counterparts, "cosmopolitan" African scholars tend to be less dismissive of nationalism, because of Africa's special position as the ultimate negative other of Europe, borne out of the Atlantic Slave Trade, which demands constant discursive redress. Also, African nationalisms were articulated at national, regional, and international levels through pan-Africanism and Pan-Arabism, and often involved protracted armed liberation struggles, which meant that the nationalist imaginary was not chained to the performance of one particular territory or the interests of the elites, so that hope could always be transferred from one failed country to another or into the possibilities of the masses being mobilized again as they had been during the liberation struggles. Indeed, the very failures of decolonization, which have been recorded with such a deep sense of anger and betrayal by African writers, were blamed less on the nationalist agenda itself than on the unwillingness or inability of the political class to implement it, abetted by international conditions and inequities. So when they come to the United States, their presence and politics are mediated by the historic African American diaspora with its long histories of nationalist struggle and Pan-African longings and solidarities, which helps temper both their infatuation with the West and the seductions of depoliticizing cultural alienation (Zeleza, 1994b).

The struggle to find a progressive politics and praxis for postcoloniality remains pressing. Writing in 2000, Quayson (2000: 8), who is keen for a radical and politicized postcolonialism, notes with evident distress: "postcolonial theory and criticism have increasingly become riven by a contradiction: The social referents in the postcolonial world call for urgent and clear solutions, but because speaking positions in a postmodernist world are thought to be always already immanently contaminated by being part of a compromised world, postcolonial critics often resort to a sophisticated form of rhetoric whose main aim seems to be to rivet attention permanently on the warps and loops of discourse....What should," he ponders with anguish, "the ultimate objectives of a responsible postcolonial discourse be? ...What, to put it bluntly and even simplistically, do academic postcolonial studies contribute to the experience of postcolonialism in the world today?" For many critics, the progressive possibilities of postcolonialism will remain limited so long as the field is tied to indiscriminate poststructuralist and postmodernist repudiations of "foundations," in which national liberation and other collective social struggles and visions are dismissed as totalizing and essentializing terrors of the Enlightenment project or its bourgeois nationalist offshoots in the South.

What, then, are the chances of postcoloniality getting a divorce from the disabling "posts?" As we saw with Lazarus, some think it possible, indeed, they have been working hard to bring materialist analysis and radical politics to postcolonial studies. Others, however, stress the limits of such efforts because of the very spatial and institutional location of postcolonial theory in the Anglo-American academy. As noted earlier, Ahmad and Dirlik attribute the rise of postcolonial theory to the arrival of "Third World" intellectuals in Western academies. In their scathing critique, postcoloniality offered a few privileged migrant Southern scholars entry into the Western academy, cheered on by their reactionary postmodernist associates. Anxious to carve out space in the crowded academic market and to leave behind the liabilities of Third World anti-imperialist radicalism, they feign collective amnesia and reduce history to contingent moments and cultural confrontations into intercultural conversations that generate ever-mutating hybridities.

The debate on the location of the producers and the production of postcolonial theory was fueled by Shohat, who located the rise of postcolonial theory and what she regarded as its ahistorical and universalizing deployment and depoliticizing implications in the contexts of North American, especially U.S. curricular and cultural battles. "The 'postcolonial' is privileged," she writes, "precisely because it seems safely distant from 'the belly of the beast', the United States" (Shohat, 1996: 329). Ahmad and Dirlik, then, picked up the gauntlet. They were joined by others, as will be shown in the next section, including most recently Spivak (1999) herself, who sees the postcolonial critic as an informant in the service of neocolonialism and contemporary global capitalism. At this juncture it will suffice to mention a few critiques of the institutional locations and politics of postcoloniality.

Leela Gandhi (1998: 141-2) has argued that in so far as postcolonial literature is privileged in postcolonial studies, where the colonial encounter is seen "primarily as a textual contest, or a bibliographic battle, between oppressive and subversive books," in the end such privileging works, "if accidentally, to privilege the role and function of the postcolonial literary critic—whose academic expertise suddenly provides the key to all oppositional and anti-colonial meanings." Located primarily in Northern metropolitan institutions and convinced of the centrality of European colonialism and the impossibility of cultural alterity after the epistemic violence of imperialism, the postcolonial intellectuals are obsessed with speaking to the West. Therefore, according to Ming-yan Lai (1998), they end up marginalizing the counter-hegemonic voices of intellectuals who are located outside the discursive and political preoccupations of the Northern metropoles, either because they are focused on power relations and politics in the postindependence nation-state, or because they were subjugated under non-European colonialism as in the case of East Asia, where Japan was the colonial power. As will be demonstrated in the next section, these charges have been greeted either with feigned silence, self-righteous anger, or liberal defenses of the universality of knowledge, according to which it does not matter where and by whom ideas are produced, as long as they are good ideas, or progressive ideas.

Let me conclude this section by noting that postcoloniality is undoubtedly a house of many mansions, that its diffuseness makes it difficult to define or to critique. Nevertheless, it is a striking fact that, typically, programmatic exegesis of postcolonial theory usually begin by telling readers how difficult it is indeed to define what the term means, or that there are many conflicting definitions, but as they proceed the postcolonial assumes a more concrete reality, referring to a particular discourse, time, world, and even a mode of subjectivity and resistance. This is to suggest that, all too often, the term "postcolonial" is used in chronological, epistemological, and concrete senses even among authors who claim otherwise. They usually discuss the experiences associated with colonialism and its present effects for both the imperial powers and the ex-colonial societies. Postcoloniality longs to be a theory of colonial and postcolonial social formations, of concrete historical processes, as well as an ideological interrogation of texts, images, and discourses.

Thus, as with postmodernism, there is a tension, a creative one in deft hands, between the temporal and typological tendencies, and the spatial and social scales of postcoloniality. Maintaining the balance between the descriptive and critical inflections, and the analytical and political agendas, is not easy for any theory, and some postcolonial scholars, unable to walk the tightrope, trip badly. As a historian and a student of development, I am struck by how uninformative the writings of literary postcolonial authors are on colonial and postcolonial societies. As will be demonstrated in a later section, to many historians the utility of post-colonial theory and the other "posts" for rigorous historical research and reconstruction is quite limited indeed, especially given its fondness for postmodernist irony, pastiche, indeterminacy and aporia and distaste for structure, collectivities, and agency. Its analytical insights are restricted the further one moves from literary studies. It has little to say about the large questions that face the world, from the environment and disease epidemics to globalization and democratization, that goes beyond the explanatory power of existing paradigms. These phenomena require structurally and historically informed paradigms, not the fragmentary and frugal discursive and textual readings of postcolonial theory. Applied to them, we usually get simplifications or banalities.

Some even contend, as Lawrence Grossberg (1996: 169) does, that even on questions it has made its own, postcolonial theory may have reached the limit "of theorizing political struggles organized around notions, however complex, of identity and difference. Politics of identity is synecdochal, taking the part (of the individual) to be representative of the whole (the social group defined by a common identity). Such a logic not only too easily equates political and cultural identities, it makes politics into a matter of representation (or its absence). Moreover the only political strategies open to it are deconstruction, strategic essentialism and an unfocused alliance." This is of course quite debatable. There are some postcolonial critics, or critics inspired by postcolonial theory, who are producing criticism that eschews the narrow preoccupations that Grossberg complains about, and who engage the larger questions of nation and nationalism. A good example of this is Suvir Kaul's (2000) study that "imperializes" eighteenth century British poetry. He shows that this poetry constituted a kind of national chorus for the emergent imperial British nation, that empire was central to the poetic imagination that, in turn, sought to provide the imperial project with literary, cultural, and iconic capital and with constructions of appropriate historical genealogies and hyperbolic visions of the future. What makes his study so compelling is its ability to weave materialist and literary analysis, to combine the cultural and historical referents and stylistic and formal properties and practices of poetry, and to present all this in lucid and imaginative prose, free of the jargon we have come to expect from postcolonial and postmodern writers. This study shows that the domesticated literatures of the imperial nations can still be reread profitably as narratives of empire.

If Kaul interrogates imperialism as the dominant material reality and textual rhetoric of the eighteenth century British nation, Adlai Murdoch (2001) and Lazarus (1990) investigate the dominant identitarian and ideological products and proclamations of difference and independence in Caribbean and Africa, respectively, while Carole Boyce Davies (1994) interposes the dynamics and demands of gender in the discursive terrains of colonialism and postcolonialism. These authors—Murdoch's dense treatise on the discourses of créolité and creliolization in the French Caribbean novel, Lazarus's informed critique of nation and nationalism in African fiction, and Davies's impassioned celebration of women's subjectivities and resistances in the Pan-African world—show the possibilities of literary theorization and explication tied to the dominant imaginaries and realities of the worlds of their chosen authors. The critical power in these studies derives from what literary scholars do best; close textual reading, combined in this case with complex understandings of the historical and cultural contexts of both the production of the texts themselves and the critical practice itself.

When, however, the aim is the facile "postcolonializing" of canonical texts, as Quayson (2000) tries to do in a shaky chapter on Shakespeare, where he mostly recounts familiar interpretations of how we can read race, othering, and imperialism through the bard (Loomba and Orkin, 1998), what we get are institutional political gestures of an ex-colonial gazing back to reaffirm the imperial canon, for while he makes numerous references to contemporary liberal and right-wing ideologies in the North, his native Africa is largely ignored as a discursive or political presence. I am reminded of Said's *Culture and Imperialism*, which promises contrapuntal reading of metropolitan canonical and "Third World" texts, but only ends up reconfirming the eternal superiority and status of the former even in the generation of one of the South's most treasured moments—anticolonial nationalism (Zeleza, 1994c). This underscores the fact that like any theory, postcoloniality inspires good and bad work, sometimes even for the same person. I have found some postcolonial criticism quite enlightening, but there is also a lot of drivel in which, aside from the infusion of eclectic historical and sociological facts, the use of self-consciously "theoretical" language, and clever if flighty comparisons of different periods and genres, the literary analysis of the texts themselves rarely goes beyond what I learnt in literature classes in the 1970s before the term postcolonial had abandoned its chronological meaning and historical-materialist references to "neocolonial" dependency and acquired its current semiotic and discursive conceits.[6]

Many of the issues raised by postcolonial re-readings of the old canonical texts, or the new texts from the South striving for scholarly legitimation, are useful but also quite familiar to social and cultural historians and historical sociologists. The practice of rewriting old social texts from contemporary concerns is of course characteristic of the historian's craft. Postcolonial literary critics, then, may simply be doing what some historians have been trying to do for decades, rewriting the past to address current questions, deconstructing and provincializing European knowledges, and expanding the boundaries and vocabularies of scholarship. In this sense, postcoloniality serves as a wedge for institutional entry for texts and literatures, scholars and sensibilities, interpretations and ideologies previously excluded from the metropolitan academy. That in itself is a positive thing, but some of the proselytizers of postcoloniality often claim much more than this; that they are dismantling Eurocentricism and the Enlightenment, as if they are the first to try it, and many of them do so with limited analytical rigor, despite their obsession with theoretical rigor, without adequately understanding the structural conditions and contexts that shape the past and the contemporary worlds they seek to analyze, and without reflecting on the formation of their own intellectual practice, on why postcoloniality has been domesticated in the Anglo-American academy with such relative ease.

Production of the 'Posts'

There is no doubt that the "posts" predominate in Northern academies and in the cultural disciplines—the humanities and the "soft" social sciences. The development of the "posts" in American universities is conditioned by intellectual, institutional, and ideological contexts in those academies that, in turn, reflect larger societal transformations. The growing distance of academics from civics, articulated in waning interest in transformative theories of society—postmodernism's so-called grand narratives—coincided with the crisis of legitimation in the wider political economy following the calamities of Vietnam and Watergate, the growth of struggles for civil rights, women's rights, and gay rights; and the proliferation of identity politics. This growing distance reflected both the loss of faith in, and fear of, profound social transformation. These crises and struggles, which were reflected on college campuses, where the so-called culture wars broke out, consumed the energies of many academics and reinforced their preoccupation with syllabuses rather than society, canons rather than class, discursive communities rather than democratic claims, and conditions of campus life rather than of community life. The "posts" captured and carried this moment forward (Bender, 1997).

Differences in national politics and university cultures in Britain and in the United States, Jonathan Culler (1988) argues, accounts for some of the differences in the academic popularity and institutionalization of postmodernism. Postmodernism has found greater succor in the United States, because with its vast capitalist university system, greater professionalization, all driven by competitive pressures for tenure for individual faculty and national rankings for departments, American scholars face enormous pressures to produce "theory", to claim theoretical and analytical novelty. This academic culture breeds channel surfing intellectualism and mass production, where theoretical claims and products are critical screening mechanisms for access to jobs, status, salaries, grants, students, and other resources.

This is particularly pressing for the cultural or literary disciplines. Relegated to the bottom of the intellectual totem pole dominated by the natural sciences, these disciplines have been suffering from disciplinary anxiety and envy for a long time; hence, their readiness to borrow theories and texts indiscriminately from diverse sources and to embrace the "posts." On the one hand, this represents a healthy attempt to transgress disciplinary boundaries, i.e., gestures towards interdisciplinarity, but on the other hand, the fetish for "theory" smacks of a desperate search for rigorism, to give the literary disciplines the gloss of theoretical and scientific complexity, to make them more abstract, more exclusive, less familiar, less accessible. This parallels the equally frantic searches by the aspiring queens of the social sciences—economics and political science—for the scientific status of the natural sciences. Postmodernism is for the cultural disciplines, with their increasingly convoluted and difficult vocabulary and their textualization of social life, what rational choice is for political science and mathematical language is for economics, a declaration of disinterested rigor befitting a professionalized and self-referential intelligentsia (Lindblom, 1997; Smith, 1997).

Postmodernism serves a larger function in the age-old struggle for intellectual capital, institutional power, knowledge production, political networks, and even moral supremacy between what Steven Ward (1995) calls the literary and scientific fields that divide academia, a division that has become wider and more vicious as resources for universities diminish and as pressures for the capitalist reorganization and corporatization of universities intensify. For the literary fields postmodernism is a powerful symbolic weapon to weaken and overturn the hegemonic sciences, as well as an organizational myth to fortify their own epistemic boundaries, regulate an internal normative order, and strengthen the sense of group identity and affiliation among their historically and institutionally aggrieved members. While postmodernism disavows the possibilities, let alone the desirability, of foundational or realist truth claims, it makes its own truth claims by proclaiming that the road to knowledge begins with the study of language and representation. All knowledge, including scientific knowledge, is declared to be textual, an assertion intended to bring down realist epistemology and its practical form, scientific methodology, upon whose pedestals the epistemic privilege of modern science rests.

The postmodernists take critiques of linear and realist models of scientific knowledge formation first articulated in the philosophy of science

(Kuhn, 1962) to the conclusion they desire, namely, that if science is a social and textual enterprise, subject to the indeterminate demands of language and interpretation, then rhetorical and cultural ways of knowing supplant empirical and rational ways of knowing. Culture and texts, the domain of the humanities, replace nature and experiments as the source of intellectual authority in the perennial battle for internal resources and external allies. Despite the proliferation of postmodernist sociologies and anthropologies of science (Aronowitz, 1988; Myers, 1990; Franklin, 1995; Fujimura, 1998, 1999), to which scientists have recently began to respond or ridicule, especially following the "Sokal hoax" perpetrated on *Social Text* (Gross and Levitt, 1994; Sokal, 1996a, 1996b, 2000; Barad, 1996; Labinger, 1997; Koertge, 1998), as sometimes happens among embattled groups fighting against stronger foes, much of the epistemological struggle has not been between the sciences and the literary disciplines, but conflicting groups in the latter camp. The divisions are particularly evident in anthropology and sociology, between the "quantitativists" and "qualitativists," the statisticians and the storytellers, as the former aspire to become more like scientists and the latter more like novelists.

Not surprisingly, then, the "posts" have proved most challenging and attractive to the literary disciplines anxious to burnish their theoretical credentials and desperately in search of new paradigms, such as cultural anthropology, qualitative sociology, and English. Besides their collective contestation with the sciences, these disciplines have, for several reasons and to varying degrees, witnessed the crumbling of their foundational projects. Needless to say, their encounters with the "posts" vary in so far as their pre-theoretical commitments, structuring the conditions of engagement with new theoretical paradigms, are different. Pretheoretical commitments are the unquestioned assumptions that establish pragmatic and programmatic foundations for any discipline, establish discursive limits on the range of theoretical propositions that characterize a discourse, and specify the range of new or external insights and critiques that can be appropriated without dismantling the field entirely (Jinks, 1997). Differences in pretheoretical commitments might also explain the resistance or receptivity to the "posts" among different scholarly or "discourse communities," as Paul Prior (1998) calls them.

Beginning with the 1960s, anthropology was assailed by attacks against many of its core assumptions: objectivity, cultural homogeneity, fact, truth, otherness, and science as an apolitical enterprise (Fischer, 1999; Greenfiled,

2000). Internal and external critiques, inspired variously by Third World, black, feminist, and postmodern scholars charged that objectivity was a myth, that the cultures of the ethnographer were not unitary wholes, that anthropological representations were interpretations not facts, that knowledge was socially constructed not revealed truth, that knowing the "other" is impossible because there is no such thing as an objective perspective and the "other" has his or her own unique perspective, and that the disciplines are political and deployed in the administration of power, more so for a discipline that was so intimately implicated with colonialism as anthropology. Even the "field," or "fieldwork," the methodological trademark of the discipline, came under increasing critique, for its spatialization of difference, the contrived separation between the "field" and "home," and the hierarchization of field sites based on their alleged purity of difference from "home" (Gupta and Ferguson, 1997).

Some anthropologist sank into self-flagellation and moved away from empirical research and making generalizations altogether. Others seized the moment with alacrity and sought to discard anthropology's conceptual, methodological, and representational tool kit, including the critical notion of culture itself, seen by some as hegemonic, elitist, and oppressive (Abu-Lughold, 1993). They celebrated the intoxicating liberties of recording multiple realities and voices, avoiding judgments and comparisons, making personal and subjective interpretations, honing their rhetorical skills and creative literary styles. Many experimented with new forms of ethnographic writing, which includes among other forms, ethnographic fiction, nonlinear texts, self-indulgent texts focused on the author, or texts engaging the ethnographer and the subject. Out of the reconfiguration of anthropological objects, subjects, methods, languages, and writing styles, the highpriests of postmodern anthropology hoped, a humane anthropology would blossom, one that would liberate human consciousness, lead to new forms of human understanding, transcendence, and self-transformation (Shweder, 1984, 1991; Clifford and Marcus, 1986; Rosaldo, 1989; Trouillot, 1991).

Postmodern anthropologists sought solace in self-referential reflexivity. They also began doing more research at home, either in communities of domestic "others"—the poor, disadvantaged, and ethnic minorities—or in "studying up" the powerful and dominant (Austin-Broos, 1998; Ortner, 1999). The production of anthropologies of prestigious fields such as science, referred to above, or medicine (Kleinman, 1995; Hann, 1995; Brown,

1998; Gaines, 1998; Joralemon, 1999; Laurie, 2000) also increased. Still largely avoided were ordinary middle class communities, to which most anthropologists belonged, a lingering homage to the ideal of detached objectivity rooted in anthropology's conviction that one cannot be objective about one's own society. The critics, many from the discipline itself, were appalled by the rhetorical excess of postmodern anthropology, its mystical and romantic aspirations, shaky logical, political, and moral grounds, retreat from society, empiricism, and the idea of reality in favor of the textualist preoccupations favored by cultural studies, increasingly the domain of studies of culture (Gellner, 1992; Reyna, 1994; Kuper, 1994; Ahmad and Shore, 1995; Moore, 1996; Peace, 1998). Charles Lindholm (1997), a particularly unsympathetic critic, is scornful of postmodern anthropology's valorization of the Enlightenment values of creativity and freedom, the very Enlightenment it wished to bury. He saw the celebration of expressive subjectivity and individuals' ability to manufacture their own identities as a marker of intellectual entrepreneurship among those eager to claim theoretical novelty and a reflection of general anomic anxieties and cravings for choice engendered by an unbridled capitalist consumer culture; a carnival of flight and forgetting as the real world burned with ever more structural inequalities, hierarchies, and conflicts.

Thus, postmodernism, whether seen as a description of the real world, a theoretical trend, or both, and whether considered as a progressive or retrogressive force, a harbinger of new forms of social and political engagement or a descent into solipsism and irrelevance, has been both a source of, and a response to, anthropology's decentering, the discipline's crises of representation and relevance. The reflexive turn in anthropology threatened to turn into naval gazing; introspection replaced empirical research, and the anthropology of anthropology assumed analytical supremacy. Inquiring into the very nature of anthropology had its limits however: in its pretheoretical commitment to the ethnographic method, anthropology still had to be done and taught, its role as an "interpretive community" remained, and its aspirations were for more authentic and theoretically informed representations, not for the abandonment of "representation" altogether (Jinks, 1997).

Postmodernism has also been divisive for sociology although it has not had the same devastating impact as in anthropology. This has partly to do with the different foundational and locational projects of the two fields. For one thing, sociology was founded to probe and prescribe the Western social self, not the non-Western other as was the case with anthropology. In sociology postmodernism was facilitated by, and reinforced, the quantitative-qualitative rift and the divide between builders of universal sociological theory and contingent social theory. Many proponents of qualitative research and social theory increasingly found succor in the "posts." According to Seidman (1994b, 1994c), one of the leading postmodern sociologists, sociological theory is a foundational and totalizing discourse whose disputes are increasingly self-referential and epistemological. Its scientific aspirations have undermined its role as an important medium of public education and advocacy. It is produced and consumed almost exclusively by the theorists themselves and has little bearing on major public debates, social conflicts, or political struggles.

With its epistemic doubt, pluralism, and contingent social narratives, Seidman argues, postmodernism offers sociology a way out of its foundational morass and misguided quest for a totalizing general theory to become more pragmatic, democratic, and publicly engaged. The social narratives of postmodern sociology should be contextual, complex, and committed; tell stories with clear temporal and spatial boundaries, stories about social development and crisis, whose efficacy is judged pragmatically on the basis of the impact of the events being narrativized on local traditions, values, and practices. Laurel Richardson (1991a, 1991b) believes story telling as a way of knowing welcomes diverse voices, those of the powerful—the scientists and scholars—as well as those of the "textually disenfranchised" (Richardson: 1991a: 36). It will allow sociologists, Denzin (1991) and Ellis (1991) contend, to get much closer to the raw, lived experiences and emotions of their subjects.

For postmodern sociologists, then, narrative and reflexivity offer innovative ways of writing sociology, of personalizing and pluralizing the authority of sociological discourse, opening up new spaces of analysis and interpretation between the traditional sociological categories and the autobiographical, and constructing a more critical rhetoric and more empowering representations, thereby liberating sociology from its sterile scientific disciplinarity and reinvigorating it with the ancient function of social thought as a moral and political practice (Bauman, 1994; Brown, 1994; Lemert, 1994; Clough, 1996). Postmodernism might even enable sociology to correct its genetic fallacy—the suppression of subjective expression, the myth of progress, and the separation of ethics and economics, which were noted by some of the founders—and reopen its closed canon to new possibilities (Siemens, 1995a).

259

As in anthropology, postmodern sociologists are often criticized by their fellow sociologists. For example, Diekema et al (1996) argues that while a critical, reflexive, and suspicious attitude toward sociological analyses is healthy, an antisytematic, event-based, local and particularistic epistemology is not justified. Sociology, he declares boldly, is more than telling stories that empathize with individual lives, their emotions and experiences, and using the language of the very people being studied. Rather, it is an enterprise that examines the experiences of people in interaction, of social transactions using concepts of a third-party standpoint that must inevitably transcend the symbols and personal languages of those studied. Ironically, he observes, in their own research many of the postmodern sociologists not only incorporate generic principles but even attempt to formulate some as Denzin (1989) does for alcoholism. It has been noted that postmodern sociologists like Seidman tend to focus on American social science almost to the neglect of developments within worldwide sociology that would contradict or challenge many of their critiques and propositions (Turner, 1996). Other critics stress that classical sociology either anticipated many of the tendencies associated with postmodernism (Kando, 1996), or that it can accommodate them without much difficulty (Kahn, 1999). Thus, beneath the veneer of theoretical innovation, there is little in postmodern sociology that is really new or incompatible with conventional social science methods and purposes. In short, despite claims about their writing styles, objects of study, and analytical perspectives, there is not much that distinguishes the postmodernists in their actual methods of social-scientific research.

It is perhaps in English studies, where texts are the quintessential objects of study, that the "posts" found their most auspicious home.[7] Ironically, as the literary increasingly became the object of desire for cultural disciplines like anthropology and sociology, the cultural became more seductive for English, the domain of the literary. The shift from the literary to the cultural, whether attributed to the social revolts of the 1960s (Bérubé , 1998), or to the rise of "theory" (Easthope, 1991), provoked intense disciplinary excitement and anxiety in English studies. To the defenders of the literary and aesthetic, English was losing its raison d'etre (Cain, 1996; Levine, 1994; Posnock, 1996); while to those who advocated the incorporation of the concerns of cultural studies—inquiring into the production, consumption, and social effectivity of literary and nonliterary texts—English was acquiring new cultural authority, ensuring its survival indeed, regaining its role as the queen of the humanities (Simpson, 1995). The aesthetic itself was of course critically interrogated; questions raised about the autonomy of aesthetic value in works of art, the articulation of aesthetic value with economic use value, the ideological interpellation of aesthetic value, and the history of aesthetic discourse. The dominant critical view increasingly dismissed the aesthetic as an ideology, an affirmation of hegemonic values. The determination of aesthetic value, it was argued, is contingent and utilitarian (Smith, 1988; Kappeler, 1986). Even if true that does not mean the aesthetic does not exist, nor can art objects—which embody both commodity and symbolic properties—simply be reduced to their exchange value.

These debates, often inflamed by ideological and intergenerational conflicts, were fueled by the explosion of the field and contraction of the market, itself a reflection, as John Guillory (1994) has argued so powerfully, of the decline of the humanities in general as cultural capital for the rising managerial-professional class, who do not require the same linguistic capital of the old bourgeoisie to mark and to maintain their newly acquired privileges. Armed with, or in need of, new sociolects, literature matters less than composition to this new class and its aspiring members on campuses. Ironically, as literature became increasingly irrelevant, literary theory assumed greater currency. Theory, specifically in its deconstructionist mold,[8] as a method of rhetorical reading and extending the properties of literariness to nonliterary (primarily philosophical) texts, became central to graduate training, supplementing and sometimes even supplanting the literary syllabus itself, in a relentless pursuit for rigor, for new technical procedure, a practice that reproduced the increasingly techno-bureaucratic restructuring of the university and the technical predilections of the new managerial-professional class.

The intensity of the canon wars in American universities, Guillory argues, were less about canon formation itself, which as an imaginary totality of texts is a continuous process, and more a reflection of the fact that the university, a critical institution of social reproduction, was the last redoubt of the political culture of liberalism. In fact, the opposing sides in this imaginary politics, i.e., the politics of images, are mutually constitutive, for both fall within the normative principles of American political culture in which politics is perceived and performed in terms of pluralism. While Guillory tends to exaggerate the demise of English and its discriminating and credentializing functions, his suggestion that there is more to the crisis of English and the humanities in general than the contents of their curricula is well taken.

The complex, sometimes contradictory, and often-contested shift from literature to culture spawned such internal heterogeneity within English that the discipline came to emblematize the crisis of the humanities and assumed the license to speak for them. The cultural turn of a preeminently literary field ensured that English would be at the center of both the literary and cultural debates, the so-called culture wars of the right-wing defenders of the canon (Bloom, 1994), and anguish about the political relevance of literary study and the public role of literary scholars among the proponents of critical tolerance (Fish, 1995). To some in the neighboring disciplines this was a mark of English's interdisciplinary flexibility to be emulated and to others a sign of intellectual fuzziness to be ridiculed (Solomon and Soloman, 1993).

The shift from the literary to the cultural, which was facilitated and reinforced by the growing influence of the "posts" in the 1980s and 1990s, was presaged by the successes and failures of the New Criticism of the 1930s and 1940s. This movement shifted the subject matter of literary studies from language to literature, changed the required skills from historical scholarship to literary criticism, and put emphasis on the elucidation of literary techniques rather than on the evaluation of texts according to some extrinsic set of measures, as part of a drive for professional consolidation and efforts to differentiate English from the neighboring disciplines. The valorization of "close reading" and the "difficulty" of literary texts that the New Critics insisted upon not only affirmed the university as an exclusive site for the consumption of high cultural artifacts but sharpened the distinction between the latter and mass cultural artifacts and their relative values as cultural capital (Graff, 1987; Guillory, 1994). Stripped of extrinsic or extraneous contextual and conceptual baggage, literature wallowed in the magnificence of its literariness.

This apparent literary self-referentiality did not last however, aside from anticipating the linguistic turn and fetishization of rigor or theory in recent times. In subsequent decades, as the field grew more self-confident and diverse, it absorbed an expanding number of critical theories derived from other disciplines (Gallagher, 1997; Berlant, 1991). English was able to traverse different disciplines partly because it provided services in the form of writing skills to students from a wide range of disciplines. It was also regarded as a critical repository of liberal education and values, and it benefitted from "the textualization of the world. As more and more objects of inquiry were said to be 'discursively constructed', the more sense it made for an expanding panorama of objects to be studied by specialists in discourse" (Hollinger, 1997: 346). As the term text expanded beyond references to conventional literary texts, the analytical skills of literary scholars were regarded as applicable to all cultural phenomena, and English departments increasingly assumed the teaching of texts and authors abandoned by other disciplines. As "one could not read Sartre in the philosophy department, Freud in the psychology department, or Luckacs in the political science department, one read them in literature departments" (Gallagher, 1997: 141). This promiscuity produced the widely publicized embarrassment of *Social Text* in 1996 (referred to earlier) when the journal published an article by a physicist parodying the literary theorist's analysis of physical theory.

By the late 1960s, intellectual boredom, critical pluralism, and eclectic theoretical borrowings, reinforced by the changing composition of student and faculty bodies and growing politicization of campuses, were beginning to erode the foundational ideas of the discipline, those of the literary, the objective status of the text, and the nature of literary language. This generated bitter intradisciplinary wars, fought in the name of "mindless theory" (Christian, 1996) and "disdainful rhetorical exchanges" (Goodheart, 1997), which encouraged the importation of terms of combat from other disciplines and discourses, as well as, in some cases, secession to and supersession by cultural studies and what some call intercultural studies (Saldìvar, 1997; During, 1993; Nelson and Gaonkar, 1996). The discipline's loss of disciplinary boundaries and consensus made it especially attractive to the antifoundational, adversarial, and deconstructive methods and rhetoric of the "posts," as well as an appealing point of entry for literatures and literary scholars from the South translocated to the North. The result for English and literary studies was both fragmentation and imperiousness, which resonated with the poststructuralist ambitions and inflections of the "posts." The New Criticism's reification of the text was carried to its logical conclusion: The author was dead, social and historical contexts were defunct, human agency was over. Only the text itself remained, now pluralized to refer to all human "performative" acts and representations (Abrams, 1997).

The foundational challenge to English also came from literatures of the ex-colonial and non-English worlds, which were clamoring for incorporation into the racialized and nationalized canons of English departments in Britain and in the United States. The new literatures in English, variously referred to as "world literature," "Third World literature," or "postcolonial literature," were also seen as opportunities for what Michael Bérubé (1998: 30-35) calls disciplinary "modernization," making English studies more cosmopolitan, more contemporary, and more cultural. Bérubé tells us that when his English Department at the University of Illinois was rewriting its by-laws the most contentious discussions focused on "literatures in English," that is, "postcolonial literatures" and "cultural studies." In the end, the revised bylaws incorporated both fields, a recognition that neither could be wished away, and that in fact they offered the department new possibilities to make literary study more cultural, and cultural study more literary, and both more complex and more global.

Clearly, to many in English departments cultural studies and postcolonial studies offered opportunities to attract new students, harness new theoretical energies, and for public advocacy and relevance in post-cold war economies, both real and rhetorical, that emphasize globalization and multiculturalism in response to the changing demographic dynamics on campuses and developmental demands in the world system. In other words, despite the shrinking job market for English, cultural studies and postcolonial studies have a marketable value. The academic marketability of postcoloniality became apparent to me when the Center for African Studies at the University of Illinois finally convinced the English department to hire an Africanist in 1996, almost three decades after Africanist historians had been hired. We did so through the rubric of postcolonial literature. Since then more postcolonial specialists, with varying degrees of African interests, have been hired. Anecdotal evidence suggests that this has happened at other institutions as well. Previously students were more likely to encounter Chinua Achebe's (1958) novel, *Things Fall Apart*, in courses in anthropology, sociology, history, and political science than in English, where it was read for its ethnographic and ideological insights not for its aesthetics. Postcoloniality has brought Achebe to more English departments where however, he is read much in the same way he has been read in the other social science and humanities disciplines whose culturalist preoccupations English has increasingly adopted.

Thus, the production and politics of postcolonial theory are tied to institutional dynamics and demands in Northern academies. In the American academy, the postcolonial represents an appropriation and reinvention of texts once considered in Britain and elsewhere under the rubrics of "Commonwealth Literature," "New Literatures in English," and "World Literature in English" (Walder, 1998: 56-83; Madsen, 1999b: 1-13). Once repackaged and popularized, many rushed to find a place in the glittering postcolonial literary kingdom, including the literatures of the old white Dominions—Australia, New Zealand, and Canada—as the sun set on Commonwealth literature on the grounds that the settler site was the space where the colonizing and colonized impulses, relations, and negotiations of imperialism were played out in all their complexities and ambivalences (Hulme, 1994; Lawson, 1995; Slemon, 1996).[9] So the literatures from Africa, Asia, and the European settler societies, all those cultures affected by imperialism from the moment of colonization to the present, were increasingly and indiscriminately embraced in the emerging postcolonial literary canon (Ashcroft et al., 1989; Thieme, 1996). Usually excluded was American literature, not to mention the literatures in the indigenous languages of Africa and Asia, or the literatures of Latin America.[10] To be sure, as we saw earlier with reference to Hulme's (1995) argument about the globality of postcoloniality, there have been efforts to consider the United States postcolonial, which further impoverishes the term of its already threadbare analytical and political meaning. More often than not, however, it is American minority literatures that are incorporated into the postcolonial paradigm (Juneja, 1995; Piper, 1999; Madsen, 1999a), thus lending credence to Ahmad's (1996:282) pithy observation that the postcolonial is a polite way of saying "not white."

Indeed, postcoloniality is still largely perceived in relation to the "Third World." To the question posed by Shohat (1996): "When exactly does the "post-colonial" begin?" Dirlik (1996: 294) answered, only half in jest: "When Third World intellectuals have arrived in the First World academe." Emerging in the mid-1980s as a "theory," it offered these intellectuals academic respectability. Their repudiation of the "master" narratives of history and social structure resonated with the prevailing celebrations of globalization, rightwing triumphalism, and the rise of identity politics. As was noted earlier, it was Shohat (1996) herself who located the rise of postcolonial theory in the contexts of North American curricular and cultural battles. It offered the academic gatekeepers, she argued, a respite from the terrorizing challenges posed by both immigrant intellectuals brandishing "neo-colonialism" and "Third World" terms of combat and restive indigenous minorities clamoring for equitable access and ethnic studies.

The role of postcolonial theory as a discursive weapon of containment against rebellious minority intellectuals can be seen in Sara Suleri's (1996: 342)

vituperous attack of "the excesses and limitations of marginal discourses," especially "black feminism's failure to move beyond the proprietary rights that can
be claimed by any oppressed discourse." Suleri is vexed by bell hooks's (1989)
caustic observation that many of the purveyors of postcolonial discourse are
often dismissive of African Americans. Henry Louis Gates (1994) also wonders whether the postcolonialists from the South are not simply sophisticated
narcissists acting out their predicament of exile and dislocation. Ruth
Frankenberg and Lata Mani (1996: 350) ask: Why is it "that Black and
Chicano critics [in the USA] have in the main not rushed to embrace the term
as adequate to their present condition?" For Gloria Davies (1998: 171) postcolonial interventions, far from being lodged at the borders of established
mainstream scholarship, are "instead constitutive of an institutionally
approved, even applauded, mode of inquiry preferred by some research funding agencies and academic publishers" in an academic and cultural market in
which "doing theory" by socially ungrounded migrant or minority professionals of color is privileged and provides an institutional sanction to reinforce, not
subvert, the system of metropolitan or neocolonial knowledge production.

Postcolonial theory's obfuscatory language and inflationary rhetoric
ensure that even its critical mappings of cultural imperialism in Euro-
American canonical texts and political claims to redress injustices are often
lost. These charges infuriate many proponents of postcolonial theory. While
Hall (1996: 243, 256) dismisses them as "politically correct grapeshots," he
refuses to address the question of why postcolonial theory is largely a product of Northern academies. Quayson (2000) offers a tortured answer, invoking the efficacy of Marxism, another Western invention, "in providing progressive ways by which non-Western nations have grasped the processes of
globalization and helping them to position themselves strategically with
regard to these processes" (Quayson, 200: 12). It is revealing that postcolonialism should be defended in the name of Marxism, to which one can only
answer that postcolonialism is not Marxism. Lest we forget, wherever
Marxism made contributions to "serious struggles for liberation," it did so
because it was tied to actual social movements and projects. What are the
social movements and projects of postcoloniality outside the small circles of
cosmopolitan intellectuals in the Northern academies?

The issue is not whether translocated intellectuals from the South and
their sympathizers in the North should or should not be pace-setters in cultural theory. Postcolonial critics have a right to be proud of the theoretical

interventions they have made that has given them entry and standing, however fleetingly, in Northern academies. They ought nevertheless to understand that their battles and successes are structured and embedded in Northern academic cultures. It does matter what, where, when, why, and by whom ideas are produced and consumed. Investigating the conditions, contexts, and content of theoretical formations is a legitimate scholarly inquiry that has wider political and ideological implications. Whatever one thinks of its strengths or weaknesses, postcoloniality has become an important episode in the history of social thought in the North especially as it concerns the constitution of the modern world and relations between the North and the South. The hostility exhibited by many postcolonial scholars to historical and sociological interrogations of postcolonial theory betrays both intellectual insecurity and arrogance, the insecurity of an insurgent intellectual movement in academies steeped in Eurocentric fantasies and the arrogance inherent in the "posts" themselves, declaring that history is over, and that they are beyond historical analysis.

Spivak's (1999) recent self-reflexive critique of postcoloniality as the handmaiden of liberal multiculturalism in the North and of transnational capitalism in the South is revealing. She contends that "the sudden prominence of the postcolonial informant on the stage of U.S. English Studies," which is being exported to Europe and other places, can be accounted for by the fact that the postcolonial informant is so focused on colonialism as securely past and culturalist that she "has rather little to say about the oppressed minorities in the decolonized nation as such....Yet the aura of identification with those distant objects of oppression clings to these informants as, again at best, they identify with the other racial and ethnic minorities in metropolitan space. At worst, they take advantage of the aura and play the native informant uncontaminated by disavowed involvement in the machinery of the production of knowledge" (Spivak, 1999: 360). They mistake "high theory" for "resistance," and their culturalist celebration of difference, as "the simulated specificity of a radical position, often dissimulate the implicit collaboration of the postcolonial in the service of neocolonialism. Today this has been displaced into hybridist postcolonial talk, celebrating globalization as Americanization" (Spivak, 1999: 361).

The denial that objective knowledge is possible is based on an extreme form of social or linguistic constructivism that is theoretically, politically, and ethically untenable. Postmodernism's suspicion of foundationalism tends to rule out the search for a nonfoundationalist theory of knowledge and the possibilities of a theory-mediated objectivity. Mohanty (1997) encourages us to abandon the positivist theoretical assumption that knowledge is truly objective only when it is shorn of all perspectives, paradigms, and mediating theories and the notion that this is the only possible image of objectivity. If we recognize that the separation of the linguistic from the real world is too contrived in that it disregards the sociality of language and the complex triadic relation between the object, the sign, and the interpretant, which interact, reference, and constitute each other in a shared social and historical space, we can begin to articulate a nonfoundationalist view of knowledge and language that can sustain a realist epistemology and progressive politics. His suggestion to go beyond the bounds of a purely text-based literary theory and to engage the substantive findings and practices of the various disciplines including history—would be well-taken by practitioners of the disciplines who are often critiqued or caricatured by the "posts."

The "Posts" and History

History and historians have had a complex and problematic relationship with the "posts," one characterized by advocacy, ambivalence, and antagonism. One of the most forceful advocates for history to embrace postmodernist approaches is Keith Jenkins (1995), who believes it is time to bury modernist history with its misguided foundationalist and essentialist beliefs in certainties, objectivity, and optimism. Jenkins writes with the impatience, passion, and occasional insights of a proselytizer. His critiques of the modernist historians E. H. Carr (1964) and Geoffrey Elton (1967, 1991) are as uncompromising as is his exaltation of the postmodernist thinkers Richard Rorty (1982, 1989, 1991) and Hayden White (1973, 1978, 1987), whose liberal pessimism, literary sensibilities, and antifoundationalist, ironic, nominalist, neopragmatic, and conversationalist philosophies, he finds appealing. To Jenkins, the opponents of postmodernist approaches are simply nostalgic for the discredited and vanishing projects of modernism and traditional history.

Another proponent of postmodernism who has made a career of trying to convert his fellow historians to each passing intellectual fad is Robert Berkhofer (1969, 1995), who in the 1960s wanted to remake history in the scientific image of behaviorism and now views salvation in what he sees as postmodernism's five provocative tendencies that disrupt historical practice: denaturalization, demystification, dehierarchization, deferentialism, and deconstruction (Haskell, 1998).

Stripped of its rhetorical heat, the analysis of Jenkins and other critics of historical objectivity, such as Leon Goldstein (1976), Peter Novick (1988), and Paul Roth (1988, 1991), offers little that is really new or subversive for historiography. They distinguish the past from history and claim that while the former did exist, history is constructed and comes to us through narrative encoded in figurative language, so that it is as much imagined and invented as found. Since the historian's "past" is transmitted through texts and reading, it cannot be a literal representation of the past or have a "true" correspondence to the past. In short, history suffers from the constraints of evidence, culture, and language, which makes all history interpretive, ideological, present-centered, or historicist. Consequently, historians should be reflexive, for they are the ones who "discipline" the "past," imposing upon it the order, coherence, structures, content, developments, processes, and meaning it never had. Little of this is really news to most historians. Indeed, Jenkins avows, the textualism of postmodernism does not offer a way of "doing" history at all, it simply encourages historians and their readers to be tolerant of various histories and become more aware of the limits and possibilities of historical understanding—good advice but not terribly profound.

Clearly, the impact of the "posts" on historiography has been more in terms of theoretical intent than in actual practice. As Willie Thompson (2000: 68) notes, the world is still awaiting the deconstructionist equivalent of *The Making of the English Working Class* (Thompson, 1963). The chances of that happening soon are not promising, because the institutional constraints, demands, imperatives, procedures, and practices of historiographical production—teaching, training, research, publishing, and employment—remain wedded to the Rankean method. Sharing Thompson's ambivalence about the historiographical import of the "posts" are Beverly Southgate (1996) and C. Bekan McCullagh (1998). They attribute the assault of the "posts" on historiography to external and internal challenges. There was the historic defeat of the Left and the debacle of Marxism in the 1970s and 1980s, while from the academy there came new psychological studies of perception, linguistic questions concerning the nature and function of language, and philosophical theories of skepticism, which emphasized the subjectivity, partiality, contingency, construction, textuality, and the relativism of historical observations, writing, and meaning. Within history itself the challenges came from feminism, the insurgent histories of racial minorities, and cultural history, which insisted on alternative modes of historical perception, expression, evaluation, narrativity, and construction. The three authors—Thompson, Southgate, and McCullagh—welcome the contributions of some of the new approaches and postmodernist questioning, but they maintain that fundamental principles of historiography remain valid.

The fact that reconstruction of the past is both difficult and problematic, they argue, does not mean it is impossible if history is to be distinguished ontologically from myth or fiction, which it should be, although historical writing is in some respects a literary artifact. Neither do the dilemmas associated with moral evaluation in historiography imply that judgment is unnecessary, as long as the basis of the judgment is made clear. The variety of historical interpretations and their subjectivity, they contend, does not exclude the possibility of their truth and fairness. Even if it is conceded that historical descriptions and explanations do not correspond to the past; they correlate with aspects of the past and can be true, or probably true, if they provide a coherent account of the world, relative to the available evidence, cultural context, and commonly accepted criteria of veracity and validity.

The "posts" may have discredited teleologies, but that does not entail the meaninglessness of history, or that historical change and movement are fictional. They may have proved congenial to feminist and ethnic studies, encouraging the study of historically despised or marginalized groups, examining how identities are constructed and constituted, exploring how situations and events are understood and represented, and emphasizing the importance of language and literary sensibility for historical writing; but historians were not blissfully unaware of these things before (Scott, 1988; Yang, 2000; Nelson and Gaonkar, 1996; During, 1985, 1993). Indeed, since the nineteenth century when the discipline emerged in its current form, new methodologies, topics, and approaches have continuously arisen and have been incorporated into historiography. This shows the strength, not the infirmity of history. Thus reports of the field's demise are premature.

There are, however, many historians who are categorically antagonistic to the "posts," which are seen as threats to the chronological, conceptual, and cultural categories and foundations of history. The attacks come from both the Right and the Left. The postmodernist notion that the past, reality, and truth are finally dead is delusionary and dangerous, so declare many of the conservative contributors to *Reconstructing History* (Fox-Genovese and Lasch-Quinn, 1999), the combative manifesto of The Historical Society, a breakaway historical association formed in the United States in 1998 by historians keen to rescue their beloved profession and scholarship from the trivialization, faddishness, tendentiousness, aestheticization, overspecialization, radical relativism, and politicization of the "posts." To them, postmodernist history—likely a passing craze—appeals to those who use identity politics and political correctness to leverage cultural and academic resources, and to young historians seduced by its avant-garde pretensions and seeking liberation from the methodological demands of modernist history (Lasch-Quinn, 1999; Fox-Genovese, 1999; Himmelfarb, 1999; Jacoby, 1999).

From the Left comes the vigorous rebuttal of Alex Callinicos (1995), who argues that the proponents of the "posts" misconstrue the nature of historical inquiry. They are mistaken in equating history with storytelling, reducing historical reconstruction to literary narrative, dismissing all historical narratives as closures, refusing to theorize about the historical process, and considering the conditions under which the so-called historical metanarratives can be an instrument of liberation rather than oppression. Reducing history to narrative ignores the fact that the typical aim of historical writing is to give an explanation, not simply a representation, of some event or episode or phenomenon in the past, and that explanation requires social theory, so that historical writing entails a continuous process of dialogue between theory and evidence.

Charges that all history is teleological are based on a confusion between theories of history and philosophies of history. Theories of history are research programs, empirical theories—theories of social structure, transformation, and directionality—that attempt to offer nonteleological explanations of the historical process, while philosophies of history seek out the meaning of history to provide some judgment of its overall moral significance. Evidence and theory are fundamental referents of historical writing. Once they have been occluded, and history is reduced to fiction, then historical events become nothing more than constructs of the historical imaginary. This is a license for politically and ethically untenable relativism, revisionism, pessimism, and even nihilism.

The dangers are brought into sharp relief with the subject of the Holocaust: How can it be transposed into a discursive construct, relativized, fictionalized, and emptied of all meaning outside of its textual representations without giving succor to neofascist revisionists? Hence, the tortuous analytical muddle in which writers like Lyotard and White find themselves when trying to apply their postmodernist insights to the Holocaust. Interestingly, the debate over Paul de Man's wartime Nazi collaboration, by his postmodernist friends and foes, in the end appealed to conventional historical standards of evidence and inference (Spitzer, 1996). It is not surprising that German historians, confronted with the historical and moral weight of the Holocaust, have apparently been more resistant to postmodernism than their counterparts elsewhere in the North. While some German historians welcome postmodernism's emphasis on self-reflexivity and plural histories, many are troubled by an approach that textualizes and relativizes everything it touches, valorizes a playful exploration of texts, ridicules historical explanation, overlooks the difference between history and memory, downplays human agency and responsibility, refuses to provide normative alternatives, and employs needlessly obfuscatory jargon (Ash, 1995; Jarausch, 1995; Steinweis, 1995, Telman, 1995; Janz, 1995a).

Given the cruel burdens of their histories, especially the traumas of the slave trade and colonialism, many African historians share similar misgivings about postmodernism. What I find intriguing is that while the postmodernists rail against "metanarratives," Eurocentric metanarratives continue to be produced for policy and popular consumption in the North, for example, about the "end of history" (Fukuyama, 1992) or the "clash of civilizations (Huntington, 1996). More importantly, in our increasingly globalizing world, dominated by rapacious corporations, totality is not simply a theoretical construct but a social reality, so that it is surely a terrible waste of intellectual energy trying to prove that all truth claims are merely power plays. The challenges and demands of human emancipation are as complex and urgent as ever, and they require forms of political and ethical engagement beyond the cynical detachment of postmodernist irony and pessimism.

The "posts" seek not simply to repudiate the intelligibility of the past in general but to take revolutions out of history and visions of fundamental social change out of the future. Hence, argues Dirlik (2000), the abandonment of two categories that were critical to earlier revolutionary discourses—nation and class—and the celebration of hybridity and borderlands, which encourages the sanitization and depiction of imperialism and colonialism as shared cultures, negotiated discursive spaces. Also, despite all the fulminations against essentialism, there is the primacy accorded to essentialized racial and ethnic identities. Thus while the "posts" seek to repudiate history, they produce metahistorical generalizations applied to ever more expansive temporal and spatial scales, thereby erasing those very prized differences. One result is the proliferation of group memories and the impoverishment of coherent histories: As specific group experiences are remembered, their larger contexts are forgotten. The erasures of revolution, nation, class, history, and reality turn the "posts," even if they may have started as critiques, into legitimating ideologies of contemporary global configurations of power and production. Foreclosed are the possibilities of visioning a world beyond the present, imagining alternatives to capitalist modernity. In so far as capitalism is not as fragmented as it is assumed, the "posts" bolster the capitalist order itself by becoming part of the ideological apparatus that sustains the inability of exploited social classes, splintered in their various cultural identities, to mobilize counterhegemonically.

Postmodernism projects its aversion to modernist utopias, especially to Marxism, to the past which is stripped of its historicity and given the attributes of the future: indeterminateness, incomprehensibility, polysemy, and the ironic play of possibilities (Epstein, 1995). Thus, the dismissal of the past ultimately entails the dismissal of the future. For the South, histories inflected by the "posts" oversimplify colonialism when Euro-American domination is depicted primarily as a cultural phenomenon, while its political and economic dynamics are ignored. The dominance of the language of culture, not political economy, leaves behind a dehistoricized and desocialized understanding of Eurocentrism, which is not just a discursive system but one embedded in structures of material power. And resistance to it has also been, and needs to be, material not simply metaphorical.

The "Posts" Encounter Women and Africa

To many in women studies and in African studies, both on the continent and in the North, the claims of the "posts" often sound both familiar and strange—familiar, because they have spent their entire careers deconstructing Western and modernist claims to truth, to the universal, and to chronicling the clashes and convergences of cultures and the loss of certainties; but also strange because many of them believe passionately, bred as they were during the era of decolonization, with its nationalist and developmentalist dreams, or by women's movements with their visions of emancipation and gender equality, in the necessity of progress, in the possibilities of historical agency. Even as the feminist aspirations were compromised by North-South divides, academic institutionalization and political incorporation of the feminist movement, and the hopes of *uhuru* began to fade as the recessions of development and democracy deepened from the 1970s and especially in the 1980s with the imposition of draconian structural adjustment programs by the international financial institutions and Africa's increasingly beleaguered dictators, the narrative of emancipation and the historical and humanistic agendas of nationalism for decolonization, nation-building, development, democracy, and regional integration retained their powerful hold on the imaginary of feminist scholars and the African intelligentsia. To be sure, some succumbed to Afropessimism, or to reactionary antifeminism, but their bitterness was more about the failures of the future than its foreclosure. That is why many Africans put their energies into the democratic struggles—struggles for the "second independence"—that began to sweep across the continent from the late 1980s.

In short, it was hard for many feminists and African intellectuals, even had they wished to, given the conditions that their countries, communities, and campuses were in, to retreat into their brick towers and to indulge in the intellectual solipsism of apolitical theorizing beloved by many adherents of the "posts." The limited appeal of the "posts" among African scholars had little to do with "the desperate plight of many universities on the continent and their continued dependence on Western institutions," as Jane Parpart (1995: 17) suggests, but more because, as she concedes, "Northern hegemony over scholarly as well as development discourse and practice is well understood and heartily disliked by many Africans." Quayson's plea for a "responsible postcolonial discourse" amply demonstrates that even African academic migrants in the Northern academies remember the histories and dreams of their societies and are anxious to recuperate a progressive mission for a theory that is not inherently so. Not surprisingly, then, the "posts," configured as they are as antirepresentational paradigms, have been treated with suspicion by many African and feminist scholars, especially those on the continent. Labeling their societies, postmodern when only recently in Western discourse they were called pre-modern or modernizing was amusing at best. The various postmodernisms—as manifested in different fields from architecture and literature to political theory—are premised on a project of transcending some aspects of a self-conscious, self-privileged project of modernism that is largely absent in Africa's construction of itself.

The ambiguous relationship between feminism and postmodernism is quite intriguing. The two share many affinities and differences. On the one hand, both question the foundational premises of Western philosophy, both see Western representations as the product of access to power not truth, both offer a critique of binarism and thinking in oppositional hierarchies. On the other, they differ about the shape and character of social criticism. The postmodern dismissal of philosophical foundations and totalizing narratives often results in the disavowal of large-scale emancipatory projects and preference for social criticism that is pragmatic, ad hoc, contextual, local, and ameliorative. While not opposed to the latter, many feminists believe that a phenomenon as pervasive and multifaceted as male domination requires social criticism based on large historical narratives and analyses of societal macrostructures, for which social-theoretical and empirical analyses are necessary. Postmodernism, for its part, faults feminism for engaging in metanarrative-like modes of theorizing in search of an essentialized female subjectivity and subordination that has cross-cultural explanatory power, even if the categories may have shifted, from sexuality and reproduction to mothering and gender identity.

To its supporters among feminists, postmodernism's decentering of the subject simply allows the problematization, not erasure, of the category of woman and the flattened concept of gender, and to record, celebrate, and mobilize the multiple registers of women's existence, experiences, and voices, thus enabling feminist alliance politics to blossom, instead of the bitter politics of imaginary unity (Alarcón, 1994). As for postmodernism's alleged murder of the subject, this should not be seen "as a conspiracy against women and other disenfranchised groups who are now only beginning to speak on their own behalf." Rather, to deconstruct the subject of feminism is "to release the term into a future of multiple significations, to emancipate it from the maternal or racialist ontologies to which it has been restricted, and to give it play as a site where unanticipated meanings might come to bear" (Butler, 1994: 165, 166). Suspicion of postmodernism as androcentric is self-defeating, because it marks the term "postmodern" as given and deprives women of an opportunity to "construct postmodern theories or aesthetics that include and account for feminist work" (Michael, 1996: 13). Instead of continuing to trade criticisms, Nancy Fraser and Linda Nicholson (1994) believe feminism and postmodernism have much to learn from each other's strengths and weaknesses. While retaining its fidelity to large narratives and its political agenda, postmodern feminism should eschew universalistic and essentialist categories and be pragmatic and fallibilistic.

Even if the two remain separate, some postmodern concepts are useful for feminist analysis and politics, declares Joan Scott (1994), who argues that the concepts of language, discourse, difference, and deconstruction productively illuminate the "equality-versus-difference" debate in the United States. Feminist postmodern perspectives have also been used in a wide range of fields, from deconstructing the narrative of women's dependence, a policy narrative that has had profound effects on social work and welfare and women's lives (East, 1998), to extending the representational possibilities of feminist communication theory by problematizing the relationship between communication and the construction of subjectivity, including gendered identities and relations, which communication researchers have left untheorized. The language of the "posts," Radha Hedge (1998) insists, not only makes communications theory transnationally responsive and more politically engaged with issues of difference, especially with reference to the representation of minorities in the West and Third World women, and it offers an avenue for feminism to be more inclusive, to overcome its universalist blinders against which both minority feminist scholars in the North and feminists in the South have railed so much. In any case, postmodern feminism eschews articulations of postmodern nihilism and aesthetics, for it is allied to oppositional or resistant postmodernism, articulated by writers like Ebert (1993) and McLaren (1994), in which "difference" is seen in relation to, or within, a system of exploitation and the social relations it engenders, and emphasizes the need to historicize and situate identities within the larger structures of power, ideology, and culture. It is indeed possible to marry materialist feminism and postmodernist approaches (Hennessy, 1993).

Critics remain unconvinced. To them postmodernism raises several red flags. Its antirealism, antihumanism, textuality, discursive pluralism, and stress on indeterminancy and instability are seen as defeatist and disempowering for ignoring the materiality of global structures and inequalities and the necessity of collective social struggles (Salleh, 1997; Harstock, 1998; Ahmed, 1996); its rejection of grand theories questions the sociostructural oppression of women (Nurius and Franklin,1998); its assumption that the more radical a textual disruption of modernist tales and telos the more radical is the political potential for feminism is indulgence in impotent symbolic politics (Pitchford, 1998); its endless deconstruction and disavowal of alternatives lead to cynicism and preclude the creation of new feminist visions and new feminist utopias to drive feminist politics (Benhabib,1991;

Laslett and Brenner, 2000); its avoidance of perspectives that have moral or transcendent vision also undermines the feminist politics of emancipation (Farganis,1992); its scholastic celebration of difference compounds the problems of creating political opposition groups based on common interests and goals; its declaration of the "death of the subject" raises fears about the repercussions of losing the female subject and suspicions as to why the subject becomes problematic just when women and others who have been silenced begin to act as subjects rather than objects of history (Hartsock, 1990; Bordo, 1990); its male theoretical masters tend to offer postmodernism as a framing discourse for feminism, as the latter is reduced to an instance of postmodern thought, a gesture, reminiscent of modernist gestures, of appropriating "femininity" at the same time as women are erased, silenced, and resubordinated to traditional male-dominated interests (de Lauretis, 1987; Modleski, 1991; Herbold, 1995); its idle contemplation of structures of cultural difference at the expense of the structures of economic exploitation gives it a colonialist gaze in the eyes of many women in the South (Stromquist, 2000); and its preoccupation with the crisis of representation is not everyone's crisis and the decentering of the unitary discourse of the Enlightenment does not necessarily promote international radicalism (Sangari, 1990).

The last point is elaborated by Philomena Okeke (1996) with specific reference to Africa. She argues that postmodern feminism has failed to confront the politics of producing feminist knowledge; while it has appropriated the critiques made by so-called marginalized voices, including those of African women, its proponents continue to act as gatekeepers keeping the subjugated voices out, now aided by renewed emphasis on theory. The quality of scholarship inspired by the "posts" does not always help their cause. Reading a self-consciously postmodernist article on a "postcolonial" subject in West Africa, I could not help but be amused by the author's facile attempts at "representing the subtle and complex relations among subjects living in a world still bleeding history" through her pathological dreams, interspersed with patronizing ethnographic notes, pretentious theorizing, personal reminiscences, and pathetic attempts at storytelling. The conclusion is convoluted, affected, and banal:

> Writing, emboldened by imagination, enables formerly colonized peoples and former colonizers to recover their humanity, to experi-

ence themselves and others as decentered, yet embodied subjects, to claim their places in the particularities of their historical, economic, and cultural allegiances. The challenge, then, is to create postcolonial and sociological theories and research methods to rhetorically and substantively incorporate a hermeneutics of liberation" (Slobin, 2000: 202).

Of course, one article cannot stand as an exemplar of a whole theoretical corpus.

But suspicions that not all is well with the encounter between the "posts" and Africa are not entirely misplaced. Even postcoloniality, which unlike postmodernity incorporates Africa in its spatial and conceptual nexus, has sometimes been seen as the latest in a long line of paradigms manufactured in the Northern academy to appropriate and to alienate Africans' intellectual and imaginative energies. The Ghanaian writer, Ama Ata Aidoo states:

Perhaps the concept [of postcoloniality] was relevant to the United States after its war of independence, and to a certain extent to the erstwhile imperial dominions of Canada, Australia, and New Zealand. Applied to Africa, India, and some other parts of the world, 'postcolonial' is not only a fiction, but a most pernicious fiction, a cover-up of a dangerous period in our people's lives" (as quoted in Mongia, 1996:1).

Aidoo is not alone.

Most African writers, artists, and other cultural producers do not describe themselves and their work as "postmodern" or "postcolonial." As Kwame Anthony Appiah (1998: 432) states so memorably in his famous essay, "Is the 'Post-' in 'Postcolonial' the 'Post-' in "Postmodern?" while all aspects of contemporary African cultural and artistic life have been influenced by colonialism, "they are not all in the relevant sense postcolonial," in so far as the "the 'post' in postcolonial, like the 'post' in postmodern, is the 'post' of the space-clearing gesture," in which one is distinguished from other producers and products, a need that derives from the underlying dynamic of a highly commodified Western cultural modernity. Indeed, African novels, which are seen as bearers of postcoloniality more than other cultural forms, are not unambiguously postcolonial. To be sure, they are novels of delegitimation, rejecting both the Western imperium and the failed nationalist project of the postcolonial national bourgeoisie, but "the basis for that project of delegitimation is very much not the postmodernist one: rather, it is grounded in an appeal to an ethical universal; indeed, it is based, as intellectual responses to oppression in Africa largely are based, in an appeal to a certain simple respect for human suffering, a fundamental revolt against the endless misery of the last thirty years" (Appiah, 1998: 435). It is a project, moreover, that appeals to a totality, the continent of Africa and its peoples, rather than to localized and relativist understandings and legitimations.

Suspicion about the "posts" reflect not only lingering discursive nationalism or materialist radicalism but also serious concerns about the quality of scholarship conducted under their conceptual auspices. It would be incorrect of course to suggest that African scholars share a unitary position on the "posts." As is the case in Northern-centered debates, one can find scholars who advocate, are ambivalent, or antagonist to the "posts." On the whole, however, it would seem that the advocates are in a distinct minority. In many instances, the "posts" are used as cultural capital in the academic marketplace. In this context, the term "postcolonial" becomes a symbolic marker for contemporary intellectual relevance, as is clearly the case in Emmanuel Eze's *Postcolonial African Philosophy*, in which for many of the contributors the postcolonial simply signifies the postindependence period (Gyeke, 1997a), the "postcolonial present" (Serequeberhan, 1997), or neocolonialism (Gordon, 1997a). All too often, the postcolonial becomes a substitute for the "Third World" without new analytical insights, as is the case with J. E. Goldthorpe's (1996) book, formerly called *Sociology of the Third World* and now retitled *The Sociology of Postcolonial Societies* in a new edition in response to the changed nomenclature of the academic market. In other cases, postcoloniality simply puts a new gloss on old studies of African pluralism as is evident in much of Richard Werbner and Terence Ranger's (1996) book, *Postcolonial Identities in Africa*.

More troubling is the propensity that the "posts" seem to give to western Africanists to write on Africa without doing much empirical research. The discursive approaches promoted by the "posts" encourage textual analyses or elevate anecdotal scholarship in the self-indulgent name of reflexivity, both of which obviate the need for extensive empirical research. Searching for what historians call "primary sources" loses its epistemological imperative with the anti-representational turn promoted by the "posts." It could be suggested then that for various reasons the postmodern turn resonated with the difficulties of conducting field research on the continent for Northern scholars. For middle-level scholars there is the mortgage factor, and for junior scholars in hope of tenure there are the increased demands for publications, which do not allow for extended research visits abroad, let alone working there as many had done in the 1960s and 1970s. In other words, given the changes and growing competitiveness in the structure of academic labor markets in the North, institutional disincentives have increased, thus discouraging Northern academics from teaching, researching, and participating in African academic exchanges and activities (Zeleza, 2000; Guyer, 1996; Fyfe, 1999; McCracken, 1993; Fage, 1989). Under such circumstances, textualized scholarship becomes quite attractive. For graduate students there has been the shrinkage of research funds both because of the increased number of Northern students studying Africa and actual declines in area studies funding, which had allowed their predecessors a generation earlier to travel to Africa with greater ease and for longer periods.

Opportunities for foreign scholars to do research or to work in Africa have also changed. The proliferation of African researchers and the Africanization of university faculties constitutes one limiting factor. Another consists of the horrific stories in the Western mass and academic media of a continent in perpetual turmoil, part of the unyielding narrative of "Afropessimism," of the pathological crisis ravaging what Achille Mbembe (1992a, 1992b) calls the "postcolony." And so it becomes appealing to substitute field research with textual discourse analyses. The same impulses make it permissible to conduct research on Africa by substitution through Africans resident in Western countries, a practice that has become popular in anthropology, whereby instead of going to an African country to do research on, say, a community, research is done on migrants of that community in European or American cities. There is of course a legitimate place for diaspora and transnational studies, but these should not be mistaken for studies of realities and developments within Africa itself.

Undoubtedly the "posts" have their intellectual believers in Africa and in African studies. In locational terms, many are to be found in South Africa. Graham Pechey (1994: 165) makes the extravagant claim that "South African writing has never been anything other than postmodern (as a whole practice, as an institution), though not always (technically, in the sense of its internal textual relations) postmodernist." Lewis Nkosi (1998) disagrees, noting that it is white, not black, South African writers who claim affinities to postmodernism; the latter are too preoccupied with nationalist (modernist) agendas and questions of agency. In fact, many black writers are either not aware they are postmodern, or they are actively hostile to postmodernism. Thus, there is a bifurcation between black and white writing rooted in the material and ideological realties, hierarchies, and differentiations of colonialism and apartheid. More generally, Nkosi (1998:84) asks, "What possible readings of indigenous African-language literature can pass unmolested through the grid of current postmodernisms?" He doubts whether the "posts" have much to contribute to the readings or creation of works of African literature written in the indigenous languages.[11]

The appeal of postmodernism and postcoloniality for many white South African scholars lies in the fact that the "posts" provide political and intellectual possibilities for the European settlers to secede from Europe and to identify with the historically oppressed majority, while simultaneously offering gestures of intimate familiarity with Western intellectual trends, thus affirming South African exceptionalism, that it remains, in discursive matters, an outpost of Western civilization on the "dark continent." The "posts" are also attractive to those who seek respite from dealing with the structural deformities of postapartheid South Africa. Postcoloniality not only foregrounds race, a familiar discourse in a country bred on apartheid, rather than class, a threatening discourse to the ruling elites, it is often celebrated for the temporal closure it marks: "We were colonial; we have become postcolonial; no further fundamental transformations are required" (Visser, 1997: 93). South African scholars who have embraced postcoloniality, Nicholas Visser (1997) suggests, seem to prefer a moderate version stripped of its more provocative and subversive assertions, thus turning it into the latest expression of liberal pluralism.

The iconoclastic intellectual climate wrought on the humanities by the postapartheid, postindustrial, postMarxist, postmodern, and postpositivist weltanschauung (ideology) is the source, argues John Bottomley (1998), of the apparent crisis affecting South African historiography. There are dangers of course, as Norman Etherington (1996: 11) warns the predominantly white academies, that if they "no longer profess to help us understand how the present state of things came to be, or to assist projects of betterment, some people may conclude they are expendable." He believes there are powerful local forces that inhibit the full development of postmodernist scholarship in South Africa. In such a politically charged, deeply divided society, it is not easy to cultivate the attitude of ironic detachment, to renounce "modernist" projects, or to pronounce oneself disillusioned with the death of apartheid, as do European former Marxists who have sought refuge in postmodernism. Also, the indiscriminate celebration of cultural and ethnic differences can facilitate the return of the intellectual ghosts of apartheid.

One of the most vocal proponents of the "posts" is the Cameroonian historian, Achille Mbembe (1992a, 1992b, 1999, 2000b, 2001a, 2001b).[12] His verbose and overexcited postmodernist fulminations essentially consist of, on the one hand, denunciations of African scholarship—except his and that of his postmodernist mentors of course—as historicist, economistic, racist, instrumentalist, opportunistic, and fatalistic; dismissal of African histories and memories of slavery, colonialism, and victimhood; disdain for nationalist and Marxist visions of liberation, progress, and development; and denial of the existence of African identity, authenticity, and difference. On the other hand, he makes fatuous declarations that imperialism is exhausted, racial identities, including whiteness in South Africa, are disappearing, and that the world is marching towards a brave new world of globalization, from which Africa risks being excluded unless it abandons its nativist claims to uniqueness, sovereignty, and self-determination. Mbembe's Africa is a conflicted sign, text, archive, or library, to use his terminology, marked by absences, by lack, whose actualization lies in its absorption into the universal. Indeed, he suggests that the classical borderlines—symbolic, cultural, structural, and territorial—of Africa or Africanity are vanishing, although every chance he gets he gratuitously stresses Africa's pathological exceptionalism, that Africa is a space marked by unusual banality, violence, and corruption.

A more intriguing assessment of postmodernism is that of Denis Ekpo (1995), who argues that postmodernism may superficially appear to be of little concern to Africans, because they did not create or did not wallow in modernism, with the materialism and deification of reason that postmodernism thematizes and wants to exorcize. However, through colonial conquest Africa was imbricated with the culture of modernity, and modern African thought was irretrievably locked in the grammar of the European logos. Consequently, from its inception modern African thought acquired an a priori isomorphic relationship to the logic, metaphysics, and rhetoric of modern European thought, so that it is vulnerable to the same postmodernist critiques. In fact, modern African thought, like modern European thought, finds itself in a performative impasse. It can only be liberated from its logocentric trap by postmodernism, since it is the most radical and disruptive critique of the various logocentric games that modern European rationality plays.

In fact, postmodernism, Ekpo contends, furnishes the modern African mind access and insight into the production mechanisms and ideologies of Western texts as well as the opportunity to get into real power games of European modernity, indeed, to gain cognitive control over the West. While Ekpo tars modern African thought with idealism and voluntarism, it is his arguments that have brushes of idealism and voluntarism written all over them. His reduction of all modern African thought to affective Afrocentric master narratives and activist moralism is truly staggering in its arrogant overgeneralizations and historical oversimplifications. His conclusion that postmodernism allows a cognitive transformation in the modern African mind from regarding the West as an awesome enemy, into an equally helpless friend, is revealing of the analytical and political bankruptcy of a postmodernism that homogenizes and dehistoricizes Africa.

There are of course more thoughtful proponents of postmodernism in Africa and African studies than Mbembe or Ekpo, among them the great Congolese scholar, V. Y. Mudimbe, (1988, 1994) whose work, despite its Gallic density, offers penetrating, fascinating, and historically grounded analyses of discourses on African societies, cultures, and peoples. Informed by Foucault's insight that knowledge is implicated with power, in *The Invention of Africa* Mudimbe interrogates the invention of Africa through categories and conceptual systems embedded in a Western epistemological order, from anthropology, and missionary discourses to philosophy, an order of knowledge constituted in the sociohistorical context of colonialism. This colonizing structure generated Eurocentrism, a dichotomizing system that produces paradigmatic oppositions and invests African societies, cultures, and bodies with the representational marginalities of alterity. African discourses and ideologies have been reacting to this epistemological ethnocentricism, whose expressive symbols, but not fundamental meanings, have mutated according to changing Western material, methodological, and moral grids, with varying degrees of epistemic domestication and defiance, in the process of which Africa' identity and alterity have been affirmed, denied, inverted, and reconstituted.

Mudimbe extends his critique of the Western epistemological order in

The Idea of Africa, an intellectual memoir to his "Americanized" children, in which he probes the constructions and fantasies of Africa in the diverse texts and times of the Western tradition. He argues that conquering Western discourses, beginning with Greek stories about Africa, through the colonial library, to contemporary postmodernist discourses, have radically silenced or converted African discourses. Even Afrocentricism, which has reactivated Greek texts, is conducted on Eurocentric grounds. Thus the African paradigm of negative difference remains intact, notwithstanding the protracted and passionate struggles for epistemological and political liberation. Mudimbe raises a fundamental question, which he does not answer: Can Africa exist outside European history, after Eurocentricism? His project of interrogating the Western invention of Africa actually recenters, not decenters, Europe and by extension Eurocentricism, the epistemological conceit that Europe invented global and regional knowledges and histories.[13]

This is to suggest that overcoming Eurocentricism requires not only a moral reorientation, an ethicopolitical critique of the existential and epistemic violence of Eurocentricism, which Mudimbe mounts effectively, but also a conceptual decentering of historical discourse by refusing to treat any region as the source and model of historical development. Mudimbe does not do that partly because he is not writing the history of African societies and also because postmodernist critiques, among which we can place many of his writings, are predicated on a repudiation of the consequences of the Enlightenment, so that they cannot avoid being centered around European history and conceptions. Ironically, the critiques of the Enlightenment are themselves "truth claims" that are utterly unprovable on a postmodernist basis, and the preoccupation with Eurocentric constructions allows for endless discussions of Euro-America, thus putting the West back onto a timeless pedestal, as a universal referent, which perpetuates the very Eurocentricism ostensibly being repudiated.

Because the "posts" suggest the pluralities but repudiate the practices, of history they are both welcomed and rejected by many African historians, who believe that it is possible to formulate historiographies that are not Eurocentric, to write history with multiple pathways, that focuses on varieties of human experiences and connections and tells stories of change without presenting linear tales of progress. For example, the renowned historian, Bethwell Ogot, whose work is analyzed in the next chapter, applauds the "posts" for emphasizing questions of identity, the production of knowledge, and discourse; but he is critical of their Eurocentric universalism, their occlusion of a radical critique of capitalism, their dismissal of collectivities that transcend essentialized identities, and their historical domain of social reality. The perceptive Africanist social historian, Frederick Cooper (2000) also embraces some of the postmodernist emphases, but argues that postmodernists suffer from a fallacy of self-centeredness in which they believe that they offer a more fundamental challenge to the ways of doing history than all previous "modernist" approaches, when in fact many of their critiques are as old as the modernist tradition itself. Moreover, celebrating fragmented histories, destabilizing narratives, or dissolving structures into fragments does little to advance the writing of history, i.e., analyzing a world in which real global power coheres around powerful multinational corporations and Euro-American states, or to promote clear thinking of political issues and large-scale organizing.

This is a common refrain among African and Africanist critics. Abiola Irele (2000: 7-8), the renowned Nigerian literary critic, sees postmodernism and its antirationalism as the "most insidious threat to the contemporary African mind," despite the fact that its radical questioning of the historical and philosophical legacy of the Enlightenment "is one that our historical experience predisposes us to understand and to rally to." The key question that Africans must ask themselves, Irele argues, is whether the postmodern project corresponds to their current intellectual and practical requirements. To him it clearly does not. On the contrary, it has no practical value, for its method of exploring the world fails to provide "a rigorous scientific understanding of our lived universe." While we indeed have to recognize the limits of science, there is no reason to jettison its real triumphs. The scientific method is "too precious an asset to be repudiated, either in a vexed reaction against the West, or in what can only be a hopeless quest for innovation." In short, the philosophical anarchy of postmodernism does not offer any real prospect of "advancing our interests in the modern world; for us, as Africans, Foucault, Derrida and their cohorts can be nothing other than false gods."

Irele's argument seems to be based on a distinction between a "bad" modernity and a "good" modernity, similar to the distinction made by the Latin American philosopher, Enrique Dussel (1995), a lapsed postmodernist who blames the terrors of the contemporary world not on modem philosophical or scientific rationality but on a distinctively modern Eurocentric irrational myth. He compares two concurrent paradigms of modernity: a

285

rational, emancipatory modernity and the negative and irrational myth with its "developmental fallacy," the assumption that Europe is the culmination of a universal developmental process, toward which all other peoples must and will go. Thus, contrary to the postmodernists who attribute the deformities and failures of modernity to reason, Dussel attributes them to irrational myth, and thereby avoids an indiscriminate and paralyzing attack on "philosophy." The separation of a rational, emancipatory modernity from a negative and irrational myth of development seems too neat however. There can be no doubt that the two were, and still are, if we agree with Dussel that it is unproductive to counterpose "modernism" and "postmodernism" too strongly, deeply entangled with each other (Lange, 1998).

Irele's concerns echo those of Kwame Gyeke (1997b: 265-267), the eminent Ghanaian philosopher who argues that postmodernism is essentially a reaction to the problems or "crisis" of modernity; it does not inaugurate new conceptually systems, social practices, institutions, habits, and outlooks that are radically different from those maintained in modern times. The skepticism against modern institutions and forms of life are as old as modernism itself. Besides the fact that the role of reason in modern life tends to be exaggerated, Gyeke doubts whether postmodernist critiques of reason are intended to debase the role of reason as such in human life or are simply to give recognition to other important features of human nature such as feeling. In any case, given the diversity of cultural traditions, what may be a postmodern idea or structure or formation for one society may not be postmodern at all for another. This suggests, he concludes, "the relative or contestable or incommensurable character of a concept of postmodernity" (Gyeke, 1997: 267).

Besides its unproductive cynicism and apparent nihilism, many Africanists simply oppose postmodernism for its "pompous and empty verbiage" (Moore, 1995); difficult theory (Harrow, 1997); inapplicability to a continent without or with a different "modernist" past (Janz, 1995b, 1995b); lack of "positive definitional content" (Lowe, 1995); the fact that its claims, jargon aside, are not new and overblown (Lowe, 1997; Chappell, 1997); because it is an externally imposed system of analysis (Steffen, 1995); and it is not a self-referential term among African writers (Dehon, 1995) or Africanist scholars (Austen, 1997a, 1997b; McClendon, 1997), especially historians who are held to high standards of evidence (Wylie, 1997) and who laugh at suggestions that history is dead (Limb, 1997). While Africanist critics of the "posts" are to be found on both sides of the Atlantic, suspicion of the "posts" is most evident on the continent.

It could, in fact, be argued that widespread perceptions among African scholars based on the continent, sometimes exaggerating the popularity of the "posts" in the North, have served to widen the intellectual, ideological, and institutional gaps between Africanist researchers based on and outside the continent. The statement by Tade Aina (1995: 2) is quite typical and deserves to be quoted at length. He argues that there is a crisis of African studies in North America and Europe that is creating

> a process of intellectual reproduction about Africa that is character-
> ized by sterility, outdated facts and information, casual and ad hoc
> observation, name-calling and sometimes wild speculation. It is our
> argument here that for an up-to-date realistic, correct and appropri-
> ate ...understanding of Africa, the most appropriate and relevant
> source is that scholarship and production emanating from or still
> directly linked to the continent in terms of research experience and
> reflection; from this living and challenging source and expression, no
> amount of post-modernist, post-industrialist, post-Marxist or 'post-
> Nativist' conceptualization or discourse can take away the relevance,
> immediacy and centrality.

These sentiments have been echoed by Thandika Mkandawire (1998b), who warns African researchers not to become seduced by the "posts" and to ignore fundamental research about their societies' complex pasts and chart-ing their developmental futures. Aina and Mkandawire were until the late 1990s head and deputy head, respectively, of the Council for the Development of Social Science Research in Africa (CODESRIA), the pre-mier social science organization in Africa. But Mkandawire's successor at CODESRIA was Achille Mbembe, the avowed postmodernist whose views we examined above. The bitter struggles witnessed during Mbembe's tenure at CODESRIA, compounded by allegations of administrative and fiscal mis-management that ended in his ignominious ouster, underscores the exac-tions of African intellectual and ideological debates.

Conclusion: Beyond the Postal Turn

The "posts" continue to be chanted, but they have lost many of their listen-ers. They never had too many sympathizers among historians, not to mention the more impenitent positivist "sciences," economics and political science. The historians' folly has been attributed to the fact that, as Hayden White (1999: 322) contends, no discipline in the human sciences "is oblivious to the 'fictionality' of what it takes to be its 'data'....History is the last refuge of that faith in common sense that culturalism in its postmodernist incarnation seeks to deconstruct." White firmly believes that the "posts" are ideologically progressive movements in their opposition to the pieties of capitalist society and bourgeois culture and are compatible with his Marxian inclinations. White was probably not thinking of Africanist historians who have been painfully aware of the "fictionality" of Eurocentric historical constructs that have dominated African societies which they have spent their lives deconstructing. To many of them the assault of the "posts" was welcome but not new. Consequently, they focused on the ideological and methodological baggage that the "posts" carried with them. Poststructuralist declarations—that all history was meaningless, that the social has no explanatory power, when the Africanists had just started constructing alternative, resistant histories for nations, social groups, and movements previously denied existence—was bound to raise suspicions.

Discomfort with the "posts," however, has not been confined to historians or to Africanists. From the early 1990s criticisms of poststructuralism, postmodernism, and postcoloniality were increasingly heard in the literary disciplines and among many Western scholars themselves. In less than a decade after Paul de Man, the influential proselytizer of deconstruction in the United States died (1983), deconstruction was being pronounced dead in literature departments. Jeffrey Nealon (1993: 22) writes almost wistfully, "deconstruction's death is usually attributed either to suicide, that deconstruction fell back into the dead-end of formalism it was supposed to remedy, or to murder at the hands of the new historicists, whose calls for rehistoricizing and recontextualizing literature have successfully challenged the supposed self-cancelling textualism of the deconstructionists." Even "more consequential than the decline of deconstruction," Guillory (1994: 256) declares, "is the current 'crisis' of theory itself, with which the name deconstruction is inseparably tangled."

In the other literary or cultural disciplines there was also a growing feeling that the cultural or linguistic turn had swung too far away from the social and the economic; that the cultural, linguistic, and representational did not explain everything; that the repudiation of social context, causes, and meanings offered no epistemological and explanatory advances over the more rigorous and systematic approaches of the maligned positivist past. Indeed, despite its privileged status, the cultural itself seemed badly in need of definition. Concluded editors of a collection entitled *Beyond the Cultural Turn:*

> Notwithstanding the many differences among them, the authors of the nine essays share a certain common stance towards the dilemmas raised by the cultural turn. All of them emphasize empirical, comparative, and theoretically informed and informing studies. They have not given up on social or causal explanation; rather, they seek better explanations....In keeping with the tenor of the times, they would probably settle for...rejecting positions that claim to explain either everything (as the positivist and Marxist paradigms once hoped to do) or nothing at all (as postmodernists sometimes seem to imply, with their rejection of explanation itself) (Bonnel and Hunt, 1999: 24-25).

It is now apparent even to some of its strongest supporters that postmodernism is being posted to mortality. Charles Altieri (1998: 1) bemoans the fact that:

> All the instruments agree that 'postmodernism' is no longer a vital concept of the arts. No artist is eager to ally with it, and even critics in the humanities now find affiliation with the term a little embarrassing. Daniel O'Hara, editor of *boundary 2*, the journal that popularized the concept, now remarks that the very notion of the 'post' seems to have become little more than the kind of self-promoting rhetorical gesture we find in university press titling a book series 'post-Contemporary Interventions.' Even the perpetrator of that title, Frederic Jameson, America's most acute and most prolific interpreter of the postmodern, acknowledges our boredom with the concept and repudiates its use....

Altieri though, is not ready to abandon his old fealties to his afflicted paradigm, for he believes that "the postmodernism that has died turns out to be an impostor who never really had title to the crown" (Altieri, 1998: 2), leading one to ask: But how do we distinguish the dead impostor from the living owner? The answer lies in the mysteries of faith, for he laments:

> I cannot give a clean definition of postmodernism. The materials
> covered by the concept are too diverse. And, more important, defi-
> nition is stymied by the fact that the very effort to define the post-
> modern is itself an instance of it. What we reveal in the effort can
> become as important to the definition as the actual formulation. It
> can even become difficult to determine whether it is we who are
> making formulations for negotiating our world, or our world that is
> speaking through us, shaping what we can say or tempting us to
> interpellations that will make life go smoothly (Altieri, 1998: 7).

With delirious friends like these, perhaps postmodernism is better off buried.
That might be true of its twin, postcoloniality, as well. They have both outlived the fifteen minutes of fame of Western pop and academic culture.

Endnotes

1. For analyses on the problems of institutionalization and theory, see
   David Kaufman (1990) who argues that institutionalization inevitably
   leads to a paralyzing impasse for theory premised on indeterminacy;
   Jonathan Culler (1988), who takes a more sanguine view about the productivity and possibilities of professionalization for critical thinking; and
   Stanley Fish (1985) whose new-pragmatist perspective leads him to dismiss anti-professionalism as naive and as a failure in appreciating its
   necessity and value for a discourse robbed of its transcendental foundations.

2. "For example, an industrial-based economy; a politics organized around
   unions, political parties, and interest groups; ideological debates centered on the relative merits of the market and state regulation to ensure
   economic growth, and the good society; institutional differentiation and
   role specialization and professionalism within institutions; knowledges
   divided into disciplines and organized around an ideology of scientific
   enlightenment and progress; the public celebration of a culture of self-
   redemption and emancipatory hope" (Seidman, 1994a:1).

3. While showing sympathy for postmodernism, West (1994: 75) is critical of a deconstructive project as manifested in the work of Derrida and his followers that "too often becomes rather monotonous, John-one-note rhetorical readings that disassemble texts with little attention to the effects and consequences these dismantling have in relation to the operations of military, economic and social powers."

4. Maulana Karenga (2000: 168), one of the founders of African American studies, dismisses postmodern critiques: "They slush and burn, undermine and overturn, but they often leave nothing in their wake except the routine competence for criticism and the urge to fondle the familiar declarations of faith against essentialism, fundamentalism, and the host of anti-isms that serve as both a pablum for the newly initiated and a prophetic engagement with illusion for the veteran." Manning Marable (2000a, 1995), seeking to retrieve a progressive role for cultural studies, the field with which the "posts" are often identified, notes that not only was the field inaugurated by the eclectic work of the great Caribbean thinker and activist C.L.R. James but also praises the grounded work of younger African American scholars influenced by cultural studies perspectives.

5. In the early days frantic attempts were made to define "postcolonial" writing and other forms of cultural production, which some said were distinguished by an oppositional attitude towards colonialism, by an ethic of resistance, or by allegory, experimentation, and innovation, or hybridization of cultures. Mukherjee (1990: 7) argued that this privileging of parodic texts "is distorting the field as it focuses on a very limited number of authors, the ones whose texts can give back what the theory is looking for." In short, these characteristics are neither necessarily common to the so-called postcolonial literatures nor confined to them.

6. Examples include Om Juneja (1995), Dennis Walder (1998), Madsen (1999a), and Lionnet (1995) on postcolonial women novelists, where the analysis of specific texts and literatures is not edified by any special insights from postcolonial theory, except in so far as texts from different postcolonial (term used in a temporal sense) societies, and U.S. minori-

ties, are carelessly juxtaposed under the same covers or are compared, making it unclear what is meant by postcolonial.

7. It is important to emphasize that there are different institutional histories of English studies in different countries. For Canada, see Murray (1995), for Kenya, see Ngugi wa Thiong'o (1972, 1986); and for India, see Viswanathan (1989).

8. As might be expected for such a slippery and promiscuous theory, there are, to quote Jeffrey T. Nealon (1993: 27) "many deconstructions: the 'rhetorical' deconstruction of Paul de Man is different from the 'pedagogical' deconstruction of Gregory Ulmer, which in turn is different from the 'political' deconstruction of Michael Ryan, the 'postcolonial' deconstruction of Gayatri Spivak, the 'philosophical' deconstruction of [Rodolphe] Gasché , or the 'feminist' deconstruction of Barbara Jordan, and the differences must be attended to."

9. As might be expected, some Canadian literary scholars object to "posts" reincorporation of "Canadian literature into a homogenizing, internationalist paradigm that occludes our 'alternative, differentiated identity'" (McDonald, 1995: 49).

10. Santiago Colas (1995: 382) informs us that "although accepted in Asian and African area studies, the concept of postcoloniality, which is identified as a product of the United States and Europe, often faces resistance from Latin Americanists for whom it is one more in a long line of foreign imports tainted by imperial origins." He obviously exaggerates its acceptance in African studies, and his attempts "to construct a more complex concept of postcoloniality" that can contribute to an understanding of Latin American culture never go far. For a contrary claim that postcolonial studies began in Latin American after World War 1, see Castro-Gomez (1998).

11. Nkosi's concerns are shared by other critics. For example, Louise Viljoen (1996) attacks the fact that Afrikaans literature has been ignored in postcolonial criticism, which largely focuses on English-language writings. Nana Wilson-Tagoe (1995) also contends that postcolonial theorizing

has not adequately grappled with the question of language in African literary production, as well as the specificities of African subjectification and the persistent imaginings of national liberation. She takes Bhabha to task for his position on colonial ambivalence and hybridity, arguing that colonialism was a space and moment of not merely negotiations, but negations.

12. My response to his editorial is reproduced in Chapter 8. Although, I sent it to Mbembe he did not publish it in *Codesria Bulletin*, claiming many months later that he had not seen it! In his recent book (Mbembe 2001a), he begins with the familiar African complaint about the devaluation and dehumanization of Africa in the Western imaginary, but the Africa he produces in his text is equally beastly. In a sympathetic review, Quayson (2001) wonders why Mbembe traffics images of Africa that are no different from those of Hegel, and concludes that this conflation is not a reflection of "any conceptual weakness in Mbembe's methodological schema as from the fact that the object of study—Africa—is being examined from the standpoint of an implicitly historicist and developmentalist perspective" under which Africa always falls short of Western benchmarks. To claim that we are doomed to produce denigratory accounts of Africa is to excuse poor scholarship by Africans who indiscriminately mimic Western narratives of their own societies.

13. Manthia Diawara (1997) argues that Mudimbe answers this question by proposing a linguistic revolution in which European languages are replaced by African languages, so that the Western ratio articulated in the European languages, even by seemingly oppositional thinkers like Foucault, will be banished from African discursive practices. Mudimbe's thoughts on this are indeed suggestive, but not adequately developed, let alone, practiced.

Chapter 6

Out of Africa: The Historical Writings of B.A. Ogot

Introduction

When I was initially approached to write this chapter as an introduction to Professor Bethwell A. Ogot's (2001) collection of selected essays between 1961 and 1998,[1] I accepted the challenge enthusiastically, thinking it could be done in a reasonably short time because I was familiar with Professor Ogot's published works. In addition, I thought that perhaps, as he was advancing in years, he had settled into a life of quiet contemplation and had not written much since January 1990, when I left Kenyatta University in Nairobi where we had taught together in the history department. When the box containing Ogot's manuscript arrived, I was overwhelmed by the sheer volume of his writings, the wide range of topics covered, and the profundity and complexity of his thoughts. I read in wonder the essays he wrote in the 1990s, commenting on everything from the impact of the end of the cold war to the current processes and patterns of globalization on Africa and the influence of postmodernism on African studies and history. Reading and commenting on the essays became a journey of intellectual pleasure for me, a rare opportunity to stand on the shoulders of one of the pioneers of African academic history, free to gaze backwards and forwards; backwards, to see from where the discipline had emerged and to appreciate the struggles that were waged, and forwards, to peer into the possibilities of the future for an enterprise that must have a mission greater than mere scholarship, that must strive to facilitate our people's liberation from oppressive pasts.

This exercise has reinforced my conviction that African scholars must read and comment on each other's work seriously, that younger scholars must build on the work of earlier generations as part of the process of constructing cumulative scholarly traditions and integrated scholarly communities across the continent and in the diaspora. I have grouped his forty-six essays into three thematic sections and divided the chapter into four parts. The first part briefly looks at Professor Ogot's times and career. The second examines his reflections on the trends in African historiography. The third focuses on the essays that reconstruct various historical processes—from precolonial state formation to the evolution of the colonial administration in Kenya and the organization, composition, and impact of the Mau Mau liberation movement. The fourth analyzes his commentaries on contemporary issues and events, including the nature and dynamics of African politics, leadership, identities, culture, development, universities, and globalization.

All I can do is to provide a mere taste of the immense feast awaiting those ready to sample the intellectual offerings by one of Africa's leading historians. It is a journey into the making of African history, as well as the life of an African public intellectual, that offers interesting contrasts to the life of a renowned African American public intellectual, Henry Louis Gates, who is examined in the next chapter. The historical writings and television series by Ogot and Gates, respectively, raise critical questions about the roles and responsibilities of public intellectuals in promoting the integrity and interests of Africa and the African diaspora.

The Man and His Times

For my generation, who went to school in the 1960s, to college in the 1970s, and began to teach in the 1980s—the existence of African history has always been taken for granted. It was not always so. In 1950, when Professor Ogot went to Makerere College to study, there was hardly any African history at that newly established, esteemed institution of higher learning. What passed for such history comprised, to quote the syllabus, "The Arab and American slave trades; Abolition; African explorers; Chartered companies; Missions; Partition and Colonization; the First World War in Africa." To the overseers and ideologues of the then hegemonic colonial state and imperial order, Africans were a primitive people without history. The little historical light that traversed this "dark continent" came from the activities and wanderings of enlightened Europeans and other outsiders. The denial of Africa's historicity facilitated the dismissal of the Africans' humanity, both of which were fundamental to the colonial project of wanton economic exploitation, political oppression, cultural subjugation, and social domination.

When Ogot returned to Makerere in 1959 as a lecturer in history, the Eurocentric syllabus had been modified slightly to accommodate the History of Tropical Africa from 1750 to the present and the History of East Africa from 1850 to the present. A decade later, half of the history courses at Makerere and the two other East African universities (Nairobi and Dar es Salaam, then constituent colleges together with Makerere of the University of East Africa) were in African history. The struggle for African history had been won. No one any longer seriously questioned that Africans had their own history or histories. The challenge now was to extend the temporal and spatial scales of these histories, their methodological and thematic dimensions, and to integrate them into other regional and global histories, as well as to expand the production and consumption of the new historical knowledge, to disseminate it to policy makers and to a public hungry for liberating ideologies and identities.

Clearly, Ogot's generation laid the foundations of African history as we currently know and practice it. They established its curricula contours, conceptual concerns, and research conventions. They founded history departments and graduate programs that trained subsequent generations of historians and associations and publishing houses that produced and promulgated knowledge about African history to various audiences. A pioneering generation it was indeed, full of energy and creativity and extremely conscious of its intellectual and ideological mission; to rehabilitate the African past and to reclaim the dignity of African peoples, to produce usable histories for the continent's newly independent nation-states. They were nationalists by context and conviction. African nationalism had produced them, brought the independent states that set up the universities that nurtured them, and demanded from its intelligentsia visions and programs of developing the "political kingdom," a project in which the intelligentsia also fervently believed.

It, later, became fashionable among the younger generation of radical African historians inspired by dependency and Marxist paradigms and subsequently feminist and environmental perspectives to attack nationalist historiography for all sorts of theoretical and ideological shortcomings. The charges were that nationalist historiography was elitist in that it largely focused on the

ruling classes rather than the on "people"; it modeled itself on European historical narratives of achievement; it focused excessively on nationalism at the
expense of explaining the exploitative dynamics of imperialism that survived
the end of formal colonial rule; and it ignored women, the environment, and
the material realities, challenges, and struggles of African societies (Zeleza,
1997a: Chapters 6-10). Some of these charges were valid and could be
applied to several historians of Ogot's generation. While the absence of
women and gender history in Ogot's collection, for example, is quite striking,
but those making the radical critiques often failed to acknowledge how much
they owed to the nationalist historians for their very presence or that they
were asking new questions precisely because the nationalist historians had
answered fundamental questions about the very existence of African history.
Also, inspired by justifiable distrust and disgust for the proliferating dictatorships, the critics became distrustful of nationalism as a whole forgetting that
their own dreams for Africa were rooted in that very nationalism and sought
to fulfill what Thandika Mkandawire (1999) calls the uncompleted historic
and humanistic tasks of African nationalism: complete decolonization,
nation-building, economic and social development, democratization, and
regional cooperation. Moreover, the critics failed to allow for the simple fact
that many nationalist historians did evolve as they responded to new questions, concerns, and perspectives as is abundantly clear from this splendid volume of Ogot's essays covering forty years. Indeed, what is remarkable about
this generation is the role they played as "public intellectuals" in terms of
addressing the burning questions of the day and their public service
functions.

Ogot was among the best of his generation. He played a leading role in
the struggle for the development and institutionalization of African history.
He taught at Makerere University between 1959 and 1964, the first professional East African historian to teach in a university. In 1964, he moved to
University College, Nairobi, later renamed the University of Nairobi, where
he served in several capacities at various times as the head of the history
department, director of the Institute of African Studies, dean of the Faculty
of Arts, and deputy vice-chancellor. In the 1980s, he began to teach at
Kenyatta University, and in the 1990s at Maseno University College, where
he was instrumental in consolidating history and other programs in the
humanities and social sciences. Outside the university Ogot served in a wide
range of organizations. He was secretary-general of the East African Institute

of Social and Cultural Affairs (1964-9), founder and chairman of the East African Publishing House (1964-74), secretary-general of the Jomo Kenyatta Foundation (1968-9), member of the East African Examinations Council (1967-74), a member of the Kenyan National Commission for UNESCO from 1968, a trustee of the National Museums of Kenya (1969-77), a member of the Executive Committee of the Association of African Universities (1972-78), a member of the Executive Council of the British Institute in Eastern Africa (1968-78), a member of the East African Legislative Council (1974-7), a founder member and chairman of the Historical Association of Kenya (1966-1985), a member of the International Scientific Committee for the Preparation of the UNESCO General History of Africa and president of the committee from 1977, a member of the Executive Council of the International Africa Institute from 1978, president of the Pan-African Association for Prehistory and Related Studies from 1977, director of the International Louis Leakey Memorial Institute for African Prehistory from 1978, and in the 1980s, he served as chairman of various parastatal organizations, including Kenya Posts and Telecommunications and Kenya Railways.

This is a truly a remarkable career. Ogot belongs to the generation of African intellectuals trained both in the regional universities that were belatedly set up during the twilight years of colonial rule and in the imperial metropoles, for whom African nationalism was articulated as much in regional as in national terms, thus producing knowledge and building institutions that were complimentary endeavors. They were, therefore, not simply narrow territorial nationalists but cosmopolitan Pan-Africanists, not merely isolated academics but public intellectuals who moved easily between the university campus and public service. They captured and represented a brief moment when African intellectuals were organic to the nationalist project, because the national elite was small, education was prized, and the universities were valued symbols for nation-building and development; the independence social contract had yet to crumble from the recessions of development and democracy, and the political class spoke and understood the language of the masses, which the intelligentsia sought to translate into modernizing political and policy claims.

There can be no doubt that Professor Ogot has been an influential figure in Kenya, in the East African region, and on the continent as whole as a teacher, researcher, university administrator, and public servant. He has trained and supervised the dissertations of hundreds of students and taught thousands more. It would be no exaggeration to say that much of the basic historical research in Kenya over the last four decades was done by his students or by students of his students, or by foreign students who were advised by him or his students. His influence on Kenyan historiography, and through his work on the UNESCO General History of Africa and other international projects on African historiography, has truly been immense. I first met him in 1977, when I was a teaching assistant and he was invited as an external examiner by the history department at the University of Malawi. I remember students were awestruck to have their papers and grades evaluated by this distinguished and famous historian. Meeting him in person I was impressed by his vast knowledge and his sense of humor. He seemed to me then the epitome of what a scholar ought to be: brilliant, witty, and personable. Years later, between 1984 and 1989, I had the privilege of working and teaching with him at Kenyatta University, where he became one of my mentors. I was always impressed by his deep love of ideas and intellectual debate, his incredible erudition, his commitment to students, and his passion for training a new generation of historians. Despite his busy schedule, he was keen to read my papers and would give me detailed and perceptive comments.

Once we wrote a joint paper on decolonization in Kenya. When the organizers of the conference tried to exclude it from the published collection because of its trenchant critique of imperialist historiography, he refused to have the paper revised. Other African historians who had participated in the conference threatened to withdraw their papers if ours was excluded. It was published as we had written it.[2] That one episode gave me a glimpse into the battles Ogot's generation had fought, and I realized how principled Ogot was as a historian and the value of standing firm for one's views and of networking, that producing knowledge is an individual and collective struggle, and each generation of African historians has a responsibility to advance the struggle from where the preceding generation left it, adding new layers of knowledge and interpretation of our varied pasts for more productive futures. Through Ogot I learnt about struggles surrounding the UNESCO General History of Africa and met many of the series' editors and other senior historians whom I hold in high regard. He inspired me to think big, to claim the whole of Africa as my heritage and my research landscape. In a critical sense, therefore, although Ogot never taught me in any formal sense, I always think of him as one of my best teachers.

Fighting Historical Dogmas

One of Ogot's key contributions to African historiography was methodological, the use of oral traditions to reconstruct history. He was among the first to depend almost entirely on oral traditions to reconstruct the precolonial history of the Luo for his Ph.D. dissertation, thereby demonstrating that there were other sources for historical writing besides written records. In addition to the oral tradition, Ogot and his colleagues resorted to other sources—including historical linguistics, historical anthropology, and of course archaeology—to take on the challenging task of mapping the historical contours of various African societies. These sources, especially oral sources, eventually gained acceptance and were employed to enrich other histories, including Western and feminist histories.

From the beginning Ogot was painfully aware of the methodological and analytical challenges that faced African history. *Ogot's Selected Essays 1961-1998* contains fourteen essays that reflect on various aspects of African historiography. Two of the essays provide fascinating overviews on the institutional development of history as a discipline in East Africa and of intellectual trends in African historiography in general over the last century. Another three offer programmatic interventions, one for social history, another for environmental history, and the third for reconceptualizing the social sciences, thus demonstrating Ogot's ability to respond creatively to changing research agendas. The rest make specific critiques against various dogmas, predominantly Eurocentric, that have bedeviled African historical studies. Let us begin with the latter.

In "Historians and East Africa" we are offered a masterful survey of European writings on East African history, demonstrating that the work of European professional historians from the 1950s was enormously influenced by the "pioneer traditions" established by amateurs—administrative officials, missionaries, and settlers. These traditions were full of misconceptions about, and contempt for, African societies and obsessed with propagating the civilizing impact of colonization. As a result East African history was reduced to an appendage of European history. In the 1950s and 1960s, European historians continued to conceive East African history in terms of invaders or outsiders, as an aspect of the expansion of Europe, although they increasingly paid attention to African responses. These biases are evident in Volume I of the *Oxford History of East Africa*, published in 1963 and edited by two renowned Africanist historians, Roland Oliver and Gervase Mathew.

Although the volume sought to provide the first comprehensive overview of precolonial East African history, but even here, Ogot shows, eight out of the twelve chapters deal with the impact of the outside world on the indigenous peoples of East Africa. Indeed, the epilogue argues that colonialism provided the stimulus for social, economic, and political advance in the region.

Preoccupation with the role of outsiders has particularly afflicted the history of the East African coast. In "The Limitations of Textual History" Ogot critiques the book *East Africa and the Orient,* based on proceedings from a conference of eminent Western scholars who met in Nairobi in 1967. None of the participants, he notes wryly, was from East Africa or from the Indian Ocean rim countries. Systematically, he attacks the book for its Eurocentric biases, shoddy scholarship, repetitiveness, spurious racial classifications, negligence of important topics such as the slave trade, and its over-reliance on problematic textual sources and anthropological evidence. The picture that emerges is one of East African coastal peoples as passive recipients of civilizing cultures and commodities, ranging from genes, words and beliefs to crops, crafts, and trade goods. Ogot shows how pervasive the notion of the civilizing outsider is in African historiography in "The Concept of the Outsider in African History." He singles out the "Hamitic myth", the tendency to equate all "civilizations" in Africa with centralized states established by outsiders, usually assumed to have Caucasoid features, a sin he finds rampant not only among European but among some African historians too.

That the Eurocentric ailment survived the nationalist onslaught is evident from Ogot's sharp reviews of two books by J. D. Fage and Roland Oliver, the doyens of African history in Britain, published in 1978 and 1991, respectively. Fage's magnun opus *A History of Africa* is taken to task in "The Dilemmas of Research in Early African History" for resurrecting the Hamitic myth by dividing the continent into the "white" North and the "black" sub-Saharan South and arguing that all the major technologies and complexes of civilization flowed from the Caucasoid to the Negroid peoples. The activities of European invaders from the fifteenth century are thereby stripped of their historic violence as they are reconstituted as the continuation of the Caucasoid factor in African history. The upshot of this racialized history, Ogot argues, is that the African, seen as the Negro, has contributed very little to the history of his own continent, let alone to human history.

Ogot finds similar shortcomings in Oliver's tome *The African Experience,* which traces the history of the continent from the emergence of hominids to the release of Nelson Mandela and is reviewed in "Reflections on an African Experience." According to Ogot, the book paints too linear a picture of human evolution and assigns crucial developments in African history to the allegedly Afroasiatic Ancient Egyptians, although like the Egyptologists he is reluctant to portray Pharaonic Egypt as an African country and its civilization as an African civilization. On the slave trade he repeats the canard of eighteenth century British slave traders that since slavery and the slave trade were allegedly an integral feature of African societies, the European slave trade merely provided new destinations and caused little harm. Similarly, he is apologetic on the impact of colonialism by depicting and sanitizing brutal conquest and stiff resistance as "colonial infiltration" and by drawing a positive "balance sheet" of empire. Predictably, too, for someone who portrays colonialism as a harbinger of progress and civilization, Oliver sees postcolonial Africa as a tragic story of disaster, economic decline, and political tyranny, which he largely attributes to internal failures, from misguided socialist policies, one-party rule, and population growth to rural-urban migration and the urban biases of African governments.

Ogot is quite critical of the tendency among Western academics and politicians to draw a racist distinction between Africa north of the Sahara— which they regard as geographically Mediterranean, culturally Arab, and historically an offshoot of Western civilization—and Africa south of the Sahara—regarded as the "real" Africa. This is the subject of "Towards a History of Relations Between African Systems," in which he urges African historians to treat the continent as a unit characterized by complex interactions between different societies and systems and to map out the nature of their relations at different moments and at various regional scales. In these essays Ogot is insistent that African historians must challenge Eurocentric historiography and its rhetoric of Afrocontempt and Afropessimism by eschewing racial or ethnic explanations and not leaving the writing of regional, continental, and global histories solely to the Europeans and others. From time to time, he advises, we must raise our heads from detailed quarrying and see the large landscape of African history and Africa's contribution to world history.

Ogot has not trained his critical gaze exclusively on Eurocentric scholars from Europe. He has also attacked African scholars prone to Afrocentric fantasies and radical sloganeering. In "Intellectual Smugglers in Africa" he questions Okot p'Bitek's sloppy dismissal of all modern scholars who have apparently "smuggled" Greek metaphysical conceptions into African religious thought. P'Bitek asserts that no African people believed in a High God and that African scholars asserting otherwise are "intellectual smugglers." His whole argument seems to rest on the spurious assumption that Africans do not think metaphysically, and that a High God must of necessity be a Christian God. Ogot expressed even greater concern about what he saw at the turn of the 1980s as "a dangerous tendency towards intellectual absolutism" among Kenyan intellectuals. In "History, Ideology and Contemporary Kenya," he singles out historians who portray those who disagree with their interpretations of Mau Mau as a heroic nationalist movement as enemies of the people. He contends that the so-called radicals' idealization of "the people" is based more on fidelity to Marxist ideology than Marxist methodology and produces bad history. Certainly these historians have oversimplified the history of the Kenyan peasantry. He concludes with a sympathetic reading of works by political scientists inspired by a clearer understanding of Marxist methodology who have demonstrated the complex and contradictory development of the Kenyan peasantry in different parts of the country.

Ogot's acute understanding of the shifting institutional and intellectual terrains in the production and content of African history and historiography is quite apparent in the following two essays, "Three Decades of Historical Studies in East Africa, 1949-1977" and "Africa: The Agenda of Historical Research and Writing." In the first essay he outlines the struggles that were fought to institutionalize African history at Makerere University and later at the University of Nairobi. He lucidly weaves an institutional and disciplinary history with personal recollections and reflections, underscoring the key moments of the struggle, the personalities involved, the issues at stake, and the successes and failures. The battles were for disciplinary respectability, receptive audiences, intellectual and ideological relevance, and for the Africanization of African history and its incorporation into truly global history.

As for the analytical trends, in the second essay Ogot succinctly traces the main interpretive traditions that have dominated African history, beginning with the imperialist school with its unabashed Eurocentrism, followed by the rise and decline of the nationalist school in the 1960s and 1970s, and the search for new directions from the 1980s. He notes with approval the emergence of new areas and themes of historical research, from the environment and health, to gender and ethnicity. He believes the growing interest in ethnicity as a historically dynamic, constantly negotiated and renegotiated, defined and redefined identity in everyday discourse, has been inspired by poststructuralism and postmodernism. For bringing questions of ethnicity and identity and the production of knowledge and discourse to the fore, Ogot applauds the "posts," but like many African historians he is troubled by postmodernism. Specifically, while disavowing universalism it is, in his view, itself a grand theory wedded to Eurocentric liberalism that offers no radical critique of capitalism. Moreover, its celebration of difference seems suspect for the historians of peoples whose difference was construed as a marker of their primitivity and backwardness. Also, the emphasis on the particularity, locality, and contingency of identities dissolves the cohesion of Africa as a historical unit and flies in the face of global forces that transcend individual agency. Finally, postmodernism threatens well-established historical methods of studying societies, for it denies the very existence or authenticity of the domain of social reality called history.

Ogot sees postmodernism as one of the main problems confronting African historical scholarship as we enter the twenty-first century. Other problems relate to developing appropriate modes of critique of historical sources as the old methodologies of historical anthropology, oral tradition, archeology, historical linguistics have come under attack. Many historians, including Ogot, now question the ability of oral tradition to provide reliable chronologies since they are synthetic products of communal and individual composition that change constantly through time. However, they still offer crucial insights into the evolution of historical consciousness, as Ogot demonstrates in "The Construction of Luo Identity and History," a probing survey of the constructions of popular and academic traditions of Luo history during the course of the twentieth century. He investigates the modes of transmission and interaction between the oral and written histories and the complex ways they are woven into the tapestry of modern Luo ethnic identity. Underlying these challenges is how to redefine the relations between popular and academic productions of history and between scholar and audience if African academic history is to transcend its fundamental conundrum, the fact that since its inception it has been modeled on, oriented towards, and sought legitimation from the historiographies of Europe and the Americas. All the major paradigms in African history—the imperialist and nationalist, dependency and Marxist, poststructuralist and postmodernist—were manufactured in the West and imported to Africa. Is autonomy of African history possible, Ogot asks.

He provides no answer for this question that has vexed generations of African historians and intellectuals. Are we condemned to eternal mimicry? Or are we asking the wrong question, uncritically accepting that the historical concepts we use and the very idea of history belongs to the West, thus inadvertently surrendering our histories and intellectual souls to the West? Is the search for authenticity a disguised cry of capitulation for a globalized intelligentsia? Shouldn't the West itself be dismembered, stripped of its universalism and provincialized as Dipesh Chakrabarty (1996) implores us to? It is encouraging that a historian of Ogot's generation and stature is still asking fundamental questions about African history. It is a testament to the boundless curiosity and creativity of his historical imagination and his readiness to stretch the boundaries of African historical scholarship. In the 1970s, he pushed for social and environmental history, as stated in the essays on "History, Anthropology and Social Change" and "African Ecology in Historical Perspectives: Problems and Prospects." Typically, he placed the two research agendas in their East African historiographical context, critiquing old approaches before outlining new ones.

In the 1990s, he turned to the issue of interdisciplinary scholarship and the social sciences. In "Social Sciences in the 21st Century: From Rhetoric to Reality," he presents a compelling analysis of the emergence and evolution of the social sciences as modes of institutionally reproduced discourse in the context of changing structures of state power, accumulation, and social organization and control. First, he maps out the development of the social sciences in Europe and in North America from the era of laissez-faire capitalism at the end of the nineteenth century, the growth of the welfare state in the mid-twentieth century, to the neoliberal era during the last two decades of the century. As to Kenya, he is critical of the tendency of African social scientists to accept uncritically concepts, theories and methodological procedures manufactured in the West, and calls for scientific creativity, through the development of innovative interdisciplinary, multidisciplinary, and transdisciplinary approaches and programs that are better equipped to analyze and understand Kenyan realities than the fragmented disciplines or approaches that currently tend to privilege development economics.

Reconstructing African Histories

As important as his historiographical reflections are, Ogot's historical work has centered on reconstructing the histories of specific societies, processes, and events. As might be expected from a generation that was committed to demonstrating the historicity of African societies, precolonial history featured prominently in his writings. His major publication in this regard was *History of the Southern Luo, Vol. 1. Migration and Settlement 1500-1900,* published in 1967. He also edited Volume V of UNESCO's General History of Africa, *Africa from the Sixteenth to the Eighteenth Century,* published in 1992. Altogether the record of his publications on a wide range of topics and subjects in Kenyan, East African, and African histories is truly staggering. In a bibliography of Ogot's work published in 1989, Hudson Liyai (1989) lists twenty-two books and monographs, forty-two chapters and contributions in books, thirty papers, lectures and reports, ten unpublished manuscripts, eighty-three articles, review articles, commentaries and letters, and forty-nine critical reviews of his work.

In this collection there are six essays dealing with various aspects of precolonial history and another four on the colonial era. "The Concept of Jok," published in 1961, is one of Ogot's earliest essays and clearly articulates what was to become his lifelong intellectual mission: an indefatigable defense of the humanity, historicity, durability, diversity, complexity, and richness of African societies and cultures. The essay begins with an indictment of Africanist scholarship that was as true then as it is now: "So far, most Africanists have avoided African philosophy." It is revealing that he begins this work with philosophy, the epitome of knowledge and reasoning in Western culture. The defense of African history had to start at that inestimable intellectual plane. Ogot is critical of studies of African customary practices and institutions that make little or no attempt to link these with African ideas of the universe, existence, and destiny. In this essay he seeks to decipher the meanings of the term *jok* or *juok*, which is found in various forms in all Nilotic languages and usually means "God," "spirit," "witchcraft," "ghost" or some form of spiritual power. What follows is a fascinating exegesis on the ontological principles embedded in the concept of jok that underlie major aspects of Nilotic cultures and societies.

Ogot's abiding interest in the history of African thought and institutional practices, especially religion, is carried further in three essays. First, in "On the Making of a Sanctuary" he examines Padhola religion, which, he contends, is monotheistic and rooted in the concept of jok and cannot be understood outside the Nilotic vision of reality. The essay also traces the changes in Padhola religion as a result of their migration southwards between 1500 and 1850, the infiltration of new people among the Padhola during the second half of the nineteenth century and the establishment of the Bura shrine as a central place of worship and unifying force among the Padhola, and the disruptive influences of Christianity and denominational rivalries during the first half of the twentieth century.

Second, "Reverend Alfayo Odongo Mango 1870-1934"presents a short biographical study of one of the leading Christian evangelists in western Kenya. Ogot gives us an intriguing portrait of the complex processes of conversion among the first African Christians in this region, their motivations, sacrifices, compromises, training, evangelical activities, intricate involvement in African struggles, and their troubled relationships with African chiefs, European missionaries and the colonial government, which in this case led Mango to break with the Anglican Church. He subsequently found his own—the Holy Ghost Church—which sought to promote the spiritual and secular aspirations of people in the region. In the end Mango was consumed by the contradictions and conflicts surrounding him, and he was murdered in January 1934 during an attack on his village.

Finally, in "A Community of Their Own" Ogot investigates the rise and impact of the Mario Legio of Africa Church, which began as a reform movement in the Roman Catholic Church in the South Nyanza District of Kenya in 1960. Its emergence is attributed to intensifying economic, political, and social insecurities among the poor who found religious and cultural comfort in the prophetic charisma and teachings of the founders, which invoked and resonated with indigenous religious beliefs, visions, rituals, and practices. By analyzing these religions on their own terms, as authentic expressions of African religious experience, Ogot is reclaiming and normalizing African cultural systems, activities, initiatives, choices, and adaptations.

The same nationalist impulse informs his essay on "Kingship and Statelessness Among the Nilotes," in which he challenges the racist hypothesis that assumes a positive correlation between the amount of Hamitic blood in a people's veins and the degree of their political evolution. Instead he suggests, referring to two cases, that the establishment of the Bunyoro and Shilluk kingdoms was facilitated by a specific conjuncture of economic, political, and military factors. Centralized kingdoms constituted only one form of political system among the Western Nilotes. The other three systems Ogot identifies included the "segmentary states" that resembled, but were less advanced than, the Bunyoro kingdom; the Ruothships of the Acholi and the Luo, in which royal clans ruled over common clans with no supreme head; and the "stateless societies" proper, such as the Dinka and Nuer.

Ogot expands his geographical canvas of political history in "The Great Lakes Region," a chapter first published in 1984 in the Volume IV of UNESCO's General History of Africa. This essay underscores the problem of sources for some regions and periods of African history. The period covered—1200 to1500—is one on which there is scant oral tradition, linguistic, or archaeological data. This makes it difficult to determine the chronology of individual states or the region as a whole. Most of the available sources are based on court traditions that tell us little about the social, economic, and political conditions of the society at large. Also, the region is riddled with myths about the nature of the relations between pastoralists and agriculturalists, the common assumption being that the former were the "civilizing conquerors" of the latter. Ogot tackles these challenges boldly, examining in considerable detail each of the four political complexes he identifies—the Kitara, Kintu, Ruhinda, and Rwanda complexes. He dispels many myths and shows that different groups of people and historical contexts were involved in the complex processes of state formation. One cannot, however, escape the tentative feel of the narrative in many places, the excessive focus on leaders and heroic individuals, and the virtual absence of information about economic and social conditions and processes. The essay's vastness of scale in temporal and spatial terms throws into sharp relief the inadequacy and inconclusiveness of oral tradition, a sentiment Ogot has come to share in recent years.

The essays on the colonial era have a more decisive edge to them, reflecting no doubt the relative abundance of sources, both written and oral. Only one essay, "British Administration in the Central Nyanza District of Kenya, 1900-1960," deals with the colonial state itself, while the rest focus on anticolonial resistance as manifested in Mau Mau, Kenya's liberation movement, thus underscoring the nationalist historian's preoccupation with African agency than the intricacies of imperial dominion. The contradictory nature of the colonial state comes through in the essay on colonial administration. The colonial state was both authoritarian and weak because as a conquest state it lacked legitimacy. He describes the fumbling efforts of the mostly ill-educated and incompetent officials to incorporate the existing segmentary system into the colonial administration and the periodic administrative reorganization and reforms, the role the missionaries played as colonial ideologues and functionaries, the impact of the First and Second World Wars, and the rise of African protest initially articulated through religious movements and later through reformist political associations formed by the educated elite. The connections between the local and national manifestations of nationalism are discussed briefly towards the end of the essay. An attempt is made to explain the relative failure of the leading nationalist party, the Kenya African Union, to establish itself in Nyanza. He attributes this to the fact that KAU leadership was largely Kikuyu and focused largely on Kikuyu land grievances which did not have the same resonance in Nyanza. Both the intensity of the nationalist struggle and fissures within the centrifugal nationalist movement increased with the outbreak of Mau Mau.

In Kenyan historiography and politics, the question of Mau Mau has been at the center of stormy debates about the country's accession to independence and its subsequent dispensation. Stripped of all the ideological and theoretical posturings, including the recent poststructuralist readings, the debate has always been polarized around whether Mau Mau was atavistic or progressive, tribalist or nationalist, successful or betrayed.[3] This mode of inquiry has not been particularly productive. Clearly, Mau Mau was militarily defeated and the movement did not provide Kenya's leadership after independence, but only a fool would argue that Mau Mau did not bring about Kenya's independence, for the Mau Mau war ruptured the colonial order in Kenya by burying the political dreams of the settlers and making constitutional and structural reforms imperative. Mau Mau fighters and their descendants may not have inherited the new political kingdom, but that does not mean they did not nourish it through their struggles.

Ogot's reflections on Mau Mau are far more cogent and nuanced than his detractors credit. As far as I can tell, he has never underestimated the historical significance of Mau Mau in the decolonization of Kenya, although he has pointed out that while its goals were nationalist, it was not a national movement because it was confined to Central Kenya. In his writings on the subject Ogot has tried to analyze the social composition and ideology of Mau Mau and its construction in the colonial and African imaginaries, as is evident in the three essays included in this volume. In the first one, "Revolt of the Elders: An Anatomy of the Loyalist Crowd in the Mau Mau Uprising, 1952-1956," he seeks to examine the composition of the "people" who supported and opposed Mau Mau among the Kikuyu. He shows that the division between the "fighters" and "loyalists" corresponded to class and ideological divisions in Kikuyu society based on relative access to land and other assets, affinities to "traditional" culture and Christianity, and attitudes towards violence and constitutionalism, all of which were articulated with the differentiations of age, the political ecologies of location, and the memories of struggle and dreams of the future.

In the next essay, "Politics, Culture and Music in Central Kenya: A Study of Mau Mau Hymns, 1951-1956," he turns to songs as critical cultural texts that embody and express deep-seated social values, visions, problems, and possibilities. He shows quite convincingly that hymns and popular songs played a crucial role in articulating and popularizing the demands of the Mau Mau struggle, mobilizing people for it, and re-enforcing the solidarity and spirits of the militants and their supporters. From these songs, he concludes, it is clear that Mau Mau was an anticolonial movement, although the fact that they were sang in Kikuyu and used Kikuyu symbols, legends and history limited their national appeal and accessibility. This raises an important question: What makes a movement nationalist in multiethnic, multicultural, and multilingual societies, as is the case in most African colonies? Except for some of the Arabic-speaking countries, there were no national languages in these colonies. The European languages spoken by the elite were not national in any meaningful sense of the term. In expressing their anticolonial nationalism ordinary people inevitably spoke in the cultural languages and addressed the grievances with which they were familiar. Did that make them any less nationalist than the elites speaking in the borrowed idioms of Europe? More important than the language of political discourse, in my view, is the content of that discourse, for after all the Kikuyu "fighters" and "loyalists" used the same language but for vastly different political goals.

From songs as a historical source, Ogot moves to the press in "Mau Mau and the Fourth Estate, 1952-1956." Mindful of the inherent biases and propagandistic uses of the press in general especially during times of conflict and of the settler-controlled press in Kenya in particular, Ogot is still able to cull important information about the conduct of the war, specifically the military aspects of the emergency, the terror and brutality meted out to the Kikuyu and all those who supported Mau Mau, who were sent to detention and forced work camps and repatriated en masse from the European farms, towns and cities, and the neighboring countries of Uganda and Tanzania, all of which had several unintended consequences. Militants used the camps and prisons to spread their political gospel, while the repatriations helped swell the numbers of Mau Mau fighters. Singling out the Kikuyu and related communities reinforced Kikuyu regional and ethnic solidarity, although it is quite clear from the press, Ogot tells us, that many more ethnic groups were involved in the Mau Mau movement than is usually acknowledged. The press, he concludes, reveals many aspects of the Mau Mau movement that historians should explore.

Confronting Contemporary Challenges

All good historians engage the pressing conditions, concerns, and challenges of their time. Indeed, history is fundamentally about the present, an attempt by historians rooted in the present to answer the questions posed by their age as filtered through their gender, class, culture, nationality, and race. Being the fine historian and intellectual that he is, Ogot has addressed many of the critical issues that have confronted African societies since their independence. In several essays in this volume we see him tussling with the work of some of Africa's leading thinkers and writers and tackling the knotty questions of African politics, leadership, identities, culture, development, the role of universities, and the impact on Africa of international developments and globalization—a mark of a versatile and truly gifted scholar who has fully lived through the tumultuous last forty years of African history.

In the 1960s, African intellectual discourse was dominated by spirited debates about the appropriate ideologies of development and governance and the regeneration and future of African societies. Specifically, scholars and politicians argued the relative merits of capitalism, Marxism, and African socialism. Kwame Nkrumah, Ghana's first president, was a towering figure in these debates. He proselytized for revolutionary change guided by Marxism and Pan-Africanism. In 1964, he published a renowned treatise outlining the philosophical principles underscoring his political ideology and vision for Africa. In the essay "Nkrumah Revisits Marx" Ogot reviews Nkrumah's book *Consciencism.* Ogot is perceptive and measured. He calls it the boldest and most comprehensive attempt so far made by an African to reconcile Marxism with the African Revolution, an honest and serious work that is destined to represent a major landmark in the history of Marxian thought in Africa. He commends the ease with which Nkrumah surveys the whole spectrum of western philosophy before Marx and his splendid defense of materialism. He is intrigued by the proposition that contemporary Africa has a triple heritage—the traditional African, Islamic, and the Euro-Christian—that needs to be reconciled; but he faults Nkrumah for not giving the "traditional" and Islamic legacies the kind of serious analysis accorded the Western one.[4] Part of Ogot's unease with Nkrumah's schema is based on doubts that there exists an exclusive and distinctive African traditional culture or a homogeneous African cultural universe, a subject that he elaborates on in "Reintroducing Man into the African World," where he examines the problematic connections between "traditional communalism" and European socialism in African politics.

Since the 1960s creative writers have provided a unique introspection into the promises, possibilities, pitfalls, and performances of independence. They have largely been critical, indeed angry, of the betrayal of the dreams of the masses by a crass ruling elite. While sympathetic to many of these critiques, Ogot calls on writers to be less idealistic, to probe deeper into the social realities that have produced the current crop of leaders, to treat the African not as a special virtuous species incapable of evil but as a normal human being. Ogot's admonition is well taken, but much of the essay offers an esoteric exposition on the definition and differences between facts and values. He is on firmer ground when he discusses specific writers' depictions of postindependence Africa in "Men of the People and the Second Independence." Ogot prefaces his remarks with the ironic observation that the portrayal of the modern African elite as corrupt and vain was presaged in the colonial fiction of writers like Elspeth Huxley, who distrusted and despised the "over-educated" African. The rest of this brief essay offers tantalizing notes on Peter Abrahams' warning in a *Wreath for Udomo* that tribalism would pave the way for dictatorship and on Chinua Achebe's acerbic incrimination in *A Man of the People* of the activities and wiles of the new "members of the establishment" parading as "men of the people." He concludes with a long quote from an essay by Wole Soyinka entitled "The Writer and the Modern African State," where the great writer states bitterly that African dictators have proven as capable of dehumanizing and degrading their victims as John Vorster in apartheid South Africa or Governor George Wallace in segregated Alabama, which shatters the romantic nationalist myth that Africans are natural humanists.

Why are African leaders so dictatorial? Ogot tries to answer this question in the essay "From Chief to President." He contends that colonialism undermined the old institutions of power and destroyed the checks and balances on chieftainship that made it difficult, except in perverted cases such as that of Shaka the Zulu, for rulers to be despots. Not only were chiefs turned into colonial administrative functionaries, the religious and spiritual basis of chiefly power was broken. Distrustful of the discredited chiefs, African nationalists invoked Western political slogans, not traditional African values, in their struggles against colonialism. The new rulers inherited states that lacked both cohesive nations and democratic traditions, for colonialism had destroyed old forms of democracy and replaced them with paternalistic authoritarian rule. The new presidents with their one-party states became chiefs with the cultural trappings of traditional chiefly authority but none of their moral sanctions and the uncontested powers of the colonial governors without their foreignness.

The tradition continues with the strongmen who emerged in the late-1980s and 1990s and who were cynically embraced by a world anxious for a new generation of African leadership. Among them is Yoweri Museveni, the president of Uganda since 1986, whose autobiography, *Sowing of the Mustard Seed,* Ogot reviews. It is a scathing appraisal. Museveni is depicted as a narcissistic tyrant who has fallen in love with his own reflection in Uganda's muddy political waters and turned Uganda's historical record into a narrative of self-justification. Ogot accuses Museveni who, apparently sees himself as the Che Guevera of Africa, of demonizing not only Milton Obote, Uganda's first prime minister and later president, but also people from the latter's ethnic group and region, of distorting and fabricating the historical record, of ignoring the role of external factors in the events he discusses, and of imposing a nonparty political system on Uganda that is no different from the one-party dictatorships of the past.

Reading this review one can only wish that Ogot will eventually write about the leaders of his native Kenya in such a candid manner. Ogot has of course commented extensively on Kenyan politics. In an address to students to commemorate Jamhuri (Independence) in December 1980, reproduced in Ogot's *Selected Essays* "Informal Education and the Kenya We Want" he states his belief that the attainment of political independence in Kenya must not only be accompanied by economic independence, but the two will be incomplete unless they are followed by cultural and intellectual independence, as well as by the democratization of culture. More substantively, in "The Siege of Ramogi: From Nationalist Coalitions to Ethnic Coalitions, 1960-1998," Ogot casts a long, critical gaze on Kenya's inability to produce a workable democratic, multiparty and multiethnic political order since independence. He attributes this to the problematic relationship between the state building project and civil society. He argues that the state has failed to construct a nation, because it has not been able to institutionalize itself and promote social integration by curtailing the centrifugal tendencies of regional, ethnic, linguistic, religious, and communal identities. The management of ethnicity has proved particularly difficult. He discusses the breakdown of the original two national party coalitions immediately after independence as power became centralized in a presidency increasingly associated with one ethnic group, the emergence of a moribund one-party system under President Kenyatta, the attempted coup of 1982, the revitalization of the one-party state under President Moi, the deployment under both presidents of legal and administrative mechanisms as well as murder to control the political process and eliminate opponents, and the return of contentious and ethnically polarized multiparty politics in the 1990s. Devoid of contending ideological visions and in the absence of strong national civil constituencies, Ogot suggests, Kenya's political elite relies on ethnic mobilization for access to state power, a critical asset in the distribution of resources and development. The result is that competition for power has been fought between ethnic coalitions around powerful individuals.

The question of identities and their political role seems to hold a particular fascination for Ogot. There are two essays that delve into this issue. The first essay, "Racial Consciousness Among Africans," broaches the subject of African racial attitudes. He is troubled by the preoccupation with racial identity among African leaders and scholars, which he ascribes to European and American colonists' and writers' denigration of Africans as racially inferior and the compensatory need for Africans to reassert their full humanity. This is what lies behind what he calls "the Africanization obsession," the attempt to Africanize institutions and concepts such as democracy and socialism, and even to develop a mythical "African personality." Unfortunately, the quest for singularity sometimes leads Africans to embrace derogatory colonial stereotypes and retrogressive politics, for example, arguing as non-Africans once did that democracy is Western and unsuitable for Africa. Ogot believes that the inverted racialism of the African scholar is likely to be transitory as African societies develop and grow in confidence and as the imperative to erect complex philosophical superstructures in defense of new or modified institutions becomes less and less.

In a later essay written in 1995, "National Identity and Nationalism: Concepts and Ideologies," Ogot abandoned the notion that development or modernization would lead to the lessening of identities, in this case ethnic identities. He observes that in reality there has been a resurgence of ethnic consciousness, chauvenisms, and conflicts all over the world, not just in Africa, thanks to the fact that modernization often reinforces unequal development that stokes the fires of ethnic identity, further fueled by the ravages of globalization as people seek refuge in the comfortable enclosures of ethnicity. The possibilities of achieving national cohesion through conquest, absorption, and forced political centralization as happened in parts of Western Europe have diminished. The rest of the essay offers a succinct analysis of the various theories of nations and nationalism. Some regard nationalism as a primordial phenomenon, others see it as an imagined political community either invented by the intelligentsia or spawned by the modernization of communications. There are also those who view nationalism as an expression of politicized ethnicity—an instrument in the struggle for power—and the Marxists who used to dismiss it as a manifestation of bourgeois ideology, of false consciousness, that was bound to disappear as the splendid solidarities of class and socialism evolved.

A related theme that has preoccupied Ogot is that of the role of culture in national development. He argues forcefully in "The Construction of a National Culture" that development should not be equated simply with raising the gross national product but also with questions of social justice; equity, and human rights. In short, development is as much an economic as it is a cultural process. The essay then examines the development of the social sector in Kenya, beginning with the heated debates in the 1960s and 1970s about cultural policy and what constitutes development in the sociocultural field. There are the traditionalists who argued for the preservation of the received cultural heritage and others who take a more dynamic view of culture and see sociocultural development in terms of supporting contemporary creative innovations. But they are all agreed that culture is critical for developing a national identity. In due course a number of cultural agencies and institutions were set up by the state and the universities to promote cultural research, development, and preservation. The study of oral literature or orature was introduced in schools and there was a vigorous controversy over the use of African and European languages spearheaded by the renowned writer Ngugi wa Thiong'o. The essay outlines the explosion of the literary arts and developments in art and music. He concludes arguing that a dynamic cultural sector is essential for developing, not a homogenized nation, but a vibrant and distinctive multicultural society.

The centrality of culture in national development is elaborated on in "Building on the Indigenous,"where he asserts that the collapse of the socialist project and the destruction of ecological habitats and social cohesion in the West underscores the need to connect the material and cultural dimensions of development and to avoid radical discontinuities and unselective delinking with the past. Development in Africa is likely to continue to be elusive as long as it does not build on the indigenous. Within the cultural sector, the arts have a special place, Ogot contends in "The Role of the Arts in a Developing Country," for they give larger meaning and purpose to life and social existence that cannot be obtained from material progress alone.

Education in general and universities in particular constitute one of the most critical cultural institutions. There are five essays in the collection that deal with the role of universities in national development. The first, "The Role of a University in the Development of National Unity and Consciousness," presents a robust defense of universities as institutions with three primary missions: teaching, research, and public service. Since independence African universities have faced the challenge of Africanizing their staff and curricula and of trying to maintain a delicate balance between civic involvement and academic freedom. Ogot believes African universities have a special responsibility to conduct painstaking research on pressing national issues, to create knowledge and myths that foster national consciousness, and facilitate the political socialization of students. He reminds those who tend to decry student radicalism that African university students played a conspicuous part in African nationalist movements.

As reservoirs of the best and brightest minds universities must, Ogot suggests in "University Development in Kenya—What Options?" always strive to be at the cutting edge of ideas, producing both professional elites required for current development and nation-building and research and knowledge for future use. Noting that as we enter the twenty-first century power is shifting from natural resources and physical strength to knowledge, and that the knowledge system itself is being transformed by the increasing quantity of data available, the growing sophistication of methodologies, and by the creation of new paradigms to understand reality, Ogot advises university planners in Kenya to put more emphasis on four major areas: information and communication, basic sciences and high technology, cultural identity and environment. Unless this is done, he states in another essay, "The Role of University in Development," the gap between the developing and developed countries will continue widening into a gulf. He gives chilling statistics on the growing gap between the two groups of countries in per capita scientific and technological personnel and research and development expenditures and the startling changes in various sectors of the new knowledge-intensive economy, from agriculture to communications. This does not mean, however, that the arts and social sciences should be ignored, for as human beings we are more than the mere sum of our economic needs. We have social, cultural, and political lives and values that need to be comprehended and nourished. African universities must strive to be centers of excellence, capable of both solving specific problems that confront their societies and contributing to global thinking, of producing highly motivated, adaptable, and technically operational graduates who are aware of their national, regional, and continental identities and understand economic, political, military, scientific and technological problems in a global context. There needs to be greater collaboration between universities, governments, and local industry to determine research priorities.

Africa has of course never been short of external advice, much of it costly and catastrophic. The university sector has been no exception. Since the 1980s the World Bank, in particular, has weighed in on African higher education with its uncompromising but misguided neoclassical zeal. In a stinging and lengthy critique, "Lessons of Experience: Higher Education Policy of the World Bank in Africa," Ogot takes on the bank. He systematically dismembers the policy prescriptions outlined in the bank's book entitled *Higher Education: The Lessons Learned.* The World Bank's policy on higher education emphasizes differentiation, privatization, diversification of funding, efficiency, relevance, and equity. Ogot maintains that neither the diagnosis nor the prognosis is new, the analysis lacks specificity, and the recommendations are overgeneralized; the regional comparisons are misleading. The bank ignores the fact that higher education in many African countries is already differentiated and diversified, that public universities cannot be fully substituted for private ones, that in the Asian countries, held up as models, private universities are subsidized by governments, and that diversification of funding sources through higher user charges, fund raising, and income generating activities cannot provide an adequate and sustainable alternative to state support.

He agrees that state control of universities must be supplanted by a more supervisory role, and in exchange for autonomy universities must develop efficient mechanisms of evaluation, quality assessment, and accountability. Internal efficiency can also be improved through greater interinstitutional coordination, while external efficiency can be achieved by ensuring programs are sufficiently flexible to meet changing labor market needs. The role of the state, however, remains fundamental to university support as part of an integrated educational system. Universities should not be envisaged and valued merely as utilitarian and technocratic institutions as the World Bank does but as critical sites for Africans to produce original thought and to conduct basic research, to create and sustain national and regional intellectual and scientific communities, and to build the continent's human capacities in all their dimensions.

For a scholar trained at a regional university—Makerere—it is not surprising that Ogot puts a high premium on university cooperation among African countries. In "University Co-operation: The East African Experience," he discusses development of the university system in East Africa, the initial support for one university among academics and governments that saw it as a rational and economic use of higher educational resources available in the region and as an essential instrument for East African cooperation and the promotion of a regional consciousness. Unfortunately, the forces of territorial nationalism combined with rising demand for higher education and diverging political ideologies and priorities led to the demise of the University of East Africa in 1970 and to the establishment of national universities. The universities in Kenya, Uganda, and Tanzania tried to maintain cooperation and student and faculty exchanges through the Inter-University Committee, but the areas of cooperation gradually dwindled, especially after the collapse of the East African Community in 1977. While development of new universities was inevitable, Ogot believes the case for regional cooperation is as strong as ever, indeed, more so now, when African countries need to pull their collective resources together to face the challenges of globalization.

The question of globalization, its conceptualization, trajectory, and impact on Africa, is tackled in a series of four captivating essays. Ever the historian, Ogot seeks to put the processes associated with globalization in their proper historical perspective. He begins with a broad survey of the relations between the rich and poor countries over the last four decades in "The Struggle for the Third World," where he tracks the emergence of the idea and geopolitical presence of the Third World and the division of the world into two hostile camps led by the United States and the former Soviet Union. While superpower rivalries formed the backdrop of international relations during this era, the essay largely focuses on the struggle for the resources and markets of Third World countries among Western countries, primarily the United States, the European Economic Community, and Japan. Deftly, Ogot unravels the way these struggles were played out with contradictory effects in Latin America, the Middle East, Africa, and Asia. Some client states, like South Korea, were able to industrialize in the process, while others like Zaire sunk deeper into economic decay. With remarkable prescience—the essay was written in 1990—he forecasts the collapse of the Soviet trading bloc, COMECON, and the USSR itself, as well as the unification of Germany and wonders about the likely impact of these developments on a Third World dissolving under the weight of uneven development and differentiation and a world drifting towards preferential trade areas. Africa, he believes, has no choice but to strengthen its already-existing regional institutions and to promote regional and continental economic cooperation. He urges the ratification and implementation of the African Economic Community treaty that stipulates a thirty-five year period for the establishment of a single African economic community.

The end of the Cold War engendered Western triumphalism and giddy expectations of a new world order. Scholars and the media scrambled to find a metaphor that would capture this brave new world. Francis Fukuyama stumbled into instant fame with his end of history hypothesis, which Ogot interrogates in "After the End of History." Fukuyama's message in his book entitled *The End of History and the Last Man* is that with the implosion of the Soviet empire Marxism no longer provided a credible guide to political and economic construction, only liberal democracy and laissez faire capitalism remained. The era of competing ideological systems had come to an end, so that while events would continue to occur, there would be no history as the purposeful movement of contending systemic ideas and visions. The belief that history as a process embracing the whole of human life could come to an end, Ogot demonstrates, goes back to Judeo-Christian ideology, and he finds secular echoes in the work of the German philosopher Friedrick Hegel and later that of Karl Marx himself, who substituted Hegel's idealistic conception of history with a materialist one. Fukuyama's argument is that there are two powerful forces at work in human history: first, the logic of modern natural science and its economic imperative of modernization, which leads to the homogenization of all human societies in the direction of capitalism; and second, what he calls the struggle for recognition, which is apparently consummated by liberal democracy. Ogot is not convinced that capitalism and liberal democracy represent the desirable ends of history. Outside the developed industrial world, he concludes, history is still very much in progress and its ultimate direction is not at all certain.

For Africa and much of the Third World, the end of the cold war has not brought peace or progress Ogot argues in two essays "African Conflicts in a Global Context: A Research Agenda" and "The Future of the Past in Africa: Reflections on the Post Cold War Era." The evidence is distressing. While there were 149 major wars in the world between 1945 and 1992, most of them proxy wars for the superpowers, in 1994 alone there were 164 armed conflicts, many of them ethnic conflicts. Thus contrary to the rosy predictions of the prophets of neo-liberalism, since the end of the cold war the world has experienced disorder beyond the control of the old, undemocratic multilateral institutions such as the World Bank, IMF, and the United Nations. There has been an intensification of violence: domestic, ethnic, sexual, religious, ideological, economic, social, and military. Ogot contends that the explosion all over the world of what some have called "complex emergences"—combining armed conflicts with the collapse of economic, political, and social institutions—environmental destruction, poverty, displacement, and massive slaughter, and "ethnic cleansing" have their roots in the worsening global political economic crisis. Neoliberals, nevertheless, celebrate globalization as desirable and inevitable, ignoring the national fragmentations and cultural fundamentalisms that it spawns.

In these two essays Ogot breathes with the kind of fire one would expect from a much younger scholar. He sharply indicts the neoMalthusians who blame the crisis of development and survival in the Third World and worsening environmental degradation on population growth. He dismisses Samuel Huntington's apocalyptic "Clash of Civilizations" thesis for its false compartmentalization of cultures and peoples. He assails the Afropessimists for writing off Africa and for promoting bewilderment and hopelessness about Africa's future. He takes the postmodernists to task for their historical frivolousness. He urges African scholars to produce their own theories, analyses, ideologies, and methodologies to explain Africa's place in the world. They should undertake extensive and critical studies of globalization and the world political economy, the impact of the cold war superpowers in the creation of African fascism and fueling low-intensity conflicts, and establish research programs in strategic studies, structural violence, and conflict formations and resolution. For Ogot, therefore, the challenge that the post-cold war era poses for Africa is as much intellectual as it is ideological, paradigmatic as well as political, epistemological and economic.

Conclusion

A rich menu indeed of ideas and reflections from a student, teacher, and architect of African history over the past half century! My generation has a lot to learn from Ogot's generation. Our work is in many ways a lot easier and a lot harder. A lot easier because although Eurocentricism is still alive and well in many corners of the Western academy, we no longer have to prove to insolent and racist outsiders, let alone our own people, that African history exists. A lot harder because, having achieved institutional respectability and in the face of so much data and so many thematic and theoretical claims, it is more difficult to find the singular inspiration to tell large, coherent, and emancipatory stories of our pasts and possible futures. One of the most tragic developments in African historical scholarship for my generation is that so few of us work on the precolonial era. Most of us concentrate on the twentieth century and are seduced by the noise and fury of current events. What Ogot's career shows is that we can do both; we can immerse ourselves into the long durée, unraveling the ebbs and flows of African history over the millennia and comment perceptively on contemporary developments. The struggle for African history, begun so energetically and brilliantly by Ogot's generation, continues. Even as we devise new theories, topics, and methodologies, we would be well served to retain the mission that inspired Ogot's generation, one that informs this volume of his collected essays, and one that is, to write histories that continue to affirm the humanity of African peoples and to illuminate Africa's contributions to and changing place in the world, for our challenges and fate have not changed much over the last half century.

Endnotes

1. All the Ogot essays referred to in the chapter are from *Selected Essays, 1961-1998.*

2. The conference entitled "African Independence: Origins and Consequences of the Transfers of Power, 1956-1980," was held in Harare, Zimbabwe, 8-14 January. See Ogot and Zeleza (1988).

3. The literature on Mau Mau is vast. Many Mau Mau combatants have written their memoirs of the war. For a flavor of the bitter debates among Kenyan historians and scholars, see William R. Ochieng and Karim Janmohamed (1977); Tabitha Kanogo (1987); Wunyabari Maloba (1993); and Maina wa Kinyatti (1991). Besides invoking Mau Mau in their fiction, Kenyan writers, especially Ngugi wa Thiong'o, have commented extensively on Mau Mau, see Sicherman, (1989) and Simatei (1999). As might be expected since Kenya was a British colony, several British historians or historians located in Britain have also been deeply engaged in the Mau Mau debate, among whom the most influential is John Lonsdale (1990, 1992); others include David Throup (1988) and Frank Furedi (1989). The subject has also attracted several American historians and political scientists, including Lonsdale's collaborator, Bruce Berman (1992), as well as Fred Cooper (1988), Presley (1992); Kennedy (1992); Kershaw (1997); Clough (1998); and Elkins (2000).

4. Mazrui has elaborated on this thesis, first suggested by Edward Blyden, in his television series *Africa: A Triple Heritage.*

Chapter 7

Out of America: The Television Wonders of a Gatekeeper

Introduction

Henry Louis Gates Jr. is one of today's most famous African American intellectuals, whose every move in academia, publishing, and public commentary is eagerly followed and chronicled. No wonder his six part documentary, *Wonders of the African World,* was eagerly anticipated, but when it premiered in the fall of 1999 it provoked a storm of commentary and controversy. Why did the series generate so much debate? I believe there are four interrelated factors. First, Africa is notable for its absence in the American popular media, especially on television, except for the occasional negative news reports about the latest calamity to befall the continent, from hunger and disease to coups and wars. Consequently, a major television series was bound to raise enormous interest, at least among African migrants in the U.S., among African Americans and Africa's assorted friends. This is connected to the second factor, namely, the number of African intellectuals in American universities has increased over the last two decades. Besieged as they often are by isolation, cultural, and racial alienation, and connected through the Internet and the conference circuit, the migrant African intellectuals are anxious and able to defend against defamations of Africa coming from any quarter. The third factor has to do with the fact that this was the first major television series by an African American on Africa. As African Americans are rarely seen in the establishment media and in the academy as experts on the continent, the series carried disproportionate weight of representation in ways that a series by a white American would not have. Connected to this, finally, is the fact that it was produced by Gates, a person less known for his African expertise than for his position as a leading figure in African American studies and for his role as a so-called "public intellectual."

The series elicited both praise and condemnation. Perhaps the most pithy critique was offered by Randall Robinson of Transafrica, who sent Gates a one-word review of the series: "SHAME!" Many others in lengthier reviews described the series—its messages, narrative style, and Gates' persona—as offensive, opinionated, disturbing, depressing, divisive, disrespectful, arrogant, rude, superficial, simplistic, self-centered, egotistical, flippant, paternalistic, uninformed, naive, sexist, racist, and even Eurocentric. Sympathy and praise for the series were in short supply, certainly among many academic commentators, and when offered they were mostly restricted to appreciation of the visual imagery it offered of Africa and for its potential as an educational tool. More positive were appraisals of the book accompanying the series. One called it "a stunning African travelogue"; another found it "an exuberant, visually stunning journey across Africa and through the history of its glorious but forgotten civilizations"; and a reviewer for the *New York Times* described it as "a subtle and absorbing narrative" (Editorial reviews, 2000).

This chapter reviews the debate the series generated, examining some of the key protagonists and issues. There are four sets of commentaries to be explored; first, those posted on two academic discussion lists, the H-Net Discussion List for African American Studies (H-Afro-Am) and the H-Net Discussion List for African History and Culture (H-Africa); second, the avalanche of e-mail messages that historian Toyin Falola moderated focusing on the Soyinka-Mazrui clash over the series; third, the special issue of *West African Review* focusing on the series; and fourth, press and public reviews garnered from newspapers and Amazon.com. There are considerable overlaps as well as differences of emphasis and tone among the discussion lists that demonstrate the varied preoccupations and politics in African and African American studies. The critique begins with a brief review of the public and press response to the series, followed by an analysis of some of the key issues that critics have addressed. In so far as Gates is a well-known figure and the series exemplifies his role as a public intellectual, the debates are placed in the context of wider debates about the possibilities and pitfalls of public intellectual production and culture.

Media Hype

As might be expected, *Wonders of the African World* was preceded by a great deal of media hype. The Public Broadcasting System (PBS) (1999) announced breathlessly:

> For centuries, the history of much of Africa has been hidden from the world, lost to the ravages of time, nature and repressive governments. Now, Harvard university professor Henry Louis Gates Jr. uncovers an Africa most people never knew existed ...Gates challenges the widespread Western view of Africa as the primitive "dark continent" civilized by white colonists. He shatters myths as he tells the true stories of proud lands filled with great civilizations, cities and centers of learning long before Europeans set foot there. He also shares his poignant personal odyssey as an African American, the great-great-grandchild of slaves, returning to the cradle of black civilization...Filmed over 12 months in 12 countries, the series takes viewers on a journey through Africa past and present. WONDERS OF THE AFRICAN WORLD is filled with unforgettable images of the breathtaking beauty of the continent and its people; the thundering falls at the source of the Blue Nile, the empty sands of the Sudan stretching to the horizon, the clove-scented shores of Zanzibar, the friendly faces of vendors in small-town market squares and the regal visage of the Queen Mother of the Ashanti royal family in Ghana.

Gushing reviews were also posted on Amazon.com, the Internet marketing warehouse, and on Africana.com, the Internet site founded by Gates. Eugene Holley, Jr.(1999) declared that the film series and the book provided answers to the old question posed by the Harlem Renaissance poet Countee Cullen, 'What is Africa to me?' for a new generation.

> A beautifully illustrated, literary companion to a PBS documentary series, Wonders traces Gates's 10-month sojourn through the African motherland, from the haunting pyramids of the Egyptian/Nubian empire in Sudan and the

ancient Christian heritage of Ethiopia to the lost city of
Timbuktu and the fabled University of Sankore. Erudite
scholar that he is, Gates uses his trip to investigate the
promise and perils of contemporary Africa, considering,
among other issues, the unifying potential of the Swahili
language and black complicity in the slave trade. Gates also
takes aim at the Enlightenment, the subsequent colonialist
occupations of European nations, and the worst aspects of
Afrocentricism. Ultimately, he reveals an unbreakable,
albeit ill-defined, relationship between Afro-Americans and
Africans.

Six of the nine reviews posted on Amazon.com (1999) gave the book a
five-star rating (out of five). One wrote: "Not since Alex Haley's historical
'novel' was released over twenty years ago has a book so enthralled me with
its information about a forgotten people...I, for one, am making plans to
visit the continent to experience the wonder and power of this most intriguing land!" Another commented: "I was especially impressed with [Gates's]
representation of Africa's intellectual traditions." Another review enthused:
"Mr. Gates did a great job of showing the truth about Blacks. Mr Gates'
video should be shown to all Black and white students. It should be required
for all class levels." Yet another declared: "Gates has literally outdone himself
(and probably every other serious scholar who has attempted to unearth the
rich historical account of Africa and its peoples)....A must read for anyone of
intellectual consequence." The remaining three reviews ranged from the
mildly critical to the censorious. One complained that "the book could have
used tighter editing in my opinion, since his discussions of this tribe's war on
that tribe and then subsequent overthrow by the other tribe gets confusing."
Another reader stated that he "would recommend this book, but not the PBS
series. Gates asked silly questions and on the whole acted very silly for such
a 'learned' man in Africa." The most negative review charged: "Shown
throughout his book and video, Gates does not in any way understand the
Afrikan experience; he blames the Afrikan people for their past and as another reviewer stated, the questions that he did ask were upsetting to the people
and plainly 'stupid', his trip to Afrika was a waste of money, time and channel thirteen's airtime."

From this rather limited sample, Jonathan Reynolds (1999a) concluded that popular responses to the series "were positive, to say the least. Given the continued disparity between academic and popular images of Africa and African History, I think the whole matter calls for some real soul-searching on the part of Africanists. I have long thought that we 'professional' Africanists have way too low a public profile—and that the fault, in no small part, is our own." There is certainly considerable informational and intellectual dissonance between Africanist scholarly knowledge and popular perceptions about Africa that show the failure of the Africanist enterprise to peel away the thick layers of public ignorance, intolerance, and indifference towards Africa. However, I am not convinced that the popular reception for the series was overwhelmingly positive, certainly not among Africans and African Americans as the analysis below makes clear.

If some of the press reports are anything to go by, my contention is probably right. Writing in *U.S. News & World Report* as the film series was airing, Jay Tolson (1999) noted that "Gates is not an Africanist by training, and the subject he tackles is fraught with pitfalls...friends and foes will be watching closely as Gates leads his tour. They might find that the film both oversells and undersells Africa's virtues and shortcomings. He makes much, for instance, of Africans' prominent role in the slave trade, even though it's hardly a revelation or even a unique blemish upon the face of Africa. And though it's partly the fault of a visual medium, Gates's celebration of architectural monuments sometimes scants Africa's other civilizing achievements, including cattle domestication and ceramics technology." Tolson captures some of the critical issues that have dominated the academic debates on *Wonders of the African World*, namely, Gates' Africanist expertise, his obsessive need to blame the European slave trade solely on Africans, and his Eurocentric view of African civilization. Debate has also centered on questions of race, gender, autobiography, and the nature and future of African—African American relations.

The Colors of Audiences

As might be expected the question of Gates' Africanist expertise was mostly raised on the African studies list. Wayne C. Jones (1999), a self-described nonacademic wrote: "From what I understand Professor Gates is an English professor. On what and who's authority did he become an expert in anything about Africa or Africans? He made statements about Africa and Africans with little or no facts being presented....We need to let Professor Gates know that he needs to stick with what he knows and that he is not an authority on Africa or Africans. I intend to write Professor Gates and PBS each a letter expressing my outrage." Opinion on the African studies list about this question ranged from indignation to introspection. Aswan Aboudre (1999) registered his disappointment with the series "given the hype. I am not familiar with Gates or his work. It was quite apparent however, that he is not an Africanist (scholar) or very knowledgeable in the field. I would guess his status [as a] (Harvard Professor) and as a writer opened doors for this production." To some lack of expertise was not an alibi for the superficiality of the series. They believed Gates had a hidden agenda. Even if Gates was neither an Africanist nor a historian, Lawrence Mbogoni argued, "I would not accuse him of not knowing what he was doing. He had a specific, may I say, ideological objective in doing this program and he knew what he was doing or wanted his program to achieve."

While not excusing Gates, others felt that the series filled a void left unattended by African studies. "The fact that there is such a vacuum of easily accessible information about African history to the general public, compared to the quantity available in academic circles to the point that the media will anoint Gates a historian of Africa," Chris Lowe (1999a) wrote, "is also an indictment of African history as a field to which I belong." John Thornton (1999a) blamed the alleged failures of Africanist history on the fact that "Africa is not yet being taught systematically at the primary and secondary school level." Then there were those who wondered whether the Africanist critiques of the series were not motivated by professional jealousy. "I'm reluctant," Timothy Burke (1999) confessed, "to give vent to these disappointments with too much zeal because I think they are tinted with unfair expectations and a certain amount of 'expertise envy', both in my case and in the case of many others who are critical of the series." Peter H. Gilliland (1999) called it academic ethnocentrism. "If the responses of this forum are indicative," he observed, "it appears that virtually none of us liked Gates' series, and for a variety of reasons. Is it possible," he asked, "that as we decry 'ethnocentrism,' there has arisen among Africanist (as among many academics) an 'ethnocentrism' of our own—which is often just as blinding as anyone else's, yet which is even less recognized?"

Africanist academic ethnocentrism occasionally veered into condescension, the arrogant argument that the stupidity of Gates' series reflected the simplicity of the American public, specifically of the African American public for whom, many white commentators assumed, the series was aimed. To John Thornton (1999b) Gates was appealing to a "barbershop version of history" acquired by African Americans through 'Roots' and to a lesser degree 'Amistad.'" For Johnathan Reynolds (1999b) the redeeming value of the series lay in the fact that it gave us an African American perspective. "Setting aside issues regarding occasional factual errors and the Harvard Big Man goes to Africa flair," he suggested,

> I do believe that Gates' perspective is a new one. His was the first such series presented from an overtly African American perspective. I found his frequent references to how the reality of Africa (as he saw it) compared to African-American barber-shop and student movement images of Africa to be very interesting. More so, I found his willingness to address popular African-American mythologies of Africa (his aggressive attack on the idea that Africans played no part in selling 'fellow Africans,' in particular, but also his repeated comparisons of African-American and African racial identity) to be most remarkable.

Similarly, Omofolabo Ajayi (1999) assuaged his anger with Gates' series by investing it with an African American authenticity. "I know I was very upset when I missed the first two episodes," he informs us,

> but after seeing the first 30 minutes of the next two, I accepted it for what it was: An African-American in Africa....So I sat down to enjoy what I got and learn what I could. Yes, I did learn about several things I did not know before, I was least concerned about what Gates was wearing and glanced over some of the disrespectful or casual attitude of Professor Gates. Having lived in this country for almost twelve years, I am beginning to understand the contentious, complex and painfully ambiguous relationship Africa and Africans have for many African Americans....So I was ready to allow some personal indulgence in the series.

It is true that Africa has complex and contradictory meanings in the African American imaginary, but Gates' series is far from representative of

331

African American popular or scholarly perspectives. Indeed, some of the most vehement criticisms against the series have come from African Americans. Anthony Cheeseborough's (1999) outrage is typical:

> As an African American and a scholar, I found the Henry Louis Gates documentary embarrassing and disappointing. Dr. Gates often makes a point of saying that his Harvard Black Studies department is a "Dream Team" of brilliant scholars....however, being black and a Ph.D. does not automatically make a person an expert on everything concerning people of similar pigmentation. The Gates series to me seems to be guilty of academic laziness.

Gwendolyn Mikell (2000), an African American and former president of the African Studies Association, declared: "We have been betrayed!" She found the series disrespectful, full of distortions and errors, and devoid of historical and cultural context.

To many African American scholars Gates was in fact not speaking on behalf of or to African Americans, but for white America. The series, declared J. Tolbert (1999),

> is not a story of one man's quest for identity, as the 'Roots' television series attempted to establish. Rather, the program must be viewed as a sonnet of white supremacist affirmation. There was no need for Gates to appear intellectual about it. He should have just come out and said, 'Boss, you is right to keep black folks down because their ancestors were solely responsible for the slavery. And Boss, don't even consider their calls for reparations. Don't even humor their concerns about economic injustice and human degradation because after all, they enslaved each other! They are the savages you said they are Boss!'....The bottom line is that,

he concluded, the series was "not made to educate blacks or whites about Africa, but to absolve whites of their guilt over the historical sins of their ancestors and their present day racist behavior."

For Molefi Asante (1999), the doyen of Afrocentric scholarship, there was no doubt that the series was irredeemably Eurocentric, ironically saved from public outcry because Gates is black.

If Gates were a white traveler in Africa commenting as he did on African society, making jokes about dignitaries, and sowing seeds of division between African people, the NAACP, NABSE, and a host of civil rights leaders would have considered this production an insult and an assault on African people. However, because he is black we must call it a travesty. This travesty will set back the intellectual discourse on the African enslavement for fifty years if the narrative is not corrected....

Specifically, Asante attacked the series for misrepresenting Africans involvement in the slave trade, trivializing African rituals and practices, reinforcing stereotypes created by generations of European travelers "that Africa is backward, inadequate, and scary."

Those who wanted to give Gates the benefit of the doubt noted that the series was worse than the book. "This suggests to me," John Burke (1999) asserted,

that Gates had to make...compromises with PBS or CBP or whoever had ultimate editorial control....Maybe the most depressing conclusion from this whole episode is that even a Harvard chair and a famous name are small potatoes against the power of the 'public' TV network and its corporate/political sponsors.

A sentiment echoed by Sara Klein (1999), who wrote apologetically,

I'm almost afraid to say this, but I am not sure Gates should have been carrying the weight of the world so to speak in representing what we wanted to see in a program on Africa -History? Sociology? Anthropology? Geography? Travel narrative? Autobiography?... (Gates and the producers/directors/editors are not one and the same thing). Without defending historical incompetence, perhaps it wasn't meant to be all things to all people.

Absolving Gates of responsibility for the composition, contents, messages, and meanings of the series on the grounds that he had little editorial control, or because of compromises required by the film medium is not convincing. There are bad and good documentaries and travelogues. Almost everyone who compared the Gates' series with the Davidson and Mazrui series found the latter two preferable in their educational value. To quote Marion Doro (1999): "Mazrui and Davidson clearly produced superior and more authentic views of Africa." Did Davidson and Mazrui have more editorial control than Gates? It is more likely that the former had better Africanist credentials and perhaps even more critically, they had greater ideological commitment to Africa than Gates. In short, being an Africanist is not in and of itself a sufficient condition for producing accurate and positive scholarship on Africa. Indeed, as several studies have amply demonstrated, and as was suggested in Chapter 4 above, Africanist scholarship has not always been a friend of Africa's; it has done much to produce and perpetuate many of the negative stereotypes that mark and marginalize the continent's peoples and societies (Owomoyela, 1994; Zeleza, 1997a; Mkandawire, 1997b; Martin and West, 1999).

It can be seen that the debate about the series was highly racialized. Those who defended it assumed Gates was speaking from an African American viewpoint and to a largely African American audience. Some even gave the series an Afrocentric glow, thus effectively absolving it of any possible white racist intentions. Cloaking the series with the badge of African American authenticity and Afrocentric epistemology serves to hide both the Eurocentricism of the series itself and the limited presence of African American voices in African studies and in the formulation of American policies towards Africa. The critics attacked the series for presenting Eurocentric stereotypes and images of both Africans and African Americans for white consumption.

Gates himself encouraged an Afrocentric reading and reception of the series, claiming in one interview that "as a black American, I know what it's like to have your history stolen from you," and that he wanted to "challenge the widespread Western view of Africa as the primitive 'dark continent' civilized by white colonists" by telling "the true story of proud lands filled with great civilizations, cities and centers of learning long before any European set foot there" and by sharing "his poignant personal odyssey as an African-American, the great-great-grandchild of slaves, returning to the cradle of black civilization" (Antenna, 1999). But his video performance contradicts his public pronouncements. As Zine Magubane (2000) has observed, the series spends as much, if not greater, energy exposing Afrocentric myths as it does Eurocentric myths about Africa.

Indeed, the purported epistemological project of rescuing Africa from racist misconceptions is constantly undermined by his caricatured and dismissive portrayal of African Americans as people whose shallow consciousness of Africa is derived from fatuous nationalism, barbershop lore, and rap music rather than from reputable academic sources. Magubane further notes that at various times the video is punctuated by Gates speaking directly into the camera in order to explain "the African American perspective" on Africa by means of anecdotes that are meant to entertain the audience and, in the process, construct African Americans as uneducated, naive, and silly. When he talks to his African informants, few of whom have much expertise, a dismissive smirk is never far from his all-knowing face. In both cases, he uses his blackness for racial entry and as license to make broad and sweeping generalizations about Africans and African Americans. In short, folk wisdom is turned into the epistemological locus of African American consciousness and knowledge about Africa, the result of which is to deny the very existence of African and African American studies. This epistemic malevolence is buttressed by the fact that although Gates is a distinguished professor at Harvard surrounded by a "dream team" of African American intellectuals, he talks and jests ignorantly; at no point does he think it fit to bring any of his colleagues or other African and African American intellectuals on camera to speak to the various issues he introduces or ridicules. Rarely are issues presented in a manner that would suggest that there are a diversity of views among Africans and African Americans, be they ordinary people or scholars.

Blaming the Natives

This was most glaring on the issue of African involvement in the slave trade, which was not presented as a historical and theoretical question open to divergent interpretations. No subject riled Gates's critics more than the allegation that Africans were largely responsible for this heinous trade. Responses to the question, as posed by Gates, of Africans selling other Africans into slavery, varied considerably. Some regarded the question as legitimate, others found it ahistorical, and many others were deeply suspicious of Gates' motives in framing the question of the slave trade in the manner he did, as is clear from the critiques quoted above by Cheeseborough (1999) and Asante (1999). The latter believed that Gates was providing an alibi for white apologists of the slave trade. Among those who credited Gates with raising an important question were Omofolabo Ajayi (1999) and John Thornton (1999b). According to Ajayi (1999)

> the most seriously indicting, actually tragically revealing aspect of the series for me was not what Professor Gates did, say, or not. It is what we Africans, as educators, politicians, government policy makers etc. have failed to do over these years, in particular since independence. We don't discuss slavery. We don't examine it, we don't educate ourselves.

The author would be on firmer grounds if he actually studied what is written and taught in history texts throughout the continent, which would indicate that his assertions are simply not true. As far as I know, the Atlantic or European slave trade constitutes a major topic in history texts used in many parts of the continent.

For John Thornton (1999b), who has written extensively on the slave trade, Gates posed a crucial historical question without

> taking us very far to either understanding it or getting past the emotional response....But in fact, getting at the root of this problem, why did Africans (or rather African rulers, merchants and other decision makers) sell slaves to Europeans when it was so obviously immoral and harmful, is in fact a central problem and one that ought to be addressed seriously. It needs to be taken as seriously as why Europeans did the buying and transporting of slaves.

Thornton's position is not surprising. In his book *Africa and Africans in the Making of the Atlantic World, 1400-1680,* he argues, "that Africans were active participants in the Atlantic world, both in African trade with Europe (including the slave trade) and as slaves in the New World" (Thornton, 1992:6-7). Thornton's history pays an underhanded homage to African agency so beloved in African nationalist historiography, while simultaneously invoking the much older European historiographical imperative to absolve Europe of responsibility for the slave trade.

The premises of Thornton's perspective were vigorously attacked on H-Africa. "I do not necessarily view," Mamaissii Dansi Hounon

(1999a) stated, "the selling of 'prisoners of war' as 'immoral' considering what their ultimate fate would have been had they remained in the hands of their enemies....The Africans did not see themselves as selling Africans (meaning) 'Blacks by Blacks,' but rather 'ethnic enemies by ethnic enemies,' hence no different from European 'ethnic wars.' Thus, the central question in my view, is not 'why did Africans (or rather African rulers, merchants and other decision makers) sell slaves to Europeans,' but rather: Why was it necessary for the Europeans to completely dehumanize the African, and create a perpetual caste system of institutional racism, and discrimination based upon the denial of the African as human, merely because they were 'prisoners of war?'"

These points are elaborated on in subsequent contributions. Jean-Claude Mporamazina (1999) reminds everyone that while

no understandable reason can justify the fact that some African rulers sold their fellow Africans to slavers...one should not forget the fact that there were more Africans who suffered from slavery of their parents than there were beneficiaries. These were not democratic or some kind of participatory societies where rulers merely apply policies accepted somehow by their people through their election or through laws voted by their representatives. Africans are still waiting for such a governing system to happen. If they had it, one could then extend the blame to the average African.

To Rhiman Rotz (1999) the seemingly Pan-Africanist basis of the question, How could Africans sell members of their own group into slavery? was actually rooted in a racist problematic. "The question is wrong," he declared. "The people doing the selling had no meaningful conception of 'African;' in other words, it wasn't Africans selling other Africans into slavery, it was folks from Oyo or Dahomey selling Ashanti or Hausa into slavery. If we still had a slave trade today, would anyone think that Serbs selling Croatians, or Kosovar Albanians into slavery (or, I hasten to add, vice versa) should need some kind of 'extra' explanation because they're all white, or all European?" The question of slavery drew its salience, some observed, not only from the history of slavery itself, its causation and contexts, but also from its aftermath. In the words of one commentator: "I seriously doubt that most

African descendants would be half as troubled over this issue had they been allowed the same dignity and autonomy as most humans during and (most importantly) 'after' their enslavement," to which John Philips (1999) added: "The 'race' problem in the United States is probably at least as much a result of the long lingering effects of the legal caste system as of slavery per se."

Most troubling to several commentators was the fact that the larger historical and economic context behind the slave trade were missing both in Gates' series and in the discussion that followed. Gloria Emeagwali (1999) argued that the Atlantic slave trade was an outgrowth, not of slavery in Africa as some European apologists, including Gates, have asserted, but of slavery in Europe.

> Slavery and slave trading were alive and well in Europe as late as the 15th century. And what seemed to have happened was that this massive slave trade and sale of Europeans by Europeans diverted into the Atlantic and Africa, taking along with it some of the physical trappings of enslavement, including shackles, branding, EuroChristianity etc. as well as racist notions of 'the Other.' In the long run what followed was a holocaust of bizarre proportions.

Kenneth Harrow (1999) reminded everyone that

> slavery took its form, its inhuman form, and spread to specific locations, because the economic system it served required certain kinds of labor which were easiest met by using slaves....It is not my intention to exculpate people in the past who carried out such evil practices by claiming that economic systems were responsible. It is just that one cannot understand their actions, motivations, practices without understanding what economic incentives were being served.

And Joseph Inikori (2000), a leading expert on the subject, noted

> that two critical conditions are needed to sustain a trade in slaves: 1. The existence of a market for slaves and a developed transportation system capable of transporting slaves to that market relatively cheaply. 2. The existence of weakly organized communities whose members can be captured and sold at little cost to the captors.

The question of the slave trade has left the cantankerous corridors of the academy and become a major international issue, as was evident at the United Nations' World Conference Against Racism, Racial Discrimination, Xenophobia and Related Intolerance, held in Durban in August and September 2001. African states and NGOs, vigorously supported by activists from the African diaspora, especially the United States, demanded an apology and reparations for the slave trade. Predictably, the European states prevaricated, and the U.S. government even withdrew from the conference on the pretext that the draft declaration was anti-Israeli. In the end, a muted apology was agreed to. The conference acknowledged

> that slavery and the slave trade, including the Atlantic slave trade, were appalling tragedies in the history of humanity not only because of their abhorrent barbarism but also in terms of their magnitude, organized nature and especially their negation of the essence of the victims and further acknowledge that slavery and the slave trade are a crime against humanity and should always have been so...

As for remedies, the conference recognized

> the need to develop programs for the social and economic development of these societies and the diaspora within the framework of a new partnership based on the spirit of solidarity and mutual respect in the following areas: debt relief, poverty eradication, building or strengthening democratic institutions, promotion of foreign direct investment, market access" (*The New York Times,* 9 September 2001).

Which side would Gates have been on? Given his thesis, he would have been quite comfortable sitting with the Europeans or walking out with the official American delegation.

Ironically, while the question of Israel dominated the Durban conference, the question of Jewish participation in the slave trade surfaced in the debate over the Gates television series. It was triggered by a remark made by Ali Mazrui, a key figure in the reparations debate, in what became the most critical intervention on the Gates series. Mazrui (2000a) wrote:

I thought that in episode three, which concerned the Trans-Atlantic slave trade, Gates would at last regard the West and the white man as relevant actors in the African tragedy....Boy! Was I wrong? Gates manages to make an African say that without the participation of Africans there would have been no slave trade! How naive about power can we get? Without the involvement of Africans, there would have been no colonialism either. Without the involvement of Africans, there would have been no apartheid. Without the involvement of African Americans, there would have been no segregationist order in the Old South. Without Jewish capital, there would have been less Trans-Atlantic slave trade. Why did Gates pick on the Asante (Ashanti) as collaborators in the Trans-Atlantic slave-trade and never mention European Jews at all as collaborators in the slave trade? (Leonard Jeffreys paid a price for involving the Jews in the trade, but will Gates pay a price for involving the Asante?).

Given the complexities of African American-Jewish relations and concerns about "black anti-semitism" (i.e., anti-Jewish), a controversy in which Gates has played a crucial role, it is perhaps not surprising that commentators would seize on Mazrui's reference to Jewish capital and Leornard Jeffreys.[1] Also remarkable is the fact that the debate about Jewish involvement in the slave trade was largely concentrated on the H-Afro-Am discussion list, while the H-Africa list focused mainly on African involvement. When Harrow broached the question of Jewish involvement on the latter list, it elicited little response. He quoted Mazrui's statement, beginning with "Without Jewish capital," and asked "whether Mazrui's defense of Jeffreys could be construed as less a defense than an unwarranted attack?" The three immediate responses offered mostly reference materials. Chris Lowe (1999b) observed that

> read one way, and particularly in connection with Leonard Jeffreys, it [Mazrui's statement] seems to have anti-Jewish overtones and to lend credence to anti-Jewish abuses of history in some quarters of U.S. intellectual life. However,

Mazrui might also be read to raise questions about the legitimacy of a) collective responsibility of ethnic groups and b) singling out any particular group in what was a huge, complex process for whom many parties of many identities bore responsibility.

The reactions on the H-Afro-Am list were more numerous and vociferous. Even people who claimed not to have seen the actual series reproached Mazrui. One commentator wondered about Mazrui's agenda was in obtruding the issue of Jewish participation when he "has a fit about the fact that Gates mentions the appalling conditions of the Arab slave market in Zanzibar...Jewish participation in the slave trade was about as central to that trade as African-Americans who owned other enslaved African-Americans were to slavery in the United States" (Casey, 1999). Another declared that: "I didn't see this episode, but this comment sounds a bit anti-Semitic to me, esp. since no other groups are mentioned" (Tanter, 1999). Robert Hinton (1999) stated that while he agreed with much of what Mazrui said about the Gates series, "his statement that 'Leonard Jeffreys paid a price for involving Jews in the slave trade,' is an outrageous understatement of Professor Jeffreys' anti-semitism." Anthony Watts (1999) contended that "Leornard Jeffreys did not pay a price for 'involving Jews in the slave trade.' It is my clear understanding Jeffreys, like Farrakhan, Tony Martin, and others of his ilk paid a price for conjuring the ugly anti-Semitic canard of the 'dirty Jew' allegedly disproportionately involved in the slave trade." Paul Finkelman (1999) castigated Mazrui for condemning Gates for not discussing Jewish involvement, arguing that "Gates did not discuss this trade because it barely existed."

There were of course a few commentators on this list who defended Mazrui's overall comments, attempting to put them in a larger context. Pysche Alethea Williams (1999) admonished: "Let's not get sidetracked by Mr. Mazrui's comment about L. Jeffreys. The real point of his comment had already been made: Gates does not adequately recognize the issues of POWER and MONEY. Yes, Africans participated willingly/unwillingly. The point is that Gates overlooks the issue of power." Abdul Alkalimat (1999), editor of H-Afro-Am, registered concern that

the criticisms have shifted from Gates to Mazrui. I happened to agree with most of Prof. Mazrui's comments. I

341

find it interesting how his mention of Jewish participation in the Atlantic Slave Trade has brought such swift reproach and determined refutations on the part of many members of this list. I hope that we are not reacting 'emotionally' to suggestions of Jewish participation in the Atlantic Slave Trade....Mazrui never states that Jews dominated or controlled the trade, at least not in his message. His point seems to be about identifying particular participants by ethnicity and balancing the presentation by giving a breakdown of other participants in the trade.

Mazrui's critique of the Gates series went beyond the question of African, let alone Jewish, involvement in the slave trade. In his preliminary critique, Mazrui also accused Gates of other sins of omission and commission, principally dis-Africanizing Egypt; ignoring Swahili experts on the Swahili people and generally relying on whites for scholarly authority; his obsession with race and imposing American conceptions of race on Africa; his insulting behavior, demonstrated most vividly in the episode on Ethiopia and his cynical search for the Ark of the Covenant; his snide remarks about other peoples' values and practices, such as female circumcision; and his general incapacity of "glorifying Africa without demonizing it at the same time." Except on the incidental question of Jewish involvement in the slave trade, most of the commentaries on H-Afro-America and H-Africa discussion lists agreed with Mazrui's critique. Debate centered on Gates' behavior and persona, his discourse on race, and his misrepresentation of some African customary practices, especially female genital mutilation.

Almost everyone who commented on Gates' behavior found it offensive. A few observations will suffice. Laura Head (1999) asked: "Why were there so many shots of his face. I would have liked to see more of Africa and less of Gates....Why did he show himself shucking and jiving so much? ...why did he spend so much time talking about his car problems." Marika Sherwood (1999) wondered "just whom Skip Gates was trying to impress with those T-shirts—Africans, the European/American viewers, or his paymasters (both Harvard and the BBC)." For Aswan Aboudre (1999), Gates was the quintessential

"Ugly American" not only in the "Africa" series but the following "Railroad" journey with his family as well....When he was introduced to the Islamic religious leader of a Malian city and asked to view the inside of a mosque, the leader, as customary, extended his faith (recruitment). Gates replied, "only if he could have four wives"...a jest which I felt was inappropriate and disrespectful in light of the theme of the program and more importantly to the Imam.

Ken Dossar (1999) singled out another example of Gates' irredeemable arrogance: "I found his quibbling over a piece of kente cloth, and saying he was a poor professor, to be insulting. In that segment he also stated that he wanted the woman to dress rather than the male. I found that his comments often bordered on sexism."

According to some commentators, even students apparently found Gates' attitude appalling. Undergraduate students of Misbahudeen Ahmed-Rufai (1999) who watched the series

> wondered if Gates is actually a professor at Harvard and whether he is a historian and which field of history...Some students said they were shocked by his arrogance in the face of obvious ignorance of African traditions and history." A student of Ahati Toure' (1999), reviewing the episode, "Road to Timbuktu," noted that "Gates was very Afrocentric in his thinking and his reasoning, but he was very Eurocentric in many of his actions....This was expressed in his complaining about the boat being late...his verbal crazing for an air conditioned room, his questioning of the functioning of the fan, by him not saying thank you for his cabin until he had approved that it was fit for him, and also by asking why they were late to Timbuktu.

Monica Schuler (1999) reported that "students who viewed some or all of the series were disappointed by the lack of explanation and by the lack of sensitivity which no amount of 'hello my brother' greeting could counteract."

Many commentators dismissed Gates' discourse on race in the series as simplistic, flippant, and arrogant. Chege Githiora (1999) noted that while "it is understandable that Bwana Gates, and any conscious North American, is obsessed by the question of race since the very foundations of the society he was born into are so racist," he wondered "why should US race discourse be transposed onto Africa, or any-where else for that matter? 'Race' is a social construction and there-fore varies, often dramatically across societies...race can exist on a continuum determined by several factors including class, phenotype and, descent...In the case of East Africa, religion (Islam) is yet anoth-er variable....So then, why does a prominent scholar like Gates who writes so well about African Americans, insist on making snide remarks about Africans who claim to be 'Arabs' or 'Persians' etc.? Has he not met Dominicans, Brazilians and others, black as I am, but who regard themselves as 'Castellano,' 'Spanish' or 'Indian' etc.?"

Gates' inability or unwillingness to probe the complex contexts and his-tories of racial constructions in Africa, Tricia Hepner (1999) asserts, is root-ed in his insufferable, self-centered arrogance. "Gates asks only his ques-tions," she observed,

always bringing the African experience directly back to his own, vis-ibly discomfiting everyone from young Persian men on Zanzibar (who don't know they are Black) to Imams and Orthodox priests with his inappropriate questions. Time and again, Gates encounters moments that illustrate the staggering complexity of racial identities and discourses of authenticity, of tangled histories and cultural bricolages that fit together in ways that he can't possibly comment upon, because he remains oblivious to anyone's concerns but his own. He misses every opportunity to unpack these categories in ways that would be relevant to broader race and ethnic relations in the United States and Africa, choosing instead to carry his own identity politics all over the continent. The series should have been called 'Skip Gates Wonders About the African World.'

No less problematic in the view of many commentators was Gates' por-trayal of African cultures and customary practices. Hounon (1999b) took exception to Gates' treatment of West African Vodoun, which he found

both condescending and stereotypical of how most in the world have been socialized to view African Traditional Religions and cos-mology. What is more tragic is that someone of Gates' professional stature, going to Africa, and publicly undermining the traditional spiritual treatment by the 'fetish' priest...has made our job, and attempt at gaining respect and visibility, even more difficult.

Ken Dossar (1999) took Gates to task for his false assertion that "Vodun was the only African religion to come into the Americas...I don't see how his research team, video tape editors, writers, whoever—could let that go over the airwave."

What attracted the most attention, however, was the question of female genital mutilation as referred to in Mazrui's 'Preliminary Critique.' Mazrui (2000a) criticized Gates for denouncing

> 'the barbarity of female circumcision.' And the institution had just been mentioned in passing. There was no attempt to introduce the viewer as to why millions of Africans belonged to this culture of female circumcision in the first place. Africans were not, after all, innate barbarians. So why had this tradition survived for so long? The institution was mentioned as a throw-away 'play to the Western feminist gallery' (I am myself opposed to female circumcision, but I do not call its practitioners barbarians).

Interestingly, this topic was debated almost exclusively on the H-Afro-Am list and virtually ignored on the H-Africa list. Some were sympathetic to, and others critical of, Mazrui's interrogation. Anthony Watts (1999) was categorical: "Frankly, it [female circumcision] does seem a barbaric practice. If it isn't, I am not quite sure what would qualify....By the way, dismissing individuals who condemn this practice as the 'Western feminist gallery' seems a bit flippant to me."

Responding to this censure, Kimberly Ellis (1999) noted that Watts had said he had not actually seen the series. She tried to put Gates' comment in its context—as an afterthought in a discussion on rites of passage for boys into manhood—noting that while Gates was quick to denounce female circumcision, he did not condemn male circumcision. While Ellis found none of the different aspects of female circumcision even remotely appealing to me as a woman, the idea of slicing off the tip of a baby boy's penis isn't an attractive option, either...In both cases, great pain is involved; and in both cases, they are reflections of what the people of that particular culture consider to be important for men and women....Male circumcision is prominent here, too. I never hear claims that Americans are 'barbaric' for this practice. And, while similar types of female circumcision are not the apparent accepted norm in the United States, I find no outrage or calls of 'barbarity' on the part of, say, white women who choose to lacerate their hips, lips, breasts and thighs to become whatever image of male sexual preference they have been socialized to internalize as the standard expression of who they are and should be.

Some questioned the right of Americans criticizing the practices of other societies when their own society is riddled with its own undesirable practices, "especially a society that 35-40 years ago," argued Lawrence Ringwald (1999),

allowed segregation on the basis of color, and continues to discriminate on the basis of class and gender. I would define barbaric as the term fitting to describe any society that does not feed its poor and ignores its history so as to let its problems persist. The preacher deals in hypocrisy unless she is the first to set example through practice.

Aswan Boudreaux (1999) was also troubled by the enthnocentricism among many critics of female circumcision, saying

I personally would avoid 'pointing fingers' when our society allows for living fetuses to be mutilated and aborted as a means of birth control...Truly there are issues regarding women's rights that should be addressed HERE as well as globally. But who/what makes us the guardians and taskmasters of morality.

The Invention of Afro-Orientalism

The debate generated by Mazrui's "Preliminary Critique" soon degenerated into vicious diatribes by Mazrui's age-old intellectual antagonists. The gauntlet was thrown by Wole Soyinka (2000a), an old foe of Mazrui and friend of Gates. Soyinka, who confessed that he had "not watched the entire series and unfortunately cannot do so before the live broadcast which is tomorrow" chided Mazrui for commenting publicly on Gates series, not for any deficiencies of observation and analysis, but solely because Mazrui had previously produced a series on Africa! In Soyinka's tortuous logic, Mazrui had forfeited his right of commentary and critique because "his happens to be the only other television series of this dimension by a black scholar on the subject of Africa's past and present. In short, Ali Mazrui has a fifty per cent stake—at least—in the reception that may be accorded to a work that, in effect, constitutes a challenge to a long-held monopoly." If Soyinka's preposterous edict were to be followed, any published writer commenting on other writers would be guilty of "crossing the ethical bounds of intellectualism" and engaging in "indecorous conduct" that "deserves the condemnation of all who believe that the virtues of criticism transcend self-interest."

Soyinka's tirade was soon followed by one from Biodun Jeyifo (2000a), a self-declared friend of Gates. Like Soyinka, Jeyifo commented on Mazrui's critique without having actually seen the series, except for one episode he saw at a private after-dinner screening at Gates' house. And so Jeyifo focused, not on the contents of Mazrui's critique, but its morality, a rather slippery critical road to travel that led him into personal attacks on Mazrui, while at the same time repeatedly and haughtily calling for the need to separate the message from the messenger, a dictum Jeyifo accused Mazrui, not himself of course, of breaching. Jeyifo called Mazrui's critique of Gates' series a "hatchet job", while doing exactly that on Mazrui as a person. Mazrui's crime? "Opportunistically using an attack on Skip Gates' series to raise the critical stock of his own series, 'The Africans: A Triple Heritage.'" The evidence? The glaring "fact that in writing about Gates' series, the ONLY other documentary that Mazrui refers to is his own series; he does not mention a SINGLE other documentary film or filmmaker." Mazrui apparently mentioned his series once in one critique and five times in another.

While Mazrui in his commentaries of the series avoided calling Gates any names or attacking him personally, Jeyifo, in his righteous anger to defend a great friend who had invited him for dinner to preview one episode, felt no such compunction. What price for dinner, for the favors of a mighty friend, who could not be criticized directly, but in the name of, or in conjunction with, guess who, Mazrui of course! And so Jeyifo faulted the episode he saw, not for its content, which he liked, but for "the FORM of the film, [which] in a very general manner, seemed very 'Mazruish.'" Jeyifo revealed that Mazrui's critique was much like the latter's newsletter that he sends to family and friends, a "monument to egoism," which he, Jeyifo, last read eight years ago. So how dare Mazrui remind him of the newsletter masquerading as a critique of Gates? How dare Mazrui accuse Gates, as an individual, of initiating "black orientalist" discourse on Africa, when none other than Edward Said, the great chronicler of orientalism himself, said "'Orientalism' was not, and could never have been, the creation of ONE man, of one DISCIPLINE, of one GENERATION of European 'Orientalists.'"

Mazrui's critique of the Gates'series as a homage to black orientalism was his second widely publicized commentary on the series (Mazrui, 2000a). According to Mazrui, Said saw Orientalism as a discursive practice that combined "cultural condescension, paternalistic possessiveness, and ulterior selectivity shown by certain Western towards non-Western societies in Asia, 'the Middle East' and Africa....The question which has been raised by Skip Gates' television series," Mazrui wondered, was whether Gates' series

> signifies the birth of BLACK ORIENTALISM....The condescension in Gates' television series might have been at its worst in Ethiopia and over the Ark of the Covenant. The paternalistic possessiveness was in Great Zimbabwe and in the wonders of the manuscripts in Timbuktu. The selectivity not only knocked out virtually the whole of North Africa; it also knocked out Nigeria, Africa's most populous country...Gates' selectivity also got the white man off the hook for the Atlantic slave trade.

Mazrui then proceeded, in his inimitable style, to interpret various episodes and themes in the series and respond to critics using the black orientalist paradigm, sometimes convincingly, sometimes less so. Mazrui's claim that Gates series initiated black orientalism was exaggerated; there has always been a strain of black orientalism in African American perceptions and discourses of Africa.

In *Orientalism,* Said showed how discursive practices of the Orient were constructed and consumed, in a complex process involving ideological and material intersections, in which particular people and geographic locations were analyzed, observed, and ultimately dominated. Magubane (2000) believes that the notion of orientalism can be put to extremely good use in understanding the production of *Wonders* as a cultural and political text. While Gates' series clearly did not give birth to orientalist practice for Africa, it is quite possible to locate it as critical to an ongoing process of producing "Africa" as outside of history—a site of self-generated chaos. The ways in which the series authorizes particular understandings of race, racism, and exploitation cannot be understood unless they are analyzed against the backdrop of the continued exploitation and marginalization of Africa reinforced by current processes of globalization. Over the last two decades African countries have been forced to undertake drastic restructuring, under the aegis of structural adjustment programs as mandated by the international financial institutions pursuing a global capitalist agenda that African states do not control. These processes of dismantling the economic and political agency of African states find their ideological articulations in the proliferation of media and other discourses that construct Africa as a "hopeless" continent. The ways that the Gates' series ultimately sanctions locating the primary responsibility for Africa's problems—historical and contemporary—with Africans themselves, while allowing the West to divest itself of that same responsibility, make it a preeminent example of "orientalist" ideological practice.

What makes this practice particularly insidious, Magubane (2000) continues, is the fact that it is enacted through a black interlocutor, thus giving it a greater degree of legitimacy and seemingly making it immune to charges of racism or orientalism. The fact that this black interlocutor is also African American is of profound significance, for it makes these texts available for use in constructing African Americans in ways that make them, rather than institutionalized racism, responsible for the increasingly marginalized status of the poor and working class majority. Constructing African Americans as people sold into slavery "by their own people," for example, works to absolve white Americans of any responsibility for the material benefits that accrued and continue to accrue to them as a result. Thus, the series must also be read and analyzed against the backdrop of the current attacks on affirmative action, on the rise of the "prison industrial complex," and on the increased tolerance for state sponsored violence and police brutality in black communities. In short, black orientalism represents the latest attempt to, in the words of Lewis Gordon (1997b:65), problematizing "black people instead of responding to the social problems that black people experience."

It was in this critique that Mazrui referred to his own series five times that so incensed Jeyifo and Soyinka. Particularly galling to Jeyifo was Mazrui's claim that the theme of his own series, Africa as a configuration of a triple heritage, was derived from the thought of two Pan-African giants, Edward Blyden and Kwame Nkrumah. Jeyifo refuted this claim, not on its merits, but on the grounds that "Mazrui is generally thought to have built his early professional career as a brash-anti-Nkrumahist pandering to the Western interests." Offering no actual proof, he quickly added, tongue-in-cheek, "I personally think that view of Mazrui is unfair and simplistic, but Mazrui certainly did much to earn it!" Mazrui's (1999) response to Jeyifo was vintage Mazrui: sarcastic, humorous, and biting. "Jeyifo admits," Mazrui scoffed,

> that he has seen only one program out of six of Skip Gates' series. With such limited exposure to Gates he feels qualified to say that 'Mazrui and Gates are so pervasive, so intrusive in their respective documentaries that I find [them] questionable.' ...Does B.J. take short cuts when it comes to judging Africanist television series? But perhaps B.J.'s reading habits are more careful than his viewing habits.

Jeyifo finally did see Gates' entire series. He sought cover for shooting his mouth off too early: "Having now watched 'Wonders of the African World,' the first question that comes to my mind is: Why didn't ANY of the commentaries on the series prepare me for what I can only describe as the 2-4 fissure in the intellectual and ideological body of the series?" (Jeyifo, 2000b). The simple answer is that he had been blinded by his abiding rage against Mazrui. He discovered that two episodes

> are relentless in the way they assail African complicity in the brutal and tragic history of modern slavery and are clearly out of sync, at least on the surface, with the other four episodes...[where] Gates confidently and exultantly reanimates cities and monuments of architecture, religion and learning that were affirmed by Europeans to be beyond the capacity of black Africans to create.

His attempts to explain this apparent fissure smacked of literary desperation. Clearly discomforted by what he saw, but mindful of his premature defense of the series in his intemperate attack on Mazrui, Jeyifo sought solace in negritude. The series, he claimed, was driven by an inner logic rooted in a reconfigured Senghorian "negritude," the obsessive need to refute European doubts about Africa, to validate Africa, in Gates' case on the grounds of achievements the West has claimed for itself as the pinnacle of civilization, culture, and humanity.

> This logic explains why five of the six episodes of the Gates series are each framed by a quotation from Western intellectual, artist or theological sources...[also] the journey motif which organizes each episode in the series often shows Gates literally on the trail of the classic journeys of Western explorers, archeologists and commentators, locked into a dialectic or discourse and counter-discourse with them, and 'rediscovering' or uncovering facts and realities whose existence or veracity they had deliberately suppressed, denied or ignored.

A rather convoluted way of saying the series was Eurocentric. Mazrui's "black orientalist" paradigm was a lot more convincing.

So, too, was Martin Kilson's (2000) reading of Gates' discursive strategy. Kilson called Gates a "master of the intellectual dodge." Kilson's critique of Gates and the series was perhaps the most ferocious and devastating. He deplored the reluctance of his younger colleagues at Harvard from joining "the ranks of Black intellectuals who have rightly challenged the intellectually atrocious film series that Henry Louis Gates has served up for American viewers— for White viewers mainly I think." He recounted the cordial relations he had with Gates until the mid-1990s when he "decided to probe Gates' modus operandi as a Black academic entrepreneur intellectual" for a chapter in a three-volume series on black intellectuals. He discovered that Gates had "an almost manic need to produce a discourse on Black realities that migrates between a 'Black put-down' or 'Black-averse' mode, on the one hand, and, on the other hand, a seemingly redeeming 'Black-friendly' mode, though in ultimate essence the redeeming posture is phony." Couched in "tough love" psychobabble, Gates' position "aims to deflect attention from the true goal that his Black put-down discourse serves—namely, the establishmentarian and conservative patterns in contemporary American society, and globally too."

Kilson attributed the filmic failure of the series, its lack of a serious didactic format, and Gates' "unbelievably arrogant irreverence that [he] exhibited at so many levels in the series" to his "myopia regarding his own self-importance." Gates' arrogance, Kilson disclosed, has been accompanied by "a convoluted autocratic component," as shown in the way he runs the W.E.B. DuBois Institute at Harvard, whose Advisory Board has not met for six years, and the privatization of the Encyclopedia Africana project, taking what was originally an DuBois Institute project to a private firm "headed by Gates and [Kwame Anthony] Appiah as sole proprietors." Gates is also, Kilson continued, "a masterful manipulator of strategic goods at his disposal as a Black academic entrepreneur....Even rather simple ones like invitations to strategic dinners at his house." Advice that came late for Jeyifo. It was the responsibility of progressive Black intellectuals to scrutinize "establishmentarian and/or conservative Black intellectuals like Henry Gates," he concluded, "because no one else will. Above all, we progressive black intellectuals still have a serious Black people agenda to attend to. Namely: protecting, advancing, and redeeming Black folks' honor, both here in the United States and elsewhere on the globe."

This trenchant critique was prompted by Gates' (2000) response to Mazrui, which exhibited much of what Kilson termed the "intellectual dodge" and "verbal trickery." Gates' defense rested on a litany of self-serving biographical details: that as a child he used to memorize the names of African countries, capitals, and leaders; that he spent the 1970-71 academic year living in an Ujamaa village in Tanzania; that he majored in history; that he befriended Soyinka at Cambridge and imbibed the great writer's notion of "tough love"—the willingness both to praise and to criticize one's people; and that he consulted many scholars, since he is "a professor of literature, not an historian, an archeologist, or an anthropologist." Nevertheless, he went on, the series remains "an autobiographical essay, narrated and written by an African American, one who has traveled extensively by land and water from Johannesburg to Cairo, from Zanzibar to Dakar, on over 50 trips to the continent."

Gates denied trying to dis-Africanize Egypt. Rather, he "sought to accord ancient Nubia its due recognition," and he promised "to deal with the question of the color of ancient Egyptians in a special one-hour documentary that will feature a wide array of experts." Color, not civilization, their melanin content, not material culture? On slavery, he roared with indignation: "Don't ask me, a descendant of slaves, to avoid addressing this complex issue, which disturbs so many of us so deeply simply because it is so confusing, so troubling, so anguishing." No one of course, asked him not to address the issue. Rather, he was urged to address it in a historically accurate and informative manner. As for the transgressions of the episode on Ethiopia, the Ethiopian Embassy in Washington, he announced gleefully, "has hailed the series 'for unveiling so many wonders of Africa and Ethiopia' and 'for combating flat superficial images.'" Being the entrepreneur and aspiring benefactor of black culture that he is, he ends

> with a piece of good news. So many people have asked me about the fate of the books at Timbuktu. When I returned from filming in Mali, I secured a grant from the Mellon Foundation to catalogue the manuscripts that we filmed, to construct a building to house them, and ultimately to digitize and translate them. The film series would have been justified, in my opinion, if this accomplishment had been the sole benefit that generated.

A very expensive way to save manuscripts indeed.

Kilson and Mazrui were unimpressed. In response Kilson wrote his fierce critique quoted above. Mazrui (2000c) produced a new commentary in which he expressed fears that the series would set back relations between Africans and African Americans and renewed his charges that it was irreverent and simplistic, that it saluted and demonized Africa at the same time. On the question of slavery, he challenged Gates: "In your TV series you seem to be asking for an apology from Africa for the slave trade. I wonder if you have ever asked in the media for an apology from descendants of white slave owners in the United States." George Nelson Preston (2000) asked even more pointedly: "Does he [Gates] rail at his wife because her ancestors sold, bought and enslaved his ancestors?" Biko Agozino (2000) asked why he did not ask the Europeans he met in Africa "if they felt guilty as the descendants of the European slave traders and whether they understood his psychological pain as one of the descendants of the survivors."

Mazrui's "Millennium Letter" provoked wrath from Soyinka (2000b), who sent a scathing personal attack with all the scorn and anger that his poetic imagination could muster. "Why does Mazrui distort, extrapolate, slander, indeed—lie, yes, lie—against the actual content of the series?" The answer: "You [Mazrui] have a vested interest in the failure of the series, and you cannot escape the charge of self-promotion." The letter rambled on accusing Mazrui of lacking "professional self-discipline"; "playing the race-emotive card" against Gates; not being "mentally African," or a "black African"; suffering from racial guilt; giving the "image of an insecure sales-man of dubious intellectual wares," adding predisposition to Islamic funda-mentalism and declaring an unannounced jihad against Gates as Mazrui had tried to do earlier against Soyinka himself; suffering from a "habit of fishing in troubled waters" like the incendiary waters of Nigeria; and a cognitive incapacity to distinguish demagogues and friends of Africa among African Americans. It was Soyinka at his worst.

The reaction was swift and censorious: Soyinka had exceeded the bounds of intellectual discourse and propriety. One charged: "Mr. Soyinka's attack on Mr. Mazrui was the pits!!! Mr. Soyinka, tragically, has in his attack ...revealed a frightening trait—he is a literary Abacha."[2] Julian Kunnie (2000) agreed: "I too found the remarks by Wole Soyinka disgusting and putrid. Professor Mazrui ought not to stoop below his dignity and respond to such vitriolic and hateful mail," a plea echoed by many others. Moyisi Majeke (2000) demand-ed that Soyinka apologize "to us who became unwilling receivers of his ire against Dr. Mazrui" and compared the outburst to the uncontrolled and childish fits of male children. To Molefi Asante (2000) Soyinka's response provided "quite a disservice to the intellectual discourse on the Wonders of Africa...the attack on Mazrui was personal, an attempt to deflect, to divert our discourse to a personal issue," a sentiment that was widely shared. Pablo Idahosa (2000) who was troubled by Soyinka's "unfortunate excoriations," wished the latter had truthfully told his friend Gates that his series was not good "in private if necessary, while staying publicly quiet and without engag-ing in ad hominem about people who it is clear you do not like." Arthur Blair (2000) drew parallels with the Kenneth Star report on President Clinton's tawdry affair with Monica Lewinsky: "How do I explain this to my children. Dr. Soyinka should think each day about the lack of credibility he will have from those who may walk in the footprints he has made."

Mazrui's (2000c) response to Soyinka's attack made sad reading. Gone were Mazrui's usual verbal playfulness and humor. Somberly and systemati-cally he dismissed accusations that he was an Islamic fundamentalist; only paranoia could make Soyinka think that Mazrui had tried to encourage Northern Nigerians to eliminate him. He vigorously defended his Africanity and accused Soyinka of racial bigotry in thinking that only "black Africans" were the real Africans. As for Nigeria, Mazrui reminded Soyinka of his family connections, that he had a Nigerian wife and children and extensive dealings with Nigerians from different regions and religions. He traced Soyinka's antipathy towards him to 1986, when Soyinka received the Nobel Prize for literature and Mazrui made his television series. "For at least a few months as many people discussed Ali Mazrui's TV series as referred to Soyinka's Nobel Prize....This was intolerable to Soyinka's monolithic pride, especially since Ali Mazrui was a Muslim." As for Soyinka's derision of the collective love Mazrui had declared for African Americans, Mazrui proclaimed: "We cannot abuse our brothers and sisters in the Diaspora by the yardstick of whether or not they are polite to Daniel Arap Moi or some other African tyrant. Before harassing African Americans who had dealings with Abacha, have you [Soyinka] resolved never to speak to hundreds of thousands of fellow Nigerians who had many more extensive dealings with Abacha?" He concluded: "You used to combine rudeness with art. Now there is only rudeness."

Everyone held their breath to see what Soyinka would do next. Many sent pleas for the Soyinka-Mazrui debate to stop. I wrote:

> I hope Mr. Wole Soyinka will heed Professor Ali Mazrui's reasoned plea and stop these embarrassing, vicious, hateful, and highly personalized attacks masquerading as debate. Let us focus on Gates' series, Wonders of the African World (which I personally consider an atrocious and third-rate travelogue), and the issues it raises. It is simply unbecoming of our 'intellectual elders' to be farting verbally in public like this"(Zeleza, 2000).

Echoing Rodney King's famous statement, S.G. Mukasa (2000) made an impassioned appeal to stop the unseemly squabble: "Can't we put this tragic saga behind? Can't we move along? Can't we just get along?" A day after Mazrui's response, Soyinka sent a terse message of closure:

> Now that we have [Mazrui's] response in the 'family' records, I think it is a high note on which to end the incestuous Internet debate—in keeping with Ali's own Millennial proposal. The work of deconstruction now belongs in individual minds. It would be most sad to ruin the symmetric arch of the exchanges—thus losing a chance of rounding off on the same elevated note as they were initiated.

Oyekan Owomoyela's (2000) "huge sigh of relief on reading Soyinka's reaction to Ali Mazrui's response to his earlier comments" was widely shared. Several days later Toyin Falola closed his e-mail discussion list on the debate.

Pitfalls of Publicity Intellectualism

In examining the debate surrounding the series, one is struck by the differences between the various discussion lists. The apparent divergence in terms of the topics and focus of discussion between the H-Afro-Am and H-Africa lists points to some of the differences in the composition and orientation of African studies and African American studies. From the late 1940s, when African studies was wrested from the historically black universities and colleges and lodged in the historically white universities, as demonstrated in Chapter 4, its practitioners and epistemic concerns changed. It became dominated by white scholars whose work shifted from the cultural preoccupations of earlier black scholars to policy prescriptions in a field now firmly tied to the cold war national-security agenda of American foreign policy. The transition in African studies from diaspora to development, culture to economy, from posing large civilizational questions to conducting empirical policy-oriented research, appropriately dressed in the theoretical flavor of the month, accompanied by the endless fears of provoking charges of Eurocentrism in a field dominated by whites, might explain the reluctance of Africanists to engage in contentious issues affecting the African diaspora in the United States, such as African and African-American-Jewish relations, and sensitive cultural questions in Africa, such as female genital mutilation. For their part, the African Africanists, ever so mindful of the cultural contempt in which things African are held, are similarly reluctant to broach such topics. Not surprisingly, leading crusaders in the female genital mutilation debate such as Alice Walker, the renowned African American author, have not come from the ranks of Africanists, although the debate has facilitated the emergence of what Nkiru Nzegwu (2001) calls "genitalia scholarship," the scholarly voyeurism on African women's bodies among Africanists.

Conversely, the cultural paradigm remains central in African American studies in large measure, because the field is centrally located in the maelstrom of multiculturalism and its cultural wars, which has facilitated and been reinforced by the ascendancy of literary studies. Combined with the culturalist tradition of earlier African American scholarship on Africa, this might explain the readiness to discuss such a controversial issue as female genital mutilation. The salience of the Jewish question arises in the context of assaults on multiculturalism whose academic site are to be found in so-called ethnic and minority studies and its utility as a litmus test of racial tolerance for scholars coming from the most racially abused population in the United States. The two discourses—the ability to question an African cultural practice and affirm another American minority constructed as the bearers of universal racial tyranny—provide crucial gestures of moderation to the academic establishment for a field created out of African American political radicalism within and outside the academy in the 1960s and 1970s and is currently faced with renewed activism.[3]

Gates has been at the center of some of these debates. His reputation as a "public intellectual" was certainly a lighting rod in the debate surrounding his television series. The notion of public intellectuals in the U.S. is quite a peculiar one. It is based on a false assumption, that one can distinguish between intellectuals who are "public" and those who are "private." As Michael Hanchard (1996) reminds us, there are no private intellectuals, all intellectuals operate in the public realm, or rather in different public realms, some are more public than others, some are organic, and others are not. In the American context, the term "public intellectual" has largely been reserved for academics in ivy league universities, although some self-anointed public intellectuals find the specialization and introverted debates of the academy intellectually stifling and pride themselves as people "writing seriously about serious matters from outside the university...to address timely questions in an accessible way" (Bawer, 1998). It is less about academics with organic links to social movements and more about those who are in the public limelight, called upon on television and in the mainstream print media to comment on whatever issue the media thinks is important. They are better described, argues Carlin Romano (1999), as publicity intellectuals, who thrust themselves upon and shmooze with the media, especially the New York-based media. The glorification of the so-called public intellectuals is rooted in, Theodore Lovi (1995) believes, media hostility to academe and impatience with sustained and logical analysis of issues in a culture of short-attention spans and instant gratification.[4] Such is the celebrity of public intellectuals that one university has even introduced a Ph.D. program to train them, thus further reinforcing the widespread view that public intellectuals are produced in the academy, not made in the crucible of public life and struggle (Schneider, 1999). The program seeks to attract students who want to merge intellectualism with activism, to participate in public conversation, but critics believe it is a prep school for media pundits (Karabell, 1999).

In the 1990s, the American mainstream media discovered black public intellectuals (BPIs), a group of about two dozen individuals, although the notion of a black public intellectual was really not new. In the 1960s Harold Cruse (1967) wrote a comprehensive critique of them as a professional class. They were rediscovered following a series of lengthy articles in "upmarket"publications, such as the *New Yorker* (9 January 1995), the *New Republic* (6 March 1995), the *Village Voice* (11 April 1995), the *Atlantic Monthly* (March 1995), the *Boston Review* (Summer 1995), not to mention the *Los Angeles Times* and the *New York Review of Books*. The articles in *New Yorker* and *Atlantic* applauded the achievements of this new celebrity intelligentsia, comparing them to an earlier generation of New York-based Jewish intellectuals, while those in *New Republic* and *Voice* dismissed them as careerist publicity hounds with little to contribute to either scholarship or public conversation. Adolph Reed's (1995) acerbic critique in the *Voice* attracted much attention and debate perhaps because Reed himself is black and seen as an aspiring public intellectual, although that is a term he would not apply to himself. Stripped of the essay's venom, Reed's essential argument was that the BPIs were anointed by whites to write social commentary about black life, to explain the mysteries of black America, to interpret "the opaquely black heart of darkness for whites."Despite their political posturing as leftists or liberals, he sees them as descendants of Booker T. Washington's conservatism and accommodationism, a club of back-slapping individualists, averse to serious internal debate, claiming black authenticity and speaking for the race. They perform blackness for whites.[5] That might explain the minstrel quality of Gates' performance in Wonders of the African World. It is certainly remarkable that none of the BPIs joined the debate about the Gates' series.

Clearly, the BPIs are valued as cultural brokers between whites and blacks, valued for their ability to mediate, represent, and deliver African American perspectives and sensibilities to European American audiences. Nevertheless, the same media that anoints them hardly ever asks for their opinions on major national political, economic, social, or foreign policy issues such as the electoral fiasco of November 2000 or the terrorist bombings of the World Trade Center and the Pentagon on 11 September 2001, and not even on the salacious stories that titillate the public, such as the

Monica Lewinsky scandal that tarnished the last years of the Clinton presidency. The forte of the BPIs is almost exclusively race and racialized discourse. The BPIs derive their authority from the fact that they are ensconced in prestigious white institutions, rather than the historically black colleges and universities, and appear mostly in prestigious white periodicals rather than popular black publications; yet they are supposed to speak for the very African American communities from which they are divorced.

Magubane (2000) argues that the social and scholarly contradiction of their position entails that the BPIs are often little more than highly paid ventriloquists, abetting white racial voyeurism. In his series, Gates is particularly adept, she demonstrates, at soliciting the gaze of the white voyeur while allowing him or her to disavow their status as voyeur and the pleasures derived therefrom. He does this by taking on the role of native informant/ethnographer, charged with the task of explication and documentation, explaining for example, the functions and importance of "barbershop" lore about Africa and intra-racial struggles over the relative weight of "African" and "American" culture in the construction of African American identities. He also sets up for ridicule Africans who claim Arab and Persian or white ancestry, as he does in the episodes on the Swahili coast and the descendants of the Portuguese slave trader, by imposing on them American racial categories and denying the validity of their own identities, thereby reaffirming long standing notions about the inability of Africans to properly reason about anything, least of all their own experiences. Gates' racial ventriloquism/voyeurism is bitterly enacted each time he addresses his African "brothers" and asks them why their forebears sold his great, great, great grandparents into slavery.

The BPIs, of course, do not think of themselves as commodified intellectual performers providing entertainment for white privileged consumers or serving as public relations intermediaries and race managers interpreting blackness for centrist and consensus politics. They prefer to think of themselves as the "grandchildren" of Du Bois' intellectual elite, the Talented Tenth, who have, Gates and Cornell West (as quoted in James, 2000: 14) declare in their book *The Future of the Race*, "responsibilities...to the larger African American community, past, present and future." Claiming a progressive agenda, they contend that "it is only by confronting the twin realities of white racism, on the one hand, and our own failures to seize initiative and break the cycle of poverty, on the other, that we, the remnants of the

Talented Tenth, will be able to assume a renewed leadership role for, and within, the black community." Reminiscent of Gates' "tough love" approach referred to earlier, they contend that "to continue to repeat the same old stale formulas, to blame 'the man' for oppressing us all, in exactly the same ways; to scapegoat Koreans, Jews, women, or even black immigrants for the failure of African Americans to seize local entrepreneurial opportunities, is to neglect our duty as leaders of our community."

Joy James (2000:14) comments wryly:

> To the extent that this passage censures black apathy, indolence, demagoguery, and bigotry it is well noted; however, simplistic assumptions appear to be embedded in its generalities. Are we to assume that if black intellectuals do not blame 'the man' then they are absolved from a critique of the state? Surely the critical analyses of black radicals and revolutionaries concerning the intersections of capitalism, imperialism, racism, patriarchy and state violence...are not yet stale, although the reductionism of such analyses into opportunistic sloganeering and performance must be tired and old.

Critical for Joyce is the wilful erasure by Gates and his fellow black public intellectuals of the fact that Du Bois later repudiated the class elitism and race leadership dogma inherent in his original notion of the Talented Tenth, which he borrowed from Christian missionary founders and funders of black higher education who wanted to create a cadre for race management. Du Bois' recantation was motivated by his political experiences and alienation and marginalization from black intellectual elites whose flaws and infidelities he came to despise and contrast to the militancy, leadership, and agency of black workers.

Even those sympathetic to the BPIs are troubled by their apparent lack of collective responsibility, in terms of both scholarly production and activist politics, to what Eugene Rivers (1995) calls "the state of emergency" in the black community. The debate about the BPIs, he laments,

> has degenerated into star-worship and name-calling, the stuff of television talk shows. The issues are too serious for that. Its time to get back on track....Black intellectuals have acquired unprecedented power and prestige. So let's quit the topic of salaries and lecture fees,

leave the fine points about Gramsci on hegemony to journals, and have a serious discussion of how intellectuals can better mobilize their resources to meet the emergency.

Specifically, he calls for a project modeled after the Atlanta Conferences on the Negro Problem, conceived by Du Bois, from which a series of serious, cooperative, and engaged studies were produced. He asks, as many have asked of the Gates series: "Why has this generation's peculiar collective genius been to produce so little from so much?" His answer is that the BPIs have embraced the failed promises of integration and abandoned the progressive black nationalist tradition.[6]

Reading debates about the BPI among the BPIs, themselves one is struck by an unsettling combination of anger, anguish, guilt, self-congratulation, and self-satisfaction, and by the contradictory and combative gestures of connectedness to the poor segments of the black community as well as to intellectual and class cosmopolitanism, sentiments, and postures that are so evident in Gates' series, in his silly elicitations of "Hello, my brother" on the streets and the ubiquitous Harvard T-shirt, and his frequent injunctions elsewhere that BPIs must "stop feeling guilty about being intellectuals and do the hard work that will lead to social transformation."[7] The problem is an old one. As Michael Eric Dyson, himself a prominent BPI, argues, black intellectuals have always been expected to speak for the race. The BPIs are caught in the political bind bred by the collectivizing and constraining propensities of racism which demands from them and other African American middle class professionals racial solidarity, political and moral commitment to community service. Indeed, unlike professionals from other racial or ethnic groups, the perverted logic of American racism routinely requires African American professionals, "to provide defenses for the personal success amidst high black unemployment, urban violence, and whatever else has been deemed to be a 'black problem,' as if their successful dance with U.S. capitalism and racism required them to explain why they had become neither middle managers, athletes, nor crackheads" (Hanchard, 1996: 258).[8]

What exacerbates the guilt and anguish of the media-anointed BPIs in contemporary American society is their physical, social, and class distance from black neighborhoods, colleges, and universities, itself a product of the limited successes of the Civil Rights movement, whose partial opening of the white-dominated public sphere was accompanied by a shrinkage of the black public sphere. In other words, the entry of African American professionals into European American dominated institutions and spaces, thanks to the integrationist opportunities opened up by the Civil Rights movement, signified both the growth of class differentiation among African Americans and the social fragmentation of African American civil society and entailed the rupture of organic links between African American professionals, especially the intelligentsia in the ivies, and working class African American communities.

In so far as the currency of the BPIs in the 1990s was a product of the resurgence of race in American politics and discourse and the rising popularity of black culture and commoditization of blackness, their limited role as spokespersons of race to a predominantly white public was reinforced. Their overexposure, despite their tiny numbers, was used cynically by opponents of affirmative action as proof that blacks had made it in the academy. While Dyson dismisses the common charges that BPIs are disconnected from their communities and their work lacks rigor, he concedes that the bright lights of celebrity can be corrupting, "making us addicted to praise and disdainful of criticism, which, by the way, every public intellectual lauds as a virtue, except when it's deflected his or her way...Equally worrisome," he continues, "too many black public intellectuals hog the ball and refuse to pass it to others on their team...a lot of black public intellectuals, despite what we say—maybe because we say we don't—really want to be HNIC," Head Negro in Charge or the Hottest Negro in the Country (Dyson, 1996:65).

Conclusion

Gates is the hottest of them all. That is why he was approached to do the television series. There are many African Americans with more expertise on African history who could have produced a much more informed but they did not have the public stature of Gates, an intellectual entrepreneur par excellence. He has been featured in numerous academic and elite periodicals. He has been praised by many, like the writer of a 1992 article in *The Chronicle of Higher Education* who described him as the person who, to quote the article's subtitle, "uses clout and flair to lead his department out of mediocrity" at Harvard who later built the "dream team" of black scholars there (Magner, 1992).[9] In a long and controversial article in *Boston Magazine* titled "Head Negro in Charge," he was called "the chief interpreter of the black experience for white America...[and] may be the most influential black man in the United States today. Having created a power base that extends deep into the nation's media-entertainment complex, Gates has brought money and glamour to the country's great racial debate" (Bentsen, 1998).[10]

Gates' detractors, especially among African American intellectuals, attribute his celebrity less to the profundity of his scholarship and more to his conservative politics. According to Reed,

> Gates didn't get to be a world-class Black Voice until he denounced the bogey of 'black anti-Semitism' all over the op-ed pieces of *The New York Times* and went on to reassure *Forbes* readership that 'Yes, there is a culture of poverty,' calling up the image of a '16-year-old mother, a 32-year-old grandmother, and a 48-year-old great-grandmother,' noting for good measure that 'It's also true that not everyone in any society wants to work, that not all people are equally motivated. There! Was that so hard to say!' He has since secured his public intellectuality in a series of essays in *The New Republic* and elsewhere whose main point is to endorse the 'vital center,' and he extols the lost Jim Crow world in *Colored People,* a memoir that could have been titled *Up from Slavery on Lake Wobegon.* (Reed, 1995:36).

In a much longer critique, Reed (1997:144) argues that Gates' conservative political position reflects an equally conservative academic project of authenticating an autonomously black intellectual tradition and literary canon, but one that is cleansed of "its association with non-academic political agendas and ideological programs."

Driven by the modernist sublimation of literature and literacy and the postmodernist tendency to subsume all texts, including political texts, into literary texts, "Gates is able to construe literary studies as a self-contained, ahistorical enterprise impelled by formalist aestheticism. Yet he can simultaneously appropriate for that endeavor the cachet and sense of moral urgency that have legitimized Afro-Americanist scholarly pursuits purporting to bear more directly on secular politics and social affairs" (Reed, 1997:150). In short, Gates seeks to dehistoricize and depoliticize both the intellectual history and popular politics of African Americans in an attempt to bring them into the center of American letters and politics. It is a desire that requires excavating and exalting black literary and material canons, as certified by Western standards of civilization, while at the same time excluding and erasing oppositional culture and politics. Hence, Gates' obsession in the series with monuments and manuscripts and blaming Africans for enslaving and oppressing each other.

The personal rewards for being a black public intellectual in the United States can be quite high, but they are sometimes compromised by the costs of playing the role of an uncritical racial ventriloquist/voyeur/translator for a predominantly white audience. Gates' *Wonders of the African World* is an opportune reminder of that. The series captures, most poignantly, the difficulties of transcending the limits that can ensnare American BPIs even in transnational contexts, in this case a context with a potentially oppositional and reaffirming Pan-African audience. If a little good is to come out of the series, it is that it should make us all more aware of the challenges of becoming public Pan-African intellectuals, promoting genuine cultural and intellectual conversations across the Atlantic, between Africa and the diaspora, on issues that really matter for the collective welfare of African peoples in this so-called age of globalization; conversations that are free from crass commercial and career considerations.

Endnotes

1. In the debate the name is spelled Jeffreys in other sources as Jeffries. Leonard Jeffries came to national attention in the early 1990s when the City College of New York, which is part of the City University of New York, tried to have his term as chairman of the Black Studies department limited to one year instead of the standard three years for a speech he had delivered in Albany, New York, which addressed the bias of New York State's public school curriculum and the history of black oppression. In the speech Jeffries apparently made several derogatory statements about Jews. Jeffries sued the university alleging that his First Amendment rights had been violated. The decision of the district court against Jeffries was later reversed on appeal, see United States Court of Appeals for the Second Circuit No. 493, August Term. 1993.

2. This message and others quoted in this section were despatched in a discussion list that Toyin Falola of the University of Texas at Austin maintained, was initially reposted to Zeleza by a friend before he joined the

list; henceforth called the "Falola Discussion List." This message was sent on Falola Discussion List, 1/24/00.

3. See the recent lead articles headlined "Taking Black Studies Back to the Streets" in *The Chronicle of Higher Education*, 20 May 2000. For brief histories of Black Studies see, Talmadge Anderson (1990) and Henry Louis Gates (1992) himself

4. He asks: "How many public intellectuals can deliver a 50-minute lecture with a complex, sustained argument? The public intellectuals whose lectures I have attended usually talk for about 15 minutes and fill most of that time with anecdotes. They then announce that they will be happy to answer questions, which simply means that the audience sets the intellectual agenda. Too often, their books are similarly composed of short sentences, short sections, and short chapters filled primarily with interesting, timely tidbits."

5. This article provoked an avalanche of commentary and criticism, including some from aggrieved BPIs. See particularly the bitter and personalized exchange between Reed and Manning Marable in *New Politics*, Summer 1996 and Winter 1996. Also see Marable (1995). The conflicts among African American intellectuals, as for most intellectual communities, are shaped as much by ideological differences as by personal jealousies, although they reflect and are rooted in broader structural, political, and social factors.

6. Robin D. G. Kelley (1995) responded that desegregation was not the same as integration, that there was no need for annual conferences, and that a lot of good work was being done by this generation of African American intellectuals.

7. See the debate between Gates and several other leading BPIs, "On the Responsibility of Intellectuals," at http://bostonreview.mit.edu/BR18.1/responsibility.html, p. 4 of 11. Also see the debate on "The Responsibility of Intellectuals in the Age of Crack," at http://bostonreview.mit.edu/BR19.1/responsibility.html.

8. Michael Hanchard (1996) agues against framing the debate about public intellectuals exclusively in U.S. terms and urges that the BPIs be compared with their hemispheric counterparts in Latin America and the Caribbean, who have, he contends, played a greater role in public discourse than their counterparts in the United States. This tantalizing line of inquiry is, unfortunately, not followed up.

9. Other prominent BPIs also featured in *The Chronicle* include Robin Kelley, "NYU Scholar Finds Himself Joining the Ranks of 'Black Public Intellectual' While Abhorring the Term," 6 February 1998; "Gloria Watkins: The Real bell hooks," 19 May 1995; "Cultural Studies Scholar Michael E. Dyson Attracts Controversy," 26 January 1996; and "Cornel West Matters: The Celebrity Philosopher," 22 September 1993.

10. The title provoked a demonstration by African American ministers outside the magazine's offices, see "Headline on Profile of Henry Louis Gates Stirs Controversy," *The Chronicle of Higher Education*, 17 April 1998.

Chapter 8

Writing and Reading Africa

1. A SOCIAL CONTRACT FOR BOOKS[1]

Introduction

I was asked to speak on "National Book Policy as a Continuous Process of Dialogue, Collaboration and Implementation." Initially, I was not quite sure what I would say, for I am neither a politician nor a publisher, both of whom I am usually wary of, although for different reasons. Nevertheless, I read books and I derive my living from teaching and prescribing books, and in the publish-or-perish world of academia I am expected to write them as well. So it began to occur to me that the topic is actually close to my heart and livelihood, that all of us, indeed, have a stake in the development of a vibrant book industry. So I decided to entitle my address "A Social Contract for Books," for what is needed is a social contract among the major stakeholders of the book industry. I have identified and will discuss six: the state, publishers, writers, educational institutions, libraries, and the reading public.

In African discourse, the value of a project, of an idea, has to be justified in terms of development if it is to be taken seriously; so let me state at the outset that books are indispensable for development. They are not a luxury in so far as the development process is underpinned by human thought, visions, planning, and organization, all of which require material and intellectual resources. The culture of reading is, of course, central to our contemporary world, to the information age in which we apparently live, an age that imprisons and impoverishes illiteracy and ignorance. This is an era when the open intimacies and prejudices of the village are possible as the boundaries of national isolation and intellectual provincialism wither away. Africa's position in the global village of book publishing is weak: Whereas in Europe nearly 800 book titles are published per million inhabitants, in Africa the figure is a miserable, i.e., fewer than 20^2. The case for developing the book industry, devising policies that promote a reading culture is therefore imperative. The risks of not doing so means greater intellectual and economic marginalization for the continent: we will be reduced to exposed pedestrians on the information highway as others, driving on the backs of powerful and prestigious publishing systems and academic enterprises of the industrialized North, who already churn out the bulk of the world's books, journals, databases, computers, software and other information technologies, and who dictate international copyright and intellectual property laws, wheeze past us, arrogantly splashing mud at our vulnerable cultures.

Where does Africa fit in the international political economy of knowledge production, dissemination, and consumption? How can our various countries and communities ensure that they are not condemned to eternal information dependency, always importing their knowledge of the world, and sometimes of themselves, from others, knowledge of history and humanity, society and science, nature and culture, and the paradigms and prescriptions of development and modernity, governance and democracy, which are often distorted and even destructive, for they are almost solely derived from Western experiences and fantasies instead of producing and sharing and, indeed, exporting our own? To answer these questions we need to assess the development and state of the continent's basic infrastructures of knowledge development and dissemination, namely, the availability of publishing houses, technical expertise, printing facilities, electronic technologies, libraries, and bodies of capable writers. Knowledge and information, whether in the form of books or newspapers, television or cinema are, of course, not created in a vacuum but in concrete contexts conditioned by economics and politics and the traditions of intellectual and cultural production. Moreover, each medium has its specific structures of production and distribution, its mode of organizing and articulating the interests of the stakeholders.

This presentation, then, focuses, first, on the political and cultural economies of the African book industry; and second on, the social contract that needs to be forged between the identified six stakeholders. I hope the reader will forgive my being rather general and prescriptive in my remarks. I am only too aware that conditions in Africa vary enormously, that the levels of book development and underdevelopment are quite uneven, that the space between prescription and implementation is filled with complex and protracted social struggles, and that, in fact, Africa has perhaps suffered more than most from cheap and careless prescriptive advice, most glaringly in recent years in the form of ill-conceived structural adjustment programs, which have wrecked havoc on African productive economies, enterprises, and energies, including the book industry. The excuse for the generality and brevity of my remarks is time. More importantly, most of you gathered here know far more about the African book trade than I do and perhaps will indeed be exploring its growth, constraints, and possibilities in the next two days.

The Cultural Economy of African Books

Books constitute crucial repositories of social memories and imaginations, containing the accumulated cultural capital of society, of its accomplishments, agonies, and aspirations. Books, therefore, are not and cannot be a luxury, a dispensable dessert on the menu of development, nationhood, or human progress. They are an essential component of these processes, indeed, their intellectual salt, spice, and starch. Through books the past is remembered, the present understood, and the future created; knowledge is codified, contested, and consumed; and communities separated by the yawning divisions of time, space, and status can and often converse with each other, and in the process sometimes exchange ideas, images, and inspirations. Thus, reading offers a singular opportunity not only to acquire the formal knowledge of the academic disciplines and the practical skills of technical knowhow, it is also a means of sharing and sampling the cultural sensibilities of other times and traditions, places and peoples, countries and classes. To read is in a large sense to partake in collective intellectual conversation crystallized over many generations, to claim, and perhaps to contribute to, the immense heritage of human social thought. That is why illiteracy is so debilitating, so destructive, so dehumanizing for the illiterate, who whatever their abilities and ambitions, wiles and wisdom, are cut-off from the written dialogues and endowment of humanity.

The written word has a complex and varied history in Africa. It has ancient roots in some of the continent's early civilizations, especially those of the Nile Valley, including Egypt, Ethiopia, and the Sudan, and the later ones of western and coastal eastern Africa. In these civilizations literacy was often confined to the state, to the commercial and religious elite, whether Christian or Islamic. This is, of course, not peculiar to Africa. Almost everywhere in the world, mass literacy is a relatively recent historical phenomenon, a product of the industrialization and democratization of social life. In many parts of Africa the written word arrived with European colonialism, although in most cases mass literacy only came with independence. In 1960, the putative year of African independence, only 9 percent of the African population was literate. Thirty years later the figure had jumped to more than 50 percent. This suggests that it is only in the period after independence that the basis for a viable book industry was established in most African countries.

The infrastructures of the industry, however, continued to carry a heavy colonial imprint either because of benign neglect or the promiscuous borrowing of models from the developed countries that were often imposed without domesticating them to the local cultural and demographic realities. Consumed as they were by the economics of development and the politics of nation-building, cultural development in general and book development in particular remained low on the policy totem pole of many African governments. Legislation affecting the book industry was either inadequate, inappropriate, or outdated. Further undermining book development were permissive or unimaginative tariff and taxation policies that either unnecessarily raised the local costs of book production or made it difficult for local publishers to compete with large, foreign, multinational publishing companies. Most importantly, perhaps, state authoritarianism bred the silences of censorship, in which critical voices were stifled, and the performances of ostentatious politics, whereby "traditional dances" and other forms of public culture, were turned into vulgar celebrations of undemocratic power.

Also unhelpful in some countries was the monopolization of critical segments of the publishing market by state-owned publishing houses for whom propaganda mattered more than probity, conformity more than creativity, the exaltation of banal power more than the efficiency of book production. In some cases the state publishing firms were established to "indigenize" the publishing industry, to supplant the foreign-owned publishing companies whose institutional loyalties, editorial networks, and re-investment outlets lay overseas, and whose commitment to local publishing often swung with foreign exchange rates and regulations. For example, when Tanzania entered a period of financial crisis in the 1980s the multinational publishing companies left, only for some of them to return later when they learned that there would be an allocation of US$60 million from the World Bank for educational supplies (Mcharazo, 1995: 245). For their part, private indigenous publishers, usually buffeted between the heavily subsidized parastatal publishers and well-resourced multinational publishing houses, found themselves further handicapped by shortages of monetary and material capital; editorial, production, promotion, and marketing skills; and limited markets. They also proved less attractive to writers—who could access the major publishers—because they were less able, or willing, to pay royalties and stroke their authors' egos.

Many African authors, brought up on a fulsome diet of colonial and Eurocentric education, displayed a marked preference for overseas publishing or with local subsidiaries of multinational firms, not only because of the pecuniary attractions of foreign exchange royalties, but also the reputational rewards of international renown: speaking tours, conference invitations, visiting appointments abroad, and so on. The relative devaluation of local publishing, certainly among academics, with whom I am most familiar, reflected the historical and prevailing relations of domination and dependency between Africa and the West, and the fact that the intellectual structures of reference, attitude, and legitimation internationally and within African universities themselves continued to be determined by Western standards and epistemologies. I remember in 1989 being denied appointment as senior lecturer both at the University of Zimbabwe and the University of Botswana, a position I already held at Kenyatta University in Nairobi, because most of my publications were in African rather than in the so-called "international" journals. The tragic irony is that the same publications earned me an appointment in Canada at the beginning of 1990.

Universities and schools constitute the fourth group of stakeholders in the book trade. Book sales to schools, colleges, and universities most likely provide the largest market for books in most African countries. Therefore, the content of curricula and canon, the composition of syllabuses and examinations matter a great deal, for they determine the books that will be sought out by schools and students, the titles that will rake in the profits to subsidize less commercially viable but equally important publications. There seem to be three main methods in which textbooks are prepared, published, and prescribed in African schools. In some countries the books are specifically prepared and published by the government itself. In such cases the writers are selected by the ministry of education from within or outside the ministry. In other countries, while the authors are not officially chosen, the ministry selects and recommends certain texts that meet the established pedagogical criteria. Finally, there are countries where books published by private and state-owned companies, commissioned and noncommissioned books, compete for the hearts and minds of teachers and students. In general, ministries of education wield enormous power and dictate the shape of the playing field. Since they can literally make or break the fortunes of publishers, especially the smaller ones, the way that power is constituted and exercised is of utmost importance.

Libraries constitute another identifiable "captive" market for books. School and university libraries are obviously critical. Certainly they form the backbone of scholarly publishing. Even in industrialized countries, where personal incomes are relatively high, libraries provide the major market for scholarly products, especially journals, which derive as much as 90 percent or more of their income from library subscriptions. Library systems in Africa expanded rapidly on the heels of the explosive growth in education after independence, but since the onset of the economic crisis and structural maladjustment in the 1980s in many countries, funding for education in general and libraries in particular has declined sharply, necessitating severe cuts in the acquisitions of books, journals, and other materials for libraries. For example, all but three out of thirty-one African university and research libraries surveyed in 1993 reported a drastic and depressing drop in their journal subscriptions from the mid-1980s, with some canceling all their subscriptions (Levey, 1993a). That is intellectual suicide. One response to the library crisis has been the growing reliance on gifts and donations of books and journals from charitable institutions and individuals, mostly in the developed countries; but much of this "book aid" is episodic. Library aid, like all aid, has strings attached, and it reinforces Africa's dependency on Western intellectual paradigms, problems, and preoccupations. It has been suggested, a little cheekily perhaps, that "many of the donations that do arrive would be far better if they were pulped. This might at least provide some new paper, a basic resource that Africa needs more urgently than other countries' cast-off books" (Sturges and Neil, 1990:79).

The last but by no means the least important group of stakeholders for the book industry consists of the general reading public, or rather publics, for readers are quite diverse in their tastes and tendencies. The potential general reading public is, of course, made up of products of the educational system. Whether or not they become regular readers depends on many factors, including their incomes and interests, occupations and orientations. Much has been said about how few read for pleasure, a view based more on anecdotal evidence than extensive research. A recent research study on Kenya revealed that a majority 39 percent of consumers bought books because of a love of reading (Nyariki and Makotsi, 1995: 11). The distinction between reading for pleasure and reading for a purpose is, in fact, quite problematic. In a sense, all reading is utilitarian; it is purposeful: It can be for immediate aesthetic pleasure or the delayed practical satisfaction of job training. In short, people read for different reasons, none of which is intrinsically superior to the others. The question that African writers and publishers should be asking themselves is how to make their books more attractive and competitive, how they can meet the diverse interests of African reading publics, from creative fiction to computer manuals. Why, for example, is Western pulp fiction so popular among many readers in African cities? Clearly, it fills a need that is not being met by our writers. For some of our writers rural life is the only subject worthy of focus, for they believe it represents African cultural authenticity, that is writing out the experiences of a third of the African people who live in cities.

Towards a Social Contract for Reading

Each of the stakeholders identified—the state, publishers, writers, educational institutions, libraries, and the reading public—has a critical role to play in the development of vibrant reading cultures and dynamic book industries. The challenges are daunting, made more so since the 1980s by the harsh economic conditions confronting many African countries, and compounded by reactionary structural adjustment programs imposed by the Bretton Woods twins—the World Bank and the IMF. These programs, which call for massive cuts in government expenditures, trade liberalization, currency devaluation, and indiscriminate privatization, all in the almighty name of the market, have wrecked havoc on education and employment, among many other sectors, that generate the literacy levels and purchasing power essential for an expanding and sustainable book trade. Currency devaluations have raised the domestic prices of imported machinery and inputs, such as paper, and thus increased the costs of local book production.

373

As with all difficult historical moments however, the present conjuncture is pregnant with contradictions and the possibilities of positive change. The winds of democratization that have been sweeping throughout Africa, from Algeria to South Africa, Djibouti to Senegal, partly spawned by the struggles of rural and urban civil societies against the frustrations and failures of postcolonial developmentalism and the discontents of structural maladjustment programs, are generating more favorable conditions for discursive freedoms, for liberating the written word from silence. As the state monopolies of politics and production are curtailed, and as the censorship boards lose their omniscient powers and the parastatal publishers their privileges, the playing field is leveled so that the pens of committed writers and the presses of independent publishers can roll with new energies.

The social contract for books, for the development of a vigorous reading culture, requires specific commitments and contributions from each of the stakeholders. African states have three primary responsibilities. First, increased state investment in education, which includes promotion of adult literacy programs and the expansion or establishment of extensive public library systems in both the urban and rural areas, is essential. Second, reading must be made less costly by lowering taxation on books and materials needed for publishing. Third, civil liberties and freedoms, including freedom of expression, need to be upheld. These freedoms are not commodities whose value shifts according to the fluctuations of cultural currency: They are fundamental human rights.

For their part, educational institutions, at all levels, from primary school to university, need to devise pedagogical practices that encourage and reward extensive reading rather than empty regurgitation, critical inquiry rather than conformist inertia, intellectual curiosity rather than indolence. All too often, school education and its regulated culture of reading are regarded as terminal rather than as stages in a continuous process of learning and living, of personal and social development, individual and collective enlightenment. As a part of this agenda, local publishing by school and university teachers should be sanctioned not censured.

As for libraries, they must aggressively and systematically collect books and materials published within their countries and the continent at large, instead of concentrating on acquiring them from Europe or North America. Research libraries need to procure the latest information technologies, such as CD-ROM capability and electronic networking, for not doing so would be reinforcing Africa's intellectual marginalization. These technologies, of course, do not come cheap. Besides the high costs of equipment and training, there are the recurrent costs of subscription to databases. Also, in so far as most of the existing databases contain Northern scholarship, not scholarship from the South, let alone Africa, the challenge is not simply one of importing electronic technologies, but of producing national, regional, and continental databases in electronic format. This requires extensive scholarly, marketing, and technical support networks that can only be built by forging interregional and international library linkages.

Without publishers and writers, of course, there would be no books and other materials to read. Publishers, especially the small indigenous ones, need to improve their promotional and marketing activities by employing trained staff; to professionalize their dealings with authors, for example, by paying them royalties at regular intervals and involving them in the publicity campaigns of their books, for without these they will be unable to attract or retain the best and brightest writers. All too often, publishers concentrate their energies on the captive school textbook market to the detriment of other areas of publishing such as scholarly and popular books. This excessively narrow base does little to promote the book industry; in fact, it reinforces dependency on foreign publications in the underpublished areas. In short, African publishers need to spread their eggs into several publishing baskets. Then too, foreign publishers operating in African countries have a responsibility to reinvest their profits locally and can assist in building local publishing infrastructures and intellectual traditions by using domestic resources for editing and reviewing manuscripts. Reliance on external reviewers based in Europe or North America, often justified in the dubious name of international standards, holds African authors hostage to conventions, conceptions, and concerns that may have little relevance, or that encourage shallow analyses and stereotypical images of African societies, cultures, and realities.

The heavy devaluation of many African currencies in the last decade has made imports of books from abroad very expensive, including those published by African authors. Recently while attending Malawi's first literary festival to celebrate the demise of Banda's dictatorship and the dawn of a more democratic order, it was quite saddening to find that the books published abroad by Malawian writers exiled during the Banda years, writers like Jack Mapanje, Frank Chipasula, and myself, were simply unaffordable. My novel,

Smouldering Charcoal, published by Heinemann sells for MK350 (US$10), well above the minimum wage. "At that price," commented one literary critic (Chirambo, 1996:9) in a paper given at the festival, "that book is as well banned." Locally produced books are not necessarily cheaper; indeed, they may be more expensive in situations where most of the inputs are imported and economies of scale do not apply. However, the "famine" of imported books offers local publishers reduced competition and an opportunity to forge creative and mutually beneficial copublishing and marketing arrangements with multinational or foreign publishers. There is a need to market African books aggressively not only within Africa itself but also abroad, for what is at stake is Africa's capacity to define and to describe itself to itself and to the rest of the world, and to see the world through its own eyes, not the warped lenses and fantasies of others. This is why the efforts of the African Books Collective (ABC) to undertake the joint promotion and distribution of African books outside the continent, and of the African Publishers Network (APNET) to encourage intra-African publishing and trade in books, must be applauded and supported.

Book reviewing is an important component of the publishing enterprise and the reading culture. Reviews, even bad ones, advertise books and mediate the reading public's critical consumption of texts. The publishing industry, therefore, working together with the mass media, needs to promote reviews in newspapers, and book discussion programs on radio and television. Also deserving support are review publications for the scholarly and general public. In this region one can mention *The Southern African Review of Books* and *The Zimbabwe Review of Books,* and on the continental level there are APNET's *African Publishing Review* and the British-based *The African Book Publishing Record.* There is room for many more of such review outlets aimed at different segments of the reading public of African books. We need, for example, an *African Review of Books,* published jointly and simultaneously in North America and in Africa for the overseas and African markets, respectively. Through such review we could give African books greater exposure in the North American market, one of the largest in the world for Africana materials, and facilitate Western Africanists' reviews of books written by African scholars based in the continent, thereby promoting serious transatlantic intellectual conversation between Africanist and African scholars and breaking the tendency towards self-referential solitude among them.

This brings us to the role of writers. Besides writing, what else can they do to promote the book industry in their respective countries and throughout the continent as a whole? Serious writers have a responsibility to be subversive, that is, to prick the public conscience, not to pacify it; to say so when the emperors are naked, not to cover them with the flowery verbiage of lies; to denounce the tyranny of state power as well as the terrors of civil society, not to give succor to the violations and violence of the intolerant chauvenisms of race, nationality, ethnicity, gender, class, religion, and sexuality, but to imagine more generous conditions of being human. Outside the often intensely lonely writing process, in the public market of ideas and subsistence, writers need the protection of collective organization against state authoritarianism and sometimes exploitation by, can one dare say, publishers.

As cultural artifacts books play an important role in the development of the cultural identities and expressive capacities of peoples, societies, and groups. In this context, the question of the language in which books are written is obviously critical, especially in Africa, where with the exception of Arab North Africa and to a smaller extent Ethiopia and Tanzania—the European languages introduced through colonialism remain the languages of national culture, government, business, and intellectual production. It is, of course, simplistic to assume that writing in the indigenous languages is intrinsically progressive: tyranny can be articulated in a native tongue, oppression can wear the expressions of tradition. Moreover, it may be historically too late to wish the colonial languages away. That does not mean they cannot be domesticated, given local accents, which, in fact, has already been happening and will continue to be the case. But neither can the need to promote writing in indigenous languages be swept aside. Can people really enjoy their democratic rights in countries where official languages are spoken by a small educated minority and the vast majority of the population is excluded from effective participation in any official business and communication, when they cannot read, write, or speak the language in which laws are inscribed and political discourse is conducted? What is the cost in terms of the development of education and a reading culture when formal education is offered in a language foreign to the child? African governments, publishers, educators, and writers need to take the question of language seriously for linguistic rights and development are an essential part of human rights and development. As Nguessan (1996: 12) states there is not a single country in the world that has developed "with a language that is foreign to the land and is unknown to the vast majority of its citizens."[3]

The reading public has an interest in all these matters, and the responsibility to patronize and promote African books. Without readers, books—however profound their contents and impressive their covers—gather dust on library or booksellers' shelves as monuments to irrelevance. Only a voracious and discriminating reading public can ensure that Africa produces not only more books, but good books, those that enlighten and enrich our lives, not debase our being and sensibilities. The privileged few can and ought to do more than simply buy and read books. Africa's wealthy capitalists could support cultural production as a whole, and the book industry in particular, by sponsoring literary prizes and arts grants. It is shameful that there is no African-sponsored equivalent of the Noma Award or the Commonwealth Prize. Culture and books are too serious to be left to sympathetic foreigners or governments. All of us have a stake in them, for they embody our cultural values, practices, and possibilities, dreams and destiny, pasts and futures, our investment in a reflective, critical, and tolerant humanity. Thank you.

2. REMEMBERING URBAN CHILDREN[4]

Introduction

In keeping with the theme of this year's book fair, I decided to focus my presentation on children. As was made abundantly clear at the Academic Workshop last week, there are of course many kinds of children; indeed, many definitions of the child. It is quite impossible to discuss children as a whole, certainly not in a presentation as short as this. So I have chosen to focus on urban children and to entitle my talk, "Towards a Sustainable Readership in Africa: Remembering Urban Children".

At first glance it may seem an act of elitist folly to suggest that we need to remember urban children. Aren't they more privileged than their rural counterparts, pampered beneficiaries of Africa's developmental urban biases, as the World Bank keeps admonishing our supposedly misguided governments? My justification for focusing on urban children is simple. Demographically they constitute one of the fastest growing segments of the African population. Over a third of our current population lives in cities, and if present trends of urbanization continue, in a couple of decades or so more than half of all Africans will be city dwellers. Given the preponderance of children—those under eighteen—in African populations, African cities will remain young, not necessarily in terms of their age, but in the age of their populations. Neveretheless, we know little about the reading habits and interests of urban children, who are destined to play an increasingly important role in determining Africa's futures. What do they like to read? What excites and empowers their imaginations and intelligence, creativity and consciousness, values and visions?

My presentation is divided into three sections. One discusses the importance of reading in general; two explores some of the reasons why urban children have tended to be ignored in African writing. This is not to suggest that all is well with the state of rural children's literature or reading cultures. On the contrary, in many ways the situation is far worse, especially in terms of supply and access. My point is simply to underscore some of the social and intellectual forces that have shaped the development of African writing in general and children's writing in particular and to underscore that children are no more homogeneous than adults. Section three examines the general structure of the book chain and suggests ways it can interface with children to promote sustainable reading among them.

The Infinite Pleasures of Reading

In the beginning was the story. Our lives are stories, narratives of being, becoming, and belonging. Stories affirm the orderliness and ordinariness of our lives in a world of unpredictable demands and infinite differences. Hearing stories helps us to overcome our existential loneliness, to connect us to experiences and expectations beyond ourselves that give more meaning to our individualities. The art of story telling, primordial and prevalent in all cultures, regales and reproduces our imaginative humanity, filling us with the memories and imaginings of pleasure, pain, pathos, and possibility. It is through storytelling that the aspirations, anxieties, affections, inquiries, ideas, information, traditions, and values of any community or any age are transmitted from one generation to another. The media of story telling, of course, evolve and overlap. Today, we have an unimaginable abundance: oral, textual, audio-visual, and electronic means for our stories to be told, shared, witnessed, and read in all their bewildering varieties.

Telling and reading stories go together. Reading is an act of narrative participation, cognitive engagement, and emotive empathy. It creates and connects social meanings, thereby furnishing us with a new imaginative potential. Different texts demand different forms of reading, of employment, of explication, of literacy. Written literacy is one of the most enchanting gifts of human communication across the spatial-temporal divides of history and culture. Written texts have the incredible ability to breathe with new life in climes and contexts beyond their original creation. They are repositories of human activities and fantasies, hopes and fears, successes and failures, insights and misconceptions; bequests of a purposeful consciousness, of creative and critical imagination. Children who read inherit the past, live the present, and imagine the future with far more inquisitive eyes than those deprived of the magic of literacy. They are able to transcend the immediate intimacies of time, place, and culture and to acquire the permissive pleasures of imagining other times, places, and cultures.

Reading cultivates and nourishes the imaginative powers of children. It titillates, as Professor Mazrui (1998) so aptly put it in his keynote address a couple of days ago, the transnatural imagination of children, through those fantastic tales of humanlike animals and animal-like humans. Reading can also stimulate children's transcultural and transnational sensibilities. Specialists of early childhood education and children's literature give us more pragmatic reasons why reading is important for children. Reading affects the child's cognitive, affective, linguistic, and literacy development. The child is exposed to the decontexualized language of books and to a world of knowledge beyond her own experiences, and she enjoys the comforts of reading with parents and other adults, acquires increased vocabulary and understanding of syntactic structures, and learns how to interpret pictures, words, and story lines. The emergent literary skills so learned should be horned with each year of schooling and growth, thereby teaching the child the love of reading and preparing her to mature eventually into a productive citizen. In short, reading and literacy are essential for development, both of the individual herself and of the society at large.

What children read also matters. Reading can empower as much as it can alienate. Empowerment comes from positive reinforcement of the familiar and affirmative domestication of the unfamiliar, while alienation can be produced by the insolent denigration of the familiar and the haughty exaltation of the unfamiliar. That was the essential criminality of colonial education, not that it tried to teach us the unfamiliar—European things and practices and values and habits and even climates—but that these were depicted as naturally superior to our own, that the familiar world around us was said to be irredeemably backward and primitive. These damaging stereotypes and the exoticization of Africa bred dangerous inferiority complexes in many students, some of them becoming frightfully alienated from their environments, from their histories; that is, colonialism sought to turn Africans into peoples without histories, into anthropological subjects. I will argue shortly that many of our own writers and intellectuals bought into this alienating dehistoricization and anthropologization of our societies and cultures, which resulted in the massive neglience of urban children as worthy subjects of literature.

Under these conditions, reading lost its enchantments and became a source of calculated duress to be abandoned gleefully after those dreadful school examinations. So the fiction was born that Africans do not like reading, that the lack of a reading culture was one of the quintessential distinguishing features of an African child from a European child. As the pleasures of reading were disavowed, in many countries children's literature was reduced to dreary textbooks, often stripped of any aesthetic delights. I can personally vouch for that. I hardly recall the textbooks I read in primary school. The only books I remember with some fondness were the comic books and the occasional novels I used to borrow from friends or from the public library. The first novel I vividly remember reading was a book my father bought for me, written in Chichewa, about the heroic exploits of a peasant man coming to the city for the first time. I was intrigued by the rural scenes, but even more fascinated by those set in the city, for after all, I was a child of the city, born here in Harare and brought up in Blantyre, Malawi's commercial capital.

The Invisibility of Urban Children

Urban children tend to be relatively invisible in African writing and in African cultural and social discourse for many reasons. They are often seen as children of privilege compared with their rural cousins, undeserving of special support or consideration. Often forgotten is the simple fact that not all urban children enjoy the secluded comforts of middle class life, and in these days of structural adjustment, middle class mobility spiraling downwards has become frighteningly common. Many urban children, in fact, live in the crowded, crummy world of working class neighborhoods, or subsist and survive in slums and on the streets, divorced from all social amenities and entitlements. Surely such children are deserving of our populist attention and moral indignation as much as the impoverished rural children. This is to suggest that urban children are not homogeneous; they are divided by the harsh hierarchies of class, not to mention the social markers of gender and genera- tion, and the imagined communities of religion, ethnicity, and race.

The invisibility and marginality of urban children articulates a discourse rooted in anthropological folklore and African cultural nationalism that depicted the city as an alien social and cultural space, where African cultur- al values were contaminated, African authenticity and agency compromised. Ironically the denigration of the city as an authentic cultural space is often expressed as much by middle class writers and ideologues as by rural tradi- tionalists and activists. For the middle class writers and scholars, this reflects the acute contradictions of their class positions in postcolonial society, where they enjoy the limited fruits of *uhuru* still denied the once beloved masses of the nationalist demagogues and the ambivalences of their cultural imagina- tions. Having recently left the peasantry, or migrated from the crowded high density suburbs, as working class neighborhoods are called here in Zimbabwe, to the low density suburbs, many of them seek cultural redemp- tion and class anonymity in a "traditional" world far removed from their daily experiences and those of their children. By denying their class and urban spaces and by affirming the rhetoric and realties of "traditional" and rural society, middle class writers have deprived us of writings that reflect the conditions of Africa in all their captivating complexities. This apparent absence of imaginative confidence reflects the impotence of a class, as Frantz Fanon once suggested, lacking a historic vision and mission, a class still uneasy with its modernist accumulations and aspirations.

Regarded as an external, colonial space, the city became an imaginary desert, empty of the nurturing and sustaining cultural reservoirs of indige- nous custom and tradition supposedly embedded in rural culture. Thus urban society as a whole tended to be dismissed or devalued in African writ- ing, as a context for African texts; as a thematic setting for African stories; as a space of imagination. So publishers, whether in Africa or abroad, often pre- ferred stories set in the rural areas over those set in the urban areas, even if, as was so often the case, the favored language of narrative was impeccable English, French, or any of the imported European colonial languages. The derivation of themes, metaphors, symbols, characters, and plots from rural culture—itself transformed by colonialism, independence, and the commer- cial and cultural circuits of globalization—deprived urban children of liter- atures that fully resonated with their complex spatial and social experiences.

As I noted earlier, as a child who was born and brought up in cities I was more enraptured by stories set in cities, especially about young people. Years later, when I became a writer, my fictional writing focused on urban life while my academic writing dwelt on the formation and struggles of the mostly urban working class. In a sense then I was telling stories of my social and creative space. All writing, all intellectual conversation is, in many ways, a form of autobiography, individual and collective biography; a creation of memories, a form of remembering. Our memories of the city, of its trials and tribulations, its pleasures and pathologies, are as real and remarkable as our memories of rural life.

It is in this sense that we need to remember urban children in our writings. Remembering implies recollection, recognition, reflection, and rethinking. We need to recollect, recognize, reflect, and rethink the complex lives of urban children. Given the constant traffic of ideas, images, institutions, and individuals between rural and urban areas, the old and the young, the narratives of the city will recollect old and new customs, ancient and modern traditions; the past, present, and future. Hence, we must also ask: What new stories, fables, proverbs, riddles are we creating and telling our urban children? It is not enough to mine the rich repertoire of creativity and wisdom left by successive generations of our ancestors. We also have a creative responsibility to make sense of our times and to live behind new artistic traditions for future generations. Culture, as we all know, is not permanently suspended in the mists of the remote past, but is a living, dynamic constellation of ever-changing social practices and processes, cognitive and concrete possibilities, moral and material imperatives, and social imaginations.

What, then, is the world of contemporary African urban children that we need to remember in our writing? It is an immensely complicated and diverse world, as I suggested earlier, differentiated by class, gender, ethnicity, religion, language, and sometimes race. While other parts of the world have recently discovered multiculturalism, most African cities are extraordinary conglomerations of multiethnic, multilinguistic, and multireligious communities. This, I would like to suggest, should give us cause to celebrate, not to moan, as is so often the case. For example, being multilingual as most of us are, especially in the cities, is an asset, not a liability, for human communication and understanding. In our writings we need to commemorate and to contemplate the incredible human stories that such multifaceted spaces of living, working, procreating, and cultural production and consumption generate.

383

The Book Chain and Children

Developing a sustainable reading culture presupposes an integrated book chain. What are the key elements of this book chain, and how does each interface with children as cultural creators and consumers? I say cultural creators and consumers for the question of children's reading is not simply one of writing for, or about children but also of writing by children. The book chain consists of many stakeholders, including, not necessarily in order of importance, the state, educational institutions, writers, publishers, distributors, libraries, and readers. Time does not allow a detailed discussion of the engagement of children with each of these stakeholders.

At the Academic Workshop we were told that many African states do not have coherent policies to promote and safeguard children's interests. At best children are regarded as helpless wards and not as active agents; as disenfranchised minors waiting to become disenchanted citizens. Besides general support for education, few governments have specific proactive policies to foster a sustainable reading culture among children, whether urban or rural. Preoccupied as they were after independence by the economics of development and the politics of nation-building, and most recently by the corrosive demands of structural adjustment and democratization, the cultural sector, including book development in general and children books in particular suffered from official neglect, as reflected in outdated or inappropriate legislation, often compounded by unimaginative tariff and taxation policies, censorship, and misguided monopolization of critical segments of the publishing industry. The recent wave of economic liberalization and democratization in many parts of Africa has opened new possibilities for the publishing industry and cultural production. If, however, these developments are to be sustainable, i.e., to set deep roots in Africa's complex cultural terrain, children ought to be specifically targeted as producers and consumers of reading texts.

Schools, of course, constitute a critical site where children acquire the skills of reading and writing. Whether they are private or public, educational institutions have a responsibility to foster a reading culture. Sufficient school funding is of course crucial to ensure the adequate provision of reading materials. So is the need for imaginative curricula that encourage a love of reading. All too often, reading in schools is turned into an insufferable chore undertaken for the all-important examinations. It becomes a source of mental pain, not intellectual and aesthetic pleasure; of dreary information, not critical knowledge, of breeding dullness, not creativity. The role of teachers cannot be overemphasized. When they appropriate or conceal reading materials donated for school use, as we heard from some workshop participants, they rob school children of their right to read. But the real villains lie in the corridors of government ministries and the international financial institutions, for it is they who have imposed draconian structural adjustment policies that have wrecked havoc on schools and other social sectors. These policies are robbing millions of children of their right to education, their right to read, their right to textual social imagination.

I have already alluded to the fact that children, especially urban children, have not been well served by our writers. While rural children often suffer from inadequate supply of books and other reading materials, urban children suffer from inadequate supply of relevant reading materials. In one of the sessions of the Academic Workshop we were told, for example, that street children find much of the available writings by African authors irrelevant. What kind of writings would attract such children if they have the skills, resources, and time to read? What do other urban children like to read when they can afford to read? Yesterday Iolanda Dube, an impressive twelve-year-old primary school student, gave us a glimpse into the reading habits of some urban children. She said she likes to read both African and European authors. Which ones and why? I wish more Iolanda Dubes had been invited to this workshop to tell us what different groups of children like to read. This is an area we need more research and understanding as writers, publishers, school teachers, and parents.

Publishers serve as indispensable midwives of the book industry, transforming private manuscripts into printed commodities for public consumption. Despite continuing facing severe challenges in terms of capital, infrastructure, and marketing the African publishing industry has expanded quite remarkably since independence when it was dominated by multinational publishing houses and later parastatals. This is mostly because of the enormous expansion of education, which remains the main market for most publishers; the divestment of foreign publishers and rising costs of book imports due to economic difficulties, including the steep devaluation of African currencies; and the rising entrepreneurial energies of the African publishers themselves. But as we heard in some of the indaba sessions over the weekend, publishers have tended to ignore children's publishing outside the school textbook market. The fact that this year's ZIBF focuses on children, and that the Kenyan children's book fair is growing, offer hopeful signs that children's books are beginning to receive the attention they deserve.

Besides encouraging writing for and about children, there is a need to encourage writing by children. During yesterday's morning session, I was gratified to hear participants encouraging Iolanda Dube and Nhamo Nyamadzawo, a secondary school student who made a presentation on his reading habits, to join the Zimbabwe Budding Writers Association. I was also gratified to learn about the Kwela books for young southern African writers and the anthologies of children's literary prizes being compiled by some adventurous advocates of children's literature. It makes marketing sense to encourage young people to write and to consult them on children's books. Above all, that is an investment for a sustainable reading and writing culture.

The role of distributors and libraries is no less important. Book sellers and distributors have not always shown the aggressiveness and creativity required to sell their wares in Africa's challenging markets, not to mention the highly competitive international markets. The recent proliferation of national, regional, and continental publishers and book distributor association and book marketing training workshops, including at the ZIBF, is reassuring. But it is not clear how much marketing efforts are directed at children above and beyond the dreaded school textbooks. As for libraries, their centrality becomes even more crucial with declining household incomes for families in many African countries due to the ravages of structural adjustment. That they should be wellstocked is obvious. The two students yesterday also mentioned the need for flexible library hours, including on weekends. In addition, the necessity for mobile libraries has long been recognized. However, such library services should not be confined to rural areas; they ought to include neglected poor urban neighborhoods. Others, including book sellers and distributors, as well as writers, could also benefit by becoming a little more mobile. School visitation programs by writers have been known to generate book sales.

Thus, readers, including children, must be actively courted by the various stake-holders in the book industry. The reading public or publics, of course, constitute a key element of the book chain. The interests and inclinations of different African reading publics, segmented according to location, class, and gender (among other considerations) need to be better understood. The commonly heard lament that Africans don't like to read, which is often based on anecdotal evidence rather than research, tends to become a self-fulfilling prophecy for publishes and writers who haven't done their homework. All the stakeholders identified should be mobilized for the development of vibrant and sustainable children's reading literatures and cultures. The difficulties cannot be underestimated, but moments of crisis can also offer windows of opportunity. The struggles for what has been called developmental democratic states in Africa are as much struggles for new modes of governance, citizenship, and economic management as they are for cultural production and development.

The development of a sustainable reading culture requires well-financed schools that produce literate students inculcated with the love of reading, states and societies that treasure free inquiry and critical citizenship, publishers and distributors who aggressively promote African books, libraries that creatively cater to children's needs, and writers whose imaginations roam across Africa's social and cultural landscapes—rural, urban, and peri-urban—recording and reshaping slices of life and experience. All of us have a responsibility to Africa's children, to make them central to our endeavors, not simply for the sake of their future as productive adults, but as current readers, as cultural producers and consumers in their own right. Lest we forget, they will bear testimony for us and our ancestors to generations yet to come. That is why they ought to be taken seriously. Thank you.

3. WRITING AS CONVERSATION[5]

As you can see, I am not Buchi Emecheta. I certainly cannot fill her large literary shoes. I don't know what she would have said this afternoon. I can, however, imagine that it would have been profound, something that would have inspired us to reflect seriously on the transformative possibilities of writing and literature. She would have shared her thoughts and insights distilled from a long and distinguished career, a versatile and rich imaginative mind, finely crafted artistic sensibilities and skills, and a passionate commitment to human freedom. Since that is clearly beyond what I can offer, the easiest thing for me to do, therefore, would simply be to declare the writers' workshop open, and let the aesthetic entertainment begin. That is what I thought I would do when alerted, around midnight last night and confirmed to my consternation this morning, to the possibility speaking in place of Ms. Emecheta. So, unlike both Dr. Ibbo Mandaza and Professor Micere Mugo, I didn't have several days to collect my thoughts, nor for that matter the courage to refuse Ms. Bamhmare's request and save myself from the embarrassment I am about to suffer this afternoon. After listening to the fascinating presentations this morning, especially the provocative and impassioned addresses by Dr. Mandaza and Professor Mugo, I changed my mind and decided to say a few things on the theme of the conference, "Transforming Africa Through Writing," to frame my thoughts around some of the issues they touched upon that emerged from the discussions. I have entitled my brief remarks, "Writing as Conversation."

Conversation entails communication that, in turn, raises questions about language, audience, media, and access, among many other things. Much has been written and debated on each of these issues and it would be pointless for me to try to summarize the debates in the literature even in the barest of outlines; in any case most of you are well informed about these issues, and the lunch hour was not long enough to do that even had I wished to. I would like to add a few thoughts on the questions of ideology, language, and responsibility in African writing.

Writing is an important form of social conversation, for while the act of writing itself is apparently an intensely personal practice, its consumption is almost invariably a public process. It is an important part of a society's conversation with itself and with other societies. Indeed, when we step back from the conceits of bourgeois individualism and its endearing fictions of the artist as a lonely genius or a raving lunatic, it is clear that all artistic production, all intellectual work represents the writer's intimate conversations with family and friends, and the mediated conversations with society through books and the media, themselves complex creations and repositories of memories, collective and conflicting memories of the society, its pasts and futures, aspirations and agonies, problems and possibilities. These written conversations between and within generations and genders, classes and communities, societies and social groups constitute granaries of memories from which various futures can be imagined and produced.

This is why writers should not simply be seen as teachers, creators, or interpreters comfortably sitting on the fences of society, soberly and quietly observing the foibles of their fellow citizens. The writer is both a student and a teacher, a creator and a chronicler, an interpreter and a participant in society, embodying within her being and creativity its social divisions and differentiations. Writers, in other words, convey and participate in different conversations, conversations that are inscribed by the grammar and accents of their gender, class, and ideological positions. In these days of post-something scholarship and sensibility it is no longer regarded important to ask about the ideological identities and messages of writers and their writing. These questions, as Professor Mugo amply demonstrated, are more critical than ever in our age of triumphalist globalization and repackaged imperialism. Artistic products are not merely aesthetic creations or texts, nor do they will themselves into being, as modernist and postmodernist critics would have us believe, but they represent critical discursive interventions in social struggles; struggles over the past, the present, and the future. Writing, in a large sense, therefore, is an ideological enterprise.

Words and images, mediated through texts, signs and symbols, are of course the weapons of composition and combat in this enterprise. This is why, in the case of writing, the question of language is so critical. As we heard this morning, this has been a central question in African literary and intellectual discourse. I have no intention of addressing the issue at length, except to observe that often the question is posed in oppositional terms: which languages should African writers use, indigenous languages or the foreign European languages inherited through colonialism; whether or not, to paraphrase Professor Ranger's statement, the languages of educational instruction and intellectual and literary production should be the Swahilis of the world, like English, or the Swahilis of our respective regions and countries? What is often forgotten is the fact that many Africans, certainly in the multicultural spaces of the cities and towns and zones of rural corporate production, are multilingual in African languages and various versions of domesticated European languages. The challenge, it would seem to me, is how to translate multilingual orality to multilingual literacy in the composition and consumption of literary texts.

Another dimension of the language question, even assuming sizeable public literacy in the language, is its intellectual accessibility. I refer here to the issues raised by Professors Tade Aina and Micere Mugo, about the construction and content of language deployed in African artistic and intellectual productions and the treacherous seductions of superficial complexity and mimicry. Each historical moment produces its own discourses that are meant to sanitize history, silence narratives of oppression and exploitation, and seize from the future possibilities of meaningful change that are demanded and embodied in prevailing social struggles. During our times, it is the calcified and contemptuous language of various posts—postmodernism, postcoloniality, post this and post that—that pose the greatest danger, in which we are assaulted with verbal violence and terror, intellectual and ideological nihilism.

This is to suggest that as African writers and intellectuals, we must always guard against the cheap thrills of mimicry, of importing faddish languages, expressions, sensibilities, styles, paradigms, and methodologies that shut us from having meaningful conversations with our own publics at home. We must not be "native interpreters" or "native ventriloquists" for the North, as those four Africans brought back from Europe to interpret and write for slavery and imperialism mentioned in Ngugi's essay on language and published in South Africa's *Weekly Mail and Guardian* three weeks ago, to which Dr. Mandaza referred.

Conversations that are not monologues require both talking and listening and appropriate silences for reflection, as well as gestures of connection, of mutual recognition. We must always ask ourselves: How much do we talk and listen to our communities and societies? Whose stories do we tell? Whose realities and conditions, hopes and dreams fill our imaginations, our voices? How much do our artistic and intellectual productions foster and facilitate intercultural literacy among our diverse peoples in our respective countries, subregions, and within the continent as a whole? And how much do we intervene in global discourses, about globalization, for example, to ensure that African intellectual views and visions are part of views and visions articulated elsewhere?

I believe that whether we are creative writers or academics, as intellectuals we have a commitment to addressing the burning questions of our day, at the local, national, continental and global levels as creatively and clearly as possible, honestly and humbly; intervening in and interrogating discourses that seek to disempower and dehumanize the poor and powerless. We must aspire to becoming public intellectuals, poised in "permanent opposition," to borrow the term Taban Lo Lyong used this morning, to the mean, brutish, and ugly in the organization and management of public affairs—economic, political, social, and cultural—at national or global levels. We must expose the nakedness of our emperors, be they despotic national governments or the unelected and unaccountable international financial institutions, such as the World Bank and IMF, that have wrecked so much havoc on our economies, societies, and polities, robbing hundreds of millions of people of fundamental rights to their livelihood, voices, and humanity. Doing anything less smacks of historical and humanistic irresponsibility, wallowing in self-indulgent and unproductive monologues.

We are living in an immensely complex period in African history, characterized by a fundamental rupturing of the postcolonial social, economic, and political order. It is a moment whose transformative possibilities echo that of the post-Second World War years, in which the colonial order began to crumble in the face of intensifying struggles in colonial towns and villages, among impoverished peasants, exploited workers, and the marginalized aspiring middle classes, all of which coalesced in what historians have named, or rather homogenized into, nationalism. Since the 1980s, Africa has been engulfed by tumultuous struggles whose historic scale and importance, in my view, compares to the decolonization era. In the last decade there have been many changes; inspiring concessions to the future, to democratic governance; but also dispiriting compromises to the past, leading in some cases to the resurrection of the bloody ghosts of history. The Africa of the 1990s, therefore, is an Africa of many stories, of the triumph of apartheid's demise in South Africa and the tragedy of genocide in Rwanda. The stories are too complex, too contradictory, to be reduced glibly to optimism or pessimism. As writers and academics we have a responsibility to understand and to explain this historical moment, with the hope that the good and the hopeful can be identified and harnessed for the future.

Let us engage in and promote literary and intellectual conversations that record the tribulations and triumphs of our people, honor their agency and aspirations, unravel the pitfalls and possibilities of modernity and globalization; conversations that enrich our multiple languages, strengthen, not weaken, our artistic traditions and intellectual capacities and communities; that deepen, not debase, our humanity. I declare the 1997 Writers Workshop open. Thank you.

4. OF GHETTOS AND ACADEMIC PIMPS[6]

Dear Achille:

I just read your editorial in *Codesria Bulletin,* Nos. 3 & 4, 1999, with interest. I was struck by your choice of title, "Getting out of the Ghetto." Now, as you know, the term "ghetto" evokes powerful images, at least in the Western world, where you are gesturing for integration, images not only of marginality, but criminal, pathological marginality. Of course you probably did not mean that; you did not mean to suggest that efforts by Africans, yes, from North to South and in the diaspora, to build independent research capacities and structures and networks of knowledge production entailed ghettoization. You know too well, I am sure, that African social science, indeed, academic knowledge in general, has been dominated by paradigms imported from elsewhere; that African scholars, like African economies, have not suffered from too little exposure to the external, or shall we use your preferred term—international—academic standards and currencies, but perhaps too much; that the agenda of "decolonizing," forgive the use of a term that to your postmodernist ears must sound shamelessly passè, African scholarship is not over.

As a student of culture and history, who surely knows that ideas reflect and reproduce contexts, you must be a little troubled, if only fleetingly, by the congruence of your plea that African scholars must abandon their intellectual ghetto and the pleas, no, the commandments by the international financial institutions that African states open their ghettoized economies. Never mind that it is not a question of opening up, for these economies, like African scholarship, have always been relatively more open than many others, including those in the North who dictate the terms. Rather it is a question of the terms of engagement; opening what, under what, and whose terms? This might sound too foundational, too nationalist, if you will, but I hope you do not believe that globalization will bring about the end of hierarchies and inequalities between regions or communities, however you configure them, in spatial or social terms.

Please do not get me wrong. It is crucial that we study globalization, as a historical process, as a constellation of contemporary trends in economy, technology, culture, and politics and as an ideology. Yes, we must confront globalization in all its manifestations and meanings. Sure, we must analyze it and try to understand its pitfalls and tease out the possibilities it holds for African societies and communities, which you would agree, cannot and will not be uniform because of the unyielding differentiations and mediations of nation, region, ethnicity, gender, class, religion, and generation. The problem, as I see it, is not the research agenda as such, but you seem to have bought the triumphalist ideology of globalization, the disempowering TINA docrtine, that there is no alternative to globalization as configured by the powerful forces of the North, so let us surrender to them, let us join them or perish. This sounds too much like unilateral surrender, almost as if our grandparents' and parents' generations said, at the moment of colonial conquest and during the heyday of empire, colonialism is too strong, so let us accept it. Of course, some did, but we do not remember them as fondly as those who resisted. These analogies, that your thesis is the intellectual equivalent of the neoliberal ideology of structural adjustment and colonial collaboration may be misplaced. Analogies are rarely exact, but I hope you get my point.

It is revealing that in order to push your ideological agenda of accommodation to the very forces that have marginalized or "ghettoized" African scholarship in the past, you choose to misrepresent the history of your own organization, CODESRIA, if only by implication. You say we must get out of the ghetto in a "methodical way." I believe we should indeed be methodical. Concretely, you suggest that we must produce "solid studies of international calibre that can help put African trajectories in perspective by comparing them with other experiences in the world." Ignoring for a minute what constitutes international in this context, if not Western scholarship, the same scholarship that has historically tended to marginalize African scholarship, despite much of it being inspired and immersed in that very western epistemological order, and whether or how matters may have changed, and also ignoring that African scholarship has always been comparative (taking any central question that has dominated African social science analysis from development and nationalism to gender and environmental studies), it is not clear how borrowing new themes, such as sexuality—popular in some cultural studies quarters of the Northern academy—or how filling African publications with such writings, will change matters. Personally I have nothing against sexuality or talking about bodies; but I am more interested in these questions as they relate to the fundamental questions of social existence in our societies, how our populations are being reproduced, how their bodies are being fed and nourished, clothed and sheltered, healed and saved, yes, the old questions of political economy.

You also tell us that getting out of our intellectual ghetto "is possible only if the tradition of field work regains its full role in research." I did not realize that African scholars had stopped doing field research, including that done for consultancy; I thought in fact that they did more of it than their Africanist counterparts who come to the continent and collect this research and process it into whatever is the theoretical flavor of the month, especially in these times of Afropessimism and post-something scholarship; one discourages extended research travel to Africa, the other encourages easy textual analysis and theorization rather than the collection of empirical data. But I may be wrong, you obviously know African researchers on the continent

393

better than I do, given our respective institutional and territorial locations.

The way forward, you continue, lies in the "reactivation of researchers' curiosity and sense of wonder." How is this to be brought about? Curiosity and a sense of wonder are of course admirable qualities. But some of the best scholarship in Africa, indeed, elsewhere in the world, has often been inspired by more than that, by a burning desire to change the world, to address the pressing issues of the times. Maybe that is why African scholars, surrounded by material poverty and political tyranny, by underdevelopment, to use a once popular term, are more preoccupied with questions of development and democracy than about gazing at their sexuality that seems to titilate the intellectual imaginations of some of our colleagues in "postmodern" societies, where, in any case, the intelligentsia has become increasingly professionalized and alienated from social movements and public culture, despite all the analytical fetish that is made about public culture.

You conclude your editorial with yet more caricatures of African scholarly production and the work of your own organization, CODESRIA. Among the cancers that you identify as having afflicted African scholarship are, first, what you call nativism, "a racist and authoritarian approach which, on the pretext of protecting cultural specificity, consists in reasoning as if black Africa were all of Africa and all Africans were Negroes." This is indeed strange coming through the pages of *Codesria Bulletin,* the organ of an organization that sought to incorporate the whole of independent Africa, not the racist sub-Saharan conconction of "international" Africanist scholarship. By the way, many of our Africanist friends in the North still think of Africa in terms of "black Africa" or "sub-Saharan Africa." Hegel's ghost is alive and well. Was Samir Amin, the renowned Egyptian economist, in fact, not CODESRIA's first executive secretary? Perhaps you are riled by the exclusion until recently of white South Africans from the councils of CODESRIA. But I hope you have not forgotten that there was a good reason for this. That beloved country was under apartheid, under which you would have been treated as a second class subject. Remember the cultural boycott of South Africa supported by all freedom-loving people and organizations in Africa and elsewhere in the world, including the OAU and UN? If you want to bring our white South African colleagues fully into CODESRIA's fold please, go ahead. But do not do it in the name of opposing some spurious nativism. You should have a better memory than that, being a historian.

The second obstacle, you claim, "has to do with territorialization of the production of knowledge, that is, the false belief that only autochthonous people who are physically living in Africa can produce, within a closed circle limited to themselves alone, a legitimate scientific discourse on the realities of the Continent." I thought the opposite was in fact the case, that African scholarship on the continent has tended to suffer from an external dependency syndrome, again, much like our economies, whereby structures of scholarly authority and validation have more often been sought from the Africanist capitals of the West than from the continent itself, an indication as clear as any of pervasive intellectual inferiority complexes, the false belief that for knowledge to be authoritative, whether in terms of themes or publication outlets, it must be from outside. To be sure, many Africans resented this and still do. But that does not mean they have fully succeeded in controlling the terms of intellectual production on the continent. Thus both your diagnosis and prognosis are misleading.

You conclude, and I cannot agree with you more, that we "must establish dialogues with both the various African diasporas and with other worlds." That, indeed, has always characterized the work of some of the continent's leading intellectuals and activists, many of whom have been pan-Africanists, people who were both nationalist and internationalist, committed to the liberation of their societies and other oppressed societies. Our generation must build on these traditions. We will be doing ourselves great disservice by forgetting the histories of our own formation as intellectuals and those of our societies across the continent and in the diaspora. Move forward, we must. But let us remember where and why the journey began.

5. THE CHALLENGES OF EDITING AFRICAN SCHOLARLY JOURNALS

Introduction

Journals constitute the lifeblood of the scholarly enterprise; they provide a medium through which scholars communicate and converse with each other, ideas are circulated and consumed, and research results are disseminated and debated. The contents, quality, and quantity of journals reflect the state of scholarship for a given community or country. The production and provision of journals are affected by many factors, including the condition of the economy and politics, the structure and size of the publishing industry, as well as the organization and vitality of the academic system itself. As these factors and processes change, so do the patterns and prospects of scholarly journal publishing.

This essay seeks to examine the forces that have contributed to and constrained the publication of scholarly journals in Africa in the last two decades. Specifically, it examines the challenges of editing journals in the social sciences and humanities, fields with which I am most familiar. The difficulties that the editors of such journals face are infrastructural, institutional, and intellectual in nature. Needless to say, they are interwoven with the performance and problems of the wider political economy, both national and international, and the changing technologies of information and cultures of education.

The essay is divided into two parts. It begins by situating scholarly journal publishing in the broader context of African political economies and the changing structures of university education and in the composition of the research communities before examining the specific challenges that confront the producers and editors of journals. It cannot be overemphasized that given the conditions of African countries, with scholarly communities being so diverse and complex, the obstacles and opportunities for publishing and editing scholarly journals vary quite considerably between countries and between disciplines. The situation in South Africa differs markedly from that in Somalia, as does that between anthropology and political science.

The Political Economy of Scholarly Knowledge Production

Scholarly journals as mediums for knowledge and information are mostly produced and patronized by intellectual communities in universities, research organizations, think tanks, and private and public policy formation agencies. In much of Africa, many of these institutions were only developed after independence. That is certainly the case with the universities, which were seen by the new states both as ivory towers for cultural modernity and factories for economic development. Charged with this mission, and committed to the protocols of scholarly discourse, journals were founded, mostly in literature, history, political science, and development economics, to trace the teleological march of the once reviled "native" subjects to respected national citizens and of their societies from underdevelopment to development. In short, the establishment of scholarly journals is largely a post-independence phenomenon, spawned and sustained by the expanding possibilities of university education, itself tethered to the dreams and demands of nationalism and developmentalism.

Many of the journals established in the 1960s enjoyed widespread circulation, reflecting, no doubt, their limited number as well as the lingering visions of pan-African integration and the structural legacies of the regional universities established during late colonialism. The postcolonial state had yet to impose its intolerant spatial and scholarly boundaries between African countries and academic communities. These were the days when *Black Orpheus* and *Transition*,[7] to mention but two of the most influential literary journals, flourished, providing writers, critics, and students an unprecedented forum to exchange ideas and to share the intoxicating moment of African independence.

The moment did not last, neither in its mood nor in its material contexts. Much has been written about the waning euphoria of the early 1970s as the challenges of development and underdevelopment, nation building, and integration became more evident, pried open by the recessions in the global economy and political liberalism. More importantly, for our purposes, was the continued expansion of universities, research institutes, and agencies in Africa. As the academic community increased in numbers, there were new opportunities and constraints for scholarly journal publishing. The size of the market grew as rising numbers of academics, anxious for personal and professional advancement, sought outlets for their intellectual products. One result was the proliferation of journals that were increasingly national and disciplinary in their clientele and audience, so that the market became more segmented and perhaps smaller for specific journals.

All was well as long as the captive library market, both at home and abroad, remained buoyant. This was, indeed, the case until the early 1980s. In the North, especially in the United States, the largest market for Africana materials outside the continent itself, African studies programs were expanding, and libraries were hurriedly building up their African monographs and serials collections. Within Africa itself, the intermittent recessions had yet to lead to the massive divestment from education and other social sectors that structural adjustment programs would do later. Many libraries were still able to order journals, especially the local and regional ones. Also, local academics could not only afford to subscribe to them, but to write for them as well.

The situation both in the North and in Africa itself began to change in the course of the 1980s, thanks to another bout of global recession and the imposition of a ferocious regime of free-market capitalism characterized by

397

structural adjustment, which entailed the dismantling of the welfare state in the North and the developmentalist state in the South. North American libraries, for example, started facing continuous cuts in their budgets, a situation made worse by the escalating costs of books and serials, which forced many of them to reduce their serials' holdings by canceling journals that had weak support among faculty or were little used by students. The constituency for African journals was feeble even among Africanists who rarely used or referenced them, as various studies indicate (Zeleza, 1997a: Chapter 4), so that they were among the most vulnerable. If the libraries in the North were suffering from a fiscal cold, those in Africa were reeling from pneumonia. Many university and research libraries reported sharp drops in their subscriptions to journals from the mid-1980s (Levey, 1993b; Zeleza, 1996, 1997a: Chapter 5); as real incomes among academics plummeted, so did their capacity to support journals, either as subscribers or as writers, for their scholarly talents were increasingly taken up by doing consultancies or by dabbling in the entrepreneurial world of the informal sector.

The political contexts for publishing became no less challenging. After the independence celebrations were over, political space was seized by an increasingly authoritarian state on the one hand and often equally intolerant forces of civil society on the other, so that the freedoms promised by decolonization began to wither. In a growing number of African countries, scholars and writers had to negotiate carefully between the impulses and demands of their intellectual calling and the crippling surveillance of both state power and civil society. Scholarly research and production was ensnared in a stifling web of censorship. Monitored especially closely were research and publications in the social sciences and humanities, with their propensity for deflating the inflationary rhetoric of development and national unity proclaimed by the new political class. In Malawi, publishers had to submit their manuscripts, including those of journal articles, to the Censorship Board before publication, a practice that terrorized both authors and publishers, as I recall from personal experience in the mid-1970s, when my book manuscript was mercilessly mutilated and I barely escaped political detention (Zeleza, 1996; Mphande, 1996). Even those who sought to publish in overseas journals or monograph series had to obtain the Board's stamp of approval to avoid recrimination later. As in Malawi, in Kenya, where I worked for many years, permission from the government had to be sought to organize an academic conference locally or to attend one abroad. Accordingly, lists of participants or the contents of articles would be scrutinized by overzealous and obtuse bureaucrats for any potential inclusion of subversive invitees and information.

Censorship sought to create a culture of silence, which was loudly enacted through the open harassment, dismissals, arrests, and even death of the errant intellectual. Such conditions were obviously not conducive to critical scholarly inquiry and productivity. In the worst-affected countries, many academics and writers, if they did not flee abroad, often learned the survival arts of self-censorship and intellectual apathy, and publishers kept their distance from potentially troublesome and unrewarding scholarly publishing, concentrating on the safer and more lucrative school textbook market. What is remarkable, however, is not the continued submission by some scholars to the silences imposed by the state and elements of civil society, but the courage of many others, who continued to research, write, and publish, both at home and abroad, at great personal and professional risk. Together with the ever restive students, they turned many universities into sites of the prodemocracy struggles that began sweeping African countries from the 1980s. Theirs was a fight against the erosion of resources and the erasure of their voices, which undermined their production and reproduction as intellectuals.

As the winds of democratization blew away one dictatorship after another, the possibilities for free speech and inquiry, scholarly research and publishing began to improve. Perhaps at no time during this century have the political conditions been so favorable in much of Africa for intellectual production and the dissemination of information as in the 1990s. The virtual explosion of newspapers, popular magazines and periodicals, and publishing houses testifies to this. The question is: To what extent have academics and scholarly journals in the newly democratic countries responded to the political opportunities presented by the demise of the old autocratic order? A full answer will have to await the passage of time and the analytical advantages of hindsight. Indications are that the results so far have been mixed; there are signs of both intellectual revitalization and continued stagnation, depending on the country and the discipline.

In most countries, the universities have yet to recover from the debilitating deprivations of the 1980s. In fact, political democratization riding on the coattails of economic liberalization has often meant less, not more, resources for the universities. Encouraged to acquire a new corporatist ethos and to sharpen their entrepreneurial skills, universities are expected to raise additional funds from hiking fees and from performing applied research for the private sector. This, added to persistent teaching pressures, threatens to erode even further the universities' mission for basic research. Thus originally conceived as brick towers for churning out professional elites, not as centers of intellectual excellence, as symbols of national prestige, rather than fundamental research, the universities are increasingly being forced to become service parks for private capital (Diouf and Mamdani, 1994; Ngara, 1995; Ajayi, Goma, and Johnson, 1996). While the problems of declining funding and increasing corporatization also afflict universities in the North (Zeleza, 1997c), in Africa the effects are much worse for universities lacking long histories and traditions of scholarly production and the protective networks of generations of generous alumni. If unchecked the current trends will reinforce the international intellectual division of labor whereby African universities and scholars will continue to import appropriate packages of "universal" theory and, at best, export empirical data; to be consumers of advanced research conducted in the metropolitan universities.

It is likely that fiscal and ideological threats to the universities may continue to erode their role as important institutional sites for the production of scholarly knowledge. In fact, in many African countries universities no longer monopolize the creation and consumption of scholarly knowledge. University funding crisis created both the need and the space for the creation of new sites of intellectual production and reproduction. Most visible was the proliferation of independent research centers; the emergence of what can be called an academic NGO sector. These research institutions and networks have become central players on the African research landscape and in the production, dissemination, and consumption of scholarly knowledge.

In addition to the internal and regional "brain drain" and "brain hemorrhage" from the universities, African academics and professionals have traversed the Atlantic and the Mediterranean in search of safer and greener pastures overseas. As might be expected the motivations and morality of their migrations are in serious dispute. The emergence of a significant African scholarly presence in African studies programs in the United States provides new possibilities for transAtlantic intellectual conversations and linkages for African scholars and publishers. This is not simply a product of increased African intellectual migration; it is connected in complex ways to the changing compositions of classrooms, curricula, and canon, itself spawned by the country's changing demographic, economic, and cultural realities and shifts in the eternal solitudes and struggles over race. The growing presence of

African scholars, some in increasingly senior academic and administrative positions in African studies programs, has, in turn, provoked complex reactions and struggles over student recruitment and faculty hiring, scholarly authority and research paradigms.

The migration of African intellectuals to the North is part of the complex processes of globalization, a process that offers both opportunities and dangers, and produces and reproduces both globality and locality in unprecedented and unpredictable ways; it is leading to the rise of new diasporic communities that often supplant and strengthen older ones. These communities, whether organized around culture, ethnicity, or religion, and in our case scholarship, connect and communicate through the very technologies and mobilities of globalization that compress the spatial and temporal divides of North and South, Africa and the West. Scholars and publishers based on the continent need to "exploit" the new African intellectual diaspora, while the latter, in turn, have a responsibility to mainstream African scholarship and publications in the countries of the North.

That there is need to develop innovative and cost-effective exchange programs between researchers in the North and within the continent is obvious. The devil, as always, is in the details, in the modes of communication and collaboration. Too often, the linkages are one-sided, used by Africanists in the North to underwrite their academic careers, leaving little intellectual benefits for African scholars. Academics, in short, ought to swear by the same democratic virtues of equality, transparency, and accountability they rightly demand from despotic politicians and governments. To facilitate this, effective scholarly media should be developed that promote intellectual conversation and accountability between African and Africanist scholarly communities. Coauthorship and copublishing should be encouraged. Also needed are extensive general and specialized review periodicals, edited and published jointly in the North and Africa. These periodicals could assist in advertizing African books in the North and vice versa, and in breaking the cycle of self-referential solitudes that currently characterizes Africanist scholarship.

It can be seen that the sites of African research and scholarly production have proliferated to include universities and independent research centers in Africa and universities in the North. Scholarly production and publishing, if they are to be fruitful and sustainable, must seek to establish mutually beneficial networks among the three, while simultaneously reinforcing the productive capacities of each. Revitalization of African universities is essential if the continent's human resources are to be developed and if the dangerous slide towards decline or continued dependency is to be reversed. This requires the restoration of adequate funding levels to the universities, and the reorientation of internal expenditure patterns and reward structures to put higher premium on research. Research centers in universities need greater financial support, administrative visibility, and outreach capacities. For their part, the independent research centers need to diversify their sources of financing and strengthen their capabilities for both basic and applied short-term and long-term research. Finally, African scholars in Northern universities can support and promote African scholarly research and production through the establishment of active collaborative linkages with their colleagues and publishers on the continent. The challenge, as always, is not the shortage of possible prescriptions but of limited material resources and political willpower.

The Joys and Tribulations of Being an Editor

No one knows for sure how many scholarly journals are published in any given year in Africa because of their high mortality rate and poor coverage by indexing and abstracting services. Jacob Jaygbay (1997:86) recites a 1996 survey conducted by CODESRIA's Documentation and Information Center (CODICE), which reported that there were nearly 200 scholarly journals in the social sciences and humanities in Africa, of which 53 percent were in English, 45 percent in French and the remaining 2 percent in Portuguese and Arabic. If correct, this represents a tiny fraction of journals published in the two fields worldwide. Damtew Teferra's (1995) data on science journals garnered from the Scientific Citation Index (SCI), indicates that Africa's share of world scientific output between 1981 and 1993 was a mere 1.3 percent, of which nearly a third came from North Africa, putting it second only to South Africa, followed by West Africa, then East Africa, and finally, Central Africa with only 2 percent of the total African output. While conceding that SCI data has shortcomings and weaknesses that result in underestimating journals published in Africa, Teferra sees a clear correlation between the amount of money invested in research and development and the contribution to knowledge; between research and development expenditures and scholarly publications.

Teferra's data also shows that, despite Africa's small global share, there was a dramatic increase in scientific publications for the continent as a whole. While in 1981 about 65 percent of the countries had fewer than fifty publications, by 1993 nearly half the countries had produced fifty or more publications, led by South Africa with 35 percent of the total, followed by Egypt and Nigeria, and then Kenya. The last three accounted for 30 percent altogether. There were considerable variations among countries: While Morocco, Ethiopia, and Algeria and Tunisia quadrupled, tripled, and doubled their respective output, there was a marked decrease in Nigeria, Liberia, Somalia, and the Sudan. Clearly the dramatic decline in Nigeria's fortunes, and civil war in the other three countries, played a crucial role. This is as clear an indication as any of the interconnections between scholarly publishing and political economy.

The challenges facing journal publishers can be grouped into five categories: first, the dependability of their institutional base; second, the availability of financial resources; third, the state of editorial capacity; fourth, the quality of submissions; and fifth, the development of marketing and distribution infrastructures. Universities, professional associations, and independent research centers constitute the three main institutional sites for African scholarly journals production. The fate of a journal is closely tied to the vitality and viability of its organizational base.

As outlined above, since the 1980s, African universities have been increasingly faced with acute financial difficulties, which reduced their capacities to support both research and its dissemination through publications. As might be expected, the better endowed universities of Southern Africa, especially those in Botswana, Lesotho, South Africa, and Zimbabwe were able to sustain and even launch new journals, while journals folded in many financially strapped universities elsewhere, including Africa's troubled giant, Nigeria. A survey of Nigerian library journals showed, for example, that of the nineteen started since 1964, ten had ceased publication by the early 1990s; the life span of the dead journals had been a mere two years. Most of them died in the 1980s (Ifidon, 1994). In contrast, Botswana's two library journals, inaugurated in 1980 and 1988, respectively, were financially healthy and enjoyed rising subscriptions. Indeed, of the sixteen library journals from nine countries that L. O. Aina (1994) surveyed, only the two from economically buoyant Botswana could boast coming out regularly and on schedule.

The fiscal fate of the universities spilled over to many professional associations. Declining incomes and morale in the universities often led to diminished interest in, and the ability to support, the professional associations among academics. Professional associations were responsible for publishing many national and sometimes regional and continental disciplinary journals. The decline or even demise of these associations for some disciplines and in some countries undermined scholarly production and productivity. Two examples will suffice. In the 1980s, the Kenyan Historical Association, once a vibrant intellectual network and forum for Kenyan historians, lost its vigor because of vicious internal ideological dissension, centered on the Mau Mau debate, which were partly fueled by wider political tensions in the country and state manipulation. There was also a rising sense of economic and epistemological deprivation among Kenyan academics in general. The result was that the association's flagship journal, *Kenya Historical Review,* ceased publication in 1978, and Kenyan historians lost a crucial outlet for their intellectual labors.

The demise of the *Kenya Historical Review* can also be attributed to the poor performance of its publisher, the Kenya Literature Bureau, a successor to the East African Publishing House, which folded after the demise of the East African Community in 1977. In the heyday of the Community and the East African Publishing House, there had been close collaboration in scholarly production among the universities of the three East African countries— Kenya, Uganda, and Tanzania—concretized among historians and developmentalists through the publication of the *Transafrican Journal of History* and the *Journal of Eastern African Research and Development.* As regional integration was sacrificed at the altar of parochial nationalism, university linkages frayed and the two journals lost their collective institutional base. They were only saved by the indomitable efforts of the late Professor Gideon Were, who took charge personally and continued to publish the journals through his own press with a subvention from the Ford Foundation.

Were's ability to sustain regular publication of the two East African journals was not replicated by the two editors of *Afrika Zamani,* originally the journal of the African Historical Association, a continental organization. As the association atrophied, the editors, two dedicated Cameroonian historians, Emmanuel Ghomsi and Mouctar Thierno, took over publication of the journal. Unfortunately, given the perennial shortages of funds and other resources, they were never able to sustain regular publication and maintain the high standards expected of a continental journal. Salvation came when CODESRIA took over the journal's publication in 1994 and reconstituted the editorial committee, bringing in historians from all the major regions of the continent and in the diaspora. While regular publication was restored and the quality raised, the absence of a vibrant institutional anchor, in the form of a historical association, continues to hinder the journal's viability. It is not clear what will happen to it once CODESRIA's subvention comes to an end.

The existence of a relatively vigorous association does not, in itself, guarantee the survival and sustainability of a journal, as the example of the African Association of Political Science (AAPS) demonstrates. Despite its overall high quality, the association's journal, the *African Journal of Political Economy,* appeared irregularly, and the editorial team was not noted for its efficiency in communicating with contributors. For example, in 1989 I submitted a review article, which was never acknowledged, let alone published. It was eventually published elsewhere. The journal also seems to have developed a "sectarian" reputation as the mouthpiece of "radical" political economists rather than as an outlet for a broad constituency of political scientists. Following the demise of actually existing socialist regimes in Central and Eastern Europe as well as in Africa from the late 1980s and the consequent ideological and epistemological crises of Marxist paradigms and politics, AAPS sought to broaden its constituency and appeal. The journal was reorganized and its name changed to the *Journal of African Political Science.*

Part of the problem for journals produced by academics based at universities or in professional associations is that editing is often an adjunct activity to their full-time work, for which they neither have adequate time nor receive remuneration. This is one reason why the independent research centers, with full-time editors, have tended to perform so much better in maintaining regular publication schedules and sustaining relatively high standards. This is quite evident when one compares the scholarly publications of such organizations as CODESRIA, OSSREA, and SAPES with those of many university departments and institutes or professional associations. To be sure, the editorial capacities of these centers could be improved. For example, authors are often not sent copy-edited versions of their forthcoming articles, with the result that one is sometimes shocked to see one's sentences, grammar, and punctuation mangled, as has happened to virtually all my articles that have appeared in *Africa Development, Codesria Bulletin,* and *Afrika Zamani* published by CODESRIA and in the *Southern Africa Political and Economic Monthly* published by SAPES.

Notwithstanding these problems, it is clear that if they are to be produced efficiently scholarly journals from universities and professional associations need to employ full-time editors, or to buy release time for them from their institutions of employment. The possibilities of doing this are, however, rather limited for most journals, for the main obstacle is lack of adequate financial resources. The financial challenges of scholarly publishing play themselves out both directly and indirectly: directly in terms of the costs of production; indirectly through the availability and size of discretionary income among potential buyers as well as the state of the educational and library infrastructures through which intellectual products are distributed and consumed.

A recurrent complaint at conferences of African publishers and in studies on African publishing centers on the ever-escalating costs of production. Already grossly undercapitalized, African journals have been faced with skyrocketing unit production costs. This is mostly because in most countries printing materials, including paper, are imported. Compounding the situation is the persistence of high import duties and the inflationary pressures of currency devaluations imposed by structural adjustment programs. One Nigerian editor reports that when his journal began in 1983, "it cost about N875 to print 250 copies. In 1985 it rose to N2,150. By the end of 1991 the cost for the same print run was N5,500, even though quality of paper and printing had declined under the impact of economic circumstances that have affected most aspects of the nation's life" (Nzotta, 1994:30). Nonetheless, vocal appeals from African publishers for the reduction of duties on printing materials, vigorously supported by UNESCO, have largely fallen on deaf ears of most governments (Bischof, 1991).

Largely locked out of commercial sources of credit, publishers have made petitions to banks and the international and regional financial institutions, including the World Bank, for concessionary credit, which have also been consistently refused. In 1993, for example, the African Publishers Network (APNET) sent a delegation to the World Bank to implore the bank to show support for the indigenous African publishing industry by abandoning its insistence on international competitive bidding for major contracts, especially of educational textbooks. The delegation returned empty-handed (Davies, 1996:14). More forthcoming have been the private foundations and official development agencies, especially from the Nordic countries and Canada, which have set up various schemes to assist in the development of sustainable publishing capacities in Africa. Publishing needs, however, far outweigh the supplies of financial support from these organizations. Moreover, as with all forms of aid, the question of sustainability after the cession of the aid always remains.

Financial constraints partly explain the reluctance of African publishers to take up journal publishing. They understandably prefer to concentrate their energies on the lucrative and captive school textbook market. In industrialized countries, production of scholarly journals has become increasingly commercialized. This usually involves joint publication by an academic association and a commercial publisher, where the former provides editorial board control, while the latter is responsible for printing, marketing, and distribution; the two share production costs as well as profits. In extreme cases, the publisher operates the journal as a commercial venture and might appoint the editorial board itself. The corporatization of journal publishing has its dangers; sales and quantity can become more important than contents and quality. The rapidly rising costs of American and European journals, especially those in the sciences, is often blamed on the corporatization of scholarly journal publishing. Cash strapped universities have responded by turning to cooperative acquisition of journals, explored greater use of document supply and electronic delivery services, and joint journal publication schemes.

Thus publishing scholarly journals through partnership with commercial publishers is fraught with difficulties and can undermine a journal's intellectual integrity and affordability. If carefully executed, however, it offers perennially impoverished editors an important source of production and marketing resources. This is an opportunity that African editors need to explore and exploit, instead of simply relying on subventions from parent organizations or donors, and subscriptions from individuals and institutions. As already noted, in most countries none of the three major sites of research and intellectual production—the universities, professional associations, and independent research centers—have the required financial resources to sustain the publication of scholarly journals. And subscriptions have proven difficult to sustain for journals with reputations for poor physical quality and sometimes low levels of scholarship, and irregular publication and delay. In situations of declining library budgets and disposable incomes, as has been the case in much of Africa, and even in North America, frustration simply turns into subscription cancellations.

Desperate African editors have resorted to two additional sources of funds to sustain their journals: paid advertisements and payment by authors. Proceeds from advertisements are usually too insignificant to make much difference or to justify the amount of time spent soliciting them (Ifidon, 1994:22; Nzotta, 1994: 230-31; Ouma, 1994:83). Similarly, charging authors does not seem to yield much. This practice appears to be particularly widespread in Nigeria. Many regard it as unethical and unprofessional, for it borders on self-publishing and buying scholarly space (Nzotta, 1994:32), although it may have helped to keep some journals afloat. Anaba Alemna (1993:50-51), in fact, argues that "journals should adopt the system of charging contributors for the cost of pages used by their articles. This system is not new, as it has been used by a number of professional journals in some developed countries." He also advises African editors to cut production costs by reducing the quality of the paper they use, even publishing in mimeographed form, and to lower their standards of acceptance. This is dangerous advice: Many African journals lack a market and respectability precisely because they are perceived as shoddy in their physical quality and scholarship. To reinforce those same features, in the name of cost savings, is a recipe for death.

A better solution would be to reduce the number of journals in fields and disciplines where journals proliferate and to rationalize their production. Also, unviable national journals ought to be folded into regional journals. That this would be difficult to implement cannot be doubted, for more often than not journals are established to promote the academic careers or ideological agendas of their founders. Ifidon (1994:21-22) goes so far as to blame the short life span of Nigerian journals on "the selfish, short-sited and short term goal of the founders," who create journals to publish their own articles and those of their colleagues to secure promotions in the fierce publish or perish world of academia, "and as soon as that short-term objective is met, the initial enthusiasm to float a journal cools off and with it comes the journal's demise."

The commitment and competence of editors is, therefore, crucial for the sustainability of journals. The road to the editor's office takes many routes: some are self-appointed, especially if they are the journal's founders; others are nominated or elected by the institution that publishes the journal. The able and conscientious editors tend to be overstretched, especially if they have full-time jobs and have few or no staff. The challenges become almost insurmountable for the inexperienced or opportunistic editors. There does not seem to be any correlation between an elective and nominated editorial position and the longevity or quality of a journal, although several editors writing in a special report by the International Federation of Library Associations and Institutions on African library journals (Wise, 1994) expressed the view that editors should be chosen on the basis of their professional standing and skills rather than of their popularity.

The contributors were also agreed that while most editorial advisers are recruited simply as publicity gimmicks, editorial boards need to play a more active role. Unfortunately, this is not always the case because of the administrative and financial problems of arranging meetings for members scattered over wide distances and engaged in full time jobs. Consequently, many editors work alone, or prefer to work with a small committee limited to, in the words of one editor, "colleagues within reach of the institution where I work" (Ouma, 1994:84). That this happens with relatively well-endowed journals, such as the revitalized *Afrika Zamani,* would seem to suggest that more than money or communication is the issue. Although a member of the journal's editorial board since 1994, I have rarely been consulted. Thus what is often missing is a professional culture of scholarly publishing and management.

In addition, the review process is poorly developed both in terms of refereeing and communicating with authors. It is the policy of most African scholarly journals that their manuscripts be refereed, but in practice some journals do not send out manuscripts for independent assessment. One former editor comments: "Some are more or less in-house journals. In some so-called refereed journals manuscripts are selectively assessed, depending on the status of the author. Consequently it is common to find bad and good quality articles in the same issue" (Aina, 1994:40). Those that do seek external referees encounter other problems. "Only a few people are genuinely interested in doing the job," states a long-time editor, "especially as it is expected to be performed gratis. Some referees take a very long time to do the job. They have to be reminded and begged several times before they do. In a few cases manuscripts have been misplaced or lost" (Nzotta, 1994:29). Contacting referees can also be even more difficult because of unreliable mail and underdeveloped communication services.

Many editors also tend to blame the widespread practice of not sending authors copy-edited manuscripts for review on poor communication. That may be true in some circumstances, but this is often used as a cover for editorial incompetence and incapacity. The frequent lack of adequate or efficient secretarial support simply makes matters worse. The problems may also arise from constant or arbitrary changes in the composition of the editorial board. Rare are those journals that promptly acknowledge manuscripts, send articles for refereeing, accept or suggest revision, or reject them. It is not unusual for articles to take several years before they see the light of day, by which time the information and interpretation may be quite dated. The case reported by Aina (1994:42) of an article written in 1984, accepted for publication in a 1987 issue that was eventually published in 1991, is probably not that exceptional. The effect is that, to quote Mary Niles Maack's (1987:48-9) apt comment on library journals,"most of these publications function as journals of record rather than providing a timely forum for the discussion of new developments or current issues."

Such delays are extremely frustrating for authors and discourage them from patronizing the journal concerned, which accelerates its demise. Thus the importance of developing the editorial capacity of journals cannot be overemphasized. It is indispensable to raise the quality and stature of a journal and to attract the best and brightest authors. That would help stem the strong tendency among African scholars to seek foreign publishing outlets. The high premium placed on publishing abroad is a sad commentary on the persistence of the external-gazing structures and ideologies of colonialism. It is not a sign of the African academics' confident universalism but of their insecure provincialism, reflecting a desperate search for intellectual legitimation from academic systems and epistemological traditions that have historically dismissed and infantalized them. It becomes a vicious circle: Weak journals attract weak contributions, which makes the journals even weaker.

Clearly, the question of the quality of submissions, which eventually determines the quality of the contents, is also central for the production of strong, influential journals. African editors are known to complain that while there is no scarcity of manuscripts, there is a dearth of quality manuscripts. The words of Briggs Nzotta, editor-in-chief of the Nigerian Library and Information Science Review, are worth quoting at length:

> Most manuscripts we receive are not based on empirical research conducted by the authors. Surprisingly, it is still much more difficult to get well-written theoretical papers making an original contribution to knowledge or thought in the field. Similarly, it is hard to find comprehensive, up to date literature reviews on any subject or aspect of the dis-

cipline. Understandably, the present economic situation has made us all out of date with current developments and literature in the field. To compound the problem, very few take the pains to ensure the grammatical and technical correctness of the manuscripts (Nzotta, 1994:27-28).

Editors can counteract this in several ways. One is to solicit submissions from distinguished scholars in a field; and the other is to participate in scholarly writing training workshops for younger scholars.

Several editors report trying the first strategy with varying degrees of success (Banjo, 1994: 52). The need for writers' workshops "to instruct potential authors in the techniques of investigation, identification of topics, and in targeting likely journals for their materials", has been recognized (Olden, 1994:62), but it has yet to be tried on a wide scale. Dissertation and scholarly writing workshops are quite common in the major North American universities, and the Rockefeller Foundation has for many years run such workshops for African students registered in these universities. Plans to introduce an annual workshop on scholarly writing for African graduate students and young academics at the Zimbabwe International Book Fair is a welcome initiative. As resource persons, it is envisaged that publishers and editors of scholarly books and journals will be invited from Africa and abroad, and so will senior academics.

These efforts will not amount to much unless African scholars, including those with distinguished reputations, publish some of their writings in African journals as a means of raising their profile and quality. As I stated on one occasion:

> [T]here can be no substitute for a vigorous publishing industry in Africa. Only by developing and sustaining our own publishing outlets can there emerge truly African intellectual traditions and communities capable of directing and controlling the study of Africa, of defining African problems and solutions, realities and aspirations, of assessing our achievements and failures, our pasts and our futures, and of seeing ourselves in our own image, not through the distortions and fantasies of others. Publishing is critical not only for the academic enterprise, but also for

411

the cultural identities of nations, peoples, classes, and groups. It provides the material basis for producing, codifying, circulating and consuming ideas, which, in turn, shape the organization of productive activities and relations in society (Zeleza, 1994d:238).

I firmly believe that African scholars, wherever they are, either on the continent or in the diaspora, must make African publishers and journals their publication media of first choice; not of last resort, only fit for rejects from elsewhere. It is unconscionable that there are still university authorities, for example, at the University of Ghana, who express reservations about journals published in Africa and do not rate articles published in them as those published in overseas journals in determining promotions (Alemna et al., 2000). Needless to say, this serves to discourages academic staff from publishing in, and using, African journals.

One also hears from African colleagues in the North that publishing in African outlets can hurt one's career in the highly competitive Northern academies. If my own personal experience is anything to go by, this may not be entirely correct. The bulk of my publications has been in Africa, but I think I have advanced in my career as fast as anyone else. I would like to believe that quality research, even when inscribed on low quality paper and bound by covers with little aesthetic value, can still speak for itself. If African migrant and diaspora intellectuals in the North were to publish regularly in African journals, they would assist enormously in promoting the quality, circulation, international acceptance, and accessibility of these journals. For one thing, they and their students would have a stronger interest in supporting and protecting such journals in the acquisition battles of the libraries.

The use of African journals by academics and students in African universities needs to be vigorously promoted by all concerned, including the academics themselves, libraries, and publishers. It is encouraging to note that about 70 percent of academics at the Universities of Ghana and Zambia surveyed for a study on the use on African journals in African universities reportedly considered Africa-published journals either equally important or more important than journals published elsewhere (Alemna et al., 2000). They found these journals more contextual and relevant to African conditions and therefore useful for research and teaching. However, the actual number and use of the African journals was rather limited. At the University of Ghana only 60 out of the 670 journals were African-published, and at the University of Zambia there were 58 out of 398. Many academics did not know the African journals that existed in their subject areas, found access to these journals was difficult, and rated some of them poorly for their quality and irregularity.

Librarians and publishers have their work cut out. Librarians need to promote library holdings, awareness, and use of African-published journals, while African journal publishers need to improve marketing and promotion, production and content quality. As more academics adopt the use of ICT for research and teaching, it is critical that African journals move to online publication as well and have a presence on the Internet. Damtew Teferra (1998: 58-9) tells us that "African scholarly journals are increasingly benefitting from current developments in information technology. E-mail, the Internet, and CD-ROM technologies are promoting the scholarly works of African scholars and their visibility and contribution to the international knowledge system."

These technologies are of course no panacea. They require costly infrastructures—reliable communications system and power supplies—and equipment, mostly imported, does not come cheap. Also, warns Hans Zell (1998), as libraries in the North increasingly move to an access rather than an ownership model and rely on electronic document delivery and interlibrary loans for journal articles, subscriptions to the often underutilized, poorly cited, and print-only African journals may be curtailed even further. These challenges are real, but African journal publishers cannot afford to be frightened into paralysis. Indeed, Zell himself believes that if used creatively the new technologies do offer African journal publishers opportunities to enhance the visibility of their products at relatively low cost.

Academics as authors and journal consumers constitute an important part of the marketing and distribution system for journals. It cannot be overemphasized that scholarly writers and publishers need to work closely together. It is encouraging that in November 1997 a crucial African Writers -Publishers Seminar was held in Arusha, Tanzania, to negotiate a new deal between the two professions. However, the primary responsibility for marketing lies with the editors and publishers. Many African journals fall awfully short on this score. Financial constraints and generally poor support infrastructure can partly be blamed for this. However, Henry Chakava, East Africa's largest indigenous publisher, believes publishers themselves bear some responsibility. "It is our view," he stated at a 1996 conference on indigenous publishing in Africa, "that the African publisher has not, in spite of these handicaps, approached his job with the energy, determination and innovativeness that would guarantee success" (quoted in Davies, 1996: 10). Singled out was poor market research and lack of strategic and sustained promotion campaigns.

Chakava's comments were directed at book publishers, but they can be applied to journals as well. Journals are sometimes established without conducting feasibility studies to ascertain their market and sustainability. Rarely does the publishing staff include a full-time marketing manager. In most cases, the editor is expected to be responsible for the actual editing of the journal and its marketing, for which he or she may not have the necessary training and skills. As noted earlier, few African journals publish jointly with a commercial publisher or appoint one as a marketing agent for the journal. Also, little advantage is taken of the marketing possibilities of international indexing and citation services. Another marketing resource that could be better exploited by African journals is direct mailing. Not only do they need to keep up-to-date lists of individuals and institutions that have subscribed to their journals or purchased other materials from them, these mailing lists could be swapped between publishers and be used for highly targeted promotional campaigns.

International mailing lists can also be rented or purchased from professional mailing list institutions. African journals could exchange space advertisements with each other and with journals elsewhere (Jaygbay, 1997). The possibilities offered by the Internet for advertising African books and journals also need to be investigated and utilized. A niche market can be cultivated by advertizing journals and their table of contents or abstracts through electronic discussion groups and bulletin boards and by establishing webpages on the Internet. This is increasingly being done for a growing number of African journals, although it is unlikely that many will be able to produce both print and online versions any time soon. There is no doubt that online publication of African journals constitutes part of the road to the future for African scholarly publishing.

Conclusion: Towards Growth and Sustainability?

The challenges are many, so are the opportunities. This essay has outlined some of the major economic, political, institutional, and intellectual trials and tribulations that face publishers and editors of African journals. Broadly speaking, African political economies in the last two decades have been dominated by two major processes, those of political democratization and economic liberalization. Both have profoundly altered the conditions and dynamics of African societies, polities, and institutions. Also transformed, sometimes for the better and sometimes for the worse, are the fortunes and prospects of the publishing industry (Altbach, 1996). It is clear that many African publishers have continued to succumb to the old challenges reinforced by the new, hence the persistence of the journal mortality syndrome of "Volume 1, Number 1." Nonetheless, many others do survive and even thrive, and new ones continues to emerge, especially in the last few years. This is a testimony to the determination of African scholars to have their intellectual voices heard; to have scholarly conversations with one another and with academic communities elsewhere.

Indeed, the question of African scholarly publishing has never been higher on the agenda as it is now. There are a plethora of programs and projects created to promote the industry at all levels, from the training of writers and editors to capitalization schemes for production and the improvement of marketing and distribution systems. Most notably they include the African Books Collective and APNET, established to promote the international and continental trade in African books (Jay, 1994, 1997; Bgoya, 1997); the Bellagio Publishing Network, an informal association of organizations dedicated to strengthening African publishing; the Donors to African Education formed by bilateral, multilateral, and nongovernmental donors and by African ministries of education and development bodies to coordinate book development and provision (Priestly, 1996). Also launched have been various book and journal donation programs, including the African Journals Distribution Program, created to facilitate the distribution of African journals within the continent; the African Periodicals Exhibit (APEX), set up to provide an international marketing service for African journal publishers and a forum for the discussion of common concerns, and the African Journals Online, which seeks to promote the awareness and use of African-published journals especially in science, technology, and medicine (Ling, 1997; Alemna et al., 2000).

Quite encouraging as well is the expansion of book fairs on the continent and the attention increasingly paid to writers and literary awards (Ling, 1997; Dekutsey, 1997). Furthermore, African publishers are beginning to explore more actively copublishing and coproduction amongst themselves

415

and to take more seriously questions of regional cooperation and the importance of scholarly publishing in order for Africa and Africans to take charge of the study of Africa. Declared Eve Horowitz Gray (1997:8, 10) of the South African publishing house Juta at an international seminar on book production and distribution in Africa, held in Norway in April 1997: "We have to extend our commissioning beyond the borders of our own countries, to include the best authors we can locate in Africa and beyond....But without a scholarly publishing industry, how does one keep African scholarship alive? Knowledge about our continent has to emanate from our continent, and for strategic reasons we cannot allow this to die." Less promising is the state of copublishing arrangements between African publishers and their Northern counterparts (Molteno, 1997). This could be used by African publishers to produce books on Africa originated in the North.

It is clear, therefore, that a lot is happening to create what Paul Brickhill (1996, 1997) calls a viable book chain; to coordinate the activities and interests of the major stakeholders of the African book and journal industry: authors and subscribers, publishers and editors, distributors and libraries. African scholars must patronize these journals by writing for them and, whenever possible, subscribing to them and by ensuring that they are acquired by their libraries and providing protection against possible library cuts and cancellations. Migrant and diasporic African intellectuals have an important role to play in promoting African scholarly production and dissemination. Some of them are founding their own journals in the North, or assuming editorial influence in Africanist and non-Africanist journals. Journal exchanges, advertizing space, ideas, and authors would enrich the scholarly communities based in Africa and the North, both African and non-African, and assist in the deparochialization of Northern scholarship and the universalization of Southern scholarship.

Besides the migration of people, a few African scholarly journals have also migrated to the North. The principal example is *Transition,* founded in Uganda in the 1960s, now relocated to Harvard University in the United States. Such journals have a special responsibility to act as a medium of serious, two-way intellectual conversation between Africa and North America. They must avoid the dangers of developing historical amnesia and of falling easy prey to the seductions of the postsomething sophistries parading in the American academy, which many African intellectuals on the continent find at best amusing and at worst dangerous. They must address the fundamental processes, issues, and questions that have shaped, connected, and differentiated African and North American societies. Through them we must remember and reconfigure the Middle Passage and the numerous ties that bind Africa and the Americas.

Endnotes

1. Keynote address, Zimbabwe International Book Fair Indaba, "National Book Policy: The Key to Long-term Development", Harare, Zimbabwe, 26-27 July 1996.

2. For the industrialized countries as a whole the figure is about 520 and for the Third World it is about 40. See Jessica Barry (1996:4).

3. The OAU Heads of State and Government adopted the Language Plan of Action in 1987, but as with most OAU resolutions, not much has been done to implement it. See Mateene (1996).

4. Speech given to the writers workshop, Zimbabwe International Book Fair, Harare, Zimbabwe, 3 August 1998.

5. Official opening of writers' workshop, "Transforming Africa Through Writing." Zimbabwe International Book Fair, 8 August 1997.

6. Response to Achille Mbembe, executive secretary of Codesria, Editorial, "Getting out of the Ghetto." Codesria Bulletin 3 & 4, 1999: 1-2.

7. According to some sources, *Transition* was apparently created by the CIA as part of the CIA's vast program of mobilizing intellectual and artistic communities during the Cold War between the United States and the former Soviet Union, in this case "to undermine Communism's claims in the former colonial world" (Sharlet, 2000).

Bibliography

AAU Newsletter 5, 2, 1997. "Breaking News... Women Researchers" 12.

___. 4, 2-3, 1998. "WGHE Holds 12th Meeting" 1-3.

___. 4, 2-3, 1998. "The International University of Africa."14.

___. 4, 2-3, 1998. "Université de Ouagadougou: Strategic Vision and Mission" 7.

___. 5, 2, 1999. "Masters Program in Human Rights and Democracy in Africa to Kick Off in 2000" 18-19.

___. 5, 2, 1999. "AAU Signs Memorandum of Understanding with the HBCU/MIC" 13-14.

___. 5, 2, 1999. "Ford Foundation to Support An Endowment Fund for AAU" 15.

___.5, 2, 1999. "AAU Evaluates NUFU Programmes in Africa" 7-8.

___. 5, 3, 1999. "AAU Programs: Graduate Education Scholarship Program" 10.

___. 6, 2, 2000. "Profile" 7-9.

___. Special Issue, March 2001, "Brief Report on the 10th General Conference" 3.

AAWORD. 2000. *1977-1999 Deconstructing Research and Development for Gender Equality. Report on AAWORD's Institutional Evolution.* Dakar: AAWORD.

Abagi, Okwach. 2001. "African Universities in the 21st Century: Vision, challenges and the Way Forward." Paper presented at the Ford Foundation Retreat on Visioning the African University in 2050, Durban, South Africa, 29 May - 1 June.

Abascál-Hildebrand, Mary. 1999a. "Public Intellectuals as Political Educators." *Educational Studies* 30 (3-4): 261-273.

___. 1999b. "Narrative and the Public Pntellectual." *Educational Studies* 30 (1): 5-18.

Abdul, Alkalimat. 1999. "A Few 'Honest' Answers About the Preliminary Critique," 2 November. *<H-AFRO-AM@H-NET.MSU.EDU> H-AFRO-AM@H-NET.MSU.EDU>*

Aboudre, Aswan. 1999. "'Wonders of the African World': Reply," 2 November.*<H-AFRICA@H-NET.MSU.EDU>*

Abrams, M. H. 1997. "The Transformation of English Studies: 1930-1995." *Daedalus* 126 (1): 105-131.

Abu-Lughold, Lila. 1993. *Writing Women's Worlds: Bedouin Stories.* Berkeley: University of California Press.

Achebe, Chinua. 1958. *Things Fall Apart.* London: Heinemann.

ADEA Working Group on Higher Education. 1998. "African Regional Networks for Graduate Training and Research," Ouagadougou, Burkina Faso, 3-5 November. *<www.adeanet.org/publications/wghe/wghereport ouaga.pdf>*

Adejumobi, Said and Abubakar Momoh, eds. 1995. *The Political Economy of Nigeria under Military Rule: 1984-1993.* Harare, Zimbabwe: Sapes Books.

Adel, Abdel M. 2000. "Battle of the Book." *World Press Review* 47 (8):42-43.

Adler, G. 1997. "New Social Movements: Democratic Struggles and Human Rights in Africa." In James H. Mittelman, ed. *Globalization: Critical Reflections.* Boulder, Colorado: Lynne Rienner: 117-43.

Adubifa, O. A, ed. 2000. "Towards the Introduction and Application of Information and Communication Technologies in African Universities: A Collaboratory Investigation of Key Issues and Guidelines by Carnegie Corporation of New York and the Association of African Universities. Unpublished.

African Regional Consultation Preparatory to the World Conference on Higher Education. 1997. Dakar, Senegal, 1-4 April. *<http://www.chet. org.za/oldsite/debates/dakar.html>*

Agozino, Biko. 2000. "Wonders of the African Crisis," *West Africa Review* 1, 2 *<Http://www.icaap.org/iuicode?101.1.2.1>*

Ahmad, Akbar and Chris Shore, eds. 1995. *The Future of Anthropology: Its Relevance in the Contemporary World.* London: Athlone Press.

Ahmad, Aijaz. 1992. *In Theory: Classes, Nations, Literatures.* London: Verso.

____.1996. "The Politics of Literary Postcoloniality." In P. Mongia, ed. *Contemporary Postcolonial Theory: A Reader.* London: Arnold: 276-293.

Ahmed, Sara. 1996. "Beyond Humanism and Postmodernism: Theorizing a Feminist Practice." *Hypatia* 405 (2): 71-93 I

Ahmed-Rufai, Misbahudeen. 1999. "'Wonders of the African World': Replies." November 5. *<H-AFRICA@H-NET.MSU.EDU>*

Aina, L. O. 1994. "The Prospects for Reducing the High Mortality Rate of African Library Science Journals." In M. Wise, ed. *Survival under Adverse Conditions: Proceedings of the African Library Science Workshop.* The Hague, Netherlands: International Federation of Library Associations and Institutions. IFLA Professional Reports, No.38.

Aina, Tade. A. 1995. "Library Acquisitions of African Books: An Academic Publishers Viewpoint."*APNET Open Forum: Library Acquisition of African Books,* Zimbabwe International Book Fair, Harare, 2 August.

____. 1997. *Globalization and Social Policy in Africa: Issues and Research*

Directions. Dakar, Senegal: Codesria Working Paper Series 6/96.

Ajami, Foaudi. 1993. "The Summoning." *Foreign Affairs* 72 (4) 2-9.

Ajayi, Omofolabo. 1999. "'Wonders of the African World': Reply." November 5.<*H-AFRICA@H-NET.MSU.EDU*>

Ajayi, J. F. Ade, Lameck K. H. Goma, and G. Ampah Johnson. 1996. *The African Experience with Higher Education.* London: James Currey.

Ajayi. O. 2000. Summary of Online Discussion. Prepared for the AAU Technical Experts Meeting in Dar es Salaam. Accra, Ghana: African Association of Universities.

Ake, Claude. 1994. "Academic Freedom and Academic Base." In Mahmood Mamdani and Mamadou Diouf, eds. *Academic Freedom in Africa.* Dakar, Senegal: Codesria Book Series: 17-25.

Ake, Claude. 1995. "The New World Order: A View from Africa." In H. Hans-Henrik and G. Sørensen, eds. *Whose World Order: Uneven Globalization and the End of the Cold War.* Boulder, Colorado: Westview: 19-42.

Akinpelu, A. Jones. 1994. "Policy Expectations and Shortfalls. Nigerian Views and Experiences." In Lalage Bown, ed. *Towards a Commonwealth of Scholars: A New Vision for the Nineties.* London: Commonwealth Secretariat: 108-115.

Alarcón, Norma. 1994. "The Theoretical Subject(s) of This Bridge Called My Back and the Anglo-American Feminism." In Steven Seidman, ed. *The Postmodern Turn: New Perspectives on Social Theory.* New York: Cambridge University Press: 140-152.

Alemna, Anaba A. 1993. "African Library Science Journals: The Missing Link." *Scholarly Publishing* 25 (October): 48-52.

Alemna, Anaba A.; Vitalicy Chifwepa; and Diana Rosenberg. 2000. "African Journal: An Evaluation of Their Use in African Universities." *African Journal of Library, Archives & Information Science* 10 (2): 93-111.

Allan, Tuzline J. 1995. *Feminist and Womanist Aesthetics: A Comparative Study.* Athens: Ohio University Press.

___. 2001. "Feminist Scholarship in Africa." In Cassandra R. Veney and Paul T. Zeleza, eds. *Women in African Studies Scholarly Publishing.* Trenton, New Jersey: Africa World Press: 65-91.

Altbach, Philip G. 1996. *The Challenge of the Market: Privatization and Publishing in Africa.* Chestnut Hill, Massachusetts: Bellagio Studies in Publishing, 7.

___. 1998. "Internationalize American Higher Education? Not Exactly." *Change* 30 (4): 36-39.

Altbach, Philip G., ed. 2001. "Universities and Globalization: Critical

Perspectives/The Globalization of Higher Education." *Journal of Higher Education* 72 (2): 254-256.

Altenstetter, C. and J. W. Bjorkman. 1997. "Global Health Policy Reform: Misleading Mythology or Learning Opportunity." In C. Altenstetter and J. W. Bjorkman, eds. *Health Policy Reform, National Variations and Globalization.* London: Macmillan Press: 348-64.

Altieri, Charles. 1998. *Postmodernisms Now: Essays on Contemporaneity in the Arts.* University Park, Pennsylvania: University of Pennsylvania Press.

Altman, Roger C. 2000. "The Nuke of the 90's." *The New York Times Magazine* 113 (3) March: 6, 34.

Amazon.com. 2000. "Editorial Reviews," <http://www.amazon.com/exec /obidos/ts/bookreviews/0375402357 /104-9778317-9435109>

Amin, Samir. 1997. *Capitalism in the Age of Globalization.* London: Zed Books.

___. 2001. "Globalism or Apartheid on a Global Scale?" Third World Forum, Dakar, Senegal. Unpublished.

Amoako. K. Y. 1999. "African Universities, the Private Sector, and Civil Society: Forging Partnerships for Development," Keynote Address, International Association of University Presidents, African Regional Council Conference. <*http://www.uneca.org/ecaresources/Speeches/amoako /99/0609es speech university.htm*>

Amory, Deborah. 1997. "African Studies as American Institution." In Akhil Gupta and James Ferguson, eds. *Anthropological Locations: Boundaries and Grounds of Field Science.* Berkeley: University of California Press: 102-116.

Amutabi, Maurice N. 2001. "African Virtual University (AVU) and the Paradox of the World Bank in Kenya." Paper presented at the 27th Annual Spring Symposium, Center for African Studies, Center for African Studies, University of Illinois at Urbana-Champaign, April 25-28.

Anderson, Perry. 1998. *The Origins of Postmodernity.* London: Verso.

Anderson, Talmadge. 1990. *Black Studies: Theory, Method, and Cultural Perspective.* Pullman, Washington: Washington State University Press.

Ann, Cecilia. 2000. "Global Transformations." *Journal of Economic Issues* 34: 247-249.

Annan, Kofi. 2000. "The Politics of Globalization." In Patrick O'Meara, Howard D. Mehlinger, and Mathew Krain, eds. *Globalization and the Challenges of a New Century.* Bloomington and Indianapolis: Indiana University Press: 125-130.

Antenna, October 1999, "Dr. Henry Louis Gates Jr., Reveals Africa's Hidden History in Wonders of the African World." <*http://www.klvx.org/aten-*

na/BlackIssues/contents/drlouis.html>

Appadurai, Arjun. 1996a. *Modernity At Large. Cultural Dimensions of Globalization*. Minneapolis: University of Minnesota Press.

___.1996b. "Diversity and Disciplinarity as Cultural Artifacts." In Cary Nelson and Dilip P. Gaonkar, eds. 1996. *Disciplinarity and Dissent in Cultural Studies*. Routledge: New York, 23-36.

___. 2001. "Grassroots Globalization and the Research Imagination." In Arjun Appadurai, ed. *Globalization*. Durham and London: Duke University Press: 1-21.

Appiah, Kwame Anthony. 1992. *In My Father's House: Africa in the Philosophy of Culture*. New York: Oxford University Press.

___. 1998. "Is the 'Post-' in 'Postcolonial' the 'Post-' in 'Postmodern'?". In Anne McClintock, Aamir Mufti, and Ella Shohat, eds. *Dangerous Liaisons: Gender, Nation, and Postcolonial Perspectives*. Minneapolis: University of Minnesota Press: 420-444.

Appleyard, Reginald. 1991. *International Migration: Challenge for the Nineties*. Geneva: International Labor Organization.

Apraku, Kofi Konadu. 1991. *African Emigres in the United States. A Missing Link in Africa's Social and Economic Development*. New York: Praeger.

Aronowitz, Stanley. 1988. *Science as Power: Discourse and Ideology in Modern Society*. Minneapolis: University of Minnesota Press.

___. 1997. "The Last Good Job in America." *Social Text* 51: 93-108.

Aronowitz, Stanley and Henry A. Giroux. 1985. *Education Under Siege: The Conservative, Liberal, Radical Debate Over Schooling*. South Hadley, Massachusetts: Bergin & Garvey.

Asamoah-Hassan, Helena and Valentina Bannerman. 2001. "From Conventional Libraries To Electronic Libraries: The Role of the African University in the Transformation." *AAU Newsletter* 7 (1): 3-6.

Asante, Molefi K. 1987. *The Afrocentric Idea*. Philadelphia: Temple University Press.

___. 1988. *Afrocentricity*. Trenton, NJ: Africa World Press.

___. 1999. "Molefi Asante on Gates' Wonders of Africa." November 17 *<H-AFRO-AM@H-NET.MSU.EDU>*

___. 2000. "Ali Mazrui: Soyinka vs. Mazrui," 24 January. *<toyin.falola@mail.utexas.edu>*

Ash, Mitchell. 1995. "Postmodern Theory in German History," 8-11-95 *<mitchash@zedat.fu-berlin.de>*

Ashcroft, Bill, Gareth Griffiths and Helen Tiffin. 1989. *The Empire Writes Back: Theory and Practice in Post-Colonial Literatures*. London: Routledge.

Atteh, Samual O. 1996. "The Crisis in Higher Education in Africa." *Issue: A Journal of Opinion* 24 (I): 36-42.

Austen, Ralph. 1997a. "Maps, Postmodernism and Knowledge: Reply." 5 November. *H-AFRICA@H-NET.MSU.EDU, <http://www.h-net2. msu.edu/logs/showlog.cgi?list=h-africa&file=h.africa.log9711a&ent=38>*

___. 1997b. "Maps, Postmodernism and Knowledge: Reply." 10 November. *H-AFRICA@H-NET.MSU.EDU,<http://www.h-net2 .msu.edu/logs/showlog.cgi?list=h-africa&file=h.africa.log9711b&ent=28>*

Austin-Broos, Diane J. 1998. "Falling Through the 'Savage Slot': Postcolonial Critique and the Ethnographic Task." *The Australian Journal of Anthropology* 9 (3): 295-309.

Axford, Barrie. 1995. *The Global System.* Cambridge: Polity Press.

Axtmann, Roland. 1997. "Collective Identity and the Democratic Nation State in the Age of Globalization." In Ann Cvetkovich and Douglas Kellner, eds. *Articulating the Global and the Local.* Boulder, Colorado: Westview.

Babaleye, Taye. 1998 (January). "Terror in the Universities." *ANB-BIA Supplement, Issue/Edition* No. 341.

Baker, Jean, Jerry Esptein, and Bob Pollin, eds. 1998. *Globalization and Progressive Economic Policy.* Cambridge: Cambridge University Press.

Balintulo, Marcus M. 2001 "Redress and Equity in the Transformation of South African Higher Education." Paper presented at the Carter Lectures 2001, "Governance and Higher Education," University of Florida, Gainesville. 22-25 March.

Banjo, A. O. 1994. "Measures at Rehabilitating a Library Journal: The Example of Nigerian Libraries, 1984-88." In M. Wise, ed. *Survival under Adverse Conditions: Proceedings of the African Library Science Workshop.* The Hague, Netherlands: International Federation of Library Associations and Institutions. IFLA Professional Reports, No.38.

Banks, William M. 1996. *Black Intellectuals: Race and Responsibility in American Life.* New York: Norton.

Barad, Karen. 1996. "Meeting the Universe Halfway: Realism and Social Constructivism Without Contradiction." In Lynn Hankinson Nelson and Jack Nelson, eds. *Feminism, Science, and the Philosophy of Science: A Dialogue.* Boston, Massachusetts: Kluwer Academic Publishers: 161-194.

Barber, Benjamin B. 1992. "Jihad vs. McWorld." *The Atlantic Monthly* (March): 53-63.

___. 1996. *Jihad vs. McWorld.* New York: Ballantine Paperback.

Barber, William J. 1997. "Reconfigurings in American Academic Economics: A General Practitioner's Perspective." *Daedalus* 126, 1: 87-103.

Barka, Lalla Ben. 2000. "Statement." Paper presented at the Regional Conference on Brain Drain and Capacity Building in Africa. UNECA, Addis Ababa, Ethiopia, 22-24 February. <*http://www.uneca.org/search_home.htm*>

Barker, C. 1999. *Television, Globalization and Cultural Identities.* Milton Keynes, England: Open University Press.

Barker, Francis, Peter Hulme, and Margaret Iversen, eds. 1994. "Introduction." *Colonial Discourse/Postcolonial Theory.* Manchester, England: Manchester University Press: 1-23.

Barraclough, Steven. 1998. "Al-Azhar: Between the Government and the Islamists." *Middle East Journal* 52 (2): 236-249.

Barrows, L. C., ed. 1997. *A European Agenda for Change for Higher Education in the Twenty-First Century.* Paris: UNESCO.

Barry, J. 1994. "Digging for Gems in a Book Lover's Paradise." *The Herald* Harare, Zimbabwe. July 24: 4.

Basinger, Julianne. 2001. "College Presidents Urged to Nurture Relationships with Business." *The Chronicle of Higher Education* June 22: A27.

Bates, Robert H. 1997. "Area Studies and Political Science: Rupture and Possible Synthesis." *Africa Today* 44 (2): 123-132.

Bates, Robert. H. V. Y. Mudimbe and Jean O'Barr, eds. 1993. *Africa and the Disciplines: The Contribution of Research in Africa to the Social Sciences and Humanities.* Chicago: University of Chicago Press.

Baum, Robert D. 1965. "Government-Sponsored Research on Africa." *African Studies Bulletin* 8 (1): 42-47.

Bauman, Zygmunt. 1994. "Is There a Postmodern Sociology?" In Steven Seidman, ed. *The Postmodern Turn: New Perspectives On Social Theory.* New York: Cambridge University Press: 187-204.

____. 1998. *Globalization and the Human Consequences.* Cambridge: Polity Press.

Bauman, Michael E. and Francis Beckwith. 1993. *Are You Politically Correct?: Debating America's Cultural Standards.* Buffalo, N.Y. : Prometheus Books.

Baumgratz-Gangl, Gisela. 1996. "Developments in the Internationalization of Higher Education in Europe." In Peggy Blumenthal et al., eds. *Academic Mobility in a Changing World. Regional and Global Issues.* London and Bristol, Pennsylvania: Jessica Kingsley Publishers:

Bawer, Bruce. 1998. "Public Intellectuals: An Endangered Species?" *The Chronicle of Higher Education* April 24: A72.

Beauchamp, Gorman. 2001. "Intellectuals Undercover." *Michigan Quarterly*

Review 40 (2): 421-430.

Becker, David G. and Richard L. Sklar. 1987. *Postimperialism: International Capitalism and Development in the Late Twentieth Century*. London: Lynne Rienner.

Beebe, Maria A. 2001. "Learning Networks in Africa: Commercial Transaction or Reciprocal Exchange?" Paper presented at the Carter Lectures 2001, "Governance and Higher Education," University of Florida, Gainesville. 22-25 March.

Bender, Thomas. 1997. "Politics, Intellect, and the American University, 1945-1995." *Daedalus* 126 (1): 1-38.

Benedict, Kennette, Caren Grown and Sharon Morris. 2000 "Initial Observations on Nigerian Higher Education." McArthur Foundation, June.

Benhabib, S. 1991. "Feminism and Postmodernism: An Uneasy Alliance." *Praxis International* 11: 137-149.

Bentsen, Cheryl. 1998. "Head Negro in Charge," *Boston Magazine* April: 64-71, 101-104, 113-122.

Berger, Suzanne. and Ronald P. Dore, eds. 1996. *National Diversity and Global Capitalism*. Ithaca, N.Y.: Cornell University Press.

Berger, Iris. 1997. "Contested Boundaries: African Studies Approaching the Millennium." *African Studies Review* 40 (2): 1-14.

Berger, Peter L. 2000. "Four Faces of Global Culture." In Patrick O'Meara, Howard D. Mehlinger, and Mathew Krain, eds. *Globalization and the Challenges of a New Century*. Bloomington and Indianapolis: Indiana University Press: 419-427.

Berkhofer, Robert F. 1969. *A Behavioral Approach to Historical Analysis*. New York: Free Press.

___. 1995. *Beyond the Great Story: History as Text and Discourse*. Cambridge: Harvard University Press.

Berlant, L. 1991. *The Anatomy of National Fantasy: Hawthorne, Utopia, and Everyday Life*. Chicago: University of Chicago Press.

Berman, Paul. 1992. *Debating P.C. : The Controversy over Political Correctness on College Campuses*. New York : Delta.

Berman, Bruce. 1992. "Bureaucracy and Incumbent Violence: Colonial Administration and the Origins of the 'Mau Mau' Emergency." In Bruce Berman and John Lonsdale. *Unhappy Valley: Conflict in Kenya and Africa*. Athens, Ohio: Ohio University Press: 227-264.

Berman, E. H. 1984. "Foundations, Philanthropy, and Neocolonialism." In Philip G. Altbach, ed. *Education and the Colonial Experience*. New Brunswick, NJ: Transaction: 253-72.

Bernstein, Alison. 2001. "Re-visioning African Universities in the 21st

Century: the Case for Bifocalism." Paper presented at the Ford Foundation Retreat on Visioning the African University in 2050, Durban, South Africa, 29 May 29 - 1 June.

Bernstein, Alina. 2000. "Things You Can See From There You Can't See from Here': Globalization, Media, and the Olympics." *Journal of Sport and Social Issues* 24 (4): 351-369.

Bertens, Hans. 1995. *The Idea of the Postmodern: A History.* London and New York: Routledge.

Bérubé, Michael. 1998. *The Employment of English: Theory, Jobs and the Future of Literary Studies.* New York: New York University Press.

Beyer, Peter. 1994. *Religion and Globalization.* Thousand Oaks, California: Sage.

Beynon, John and David Dunkerley, eds. 2000. *Globalization: The Reader.* New York: Routledge.

Bgoya, Walter. 1997. "How Can Independent African Publishers Survive Against National Monopolies and Transnational Corporations?" Paper presented at the International Seminar on Book Production and Distribution in Africa. Chr. Michelsen Institute, Bergen, Norway, 10-11 April.

Bhabha, Homi K. 1989. "Remembering Fanon: Self, Psyche, and Colonial Condition." In Barbara Kruger and Phil Mariani, eds. *Psychoanalysis and Cultural Theory: Thresholds.* Seattle: Bay Press: 131-148.

____. 1990. *Nation and Narration.* London and New York: Routledge.

____. 1994. *The Location of Culture.* London: Routledge.

Bhalla, A. S. and A. Berry. 1998. "Regional Perspectives: An Overview." In A. S. Bhalla, eds. *Globalization, Growth and Marginalization.* New York: St. Martin's Press: 168-189.

Biever, Joan L; Cynthia de las Fuentes, Lisa Cashion, and Cynthia Franklin. 1998. "The Social Construction of Gender: A Comparison of Feminist and Postmodern Approaches." *Counseling Psychology Quarterly* 11 (2): 163-179.

Bindé, Jérôme. 2001. "Toward an Ethics of the Future." In Arjun Appadurai, ed. *Globalization.* Durham and London: Duke University Press: 90-113.

Binyan, Liu. 1996. "Unique Spiritual Engineers: The Infighting Among Chinese Intellectuals." *Journal of International Affairs* 49 (2): 348-354.

Birchard, Karen. 2001. "European Nations Promote Online Education." *The Chronicle of Higher Education* 47 (33) 27 April: A46.

Bischof, Phyllis B. 1991. "Publishing and the Book Trade in Sub-Saharan Africa: Trends and Issues and Their Implication for American Libraries."

The Journal of Academic Librarianship 16 (6): 340-347.

Black Caucus Statement, 1968 and 1969. *Africa Today* 16 (5&6):18-19.

Blair, Arthur. 2000. "Various Issues and Opinions," 2 February. <*toyin.falo-la@mail.utexas.edu*>

Bloom, Allan. 1988. *The Closing of the American Mind.* New York: Touchstone Books.

Bloom, Harold. 1994. *The Western Canon: The Books and School of the Ages.* New York: Harcourt Brace.

Bloomberg, Charles. 1989. *Christian Nationalism and the Rise of the Afrikaner Broederbond in South Africa, 1918-48.* Bloomington: Indiana University Press,

Bluestone, Barry and Bennett Harrison. 1982. *The Deindustrialization of America.* New York: Basic Books.

Blumenstyk, Goldie. 1999. "The Marketing Intensifies in Distance Learning" *The Chronicle of Higher Education* 45 (31) 9 April: A27-A30.

___. 2001a. "Some Universities With Similar Ventures Say They Can Still Make Money." *The Chronicle of Higher Education* 20 July: A29.

___. 2001b. "A New Web Site Details the Corporate Ties of Some Researchers." *The Chronicle of Higher Education* 47 (38) 1 June: A25.

Blumenstyk, Goldie and Beth McMurtrie. 2000. "Educators Lament a Corporate Takeover of International Accreditor." *The Chronicle of Higher Education* 27 October: A57.

Bollag, Burton. 1998. "International Aid Groups Shift Focus to Higher Education in Developing Countries," *The Chronicle of Higher Education* 30 October.

___. 2000a. "4 Foundations Start $100-Million Effort to Help Universities in Africa." *The Chronicle of Higher Education* May 5 : A56.

___. 2000b. "The New Latin: English Dominates in Academe." *The Chronicle of Higher Education* 47 (2) 8 September: A73-A77.

___. 2001a. "An African Success Story at the U. of Dar es Salaam." *Chronicle of Higher Education* 47 (30): A53-A55.

___. 2001b. "African Universities Begin to Face the Enormity of Their Losses to AIDS." *Chronicle of Higher Education* 47 (25): A45-A47.

___. 2001c. "East African Universities Will Gain Journal Access in New Online Project." *The Chronicle of Higher Education* 39 (27): A39.

Bonnell, Victoria E., and Lynn Hunt, eds. 1999. *Beyond the Cultural Turn.* Berkeley and Los Angeles: University of California Press.

Bordo, S. 1990. "Feminism, Postmodernism and Gender-Scepticism." In L. J. Nicholson, ed. *Feminism/Postmodernism.* New York: Routledge: 133-156.

Bottomley, John. "CFP: Idealization in History." *H-SAFRICA@H-NET.MSU.EDU*, <*http://www.h-net.msu.edu/logs/showlog.cg...safrica &file=h.safrica.log9806c/11&ent=0*>

Boudreaux, Aswan. 1999. "Female Circumcision." 16 November.<*H-AFRO-AM@H-NET.MSU.EDU*>

Bowen, John R. 2000. "The Myth of Global Ethnic Conflict." In Patrick O'Meara, Howard D. Mehlinger, and M. Krain, eds. *Globalization and the Challenges of a New Century.* Bloomington and Indianapolis: Indiana University Press: 79-89.

Boyd-Barret, J. O. 1997. "Global News Wholesalers as Agents of Globalization." In Annabelle. Sreberny-Mohammadi, D. Winseck, J. McKenna, and O. Boyd-Barrett, eds. *Media in Global Context: A Reader.* New York: Arnold.

Boyer, R., and D. Drache. 1996. "Introduction." In R. Boyer and D. Drache, eds. *States and Markets: The Limits of Globalization.* London and New York: Routledge: 1-27.

Brainard, Jeffrey. 2000. "At NIH Meeting, Scientists Debate When They Should Reveal Financial Interests to Volunteers." *The Chronicle of Higher Education* 30 March: A43.

Brass, Tom. 1997. "The Agrarian Myth, the 'New' Populism and the 'New' Right." *Journal of Peasant Studies* 24 (4): 201-245.

Brecher, Jeremy, Tim Costello, and Brendan Smith. 2000a. "Globalization from Below." *The Nation* 271 (18 Dec.): 19-22.

____. 2000b. *Globalization From Below.* Boston and London: South End.

Brender, Alan. 2001. "Distance-Education Road Show." *The Chronicle of Higher Education* 47 (29) 8 September: A43, 47.

Brickhill, Paul. 1996. "The Transition from State to Commercial Publishing Systems in African Countries." In Philip G. Altbach, ed. *The Challenge of the Market: Privatization and Publishing in Africa.* Chestnut Hill, Massachusetts: Bellagio Studies in Publishing, 7.

____. 1997. "How Can Publishers, Booksellers and Librarians Cooperate to Stimulate Book Production and Distribution in Africa?" Paper presented at the International Seminar on Book Production and Distribution in Africa. Chr. Michelsen Institute, Bergen, Norway, 10-11 April.

Broad, Dave. 1995. "Globalization Versus Labor." *Monthly Review* 47 (7): 20-31.

Brown, Mercy. 2000. "Using the Intellectual Diaspora to Reverse the Brain Drain: Some Useful Examples." Paper presented at the Regional Conference on Brain Drain and Capacity Building in Africa. UNECA, Addis Ababa, 22-24 February. <*http://www.uneca.org/search_home.htm*>

Brown, Peter J., ed. 1998. *Underlying and Applying Medical Anthropology.* Mountain View, California: Mayfield.

Brown, Richard H. 1994. "Rhetoric, Textuality, and the Postmodern Turn in Sociological Theory." In Steven Seidman, ed. *The Postmodern Turn: New Perspectives on Social Theory.* New York: Cambridge University Press: 229-241.

Buchbinder, Howard 1993. "The Market Oriented University and the Changing Role of Knowledge." *Higher Education* 26 (3): 331-347

Buchbinder, Howard & Newson, Janice. 1992. "The Service University and Market Forces." *Academe* 78 (4): 13-15.

Burbach, Roger, Orlando Núñez Soto, and Boris Kagarlitsky. 1997. *Globalization and its Discontents: The Rise of Postmodern Socialisms.* London and Chicago: Pluto Press.

Burbules, Nicholas C., and Thomas A. Callister. 2000. "Universities in Transition: The Promise and the Challenge of New Technologies." *Teachers College Record* 102 (2): 271-293.

Burgmann, Verity. 1993. *Power and Protest: Movements for Change in Australian Society.* St. Leonards, NSW, Australia: Allen and Unwin.

Burke, Timothy. 1999. "Mainstreaming Africa: Reply." November 8. *<H-AFRICA@H-NET.MSU.EDU>*

Burke, Fred G. 1969a. "The Meaning of Montreal." *Africa Today* 16 (5&6): 8-9.

___. 1969b. "The Future of African Studies After Montreal." *Africa Report* 14 (12): 25.

___. 1999. "Ali Mazrui on Gates." 1 November *<H-AFRO-AM@H-NET.MSU.EDU>*

Buschman, Jim. 2000. "Study Abroad in Africa: A Personal Memoir." *African Issues* 28 (1&2): 130-132.

Busia, Abena. 1989-90. "Silencing Sycorax: On African Colonial Discourse and the Unvoiced Female." *Cultural Critique* 14 (Winter): 81-104.

Business Week. 2000. "Global Capitalism: Can It be Made to Work Better?" Special Report. November 6: 72-100.

Butler, Judith. 1994. "Contingent Foundations: Feminism and the Question of 'Postmodernism." In Steven Seidman, ed. *The Postmodern Turn: New Perspectives on Social Theory.* New York: Cambridge University Press: 153-170.

Cable, Vincent. 1995. "The Diminished Nation-State: A Study in the Loss of Economic Power." *Daedalus* 124 (2): 25-53.

Cain, William. 1996. "A Literary Approach to Literature: Why English Departments Should Focus on Close Reading, Not Cultural Studies."

Chronicle of Higher Education December 13: B4-B5.

Callari, Antonio; Stephen Cullenberg; and Carole Biewner, eds. 1995. *Marxism in the Postmodern Age: Confronting the New World Order.* New York: The Guilford Press.

Callinicos, Alex. 1989. *Against Postmodernism: A Marxist Critique.* Cambridge: Polity Press.

___. 1995. *Theories and Narratives: Reflections on the Philosophy of History.* Durham: Duke University Press.

Camara, Mohamed S. 2000. "Africa-to-Africa: A Responsible Alternative to Study Abroad for 21st Century African Scholarship." *African Issues* 28 (1&2): 61-64.

Carnevale, Dan. 2000. "A Study Produces a List of 24 Benchmarks for Quality Distance Education," *"The Chronicle of Higher Education* 7 April: A45.

___. "Report Urges Canada to Invest in Online Learning." *The Chronicle of Higher Education* 47 (24) 23 February: A44.

___. 2001b. "Teachers' Union Report Criticizes Businesslike Approach to Distance Education." *The Chronicle of Higher Education* 31 August.

Carr, E. H. 1964. *What Is History?* 2nd ed. London: Macmillan.

Carr, Susan. 2000. "As Distance Education Comes of Age, the Challenge if Keeping Students," *The Chronicle of Higher Education* 11 February: A 39.

___. 2001a. "With National e-University, Britain Gets in on the Online-Education Game." *The Chronicle of Higher Education* 17 August: A27.

___. Carr, Susan. 2001b. "Is Anyone Making Money on Distance Education?" *The Chronicle of Higher Education* 16 February: A41.

Carter, Gwendolyn M. 1976. "African Studies in the United States: 1955-1975." *ISSUE: A Quarterly Journal of Africanist Opinion* 6 (2/3): 2-4.

Casey, Leo. 1999. "A Few 'Honest' Answers About the Preliminary Critique," *<H-AFRO-AM@H-NET.MSU.EDU>*, November 2.

Castells, Manuel. 1996. *The Rise of Network Society.* Oxford: Blackwell.

Castillo, Daniel Del. 2001. "A 1,000-Year-Old University Takes on a New and Troubling Role." *Chronicle of Higher Education* 47 (35): A47-A48.

Castro-Gomez, Santiago. 1998. "Latin American Postcolonial Theories." *Peace Review* 10 (1): 27-33.

Cerych, Ladislav. 1996. "East-West Academic Mobility Within Europe: Trends and Issues." In Peggy Blumenthal et al, eds., *Academic Mobility in a Changing World. Regional and Global Issues.* London and Bristol, Pa: Jessica Kingsley Publishers.

Chachage, C. S. L. 1999. "Higher Education Transformation and Academic Extremism." Department of Sociology: University of Cape Town, April.

Chakrabarty, Dipesh. 1996. "Postcoloniality and the Artifice of History: Who Speaks for 'Indian' Pasts?" In Padmini Mongia, ed. *Contemporary Postcolonial Theory: A Reader.* New York: Arnold: 223-47.

Challenor, H. S. 1969. "No Longer at Ease: Confrontation at the 12th Annual African Studies Association Meeting at Montreal." *Africa Today* 16 (5&6): 4-7.

Champlin, Dell, and Paulette Olson. 1999. "The Impact of Globalization on U.S. Labor Markets: Redefining the Debate." *Journal of Economic Issues* 33 (2): 443-452.

Chapman, Savid W. and Joan M. Claffey. 1998. "A New Wealth of Opportunities Overseas." *The Chronicle of Higher Education* 25 September: B6.

Chappell, David A. 1997. "Re: Postmodernism in Historiography," 12 November. *H-AFRICA@H-NET.MSU.EDU, <http://www.h-net2.msu. edu/logs/showlog.cgi?list=h-africa&file=h.africa.log9711b &ent=46>*

Cheater, Angela P. 1991. "The University of Zimbabwe: University, National University, State University, or Party University?" *African Affairs* 90: 189-205.

Cheeseborough, Anthony. 1999. "'Wonders of the African World': Replies," November 5. *<H-AFRICA@H-NET.MSU.EDU>*

Chege, Michael. 1996-97. "Africa's Murderous Professors." *National Interest* 46: 32-40.

___. 1997. "The Social Science Area Studies Controversy from the Continental African Perspective." *Africa Today* 44 (2): 133-142.

___. 1998. "Academic Apparatchiks in the New Kenya." *The Chronicle of Higher Education* 23 January: B9.

Chigudu, Hope and Ezra Mbogori. 2001. "The African University of the 21st Century — What Do We Desire?" Paper presented at the Ford Foundation Retreat on Visioning the African University in 2050, Durban, South Africa, 29 May - 1 June.

Chilcote, Ronald H., and Martin Legassick. 1971. "The African Challenge to American Scholarship in Africa."*Africa Today* 18 (1): 4-11.

Ching, Leo. 2001. "Globalizing the Regional, Regionalizing the Global: Mass Culture and Asianism in the Age of Late Capital." In Arjun Appadurai, ed. *Globalization.* Durham and London: Duke University Press: 279-306.

Chirambo, R. M. 1996. "Malawian Literature Under Dr. Kamuzu Banda and Its Place in the New Democratic Malawi." Paper presented at the Symposium on Malawian Literature. Malawi Literacy Festival. Blantyre, 15-20 July.

Chitoran, Dumitru. 1996. Increasing Demands and Diminishing Resources in Higher Education: The Role of International Academic Cooperation." *The Courier ACP-EU* 159 (Sept.-Oct.): 56-58.

Chossudovsky, Michel. 1998. "Global Poverty in the Late 20th Century." *Journal of International Affairs* 52 (1): 293-311.

Christian, Barbara. 1996. "The Race for Theory." In Padmini Mongia, ed. *Contemporary Postcolonial Theory: A Reader.* London: Arnold: 148-157.

Clark, Burton R. 1995. *Creating Entrepreneurial Universities: Organizational Pathways of Transformation.* Oxford: IAU Press and Pergamon.

Clark, Gordon L. and Kevin O'Connor. 1997. "The Informational Content of Financial Products and the Spatial Structure of the Global Finance Industry." In Kevin R. Cox, *Spaces of Globalization: Reasserting the Power of the Local.* New York: The Guilford Press: 89-113.

Clark, Ian. 1997. *Globalization and Fragmentation: International Relations in the Twentieth Century.* New York: Oxford University Press.

Clark, Jan Guynes and Vincent Lai. 1998. "Internet Come to Morocco." *Communication of the ACM* 41 (2): 21-23.

Clarke, John Henrik. 1969. "The Future of African Studies after Montreal." *Africa Report* 14 (12): 23-24.

___. 1976. "The African Heritage Studies Association (AHSA): Some Notes on the Conflict with African Studies Association (ASA) and the Fight to Reclaim African History." *ISSUE: A Quarterly Journal of Africanist Opinion* 6 (2/3): 5-11.

Clifford, James and George E. Marcus, eds. 1986. *Writing Culture: The Poetics and Politics of Ethnography.* Berkeley: University of California Press.

Cloete, Nick and Ian Bunting. 2000. *Higher Education Transformation: Assessing Performance in South Africa.* Pretoria: CHET.

Clough, Marshall S. 1998. *Mau Mau Memoirs: History, Memory, and Politics.* Boulder, Colorado: Lynne Rienner.

Clough, Patricia T. 1996. "A Theory of Writing and Experimental Writing in the Age of Telecommunications: A Response to Steven Seidman." *The Sociological Quarterly* 37: 721-733.

Codesria Bulletin, 2, 1998. "Codesria's Activities: 9th General Assembly" 2-6.

Coffie, Amanda J. 2001. "Vision for Africa Universities in the 21st Century and Beyond." Paper presented at the Ford Foundation Retreat on Visioning the African University in 2050, Durban, South Africa, 29 May - 1 June.

Coffman, Jennifer E. 2000. "Study Abroad in Africa Considered Within the New World Economy." *African Issues* 28 (1&2): 49-53.

Cohen, David. 1996. "Educators Push to Expand Academic Exchanges and

University Partnerships in the Pacific." *The Chronicle of Higher Education* 43 (3): A49-A50.

Colas, Santiago. 1995. "Of Creole Symptoms, Cuban Fantasies, and Other Latin American Postcolonial Ideologies." *PMLA: Publications of the Modern Language Association* 110 (3): 382-396.

Coleman, Peter. 1999. "Supporting the Indispensable." *The New Criterion* 18 (1): 62-65.

Comaroff, John L. and Jean Comaroff, eds. 1999. *Civil Society and the Political Imagination in Africa: Critical Perspectives.* Chicago: University of Chicago Press.

Cooper, Frederick. 1988. "Mau Mau and the Discourses of Decolonization." *Journal of African History* 29: 313-320.

____. 1993. "Postscript: Africa and the World Economy." In Frederick Cooper et al. *Confronting Historical Paradigms.* Madison, Wisc: University of Wisconsin Press: 187-201.

____. 1994. "Conflict and Connection: Rethinking Colonial African History." *American History Review* 99 (5): 1516-1545.

____. 2000. "Africa's Pasts and Africa's Historians." *Canadian Journal of African Studies* 34 (2): 298-336.

____. 2001. "What Is the Concept of Globalization Good For? An African Historian's Perspective." *African Affairs* 100: 189-213.

Coovadia, Hoosen M. 1999. "Sanctions and the Struggle for Health in South Africa." *American Journal of Public Health* 89 (10): 1505-1508.

Costantino, Renato. 1997. "Globalization and the Intellectual Tradition." *Journal of Contemporary Asia* 27 (2): 275-283.

____. 2000. "Comprador Intellectuals." *Journal of Contemporary Asia* 30 (3): 424-425.

Court, David. 1990. "Universities and Academic Freedom in East Africa: Random Reflections From A Donor Perspective." CODESRIA Symposium on Academic Freedom, Research and Responsibility of the Intellectual in Africa," Kampala, Uganda, November.

Cowan, L. Gray. 1969. "Ten Years of African Studies." *African Studies Bulletin* 12 (1): 1-7.

____. 1970. "President's Report." *African Studies Review* 11 (3): 343-52.

Cox, Robert W. 1997. "A Perspective on Globalization." In James H. Mittelman, ed. *Globalization: Critical Reflections.* Boulder, Colorado: Lynne Rienner: 21-30.

Cressey, William W. 2000. "Study Abroad and Area Studies." *African Issues* 28 (1&2): 46-48.

Crook, S.; J. Pakulski, and M. Waters. 1992. *Postmodernization.* London:

Sage.

Cruse, Harold. 1967. *The Crisis of the Negro Intellectual: A Historical Analysis of the Failure of Black Leadership.* New York: Quill.

Culler, Jonathan. 1988. *Framing the Sign: Literature and Its Institutions.* Oxford: Basil Blackwell.

Currie, Jan and Janice Newson, eds. 1998. *Universities and Globalization: Critical Perspectives.* Thousand Oaks, Calif: Sage.

Curtin, Philip D. 1971. "African Studies: A Personal Assessment." *African Studies Review* 14 (3): 357-368.

Czetkovich, A., and D. Kellner, eds. 1997. *Articulating the Global and the Local.* Boulder, Colorado: Westview.

D'Souza, Dinesh. 1991. *Illiberal Education: The Politics of R ace and Sex on Campus.* New York: Vintage Books.

___. 2000. *The Virtue of Prosperity: Finding Values in an Age of Techno-Affluence.* New York: Free Press.

Daddieh, Cyril Koffie. 1996. "Universities and Political Protest in Côte d'Ivoire." *Issue: A Journal of Opinion* 24 (I): 57-60.

Darkwa, Osei, and Fikile Mazibuko. 2000. "Creating Virtual Learning Communities in Africa: Challenges and Prospects." First Monday, *<http://firstmonday.org/issues/issue5_5/darkwa>*

Daves, Bryan R. 2000. "A Small World After all? The Reach and Grasp of the Globalization Debate."*Journal of International Studies & World Affairs* 42 (2): 109-121.

Davies, Carole Boyce. 1994. *Black Women, Writing Idenity: Migrations of the Subject.* London and New York: Routledge.

Davies, Gloria. 1998. "Professing Postcoloniality: The Perils of Cultural Legitimation." *Postcolonial Studies* 1 (2): 171-182.

Davies, Wendy. 1996. *The Future of Indigenous Publishing in Africa. Seminar Report.* Stockholm: Dag Hammarskjöld Foundation.

Davis, Jim. 1998. "Rethinking Globalization." *Race and Class* 40 (2 / 3): 37-48.

Davis, R. Hunt. 1997. "For African Studies, Race Still Matters." *Africa Today* 44 (2): 133-142.

Dawkins, Richard. 1998. "Postmodernism Disrobed." *Nature* 9 (394 July): 141-143.

Dawson, Nancy J. 2000. "Study Abroad and African American College Students at Southern Illinois University at Carbondale." *African Issues* 28 (1&2): 124-129.

Daymond, M. J., ed. 1996. *South African Feminisms: Writing, Theory, and Criticism, 1990-1994.* New York and London: Garland.

de Lauretis, Teresa. 1987. *Technologies of Gender.* Bloomington: Indiana University Press.

De Vroey, M. 1984. "A Regulation Approach Interpretation of Contemporary Crisis." *Capital and Class* 23.

De Neufville, Robert. 2000. "The Cultural Cold War." *The Washington Monthly* 32 (5): 52-54.

Debray, Régis. 2001. "The Terminal Intellectual." *New Perspectives Quarterly* 18 (2): 59-62.

Deen, Thalif. 1999. "Best and Brightest Head West." InterPress Third World News Agency (IPS). 10 February. <*http://www.hartford-hwp.com/archives/30/098.html*>

Dehon, Claire. 1995. "Postmodernism and Modern Africa," 25 May. *H-AFRICA@H-NET.MSU.EDU*, <*http://www.h-net.msu.edu/~africa/threads/pomothread.html*>

Dekutsey, Woeli. 1997. "Stimulating Writing in Africa." Paper presented at the International Seminar on Book Production and Distribution in Africa. Chr. Michelsen Institute, Bergen, Norway, 10-11 April.

Delahanty, James M. and Joan A. Raducha. 2000. "American Study-Abroad Programs and the African University." *African Issues* 28 (1&2): 65-68.

Dent, David J. 1993. "African Ties Help HBCUs." *Black Enterprise* 23 (8): 20.

Denzin, Norman K. 1989. *The Alcoholic Self.* Newbury Park, Calif.: Sage.

___. 1991. "Representing Lived Experiences in Ethnographic Texts." In Norman K. Denzin, ed. *Studies in Symbolic Interaction.* Greenwich, Conn.: JAI Press 12, 59-70.

Derrida, Jacques. 1976. *Of Grammatology.* Baltimore: Johns Hopkins University Press.

Desruisseaux, Paul. 1995a. "Agreement on Academic Exchanges Signed by U.S., European Union." *The Chronicle of Higher Education* 14 (37) 26 May: A40.

___. 1995b. "Canada and Mexico Join U.S. in Academic-Exchange Project." *The Chronicle of Higher Education* 41 (41) 23 June: A35.

___. 1998. "Intense Competition for Foreign Students Sparks Concerns About U.S. Standing." *The Chronicle of Higher Education,* 9 October: A 55.

___. 1999. "15% Rise in American Students Abroad Shows Popularity of Non-European Destinations." *The Chronicle of Higher Education,* 10 December: A60.

___. 2000. "As Exchanges Lose a Political Rationale, Their Role if Debated." *The Chronicle of Higher Education* 11 February: A52.

DeVotta, Neil. 2000. "Review Article: Arresting the Post-Cold War Sisyphean Quandary: Ethnonationalism, Internal Conflicts, and the

Quest for Conflict Resolution." *Journal of Third World Studies* 17 (1): 177-196.

Diaw, Aminata. 2001. "The African University of the Future." Presented at the Ford Foundation Retreat on Visioning the African University in 2050, Durban, South Africa, 29 May - 1 June.

Diawara, Manthia. 1997. "Reading Africa Through Foucault: V. Y. Mudimbe's Reaffirmation of the Subject." In Anne McClintock, Aamir Mufti, and Ella Shohat, eds. *Dangerous Liaisons: Gender, Nation, and Postcolonial Perspectives.* Minneapolis: University of Minnesota Press: 456-467.

Diekema, David A., Carl J. Couch, and Joel O. Powell. 1996. "The Third Party Standpoint, Postmodernism, and the Study of Social Trans-actions." *Sociological Perspectives* 39: 111-127.

Diouf, Mamadou. 1994. "Intellectuals and the State in Senegal: The Search for a Paradigm." In Mahmood Mamdani and Mamadou Diouf, eds. *Academic Freedom in Africa.* Dakar: Codesria Book Series: 212-246.

Diouf, Mamadou and Mahmood Mamdani, eds. 1994. *Academic Freedom in Africa.* Dakar, Senegal: Codesria Book Series.

Dirlik Arif. 1996. "The Postcolonial Aura: Third World Criticism in the Age of Global Capitalism." In Padmini Mongia, ed. *Contemporary Postcolonial Theory: A Reader.* London: Arnold: 294-320.

____. 1997. *The Postcolonial Aura.* Boulder, Colo.: Westview Press.

____. 2000. *Postmodernity's Histories: The Past as Legacy and Project,* New York: Rowman and Littlefield Publishers.

Dolphyne, Florence A. 2000. "African Perspectives on Programs for North American Students in Africa: The Experience of the University of Ghana-Legon." *African Issues* 28 (1&2): 28-33.

Domatob, Jerry Komia. 1996. "Policy Issues for African Universities." *Issue: A Journal of Opinion* 24 (I): 29-35.

Dominguez, Virginia R. 1996. "Disciplining Anthropology." In Cary Nelson and Dilip P. Gaonkar, eds. *Disciplinarity and Dissent in Cultural Studies.* Routledge: New York: 37-61.

Doremus, Paul N., William W. Keller, Louis W. Pauly, and Simon Reich et al. 1998. *The Myth of the Global Corporation.* Princeton, N.J.: Princeton University Press.

Doro, Marion. 1999. "'Wonders of the African World': Replies." November 3 <*H-AFRICA@H-NET.MSU.EDU*>

Dossar, Ken. 1999. "'Wonders of the African World': Reply." November 3 <*H-AFRICA@H-NET.MSU.EDU*>

Drakulic, Slavenka. 1999. "Intellectuals as Bad Guys." *East European Politics and Societies* 13 (2): 271-277.

Draper, Roger. 2000. "Secrets of State." *The New Leader* 83 (2): 15-17.

Dressel, Carol A. 1966. "The Development of African Studies in the United States." *African Studies Bulletin* 9 (3): 66-73.

Dubois, Demerise R. 1995. "Responding to the Needs of Our Nation: A Look at the Fulbright and NSEP Education Acts." *Frontiers: The Interdisciplinary Journal of Study Abroad* 1.

Duderstadt, James J. 1999/2000. "New Roles for the 21st Century University." *ASEE Prism* 5 (February): 20-24.

Dunning, J. H. 1993. *Multinational Enterprises and the Global Economy.* Workingham, UK: Addison-Wesley.

Durac, Vincent. 1999. "Islam and Modernity: Intellectuals Respond/Defining Islam for the Egyptian State: Muftis and Fatwas of the Dar Al-Ifta." *British Journal of Middle Eastern Studies* 26 (2): 350-352.

During, Simon. 1993. "Introduction." In Simon During, ed. *The Cultural Studies Reader.* London and New York: 1-25.

___. 1995. "Postmodernism or Postcolonialism?" *Landfill* 39 (3): 366-380.

Dussel, Enrique. 1995. *The Invention of the Americas: Eclipse of "the Other" and the Myth of Modernity.* Translated by Michael D. Barber. New York: Continuum.

Dyson, Michael Eric. 1996. *Race Rules: Navigating the Color Line.* New York: Addison-Wesley.

Eakin, Emil. 1999. "Inside Publishing: The Importance of Being Jacques." *Lingua Franca* 9 (6).

East, Jean F. 1998. "In-dependence: A Feminist Postmodern Deconstruction." *Affilia* 13 (3): 273-288.

Easthope, Antony. 1991. *Literary into Cultural Studies.* New York: Routledge.

Ebert, Teresa. 1993. "Ludic Feminism, the Body, Performance and Labor: Bringing Materialism Back Into Feminist Cultural Studies." *Cultural Critique* 22: 5-50.

Eder, Klaus 1993. *The New Politics of Class: Social Movements and Cultural Dynamics in Advanced Societies.* London: Sage

Ejiaga, Romanus. 2001. "Higher Education and the Academic Labor Market: The Effectiveness of Rewards and Incentives in Nigerian Universities." Paper presented at the Carter Lectures 2001, "Governance and Higher Education," University of Florida, Gainesville. 22-25 March.

Ekpo, Denis. 1995. "Towards a Post-Africanism: Contemporary African Thought and Postmodernism." *Textual Practice* 9 (1): 121-135.

El Kenzi, Ali. 1996. "Algeria: From Development Hope to Identity Violence." In *Codesria: The State of Academic Freedom in Africa 1995.* Dakar: Codesria.

Elkins, Caroline. 2000. "The Struggle for Mau Mau Rehabilitation in Late Colonial Kenya." *International Journal of African Historical Studies* 33 (1): 25-57.

Ellis, Carolyn. 1991. "Emotional Sociology." In Norman K. Denzin, ed. *Studies in Symbolic Interaction.* Greenwich, Conn.: JAI Press 12: 123-145.

Ellis, Kimberly C. 1999. "A Few 'Honest' Answers About the Preliminary Critique." 3 November. *<H-AFRO-AM@H-NET.MSU.EDU.>*

Elton, Geoffrey. 1967. *The Practice of History.* London: Fontana.

____. 1991. *Return to Essentials.* Cambridge: Cambridge University Press.

Emeagwali, Gloria. 1999. "Mainstreaming Africa: Reply." 20 November. *<H-AFRICA@H-NET.MSU.EDU>*,

Emerson, Rupert. 1969. "Letter Sent to All ASA Members." *Africa Today* 16 (5&6): 17.

Epstein, Mikhail. 1995. *After the Future: The Paradox of Postmodernism and Contemporary Russian Culture.* Translated with an Introduction by Anesa Miller-Pogacar. Amherst, MA: The University of Massachusetts Press.

Epstein, Joseph. 2000. "Intellectuals - Public and Otherwise." *Commentary* 109 (5): 46-51.

Ercolano, Vincent. 1996. "Exporting Engineering Education." *The Chronicle of Higher Education* 10 December: A60.

Eribo, Festus. 1996. "Higher Education in Nigeria: Decades of Development and Decline." *Issue: A Journal of Opinion* 24 (I): 64-67.

Escobar, Arturo. 1955. *Encountering Development: The Making and Unmaking of the Third World.* Princeton, NJ: Princeton University Press.

Etherington, Norman. 1996. "Post-Modernism and South African History." *Southern African Review of Books* 44, July/August. *<http://www. uni-ulm.de/~rturrell/antho4html/Eherington.html>*

Etuk, Emma S. 1996. "Problems in African University Administration." *Issue: A Journal of Opinion* 24 (I): 43-44.

Eyoh, Dickson. 1996. "From Economic Crisis to Political Liberalization: Pitfalls of the New Political Sociology for Africa." *African Studies Review* 39 (3): 43-80.

Eze, Emmanuel C., ed. 1997. *Postcolonial African Philosophy: A Critical Reader.* Cambridge, MA: Blackwell.

Fagan, B. M. 1970. "Review of G. M. Carter and A. Paden, eds., Expanding Horizons in African Studies." *Africa Report* 15 (5).

Fage, John. D. 1989. "British African Studies Since the Second World War: A Personal Account." *African Affairs* 88 (352): 397-413.

Falk, Peter. 1999. "The Future of Sovereign States and International Order." *Harvard International Review* 21 (3): 30-35.

Falola, Toyin. 2001. *Nationalism and African Intellectuals.* Rochester, N.Y.: University of Rochester Press.

Farganis, S. 1992. "Feminism and the Reconstruction of Social Science," In A. M. Jaggar and S. R. Bordo, eds. *Gender/body/knowledge: Feminist Reconstruction of Being and Knowing.* New Brunswick, NJ: Rutgers University Press, 207-223.

Featherstone, M. 1993. "Global and Local Cultures." In J. Bird, B. Curtis, P. Putnam, G. Robertson and L. Tickner, eds. *Mapping the Futures: Local Culture, Global Change.* London and New York: Routledge.

____. 1996. "Localism, Globalism and Cultural Identity." In R. Wilson and W. Dissanayake, eds. *Global-Local: Cultural Production and the Transnational Imaginary.* Durham and London: Duke University Press.

Featherstone, M., S. Lash and R. Robertson, eds. 1995. *Global Modernities.* London: Sage.

Feld, Steven. 2001. "A Sweet Lullaby for World Music." In Arjun Appadurai, ed. *Globalization.* Durham and London: Duke University Press: 189-216.

Felix, David. 1998. "Is the Drive Toward Free-market Globalization Stalling?" *Latin American Research Review* 33 (3): 191-216.

Findlay, Allan M. 1995. "Skilled Transients: The Invisible Phenomenon." In R. Cohen, eds. *The Cambridge Survey of World Migration.* Cambridge University Press: 515-522.

Findlay, A.M; F.L.N. Li; A.J. Jowett; and R. Skeldon. 1996. "Skilled Migration and the Global City: A Study of Expatriates in Hong Kong." *Transactions Institute of British Geographers* 2:51-67.

Finkelman, Paul. 1999. "A Preliminary Critique of 'Wonders of the African World.'" 1 November <*H-AFRO-AM@H-NET.MSU.EDU.*>

Fischer, Michael M. 1999. "Emergent Forms of Life: Anthropology of Late or Postmodernities." *Annual Review of Anthropology* 28: 455-478.

Fish, Stanley. 1985. "A Reply to Gerald Graff." *New Literary History* 17 (1): 119-127.

____. 1995. *Professional Correctness: Literary Studies and Political Change.* New York: Oxford University Press.

Fisher, Donald. 1993. *Fundamental Development of the Social Sciences: Rockefeller, Philanthropy, and the United States Social Science Research Council.* Ann Arbor: University of Michigan Press.

Fobih, D. K. "Sustainability of Higher Education Partnerships." Proceedings of the African Partnerships USAID UDLP Higher Education Conference, "Factors that Contribute to Successful International Partnerships: Results of Higher Education Linkages," Elmina, Ghana, 18-11 February. <http://www.cehd.ewu.edu/cehd/faculty/ntodd/GhanaUDLP/conference/Proceedings.html>

Foster, John B. 2000. "Marx and Internationalism." *Monthly Review*, 52 (3): 11-22.

Foucault, Michel. 1976. *The Archaeology of Knowledge*. New York: Harper and Row.

___. 1980. *Power/Knowledge: Selected Interviews and Other Writings, 1972-1977*. New York: Pantheon.

Fourie, M. J. and R. Joubert. 1998. *Emigration's Influence on South Africa: A Human Capital Theory Approach*. Pretoria: University of South Africa.

Fox-Genovese, Elizabeth. 1999. "History in a Postmodern World." In Elizabeth Fox-Genovese, and Elisabeth Lasch-Genovese, eds. *Reconstructing History: The Emergence of a New Historical Society*. New York: Routledge: 35-39.

Fox-Genovese, Elizabeth, and Elisabeth Lasch-Genovese, eds. 1999. *Reconstructing History: The Emergence of a New Historical Society*. New York: Routledge.

Frankenberg, R., and L. Mani. 1996. "Crosscurrents, Crosstalk: Race, "Postcoloniality" and the Politics of Location." In P. Mongia, ed. *Contemporary Postcolonial Theory: A Reader*. London: Arnold: 347-364.

Franklin, Sarah. 1995. "Science as Culture, Cultures of Science." *Annual Review of Anthropology* 24: 165-184.

Fraser, Nancy and Linda Nicholson. 1994. "Social Criticism Without Philosophy: An Encounter Between Feminism and Postmodernism." Steven Seidman, ed. *The Postmodern Turn: New Perspectives on Social Theory*. New York: Cambridge University Press: 242-261.

Friedman, J. 1997. "Simplifying Complexity: Assimilating the Global in a Small Paradise." In K. F. Olwig and K. Hastrup, eds. *Sitting Culture: The Shifting Anthropological Object*. London: Routledge.

Frost-Smith, Brian. 1994. "European Union: Fresh Tracks for Academic Exchanges." *Science* 266 (5186): 743-745.

Fujimura, Joan A. 1999. "Authorizing Science Studies and Anthropology." *American Anthropologist* 101 (2): 381-384.

Fujimura, Joan A. 1998. "Authorizing Knowledge in Science and Anthropology." *American Anthropologist* 100 (2): 347-360.

Fukuyama, Francis. 1989. "The End of History?" *The National Interest* (Summer).

___. 1992. *The End of History and the Last Man.* London: Hamish.

Furedi, Frank. 1989. *The Mau Mau War in Perspective.* Athens: Ohio University Press.

Fyfe, C. 1999. "The Emergence and Evolution of African Studies in the United Kingdom." In William G. Martin and Michael O West, eds. 1999. *Out of One, Many Africas: Reconstructing the Study and Meaning of Africa.* Urbana, Ill.: University of Illinois Press: 54-61.

Gaillard, Jacques, and A. Gaillard. 1997. "Introduction: The International Mobility of Brain: Exodus or Circulation." *Science, Technology and Society* 2 (2).

Gaines, Atwood D. 1998. "From Margin to Center: From Medical Anthropology to Cultural Studies of Science." *American Anthropologist* 100 (1): 191-194.

Gallagher, Catherine. 1997. "The History of Literary Criticism." *Daedalus* 126 (1): 133-153.

Gamson, Zelda F. 1997. "The Stratification of the Academy." *Social Text* 51: 67-73.

Gandhi, Leela. 1998. *Postcolonial Theory: A Critical Introduction.* New York: Columbia University Press.

Gaonkar, Dilipp, ed. 2001. *Alternative Modernities.* Durham and London: Duke University Press.

Gappert, G. 1969. "In Defense of the Black Caucus of the ASA." *Africa Today* 16 (5&6): 16.

Garber, Marjorie. 2001. "Coveting Your Neighbor's Discipline." *The Chronicle of Higher Education* 12 January: B7-B9.

Garnier, Phillipe. 1998. *International Trade in Services: A Growing Trend Among Highly Skilled Migrants With Special Reference to Asia.* Geneva: ILO.

Gates, Henry L. 1992. "Ethnic and Minority Studies." In Joseph Gibaldi, ed. *Introduction to Scholarship in Modern Languages and Literatures.* New York: MLA.

___. 1994. "Critical Fanonism." In Robert C. Davis and Ronald Schleifer, eds. *Contemporary Literary Criticism.* New York: Longman.

___. 2000. "A Preliminary Response to Ali Mazrui's Preliminary Critique of Wonders of the African World." *West Africa Review* 1, 2. *<Http://www.icaap.org/iuicode?101.1.2.6>*

Gelernter, David H. 1997. "The Intellectuals." *Commentary* 103 (June): 5-10.

Gellner, Ernest. 1992. *Postmodernism, Reason and Religion.* London: Routledge.

Gereffi, G. 1997. "The Elusive Last Lap in the Quest for Developed-Country Status." In James H. Mittelman, ed. *Globalization: Critical Reflections.* Boulder, Colo.: Lynne Rienner: 53-81.

Gertler, M. S. 1997. "Between the Global and the Local: The Spatial Limits to Productive Capital." In Kevin R. Cox, *Spaces of Globalization: Reasserting the Power of the Local.* New York: The Guilford Press: 45-63.

Giddens, Anthony. 1990. *The Consequences of Modernity.* Stanford: Stanford University Press.

Gill, Stephen. 1997. "Democratization, Globalization, and the Politics of Indifference." In James H. Mittelman, ed. *Globalization: Critical Reflections.* Boulder, Colo.: Lynne Rienner: 205-228.

Gilliland, Peter H. 1999. "'Wonders of the African World': Reply." 5 November. *<H-AFRICA@H-NET.MSU.EDU>*

Gilroy, Paul. 2000. *Against Race: Imagining Political Culture Beyond the Color Line.* Cambridge, Mass.: Harvard University Press.

Githiora, Chege. 1999. "'Wonders of the African World': Replies." 5 November. *<H-AFRICA@H-NET.MSU.EDU>*

Goldstein, Leon J. 1976. *Historical Knowing.* Austin: University of Texas Press.

Goldthorpe, J. E. 1996. *The Sociology of Post-Colonial Societies.* Cambridge: Cambridge University Press.

Goodheart, Eugene. 1997. "Reflections on the Culture Wars." *Daedalus* 126 (4): 153-175.

Gordon, Lewis. 1997a. *His Majesty's Other Children: Sketches of Racism in a Neocolonial Age.* New York: Rowman and Littlefield.

____. 1997b. "Tragic Dimensions of our Neocolonial 'Postcolonial' World." In Emmanuel Chukwudi Eze, ed. *Postcolonial African Philosophy: A Critical Reader.* Cambridge, Mass.: Blackwell: 241-251.

Graff, Gerald. 1987. *Professing Literature: An Institutional History.* Chicago: University of Chicago Press.

Granovetter, Mark and Richard Sweedberg. 1992. *The Sociology of Economic Life.* San Francisco: Westview Press.

Gray, Eve Horowitz. 1997. *"Strategies of Survival and African Academic Publishers."* Paper presented at the International Seminar on Book Production and Distribution in Africa. Chr. Michelsen Institute, Bergen, Norway, 10-11 April.

Gray, Herman. 1996. "Is Cultural Studies Inflated? The Cultural Economy of Cultural Studies in the United States." In Cary Nelson and Dilip P. Gaonkar, eds. *Disciplinarity and Dissent in Cultural Studies.* Routledge: New York: 203-216.

Greenberg, Daniel S. 2001. "Science in the Public Sector: Who's Making the Decisions?" *The Chronicle of Higher Education* 19 January: B10.

Greene, Sandra E. 1999. "Symbols and Social Activism: An Agenda for African Studies and the ASA." *African Studies Review* 42 (2): 1-14.

Greenfiled, Patricia A. 2000. "What Psychology Can Do for Anthropology, or Why Anthropology Took Postmodernism on the Chin." *American Anthropologist* 102 (3): 564-576.

Gross, Paul R., and Norman Levitt. 1994. *Higher Superstition: The Academic Left and Its Quarrels With Science.* Baltimore: Johns Hopkins University.

Grossberg, Lawrence. 1996a. "The Space of Culture, the Power of Space." In Iain Chambers and Lidia Curti, eds. *The Post-Colonial Question: Common Skies, Divided Horizons.* London and New York: Routledge:169-188.

___. 1996b. "Toward a Genaology of the State of Cultural Studies." In Cary Nelson and Dilip P. Gaonkar, eds. *Disciplinarity and Dissent in Cultural Studies.* Routledge: New York: 131-147.

Guidice, Barbara. 1997. "An Era of Soul-searching for France's Intellectuals." *The Chronicle of Higher Education* 43 (40): A41-A42.

Guillory, John. 1994. *Cultural Capital: The Problem of Literary Canon Formation.* Chicago:University of Chicago Press.

Gupta, Akhil and James Ferguson. 1997. "Discipline and Practice: 'The Field' as Site, Method, and Location in Anthropology." In Akhil Gupta and James Ferguson, eds. *Anthropological Locations: Boundaries and Grounds of Field Science.* Berkeley: University of California Press: 1-46.

Guterman, Lila. 2001. "In a Shift, 'Nature' Will Ask Authors to Reveal Potential Conflicts of Interest." *The Chronicle of Higher Education* 23 August: A22.

Guyer, Jane I. 1996. "Distant Beacons and Immediate Steps: Area Studies, International Studies, and the Disciplines in 1996." *Africa Today* 44, 2: 149-154.

Guyer, Jane I. with the assistance of Akbar M. Virmani and Amanda Kemp. 1996. *African Studies in the United States: A Perspective.* Atlanta, Ga.: African Studies Association Press.

Gyeke, Kwame. 1997a. "Philosophy, Culture, and Technology in the Postcolonial." In Emmanuel Chukwudi Eze, ed. *Postcolonial African Philosophy: A Critical Reader.* Cambridge, MA: Blackwell: 25-44.

___. 1997b. *Tradition and Modernity: Philosophical Reflections on the African Experience.* New York: Oxford University Press.

Hall, Catherine. 1996. "Histories, Empires and the Post-Colonial Moment." In Iain. Chambers and Lidia Curti, eds. *The Post-Colonial Question:*

Common Skies, Divided Horizons. London and New York: Routledge: 65-77.

Hall, Perry A. 1991a. "Beyond Afrocentricity: Alternatives for African American Studies." *The Western Journal of Black Studies* 15, 4: 207-212.

Hall, Peter A. and Sidney Tarrow, 1998. "Globalization and Area Studies: When Is Too Broad Too Narrow?" *The Chronicle of Higher Education* 44, 20 (January 23): B4-B5.

Hall, Stuart. 1991b. "The Local and the Global: Globalization and Ethnicity." In A. D. King, ed. *Culture, Globalization and the World System.* New York: State University of New York: 19-39.

____. 1996. "When Was 'the Post-colonial'? Thinking at the Limit." In Iain Chambers and Lidia Curti, eds. *The Post-Colonial Question: Common Skies, Divided Horizons.* London and New York:Routledge: 242-260.

____. 1999. "A Conversation with Stuart Hall." *The Journal of the Humanities Institute* University of Michigan, 7 (1): 14-15.

Hamilton, Georgina. 2001. "African Universities in the 21st Century and Beyond." Paper presented at the Ford Foundation Retreat on Visioning the African University in 2050, Durban, South Africa, 29 May - 1 June.

Hamilton, Nora, and Norma S. Chinchilla. 1996. "Global Economic Restructuring and International Migration." *International Migration* 34 (2): 195-227.

Hance, William and Philip Curtain. 1996. "African Studies in Africa and the American Scholar." *African Studies Bulletin* 9,1:24-32.

Hanchard, Michael. 1996. "Cultural Politics and Black Public Intellectuals." In Cary Nelson and Dilip P. Gaonkar, eds. *Disciplinarity and Dissent in Cultural Studies.* New York and London: Routledge: 251-263.

Hanke, Steve H. 1996. "Globalization Is Globaloney." *Forbes* 157 (1 Jan.1): 56.

Hann, Robert A. 1995. *Sickness and Healing: An Anthropological Perspective.* New Haven, Conn.: Yale University Press.

Haricombe, Lorraine J. and F. W. Lancaster. 1995. *Out in the Cold: Academic Boycotts and the Isolation of South Africa.* Champaign, Ill.: Information Resources Press.

Harnnez, U. 1991. "Scenarios for Peripheral Cultures." In A. D. King, ed. *Globalization and the World System.* London: Macmillan.

Harris, Jerry. 1998. "Globalization and the Technological Transformation of Capitalism." *Race and Class 40* (October):21-35.

Harrow, Ken. 1999a. "Mainstreaming Africa: Reply." 22 November. *<H-AFRICA@H-NET.MSU.EDU>*,

____. 1999b. "'Wonders of the African World': Reply." 4 November. *<H-AFRICA@H-NET.MSU.EDU>*

___. 1999c. "Maps, Postmodernism and Knowledge: Reply." 9 November. *H-AFRICA@H-NET.MSU.EDU,<http://www.h-net2.msu.edu /logs/showlog.cgi?list=h-africa&file=h.africa.log9711b&ent=9>*

Hart, Jeffrey and Aseem Prakash. *Globalization and Regionalization: Conceptual Issues and Reflections.* Bloomington, Indiana: Indiana Center for Global Business, Graduate School of Business, Indiana University.

Hartsock, Nancy 1990. "Foucault on Power: A Theory for Women?" in L. J. Nicholson, ed. *Feminism/Postmodernism.* New York: Routledge: 157-175.

___. 1998. *The Feminist Standpoint Revisited and Other Essays.* Boulder, Colo.: Westview Press.

Harvey, David. 1989. *The Condition of Postmodernity: An Inquiry Into the Origins of Cultural Change.* Cambridge: Blackwell.

Haskell, Thomas L. 1998. "Farewell to Fallibilism: Robert Berkhofer's Beyond the Great Story and the Allure of the Postmodern." *History and Theory* 37 (3): 347-369.

Hassan, Mohamed H. A. 2000. "Challenges, Opportunities and Strategies for South-South Co-operation in Science and Technology in the 21st Century." Paper presented to the High-Level Forum on South-South Co-operation in Science and Technology. *<http://wmy2000.math.jussieu. fr/92000Feb-KOREA.htm>*

Hassim, Shireen and Cherryl Walker. 1993. "Women's Studies and the Women's Movement in South Africa: Defining a Relationship." *Women Studies International Forum* 16 (5): 523-534.

Hayes, Floyd W. 1994. "Taking Stock: African American Studies at the Edge of the 21st Century." *The Western Journal of Black Studies* 18, 3:153-163.

Head, Laura. 1999. "Gates Series." 29 October. *<H-AFRO-AM@H-NET.MSU.EDU.>*

Hefner, Robert W. 1998. "Multiple Modernities: Christianity, Islam, and Hinduism in a Globalizing Age." *Annual Review of Anthropology* 27:83-104.

Hegde, Radha S. 1998. "A View From Elsewhere: Locating Difference and the Politics of Representation from a Transnational Feminist Perspective." *Communication Theory* 8 (3): 271-292.

Heginbotham, S. J. 1994. "Rethinking International Scholarship." *Items* 48 (2-3): 33-40.

Held, D. 1991. "Democracy and the Global System." In D. Held, ed. *Political Theory Today.* Cambridge, UK: Polity: 197-235.

Held, D., A. McGrew; D. Goldblatt; and J. Perraton, eds. 1999. *Global Transformations: Politics, Economics and Culture.* Cambridge: Polity.

Henderson, M. G. 1996. "'Where, By the Way, Is This Train Going?' A Case for Black (Cultural) Studies." *Callaloo* 19, 1:60-67.

Hennessy, Rosemary. 1993. *Materialist Feminism and the Politics of Discourse.* New York: Routledge.

Hepner, Tricia Redeker. 1999. "'Wonders of the African World': Replies." 3 November. *<H-AFRICA@H-NET.MSU.EDU>*

Herbold, Sarah. 1995. "Well-Placed Reflections: (Post)modern Woman as Symptom of (Post)modernman." *Signs: Journal of Women in Culture and Society* 21 (1): 83-115.

Herod, Andrew. 1997. "Labor as an Agent of Globalization and as a Global Agent." In K. R. Cox, *Spaces of Globalization: Reasserting the Power of the Local.* New York: The Guilford Press: 167-200.

Herod, Andrew; Gearóid Ó Tuathail; and Susan Roberts, eds. 1998. *An Unruly World? Globalization, Governance and Geography.* London and New York: Routledge.

Herskovits, Melville. 1958. "Some Thoughts on American Research in Africa." Presidential Address, First Annual Meeting, African Studies Association, *African Studies Bulletin* 1, 2: 1-11.

Hesse, Reinhard. 1995. "Egypt's Intelligentsia Fights Back." *World Press Review* 42, (2): 48-50.

Higgins, John. 2000 (Spring). "Academic Freedom in the New South Africa." *Boundary* 27, 1: 97-119.

Hill, F. W. G. 1999. "Challenges Facing African Universities Entering the New Millennium - An Institutional Point of View." Paper presented on the occasion of the 20th Anniversary Seminar for the University of Oslo's Committee for North-South Cooperation, Oslo, 15 December. *<http://www.admin.uio.no/sfa/sip/nord-sor/jubileum/hill.html>*

Himmelfarb, Gertrude. 1999. "Postmodernist History." In Elizabeth Fox-Genovese, and Elisabeth Lasch-Genovese, eds. *Reconstructing History: The Emergence of a New Historical Society.* New York: Routledge: 71-93.

Hinton, Robert. 1999. "Ali Mazrui on Wonders of the African World." 1 November. *<H-AFRO-AM@H-NET.MSU.EDU>*

Hirji, K.F. 1990. "Academic Pursuits Under the Link." *Codesria Bulletin* 1:9-16.

Hirst, Paul Q. 1997. *From Statism to Pluralism.* Bristol, Pa: UCL Press.

Hirst, Paul, and Grahame Thompson. 1996. *Globalization in Question.* Cambridge, UK: Polity Press.

Hobsbawm, Eric. J. 1994. *Age of Extremes: The Short Twentieth Century, 1914-1991.* London: Michael Joseph.

Hollander, Paul. 1998. "Intellectuals, Estrangement, and Wish Fulfillment." *Society* 35 (2): 258-268.

___. 2000. "Marxism and Western Intellectuals in the Post-communist Era."

Society 37 (2): 22-28.

Holley, Eugune. 2000. "Editorial Reviews," Amazon.com, May.*http://www. amazon.com/exec/obidos/ts/book-reviews/0375402357 /104-9778317- 9435109*

Hollinger, D. A. 1997. "The Disciplines and the Identity Debates, 1970- 1995." *Daedalus* 126, (1): 333-351.

Holm, Hans-Henrik, and Georg Sørenson. 1995. "Introduction: What Has Changed?" In H-H. Holm and G. Sørenson, eds. *Whose World Order? Uneven Globalization and the End of the Cold War.* Boulder, Colo.: Westview: 1-17.

Holzner, Burkart and Mathew Harmon. 1998. "Intellectual and Organizational Challenges for International Education in the United States: A Knowledge System Perspective." In John Hawkins et al., eds. *International Education in the New Global Era.* Los Angeles: International Studies and Overseas Programs, University of California: 31-63.

Hoogvelt, Ankie. 1997. *Globalization and the Postcolonial World: The New Political Economy of Development.* Baltimore, Md.: The Johns Hokins University Press.

Hooks, Bell. 1989. *Yearning: Race, Gender, and Cultural Politics.* Boston, Mass.: South End Press.

Hormats, R. D. 1999. "High Velocity: International Business in the 21st Century." *Harvard International Review* 21 (3): 36-41.

Horseman, M., and A. Marshall. 1994. *After the Nation State.* London: Harper Collins.

Hounon, Mamaissii Dansi. 1999a. "Mainstreaming Africa: Reply." 20 November. <*H-AFRICA@H-NET.MSU.EDU*>

___. Dansi. 1999b. "'Wonders of the African World': Reply." 5 November. <*H-AFRICA@H-NET.MSU.EDU*>

Hountodji, Paulin. 1997. "Introduction: Recentering Africa." In *Endogenous Knowledge: Research Trails.* Dakar: Codesria Book Series: 1-39.

___. 2001 (June). "Manufacturing Unemployment: The Crisis of African Universities." Paper presented at the Ford Foundation Retreat on Visioning the African University in 2050, Durban, South Africa, 29 May - 1 June.

Howard, L., and P. West. 2000. "The African Digital Library For Lifelong Learners." *AAU Newsletter* 6 (1): 2-3.

Howe, Florence, ed. 2000. *The Politics of Women's Studies: Testimony from Thirty Founding Mothers.* New York: Feminist Press.

http://www.wiz.uni-kassel.de/gear/newsletter/gnews1.htm German-Egypt-

Arab-Region Inter-Alumni-Net Newsletter, July 1999.

http://www.rks.dk/rektorkollegiet/sydafrika/southafr.htm "Cooperation with South African Universities. Report on Visits to South African Universities by Representatives from The Danish Rector's Conference, March 1996."

http://www.worldbank.org/wb/aerc/aerc.htm "The African Economic Research Consortium."

http://www.umich.edu/~saioum/IIJournal.html "U-M's South Africa Initiative Office (SAIO)."

http://www.unam.na/vcdesk/presjune.html "University of Namibia Press Releases."

http://www.milasfrica.org/accra e.htm "Communiqué of the International Conference Organized By the Independent Commission on Africa and the Challenges of the Third Millennium and the United Nations University."

http://www.acbf-pact.org/ "ACBF: Profile."

http://tony.csd.unp.ac.za/links/links.htm "University of Natal International Office: International Links Report."

http://www.founders.howard.edu/hursap9798.htm "Howard University Republic of South Africa Project. Accomplishments 1997-1998.

http://www.matrix.msu.edu/connect/finalreport1998.html "Building Scholarly Networks in Southern Africa: Solving Problems of Communication Through the Internet. A Final Report."

http://www.matrix.msu.edu/sacapacity/reports/part-research.html "Partnerships for Research and Graduate Programs."

http://nairobi.daad.de/subsharan-sec1.htm "DAAD in Sub-Saharan Africa (Tasks and Figures).

Hugo, Pierre. 1998. "Transformation: The Changing Context of Academia in Post-Apartheid South Africa." *African Affairs* 9: 5-27.

Hulme, Peter. 1994. "The Locked Heart: The Creole Family Romance of Wide Sargasso Sea." In Francis Barker, Peter Hulme, and Margaret Iversen, eds. *Colonial Discourse/Postcolonial Theory*. Manchester, UK: Manchester University Press: 72-88.

____. 1995. "Including America." *ARIEL: A Review of International English Literature* 26 (1): 117-123.

Huntington, Samuel. 1993. "The Clash of Civilizations." *Foreign Affairs* 72 (3): 186-194.

____. 1996. *Clash of Civilizations*. New York: Simon and Schuster.

Hutton, Will and Anthony Giddens. 2000. "Is Globalization Americanization?" *Dissent* 47 (3): 58-63.

Idahosa, Pablo. 2000. "Reconcile Soyinka and Mazrui: Public Discourse," 25 January. <*toyin.falola@mail.utexas.edu*>

Ifidon, Sam E. 1994. "Overview of the State of Nigerian Journal Publishing." In M. Wise, ed. *Survival Under Adverse Conditions: Proceedings of the African Library Science Workshop.* The Hague, Netherlands: International Federation of Library Associations and Institutions. IFLA Professional Reports, No.38.

Ikenberry, Stanley O. 2001. "Higher Education and Market Forces." *USA Today* 129 (2670) March: 34-35.

Imam, Ayesha, and Amina Mama. 1994. "The Role of Academics in Limiting and Expanding Academic Freedom." In Mahmood Mamdani and Mamadou Diouf, eds. *Academic Freedom in Africa.* Dakar, Senegal: Codesria Book Series: 73-107.

Iman, Ayesha; Amina Mama; and Fatou Sow, eds. 1997. *Engendering African Social Sciences.* Dakar: Codesria Book Series.

Inikori, Joseph. 2000. "The 'Wonders of Africa' and the Trans-Atlantic Slave Trade," *West Africa Review* 1, 2. <*Http://www.icaap.org/iuicode?101.1.2.7*>.

Iredale, Robyn. 1999. "The Need to Import Skilled Personnel: Factors Favoring and Hindering its International Mobility." *International Migration* 37,1:89-123.

Irele, Abiola F. 1991. "The African Scholar. Is Black Africa Entering the Dark Ages of Scholarship?" *Transition* 51: 56-69.

___. 2000. "The Political Kingdom: Toward Reconstruction in Africa." <wysiwyg://39/http://www.africahome.com/scholar/stories/irele_recon-struct.shtml>

Iskandar, Laila. 2001 (June). "New Vision for Higher Education in Africa." Paper presented at the Ford Foundation Retreat in Durban, South Africa.

Iurevich, Aleksandr V. 2000. "Academics in Politics." *Russian Politics and Law* 38 (3): 24-48.

Jacoby, Russell. 1987. *The Last Intellectuals: American Culture in the Age of Academe.* New York: Noonday Press.

Jacoby, Russell. 1999. "A New Intellectual History?" In Elizabeth Fox-Genovese, and Elisabeth Lasch-Genovese, eds. *Reconstructing History: The Emergence of a New Historical Society.* NewYork: Routledge: 94-118.

James, Joy. 2000. "Transcending the Talented Tenth." <*http://spot.colorado.edu/~hudehart/talented_tenth.html*>

Jameson, Fredric. 1991. *Postmodernism. Or the Cultural Logic of Late Capitalism.* Durham, N.C.: Duke University Press.

___.1998a. "Preface." In Fredric Jameson and Masao Miyoshi, eds. *The Cultures of Globalization*. Durham and London: Duke University Press: xi-xvii.

___. 1998b. "Notes on Globalization as a Philosophical Issue." In Fredric Jameson and Masao Miyoshi, eds. *The Cultures of Globalization*. Durham and London: Duke University Press: 54-77.

Janz, Bruce. 1995a. "Postmodernism." 6 April. *<janz@corelli.augustana. ab.ca>*

___. 1995b. "Postmodernism and Modern Africa," 29 May. *H-AFRICA@H-NET.MSU.EDU,<http://www.h-net.msu.edu/~africa /threads/pomothread.html>*.

Jarausch, Konrad. 1995. "Postmodern theory: Konrad Jarausch responds." 4 April. *<jarausch.ham@mhs.unc.edu>*

Jarvis, Peter. 1999. "Global Trends in Lifelong Learning and the Response of the Universities." *Comparative Education* 35 (2): 249-257.

Jason, Pini. 1998. "Secret Cults Terrorise Nigerian Universities." *New Africa* April.

Jay, Mary. 1994. "African Books Collective: Its Contribution to African Publishing." *Africa Bibliography 1992. Works on Africa Published During 1992*. Edinburgh: Edinburgh University Press.

___. 1997. "How Can Publishers Effectively Distribute Books in and out of Africa?" Paper presented at the International Seminar on Book Production and Distribution in Africa. Chr. Michelsen Institute, Bergen, Norway, April 10-11.

Jaygbay, Jacob. 1997. "African Scholarly Journals: Slow Decline on Quantum Jump?" *Logos* 8(2): 85-89.

Jega, Attahiru. 1996. "Unions and Conflict Management in Nigeria's Tertiary Institutions." *Issue: A Journal of Opinion*. 24 (I): 61-63.

Jenkins, Keith. 1995. *On 'What is History?': From Carr and Elton to Rorty and White*. London and New York: Routledge.

Jensen, Mike. 1998 (October). *The African Internet Connectivity*. *Mikej@sn.apc.org*

___. 2001 (May). *The African Internet-A Status Report. Mikej@sn.apc.org*

Jessop, B. 1989. "Conservative Regimes and the Transition to Post-Fordism: The Case of Great Britain and West Germany." In M. Gottdiener and N. Komninos, eds. *Capitalist Development and Crisis Theory*. New York: St. Martin's Press.

Jeyifo, Biodun. 2000a. "On Mazrui's 'Black Orinetalism': A Cautionary Critique," *West Africa Review* 1, 2. *<Http://www.icaap.org/iuicode?101. 1.2.19>*

____. 2000b. "Greatness and Cruelty: 'Wonders of the African World' and the Reconfiguration of Senghorian Negritude." *West Africa Review* 1, 2. <*Http://www.icaap.org/iuicode?101.1.2.9*>

Jinks, Derek P. 1997. "Essays in Refusal: Pre-theoretical Commitments in Postmodern Anthropology and Critical Race Theory." *Yale Law Journal* 107 (2): 499-528.

Johnson, David. 2000. "Africa's Brain Drain Slows Development."<http://216.239.39.100/search?q=cache:ZPmpAetp4ymc.www.afri...>

Johnson, Hazel. 1992. *Dispelling the Myth of Globalization: The Case for Regionalization.* New York: Praeger Publishers.

Johnson, Paul. 1990. *Intellectuals.* New York: HarperPerennial.

Johnson, W. R. 1971. "The Responsibility of Africanists - A Board Candidate's Platform."*Africa Today,* 18, 1: 23-25.

Johnston, Robert D. 2000. "Where Have All the Tenured Radicals Gone." *Social Policy* 30 (4): 19-22.

Jomo, K. S. 2000. "Economic considerations for a Renewed Nationalism." *Journal of Contemporary Asia* 30 (3): 338-368.

Jones, Wayne C. 1999. "Gates PBS Series." 29 October. <*H-AFRO-AM@H-NET.MSU.EDU*>

Joralemon, Donald. 1999. *Exploring Medical Anthropology.* Boston: Allyn and Bacon.

Juan, E. S. 1998. *Beyond Postcolonial Theory.* New York: St. Martin's Press.

Juneja, O. P. 1995. *Postcolonial Novel: Narratives of Consciousness.* New Delhi: Creative Books.

Kahn, Peter H. 1999. "Reinstating Modernity in Social Science Research - Or - The Status of Bullwinkle in a Postmodern era." *Human Development* 42 (2): 92-108.

Kalinga, Owen J. M. 1998. "The Production of History in Malawi in the 1960s: The Legacy of Sir Harry Johnston, The Influence of the Society of Malawi and the Role of Dr. Kamuzu Banda and His Malawi Congress Party." *African Affairs* 97 (389): 523-549.

Kanani, Simeon S. 2000. "Study Abroad in Kenya: Now and in the Future." *African Issues* 28 (1&2): 84-88.

Kandeh, Mori. 2001 (April). "Propaganda on AIDS in Africa." <*http://chronicle.com/weekly/v47/i30/30b02201.htm*>

Kando, Tom. 1996. "Postmodernism: Old Wine in New Bottles?" *International Journal on World Peace* 13 (3).

Kang, Liu. 1998. "Is There an Alternative to (Capitalist) Globalization? The Debate about Modernity in China." In F. Jameson and M. Miyoshi, eds. *The Cultures of Globalization.* Durham, N.C.: Duke University Press:

164-188.

Kanogo, Tabitha. 1987. *Squatters and the Roots of Mau Mau.* Nairobi and London: James Currey and Heinemann Kenya.

Kaplan, R. D. 1994. "The Coming Anarchy." *The Atlantic Monthly* 273 (2) (December): 44-76.

___. 2000. "Was Democracy Just a Moment." In Patrick O'Meara, Howard D. Mehlinger, and Mathew Krain, eds. *Globalization and the Challenges of a New Century.* Bloomington and Indianapolis: Indiana University Press: 196-214.

Kappeler, Suzanne. 1986. *The Pornography of Representation.* Minneapolis: Minnesota University Press.

Kapur, G. 1998. "Globalization and Culture: Navigating the Void." In F. Jameson and M. Miyoshi, eds. *The Cultures of Globalization.* Durham, N.C.: Duke University Press: 191-217.

Karabell, Zachary 1999. "The Uncertain Value of Training Public Intellectuals." *The Chronicle of Higher Education* 24 September.

Karenga, Maulana. 2000. "Black Studies: A Critical Reassessment." In Manning Marable, ed. *Dispatches From the Ebony Tower.* New York: Columbia University Press:162-170.

Karp, Ivan. 1997. "Does Theory Travel? Area Studies and Cultural Studies." *Africa Today* 44 (3): 281-296.

Kassimir, Ron. 1997. "Internationalization of African Studies: A View from the SSRC." *Africa Today* 44 (2):155-162.

Katjavivi, Peter H. 2001 (June). "Breasting the Challenge and Seizing the opportunities: The Vision of Higher Learning Institutions in Developing Countries." Paper presented at the Ford Foundation Retreat on Visioning the African University in 2050, Durban, South Africa, 29 May - 1 June.

Kaufman, David. 1990. "The Profession of Theory." *PMLA* 105 (3): 519-530.

Kaul, Suvir. 2001. *Poems of Nation, Anthems of Empire.* Charlottesville, Va.: University of Virginia Press.

Kazanjian, Miriam A.. 1998. "Charge of the Conference." In John Hawkins, et al., eds. *International Education in the New Global Era.* Los Angeles: International Studies and Overseas Programs, University of California: 19-22.

Kebede, Abebe. n.d. "The Transition from Brain Drain to Brain Gain." *<http://trigonal.ncat.edu/AAU-Network/aau/feature/brain.html>*

Keck, Margaret and Kathryn Sikkink. 2000. *Activists Beyond Borders: Advocacy Networks in International Politics.* Ithaca, NY: Cornell

University Press.

Keen, D. 2000. "Organized Chaos: Not the New World We Ordered." In Patrick O'Meara, Howard D. Mehlinger, and Mathew Krain, eds. *Globalization and the Challenges of a New Century.* Bloomington and Indianapolis: Indiana University Press: 140-148.

Keller, Edmond J. and Donald Rothchild, eds. 1996. *Africa in the New International Order.* Boulder and London: Lynne Rienner.

Kelley, Robin D.G. 1995. "To the Editors." *Boston Review* Forum, Black Nationalism. *http://bostonreview.mit.edu/bro20.4/Kelley.html*

Kellogg, Alex P. 2001. "Leading Medical Journals Hope to Curb Drug Companies' Publishing Influence." *The Chronicle of Higher Education* 6 August.

Kelly, M. J. 2001. *Challenging the Challengers: Understanding and Expanding the Response of Universities in Africa to HIV/AID.* <*http://chronicle. com/weekly/documents/v47/i25/4725hiv.htm*>

Kempner, Ken. 2000. "Education and the Rise of the Global Economy." *Journal of Higher Education* 71 (5): 624-627.

Kennedy, Dane. 1992. "Constructing the Colonial Myth of Mau Mau." *International Journal of African Historical Studies* 25 (2): 241-60.

Keohane, R. O. and H. V. Milner, eds. 1996. *Internationalization and Domestic Politics.* Cambridge: Cambridge University Press.

Kershaw, Greet. 1997. *Mau Mau From Below.* Athens, Ohio: Ohio University Press.

Khan, Amin. 1994. "Algerian Intellectuals: Between Identity and Modernity." In Mahmood Mamdani and Mamadou Diouf, eds. *Academic Freedom in Africa.* Dakar, Senegal: Codesria Book Series: 274-298.

Ki-Zerbo, Joseph. 1994. "The Need for Creative Organizational Approaches." In Mamadou Diouf andMahmood Mamdani, eds., *Academic Freedom in Africa.* Dakar, Senegal: Codesria Book Series: 26-38.

Kiangi, G. E and K. E. Mshigeni. 2001. "The Status of ICT and its Use in Higher Education and Research in the Southern African Region. Paper presented at the Carter Lectures 2001, "Governance and Higher Education," University of Florida, Gainesville. 22-25 March.

Kilson, Martin. 2000. "Master of the Intellectual Dodge: A Reply to Henry Louis Gates." West Africa Review 1, 2. <*Http://www.icaap.org/iuicode? 101.1.2.10*>

Kimball, Roger. 1990. *Tenured Radicals: How Politics Has Corrupted Higher Education.* New York: Harper and Row.

Kirkaldy, Alan. 1996. "History Teaching in Rural Areas: The University of Venda." *Issue: A Journal of Opinion.* 24, (1): 17-23.

Klare, Michael. 2000. "Redefining Security: The New Global Schisms." In Patrick O'Meara, Howard D. Mehlinger, and Mathew Krain, eds. *Globalization and the Challenges of a New Century*. Bloomington and Indianapolis: Indiana University Press: 131-139.

Klein, Sarah. 1999. "Gates PBS Series & History of Slavery." 1 November. <*H-AFRO-AM@H-NET.MSU.EDU*>

Kleinman, Arthur. 1995. *Writing at the Margins: Discourse Between Anthropology and Medicine*. Berkeley: University of California Press.

Knoch, Cartsen. 1997. "Uninet - The South African Academic and Research Network." <*http://www.idrc.ca/acacia/outputs/op-unim.htm*>

Knox, P. L. 1995. "World Cities and the Organization of Global Space." In R. J. Johnson, P. J. Taylor, and M. J. Watts, eds. *Geographies of Global Change*. Cambridge, Mass.: Blackwell.

Koechlin, Timothy. 1995. "The Globalization of Investment." *Contemporary Economic Policy* 13 (1): 92-100.

Koertge, Noretta. 1998. *A House Built on Sand: Exposing Postmodernist Myths about Science*. New York: Oxford University Press.

Kreps, David M. 1997. "Economics - The Current Position." *Daedalus* 126, 1: 59-85.

Krugman, Paul R. 1996. "The Adam Smith Address: What Difference Does Globalization Make?" *Business Economics* 31 (7): 7-10.

Kuhn, Thomas. 1962. *The Structure of Scientific Revolutions*. Chicago: University of Chicago Press.

Kuper, Adam. 1994. "Culture, Identity and the Project of a Cosmopolitan Anthropology." *Man* 29:536-554.

Kuryluk, Ewa. 1995. "Intellectuals, Be Intelligent." *TriQuarterly* 94 (Fall): 131-136.

Labinger, J. A. 1997. "The Science Wars and the Future of the American Academic Profession." *Daedalus* 126 (4): 201-220.

Lai, Ming-yan. 1998. "The Intellectual's Deaf-Mute, or (How) Can We Speak Beyond Postcoloniality?" *Cultural Critique* 39: 31-58.

Lajos, Tamas. 1996. "The Hungarian Experience of Academic Cooperation with North America and the European Community." In Peggy Blumenthal et al., *Academic Mobility in a Changing World. Regional and Global Issues*. London and Bristol: Jessica Kingsley Publishers.

Lamont, Michèle. 1987. "How to Become a Dominant French Philosopher: The Case of Jacques Derrida." *American Journal of Sociology* 93: 584-622.

Lange, Lynda. 1998. "Burnt Offerings to Rationality: A Feminist Reading of the Construction of Indigenous Peoples in Enrique Dussel's *Theory of Modernity*." *Hypatia* 405 (3): 132-145.

Lapham, Lewis H. 1998. "Kulturkampf." *Harper's* 300 (1800, May): 9-11.

Lasch-Quinn, Elisabeth. 1999. "Democracy in the Ivory Tower? Toward the Restoration of an Intellectual Community." In Elizabeth Fox-Genovese, and Elisabeth Lasch-Genovese, eds. *Reconstructing History: The Emergence of a New Historical Society.* New York: Routledge: 23-34.

Lash, Scott, and John Urry. 1994. *Economies of Signs and Space.* London: Sage.

Laslett, Barbara and Johanna Brenner. 2000. "Twenty-First-Century Academic Feminism in the United States: Utopian Visions and Practical Actions." *Signs: Journal of Women in Culture and Society* 25 (4): 1231-1235.

Laurie, Price J. 2000. "Exploring Medical Anthropology." *Medical Anthropology Quarterly* 14 (1): 109-112.

Law, Murray. 1997. "Representation Unbound: Globalization and Democracy." In K. R. Cox, *Spaces of Globalization: Reasserting the Power of the Local.* New York: The Guilford Press: 240-280.

Lawrence, Nicholas Benjamin. 2001 (March). "Jeunes Pour Jeunes: Strategies for Combating the Spread of HIV/AIDS Among African Students: Lessons from a Project at the Universite du Benin in Togo." Paper presented at the Carter Lectures 2001, "Governance and Higher Education," University of Florida, Gainesville. March 22-25.

Lawson, Alan. 1995. "Postcolonial Theory and the 'Settler' Subject." *Essays on Canadian Writing* 56: 20-36.

Lazarus, Neil. 1990. *Resistance in Postcolonial African Fiction.* New Haven: Yale University Press.

___. 1994. "National Consciousness and the Specificity of (Post) colonial Intellectualism." In Francis Barker, P. Hulme, and M. Iversen, eds. *Colonial Discourse/Postcolonial Theory.* Manchester and New York: Manchester University Press: 197-220.

___. 1999. *Nationalism and Cultural Practice in the Postcolonial World.* Cambridge: Cambridge University Press.

Lechner, F. J. 1993. "Global Fundamentalism." In William H. Swatos, ed. *A Future for Religion.* Newbury Park, Calif.: Sage.

Lee, Benjamin. 1995. "Critical Internationalism." *Public Culture* 7 (3): 559-592.

___. 1996. "Between Nations and Disciplines." In Cary Nelson and Dilip P. Gaonkar, eds.1996. *Disciplinarity and Dissent in Cultural Studies.* Routledge: New York: 217-233.

LeMelle, T. J. 1969. "Where Was the Racism in Montreal?" *Africa Today* 16 (5&6): 3.

___. 1971. "ASA - Going Nowhere." *Africa Today* 18 (1): 18-20.

Lemert, Charles C. 1994. "Post-structuralism and Sociology." In Steven

Seidman, ed. *The Postmodern Turn: New Perspectives On Social Theory.* New York: Cambridge University Press: 265-281.

Letgers, Lyman H. 1964. "The National Defense Act and African Studies." *African Studies Bulletin* 7,3:3-10.

Levey, Lisbeth A., ed. 1993a. *A Profile of Research Libraries in Sub-Saharan Africa: Acquisition, Outreach, and Infrastructure.* Washington, D.C.: America Association for the Advancement of Science, 1993.

___. 1993b. *Profile of Research Libraries in Sub-Saharan Africa: Acquisitions, Outreach, and Infrastructure.* Washington, D.C.: American Association for the Advancement of Science.

Levi, M., and D. Olson. 2000. "The Battles in Seattle." *Politics and Society* 28 (3): 309-329.

Levine, George, ed. 1994. *Aesthetics and Ideology.* New Brunswick, N.J.: Rutgers University Press.

Lewsen, Phyllis. 1996. *Reverberations: A Memoir.* Cape Town, South Africa: University of Cape Town Press.

Lie, John. 1996. "Globalism and Its Discontents." *Contemporary Sociology* 25 (5): 585-587.

Lim, Linda Y. C. 1998. "Whose 'Model' Failed? Implications of the Asian Economic Crisis." *Washington Quarterly* 21 (3): 25-36.

Limb, Peter. 1997. "Postmodernism and Africa: Reply." 12 November. <"Postmodernism and Modern Africa," *H-AFRICA@H-NET.MSU .EDU*, <*http://www.h-net2.msu.edu/logs/showlog.cgi?list=h-africa&file= h.africa.log9711b&ent=36*>

Lindblom, Charles E. 1997a. "Political Science in the 1940s and 1950s." *Daedalus* 126 (1): 225-252.

___. 1997b. "Logical and Moral Dilemmas of Postmodernism." *Journal of the Royal Anthropological Institute* 3: 747-760.

Lindsay, Beverly. 1997. "Toward Conceptual, Policy, and Programmatic Frameworks of Affirmative Action in South African Universities." *Journal of Negro Education* 66 (4): 522-538.

Ling, Margaret. 1997. "How Can an International Book Fair Stimulate African Book Production?" Paper presented at the International Seminar on Book Production and Distribution in Africa. Chr. Michelsen Institute, Bergen, Norway, 10-11 April.

Lionnet, Françoise. 1995. *Postcolonial Representations: Women, Literature, Identity.* Ithaca, N.Y.: Cornell University Press.

Lively, Kit. 1999. "Carnegie Corporation Plans Renewed Emphasis on Higher Education." *The Chronicle of Higher Education* 45, 28: A41.

Liyai, H. A. 1989. "The Historical Writings of B. A. Ogot." In William R.

Ochieng', ed. *A Modern History of Kenya, 1895-1980. In Honor of B.A. Ogot.* London and Nairobi: Evans Brothers: 245-255.

Llyod, John. 1996. "Are Intellectuals Useless?" *New Statesman* 127 (4409, 30 October): 11-12.

Lombardi, J. V. 1993. *A Changed World : NASULGC's Commission on International Affairs and the Post-Cold War Era.* Washington, D.C.: National Association of State Universities and Land-Grant Colleges.

Lonsdale, John. 1990. "Mau Maus of the Mind: Making Mau Mau and Remaking Kenya." *Journal of African History* 31: 393-421.

___. 1992. "The Moral Economy of Mau Mau: The Problem." In Bruce Berman and John Lonsdale. *Unhappy Valley: Conflict in Kenya and Africa.* Athens, Ohio: Ohio University Press: 265-504.

Loomba, Ania. 1998. *Colonialism/Postcolonialism.* London and New York: Routledge.

Loomba, Ania and M. Orkin, eds.1998. *Post-Colonial Shakespeares.* London: Routledge.

Loriaux, M.; M. Woo-Cummings; K. Calder; S. Maxfield; and S. Perez. 1997. *Capital Ungoverned. Liberalizing Finance in Intervention States.* Ithaca, NY: Cornell University Press.

Lovi, Theodore J. 1995. "Media Fascination with Self-Styled Public Intellectuals." *The Chronicle of Higher Education* 27 January.

Lowe, Chris. 1995. "Postmodernism and Modern Africa." 27 May. *H-AFRICA@H-NET.MSU.EDU,<http://www.h-net.msu.edu/-africa/threads/pomothread.html>*

___. 1997a. "Unexamined Consequences of Academic Globalism in African Studies." *Africa Today* 44 (3): 297-307.

___. 1997b. "Maps, Postmodernism and Knowledge." 31 October. *H-AFRICA@H-NET.MSU.EDU,<http://www.h-net2.msu. edu/logs/showlog. cgi?list=h-africa&file=h.africa.log9711b&ent=7>*

___. 1999a. "'Wonders of the African World': Reply." 2 November. *<H-AFRICA@H-NET.MSU.EDU>*

___. 1999b. "'Wonders of the African World': Replies." 5 November. *<H-AFRICA@H-NET.MSU.EDU>*

Lubiano, Wahneema. 1996. "Mapping the Interstices Between Afro-American Cultural Discourse and Cultural Studies: A Prolegomenon." *Callaloo*, 19 (1): 68-77.

Luke, T. W. 1995. "New World Order or Neo-World Orders." In M. Featherstone, S. Lash, and R. Robertson, eds. *Global Culture: Nationalism, Globalization and Modernity.* London: Sage.

Lull, J. 1995. *Media, Communication, Culture: A Global Approach.*

Cambridge: Polity Press.

Lurry, C. 1996. *Consumer Culture.* Cambridge: Polity Press.

Lykes, M. Brinton. 2001 (June). "Envisioning African Higher Education at Mid-Century." Paper presented at the Ford Foundation Retreat on Visioning the African University in 2050, Durban, South Africa, 29 May - 1 June.

Lyotard, Jean-Francois. 1984. *The Postmodern Condition.* Minneapolis: University of Minnesota Press.

Ma, Shu-Yun. 1998. "Clientelism, Foreign Attention, and Chinese Intellectual Autonomy." *Modern China* 24 (4): 445-471.

Maack, Mary Niles. 1987. "Library Research and Publishing in Francophone Africa." *IFLA Journal* 13(1): 45-53.

Mabokela, Reitumetse Obakeng. 2000. "'We Cannot Find Qualified Blacks': Faculty Diversification Programmes at South African Universities." *Comparitive Education* 36, 1 (February): 95-112.

Macnaghten, Phil and John, Urry, 1998. *Contested Natures.* Thousand Oaks, Calif.: Sage.

Madsen, Deborah L, ed. 1999a. *Post-Colonial Literatures: Expanding the Canon.* London: Pluto Press.

Madsen, Deborah L. 1999b. "Beyond the Commonwealth: Post-Colonialism and American Literature." In Deborah L. Madsen, ed. *Post-Colonial Literatures: Expanding the Canon.* London: Pluto Press: 1-13.

Mafeje, Archie. 1994. "Beyond Academic Freedom: The Struggle for Authenticity in African Social Science Discourse." In Mamadou Diouf and Mahmood Mamdani, eds., *Academic Freedom in Africa.* Dakar, Senegal: Codesria Book Series: 59-71.

Magner, Denise K. 1992. "Nomadic Scholar of Black Studies Puts Harvard in the Spotlight." *The Chronicle of Higher Education* 15 July.

Magubane, Zine. 2000. "The Interplay of Text, Audience, and Narrator in *Wonders of the African World.*" Unpublished.

Mair, A. 1997. "Strategic Localization: The Myth of the Postnational Enterprise." In K. R. Cox, *Spaces of Globalization: Reasserting the Power of the Local.* New York: The Guilford Press: 64-88.

Mallon, S., J. Stern, A. F. Isaacman, and W. Rosebury. 1993. *Confronting Historical Paradigms.* Madison: The University of Wisconsin Press: 187-201.

Maloba, Wunyabari O. 1993. *Mau Mau and Kenya: An Analysis of a Peasant Revolt.* Bloomington: Indiana University Press.

Mamdani, Mahmood. 1994. "The Intelligentsia, the State and Social Movements in Africa." In Mahmood Mamdani and Mamadou Diouf, eds. *Aca-*

demic Freedom in Africa. Dakar, Senegal: Codesria Book Series: 247-261.

___. 1995. "Critique of the State and Civil Society Paradigm in Africanist Studies." In Mahmood Mamdani and Wamba-dia-Wamba, eds. *African Studies in Social Movements and Democracy*. Dakar: Codesria Book Series: 602-616.

___. 1998a. "Teaching Africa at the Post-Apartheid University of Cape Town: A Critical View of the 'Introduction to Africa's Core Course in the Social Sciences and Humanities Faculty's Foundation Semester." *Social Dynamics* 24 (2):1-32.

___. 1998b. "Is African Studies to be turned into a new home for Bantu Education at UTC?" *Social Dynamics* 24(2):63-75.

___. 2001. *When Victims Become Killers: Colonialism, Nativism, and the Genocide in Rwanda*. Princeton, New Jersey: Princeton University Press.

Mandel, E. 1978. *Late Capitalism*. London: New Left Books.

Mandle, Joan D. 2000. *Can We Wear Our Pearls and Still Be Feminists? Memoirs of a Campus Struggle*. Columbia: University of Missouri Press.

Mani, Lata. 1992. "Cultural Theory, Colonial Texts: Reading Eyewitness Accounts of Widow Burning." In Lawrence Grossberg, Cary Nelson and P. Treicher, eds. *Cultural Studies*. Urbana: University of Illinois Press:

Manuh, Takyiwaa. 2001 (June). "Envisioning the African University in 2050 AD." Paper presented at the Ford Foundation Retreat on Visioning the African University in 2050, Durban, South Africa, 29 May - 1 June.

Marable, Manning. 1995a. "Black Studies, Multiculturalism, and the Future of American Education." *Items* 49, 2/3: 49-57.

___. 1995b. "Black Intellectuals in Conflict." In Manning Marable, ed. *Beyond Black and White*. London: Verso, 167-173.

___. ed. 2000a. "Introduction: Black Studies and the Racial Mountain." In Manning Marable, ed. *Dispatches from the Ebony Tower: Intellectuals Confront the African-American Experience*. New York: Columbia University Press, 1-28.

___. ed. 2000b. *Dispatches from the Ebony Tower: Intellectuals Confront the African American Experience*. New York: Columbia University Press.

Marcuse, Peter. 2000. "The Language of Globalization." *Monthly Review* 52 (3): 23-27.

Marcuse, Peter and Ronald van Kampen, eds. 2000. *Globalizing Cities: A New Spatial Order?* Malden, Mass.: Blackwell.

Marshall, D. 1996. "National Development and the Globalization Discourse: Confronting 'Interpretive' and 'Convergence' Notions." *Third World Quarterly* 17: 875-901.

Martin, William G. and Michael O. West. 1995. "The Decline of the

Africanists' Africa and the Rise of New Africas." *ISSUE: A Quarterly Journal of Africanist Opinion* 23 (1): 24-26.

___. 1999a. "Introduction: The Rival Africa's and Paradigms of Africanists and Africans at Home and Abroad." In W. G. Martin and M. O. West, eds. *Out of One, Many Africas: Reconstructing the Study and meaning of Africa*. Urbana and Chicago: University of Illinois: 1-36.

___. 1999b. "The Ascent, Triumph and Disintegration of the Africanist Enterprise, USA." In W. G. Martin and M. O. West, eds. *Out of One, Many Africas: Reconstructing the Study and Meaning of Africa*. Urbana and Chicago: University of Illinois: 85-122.

Martinez, Ruben O. 1998. "Globalization and the Social Sciences." *The Social Science Journal* 35, 4: 601-13.

Massey, Doreen. 1994. *Space, Place, and Gender*. Minneapolis: University of Minnesota Press.

Mateene, K. 1996. "OAU's Resolutions on African Languages and the State of Their Implementation." Colloquium on Language Legislation and Linguistic Rights, University of Illinois at Urbana-Champaign, March 21-23.

Mathieu, James. 1996. "Reflections on Two African Universities." *Issue: A Journal of Opinion* 24 (I): 24-28.

Mattson, Kevin. 1999. "Where Are the Young Left Intellectuals?" *Social Policy* 29 (3): 53-58.

Mazrui, Ali A. 1978. *Political Values and the Educated Class in Africa*. London: Heinemann.

___. 1994. "The Impact of Global Changes on Academic Freedom in Africa: A Preliminary Assessment." In Mamadou Diouf and Mahmood Mamdani, eds., *Academic Freedom in Africa*. Dakar, Senegal: Codesria Book Series: 118-140.

___. 1998. "Fewer Heroes and More Martyrs in Africa's Post-Colonial Experience: Implications for the African Child." Keynote Address at the Indaba of the Zimbabwe International Book Fair on "Books and Children," 1 August.

___. 1999. "Mazrui Replies to Jeyifo." 18 November. *<H-AFRO-AM@H-NET.MSU.EDU>*

___. 2000a. "A Preliminary Critique of the TV Series By Henry Louis Gates, Jr." *West Africa Review* 1,2 *http://www.icaap.org/iuicode?101.1.2.11*.

___. 2000b. "A Millennium Letter to Henry Louis Gates Jr.: Concluding a Dialogue." *West Africa Review* 1, 2. *<Http://www.icaap.org/iuicode?101.1.2.13>*

___. 2000c. "Black Orientalism?: Further Reflections on 'Wonders of the

African World.' " *West Africa Review* 1, 2. <*http://www.icaap.org/iuicode? 101.1.2.12*>

___. 2000d. "Soyinka vs. Mazrui?" 24 January.*toyin.falola@mail.utexas.edu"*

Mbembe, Achille. 1992a. "Provisional Notes on the Postcolony." *Africa*, 62: 3-37.

___. 1992b. "The Banality of Power and the Aesthetics of Vulgarity in the Postcolony." *Public Culture* 4: 1-30.

___. 1998. Editorial. *Codesria Bulletin* 3&4: 3-5.

___. 1999. Editorial, "Getting out of the Ghetto." *Codesria Bulletin* 3 & 4: 1-2.

___. 2000. "African Modes of Self-Writing." *Codesria Bulletin* 1: 4-19.

___. 2001a. *On the Postcolony*. Berkeley: University of California Press.

___. 2001b. "At the Edge of the World: Boundaries, Territoriality, and Sovereignty in Africa." In Arjun Appadurai, ed. *Globalization*. Durham and London: Duke University Press: 22-51.

Mbogoni, Lawrence. 1999. "'Wonders of the African World': Reply." 2 November. < *H-AFRICA@H-NET.MSU.EDU*>

McCarthy, JoAnn S. 1998."Continuing and Emerging National Needs for the Internationalization of Undergraduate Education." In John Hawkins et al., eds. *International Education in the New Global Era*. Los Angeles: International Studies and Overseas Programs, University of California: 65-75.

McClendon, Thom. 1997. "Maps, Postmodernism and Knowledge: Reply." 9 November. *H-AFRICA@H-NET.MSU.EDU,<http://www.h-net2. msu.edu/logs/showlog.cgi?list=h-africa &file=h.africa.log 9711b&ent=15*>

McClintock, A. 1994. "The Angel of Progress: Pitfalls of the Term 'Post-Colonialism." In Francis Barker, P. Hulme, and M. Iversen, eds. *Colonial Discourse/Postcolonial Theory*. Manchester and New York: Manchester University Press: 253-266.

McCoy, Molly. 2000. "Experiencing Race and Class Social Structures." *African Issues* 28 (1&2): 133.

McCracken, J. 1993. "African History in British Universities: Past, Present, and Future." *African Affairs* 92 (367): 239-253.

McCullagh, C. Behan. 1998. *The Truth of History*. London and New York: Routledge.

McDonald, Larry. 1995. "I Looked for It and There It Was - Gone: History in Postmodern Criticism." *Essays on Canadian Writing* 56: 37-50.

Mcharazo, A. A. S. 1995. "Summary of S. Arunachalam's 'Accessing Information Published in the Third World: Should Spreading the Word from the Third World Always Be Like Swimming Against the Current,'

Workshop on Access to Third World Journals." *The African Book Publishing Record* 20 (4): 245.

McLaren, P. 1994. "Multiculturalism and the Postmodern Critique: Towards a Pedagogy of Resistance and Transformation." In H. Giroux and P. McLaren, eds. *Between Borders: Pedagogy and the Politics of Cultural Studies.* New York: Routledge. 192-222.

McMichael, Philip. 1996. "Globalization: Myth and Realities." *Rural Sociology* 61 (1): 25-55.

McMurtrie, Beth. 2000. "America's Scholarly Societies Raise Their Flags Abroad." *The Chronicle of Higher Education* 28 January: A53.

Meena, Ruth. 2001. "Women's Participation in Higher Levels of Learning in Africa: Interventions to Promote Gender Equity." Paper presented at the Carter Lectures 2001, "Governance and Higher Education," University of Florida, Gainesville. 22-25 March.

Mengisteab, Kidane. 1996. *Globalization and Autocentricity in Africa's Development in the 21st Century.* Trenton, N.J.: Africa World Press.

___. 1999. "Globalization and the Struggle for Democratization in Africa." Paper presented to Annual Spring Symposium, "Human Rights and the Rule of Law in Africa," University of Illinois at Urbana Champaign, June.

Merkx, Gilbert W. 1998. "Graduate Training and Research." In John Hawkins, et al., eds. *International Education in the New Global Era.* Los Angeles: International Studies and Overseas Programs, University of California: 76-86.

Metzler, John. 2000. "Strengthening Reciprocity in Study-Abroad Programs." *African Issues* 28 (1&2): 13-19.

Meyer, et.al. 19997. "Turning the Brain Drain: The Case for Utilizing South Africa's Unique Intellectual Diaspora." *Science, Technology and Society* 2 (2).

Mhone, Guy C. Z. 1971. "The Case Against Africanists." *ISSUE: A Journal of Opinion* 3: 8-13.

Michael, Magali Cornier. 1996. *Feminism and the Postmodern Impulse: Post-World War II Fiction.* Albany, N.Y.: State University of New York Press.

Mikell, Gwendolyn. 1999. "Forging Mutuality: The ASA and Africa in the Coming Decades." *African Studies Review* 42 (1): 1-21.

___. 2000. "Deconstructing Gates' 'Wonders of the African World.'" *West Africa Review* 1, 2, 2000. <*Http://www.icaap.org/iuicode?101.1.2.14.*>

Miles, Jack. 1999. "Three Differences Between an Academic and an Intellectual: What Happens to the Liberal Arts When They Are Kicked off Campus?" *Cross Currents* 49 (3): 303-318.

Miller, Christopher. 1990. *Theories of Africans: Francophone Literature and*

Anthropology in Africa. Chicago: University of Chicago Press.

Minh-ha, T. T. 1996. "The Undone Interval." In Iain Chambers and Lidia Curti, eds. *The Post-Colonial Question: Common Skies, Divided Horizons.* London and New York: Routledge: 3-16.

Mittelman, James H. 1997a. "The Dynamics of Globalization." In James H. Mittelman, ed. *Globalization: Critical Reflections.* Boulder, Colorado: Lynne Rienner: 1-19.

___. 1997b. "How Does Globalization Really Work?" In James H. Mittelman, ed. *Globalization: Critical Reflections.* Boulder, Colorado: Lynne Rienner: 229-241.

___. 1998. "Globalization and Environmental Resistance Politics." *Third World Quarterly* 19 (5): 847-872.

Miyoshi, Masao. 1998. "'Globalization,' Culture, and the University." In F. Jameson and M. Miyoshi, eds. *The Cultures of Globalization.* Durham, N.C.: Duke University Press: 247-270.

Mkandawire, Thandika. 1989. "Problems and Prospects of the Social Sciences in Africa." *Eastern Africa Social Science Review* 5:1-17.

___. 1997a. "Globalization and Africa's Unfinished Agenda." *Macalaster International* 7: 71-107.

___. 1997b. "The Social Sciences in Africa: Breaking Local Barriers and Negotiating International Presence." *African Studies Review* 40, 2: 15-36.

___. 1998a. *Thinking About Development in Africa.* Study No. 9. African Development in a Comparative Perspective. Geneva: United Nations Conference on Trade and Development.

___. 1998b. "The Claude Ake Memorial Lecture," *Codesria General Assembly,* Dakar, Senegal, 14-18 December.

___. 1999. "African Intellectuals and the Changing Global Context." Paper presented as Keynote Address at the African Studies Association of Australasia and the Pacific, Perth, Australia, 26-28 November.

___. 2000. "Globalization-A Social Development Perspective." Unpublished paper.

Mkandawire, Thandika, and Charles C. Soludo. 1999. *Our Continent Our Future.* Trenton, NJ: Africa World Press.

Mkude, D. .J. 2001 (March). Reforming Higher Education: Change and Innovation in Finance and Administration: A Case Study of the University of Dar es Salaam. Paper presented at the Carter Lectures 2001, "Governance and Higher Education," University of Florida, Gainesville. 22-25 March.

Mlama, Penina. 2000. "African Perspectives on Programs for North American Students in Africa: The Experience of the University of Dar es

Salaam." *African Issues* 28 (1&2): 24-27.

Modleski, Tania. 1991. *Feminism Without Women: Culture and Criticism in a "Postfeminist" Age.* New York and London: Routledge.

Mohammadi, Ali. 1997. "Communication and the Globalization Process in the Developing World." In Ali Mohammadi, ed. *International Communication and Globalization.* London: Sage.

Mohanty, Satya P. 1997. *Literary Theory and the Claims of History: Postmodernism, Objectivity, Multicultural Politics.* Ithaca: Cornell University Press.

Moja, Teboho. 2000. "An Assessment of the Ford Foundation's Impact on Higher Education in Africa." Paper presented at the Ford Foundation Meeting on Higher Education Initiative in Africa, Johannesburg, South Africa, 6-7 April.

___. 2001. "African Universities of the Future." Paper presented at the Ford Foundation Retreat on Visioning the African University in 2050, Durban, South Africa, 29 May - 1 June.

Moja, Teboho, and Nico Cloete. 1996. "Transforming Higher Education in South Africa: A New Approach to Governance?" *Issue: A Journal of Opinion* 24 (I) : 10-16.

Molteno, Robert. 1997. "Copublishing and Coproduction as an Answer to Sustainable Book Production in Africa." Paper presented at the International Seminar on Book Production and Distribution in Africa. Chr. Michelsen Institute, Bergen, Norway, April 10-11.

Momoh, Abubakar. 1995. "The Political Economy of Transition to Civil Rule." In Said Adejumobi and Abubakar Momoh, eds. *The Political Economy of Nigeria Under Military Rule.* Harare: Sapes Books: 16-56.

Mongia, Padmini. 1996. "Introduction." In Padmini Mongia, ed. *Contemporary Postcolonial Theory: A Reader.* London: Arnold: 1-18.

Moore, David. 1995. "Postmodernism and Modern Africa." 23 May. *H-AFRICA@H-NET.MSU.EDU, <http://www.h-net.msu.edu/~africa/threads/pomothread.html>*

Moore, Henrietta, ed. 1996. *The Future of Anthropological Knowledge.* New York: Routledge Press.

Moreiras, Alberto. 1998. "Global Fragments: A Second Latinamericanization." In Fredric Jameson and Masao Miyoshi, eds. *The Cultures of Globalization.* Durham and London: Duke University Press: 81-102.

Morgan, Gordon D. 1991. "Afrocentricity in Social Science." *The Western Journal of Black Studies* 15, 4:197-205.

Morley, David and Kevin Robins. 1995. *Spaces of Identity: Global Media, Electronic Landscapes and Cultural Boundaries.* London and New York: Routledge.

Morley, David and Kuan-Hsing Chen, eds. 1996. *Stuart Hall: Critical Dialogues in Cultural Studies.* London and New York: Routledge.

Morna, Colleen L. 1995. "The Plight of Universities." *Africa Report* 40,2:30-33.

Morris, Sarah. 1996. "International Academic Cooperation in the Arab Region. Past, Present and Future." In Peggy Blumenthal et al., eds. *Academic Mobility in a Changing World: Regional and Global Issues,* London and Bristol, Pa: Jessica Kingsley Publishers: 300-319.

Mphande, Lupenga. 1996. "Dr. Hastings Banda and the Malawi Writers Group: The (Un)Making of a Cultural Transition." *Research in African Literatures* 27:80-101.

Mporamazina, Jean-Claude. 1999. "Mainstreaming Africa: Reply." 22 November. *<H-AFRICA@H-NET.MSU.EDU>*

Mshomba, Richard E. *Africa in the Global Economy.* Boulder and London: Lynne Rienner.

Mudimbe, V. Y. 1988. *The Invention of Africa: Gnosis, Philosophy, and the Order of Knowledge.* Bloomington and Indianapolis: Indiana University Press.

___. 1994. *The Idea of Africa.* Bloomington and Indianapolis: Indiana University Press.

Mukasa, G. 2000. "Soyinka-Mazrui-Gates etc.," 5 February *<toyin.falola@mail.utexas.edu>*

Mukherjee, Arun P. 1990. "Whose Post-Colonialism and Whose Postmodernism?" *World Literature Written in English* 30 (2): 1-9.

Murdoch, J. 1997. "Towards a Geography of Heterogeneous Associations." *Progress in Human Geography* 21 (3): 321-337.

Murdoch, H. Adlai. 2001. *Creole Identity in the French Caribbean Novel.* Gainesville: University of Florida Press.

Murray, Bruce K. 1997. *Wits: The "Open" Years: A History of the University of the Witwatersrand.* Johannesburg, South Africa: Witwatersrand University Press.

Murray, Heather. 1995. "English Studies in Canada and the Case of Postcolonial Culture." *Essays on Canadian Writing* 56: 51-77.

Mwangi Wambui. 2001 (June). "To Play the Fool: What's "African" about Universities, Anyways?" Paper presented at the Ford Foundation Retreat in Durban, South Africa.

Mwaura, Peter. 1999. "UNESCO Pushes for Science in Africa." *African Recovery* 12,4:30.

Myers, Greg. 1990. *Writing Biology: Texts in the Social Constitution of Scientific Knowledge.* Madison: University of Wisconsin Press.

Nabudere, Dani W. 2000. "Globalization, The African Post-Colonial State, Post-Traditionalism, and the New World Order." In Dani W. Nabudere, ed. *Globalization and the Post-Colonial African State.* Harare, Zimbabwe: Sapes Books: 7-55.

Najjar, Fauzi M. 1998. "Islamic Fundamentalism and the Intellectuals: The Case of Naguib Mahfouz." *British Journal of Middle Eastern Studies* 25,1:139-162.

National Summit on Africa. 1998a. *Economic Development, Trade and Investment, and Creation. Thematic Working Paper Series.* Washington, D.C.: The National Summit on Africa.

____. 1998b. *Bird's Eye View of Midwest-Africa Trade Linkages.* Washington, D.C.: National Summit on Africa.

Nazer, H. M. 1999. *Power of a Third Kind: The Western Attempt to Colonize the Global Village.* Westport, Conn.: Praeger.

Næste, Indhold Forrige. 1997. "Nordic Africa Institute. Chapter 3. Assessment of NAI's Activities."<http://www.um-dk/danida/evalueringsrapporter/1997-5/kap3.asp>

Ndebele, Njabulo S. 2001 (June). "The African University of the 21st Century." Paper presented at the Ford Foundation Retreat on Visioning the African University in 2050, Durban, South Africa, 29 May - 1 June.

Nealon, Jeffrey T. 1993. *Double Reading: Postmodernism After Deconstruction.* Ithaca, N.Y.: Cornell University Press.

Nelson, Cary. 1996. "Literature as Cultural Studies. 'American' Poetry of the Spanish Civil War." In Cary Nelson and Dilip P. Gaonkar, eds. *Disciplinarity and Dissent in Cultural Studies.* New York: Routledge: 63-102.

Nelson, Cary and Dilip P. Gaonkar, eds. 1996. *Disciplinarity and Dissent in Cultural Studies.* NewYork: Routledge.

Nelson, Charles M. 1996. "PAT 101 Principles of Patronage." *Issue: A Journal of Opinion* 24 (1): 45-51.

Newman, Frank. 2000. "Saving Higher Education's Soul." *Change* 32 (5): 16-23.

Ngara, Emmanuel. 1995. *The African University and Its Mission.* Roma, Lesotho: Institute of Southern African Studies.

Nguessan, M. 1996. "Language and Human Rights in Africa." Colloquium on Language Legislation and Linguistic Rights, University of Illinois at Urbana-Champaign, 21-23 March.

Niang, Souleymane. 1997. "African Universities and Globalization." Keynote address, African Regional Consultation Preparatory to the World Conference on Higher Education. Dakar, Senegal, 1-4 April.

Nimer, B. 1970. "Politics and Scholarship in African Studies in the United States." *African Studies Review* 13 (3): 353-361.

Njisane, Mlahleni. 1971. "The African Studies Association: Priority Issues." *ISSUE: A Journal of Opinion* 1: 2-5.

Nkosi, Lewis. 1998. "Postmodernism and Black Writing in South Africa." In Derek Attridge and Rosemary Jolly, eds. *Writing South Africa: Literature, Apartheid and Democracy 1970-1995.* New York: Cambridge University Press: 75-90.

Nkrumah, Gamal. 2001. "Building Cultural Bridges." 24-30 May. Al-Ahram Weekly Online. <http://www.ahram.org.eg/weekly/2001/535/fe3.htm>

Novick, Peter. 1988. *That Noble Dream: The 'Objectivity Question' and the American Historical Profession.* Cambridge: Cambridge University Press.

Ntaragwi, Mwenda. 2000. "Education, Tourism, or Just a Visit to the Wild?" *African Issues* 28 (1&2): 54-60.

Nurius, P. and C. Franklin. 1998. "The Role of Gender in Practice Knowledge Research." In A.Casebolt, F. E. Netting, and J. Figueira-McDonough, eds. *The Role of Gender in Practice Knowledge: Claiming Half of the Human Experience.* New York: Longman.

Nwamuo, Chris. 2001. "Increasing Access to Higher Education in Africa: Emerging Issues." *AAU Newsletter* 6 (2): 1-3.

Nwauwa, Apollos O. 1997. *Imperialism, Academe and Nationalism: British and University Education for Africans 1860-1960.* London: Frank Cass.

Nyang'oro, Julius E. 1997. "Funding African Studies in the Twenty-First Century." *Africa Today* 44, 2 :163-167.

Nyariki, L. and R. Makotsi. 1995. "Problems of Book Marketing and Distribution in Kenya." *African Publishing Review* 4 (2): 11.

Nzegwu, Nkiru. 2001. "The Politics of Gender in African Studies." In Cassandra R. Veney and Paul T. Zeleza, *Women in African Studies Scholarly Publishing.* Trenton, N.J.: Africa World Press: 111-146.

Nzotta, Briggs C. 1994. "Journal Publishing in Nigeria: An Editor's View." In M. Wise, ed. *Survival Under Adverse Conditions: Proceedings of the African Library Science Workshop.* The Hague, Netherlands: International Federation of Library Associations and Institutions. IFLA Professional Reports, No.38.

O'Neill, J. 1990. "AIDS as a Globalizing Panic." In M. Featherstone, ed. *Global Culture.* London: Sage: 329-42.

O'Sullivan, T., B. Dutton, and P. Rayner. 1994. *Studying the Media: An Introduction.* New York: Edward Arnold.

Ochieng, William R. and Karim K. JanMohamed, eds. 1977. *Some Perspectives on the Mau Mau Movement.* Special Issue of *Kenya Historical Review* 5 (2).

Ogot, Bethwell A. 2001. *Selected Essays, 1961-1998.* Trenton, NJ: Africa World Press (forthcoming).

Ogot, Bethwell Alan and Paul Tiyambe Zeleza. 1988. "Kenya's Bumpy Road to Independence and After." In P. Gifford and W. R. Louis, *Decolonization and African Independence.* New Haven: Yale University Press: 401-426

Ohmae, Kenichi. 1990. *The Borderless World: Power and Strategy in the Interlinked Economy.* New York: Harper Business.

____. 1996. *The End of the Nation State.* New York: Harper Collins.

Okeke, Philomena E. 1996. "Postmodern Feminism and Knowledge Production: The African Context."*Africa Today* 43 (3): 223-233.

Olagunju, Tunji, Adele Jinadu, and Sam Oyovbaire. 1993. *Transition to Democracy in Nigeria (1985-1993).* Ibadan: Safari Books.

Olden, Anthony. 1994. "What Gets Published Overseas on Africa: Articles in Library Journals Compared and Contrasted with Academic Books that Win Awards." In C. Wise, ed. *Survival Under Adverse Conditions: Proceedings of the African Library Science Workshop.* The Hague, Netherlands: International Federation of Library Associations and Institutions. IFLA Professional Reports, No. 38.

Olukoshi, Adebayo. 2001 (June). "The African University of My Dream." Paper presented at the Ford Foundation Retreat in Durban, South Africa.

Omvedt, Gail. 1993. *Reinventing Revolution: New Social Movements and the Socialist Tradition in India.* Armonk, N.Y.: M. E. Sharpe.

Ong, Aihwa. 1996. "Anthropology, China and Modernities: The Geopolitics of Cultural Knowledge." In Henrietta L. Moore, ed. *The Future of Anthropological Knowledge.* London: Routledge: 60-93.

Oni, Bankole. 2000. "Capacity Building Effort and Brain Drain in Nigerian Universities." Paper presented at the Regional Conference on Brain Drain and Capacity Building in Africa. UNECA, Addis Ababa, 22-24 February. <http://www.uneca.org/search-home.htm>

Oppenheim, Lois. 2001. "France Takes Its Intellectuals to Heart, Even as They Doubt Themselves." *The Chronicle of Higher Education* 7 September: B7-B10.

Ortner, Sherry B. 1999. "The Future of Anthropological Knowledge." *American Ethnologist* 26 (4): 984-991.

Osundina, Oyeniyi. 1995. "Networking and Information Capacities in Africa." In J. van Laar, ed. *Capacity Building for Development Information.* Maastricht, Netherlands: ECDPM: 25-31.

Ouma, Symphrose. 1994. "Publishing Library Science Journals: The Case of Maktaba and Other Kenyan Library Association Publications." In M. Wise, ed. *Survival Under Adverse Conditions: Proceedings of the African Library Science Workshop.* The Hague, Netherlands: International Federation of Library Associations and Institutions. IFLA Professional Reports, No.38.

Ouma, Gerald Wangenge. 2001 (June). "The African University of the Year 2050." Paper presented at the Ford Foundation Retreat in Durban, South Africa.

Owomoyela, Oyekan. 1994. "With Friends Like These ... A Critique of Pervasive Anti-Africanisms in Current African Studies Epistemology and Methodology." *African Studies Review* 37 (3): 77-101.

___. 2000. "Soyinka: A Perfect Symmetry?" 6 February. *<toyin.falola@mail.utexas.edu>*

Owusu, Maxwell. 1971. "Anthropology: New Insights...or Just New Stereotypes." *Africa Report* 16 (7): 23-24.

Parpart, Jane L. 1995. " Is Africa A Postmodern Invention?" *Issue: A Journal of Opinion 23,* (1):16-18.

Parry, Benita. 1994. "Resistance Theory/Theorising Resistance, or Two Cheers for Nativism." In Francis Barker, Peter Hulme and Margaret Ives, eds. *Colonial Discourse/Postcolonial Theory.* Manchester: Manchester University Press: 172-196.

Patai, Daphne. 2000. "Will the Real Feminists in Academe Please Stand Up?" *The Chronicle of Higher Education* 47 (6) Oct 6: B6-B9.

PBS, 1999. "Wonders of the African World - Behind the Scenes." <wysi-wyg://496/http://www.pbs.org/wonders/BehindSc/behind.htm>

Peace, Ade. 1998. "Anthropology in the Postmodern Landscape: The Importance of Cultural Brokers and Their Trade." *Australian Journal of Anthropology* 9 (3): 274-284.

Pechey, Graham. 1994. "Post-Apartheid Narratives." In Francis Barker, Peter Hulme, and Margaret Iversen, eds. *Colonial Discourse/Postcolonial Theory.* Manchester, UK.: Manchester University Press: 151-171.

Peil, Margaret. 1996. "Ghana's Universities and Their Government: An Ambiguous Relationship." *Issue: A Journal of Opinion* 24 (1): 52-56.

Pendleton, Denise C. 2000. "A Broad Perspective: Reflections of an African Study Abroad." *African Issues* 28 (1&2): 117-118.

Peterson, Patti M. 2001. "The Balance of Trade in International Education: A New Model of Globalization." *Vital Speeches of the Day* 67 (20): 638-640.

Petras, James. 1990. "Metamorphosis of Latin American Intellectuals."

470

CODESRIA Bulletin 1: 7-8.

Petras, James. 1999. "Globalization: A Critical Analysis." *Journal of Contemporary Asia* 29 (1): 3-37.

Philips, Howard. 2000. "What Did Your University Do During Apartheid?" *Journal of Southern African Studies* 26 (1): 173-177.

Philips, John Edward. 1999. "Mainstreaming Africa: Reply." 23 November. <H-AFRICA@H-NET.MSU.EDU>

Philip, Mary-Christine. 1994. "25 Years of Black Studies: Pondering Strategies for the Future." *Black Issues in Higher Education* 11, 5: 14-19.

Pieterse, J. N. 1995. "Globalization as Hybridization." In M. Featherstone, S. Lash, and R. Robertson, eds. *Global Culture: Nationalism, Globalization and Modernity.* London: Sage.

Piper, Karen. 1999. "Post-Colonialism in the United States: Diversity or Hybridity?" In Deborah L. Madsen, ed. *Post-Colonial Literatures: Expanding the Canon.* London: Pluto Press: 14-28.

Pires, Mark. 2000. "Study Abroad and Cultural Exchange Programs to Africa: America's Image of a Continent." *African Issues* 28 (1&2): 39-45.

Pires, Mark, Ron Kassimir, and M. Brhane. 1999. *Investing in Return: Rates of Return of African Ph.D.'s Trained in North America.* New York: Social Science Research Council.

Pires, Mark with Oumatie Marajh and John Metzler. 2000. "Study Abroad in Africa: A Survey." *African Issues* 28 (1&2): 4-12.

Pitchford, Nicola. 1998. "The Decentered Subject in Opposition." *Contemporary Literature* 39 (1):140-145.

Piven, Frances F. and Richard A. Cloward. 1998. "Eras of Power." *Monthly Review* 49 (January): 11-23.

___. 2000. "Power Repertoires and Globalization." *Politics & Society* 28 (3): 413-430.

Pogue, Frank G. 1993. "The Future of Black Studies." *Vital Speeches of the Day* 59: 536-540.

Posnock, Ross. 1996. "A View from an English Department." *Intellectual History Newsletter* 18:18-20.

Prah, Kwesi K. 1997. *Beyond The Colour Line: Pan-Africanist Disputations.* Lea Glen, Florida: Vivlia Publishers.

Prakash, Gyan. 1995. "Introduction: After Colonialism." In Gyan Prakash, ed. *After Colonialism: Imperial Histories and Postcolonial Displacements.* Princeton, NJ: Princeton University Press.

Prakash, Aseem and Jeffrey A. Hart. 1999. *Globalization and Governance.* London and New York: Routledge.

Presley, Cora Ann. 1992. *Kikuyu Women, the Mau Mau Rebellion, and Social*

Change in Kenya. Boulder, Colo.: Westview Press.

Preston, George Nelson. 2000. "Wondergates." *West Africa Review* 1, 2 <Http://www.icaap.org/iuicode?101.1.2.17>

Prewitt, Kenneth. 1996a. "Presidential Items." *Items* 50, 1:15-18.

___. 1996a. "Presidential Items." *Items* 50 (2-3): 1-9

Priestly, Carol. 1996. "Publishing and Library Support for Africa: An Update." London: International Africa Institute. Unpublished.

Prior, Paul A. 1998. *Writing/Disciplinarity: A Sociohistoric Account of Literate Activity in the Academy*. London: Lawrence Erlbaum Associates.

Puddington, Arch. 2000. "Sulking Above the Fray." *American Spectator* 33,5:71-73.

Quayson, Ato. 2000. *Postcolonialism: Theory, Practice or Process*. Cambridge: Polity Press.

___. 2001. "Breaches in the Commonplace: Achille Mbembe's *On the Postcolony*." 16 August <*www.h-net.msu.edu*>

Rafael, Vincente L.1994. "The Cultures of Area Studies in the United States." *Social Text* 38 : 92-111

Ranger, Terence. 1983. "The Invention of Tradition in Colonial Africa." In Eric Hobsbawm and Terence Ranger, eds. *The Invention of Tradition*. Cambridge: Cambridge University Press: 211-262.

Ray, Larry. J. 1993. *Rethinking Critical Theory: Emancipation in the Age of Global Social Movements*. Newbury Park, Calif.: Sage.

Redcliffe, Quinton P., and Lesley Y. Shackleton. 2000. "The Southern Gateway to Africa." *African Issues*, 28 (1&2): 108-111.

Reed, Adolph. 1995. "What Are the Drums Saying, Booker? The Current Crisis of the Black Intellectual." *Village Voice* 11 April: 31-36.

___. 1997. *W.E.B. DuBois and American Political Thought: Fabianism and The Color Line*. New York: Oxford University Press.

Reich, Robert B. 1991. *The Work of Nations*. New York: Alfred Knopf.

Reinsch, Lamar N. 1996. "New Times Demand New Degree Programs." *Vital Speeches of the Day* 62 (19): 592-594.

Resnick, I. N. 1969a. "The Future of African Studies After Montreal." *Africa Report* 15 (9):

___. 1969b. "Crisis in African Studies." *Africa Today* 16 (5&6): 14-15.

Reyna, S. P. 1994. "Literary Anthropology and the Case Against Science." *Man* 29 (3): 555-582.

Reynolds, Jonathan. 1999a. "Mainstreaming Africa: Replies." 15 November. <*H-AFRICA@H-NET.MSU.EDU*>,

___. 1999b. "'Wonders of the African World': Reply." 2 November. <*H-AFRICA@H-NET.MSU.EDU*>

Rhoades, Gary and Slaughter, Sheila. 1997. "Academic Capitalism, Managed Professionals, and Supply-Side Higher Education." *Social Text* 51: 9-38.

Richardson, Laurel. 1991a. "Postmodern Social Theory: Representational Practices. *Sociological Theory* 9: 173-179.

____. 1991b. "Speakers Whose Voices Matter: Toward a Feminist Postmodernist Sociological Praxis." In Norman K. Denzin, ed. *Studies in Symbolic Interaction.* Greenwich, Conn.: JAI Press, 12: 29-38.

Riggs, Alma. 2000. "Akwaaba! My Welcome to Ghana." *African Issues* 28 (1&2): 134-139.

Ringwald, Lawrence. 1999. "Female Circumcision." 16 November. <*H-AFRO-AM@H-NET.MSU.EDU*>

Rivers, Eugene F. 1995. "Beyond the Nationalism of Fools: Toward an Agenda for Black Intellectuals." *Boston Review* xx, 3. <*http://bostonreview.mit.edu/BostonReview/BR20.3/rivers.html*>

Robertson, Roland. 1992. *Globalization: Social Theory and Global Culture.* London: Sage.

____. 1995. "Globalization." In M. Featherstone, S. Lash, and R. Robertson, eds. *Global Culture: Nationalism, Globalization and Modernity.* London: Sage.

Robertson, R. and J. A. Chirico. 1985. "Humanity, Globalization and World-Wide Religious Resurgence." *Sociological Analysis* 46 (3): 219-241.

Robinson, Pear T. 1997. "Local/Global Linkages and the Future of African Studies." *Africa Today* 44 (2): 169-178.

Robinson, Pearl T., with Andrew Kiondo and Hail Seif Mohamed. 2001. "Curriculum Co-Development: Asynchronous Networks for Bringing International Perspectives to Learning." Paper presented at the Carter Lectures 2001, "Governance and Higher Education," University of Florida, Gainesville. 22-25 March.

Robotham, Don. 2000. "Postcolonialities: The Challenge of New Modernities." *International Social Science Journal* 52: 357-371.

Rodriguez, Linda A. 1998. "Immigration, Ethnic Groups, and Area Studies." In John Hawkins et al., eds. *International Education in the New Global Era.* Los Angeles: International Studies and Overseas Programs, University of California: 155-163.

Rodrik, Dani. 1996. "Why Do More Open Economies Have Bigger Government?" NBER Working Paper No.5537. Cambridge, Mass.: NBER, March.

____. 1997. "Sense and Nonsense in the Globalization Debate." *Foreign*

Policy 107 (Summer): 19-37.

Roeloffs, Karl. 1996. "Academic Mobility Programmes in a Regional Context. A German Viewpoint." In Peggy Blumenthal et al., *Academic Mobility in a Changing World. Regional and Global Issues.* London and Bristol, Pa: Jessica Kingsley Publishers.

Romano, Carlin. 1999. "The Dirty Little Secret About Publicity Intellectuals." *The Chronicle of Higher Education* 19 February: B4.

Rorty, Richard. 1982. *Consequences of Pragmatism.* Minneapolis: University of Minnesota Press.

___. 1989. *Contingency, Irony, and Solidarity.* Cambridge: Cambridge University Press.

___. 1991. *Essays on Heidegger and Others.* Cambridge: Cambridge University Press.

___. 1997. "Intellectuals and the Millennium." *The New Leader* 80 (24 February): 10-11.

Rosaldo, Renato.1989. *Culture and Truth: The Remaking of Social Analysis.* Boston: Beacon Press.

Roseneau, James N. 2000. "The Challenges and Tensions of a Globalization World." *American Studies International* 38 (2): 8-22.

Ross, Andrew. 1996. "Cultural Studies and the Challenge of Science." In Cary Nelson and Dilip P. Gaonkar, eds. 1996. *Disciplinarity and Dissent in Cultural Studies.* Routledge: New York: 171-184.

Roth, Paul A. 1988. "Narrative Explanations: The Case of History." *History and Theory* 27:1-13.

___. 1991. "Truth in Interpretation." *Philosophy of the Social Sciences* 21:175-195.

Rothenberg, Paula S. 2000. *Invisible Privilege: A Memoir About Race, Class, and Gender.* Lawrence, Kansas: University Press of Kansas.

Rothkopf, D. 2000. "In Praise of Cultural Imperialism?" In Patrick O'Meara, Howard D. Mehlinger, and Mathew Krain, eds. *Globalization and the Challenges of a New Century.* Bloomington and Indianapolis: Indiana University Press: 443-453.

Rotz, Rhiman. 1999. "Mainstreaming Africa: Reply." 27 November. <*H-AFRICA@H-NET.MSU.EDU*>

Rubin, Amy M. 1995. "Defending Academic Exchanges." *The Chronicle of Higher Education* 41 (23): A41-A42.

Sachs, Jeffrey D. 1995. "Consolidating Capitalism." *Foreign Affairs* 98 (Spring): 50-64.

___. 2000. "A New Map of the World." *The Economist* 24 June.

Sacks, Peter. 1996. *Generation X Goes to College: An Eye-Opening Account of*

Teaching in Postmodern America. Chicago: Open Court.

Sadawoski, Y. 1998. *The Myth of Global Chaos.* Washington, D.C.: Brookings Institution Press.

Said, Edward W. 1979. *Orientalism.* New York: Vintage Books.

____. 1993. *Culture and Imperialism.* New York: Alfred Knopf.

Sakakibara, Eisuke. 1995. " The End of Progressivism: A Search for New Goals." *Foreign Affairs* 74 (5): 8-14.

Saldívar, J. D. 1997. "Tracking English and American Literary and Cultural Criticism." *Daedalus* 126, (1): 155-174.

Salih, M.A. Mohamed. 2001 (June). "A Breakaway African University." Paper presented at the Ford Foundation Retreat in Durban, South Africa.

Salleh, Ariel. 1997. *Ecofeminism as Politics: Nature, Marx and the Postmodern.* London: Zed Books.

Sandenburgh, Polly and Acacia Schut. 2000. "Teaching in Africa: Two Programs for Educators." *African Issues* 28 (1&2): 93-102.

Sanders, Mark. 1999. "'Problems of Europe': N.P. van Wyk Louw, the Intellectual and Apartheid." *Journal of Southern African Studies* 25, 4: 607-631.

Sangari, K. 1990. "The Politics of the Possible." In A. R. JanMohamed and D. Lloyd, eds. *The Nature and Context of Minority Discourse.* Oxford: Oxford University Press: 216-245.

Sassen, Saskia. 1991. *Global City.* Princeton, NJ: Princeton University Press.

____. 1997. "The Spatial Organization of Information Industries: Implications for the Role of the State." In James H. Mittelman, ed. *Globalization: Critical Reflections.* Boulder, Colo.: Lynne Rienner: 33-52.

____. 2001. "Spatialities and Temporalities of the Global: Elements for a Theorization." In Arjun Appadurai, ed. *Globalization.* Durham and London: Duke University Press: 260-278.

Saunders, Frances Stonor. 1999. *The Cultural Cold War: The CIA and the World of Arts and Letters.* New York: The New Press.

Scarfo, Richard D. 1998. "History of Title VI/Fulbright-Hays." In John Hawkins et al., eds. *International Education in the New Global Era.* Los Angeles: International Studies and Overseas Programs, University of California: 23-25.

Schlegel, Markus. 1994. "Fostering Brain Drain: Data-communications in the Developing World With Special Regard to the Situation on the African Continent." *<http://www.sas.upenn.edu/AfricanStudies/ArticlesGen/BrainDrain.html>*

Schneider, Alison. 1999. "Florida Atlantic U. Seeks to Mold a Different

Kind of Public Intellectual." *The Chronicle of Higher Education* 29 October: A18.

Schuler, Monica. 1999. "'Wonders of the African World': Replies." 3 November. *<H-AFRICA@H-NET.MSU.EDU>*

Scott, Alan. 1997. "Introduction." In A. Scott, ed. *The Limits of Globalization.* London and New York: Routledge.

Scott, Joan W. 1988. *Gender and the Politics of History.* Ithaca, NY: Cornell University Press.

____. 1994. "Deconstructing Equality-Versus-Difference: Or, the Uses of Poststructuralist Theory for Feminism." In Steven Seidman, ed., *The Postmodern Turn: New Perspectives On Social Theory.* New York: Cambridge University Press: 282-298.

Scott, Peter, ed. 1998. *Globalization and Higher Education.* Buckingham, UK: Open University Press.

Seidman, Steven. 1994a. "Introduction." In Steven Seidman, ed. *The Postmodern Turn: New Perspectives on Social Theory.* New York: Cambridge University Press: 1-23.

____. 1994b. "The End of Sociological Theory." In Steven Seidman, ed. *The Postmodern Turn: New Perspectives On Social Theory.* New York: Cambridge University Press: 119-139.

____. 1994c. *Contested Knowledge: Social Theory in the Postmodern Era.* Oxford: Blackwell.

Semambo, Clare. 2001 (June). "Vision 2050: African Universities 'Education for All' with Special Reference to Special Needs Education." Paper presented at the Ford Foundation Retreat on Visioning the African University in 2050, Durban, South Africa, 29 May-1 June.

Serequeberhan, Tsenay. 1997. "The Critique of Ethnocentrism and the Practice of African Philosophy." In Emmanuel Chukwudi Eze, ed. *Postcolonial African Philosophy: A Critical Reader.* Cambridge, Mass.: Blackwell: 141-161.

Serfontein, J. H. P. 1978. *Brotherhood of Power: An Exposé of the Secret Afrikaner Broederbond.* London: R. Collings.

Shami, Seteney. 2001. "Prehistories of Globalization: Circassian Identity in Motion." In Arjun Appadurai, ed. *Globalization.* Durham and London: Duke University Press: 220-250.

Sharlet, Jeff. 2000. "Tinker, Writer, Artist, Spy: Intellectuals During the Cold War." *The Chronicle of Higher Education* 46 (30) 31 March: A19-A20.

Shaw, Timothy M. 1993. *Reformism and Revisionism in Africa's Political Economy in the 1990s.* New York: Macmillan's Press.

Shear, Mervyn. 1996. *Wits: A University in the Apartheid Era.* Johannesburg, South Africa: Witwatersrand University Press.

Shepherd, G. W. 1969. "Pluralism and Parity in African Studies." *Africa Today* 16 (5&6): 1-2.

Sherwood, Marika. 1999. "'Wonders of the African World': Replies." 3 November. *<H-AFRICA@H-NET.MSU.EDU>*

Shohat, E. 1996. "Notes on the 'Post-Colonial.'" In P. Mongia, ed., *Contemporary Postcolonial Theory: A Reader.* London: Arnold: 321-334.

Shweder, Richard A. 1984. "Anthropology's Romantic Rebellion Against the Enlightenment, or There Is More to Thinking than Reason and Evidence." In R. Shweder and R. Levine, eds. *Culture Theory: Essays on Mind, Self and Emotion.* Cambridge: Cambridge University Press.

Shweder, Richard A, ed. 1991. *Thinking Through Cultures: Expeditions in Cultural Psychology.* Cambridge, Mass.: Harvard University Press.

Sibley, E. 1974. *Social Science Research Council: The First Fifty Years.* New York: Social Science Research Council.

Sicherman, Carol M. 1989. "Ngugi wa Thiong'o and the Writing of Kenyan History." *Research in African Literatures* 20 (3): 347-70.

Siemens, Robert. 1995a. "Henry George: An Unrecognized Contributor to American Social Theory." *The American Journal of Economics and Sociology* 54: 107-127.

___. 1995b. "Henry George and Social Theory: Part II, Consequences of Inattention to His Contributions." *The American Journal of Economics and Sociology* 54: 249-256.

Simanovsky, Stanilav, Margarita P. Strepetova, and Yu G. Naido. 1995. *Brain Drain From Russia: Problems, Prospects, and Regulation.* Commack, New York: Nova Science Publishers.

Simatei, Peter. 1999. "Versions and Inversions: Mau Mau in Kahiga's Dedan Kimathi: The Real Story." *Research in African Literatures* 30 (1): 154-61.

Simpson, David. 1995. *The Academic Postmodern and the Rule of Literature: A Report on Half-Knowledge.* Chicago: University of Chicago Press.

Sivanandan, A. 1998. "Globalism and the Left." *Race and Class* 40 (2 / 3): 5-19.

Sivier, D. J. 1997. "The Lost Intellectuals of Blair's Britain." *Contemporary Review* 27 (1581): 188-191.

Skidelsky, Edward. 1996. "Perry Anderson: He's One of Britain's Great Marxist Intellectuals, Yet Now He Seems a Strangely Conservative Figure." *New Statesman* 129 (4428) 19 March: 18-19.

Sklair, Leslie. 1991. *The Sociology of the Global System.* New York: Prentice Hall.

____. 1998. "Social Movements and Global Capitalism." In F. Jameson and M. Miyoshi, eds. *The Cultures of Globalization*. Durham, N.C.: Duke University Press: 291-311.

Sklar, R. L. 1969. "Politics and Scholarship." *Africa Today* 16 (5&6): 11-12.

Slemon, Stephen. 1996. "Unsettling the Empire: Resistance Theory for the Second World." In Padmini Mongia, ed. *Contemporary Postcolonial Theory: A Reader*. London: Arnold: 72-83.

Slobin, Kathleen. 2000. "Tracking the Imaginary, Postcolonial Subject in West Africa." *Qualitative Inquiry* 6 (2): 188-211.

Smallwood, Anthony and T. L. Maliyamkono. 1996. "Regional Cooperation and Mobility in Higher Education. The Implications for Human Resource Development in Sub-Saharan Africa and the Relevance of Recent Initiatives in Europe." In Peggy Blumenthal et al.,eds. *Academic Mobility in a Changing World. Regional and Global Issues*. London and Bristol: Jessica Kingsley Publishers.

Smith, Alan. 1996. "Regional Cooperation and Mobility in Global Setting. The Example of the European Union." In Peggy Blumenthal et al., *Academic Mobility in a Changing World. Regional and Global Issues*. London and Bristol: Jessica Kingsley Publishers, 1996.

Smith, Barbara H. 1988. *Contingencies of Value: Alternative Perspectives for Critical Theory*. Cambridge, Mass.: Harvard University Press.

Smith, Jeremy. 1997. "Faculty, Students, and Political Engagement." *Social Text* 51:131-142.

Smith, Rogers M. 1997. "Still Blowing in the Wind: The American Quest for a Democratic, Scientific Political Science." *Daedalus* 126 (1): 253-287.

Smock, Audrey C. 1970. "A Critical Look at American Africanist." *Africa Report* 15,9:23-24.

Smyth, John and Robert Hattam. 2000. "Intellectual as Hustler: Researching Against the Grain of the Market." *British Educational Research Journal* 26 (2): 157-175.

Sokal, Alan D. 1996a. "Transgressing the Boundaries: Towards a Transformative Hermeneutics of Quantum Gravity." *Social Text* 11 (November).

____. 1996b. "A Physicist Experiments with Cultural Studies." *Lingua Franca* (May/June): 62-64.

____. 2000. *The Sokal Hoax: The Sham That Shook the Academy*. Lincoln: University of Nebraska Press.

Solomon, Robert, and Jon Solomon. 1993. *Up the University: Re-Creating Higher Education in America*. Reading, Mass.: Addison-Wesley.

Solow, Robert M. 1997. "How Did Economics Get That Way and What Way Did it Get?" *Daedalus* 126, 1:39-57.

Soros, George. 1998. *The Crisis of Global Capitalism.* New York: Public Affairs.

Southgate, Beverley. 2001. *History: What and Why: Ancient, Modern, and Postmodern Perspectives.* London and New York: Routledge.

Soyinka, Wole. 2000a. "Ali Mazrui and Skip Gates' Africa Series." *West Africa Review* 1, 2. <*Http://www.icaap.org/iuicode?101.1.2.19*>

___. 2000b. "The Problem With You, Ali Mazrui! Response To Ali's Millenial Conclusion." *West Africa Review* 1, 2 <*Http://www.icaap. org/iuicode?101.1.2.20*>

Spitzer, Alan B. 1996. *Historical Truth and Lies About the Past.* Chapel Hill: University of North Carolina Press.

Spivak, Gayatri C. 1988a. *In Other Worlds: Essays in Cultural Politics.* New York and London: Routledge.

___. 1988b. "Can the Subaltern Speak?" In Cary Nelson and Lawrence Grossberg, eds. *Marxism and the Interpretation of Culture.* Urbana: University of Illinois Press: 271-313.

___. 1999. *A Critique of Postcolonial Reason: Toward a History of the Vanishing Present.* Cambridge: Harvard University Press.

Spring, Joel. 1998. *Education and the Rise of the Global Economy.* Mahwah, N.J.: Lawrence Erlbaum.

Ssebuwufu, P.J.M. 2001 "Reforming Higher Education: Change and Innovation in Finance and Governance." Paper presented at the Carter Lectures 2001, "Governance and Higher Education," University of Florida, Gainesville. 22-25 March.

Stallings, Barbara, ed. 1995. *Global Change, Regional Response: The New International Context of Development.* Cambridge: Cambridge University Press.

Staniland, M. 1983. "Who Needs African Studies?" *African Studies Review* 26: 77-97.

Steinberg, Michael P. 1996. "Cultural History and Cultural Studies." In Cary Nelson and Dilip P. Gaonkar, eds. *Disciplinarity and Dissent in Cultural Studies.* Routledge: New York: 103-129.

Steinweis, Alan. 1995. "Postmodernism and German History." 8-9-95 <*aes@unlinfo.unl.edu*>

Stone, M. Priscilla. 1997. "The Remaking of African Studies." *Africa Today* 44, 2: 179-184.

Storper, M. 1997. "Territories, Flows, and Hierarchies in the Global Economy." In K. R. Cox, *Spaces of Globalization: Reasserting the Power of the Local.* New York: The Guilford Press: 19-44.

Straubhaar, J. D. 1997. "Distinguishing the Global, Regional and National Levels of World Television." In A. Sreberny-Mohammadi, D. Winseck, J. McKenna, and O. Boyd-Barrett, eds. *Media in Global Context: A Reader.* New York: Arnold.

Street, J. 1997. "'Across the Universe': The Limits of Global Popular Culture." In A. Scott, ed. The *Limits of Globalization.* London and New York: Routledge.

Streeten, Paul. 1993. "Markets and States: Against Minimalism." *World Development* 21 (8): 1,281-1,298.

____. 1998. "Globalization: Threat or Salvation." In A. S. Bhalla, eds. *Globalization, Growth and Marginalization.* New York: St. Martin's Press: 13-47.

Stromquist, Nelly P. 2000. "Voice, Harmony, and Fugue in Global Feminism." *Gender and Education* 12 (4): 419-433.

Sturges, P., and R. Neil. 1990. *The Quiet Struggle: Libraries and Information for Africa.* London: Mansell.

Suleri, S. 1996. "Women Skin Deep: Feminism and the Postcolonial Condition." In P. Mongia, ed. *Contemporary Postcolonial Theory: A Reader.* London: Arnold: 335-346.

Sutton, F. X. and D. R. Smock. 1976. 'The Ford Foundation and African Studies.' *ISSUE: A Quarterly Journal of Africanist Opinion* 7 (2/3): 68-72.

Swyngedouw, E. 1997. "Neither Global nor Local: 'Glocalization' and the Politics of Scale." K. R. Cox, *Spaces of Globalization: Reasserting the Power of the Local.* New York: The Guilford Press: 137-66.

Synott, Thomas. 2000. "Remaking the World Financial System." *Business Economics* 35 (3): 42-52.

Tabifor, Henry. 2001 (June). "A Personnal Narrative for the Facilitated Dialogue South Coast of Durban-South Africa." Paper presented at the Ford Foundation Retreat on Visioning the African University in 2050, Durban, South Africa, May 29-June 1.

Taiwo, Olufemi. 1997. "Exorcizing Hegel's Ghost: Africa's Challenge to Philosophy." *African Studies Quarterly* 1, 4. *http://web.africa.ufl.edu/asq/*

Tamale, Sylvia. 2001. "My Dream African University." Paper presented at the Ford Foundation Retreat on Visioning the African University in 2050, Durban, South Africa, 29 May - 1 June.

Tangian, S. A. 2001. "Higher Education in the Perspective of the Twenty-First Century." *Russian Education and Society* 43 (4): 28-42.

Tanter. 1999. "A Preliminary Critique of 'Wonders of the African World.'"

1 November. <*H-AFRO-AM@H-NET.MSU.EDU*>

Tanzer, Michael. 1995. "Globalizing the Economy: The Influence of the International Monetary Fund and the World Bank." *Monthly Review* 47 (4): 1-15.

Taylor, Ronald A.1995. "Black Studies in Whiteface." *Black Issues in Higher Education* 12, November : 25-27.

Taylor, P. J., J. Watts, and R. J. Johnston. 1995. "Re-mapping the World: What Sort of Map? What Sort of World." In P. J. Taylor, J. Watts, and R. J. Johnston, eds. *Geographies of Global Change: Remapping the World in the Twentieth Century.* Cambridge, Mass.: Blackwell.

Teferra, Damtew. 1995. "The Status and Capacity of Science Publishing in Africa." *Journal of Scholarly Publishing* 27(October): 28-36.

Teferra, Damtew. 1998. "The Significance of Information Technology for African Scholarly Journals." In Philip G. Altbach and Damtew Teferra, eds. *Knowledge Dissemination in Africa: The Role of Scholarly Journals.* Chestnut Hill, Mass.: Bellagio Studies in Publishing, 39-61.

____. 2000. "Revisiting the Brain Mobility Doctrine in the Information Age." Paper presented at the Regional Conference on Brain Drain and Capacity Building in Africa. UNECA, Addis Ababa. 22-24 February. <http://www.uneca.org/search_home.htm>

Teffen, George. 1995. "Postmodernism and Modern Africa." 30 May. *H-AFRICA@H-NET.MSU.EDU* <*http://www.h-net.msu.edu/~africa/threads/pomothread.html*>

Tehranian, M., and K. K. Tehranian, 1997. "Taming Modernity: Towards a New Paradigm." In Ali Mohammadi, ed. *International Communication and Globalization.* Thousand Oaks, Calif.: Sage.

Tehranian, Majid. 1999. *Global Communication and World Politics: Domination, Development, and Discourse.* Boulder, Colo.: Lynne Rienner.

Telman, Jeremy. 1995. "Postmodern Theory in German History and a Query." <*telmand@cofc.edu*> 8-8-95.

Tempo (Lagos). 1999. Editorial, "Save Universities From Cults and Dictators." July 21.

The Chronicle of Higher Education. 29 September 1995. "Black U.S. Medical Schools to Help in South Africa."

____. 10 December 1999. "Foreign Students at U.S. Institutions."

____. 22 September 2000. "American College Finds Challenges in Delivering Distance Education Abroad": A41.

____. 17 November 2000. "International Section."

____. 29 June 2001. "Popular Thai Singer Defends Distance Education in Face of Government Skepticism": A28.

___. *Almanac 2001-2.* 78 (1) 31 August 31 2001.

The Economist. 2000. "The Case For Globalization." Survey. 23 September.

The New York Times. 9 September 2001. "Excerpts From U.N. Declaration."

Thieme, John, ed. 1996. *The Arnold Anthology of Post-Colonial Literatures in English.* London: Edward Arnold.

Thompson, Edward P. 1963. *The Making of the English Working Class.* New York: Vintage Books.

Thompson, Willie. 2000. *What Happened to History?* London: Pluto Press.

Thornton, John. 1992. *Africa and Africans in the Making of the Atlantic World, 1400-1680.* New York: Cambridge University Press, 1992.

___. 1999a. "'Wonders of the African World': Reply." 7 November. *<H-AFRICA@H-NET.MSU.EDU>*

___. 1999b. "Mainstreaming Africa: Reply." 9 November. *<H-AFRICA@H-NET.MSU.EDU>*

Throup, David W. 1988. *Economic and Social Origins of Mau Mau, 1945-53.* Athens, Ohio: Ohio University.

Tirelli, Vincent. 1997. "Adjuncts and More Adjuncts: Labor Segmentation and the Transformation of Higher Education." *Social Text* 51: 75-91.

Tolbert Jr, J. 1999. "Henry Louis Gates Is No Alex Haley." 23 November. *<H-AFRO-AM@H-NET.MSU.EDU.>*

Tolliver, Derise E. 2000. "Study Abroad in Africa: Learning about Race, Racism and the Racial Legacy of America." *African Issues* 28 (1&2): 112-116.

Tolson, Jay. 1999. "Telling the Story of Africa: Scholar-Entrepreneur Henry Louis Gates Jr. Take on a New continent." U.S. News Online, <wysi-wyg://513/http://www.usnews.com/usnews/issue/991101/gates.htm> 1 November.

Tomlinson, J. 1991. *Cultural Imperialism.* London: Pinter Publishers.

Torres, Carlos Alberto. 1998. "Immigration, Ethnic Groups, and Area Studies." In John Hawkins et al., eds. *International Education in the New Global Era.* Los Angeles: International Studies and Overseas Programs, University of California.

Touré, Ahati N. 1999. "Reactions of Students to 'Wonders of the African World'." 19 November. *<H-AFRO-AM@H-NET.MSU.EDU>*

Trouillot, Michel-Rolph. 1991. "The Savage Slot in Anthropology." In Richard Gabriel Fox, ed. *Recapturing Anthropology: Working in the Present.* Sante Fe, N.M.: School of American Research Press: 17-44.

Tuathail, Gearoid O. and Derek McCormack. 1998. "The Technoliteracy Challenge: Teaching Globalization Using the Internet." *Journal of Geography in Higher Education* 22 (3): 347-361.

Tugend, Alina. 1996. "Group Seeks to Compare Academic Programs from Nation to Nation." *The Chronicle of Higher Education.* 27 September 1996

Turner, Bryan S. 1996. "Cultural Criticism in the Late Twentieth Century - Contested Knowledge: Social Theory in the Postmodern Era by Steven Seidman." *Contemporary Sociology* 25 (1): 6-8.

Turner, J., and R. Murapa. 1969. "Africa: Conflict in Black and White." *Africa Today* 16 (5&6): 13-14.

Uchendu, Victor. 1977. "Africa and the Africanist: The Challenge of a Terminal Colonial Order." *ISSUE: A Journal of Opinion* 7, 1: 5-11.

Underhill, G. R. D. 1994. "Conceptualizing the Changing Global Order." In R. Stubbs and G. R. D. Underhill, eds. *Political Economy and the Changing Global Order.* New York: St. Martin's Press: 17-44.

UNDP. 2000. *Human Development Report 2000.* New York: UNDP.

UNESCO. 1998. World Conference on Higher Education. Higher Education in the Twenty-First Century: Vision and Action, Volume III - Commissions, Part I and II. UNESCO, Paris, 5-9 October.

____. 2000. World Conference on Higher Education: A Review of Progress Since 1998. Paper for the AED Conference, Washington, D.C. December.

USAID, 1999. Proceedings of the African Partnerships USAID UDLP Higher Education Conference. Factors that Contribute to Successful International Partnerships: Results of Higher Education Linkages. Elmina, Ghana. 8-11 February. *<http://www.cehd.ewu/cehd/faculty/ntodd/GhanaUDLP/conference/Proceedings.html>*

Useem, Andrea. 1997. "An Era of Painful Self-Examination for Many Intellectuals in Africa." *The Chronicle of Higher Education* 44 (7): A47-A48.

____. 1999. "How 2 African Universities Have Moved Ahead in Information Technology." *The Chronicle of Higher Education* 45 (30): A52.

Van Ginneken, Jaap. 1998. *Understanding Global News: A Critical Introduction.* Thousand Oaks, Calif.: Sage.

Van den Berghe, P. L. 1969. "The Montreal Affair: Revolution or Racism?" *Africa Today* 16 (5&6):10-11.

Van Wolferen. K. 2000. "The United Nations and the Conceptual Challenges of a Globalizing Economy." *UN Chronicle* 37 (1): 64-67.

Vargas-Baron, Emily. 1998. "Higher Education Partnerships for Development." In UNESCO, World Conference on Higher Education. Higher Education in the Twenty-First Century: Vision and Action, Volume III - Commissions, Part II. UNESCO, Paris, 5-9 October.

Vaughn, Megan. 1991. *Curing Their Ills: Colonial Power and African Illness.* Cambridge: Polity Press.

Veltmeyer, H. 1997. "New Social Movements in Latin America: The Dynamics of Class and Identity." *Journal of Peasant Studies* 25 (1): 139-169.

Veney, Cassandra Rachel and Paul Tiyambe Zeleza. 2000. "The U.S. Elections, Political System and Africa." *USAfrica Online* <*www.USAfricaonline.com*> 24 November 2000.

Vergnani, Linda. 1998a. An Elite South African University Seeks to Make Itself More 'African.'" *Chronicle of Higher Education* 45 (12): A42-A44.

___. 1998b. "South African Universities Move to Cast Aside Legacy of Apartheid." *Chronicle of Higher Education* 45 (2): A73-A74.

___. 2000a. "Corruption alleged at South African College." *The Chronicle of Higher Education,* 47 (11): A56.

___. 2000b. "South African Universities Grapple with the Growth of Distance Learning." *The Chronicle of Higher Education* 46 (42): A45-A47

Veseth, Michael. 1998. *The Myth of the Global Economy.* Boulder, Colorado: Lynne Rienner.

Vidovitch, Lesly et al. 2000. "Quality Teaching and Learning in Australian and South African Universities: Comparing Policies and Practices. *Compare* 30 (2): 193-209.

Viljoen, Louise. 1996. "Postcolonialism and Recent Women's Writing in Afrikaans." *World Literature Today* 70 (1) 63-72.

Visser, Nicholas. 1997. "Postcoloniality of a Special Type: Theory and Its Appropriations in South Africa." *The Yearbook of English Studies* 27: 79-94.

Viswanathan, Gauri. 1989. *Masks of Conquest: Literary Study and British Rule in India.* New York: Columbia University Press.

Vubo, E. Yenshu. 2001 (June). "A Society-Centered Vision for the African University by the Year 2050." Paper presented at the Ford Foundation Retreat in Durban, South Africa.

Wa Thiong'o. Ngugi. 1986. *Decolonizing the Mind: The Politics of Language in African Literature.* London: James Currey.

Wa Kinyatti, Maina. 1991. *Mau Mau: A Revolution Betrayed.* New York: Mau Mau Research Center.

Wa Thiong'o. Ngugi. 1972. "On the Abolition of the English Department." *Homecoming: Essays on African and Caribbean Literature, Culture and Politics.* London: Heinemann, 145-150.

Walder, Dennis. 1998. *Postcolonial Literatures in English: History Language Theory.* Oxford: Blackwell.

Walfish, Daniel. 2001. "Chinese Government Predicts Strong Growth in Online Education." *The Chronicle of Higher Education* 21 May.

Walker, Melanie. 1997. "Women in the Academy: Ambiguity and Complexity in a South African University." *Gender & Education* 9 (3): 65-381.

___. 1998. "Academic Identities: Women on a South African Landscape." *Journal of Sociology of Education* 19 (3): 335-354.

Wallerstein, Emmanuel. 1969. "Africa, America and the Africanists." *Africa Today* 16 (5&6): 12-13.

___. 1995. "Africa in the Shuffle." *ISSUE: A Journal of Opinion,* 23, 1:22-23.

___. 1999. *The End of the World As We Know It: Social Science for the Twenty-First Century.* Minneapolis: University of Minnesota Press.

Ward, Steven C. 1995. "The Revenge of the Humanities: Reality, Rhetoric and the Politics of Postmodernism." *Sociological Perspectives* 38: 109-128.

Waters, Malcolm. 1995. *Globalization.* London and New York: Routledge.

Watkins, John J. 2000. "Kumusha Tales: Messages from Msengezi and Other Stories." *African Issues* 28 (1&2): 140-144.

Watts, Anthony. 1999. "A Few 'Honest' Answers About the Preliminary Critique." 2 November <*H-AFRO-AM@H-NET.MSU.EDU*>

Weir, Jennifer, Alex Radloff, and Heidi Hudson. 2001. "Project-Based Professional Development for Quality Teaching and Learning in South African Further and Higher Education." Paper presented at the Carter Lectures 2001, "Governance and Higher Education," University of Florida, Gainesville. 22-25 March.

Weiss, L. 1997. "Globalization and the Myth of the Powerless State." *New Left Review* 225 (September/October): 3-27.

Welsh, Frank. 1999. *Dangerous Deceits.* London : HarperCollins Publishers.

Werbner, Richard and Terence Ranger, eds. 1996. *Postcolonial Identities in Africa.* London: Zed Books.

West, Cornell. 1994. "The New Cultural Politics of Difference." In Steven Seidman, ed. *The Postmodern Turn: New Perspectives On Social Theory.* New York: Cambridge University Press: 65-81.

West, Michael O., and William G. Martin. 1997. "A Future with a Past: Resurrecting the Study of Africa in the Post-Africanist Era." *Africa Today* 44 (3): 297-326.

West Africa. 1995. "Africa's Costly Human Export." 1424-1425.

Wheeler, David L. 2000. "More Students Study Abroad, But Their Stays Are Shorter." *The Chronicle of Higher Education* November 17: A74.

White, Hayden. 1973. *Metahistory: The Historical Imagination in Nineteenth*

Century Europe. Baltimore: Johns Hopkins University Press.

___. 1978. *Tropics of Discourse.* Baltimore: Johns Hopkins University Press.

___. 1987. *The Content of the Form.* Baltimore: Johns Hopkins University Press.

___. 1999. "Afterward." In Bonnell, V. E. and L. Hunt, eds. *Beyond the Cultural Turn.* Berkeley and Los Angeles: University of California Press: 315-324.

Wiley, David. 1998. "The Conference Rapporteur's Synthesis of the Findings of the National Policy Conference on Title VI of the Higher Education Act and Fulbright-Hays Programs." In John Hawkins et al., eds. *International Education in the New Global Era.* Los Angeles: International Studies and Overseas Programs, University of California: 213-225.

Wiley, David and John Metzler. 2000. "Building a National Focus for Student Exchange with Africa: The National Consortium for Study in Africa." *African Issues* 28 (1&2): 34-38.

Wilhelm, D. 1971. "The Crisis in Area Studies Programs: A Time for Innovation." *African Studies Review* 14 (2): 171-178.

Wilkin, P. 1997. "New Myths for the South: Globalization and the Conflict Between Private Power and Freedom." In C. Thomas and P. Wilkin, eds. *Globalization and the South.* New York: St. Martin's Press.

Wilkins, Ivor, and Strydom, Hans. 1979. *Broederbond: The Super-Afrikaners.* London: Corgi Books.

Williams, Jeffrey. 1995. *PC Wars: Politics and Theory in the Academy.* New York: Routledge.

Williams, Pysche Aletheia. 1999. "About the Preliminary Critique." 2 November. *<H-AFRO-AM@H-NET.MSU.EDU>*

Wilson-Tagoe, Nana. 1995. "Post-Colonial Literary Theory and the Theorizing of African Literature." *Yearbook of Comparative Literature and General Literature* 43: 110-119.

Wise, Christopher. 1998. "Chronicle of a Student Strike in Africa: The Case of Burkina Faso, 1996-1997."*African Studies Review* 41 (2): 19-36.

Wise, Michael, ed. 1994. *Survival Under Adverse Conditions: Proceedings of the African Library Science Workshop.* The Hague, Netherlands: International Federation of Library Associations and Institutions. IFLA Professional Reports, No.38.

Wissoker, K. 2000. "Negotiating a Passage Between Disciplinary Borders." *The Chronicle of Higher Education* (April 14): B4-B6.

Wolf, Michael. 1997. "Universities Vital to Democracy in Africa." *The Chronicle of Higher Education* 10 October: B13.

Wolferen, Karel G. van. 1999. "The Global Conceptual Crisis." *New Perspectives Quarterly* 16 (1): 17-24.

Woo, Wing. 2000. "Coping with Accelerated Capital Flows From the Globalization of Financial Markets." *Asean Economic Bulletin* 17 (2): 193-204.

Wright, Robert. 2000. "Will Globalization Make You Happy?" *Foreign Policy* 120 (Sep/Oct): 54-64.

Wood, Jennifer and Clifford Shearing. 1991. "Reinventing Intellectuals." *Canadian Journal of Criminology* 41 (2): 311-320.

World Bank. 1988. *Education in Sub-Saharan Africa: Policies for Adjustment, Revitalization, and Expansion.* Washington, DC: World Bank.

___. 1994. *Higher Education: The Lessons of Experience.* Washington, DC: World Bank

___. 2000. *Higher Education in Developing Countries. Peril and Promise.* Washington, D.C.: World Bank.

www.arabicnews.com "45,000 Egyptian Scientists Migrate in 50 Years," Egypt, Science, 7/14/2000.

www.siu.no/vev.nsf/ "Pro 07/96 Administration - Africa: Politics of Administration, Bureaucracy, Professionalization and Good Governance."

Wylie, Ken. 1997. "Postmodernism and Africa: Reply." 11 November. <"Postmodernism and Modern Africa," *H-AFRICA@H-NET.MSU. EDU,<http://www.h-net2.msu.edu/logs/showlog.cgi?list=h-africa&file=h. africa.log9711b&ent=34> <http://www.h-net.msu.edu/~africa/threads/ pomothread.html>*

Yach, D. and D. Bettcher. 1998. "The Globalization of Public Health, 1: Threats and Opportunities." *American Journal of Public Health* 88 (5): 735-738.

Yang, Philip Q. 2000. *Ethnic Studies: Issues and Approaches.* Albany, NY: State University of New York Press.

Yavo, Noel. 1999. *Top 50 African Websites: Analytical Report.* 27 November. <http://www.woyaa.com/topweb>

Yeager, R. 1970. "The Legitimacy of Area Studies" Paper prepared for presentation at the thirteenth annual meeting of the African Studies Association, Boston, October.

Yisak, Wolde-Ab. 2001. "The Role of Higher Education in Nation Building: The Eritrean Experience." Paper presented at the Carter Lectures 2001, "Governance and Higher Education," University of Florida, Gainesville. 22-25 March.

Yizengaw, Teshome. 2001. "The Future of African Higher Education." Paper presented at the Ford Foundation Retreat in Durban, South

Africa, 29 May - 1 June.

Young, Jeffrey R. 2000. "Faculty Report at U. of Illinois Casts Skeptical Eye on Distance Education." *The Chronicle of Higher Education* 14 January: A48.

Zachernuk, Philip S. 1999. "African Intellectuals and the Reconceptualization of Africa." In Misty Bastian and Jane Parpart, eds. *Great Ideas for Teaching Africa*. Boulder, Colo.: Lynne Rienner Press: 211-218.

____. 2000. *Colonial Subjects: An African Intelligentsia and Atlantic Ideas.* Charlottesville, Va. : University Press of Virginia.

Zack-Williams, Alfred. 1995. "Development and Diaspora: Separate Concerns?" *Review of African Political Economy* 65: 349-358.

Zakaria, Fareed. 2000. "The Rise of Illiberal Democracy." In Patrick O'Meara, Howard D. Mehlinger, and Mathew Krain, eds. *Globalization and the Challenges of a New Century*. Bloomington and Indianapolis: Indiana University Press: 181-195.

Zalewski, David A. 2000. "Globalization and Progressive Economic Policy." *Journal of Economic Issues* 34 (1): 241-244.

Zeleza, Paul Tiyambe 1987a. *Imperialism and Labor: The International Relations of the Kenyan Labor Movement*. Kisumu: Anyange Publications.

____. 1987b. "Trade Union Imperialism: American Labor, the ICFTU and the Kenyan Labor Movement." *Social and Economic Studies* 36 (2):145-170.

____. 1994a "African Studies and the Disintegration of Paradigms." *Africa Development* 19 (4): 179-93.

____. 1994b. "The Democratic Transition and the Anglophone Writer." *Canadian Journal of African Studies* 28 (3): 472-497.

____. 1994c. "The Tribulations of Undressing the Emperor." *Canadian Journal of African Studies* 28 (1): 106-20.

____. 1994d. "1994 Noma Award Presentation." *The African Book Publishing Record* 20 (4): 237-238.

____. 1996. "Manufacturing and Consuming Knowledge: African Libraries and Publishing." *Development and Practice* 6(4): 293-303.

____. 1997a. *Manufacturing African Studies and Crises*. Dakar, Senegal: Codesria Book Series.

____. 1997b. "The Perpetual Solitudes and Crises of African Studies in the United States." *Africa Today* 44, 2 : 193-210.

____. 1997c. "Academic Freedom in the North and South: An African Perspective." *Academe: Bulletin of the American Association of University Professors* 83 (6): 16-21.

____. 1998. "African Migrant Intellectuals: Constructing New Trans-Atlantic

Bridges." Paper presented at the Symposium on African and African American Intellectuals." University of California, San Diego, 22 May.

___. 1999a. "Africa's Bumpy Road to Democracy." Paper presented at the Production School, Hopes on the Horizon Project, Blackside Inc., Boston, June 1999.

___. 1999b. "The Challenges of Writing African Economic History." In George Clement Bond and Nigel Gibson, eds. *Issues in African Studies*, Boulder, Colorado: Westview Press (in press).

___. 2000a. "Challenges of Research in African Universities: Potential Partnerships Between African and American Universities." Paper presented at Ford Foundation Meeting on Higher Education Initiative in Africa, 6-7 April, 2000, Johannesburg, South Africa.

___. 2000b. "Mazrui-Soyinka Controversy." 24 January *<toyin.falola@mail. utexas.edu>*

___. 2001. "The Chronicles of Elsewhere." Paper Presented at the Ford Foundation on Visioning the African University in 2050, Durban, South Africa, 29 May-1 June.

Zeleza, Paul Tiyambe and Ezekiel Kalipeni, eds 1999. *Sacred Spaces and Public Quarrels: African Cultural and Economic Landscapes.* Trenton, N.J.: Africa World Press.

Zeleza, Paul Tiyambe and Phil McConnaughay, eds. 2002. *Human Rights, Development, and the Rule of Law in Africa.* University of Pennsylvania Press (forthcoming).

Zeleza, Paul Tiyambe, Ilesanmi Adesida, and Ibulaimu Kakoma, eds. 2002. *Science, Technology, and Development in Africa.* Trenton, New Jersey: Africa World Press, (forthcoming).

Zell, Hans. 1998. "African Journal Publishers in a Digital Environment." In Philip G. Altbach and Damtew Teferra, eds. *Knowledge Dissemination in Africa: The Role of Scholarly Journals.* Chestnut Hill, Mass.: Bellagio Studies in Publishing: 85-97.

Zevin, R. 1992. "Our World Financial Market Is More Open? If So, Why and with What Effect?" In T. Banuri and J. B. Schor, eds. *Financial Openness and National Autonomy: Opportunity and Constraints.* New York: Oxford University Press.

Zhao, Suisheng. 1997. "Chinese Intellectuals' Quest for National Greatness and Nationalistic Writing in the 1990s." *China Quarterly* 152 (December): 725-745.

Zimmerer, Karl. 2000. "Commentary: Social Science Intellectuals, Sustainable Development and the Political Economies of Bolivia." *Journal of Latin American Anthropology* 5 (2): 179-189.

Zinyemba, Ranga. 2000. "African Perspectives on Programs for North American Students in Africa: The Experience of the University of Zimbabwe." *African Issues* 28 (1&2): 20-23.

Zlotnik, H. 1999. "Trends of International Migration Since 1965: What Existing Data Reveal." *International Migration* 37 (1): 21-59.

Index